Fodor's

1st EDITION

Michigan Wisconsin Minnesota

Don Davenport

Fodor's Travel Publications, Inc.
New York and London

KT-383-368

Copyright © 1989
by Fodor's Travel Publications, Inc.

Fodor's is a trademark of Fodor's Travel Publications, Inc.

All rights reserved under International and Pan-American Copyright Conventions. Published in the United States by Fodor's Travel Publications, Inc., a subsidiary of Random House, Inc., New York, and simultaneously in Canada by Random House of Canada, Limited, Toronto. Distributed by Random House, Inc., New York.

"A Minnesota Childhood" by Shirley Schoonover is abridged from the essay "Route 1, Box 111, Aurora" in *Growing Up in Minnesota*, edited by Chester G. Anderson and published by the University of Minnesota Press. © 1976 by the University of Minnesota. Reprinted by permission of the University of Minnesota Press.

No maps, illustrations, or other portions of this book may be reproduced in any form without written permission from the publisher.

First Edition

ISBN 0-679-01718-6

Fodor's Michigan, Wisconsin, Minnesota

Editors: Christopher Billy, Holly Hughes, Vernon Nahrgang
Associate Editors: Barbara A. Koeth, Max Lowenthal
Editorial Contributors: Jeremy Iggers, Anne Schamberg, Donna G. White, Karin Winegar
Art Director: Fabrizio La Rocca
Cartographer: David Lindroth
Illustrator: Karl Tanner
Cover Photograph: Stroheim/West Light

Design: Vignelli Associates

About the Author

Don Davenport is a freelance writer and photographer based in Verona, Wisconsin. He is the author of *Shipwreck on Lake Michigan,* he writes on travel and Great Lakes subjects for a number of magazines and newspapers, and he contributes annually to *Fodor's United States of America.*

Special Sales

MANUFACTURED IN THE UNITED STATES OF AMERICA

10 9 8 7 6 5 4 3 2 1

Contents

Foreword

This is an exciting time for Fodor's, as it begins a three-year program to rewrite, reformat, and redesign all 140 of its guides. Here are just a few of the exciting new features:

★ Brand-new computer-generated maps locating all the top attractions, hotels, restaurants, and shops

★ A unique system of numbers and legends to help readers move effortlessly between text and maps

★ A new star rating system for hotels and restaurants

★ Restaurant reviews by major food critics around the world

★ Stamped, self-addressed postcards, bound into every guide, give readers an opportunity to help evaluate hotels and restaurants

★ Complete page redesign for instant retrieval of information

★ FODOR'S CHOICE—Our favorite museums, beaches, cafes, romantic hideaways, festivals, and more

★ HIGHLIGHTS '89—An insider's look at the most important developments in tourism during the past year

★ TIME OUT—The best and most convenient lunch stops along the shopping and exploring routes

★ Exclusive background essays create a powerful portrait of each destination

★ A mini-journal for travelers to keep track of their own itineraries and addresses

While every care has been taken to assure the accuracy of the information in this guide, the passage of time will always bring change, and consequently the publisher cannot accept responsibility for errors that may occur.

All prices and opening times quoted here are based on information available to us at press time. Hours and admission fees may change, however, and the prudent traveler will avoid inconvenience by calling ahead.

Fodor's wants to hear about your travel experiences, both pleasant and unpleasant. When a hotel or restaurant fails to live up to its billing, let us know and we will investigate the complaint and revise our entries where the facts warrant it.

Send your letters to the editors of Fodor's Travel Publications, 201 E. 50th Street, New York, NY 10022, or 30-32 Bedford Square, London WC1B 3SG, England.

Highlights '89 and Fodor's Choice

Highlights '89

Michigan   Detroit remains a front-runner among cities on the move in the Upper Great Lakes region.

A $25-million remodeling project at the **Renaissance Center** has attempted to cure the ills of an ultramodern glass-and-concrete impersonality. New storefronts, color-coded areas, and easier access are the results. Reports are that tourists still get lost, but what else can you expect from a building that has its own ZIP Code and more than 12,000 people working there? After years of struggle and controversy, the **People Mover** finally got on the right track in late 1987. The 2.9-mile monorail encircles downtown Detroit in about 15 minutes. With homegrown art in all 13 of its stations, the People Mover has already become a major tourist attraction *and* one of the best transportation buys in the Upper Great Lakes.

On the restaurant front, the opulent **Whitney** opened in late 1987. Housed in a 46-room pink granite mansion, the restaurant features Tiffany windows, Delft pottery fireplace mantels, rich wood paneling, and a number of small, intimate dining rooms. It's already become a Motor City favorite. **Opus One** opened on East Larned in Detroit's Bricktown area in February of 1988. Start-up costs came to $3.5 million, providing for marbled floors, etched glass, mirrored panels, and tapestry banquettes. Also new is the **Rattlesnake Club,** a fine-dining spot that opened in the Stroh Riverplace development in July of '88.

On the hotel scene, the new **Riverplace Inn** was scheduled to open in the spring of 1989. The 111-room hotel will offer Tudor-mansion styling and super-deluxe facilities. The 73-story **Westin Hotel,** in the Renaissance Center, has extensively remodeled its public spaces and eight-story-high lobby, largely to counteract complaints that hotel patrons couldn't tell the lobby from other sections of the Ren Cen. In suburban Dearborn, the **Dearborn Inn,** originally built in 1931 by Henry Ford, is slated to reopen in the spring of 1989. Closed for more than a year, the inn has undergone an $18.5-million renovation that added 54 new rooms. Sportswise, the **Detroit Pistons** were scheduled to move from the Pontiac Silverdome and begin the 1988–89 season at the Palace in Auburn Hills.

A $225-million remodeling project giving the Civic Center's **Cobo Conference/Exhibition Center** a total of 700,000 square feet of exhibit space was scheduled for completion in early 1989. It is one of the People Mover stops, and the monorail now goes *through* the building. The **Detroit Trolley,** which was shut down for the first six months of 1988 by the construction project, is back in service and operating year-round.

The newest building on the Detroit skyline is a 28-story office tower called **150 West Jefferson.** The long-neglected **Fox Theater,** located on Woodward Avenue just north of Grand Circus Park, has been completely refurbished and a grand reopening ceremony was held in November 1988. The 5,000-seat theater once played host to many early Motown acts; the hallowed halls will now serve mainly as a performing arts theater. The **Museum of African-American History,** which has struggled to survive for 20 years, moved into new digs on Frederick Douglass Avenue in the Cultural Center in late 1987. The **Henry Ford Museum and Greenfield Village** in suburban Dearborn opened its first major new exhibit in decades in late 1987. Entitled *The Automobile in American Life,* the exhibit—like the museum itself—is nothing short of spectacular.

The famed **Grand Hotel** on Mackinac Island completed a 10-year program that remodeled the facility from top to bottom for its 100th anniversary celebration in 1987.

Wisconsin   In Milwaukee, the new **Milwaukee Center,** on the banks of the river downtown, was scheduled to be completely finished in early 1989. Showcasing the **Milwaukee Repertory Theater's** three new theaters, the center's latest addition is the 221-room **Wyndham Hotel.** The hotel's **Kilbourn Cafe** opened in late summer 1988. The Milwaukee Center allows patrons to go from lodging to dining, theater, and shopping in a shirt-sleeve environment year round.

Sports fans are enthusiastic about Milwaukee's new **Bradley Center,** scheduled to open by the end of 1988. The 20,000-seat arena will be the new home to the NBA's Milwaukee Bucks and the Milwaukee Admirals of the International Hockey League; it will also host conventions and other large gatherings. Unlimited hydroplane racing—the big time of boat racing—is reportedly in the works for Milwaukee, but no dates or location had been set at press time. A new visitors center has been completed at the **Milwaukee Zoo.** And beginning in January 1989, Milwaukee will be hosting a brand-new four-day-long winter festival: **Ice Breaker '89.**

Minnesota   St. Paul has come to the end of a decade of major renovations, so things are a bit quiet on the construction scene there for the time being, but the 1990s should see major renovation projects taking place along its downtown riverfront. The newest building on the skyline, the **Minnesota World Trade Center,** opened in August of 1987. The **Como Park Conservatory,** in St. Paul's most popular park, is undergoing a major renovation slated for completion in mid-1989. The conservatory will remain open; annual flower shows and special events will be scheduled around the construction. On the hotel scene, the **Radisson St. Paul** extensively renovated guest rooms a year ago; it has now completed remodeling many public spaces, including the swimming pool area. Le Carrousel, the hotel's rooftop restaurant, reopened in mid-1988 after having been closed for renovations. The downtown **Holiday Inn Town Square** changed its name during the summer of 1988—it is now the **Holiday Inn St. Paul Center.** The **Cathedral Hill District,** west of Selby and Western, continues to add new boutiques and shops. **Tommy K's Restaurant,** which opened in late '87 in the **Blair Arcade,** is typical of the new, upscale restaurants that have opened on the fringes of downtown St. Paul.

In Minneapolis, indoor soccer enthusiasts mourn the loss of the **Minnesota Strikers,** who threw in the towel after years of struggle to make the franchise financially successful. Basketball fans, however, should note that the **Minnesota Timberwolves,** one of the newest teams in the NBA, are scheduled to begin

play in the autumn of 1989. Construction of a new arena is
planned, but the team may play its first season in other digs.
The first phase of a new $200-million **Convention Center** down-
town on Grant Street is slated to open in late spring of 1989.
When completed, the 720,000-square-foot facility will offer
353,000 square feet of exhibit space. There are plans for a new
800-room hotel to be located near the center; construction is not
yet under way. A new bus trolley system that will run from the
Convention Center to various downtown areas was slated to go
into operation in March of 1989.

New faces on the Minneapolis skyline are the **Opus buildings**
(two of them) and the **Norwest Tower,** all of which opened for occupancy during the summer of 1988. On the shopping scene,
Saks Fifth Avenue is scheduled to open a downtown store in the
spring of 1989. The elegant new 97-room **Whitney Hotel,** on
Portland Avenue overlooking the Mississippi River and the
Falls of St. Anthony, opened in early 1988, and in late summer
of 1988 the **Nicolet Inn,** a 13-room country inn, opened on
Nicolet Island in the Mississippi. Renovation of the riverfront
area continues, although the summer drought of 1988 raised
havoc with new plantings.

New restaurants in Minneapolis include **Chez Bananas,** a
trendy after-hours restaurant in the Warehouse District, and
the **Fine Line Music Cafe,** which also features live music, on 1st
Avenue North. **The Whitney Grille,** in the Whitney Hotel, has
become a popular upscale dining spot. In September 1988, the
Walker Arts Center opened its **Minneapolis Sculpture Garden,**
billed as the largest outdoor urban sculpture garden in the nation.

Fodor's Choice

No two people will agree on what makes a perfect vacation, but it's fun and helpful to know what others think. We hope you'll have a chance to experience some of Fodor's Choices yourself while visiting the Great Lakes states. For detailed information about each entry, refer to the appropriate chapters within this guidebook.

Sights

Henry Ford Museum and Greenfield Village, Dearborn, MI

The People Mover, Detroit, MI

The Mackinac Bridge, Mackinaw City–St. Ignace, MI

Circus World Museum, Baraboo, WI

Big Manitou Falls, Pattison State Park, Superior, WI

The Depot Museum, Duluth, MN

Charles A. Lindbergh Home, Little Falls, MN

American Swedish Institute, Minneapolis, MN

The Science Museum, St. Paul, MN

Special Moments

The view, day or night, from the Summit Restaurant at the top of the Westin Hotel, Detroit, MI

Sunset on the beach at Grand Marais, MI

The ferry ride from Bayfield to Madeline Island, WI

Thousands of Canada geese at Horicon Marsh, WI

Any opening night at the Guthrie Theater, Minneapolis, MN

People-watching at Rice Park, St. Paul, MN

Taste Treats

Coney Islands at the American Coney Island, Detroit, MI

A fish boil at the White Gull Inn, Fish Creek, WI

Homemade chocolates at Beernsten's Chocolates, Manitowoc, WI

Sour-cream raisin pie at the Norske Nook, Osseo, WI

Tenderloin of beef topped with Béarnaise sauce, Whitney Grille, Minneapolis, MN

Champagne brunch at the Deco Restaurant, St. Paul, MN

Off the Beaten Track

Motown Museum, Detroit, MI

John K. King Bookstore, Detroit, MI

Merrimac Ferry, Merrimac, WI

Split Rock Lighthouse State Park, MN

Schubert Club Piano Museum, St. Paul, MN

After Hours

Monroe's in Trappers Alley, Detroit, MI

Mykonos Supper Club, Detroit, MI

The Safe House, Milwaukee, WI

First Avenue Club, Minneapolis, MN

Pacific Club, Minneapolis, MN

Dakota Bar and Grill, St. Paul, MN

The cocktail lounge at the Saint Paul Hotel, St. Paul, MN

Speak Easy Restaurant and Lounge, Moorhead, MN

Hotels

The Grand Hotel, Mackinac Island, MI *(Very Expensive)*

The Westin Hotel, Detroit, MI *(Very Expensive)*

The American Club, Kohler, WI *(Very Expensive)*

Mansion Hill Inn, Madison, WI *(Very Expensive)*

St. James Hotel, Red Wing, MN *(Very Expensive)*

The Saint Paul Hotel, St. Paul, MN *(Very Expensive)*

The Whitney Hotel, Minneapolis, MN *(Very Expensive)*

Hyatt Regency, Dearborn, MI *(Expensive)*

The Mayflower Bed & Breakfast Hotel, Plymouth, MI
(Expensive–Moderate)

Hotel Chequamegon, Ashland, WI *(Moderate–Inexpensive)*

Stage Coach Inn, Cedarburg, WI *(Moderate)*

Restaurants

The Whitney, Detroit, MI *(Very Expensive)*

Old Rittenhouse Inn, Bayfield, WI *(Very Expensive)*

The Whitney Grille, Minneapolis, MN *(Very Expensive)*

The Fess Hotel Dining Room, Madison, WI *(Expensive)*

Mason-Girardot Alan Manor, Windsor, Ont. *(Expensive)*

Zehnder's Restaurant, Frankenmuth, MI *(Inexpensive)*

The Common House, Bailey's Harbor, WI *(Inexpensive)*

Michigan, Wisconsin, and Minnesota

MANITOBA

ONTARIO

Lake of the Woods

Rainy Lake

Upper Red Lake

International Falls

71

53

Grand Portage

Lower Red Lake

2

Bemidji

Hibbing

Apostle Islands

Chequamegon Bay

Iron Wood

71

Leech Lake

169

2

Duluth

Superior

2

Ashland

ND

Fargo

10

M I N N E S O T A

Mille Lacs Lake

35

53

13

51

94

St. Cloud

10

St. Croix River

8

Prentice

S D

Minneapolis

St. Paul

53

Eau Claire

Wausau

7

Minnesota River

169

35

Mississippi River

W I S C O N

14

Mankato

Rochester

Winona

94

51

71

14

La Crosse

90

13

94

90

14

Madison

151

I O W A

Des Moines

80

II

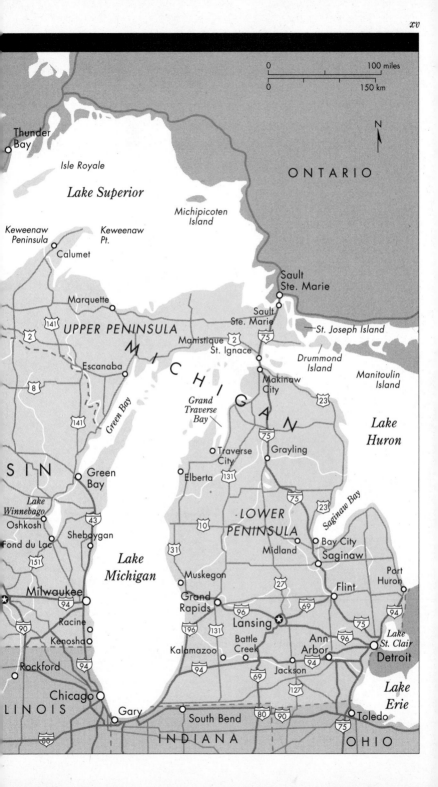

World Time Zones

Numbers below vertical bands relate each zone to Greenwich Mean Time (0 hrs.).
Local times frequently differ from these general indications,
as indicated by light-face numbers on map.

-1 0 +1 +2 +3 +4 +5 +6 +7 +8 +9 +10
Greenwich
Mean Time

Stockholm, **32**
Copenhagen, **33**
Berlin, **34**
Vienna, **35**
Warsaw, **36**
Budapest, **37**
Madrid, **38**

Rome, **39**
Istanbul, **40**
Athens, **41**
Jerusalem, **42**
Nairobi, **43**
Johannesburg, **44**
Moscow, **45**
Baghdad, **46**

Mecca, **47**
Delhi, **48**
Rangoon, **49**
Bangkok, **50**
Saigon, **51**
Singapore, **52**
Djakarta, **53**
Beijing, **54**
Shanghai, **55**

Hong Kong, **56**
Manila, **57**
Perth, **58**
Seoul, **59**
Tokyo, **60**
Sydney, **61**

Introduction

T he French were the first Europeans to visit the Upper Great Lakes, early in the 17th century. They came searching for the Northwest Passage, the fabled water route that would take them to the Orient. In the process, they reached the heart of North America, discovered the five Great Lakes, and established a fabulous fur trade.

The role of French exploration in the Midwest is often overlooked; many travelers are surprised to find communities in the Upper Great Lakes that predate the American Revolution by nearly a century. The Jesuit mission on the Fox River at De Pere, today a suburb of Green Bay, Wisconsin, was built in 1672. By 1680, Green Bay itself had emerged as an outpost prominent in the fur trade and mission activity. Sault Ste. Marie (1668) and St. Ignace, Michigan (1671), were missions founded by Father Jacques Marquette, who, along with Louis Jolliet, discovered the Upper Mississippi River. Detroit stood guard over the straits between Lake Erie and Lake Huron for three-quarters of a century before the Minutemen fired "the shot heard round the world" at Concord's North Bridge in 1775. In many communities in the region, French was the principal language until well into the 19th century. French names dot the maps of all three states.

But what gave (and still gives) the Upper Great Lakes region its true flavor was the Great Migration of the mid-19th century, when millions of Europeans came to the United States. Many of those millions—Swedes, Dutch, Germans, Norwegians, and scores of others—came to Michigan, Wisconsin, and Minnesota. The German communities of New Ulm, Minnesota, and Frankenmuth, Michigan; the Swiss settlement of New Glarus, Wisconsin; the Dutch settlements at Holland, Michigan, and Oostburg, Wisconsin, are but a few of many places where ethnic heritage remains a vital part of everyday life. Milwaukee has strong German traditions and, as does Detroit, claims more than 50 ethnic groups. Throughout the region, annual festivals, religious customs, ethnic foods, and in some cases Old World architecture keep the heritage alive today. You'll find some sort of ethnic festival (serving deliciously authentic foods) being held most months of the year, especially in the major cities.

Geographically the three states are bound together by the Great Lakes—the largest body of fresh water in the world—and the St. Lawrence Seaway, an engineering marvel of canals and locks that connects the lakes with the Atlantic Ocean. Although Duluth, Minnesota, and Superior, Wisconsin, are more than 2,000 miles from the Atlantic, they are nevertheless seaports, with a direct water connection to the rest of the world. Together they constitute the largest port on the Great Lakes and, at times, one of the busiest ports in the nation. The Great Lakes shipping industry may have fallen on hard times in recent years, yet millions of tons of bulk commodities are still shipped via the lakes each year. Freighters heavy with iron ore from the ranges in Minnesota steam out of Duluth–Superior for the lower-lakes steel-producing ports of Detroit, Cleveland, or Gary, Indiana. Millions of bushels of grain from the western prairies pass through Duluth–Superior each year on their way to nations around the world. Minneapolis and St. Paul, set at the head of navigation on the Mississippi River, are active ports as well.

The Great Lakes disrupt the geographical unity of this widespread region. Detroit actually lies closer to New York City than to Minneapolis, and Milwaukee is nearly as close to St. Louis, Missouri, as it is to Detroit. Minneapolis is much closer to Omaha, Nebraska, than to Detroit. But in the north, where Michigan's Upper Peninsula and eastern Minnesota border Wisconsin, a two-hour drive can take you to all three states. Residents of the northern reaches, perhaps drawn together by the harsh winters, have closer ties to each other than to other sections of their own state and especially to the southern cities, which northerners tend to look upon askance.

"Up north" you'll find millions of acres of piney green forest, more than 30,000 lakes, and thousands of miles of rivers and trout streams. There are deer and bear in the forests and big fish in the waters. This is the land of Paul Bunyan and Babe the blue ox, Longfellow's Hiawatha and Gitche Gumee, crystal streams and thundering waterfalls, jeans and flannel shirts, polka bands, and roadhouses with deer heads mounted behind the bar. It is a place to escape from the crowds, not to join them, and there are spots in all three states that seem untouched since the days of the fur traders and explorers.

Much of the mineral wealth of the region lies in the north, and scars from iron and copper mining are prominent in certain areas, but this is also hunting, fishing, and camping country. From May through September the start of each weekend sees thousands of boats being trailered northward; the flow reverses late on Sunday. The annual autumn deer season draws hundreds of thousands from the cities and surrounding states into the woods—farmers have been known to paint the letters C-O-W on the sides of their bovine livestock. In winter, snowmobiles replace the boats on the trailers heading northward each Friday, and thousands of miles of trails crisscross each of the states. Ice fishing has its hardy aficionados, and skiing—both alpine and Nordic —has grown in popularity in the last decade, with ski slopes and trails being opened throughout the region.

If you'd rather watch than participate, the Detroit Tigers, Milwaukee Brewers, and Minnesota Twins annually draw millions of big-league baseball fans. Professional-football fans flock to see the Detroit Lions, Green Bay Packers, and Minnesota Vikings. In this era of domed stadiums, Green Bay still plays outdoors; late autumn games at Lambeau Field are viewed with horror by warm-climate opponents yet are part of the stuff of which the Packer legend is made. The Detroit Pistons and the Milwaukee Bucks are long established in the National Basketball Association, and one of the newest NBA teams, the Minnesota Timberwolves, will begin play in Minneapolis in the autumn of 1989. Hockey fans thrill to the exploits of the Minnesota North Stars and the Detroit Red Wings.

Most professional sports events take place in the southern parts of the region, near the industrial and population centers of each state. Here, too, are the state capitals Lansing, Madison, and St. Paul, and the major universities: the University of Michigan at Ann Arbor, Michigan State University at East Lansing, the University of Wisconsin at Madison, and the University of Minnesota at Minneapolis.

You will do yourself a grave injustice if you limit your visit to the Upper Great Lakes either to the cities or to the great outdoors, for both have many pleasures to offer. Detroit, Milwaukee, and Minneapolis/St. Paul have renowned symphony orchestras, ballet and opera companies, touring Broadway shows, popular entertainers, galleries and museums, festivals, sports events, and restaurants and hotels that will hold their own with those of any major city in the country. Be sure not to overlook such smaller cities as Ann Arbor, Grand Rapids, and Lansing in Michigan; Madison and Green Bay in Wisconsin; and Duluth and Rochester in Minnesota. The scale is smaller and the pace a little slower, but the same delights can be found.

The Upper Great Lakes have long been a favorite summer tourist spot, especially for residents of the lower Midwest, but until recent decades tourism was mostly a Memorial Day-to-Labor-Day and weekends-through-October affair. Then the snowmobilers and skiers created the winter tourist season—almost single-handedly—and now more and better north-country dining and lodging facilities are open in the winter, making tourism in the Upper Great Lakes a year-round business. The only slow times are from the end of the autumn color season until the first snowfalls, and late in March and April.

Michigan, Wisconsin, and Minnesota offer what most tourists value highly: good toll-free highways, excellent state park systems, and some of the lowest vacation costs in the nation. They present a promise of sunshine and seascapes, sparkling waters, majestic forests, urban delights, snowy hills, and warm hospitality that is always fulfilled.

1 Essential Information

Before You Go

Visitor Information

Contact the following travel bureaus for a free travel information packet and additional tourist information:

Michigan Travel Bureau, 333 S. Capitol Avenue, Town Center Building, Suite F, Lansing, MI 48933, tel. 517/373–1195 (to speak to a travel representative) or 800/543–2937 (for a free information packet).
Wisconsin Division of Tourism, Box 7606, Madison, WI 53707, tel. 608/266–2161 or 800/ESCAPES in MN, IA, IL, MI, and WI.
Minnesota Office of Tourism, 375 Jackson St., Room 250, St. Paul, MN 55101, tel. 612/296–5029 (to speak to a travel representative) or 800/328–1461 (for a free information packet).

Tour Groups

General-Interest Tours
Maupintour (Box 807, Lawrence, KA 66044, tel. 913/843–1211 or 800/255–4266) offers a Fall Foliage package that tours Minnesota, the Ozarks, Pennsylvania, and New England.
Talmadge Tours (1223 Walnut St., Philadelphia, PA 19107, tel. 215/923–7100) has put together a unique itinerary that starts in Canada and proceeds to Niagara Falls, Lake Michigan, Mackinac Island, and Michigan.

Tips for British Travelers

Tourist Information
Contact the **U.S. Travel and Tourism Administration** (22 Sackville St., London WIX 2EA, England, tel. 01/439–7433) for useful touring tips.

Passports
You will need a valid passport (cost £15) and a U.S. Visitor's Visa that you can get either through your travel agent or by post from the United States Embassy, Visa and Immigration Dept., 5 Upper Grosvenor St., London W1A 2JB, tel. 01/499–3443. The embassy no longer accepts visa applications made by personal callers. No vaccinations are required.

If you decide to visit Canada from Michigan, Wisconsin, or Minnesota, you won't need any additional documentation.

Customs
Visitors 21 or over can take in 200 cigarettes or 50 cigars or three pounds of tobacco; one U.S. quart of alcohol; duty-free gifts to a value of $100. Be careful not to try to take in meat or meat products, seeds, plants, fruits, etc. Avoid illegal drugs like the plague.

Returning to Britain, you may bring home (1) 200 cigarettes or 100 cigarillos or 50 cigars or 250 grams of tobacco; (2) two liters of table wine and, in addition, (a) one liter of alcohol over 22% by volume (most spirits), (b) two liters of alcohol under 22% by volume (fortified or sparkling wine), or (c) two more liters of table wine; (3) 50 grams of perfume and 1/4 liter of toilet water; and (4) other goods up to a value of £32.

Insurance
We recommend that you insure yourself against health and motoring mishaps. **Europ Assistance** (252 High St., Croydon, Surrey CRO 1NF, tel. 01/680–1234) is a firm that offers this service.

It is also wise to take out insurance to cover loss of luggage (but check that this isn't already covered by any existing home-owner's policy you may have). Trip cancellation is another good buy. **The Association of British Insurers** (Aldermary House, Queen St., London EC4N 1TT, tel. 01/248–4477) will give comprehensive advice on all aspects of vacation insurance.

Airfares **British Airways** (Box 10, London-Heathrow Airport, Hounslow, Middlesex TW6 2JA, tel. 01/897–4000); **Northwest Airlines** (49 Albermarle St., London W1X 3FE, tel. 01/629–5353); **Pan Am** (193 Piccadilly, London, tel. 01/409–3377); and **TWA** (214 Oxford St., London W1N 0HA, tel. 01/636–4090) are among the major airlines serving leading cities in Michigan, Wisconsin, and Minnesota. Check out the APEX and other money-saving fares offered by the major airlines: in mid-1988, APEX round-trip fares from London to Detroit cost about £419; to Milwaukee, about £409; and to Minneapolis, about £469. Certain restrictions apply to APEX tickets, mainly length of stay, and you may lose money if you alter your travel plans, but they can be a good value.

We also suggest that you investigate budget flights. Look in the small ads of the newspapers. Some of these cut-rate fares can be extremely difficult to come by, so try to book well in advance. Check that the price quoted is the final price, because extras such as supplements and airport taxes can increase the fare considerably. Last-minute flights to Detroit offered in the small ads cost about £280.

For greater independence, look for fly-drive offers, as these usually are an excellent value for the money, giving you freedom and flexibility. **Northwest Fly-Drive USA** (Box 45, Bexhill-on-Sea, East Sussex TN40 1PY, tel. 0424/224400) offers fly-drive vacations to Detroit from £343 and to Minneapolis from £454; both include seven days free car rental. Pay for your accommodations with hotel vouchers from as little as £24 per night.

Electricity The electrical current in the United States is 110 volts. You should take along an adaptor because American razor and hair-dryer sockets require flat two-prong plugs.

When to Go

For most people, May through October is the favored time to visit Michigan, Wisconsin, and Minnesota. Even then, there is considerable weather difference between north and south in all three states. It is not uncommon in spring, for example, for southern Wisconsin farmers to be plowing their fields while early-season joggers in Minneapolis/St. Paul run beside frozen lakes, and skiers in the Big Snow Country of Upper Michigan are squeezing in a final weekend on the slopes.

Memorial Day traditionally kicks off the travel season in Michigan, Wisconsin, and Minnesota. Seasonal attractions tend to open between May 1 and May 15 in the southern sections of the states, and somewhat later in the north. In the last decade, heavy promotion of the autumn color season has extended the traditional Labor Day closing to early October in the north, and to mid- to late October in the south. One sees more and more autumn travelers in the Great Lakes states, especially older tourists.

Winter is a specialized season here. Cross-country skiing has
become increasingly popular throughout the region, and most
ski resorts are in operation by Thanksgiving or shortly after. A
vast system of snowmobile trails draws thousands to that
sport. Roads throughout the region are well maintained year-
round, so winter travel by car is usually not difficult. But with
the exception of events like St. Paul's Winter Carnival, held
late January to early February, winter in the region is basically
quiet unless you're a winter-sports enthusiast.

Summer still draws the most visitors. The days are warm (they
can be hot from mid-May on); nights are pleasantly cool, and
attractions are going full tilt. Many attractions offer extended
hours in July and August. The fish are biting, the waters are
warm for swimmers and boaters (except the Great Lakes,
which are never warm), and festivals and special events
abound: Traverse City, Michigan's National Cherry Festival in
early June; Milwaukee, Wisconsin's Summerfest in late June
and early July; and Minneapolis, Minnesota's Aquatennial in
July are typical of the events that draw hundreds of thousands
of visitors each summer.

Climate　What follows are the average daily maximum and minimum
temperatures for major cities in Michigan, Wisconsin, and Minnesota.

Detroit	**Jan.**	31F	−1C	**May**	67F	19C	**Sept.**	73F	23C
		19	−7		48	9		55	13
	Feb.	32F	0C	**June**	77F	25C	**Oct.**	60F	16C
		18	−8		58	14		44	7
	Mar.	42F	6C	**July**	82F	28C	**Nov.**	46F	8C
		27	−3		63	17		33	1
	Apr.	55F	13C	**Aug.**	80F	27C	**Dec.**	35F	2C
		37	3		62	17		24	−4

Milwaukee	**Jan.**	31F	−1C	**May**	65F	18C	**Sept.**	72F	22C
		14	−10		45	7		54	12
	Feb.	32F	0C	**June**	76F	24C	**Oct.**	63F	17C
		18	−8		56	13		43	6
	Mar.	40F	4C	**July**	81F	27C	**Nov.**	45F	7C
		25	−4		61	16		31	−1
	Apr.	56F	13C	**Aug.**	81F	27C	**Dec.**	34F	1C
		38	3		61	16		20	−7

Minneapolis	**Jan.**	22F	−6C	**May**	68F	20C	**Sept.**	72F	22C
		6	−14		48	9		52	11
	Feb.	25F	−4C	**June**	77F	25C	**Oct.**	59F	15C
		8	−13		58	14		41	5
	Mar.	38F	3C	**July**	83F	28C	**Nov.**	40F	4C
		22	−6		63	17		26	−3
	Apr.	56F	13C	**Aug.**	80F	27C	**Dec.**	27F	−3C
		36	2		61	16		12	−11

Updated hourly weather information in 235 cities around the
world—180 of them in the United States—is only a phone call
away. Telephone numbers for WeatherTrak in the 12 cities
where the service is available may be obtained by calling

800/247–3282. A taped message will tell you to dial the three-digit access code to any of the 235 destinations. The code is either the area code (in the United States) or the first three letters of the foreign city name. For a list of all access codes send a stamped, self-addressed envelope to Cities, Box 7000, Dallas, TX 75209. For further information, tel. 214/869–3035 or 800/247–3282.

Festivals and Seasonal Events

The following list is a sample of festivals and seasonal happenings throughout Michigan, Wisconsin, and Minnesota. For exact dates and details and more complete listings, contact the department of tourism in each state.

Mid-Jan. The World's Championship Snowmobile Derby, Eagle River, Wisconsin, features nationally famous racers on the half-mile banked ice track. Tel. 715/479–4424.

Late Jan.–early Feb. St. Paul Winter Carnival is a famous spectacle of ice sculptures, entertainment, and parades in Minnesota's St. Paul. Tel. 612/297–6955.

Late Feb. American Birkebeiner cross-country ski races at Hayward, Wisconsin, award points for world championships. Tel. 715/634–5025.

Early Mar. The Milwaukee Sentinel Sports, Boat, and Travel Show in Milwaukee, Wisconsin, previews the coming year in outdoor Wisconsin. Tel. 414/224–2427.

Mid-Mar. An Irish Celebration in St. Paul, Minnesota, includes music, entertainment, and food, following a huge St. Patrick's Day Parade. Tel. 612/224–5891.

Late April–early May. Spring Flower Show has more than a thousand Easter lilies in Milwaukee, Wisconsin's Mitchell Park Conservatory. Tel. 414/649–9800.

Early May. Festival of Nations in Minnesota is three days of food demonstrations, exhibits, and cultural events, involving more than 50 countries, at the St. Paul Civic Center (I.A. O'Shaughnessy Plaza), tel. 612/224–7361.

Late May. On **State Parks Open House Day,** free admission is offered to all Wisconsin state parks and various activities, statewide. Tel. 608/266–2181.

Mid-June. Summerfest at Milwaukee, Wisconsin, is 10 days of jazz, country, and rock music on 10 different stages along the Lake Michigan waterfront. Tel. 414/273–2680.

Late June–early July. International Freedom Festival in Detroit, Michigan, and Windsor, Ontario, is a celebration of freedom and friendship between Canada and the United States that encompasses Canada Day and Independence Day.

Early July. Taste of Minnesota is four days of feasting on food from Minnesota restaurants, plus entertainment and a gigantic fireworks display on the Fourth, at the Minnesota State Capitol Mall in St. Paul.

July. Wisconsin Shakespeare Festival, at the University of Wisconsin–Platteville, is a month of excellent Shakespearean theater productions. Tel. 608/342–1198 or 342–1298.

Early Aug. The EAA Fly-In and Convention, Oshkosh, Wisconsin, features the largest aviation event of its kind with a week of air shows and acres of airplanes. Tel. 414/426–4800.

Early Aug. The Wisconsin State Fair at West Allis, Wisconsin, has 10 days of big-name entertainment, livestock shows, and agricultural displays. Tel. 414/257–8800.

Mid-Aug.–late Sept. Minnesota Renaissance Festival is held on weekends in Shakopee. Tel. 612/445–7361.

Late Aug. Minnesota State Fair is one of America's oldest and largest. It takes place at the Minnesota State Fairgrounds in St. Paul. Tel. 612/642–2200.

Early Sept. Michigan State Fair takes place at Michigan State Fairgrounds in Detroit. Tel. 313/368–1000.

Early Sept. Stroh's Montreux Detroit Jazz Festival lures the legends of jazz to Hart Plaza in downtown Detroit. Tel. 313/259–5400.

Sept. Festival of the Lakes, Madison, Wisconsin, is a week-long celebration of the performing arts, held in even-numbered years. Tel. 608/257–2527, ext. 565.

Month of Sept. Michigan Renaissance Festival is a re-creation of a 16th-century village, plus food and entertainment, during three weekends in Holly. Tel. 313/645–9640.

Mid-Sept. Michigan State Potato Festival is held in Edmore Park. Tel. 517/427–3401.

Early Oct. Autumn Harvest Festival is celebrated at Dearborn's Greenfield Village, Michigan. Tel. 313/271–1620.

Mid-Oct. Twin Cities Marathon runs from downtown Minneapolis to the state capitol area of St. Paul.

Month of Dec. Christmas Past and Present includes ongoing festivities at Greenfield Village in Dearborn, Michigan. Tel. 313/271–1620.

Dec. The Christmas Flower Show, Mitchell Park Conservatory, Milwaukee, Wisconsin, features a traditional display of poinsettias in the show dome. Tel. 414/649–9800.

New Year's Eve. Minneapolis New Year's Eve Party is held on the riverfront. Tel. 612/379–4540.

What to Pack

Pack light because porters and luggage trolleys are hard to find. Luggage allowances on domestic flights vary slightly from airline to airline. Most allow three checked pieces and one carry-on. Some give you the option of two checked and two carry-on. In all cases, check-in luggage cannot weigh more than 70 pounds each or be larger than 62 inches (length + width + height). Carry-on luggage cannot be larger than 45 inches (length + width + height) and must fit under the seat or in the overhead luggage compartment.

Michigan, Wisconsin, and Minnesota have extremely cold, snowy winters. Be certain to pack snow boots or sturdy, warm shoes with a good grip for icy sidewalks. Summers can be hot and humid. The three states are known for their beautiful farmland, woods, and lakes, which are especially appealing in the spring and fall. Take sturdy walking shoes and a lightweight raincoat for walks through the woods in the spring and fall, and sweaters for evenings which turn cool. In the summer, take insect repellent if you plan to be outdoors a lot.

In general, pack for cities in the Great Lakes states as you would for any American city: slightly dressy outfits for elegant restaurants, casual outfits for informal dining. Detroit and Minneapolis/St. Paul, for example, tend to be casual, but you'll need a jacket and tie for the expensive restaurants. For the theaters and concert halls, people tend to wear informal yet conservative clothes.

Cash Machines

Virtually all U.S. banks belong to a network of ATMs (Automatic Teller Machines) that dispense cash 24 hours a day in cities throughout the country. There are some eight major networks in the United States, the largest of which are Cirrus, owned by MasterCard, and Plus, affiliated with Visa. Some banks belong to more than one network. These cards are not issued automatically; you have to ask for them. Cards issued by Visa and MasterCard may also be used in the ATMs, but the fees are usually higher than the fees on bank cards (and there is a daily interest charge on the "loan" even if monthly bills are paid on time). Each network has a toll-free number you can call to locate its machines in a given city. The Cirrus number is 800/424–7787; the Plus number is 800/843–7587. Contact your bank for information on fees and the amount of cash you can withdraw on any given day.

Traveling with Film

If your camera is new, shoot and develop a few rolls before leaving home. Pack some lens tissue and an extra battery for your built-in light meter. Invest about $10 in a skylight filter and screw it onto the front of your lens; it will protect the lens and also reduce haze.

Film doesn't like hot weather. When you're driving in summer, don't store film in the glove compartment or on the shelf under the rear window. Put it behind the front seat on the floor, on the side opposite the exhaust pipe.

On a plane trip, never pack unprocessed film in check-in luggage; if your bags are X-rayed, you can say goodbye to your pictures. Always carry undeveloped film with you through security and ask to have it inspected by hand. (It helps to isolate your film in a plastic bag, ready for quick inspection.) Inspectors at American airports are required by law to honor requests for hand inspection; abroad, you'll have to depend on the kindness of strangers.

The airport scanning machines used in all U.S. airports are safe for anything from five to 500 scans, depending on the speed of your film. The effects are cumulative; you can put the same roll of film through several scans without worry. After five scans, though, you're asking for trouble.

If your film gets fogged and you want an explanation, send it to the National Association of Photographic Manufacturers, 600 Mamaroneck Ave., Harrison, NY 10528. They will try to determine what went wrong. The service is free.

Car Rentals

Michigan Probably no place outside southern Florida and California offers as many rental car options as Detroit, traditional center of the nation's automobile industry. Expect to pay $35–$45 daily for a subcompact, with 75–100 free daily miles and 30¢ per mile thereafter, with most major companies.

Avis (tel. 800/331–1212), **Hertz** (tel. 800/654–3131), **Budget** (tel. 800/527–0700), **National** (tel. 800/328–4567), **American Inter-**

national (tel. 800/527–0202), **Dollar** (tel. 800/421–6868), **Sears** (tel. 800/527–0770) and **Rent-A-Wreck** (tel. 800/221–8282) have airport and downtown Detroit offices. Local and regional discount rental firms include: **Americar** (tel. 313/839–7700, with 14 greater Detroit locations), **McDonald** (tel. 313/326–3600), **American** (tel. 313/259–1440), **Jiffy** (313/352–6600), **Automate** (313/644–1640), **Host** (313/562–5310), **Snappy** (tel. 800/762–7791) and **Rent-A-Beast** (tel. 313/885–6300). Nearby Ann Arbor has the same national companies plus **Econo-Car** (tel. 313/663–2033), **Campus** (tel. 313/761–3768) and **Rent-A-Heap** (tel. 313/287–8888, five locations). Lansing's budget companies include **Rent-A-Heap** (tel. 517/484–7845, 11 locations), **Astro** (tel. 517/323–9200), **Ugly Duckling** (tel. 517/372–7650), and **Discount** (tel. 517/485–4310). Grand Rapids has most major companies plus **V.I.P.** (tel. 616/245–3900), **Ugly Duckling** (tel. 616/698–7070) and **Rent-A-Wreck** (tel. 616/957–2613). Some of the local companies listed above will rent without credit cards and to drivers ages 18–25.

Wisconsin Milwaukee and Madison are the state's two best rental car bargains for variety and price. Expect to pay $30–$40 daily there and $35–$50 daily in cities like Appleton, Green Bay, and Eau Claire, with 100 free miles daily the norm and the unlimited mileage weekly special—usually around $140–$160—the exception.

National (tel. 800/328–4567), **Hertz** (tel. 800/654–3131), **Avis** (tel. 800/331–1212), **Sears** (tel. 800/527–0770), **Budget** (tel. 800/527–0700), **Dollar** (tel. 800/421–6868), **American International** (tel. 800/527–0202), **Thrifty** (tel. 800/367–2277) and **Rent-A-Wreck** (tel. 800/221–8282) have Milwaukee offices; the first four have airport and in-town locations. Lesser-known budget and regional companies, some with lower rates than the biggies, include: **Ajax** (tel. 800/421–0896), **Econo-Car** (tel. 800/228–1000), **Rent-A-Heap** (tel. 414/541–3650), and Wisconsin Car Rental (tel. 414/425–9010). Madison has Budget, Sears, Hertz and Rent-A-Wreck, plus Ajax (see above) and **Rental Wheels** (tel. 608/831–2600). Racine has **Avis** (tel. 800/331–1212) and **American International** (tel. 800/527–0202), plus **Agency** (tel. 800/321–1972) and **All-American** (tel. 414/259–9950).

Minnesota Unlimited mileage specials are worth seeking out in spacious Minnesota, especially since Minneapolis is a natural gateway for attractions outside the state—you might want to follow the historic Mississippi River Road maintained by Minnesota, Wisconsin and Illinois, for example, or drive from Minneapolis out to South Dakota's Black Hills, some 800 miles away. Expect to pay $30–$40 daily in Minneapolis and $35–$45 daily in Duluth and other midsize cities for a subcompact with 75 free miles daily. Occasional unlimited mileage weekly rates average around $150.

All major companies rent out of the Minneapolis/St. Paul airport and some of the following downtown as well: **National** (tel. 800/328–4567; because this is National's headquarters, it often has special promotional rates), **Avis** (tel. 800/331–1212), **Hertz** (tel. 800/654–3131), **Budget** (tel. 800/527–0700), **American International** (tel. 800/527–0202), **Dollar** (tel. 800/421–6868), **Sears** (tel. 800/527–0770) and **Rent-A-Wreck** (tel. 800/221–8282). Regional and local budget and used rental firms include: **Alamo** (tel. 800/327–9633), **Ajax** (tel. 800/367–2529), **Almost New** (tel. 612/535–2933), **Jiffy** (tel. 800/245–4339) and **Premier** (tel. 612/379–0131). Duluth has **Avis** (tel. 800/331–1212), **Hertz** (tel. 800/654–3131), **Budget** (tel. 800/527–0700), **National** (tel. 800/328–4567) and **Sears** (tel. 800/527–0770), with no "cheapie" outfits. National, Hertz, and Avis generally have offices in Minnesota's smaller cities.

It's always best to know a few essentials *before* you arrive at the car rental counter. Find out what the collision damage waiver (CDW, usually an $8–$12 daily surcharge) covers and whether your corporate or personal insurance already covers damage to a rental car (if so, bring a photocopy of the benefits section along). More and more companies are now also holding renters responsible for theft and vandalism damages if they don't buy the CDW; in response, some credit card and insurance companies are extending *their* coverage to rental cars. These include **Dreyfuss Bank Gold** and **Silver MasterCards** (tel. 800/847–9700), **Chase Manhattan Bank Visa** (tel. 800/645–7352), and **Access America** (tel. 800/851–2800). Find out, too, if you must pay for a full tank of gas whether you use it or not; and make sure you get a reservation number.

Traveling with Children

Publications *Family Travel Times* is an 8- to 12-page newsletter published 10 times a year by TWYCH (Travel with Your Children, 80 Eighth Ave., New York, NY 10011, tel. 212/206–0688). A subscription includes access to back issues and twice-weekly opportunities to call in for specific advice. *Great Vacations with Your Kids: The Complete Guide to Family Vacations in the U.S.*, by Dorothy Ann Jordon and Marjorie Adoff Cohen (E.P. Dutton, 2 Park Ave., New York, NY 10016; $9.95), details everything from city vacations to adventure vacations to childcare resources. Another helpful book is *Exploring the Twin Cities with Children* by Elizabeth French (Nodin Press, 525 N. Third St., Minneapolis, MN 55401, tel. 612/333–6300).

Monthly newspapers for parents, filled with events listings, resources, and advice, are available free at such places as libraries, supermarkets, museums. *Minnesota Parent* (100 W. Franklin Ave., Minneapolis, MN 55404, tel. 612/874–1155) covers the Twin Cities and *Metropolitan Parent Magazine* (140 Madison SE, Grand Rapids, MI 49503, tel. 616/459–5577) covers western Michigan. For a small fee, you can usually have an issue sent to you before your trip.

Hotels **The Grand Traverse Resort Village** (Grand Traverse Village, MI 49610-0404, tel. 616/938–2100) has organized children's activities and allows all kids to stay free in a room or condo with two adults.

The following Minnesota resorts welcome families with special children's programs: **Brookside Resort** (HC 05, Box 240, Park Rapids, MN 56470, tel. 218/732–4093), **Grand View Lodge and Tennis Club** (Rte. 6, Box 22, Brainerd, MN 56401, tel. 218/963–2234), **Gunflint Lodge** (Box 100 GT, Grand Marais, MN 55604, tel. 218/388–2294, 800/328–3325), **Ludlow's Island Lodge** (Box 87 MRA, Cook, MN 55732, tel. 218/666–5407), **North Star Lake Resort** (Box 128, Marcell, MN 56657, tel. 218/832–3131).

Home Exchange See *Home Exchanging: A Complete Sourcebook for Travelers at Home or Abroad* by James Dearing (Globe Pequot Press, Box Q, Chester, CT 06412, tel. 800/243–0495; in CT, 800/962–0973).

Getting There On domestic flights, children under 2 not occupying a seat travel free. Various discounts apply to children 2–12. Reserve a seat behind the bulkhead of the plane, which offers more leg room and can usually fit a bassinet (supplied by the airline). At the same time, inquire about special children's meals or snacks, offered by most airlines. (See "TWYCH's Airline Guide," in the Feb. 1988 issue of *Family Travel Times* [see above], for a rundown on the services offered by 46 airlines.) Ask the airline in advance if you can bring aboard your child's car seat. (For the booklet *Child/Infant Safety Seats Acceptable for Use in Aircraft,* write the Community and Consumer Liaison Division, APA–400 Federal Aviation Administration, Washington, DC 20591, tel. 202/267–3479.)

Baby-sitting Services Make child-care arrangements with the hotel concierge or housekeeper.

Hints for Disabled Travelers

The **Information Center for Individuals with Disabilities** (20 Park Plaza, Room 330, Boston, MA 02116, tel. 617/727–5540) offers useful problem-solving assistance, including lists of travel agents that specialize in tours for the disabled.

Moss Rehabilitation Hospital Travel Information Service (12th St. and Taber Rd., Philadelphia, PA 19141, tel. 215/329–5715) provides information on tourist sights, transportation, and accommodations in destinations around the world. The fee is $5 for each destination. Allow one month for delivery.

Mobility International (Box 3551, Eugene, OR 97403, tel. 503/343–1284) has information on accommodations, organized study, and other resources around the world.

The **Society for the Advancement of Travel for the Handicapped** (26 Court St., Brooklyn, NY 11242, tel. 718/858–5483) offers access information. Annual membership costs $40, or $25 for senior travelers and students. Send $1 and a stamped, self-addressed envelope.

The Itinerary (Box 1084, Bayonne, NJ 07002, tel. 201/858–3400) is a bimonthly travel magazine for the disabled.

Greyhound/Trailways (tel. 800/531–5332) will carry a disabled person and companion for the price of a single fare. **Amtrak** (tel. 800/USA–RAIL) requests 24-hour notice to provide redcap service, special seats, and a 25% discount.

Hints for Older Travelers

The **American Association of Retired Persons** (AARP, 1909 K St. NW, Washington, DC 20049, tel. 202/662–4850) has two programs for independent travelers: (1) The Purchase Privilege Program offers discounts on hotels, airfare, car rentals, and sightseeing; and (2) The AARP Motoring Plan offers emergency aid and trip routing information for an annual fee of $29.95 per couple. The AARP also arranges group tours, including apartment living in Europe, through two companies: Olson-Travelworld (5855 Green Valley Circle, Culver City, CA

90230, tel. 800/227–7737) and RFD, Inc. (4401 W. 110th St., Overland Park, KS 66211, tel. 800/448–7010). AARP members must be 50 or older. Annual dues are $5 per person or couple.

When using an AARP or other identification card, ask for a reduced hotel rate at the time you make your reservation, not when you check out. At restaurants, show your card to the maître d' before you're seated, since discounts may be limited to certain set menus, days, or hours. When renting a car, remember that economy cars, priced at promotional rates, may cost less than cars that are available with your ID card.

Elderhostel (80 Boylston St., Suite 400, Boston, MA 02116, tel. 617/426–7788) is an innovative 13-year-old program for people 60 and older. Participants live in dorms on some 1,200 campuses around the world. Mornings are devoted to lectures and seminars, afternoons to sightseeing and field trips. The all-inclusive fee for trips of two to three weeks, including room, board, tuition, and round-trip transportation, is $1,700–$3,200.

Travel Industry and Disabled Exchange (TIDE, 5435 Donna Ave., Tarzana, CA 91356, tel. 818/343–6339) is an industry-based organization with a $15 per person annual membership fee. Members receive a quarterly newsletter and information on travel agencies and tours.

National Council of Senior Citizens (925 15th St. NW, Washington, DC 20005, tel. 202/347–8800) is a nonprofit advocacy group with some 4,000 local clubs across the country. Annual membership is $10 per person or $14 per couple. Members receive a monthly newspaper with travel information and an ID card for reduced rates on hotels and car rentals.

Mature Outlook (Box 1205, Glenview, IL 60025, tel. 800/336–6330), a subsidiary of Sears, Roebuck & Co., is a travel club for people over 50, with hotel and motel discounts and a bimonthly newsletter. Annual membership is $7.50 per couple. Instant membership is available at participating Holiday Inns.

Travel Tips for Senior Citizens (U.S. Dept. of State Publication 8970, revised Sept. 1987) is available for $1 from the Superintendent of Documents, U.S. Government Printing Office, Washington, DC 20402.

Golden Age Passport is a free lifetime pass to all parks, monuments, and recreation areas run by the federal government. People over 62 should pick them up in person at any national park that charges admission. A driver's license or other proof of age is required.

Further Reading

Historical novels set in the area include *The Big Knives* by Bruce Lancaster, which takes place during the Revolutionary War; *Spoon* by John Christgan, which describes the Sioux-Santee uprising in 1862; and Ida Fuller's *The Loon Feather*, which is set in the 1880s.

Arthur Hailey's *Wheels* looks at the auto industry. Small-town, middle-American life is examined in Sinclair Lewis's *Main Street* and in Garrison Keillor's stories about an imaginary Minnesota town, *Lake Wobegon Days*.

Other suggested titles are: Judith Guest's *Second Heaven*, Marge Piercy's *Braided Lives, Northern Lights* by Tim O'Brien, and Glenway Wescott's *The Grandmothers*.

Arriving and Departing

By Car

The auto is still king in the Great Lakes states, and unless your trip is extremely limited in scope, you will need a car to get around. Michigan, Wisconsin, and Minnesota all have extensive networks of good roads. Roads tend to be less numerous in the northern regions, and secondary roads are often gravel or dirt, especially in northern Michigan and Minnesota. Getting off the main routes and touring some of the smaller communities is most rewarding and will show you scenes many travelers in the region miss. Wisconsin has charted and marked 32 back roads as Rustic Roads. For a map and more information, contact **Rustic Roads Board, Wisconsin Dept. of Transportation,** Box 7913, Madison, WI 53707, tel. 608/266–0639.

Circle tours of Lake Michigan and Lake Superior have been mapped and marked. The routes often leave main highways and wind through lakeshore communities and scenic areas. The Lake Michigan Circle will take you through Wisconsin, Upper and Lower Michigan, and small sections of Illinois and Indiana. The Lake Superior Circle Route takes you through Michigan's Upper Peninsula, northern Wisconsin, northeastern Minnesota, and Ontario, Canada, and is 1,300 miles long. The route is crowded with fishermen and campers during the summer. Both Circle Routes are marked with prominent green-and-white signs.

The speed limit is 55 mph in Michigan, Wisconsin, and Minnesota. Interstate speed limits in all three states are 65 mph in rural areas, 55 mph in urban areas. The minimum driving age in all three states is 16.

The AAA Emergency Road Service number is listed in local telephone directory white pages. If no number is listed, tel. 800/336–HELP.

By Train

Amtrak (tel. 800/872–7245) serves major cities and larger communities in all three states, but service is somewhat limited. Call for current schedule information.

By Plane

Air service into Detroit, Milwaukee, and Minneapolis/St. Paul is good and is provided by a large number of carriers. Cities like Grand Rapids, Madison, and Duluth are fairly easy to reach by air, but once there you will need a car to get around. Regional carriers serve most areas of all three states, but touring the Great Lakes states by air is difficult unless your stay is limited to the principal cities.

Smoking If smoking bothers you, ask for a seat in the nonsmoking section. If the airline tells you there are no nonsmoking seats, insist on one: FAA regulations require U.S. airlines to find seats for all nonsmokers.

Carry-on Luggage New rules have been in effect since January 1, 1988, on U.S. airlines in regards to carry-on luggage. The model for these new rules was agreed to by the airlines in December 1987 and then circulated by the Air Transport Association with the understanding that each airline would present its own version.

Under the model, passengers are limited to two carry-on bags. For a bag you wish to store under the seat, the maximum dimensions are 9″ × 14″ × 22″, a total of 45″. For bags that can be hung in a closet or on a luggage rack, the maximum dimensions are 4″ × 23″ × 45″, a total of 72″. For bags you wish to store in an overhead bin, the maximum dimensions are 10″ × 14″ × 36″, a total of 60″. Your two carry-ons must each fit one of these sets of dimensions, and any item that exceeds the specified dimensions will generally be rejected as a carry-on and handled as checked baggage. Keep in mind that an airline can adapt these rules to circumstances; don't be surprised if you are allowed only one carry-on bag on an especially crowded flight.

In addition to the two carry-ons, the rules list eight items that may also be carried aboard: a handbag (pocketbook or purse), an overcoat or wrap, an umbrella, a camera, a reasonable amount of reading material, an infant bag, an infant/child safety seat, and crutches, cane, braces, or other prosthetic device upon which the passenger is dependent.

Note that these regulations are for U.S. airlines only. Foreign airlines generally allow one piece of carry-on luggage in tourist class, in addition to handbags and bags filled with duty-free goods. Passengers in first and business class are also allowed to carry on one garment bag. It is best to check with your airline in advance to learn its exact rules regarding carry-on luggage.

Checked Luggage U.S. airlines allow passengers to check in two suitcases whose total dimensions (length + width + height) do not exceed 60″. There are no weight restrictions on these bags.

Rules governing foreign airlines vary from airline to airline, so check with your travel agent or the airline itself before you go. All airlines allow passengers to check two bags. In general, expect the weight restriction on the two bags to be not more than 70 lbs. each, and the size restriction to be 62″ total dimensions on the first bag and 55″ total dimensions on the second bag.

Lost Luggage Airlines are responsible for lost or damaged property only up to $1,250 per passenger on domestic flights; $9.07 per pound (or $20 per kilo) for checked baggage on international flights, and up to $400 per passenger for unchecked baggage on international flights. When you carry valuables, either take them with you on the airplane or purchase additional insurance for lost luggage. Some airlines will issue additional luggage insurance when you check in, but many do not. American Airlines is one that does. Its additional insurance is only for domestic flights or flights to Canada; rates are $1 for every $100 valuation, with a maximum of $400 valuation per passenger. Hand luggage is not included.

Insurance for lost, damaged, or stolen luggage is available through travel agents or directly through various insurance companies. Two that issue luggage insurance are Tele-Trip, a subsidiary of Mutual of Omaha, and The Travelers Insurance Co.

Tele-Trip (tel. 800/228–9792) operates sales booths at airports, and also issues insurance through travel agents. Tele-Trip will insure checked luggage for up to 180 days and for $500 to $3,000 valuation. For 1–3 days, the rate for a $500 valuation is $8.25; for 180 days, $100. **The Travelers Insurance Co.** will insure checked or hand luggage for $500 to $2,000 valuation per person, for a maximum of 180 days. For 1-5 days, the rates for a $500 valuation are $10; for 180 days, $85. For more information, write The Travelers Insurance Co., Ticket and Travel Dept., 1 Tower Sq., Hartford, CN 06183. The two companies offer the same rates on domestic and international flights.

Consult the travel pages of your Sunday newspaper for the names of other companies that insure luggage. Before you travel, itemize the contents of each bag in case you need to file an insurance claim. Be certain to put your home address on each piece of luggage, including carry-on bags. If your luggage is stolen and later recovered, the airline must deliver the luggage to your home free of charge.

By Bus

Greyhound (tel. 800/528–0447) and **Trailways** (tel. 800/242–2935) are the two major bus lines serving the region. There are smaller intrastate lines connecting many smaller cities and towns in all three states.

By Bike

Touring by bicycle has become popular in recent years. **Bike Wisconsin, Ltd.** (Box 9309, Madison, WI 53715, tel. 608/238–BIKE) offers guided tours to scenic parts of Wisconsin. Meals and accommodations are included in the tour price.

SpokeSongs (130 Fir St., Mahtomedi, MN 55155, tel. 612/429–2877) offers biking tours of Minnesota for casual and experienced cyclists alike. The trips range from weekends to five days in length.

Staying in the Great Lakes States

Shopping

Late summer and early autumn brings good buys in farm-fresh produce. You'll find roadside produce stands in smaller communities and rural areas in all three states. Look for especially good buys on fresh fruit in southwestern Michigan and tart cherries in the Grand Traverse region. The orchards of Bayfield, Wisconsin, produce beautiful apples. Door County fruit-growers offer bargains on apples and tart cherries. Jams, jellies, maple syrup, sweet corn, pumpkins, and squash are offered seasonally in all three states.

Michigan offers two brochures on fruit and produce in the southwestern region of the state—*Pick Michigan* and *A Cook's*

Tour. For a free copy contact Michigan Travel Bureau (Box 30226, Lansing, MI 48909, tel. 800/543–2937).

For a free copy of the *Wisconsin Farm Market Shopping Guide* write Wisconsin Farm Market Association (7010 Mineral Point Rd., Box 5550, Madison, WI 53705).

The booklet *Take Something Home From Wisconsin* contains a directory of roadside markets, farm markets, and maple syrup and honey producers. For a free copy write Wisconsin Department of Agriculture (Marketing Division, Dept. S, Box 8911, Madison, WI 53708).

There are bargains in Native American art and crafts, if you shop carefully. Best bets are art museum gift shops or Indian reservation outlets. Woolens from mills in Michigan, Wisconsin, and Minnesota mills are sometimes found at bargain prices.

Beaches

With thousands of lakes and rivers, there are no shortages of beaches in the Great Lakes states. In resort areas, many beaches are private. Remember the waters of the Great Lakes are cold and seldom reach 70 degrees, even late in the summer. Except for the very shallowest of bays, Lake Superior waters are dangerously cold; even with air temperatures in the 90s, it is usually too cold for swimming.

In Michigan, **P.J. Hoffmaster State Park** at Muskegon has a fine beach on Lake Michigan. **Tawas Point State Park** at East Tawas offers a two-mile-long sand beach on Lake Huron. The community of **Grand Marais,** on Lake Superior in Michigan's Upper Peninsula, has a choice sand beach.

Newport State Park, at the tip of Wisconsin's Door Peninsula, has a fine beach on Lake Michigan. **Bradford Beach** in Milwaukee is one of the better urban beaches on Lake Michigan.

The sand beaches on Duluth's **Minnesota Point** are interesting because of their location in the harbor area. Inland, Minnesota's **Itasca State Park,** at Lake Itasca, offers swimming in the lake where the Mississippi River rises, and **Thomas Beach,** on Lake Calhoun in Minneapolis, is one of the Twin Cities' finest. **Geneva Lake,** at Lake Geneva in far southern Wisconsin, has several good swimming beaches. Michigan's **Young State Park,** at Boyne City, has one of the state's finest beaches on Lake Charlevoix.

Participant Sports

Biking There are tens of thousands of miles of back roads for biking in Michigan, Wisconsin, and Minnesota, plus specifically marked bicycle trails. For information on bike touring events in Michigan, contact Michigan Bicycle Touring, Inc., 3512 Red School Rd., Kingsley, MI 49649, tel. 616/263–5885.

The *Wisconsin Bicycle Escape Guide* consists of two maps that outline over 10,000 miles of recommended roads. It is available from the Wisconsin Division of Tourism (Box 7606, Madison, WI 53707, tel. 800/ESCAPES).

The brochure *Explore Minnesota Biking* is available from the Minnesota Office of Tourism (375 Jackson St., 250 Skyway Level, St. Paul, MN 55101, tel. 800/328–1461).

Canoeing The Upper Great Lakes offer waters for every level of canoeists' skills. In Wisconsin, the Wisconsin River is a favorite, especially in the lower third where there are no portages. A list of places where you can rent a canoe is included in the *Wisconsin Attractions & Recreation Guide*, available free from Wisconsin Department of Tourism Development (Box 7606, Madison, WI 53707, tel. 608/266–2161 or 800/372–2737 in Wisconsin and neighboring states).

The Au Sable, Kalamazoo, and Pere Marquette are among the many popular canoeing rivers in Michigan. A free *Michigan Canoeing Directory* is available from Recreational Canoeing Association (Box 926, Montague, MI 49437).

The Boundary Waters Canoe Area is a favorite with canoeists in Minnesota. Two brochures, *Canoe Outfitters* and *Canoeing, Hiking, and Backpacking*, are available from the Minnesota Office of Tourism (375 Jackson St., 250 Skyway Level, St. Paul, MN 55101, tel. 800/328–1461).

Fishing Fishing is a big-league sport in the Upper Great Lakes, whether you're wetting a line in a backwoods stream or trolling for lake trout and salmon on one of the big lakes. Fishing is good throughout all three states but many a vacation is built around going "up north" after the big ones. License fees, fishing seasons, and regulations vary from state to state. For additional information contact Department of Natural Resources, Information Services Center (Box 30028, Lansing, MI 48909, tel. 517/373–1220), Wisconsin Department of Natural Resources (Box 7921, Madison, WI 53707, tel. 608/266–2105), DNR Information Center (500 Lafayette Rd., Box 40, St. Paul, MN 55155, tel. 612/297–3000).

For a free copy of the 64-page *Michigan Charterbook* listing charter-boat operators throughout the state, contact Michigan Travel Bureau (Box 30226, Lansing, MI 40909, tel. 800/543–2937).

A packet of Minnesota fishing information, including a state fishing waters map, is available free from the Minnesota Office of Tourism (375 Jackson St., 250 Skyway Level, St. Paul, MN 55101, tel. 800/328–1461).

Golf There are more courses (565 at last count) in Michigan than in any other state, and Michigan is nicknamed the "Golf Coast" because of the number and quality of its public courses. But golf courses abound throughout the Great Lakes states, and you'll find courses designed by such famous names as Jack Nicklaus, Arnold Palmer, and Robert Trent Jones in all three states.

For a free copy of the 96-page *Golf in Michigan*, contact Michigan Travel Bureau (Box 30226, Lansing, MI 48909, tel. 800/543–2937).

For the *Wisconsin Golf Course List*, send a stamped, self-addressed # 10 envelope to Milwaukee Journal Travel Bureau (Box 661, Milwaukee, WI 53201).

Hiking Nearly every state park in Michigan, Wisconsin, and Minnesota offers hiking, walking, or nature trails; a favorite with wilderness backpackers is **Porcupine Mountains State Park,** on Lake Superior, in the western Upper Peninsula of Michigan. The park has 85 miles of trails. All three states have bicycle, skiing, and snowmobile trails that are used by hikers. Wisconsin's **Elroy-Sparta Trail** is on a former railroad right-of-way and passes through several tunnels. The **Minnesota Trailer Explorers Club** will make you a member (free) and send free information packets on hiking. Contact Trail Explorers Club (DNR Information Center, Box 40, 500 Lafayette Rd., St. Paul, MN 55155, tel. 612/297–3000).

Hunting Whitetail deer, small game, pheasant, and waterfowl are abundant in the Great Lakes states, and all three states have vast areas of public hunting grounds. The autumn deer season sees hundreds of thousands of hunters in the woods in the three states, and draws hunters from throughout the Midwest. License fees, seasons, and hunting regulations vary from state to state. For additional information contact Department of Natural Resources, Information Services Center (Box 30028, Lansing, MI 48909, tel. 517/373–1220), Wisconsin Department of Natural Resources (Box 7921, Madison, WI 53707, tel. 608/266–2105), DNR Information Center (500 Lafayette Rd., Box 40, St. Paul, MN 55155, tel. 612/297–3000).

Skiing The Big Snow Country of northeastern Wisconsin and western Upper Michigan offers some of the finest skiing in the Midwest. There is good skiing throughout all three states, with a wide assortment of facilities that range from single hills with rope tows and simple warming huts to plush resorts offering dining, lodging, and a host of amenities, ski-related and otherwise. Thousands of miles of cross-country ski trails are also available in the region—in city parks, golf courses, and arboretums, state parks, and on state ski trails.

The *Michigan Winter Travel Planner* has a list of both downhill and cross-country ski areas. For a free copy contact Michigan Travel Bureau (Box 30226, Lansing, MI 48909, tel. 800/543–2937).

The 48-page *Wisconsin Fall and Winter Recreation Guide* lists the state's downhill and cross-country ski areas and is free from Wisconsin Department of Tourism Development (Box 7606, Madison, WI 53707, tel. 608/266–2161, or 800/372–2737 in Wisconsin and neighboring states).

Two ski booklets, *Explore Minnesota Skiing* (alpine), and *Explore Minnesota on Skis, A Guide to Cross Country Ski Trails,* are available free from Minnesota Office of Tourism (375 Jackson St., 250 Skyway Level, St. Paul, MN 55101, tel. 800/328–1461).

Tennis While tennis is not a major sport in the Great Lakes states, you'll find courts in parks in most communities. Large resorts often have courts for their guests, and there are indoor courts in some of the larger cities.

State and National Parks

State Parks Michigan has 94 state parks located in all parts of the state, in-
Michigan cluding 23 in the Upper Peninsula, where a number feature spectacular waterfalls. Camping is allowed in 78 parks, and there are more than 14,000 campsites where you can pitch a

tent or park your RV. Facilities vary from modern sites with electricity, flush toilets, and showers, to rustic with no electricity and outdoor privies. At 14 parks, including **Brimley,** on Lake Superior's Whitefish Bay, you may rent a tent already set up on a lot and equipped with two cots and two sleeping pads. Thirteen other parks, including **Porcupine Mountains,** on Lake Superior, and **J. W. Wells,** on the western shore of Lake Michigan, have more than 60 cabins available to rent. They are rustic, with single beds or bunks with mattresses, and wood stoves for heat. There are outside hand pumps for water and vault toilets. Reservations must be made well in advance at individual parks. Campgrounds are open year-round, although facilities may be reduced November 1–May 1.

Many parks have interpretive programs and exhibits; **Fort Michlimackinac, Fort Mackinac,** and **Fort Wilkins** contain historic, reconstructed forts. **Fayette State Park** has a ghost town.

Some parks do not allow alcohol and others do not allow visitors in the campgrounds. Regulations and recreation rules are posted at all state parks. A motor vehicle permit, available at each park entrance, is required for admission. The cost is $2 daily, or $10 for an annual permit. Camping fees vary. For additional information contact **Michigan Travel Bureau** (Box 30226, Lansing, MI 48909, tel. 800/543–2937).

Wisconsin Wisconsin's State Park system includes 52 parks, 9 state forests, and 12 state trails. Camping is allowed in 36 state parks and 9 state forests. Facilities range from sites with electricity, flush toilets, and showers, to sites with no electricity and pit toilets. A number of Wisconsin parks get heavy use, especially from Illinois visitors, and **Devil's Lake, Governor Dodge, Peninsula,** and the **Kettle Moraine State Forest** are usually crowded. Campground reservations must be made well in advance. For alternatives try **Blue Mound, Mirror Lake, Potawatomi,** and **Point Beach State Forest.** In the north, **Copper Falls** and **Pattison** have outstanding waterfalls. **Perrot** (Pa-ROW) and **Wyalusing** offer great Mississippi River scenery, and **Kohler-Andre** fronts Lake Michigan. **First Capitol** is the site of Wisconsin's first territorial capital, when the Wisconsin Territory included all of present-day Wisconsin, Iowa, Minnesota, and parts of the Dakotas.

In Wisconsin a vehicle permit is required for admission: the daily fee is $3.50 for state residents, $6 for nonresidents; the annual fee is $14 for residents, $30 for nonresidents. Camping fees vary. For additional information contact **Wisconsin Department of Natural Resources** (Bureau of Parks and Recreation, Box 7921, Madison, WI 53703, tel. 608/266–2181).

Minnesota Minnesota has 64 state parks, with 51 offering camping facilities which vary from modern, with electricity, flush toilets, and showers, to primitive sites with no electricity and pit toilets. Campsites may be reserved; all parks are open year-round. Most parks have a variety of interpretive programs during the summer months, ranging from guided walks and campfire talks to natural-craft programs and guest speakers. Eight parks, including **Fort Snelling** and **Itasca,** have interpretive programs year-round. **Tower Soudan,** in the iron range county, offers guided tours of the oldest and deepest underground iron mine in the country. **Split Rock Lighthouse,** on the Lake Superior shore, has tours of a historic lighthouse, and

Charles A. Lindbergh contains the boyhood home of the famous aviator; the Mississippi River rises in Lake Itasca, and there are spectacular waterfalls at Gooseberry Falls and Temperance River (*see* Chapter 4).

A daily vehicle admission of $3.50 is charged to enter a Minnesota state park; the annual vehicle permit is $16. For additional information contact **DNR Information Center** (500 Lafayette Rd., Box 40, St. Paul, MN 55155, tel. 612/297–3000).

National Parks   **Isle Royale National Park,** 48 miles off the Michigan coast in Lake Superior, is a wilderness park and can be reached by ferry from Houghton or Copper Harbor, Michigan, or by seaplane from Houghton.

Voyageurs National Park, in far northern Minnesota near International Falls, has 30 major lakes and is part of the watery highway that makes up Minnesota's northeastern border with Canada.

Sleeping Bear Dunes National Lakeshore lies along 33 miles of Lower Michigan's Lake Michigan shore and includes the Manitou Islands. The 71,000-acre preserve has the highest sand dunes outside the Sahara.

Pictured Rocks National Lakeshore in the Upper Peninsula extends 40 miles along the Lake Superior shore between Munising and Grand Marais.

Apostle Islands National Lakeshore takes in a portion of Wisconsin's Bayfield Peninsula shoreline and 20 of the 22 Apostle Islands that lie offshore. Primitive camping and hiking are allowed on most of the islands.

In addition, the **Hiawatha, Huron, Manistee,** and **Ottawa National Forests** in Michigan, the **Chequamegon** and **Nicolet** in Wisconsin, and the **Chippewa** and **Superior National Forests** in Minnesota offer millions of acres for backcountry hiking, primitive camping, fishing, canoeing, and skiing. For more information contact **Chippewa National Forest** (Supervisor's Office, Cass Lake, MN 56633), **Superior National Forest** (Box 338, Duluth, MN 55804); for forests in Michigan and Wisconsin, **U.S. Forest Service** (Eastern Region, 310 W. Wisconsin Ave., Suite 500, Milwaukee, WI 53203, tel. 414/291–3693).

Dining

People in the Great Lakes states like to eat—perhaps it's what gets them through those cold, snowy winters. Dining is more formal in the larger cities, and quite casual in outlying regions of the three states.

Look for fish dishes everywhere on the lakeshore. Locally caught whitefish and trout are specialties. Fish boils are a specialty in Wisconsin's Door County. Tender chunks of whitefish are boiled with salt and onions in a caldron over an open fire, then served steaming hot with boiled potatoes, homemade bread, and cherry pie for dessert. In Wisconsin, the Friday-night fish fry is a ritual, and you'll have to search to find a restaurant that doesn't offer one. Cod and haddock are the mainstays, with local variations.

The German influence is strong, especially in Milwaukee and New Glarus, Wisconsin; Frankenmuth, Michigan; and New Ulm, Minnesota. You might want to try sauerbraten or Wiener schnitzel. In Norwegian enclaves, *lefse* (a type of rolled pastry) and *lutefisk* (a boiled fish dish) are popular, especially around the holidays.

Detroit, Milwaukee, and Minneapolis/St. Paul have large numbers of ethnic groups in their populations, and you can find specialties from virtually every region of the world.

Steak, prime rib, and seafood are the core of menus throughout the Great Lakes states, both in the cities and in the rural areas. As you drive through the countryside, keep an eye peeled for rural steak houses and supper clubs in the woods, especially in the northern sections of the region. A crowd often means good food, and lots of it.

The cost of dining varies widely throughout the three states. Costs are higher in the larger cities, but you can find large numbers of good inexpensive and moderately priced urban restaurants.

The restaurant price categories used throughout this book are based on the average cost of a three-course dinner (à la carte) for one person, food alone, not including beverages, tax, and tip.

Lodging

Accommodations vary widely in the Great Lakes states. In general, rooms are more expensive in the larger cities than in rural areas, but not always. You'll find some first-class facilities in rural areas, and there are bargain lodgings to be found in the cities. The old adage, you pay for what you get, holds true. More and more hotels and motels are offering nonsmoking rooms.

Michigan offers the following accommodation booklets: *Michigan Guide to Hotels and Motels; Michigan's Bed and Breakfast and Historic Inns;* and *Michigan Guide to Cabins and Cottages.* Contact Michigan Travel Bureau, Box 30226, Lansing, MI 48909, tel. 800/543–2937.

For a list of accommodations in Wisconsin, send $2 to Wisconsin Innkeepers Association (509 W. Wisconsin Ave., Suite 619, Milwaukee, WI 53203).

Minnesota offers the following free brochures on accommodations: *Explore Minnesota Hotels; Explore Minnesota Hotel/ Motor Hotels; Bed and Breakfast/Historic Inns Guide; Explore Minnesota Resorts;* and *Minnesota Campgrounds.* Contact Minnesota Office of Tourism, 375 Jackson St., 250 Skyway Level, St. Paul, MN 55101, tel. 800/328–1461.

Hotels Most lodging downtown in the larger cities is available in hotels, and hotels are becoming popular with travelers in some of the smaller cities, too. Many larger hotels offer numerous amenities, including restaurants and dining rooms, cocktail lounges, entertainment, swimming pools, exercise equipment, and even shopping. Accommodation packages—for weekend getaways, local sports and cultural events, or other reasons— are becoming popular with hotel operators and patrons. Check with individual hotels about package possibilities.

Motels Motels are still the mainstay for people who travel by car. The simplicity of the "yes-no" vacancy sign out front, the car park at the door, and the ease of checking in and out has great appeal for many, especially those traveling with children. Facilities vary widely, from no frills, offering little more than a bed and shower, to plush accommodations with indoor pools, exercise facilities, dining rooms, cocktail lounges, and entertainment. While motel rooms are generally priced lower than hotels, large motels in the bigger cities charge about the same as hotels with equal facilities.

Inns While both hotels and motels use the word "inn" in their names, true inns are smaller than hotels, with about eight to 20 rooms. Many are restored buildings, often with historical significance. Breakfast is often included in the price of the room, but not always. In many inns, some rooms have shared baths. Service at an inn is usually much more personal than at a motel or hotel.

Guide to the Recommended Country Inns of the Midwest, by Bob Puhala (Globe Pequot Press; $9.95), evaluates 152 inns in the Midwest, including 63 in the Great Lakes states.

Bed-and-Breakfast B&Bs are located in private homes where the owners share their home and strive to make you feel like a guest of the family. They are small, generally from two to five rooms, and often have shared baths. Breakfast is included in the price of the room.

Bed and Breakfast, Inns, Homes, and Little Out of the Way Places in Wisconsin (CJB Enterprises, 458 Glenway St., Madison, WI 53711; $5) lists 79 such establishments.

Room at the Inn—Wisconsin (Down to Earth Publications, 1426 Sheldon, St. Paul, MN 55108, tel. 612/644–3047; $11.95) lists 86 B&Bs and inns.

Resorts From large to small, and plush to plain, there are thousands of resorts in the Great Lakes states. Bear in mind, "resort" to most residents of the region means housekeeping cabins or cottages on a lake "up north." Facilities usually include a boat with a cottage/cabin, a beach area, a playground for the kids, and a central lodge building with games and a bar. There may be some organized activities (evening campfires or a weekly cookout for all the guests), but fishing is the prime activity. The resorts are fairly small, from five to 15 units, family oriented, and often the same families return to the same resort year after year. Most often these smaller resorts close during the winter or keep only a few cottages/cabins open for snowmobilers and skiers.

The Great Lakes states have their share of big, plush, pricey resorts as well. The orientation may still be toward fishing, especially in the northern regions, but facilities may also include exercise facilities, pools, saunas, golf, tennis, skiing, bicycling, restaurants, lounges, and big-name entertainment. Even these more expensive resorts tend to be fairly informal.

Camping Camping is a reasonably inexpensive way to tour the Great Lakes states if you don't mind the occasional bouts with bugs and bad weather. State parks are among the best camping bets in all three states, in terms of campground facilities, park interpretive programs, and scenery. (*See* State Parks section, above.) In addition, there is a host of private campgrounds throughout the region, many of which offer laundry facilities, showers, flush toilets, swimming pools, game rooms, and organized activities for the youngsters. Campers are among the friendliest of travelers and are often willing to share travel tips and campground information.

For a free copy of the *Michigan Campground Directory*, which lists private campgrounds and camping sites in local, county, and state parks and forests, write Michigan Association of Campground Owners (Box 3384, Ann Arbor, MI 48106-3384).

A booklet on private campgrounds in Wisconsin is available for $1 from Wisconsin Association of Campground Owners (Box 1770, Eau Claire, WI 54702).

2 Portraits of Michigan Wisconsin Minnesota

A Minnesota Childhood

by Shirley Schoonover

Born in Biwabik, Minnesota, in the Iron Range country, novelist Shirley Schoonover recalls her ethnic Finnish upbringing in the 1940s.

I was born on a small farm that scrabbled and sprawled along the long lively road to Aurora, that brawling, Saturday night town. The ore-red road cut like a wound through the black wood of northern Minnesota, my black wood where mysterious gods hooted and squalled, the black wood that edged our farm. I'd follow the farm dogs down rabbit trails and around fallen trees where bears were sure to be lurking, those sullen bears, scruffy and baggy at the knees, foul-breathed, looking boozy, swearing bitterly when startled out of a nap. The black wood, where even in highest summer there'd be snow sulking in the knee-deep moss, and ice glittering within the moss so that a child could freeze her legs to the bone in July and throw snowballs at the dogs who'd blink reproachfully and nip off for home. The black wood, ominous with those big pawed bears, haunted by dawn gray owls who spat up mouse bones in furry cuds; the black wood with its old tall trees and many secret places and green halls where deer and unicorn grazed and gazed and the rare doves would make a pale lament. And I, brash and sassy, innocent as an egg, tough as rawhide, would yell, "Hello!" and the echo rang until I wished I hadn't said it at all because it roused ghosts and the loon whose voice stopped the spit in my throat and made my knobby knees leap high and wide for home.

The memories of childhood have no order at all but come lilting and spilling like the snows of all those winters. The snows of my childhood came shaking down the sky, mute thunderstorms that shawled the trees and capped the fence posts. Snowstorms that howled and nagged at the windows and drove the smoke back down the chimneys. Our snows made castles of haystacks and, one year, a turret on the outhouse. Our snows made royalty of us all, for we had crystal hanging from the eaves and frost-brocaded windows, not to mention the icy lace on our lashes and brows.

If there were snows to remember, there were the dazzling nights when your breath crisped inside your nostrils and the moon had blazing rings around it. Such clear nights that the stars sprang up at the edges of the pasture. And the Northern Lights spangled in silent fireworks all across the sky. Those cold clear nights so still that if you sang while carrying firewood, the man three farms away could hear you and yodel back.

Out of the clutter of memory comes the recollection of how we Finns fought the long winters: the sauna. If we didn't heat our own sauna, we'd wallow through the snow to someone else's sauna. Saturday nights and fifty below zero, we'd bundle our clean clothes together and be off to Aunt Martha's or Aunt Anna's, there to mingle and joke in the blustery, hot little kitchen as the children found each other and started to scrap under the

Abridged from a chapter of Growing Up in Minnesota: Ten Writers Remember Their Childhoods, *edited by Chester G. Anderson, The University of Minnesota Press.*

table or under the feet of the red-faced fathers and the knitting mothers. We'd come in from the cold and have our coats, scarves, and mittens snatched away from us and be sent to behave ourselves, we uncorked, unruly children. The adults would sort themselves out for coffee and a chat before the ritual sauna began. And it seemed that just when we brawling brats would get a good fight going, that was when a mother would appear and haul the little girls off, usually by an ear, to the sauna where we'd be peeled like onions and stuck into the steam room to stew until we were scoured and scrubbed, our ears turned inside out, our necks, knees, and elbows scraped. Then we were rinsed with cold water and what was left of our skin was sanded off with the rough towels. A child had no privacy in the sauna. The slightest sniffle, the gentlest clearing of the throat, hinting at a cold (much wished for on Monday mornings!) exposed you. Your mouth was pried open for mother and aunts to examine; that sore throat you'd been encouraging by sucking icicles was revealed. Eyes glinting, my mother brought forth the jar of Musterole, which I thought I'd destroyed, and slathered me fore and aft. Then, deaf to my squalls, she forced me into the much despised long woolen underwear that chafed and itched even without the stinking Musterole. I raged and balked, but she had her way with me until it was time to put on my suspenders and long stockings.

"I ain't wearing that contraption!"

"You have to. You have a cold."

"Just socks," I begged. "Not the garter belt and stockings."

"Don't you want to get better?"

"It looks like hell."

"Don't swear. Here." And she snaked me into the suspenders, the garters snapping around my ears, the stockings lumping around my ankles.

I was done for and I knew it. Surly, greased, and gartered, I quit the sauna and went back to my aunt's kitchen, hoping no one would get downwind of me. But no wind was needed to carry my stench. My boy cousins were in the parlor telling dirty stories, and I tried to weasel in without being noticed.

"Boy, you stink!" Joel blatted, holding his nose at me. The other boys chortled, snorted, and backed away from me. "Stink! Ink, pink, stink!"

I lammed Joel one in the middle of his forehead, and he whacked me in the belly. Quicker than a cat could sneeze, we were rolling on the floor, gouging, kicking, and biting, our Finnish bloodlust rampaging. But then my father plucked me by the scruff of my neck and dumped me into the kitchen to sit behind the stove, where I glowered and sulked, one eye swelling shut and the smell of Musterole rising about me.

Winter. If I write more about winter than anything else, it's because I know more about winter. Laskiainen, the winter festival when the Finns came skiing in lyric patterns down the milky hills and from the snow-ruffed woods. Lakes with snow beaches where we left trails that ice dinosaurs might have en-

vied and where the winter birds feathered the crusted snow
with the whisper kisses of their landings. Winter in northern
Minnesota where midday shone as bright and dark as midnight
with all the sky shattered and falling into rings around the sun
and moon. And, we children, stuffed and muffled with woolen
mitts and scarves and the eternal long underwear, came trum-
peting down the hills with wooden sleds and homemade skis
and got in the way of the people with store-bought skis and fancy bindings, people who could ski the slalom. The slalom! Those
whip turns marked by flags and fallen bodies. But anyone could
do the ski jumps, even on homemade skis. And we Finns knew
we could fly anyway, once launched on wax and supple wood
and our own flaming arrogance. We'd take the downhill dare-
devil ice slide and, lifting from the lip of the slide, we would
flatten along the skis, nose to tip, to soar in silence and then
come down, baffling the wind with our bodies, hissing along
above the snow to land with flexed knees and a flourishing
snowplow.

Not just skiing, those Laskiainen days. Skating, not the
figures, but the blood battles of hockey and racing.
The lean black skates laced up the ankles and sharp-
ened so that we flew on knife-edges, and when the game got
rough we'd kick and gouge. The figure skaters were all indoors.
But we took the Minnesota winds and snow squalls straight,
out on the lakes, and came home frozen across the face, brows
silvered with frost, even frost moustaches. And me, at six and
seven, I had learned to skate on clear patches in the swamp,
falling and bruising myself twenty-seven times in one day. And
I would slip into a game of hockey, snatching the puck from the
older kids, cutting it in and out between longer legs, and bash-
ing it into the net, only to be snuffed out by the goalie who
wouldn't let a punk kid play!

Snow and ice were our native territory. If we couldn't fly over
the lakes, we'd swim under the ice on Laskiainen. That was the
best, I thought. The brave boys and the whiskey-breathed men
would gather before noon in the sauna to brag and bully and
drink Old Crow or Teacher's, puffing up their courage to the
swimming point.

"I could do more'n a hundred yards easy," one of the boys would
say.

"Nah, a hundred's enough," the red-nosed gin drinker would
answer.

"Oiva did more last year," the boys would claim.

And the rude sounds of belching and disbelief would belly
around the sauna. But it would be settled there where the
temperature was one hundred and ninety plus as they sat
around the bottles and the stove while the steam frisked over
their heads and they scratched and stretched before the plunge
into the mother heart of winter, the lake. Earlier someone
would have gone out to the lake to ax two holes in the ice a hundred yards apart. And now the brave boys would drink straight
whiskey or gin at a gulp and run naked, high-kneeing it
through the snow, to haul the harsh air into their lungs and
then dive headfirst into the first hole.

"Don't forget where you are," someone would advise them. "Don't let the shock make you inhale."

Advice was dimly remembered at that first shock of icy water. Then the garbled silence and the ice-gray world beneath. The first to go were the toes; they turned lumpen dull. Ice formed over the open eyes, it seemed; and one's genitals crept up to a safe warm place in the bowel. Sounds from the outside world were shrill, steps thumped overhead, the world drew skin-close, and the pulse of life was in your ears. Breaststroke was best, a long flat stroke and kick that took you a fifth of the way, the water purring around you like syrup, but cold! The breath came sliding through your nose, unwilled. Another gathering of muscles, contracting and stretching in the stroke, and the long glide while turning the eyes upward to measure how far, oh God! how far now? Not even half the distance and the god of death, Kalma, was breathing cold along your spine. A glance downward and there were all the pickerel and trout you'd never caught, asleep at the bottom of this ice-trapped world. You reached down and touched them: the spine of the sleepy pickerel, the fanning tail of the trout, all jeweled with cold, not moving, the gills and fins transparent. The sand beneath them dew-pearled with ice, prickling with air bubbles, the water-weeds drifting dark green and cold, slowly . . . slowly . . . and crawdaddies on the half shell with claws grasping at underwater dreams. The water world tucked up for the winter's night, and you, icy lunged, kicked off again to reach for the gray day world ahead. Heavy, the calves of your legs, the upper arms . . . heavy. Breath seethed from your nostrils, warming your belly in bubbles that rose and glimmered silver under the ice.

And then you broke for the surface, that shining circle of light, and you crawled and sprawled out of the water onto the ice and the brisk, rough clasp of the other Finns who had cursed and sworn and worried. You had come this long cold distance in silence and fear, and now they carried you, breathless, to the sauna and slopped more whiskey into you, doused you with hot water, scraped you with towels, and helped you into the bravado you now deserved.

Winter and water were our domain. We Finns were good at both. And after the sauna, at any time of the year, it was the lake or the river we sought. The sauna, for the child, was the baptismal, the place for laundering and scrubbing the soul. I, as a child, first saw my mother and father, soap-lathered and splendid, he with his fierce Finnish pride and my mother with her perky blue eyes and that biting scrub brush. Then, when I was seven or so, I was banished to bathe with only womenfolk: aunts, grandmother, girl cousins, and mothers. The men and boys kept apart, and I sulked under the blandishments of Aunt Anna, who pinched my fanny and chucked my chin. The sauna was just gab and gossip then, but I still had the coeducational juxtaposition of the sexes in the lake after the sauna. Then we were eels under the moon, diving from the sauna door to flash silver and black-wet under the stars. We all were hairless fauns then, I remember, with flat chests and just a cockleshell of sex. It was our time of innocence, and we were randy as lambs; the boys would pee from the tree branches and sprinkle our legs warm and laughing . . . we girls would trickle slyly into the lake, always knowing that we somehow had the magic of new life. Not for us, then, were the hooded eyes of lust. No, we kicked up our heels and danced back from the serious material of life. The glitterswim of the lake, the wreathing of waterweeds around our heads, the green gossip of fishes: those were our world. We wrote with scabby fingers on the sands and dreamed the dreams that lifted and billowed around us.

And what is left now, spinning from the wild and woolly skein of childhood memory? Spring! When the snow foamed in the gullies, scorched by the resurrected sun. The crooked-fingered trees threw off their widows' weeds to flirt green and tender on the hilltops. Spring, when my weeping willow trailed green ribbons and chuckled seductively, holding hands with the wind.

Minnesota spring mornings that shone clear and calm so that I always wakened clean and newborn, sassy as an Easter egg. And bounding out of bed to yodel and sing through breakfast, wearing my knees bare, the long underwear abandoned, the suspenders dangling from a doorknob. Somewhere along the knotted string of growing up I had eased out of my patchwork, prickly kidhood into adolescence, that time of moods and daymares when I was thistle-witted and hiccuping inside while my legs and arms went spidering off beyond control. My parents, who must have wondered at the fate that dumped me down their chimney, quit giving me chores to do: I would forget myself while whipping cream and churn it into butter, or sitting at the table with my long legs I would spill the table leaf and send the mashed potatoes into my father's lap along with the gravy and the green beans, or I would slam the barn door on my own head, or sent to fetch the cows I would idle and dream in the pasture until the cows, painful and heavy with milk, would come home by themselves. Minnesota spring days when I thought I could reach out of myself and touch everything around me, could somehow hold the morning song of the lark, could always taste those wild rose days, would never lose my cockleshell dreams.

One of those spring mornings I can remember waking before the rest of the world and climbing to the top of the barn, its corrugated roof dew-iced and silver, to look at the farm and our farmhouse, smoke wisping from the sleeping chimney, the windows heavy-lidded, the house itself still asleep with my parents inside, their dreams quilted close around them.

And down the road, my grandmother sleeping too, in her little salt-white house. I wondered if she dreamed fresh dreams or slept with her heart rocking with ancient loves now gone. Did she dream even now of the cuckoos and their round-songs, so long ago heard in the forests of Savonlinna, that castle, a real castle, where she had been a girl? Those ancient loves, were they safe and chaste within her memory, as my yet unknown loves were untouched, our griefs known and unknown, still pulsing, past and future and not in our arms? She always wore her hair in a bun during the day, but at night it fell across her pillow like silver seaweed drifting from the warm, worn, time-carved ivory of her brow. She was my moon, my grandmother, the light that gleamed always across the darkest moments of my childhood. All the times I had run away from the grown-up world, I had never run away from her, but rather I spun her coronets of ferns and violets and clover buds, wrapping myself close to her in the silken loops of love and trust. And she, ancient yet ageless, had time and place for me, rocking me in her chair or letting me comb her long ash-silver hair with her ivory comb and braid it, or letting me parade her back and forth between the lilacs and bleeding hearts that magicked under the shining birch trees. And she was always there with the glowing night-light when nightmares shrieked me out of bed; and she saved for me the broken beads from lost necklaces, even a teal's wing I had found, and the old glass doorknobs, so old they were lavender and shadowed with memories she might have known.

Minnesota childhood. The mornings of my life, moving out of darkness and sleep into the newly born, innocent, exuberant-as-roses days of love, leaving behind me the pillows where kisses feathered my cheeks. The memories of childhood, lilting as candles, come chuckling like the rain, with no order and no end.

Fishing on the Big Lake

by Don Davenport

The cry is lusty, age-old, primeval. "Fish on!" A fisherman in a baseball-type cap grabs one of a dozen rods that bristle from the open stern of the charter boat and sets the hook with a sharp jerk. The boat's skipper throttles back and swiftly positions the boat, while a young first mate scrambles to clear rods and lines so that there will be room to play the fish.

At the urging of the captain, the fisherman holds the rod tip high, then lowers it swiftly, reeling in slack. Then he raises the tip and repeats the motion. "Big one," he grunts. Minutes pass like hours.

The fish jumps, silver scales flashing in the sun a dozen yards behind the boat. "It's a king," several voices call at once. The fisherman continues to reel his prize toward the boat. "Easy now," the captain cautions. "Don't rush him."

The fisherman nods. His mouth is dry, his arms heavy, and still the fish resists. With the captain's prodding reminder, he keeps the rod tip high and cranks the reel slowly. He would disgrace himself if he lost the fish at this point. His colleagues would offer sympathy, but the condolences would be tinged with scorn.

"When I tell you, stop reeling him in and walk straight backwards," the captain says. The first mate leans over the back of the boat with a net. "Now!" comes the command, and the fisherman steps back until he strikes the cabin. "Got 'im," says the mate, raising the net over the stern and lowering it gently to the deck.

Five pounds of silver fish flops about, a green lure dangling from its jaw. As the grinning fisherman accepts his colleagues' congratulations, the mate dispatches the fish with one swift blow of a lead-pipe sap. The fish quivers once and is motionless. The mate pulls the lure from its mouth, and the fisherman takes the salmon from the net. He holds it high with his right hand and draws in his stomach while someone snaps a picture. The bony gills where he holds the fish are sharp and cut into his fingers. The fisherman knows he is bleeding, but he does not care. He has put a respectable fish in the box.

From early spring until late autumn, this scenario is repeated hundreds of times a day on the Great Lakes, especially on Lake Michigan. It is called charter boat fishing, and the prized fish are coho and chinook salmon, two fish that belong in the ocean, not in Lake Michigan. It is, for the most part, put-and-take fishing, a carefully managed, computer-modeled fish-stocking experiment, as artificial as making babies in test tubes. But the lure of the big fish brings millions and millions of dollars into the Great Lakes region each year and has saved the economies of dozens of lakeshore communities. A whole new industry has been created, and the big lake produces some of the best fishing you'll find. And like most good things in life, it was virtually unexpected.

When the first Europeans arrived on the scene almost 350 years ago, about half of the lakes' biomass—half of all living creatures in the waters—consisted of fish weighing more than 10 pounds. Individuals among all species of the larger predator fish topped out at more than 20 pounds. Most Native Americans in the lakes region depended on fish to one degree or another. Dip-netting from canoes was a favorite Indian fishing method, and they also speared fish and caught them with baited bone hooks and lines. Fish soon became a staple in the diets of the early European fur traders, missionaries, and settlers. By 1784 the North West Company was shipping barrels of Lake Superior fish to supply its remote fur-trading outposts.

T he first true commercial fishing began in the 1830s when John Jacob Astor's American Fur Company established fishing stations on Lake Superior. A decade later, in the closing years of the Great Lakes fur trade, the company was shipping a million pounds of fish a year. Immigrants from Europe, especially the Scandinavian countries, began to establish fishing communities on Lake Michigan, too.

By 1899, the year the Great Lakes commercial fish harvest peaked with a total catch topping 119 million pounds, there were 10,000 commercial fishermen on the Great Lakes. Yet the fishery, severely overfished, was on the decline. Within 40 years it would virtually collapse.

The reasons for the decline were many and varied. Scientists now know that massive clear-cut logging practices did severe damage to the fishery. Thousands of tons of soil from denuded lands blew or washed into the lakes, polluting the waters. Log drives destroyed fish spawning grounds in the rivers, and increased water temperatures caused the growth of aquatic plants that depleted the oxygen fish needed. Sawdust from mills along the shore or on rivers that fed into the lake choked the waterfronts and bays, and sawdust islands floated miles out to sea. Great forest fires destroyed all living creatures in streams and lakes that remained barren for years afterward. The Industrial Age brought industrial waste, and lakeshore industries found the lakes a convenient place to deposit it. Many municipalities followed suit. Untreated pulp and papermill wastes, dumped into rivers far from the lakes, killed fish spawning in the rivers and eventually made their way into the lakes.

As catches dwindled, Great Lakes fishermen worked harder, ranging farther afield and working longer hours. They turned to new technology such as steam-powered fishing boats and net-lifting devices and smaller mesh nets made of finer twine. All took their toll. But the coup de grace was administered by a prehistoric saltwater fish called a sea lamprey.

The foot-long, snakelike lamprey belongs to an ancient family that dates back 250 million years—the jawless fish. The lamprey feeds by attaching itself to the side of a large fish, rasping a hole in the skin, and sucking out blood and body fluids until it is no longer hungry or until its victim dies. The process can last hours, days, even weeks. Native to the Atlantic Ocean, the sea lamprey is found from Canada to Florida. Like a salmon, it lives its adult life in the ocean and runs up freshwater streams to spawn. And like a salmon, it can live its entire life in fresh water.

The sea lamprey was first spotted in Lake Erie in 1921, apparently having made its way along the route of the Erie Canal. But Lake Erie—perhaps because it was too warm, or too polluted—was not to the lamprey's liking. Unfortunately, the upper lakes were. Sea lampreys were first seen in Lake Huron in 1932, Lake Michigan in 1934, and Lake Superior in 1938. With no natural predator to control it, the parasite ran rampant. It decimated the lake trout and whitefish populations, then turned to burbot, walleye, and suckers. Within 15 years the fisheries collapsed. The Lake Michigan lake trout catch dropped from 11 million pounds to less than 200,000 pounds, and scores of commercial fishermen were forced out of business.

Following in the wake of the sea lamprey was the alewife, another ocean fish that wreaked havoc. Alewives eat the eggs of other fish and compete for food. They were first reported in Lake Michigan in 1949. With the major predator fish gone, there was no stopping the prolific alewife, and by the 1960s it was more than 80% of all fish in the lake and more than half of the total biomass. The lake herring, once the most abundant commercial fish in Lake Michigan, disappeared completely.

By the late 1960s the Great Lakes ecosystem was a shambles. The low point came in 1967, with a massive die-off of alewives in Lake Michigan. Hundreds of millions of silvery, rotting, sardine-sized fish washed up on the beaches. People began to speak of the Great Lakes as being dead, and the lakes certainly smelled like it.

The Canadian and American bureaucracies dealing with the Great Lakes fishery had never been particularly coordinated. But to their credit, they rose to the occasion. The Great Lakes Fishery Commission, charged with finding a solution to the sea lamprey problem, was created by international treaty between the United States and Canada in 1955.

The first attempt was to control lampreys with mechanical and electrical barriers in the streams where they spawned; this was mostly unsuccessful. Scientists then began searching for a chemical that would kill the lamprey larvae, which spend from three to 14 years in the streambeds they were spawned in before going to the lakes as mature adults. After testing some 6,000 chemicals, U.S. Fish and Wildlife scientists in 1958 found an obscure chemical called TFM that selectively killed sea lamprey larvae without apparent harm to other fish and aquatic life.

Because Lake Superior had small remaining stocks of native lake trout, it was the first lake to get intensive treatment with TFM. Within two years, the number of adult lampreys returning to spawn had dropped by a remarkable 85%. Regular treatment began on Lake Michigan in 1963, on Lake Huron in 1970, and Lake Ontario in 1972—all with similarly successful results.

With the lampreys under control, a massive predator fish plant-ing program was begun. Some four million lake trout are stocked each year, but to the disappointment of all, the stocked trout have not reproduced successfully in the Great Lakes.

After the massive Lake Michigan alewife die-off in 1967, the states of Michigan and Wisconsin began to stock the lakes with thousands of coho salmon, then with millions of chinook salmon —predators imported from the Pacific Ocean to prey on the ale-wives. With all those alewives to feed on, the salmon and trout quickly put on the pounds, and some pretty big fish were swim-ming in the lakes. Within a couple of years another malady swept the lakes (particularly Lake Michigan); called "salmon fever," it ran epidemic among sport fishermen.

The Great Lakes sport fishery, virtually nonexistent 20 years ago, now brings an estimated $1.1 billion into the Great Lakes economy each year. And it has given birth to the charter boat industry. In Wisconsin there were barely a handful of charter operators on Great Lakes waters in the early 1970s; today there are nearly 600 of them. The story is much the same in Michigan, Minnesota, and the other Great Lakes states.

While charter boat fishing does not guarantee a fish, it certain-ly increases the odds in your favor. The good skippers have taken time to learn about the fishery and the various fish spe-cies, and they know where to seek fish under a variety of weather conditions. Their boats carry sophisticated electronic gear to aid in the search: outriggers to hold fishing lines off to the side of the boat; downriggers to take lines to the bottom; devices that hold a lure at a certain depth; gadgets that mea-sure the speed of the lure through the water or the temperature of the water at the lure and at the surface; and "locators," which give a profile of the lake bottom on a computer-like screen and measure the depth of the water. These instruments are so sen-sitive as to show fish swimming in schools or individuals making passes at the lure (they appear as thin lines). This is called "marking fish," and it occasions considerable excitement among the fishermen and considerable talking back and forth on the radios by the charter skippers. Charter boats run the maximum number of lines the regulations allow, and they have an arsenal of brightly colored lures and baits. But what caught fish yesterday won't necessarily catch them today, and there is considerable experimentation with lures and equipment when the action is slow in coming.

"I can't guarantee you a fish," one veteran Lake Michigan char-ter skipper said, "but I'll guarantee you a good time. I'll reschedule you for free if the weather is too rough to go out on the day of your charter, and I'll do my damnedest to put fish in the box."

And fish in the box is why the game is played.

The Birthplace of the Shopping Mall

by Donna G. White

A freelance writer and editor of The Oak Leaf *magazine, Donna G. White has lived in Rochester, Michigan, for more than 20 years.*

In 1954 the nation's first regional shopping mall, Northland Center, opened its doors in what was then rural Southfield, Michigan, just north of the city limits of Detroit. This event ushered in a revolution in American shopping habits.

Two years before Northland's grand opening, the architect Victor Gruen delivered a lecture to the Detroit chapter of the American Institute of Architects in which he listed 10 prerequisites for a successful shopping center. "It must be in the right city, in the right area, on the right spot, and of the right size. It must be easily accessible, offer complete services and the highest degree of obtainable shopping convenience. It must lease to the right tenants on the right terms. It must offer the most attractive shopping surroundings obtainable." *That* was how Northland was born.

In the early 1950s the Webber brothers, owners of downtown Detroit's J.L. Hudson's, were looking for a suburban area in which to build Hudson's first branch store. After extensive demographic studies, Southfield became the chosen city. Victor Gruen designed the mall, utilizing a classic marketplace concept. The June 1954 *Architectural Forum* said, "Northland is a planning classic because it is the first modern pedestrian commercial center to use an urban 'market town' plan, a compact form physically and psychologically suited to pedestrian shopping."

Hudson's four-story branch was not only the biggest branch department store ever built at that time, it was the largest department store of any kind built since the 1920s. This structure centered the mall; the other 80 stores, mostly specialty shops in direct competition with Hudson's, were placed around three sides of its perimeter. In all there were six other buildings, each one story high, with additional levels underground.

To complete the atmosphere of a medieval marketplace, the architect planned an extensive landscaping program that was carried out by the landscape architect Edward A. Eichstedt. Six mini-malls or courts each had distinctive plantings: In the North Mall were Japanese cherry trees and tulips; Fountain Court had redbud, rhododendron, and azaleas; and the Great Lakes Court had wildflowers and birches. In all, the plantings included 1,500 shade trees, 625 flowering trees, 1,900 evergreens, 5,000 shrubs, 18,000 ground cover plants, and 23,000 bulbs, giving the mall a parklike atmosphere. The floral displays were changed with the season.

No aesthetic aspect was overlooked in the planning of the open-air mall. An intrinsic part of the landscaping was the work of six well-known sculptors, Marshall Fredericks, Richard Hall Jennings, Gwen Lux, Malcolm Moran, Lily Saarinen, and Arthur Kraft, who were commissioned for the project. Their works became permanent exhibitions. *Life* magazine for August 30, 1954, showed pictures of Northland Center, describing it as a "fantastic combination of modern efficiency and physical form . . . fine architecture and pure gaiety. Courts and malls are full of flowers, fanciful sculptures, and music giving the air of a bazaar."

There was no glitzy grand opening for Northland Center on March 22, 1954. In fact, the Webber brothers brought in the press a week before to view the mall so that the actual opening day would not be played up too much. Yet the shopping center became an immediate success, with attendance averaging 40,000 to 50,000 a day (against an estimate of 30,000). The mall reported $88 million in sales during its first full fiscal year. Hudson's, which had invested $30 million, chalked up about $50 million of this amount. At the same time, many retailers in downtown Detroit were pleading for tax relief because of declining sales.

Hudson's built three more regional shopping centers: Eastland in Harper Woods in 1957; Westland in suburban Westland in 1965; and Southland in Taylor in 1970. None of these centers was on the grand scale of Northland, but all were similar in layout. And some 120 other shopping centers have opened across southeastern Michigan, cornering the bulk of the consumer goods market.

Eight years after the opening of Northland Center, the Detroit-based S.S. Kresge opened the country's first K Mart in Garden City, Michigan. This experiment with a supermarket shopping concept proved so successful that in 1977 S.S. Kresge changed its name to K Mart Inc., with world headquarters in suburban Troy, Michigan. Today K Mart is the second-largest retailer in the world after Sears.

Today, 35 years after its grand opening, competition from other major malls has taken its toll on the once-supreme Northland Center. The original open-air mall has since been enclosed, and the magnificent gardens are no more. The anchor stores remain Hudson's and J.C. Penney, with some 170 other apparel and specialty shops and restaurants. But demographics have changed significantly since the early 1950s, causing a decline in sales. Crime in the area has been serious enough to warrant valet parking for Hudson's customers. Still, Northland maintains a special standing in metro Detroit, undoubtedly because of its top-quality Hudson's store, the prototype for all the regional Hudson's stores, which has never been matched.

Twenty-five years after the opening of Northland, Victor Gruen, widely credited as the father of the modern shopping center, lamented what had been wrought in the suburban centers, contending that his idea had been perverted by "fast-buck promoters and speculators." Regional shopping centers, he said, were supposed to be "not just selling machines but crystallization points for anonymous residential areas; they created opportunities for social and cultural events."

In an interview for a *Detroit News* magazine article on malls in 1979, Gruen explained: "What happened in many (but by no means all) cases was that shopping centers promoted disintegration. They were built somewhere on the cheapest land available, with the aim of dragging customers over long distances because of department and other stores. In erecting these selling machines, the cultural and social functions of a center were neglected. Thus, they became actually monofunctional ghettos which, instead of bringing central urban facilities to the people, tried to hold people away from their living spaces and draw them to ever larger conglomerations of stores."

In the same article, taking a different tack, Professor Neil Harris, a cultural historian at the University of Chicago, said, "Although it's not their purpose—malls are constructed to make money—they give focus to communities which are sprawling and have no cultural center."

Somewhere in the middle of these two viewpoints may be what happened in Novi, once a rural community 40 minutes due west of Detroit. Twelve years ago Novi residents had to commute for their groceries, clothing, and dinners out. Then Twelve Oaks Mall—anchored by Hudson's, Lord & Taylor, J.C. Penney, and Sears—opened on 230 acres of land just outside the town, changing forever Novi's small-town atmosphere. Real-estate prices skyrocketed, the population quadrupled, and the apple orchards were subdivided. Novi became a retail center for the region, drawing shoppers from Lansing, Grand Rapids, even Toledo, Ohio. Twelve Oaks Mall and the town called Novi have become synonymous, and two more malls have opened there recently.

In January 1983 the downtown J.L. Hudson's—a venerable fixture in Detroit's Woodward Avenue shopping district—closed its doors for the last time, ending a 101-year history. Occupying one entire city block and 21 floors, Hudson's at its zenith had 1,800 employees and was always among the nation's top 10 giant department stores, along with Macy's in New York and Marshall Field in Chicago. Hudson's was the last of the large Detroit department stores to close its downtown store, having been preceded by Crowley's, D. J. Healy's, Himelhoch's, and Kern's.

Some claim that the suburban shopping malls tolled the knell for the downtown stores. Others point to the Eisenhower Interstate Bill of the 1950s, which allocated money for suburban expressways in, out, and around the city. Originally intended to ease congestion in the cities, the highways instead provided a quick route out of the city and into the fast-growing suburbs where, by 1960, 22 Michigan malls offered convenient parking plus shopping in air-conditioned comfort.

Malls come in all sizes, ranging from a small strip of land containing a few assorted stores to a "megamall" like Fairlane Town Mall in Dearborn. This three-level, 270-acre complex is southeast Michigan's largest in land area and number of stores (220). Fairlane has even produced clones—sister malls somewhat smaller in size but much the same in layout, appearance, and types of stores. These include Briarwood in Ann Arbor, Lakeside in Sterling Heights, and Twelve Oaks in Novi. Most of the larger malls are anchored by big department stores such as Hudson's, Lord & Taylor, J.C. Penney, Sears, and Crowley's. Small strip malls may have no anchor at all other than a grocery store or a Woolworth. Medium-size malls could have a Montgomery Ward or a K Mart as major stores. But the K Marts do not share ground with the Hudson's or the Lord & Taylor's in malldom's caste system. Saks Fifth Avenue, for example, is choosy about where it vends its wares and has opted for only two malls in Michigan: Fairlane Town Mall and the exclusive Somerset Mall in Troy.

Shopping malls may be one of the most profound transformers of our lifestyle since World War II. They are like enclosed town squares, drive-in cities with climate control. Physicians prescribe for elderly patients to walk the flat, tiled paths of the malls, where no blasts of cold air can cause angina and where there are plenty of benches for resting. Both young and old fitness seekers can walk the malls in comfort—in southern Michigan some 12 malls open their doors early for walkers to work out before the shopping crowd arrives. Many have the mileage marked on the walls.

A mall is where you can go to do your banking, be fitted for glasses, have your teeth cleaned, check your cholesterol, meet your favorite soap opera star, buy a take-out gourmet meal (together with a floral bouquet for the dining room table), have your shoes resoled, and take in a movie in rocking-chair comfort—all in just a few hours. The mall has replaced the street corner for teenage hangouts, who go in droves to see and be seen and to check out the latest fashion trends.

In southeastern Michigan, with its proliferation of suburban malls, competition is fierce for the consumer dollar. While shoppers frequent certain malls simply because of proximity, other malls seem worth an hour's (or more) journey because of some unique quality such as specialty stores or bargains. Show shoppers a good bargain, and they'll beat a path to your door. Show them a complex of 70 discount factory outlet stores, and you'll have a stampede.

Opened in 1986, Manufacturers Marketplace Mall, Michigan's largest factory-direct mall, has been a financial success from the start. Although it is a 90-minute trip from Detroit straight north on I-75, this has not been a deterrent to intrepid shoppers searching for quality goods at bargain prices. Clothing and apparel outlets are in the majority here, with such well-known labels as Jonathan Logan, Izod, Van Heusen, and Carters. Looking for shoes? Bass has them, along with Mushrooms, Totes, and Sneakers and Cleats. Socks Galore offers 60,000 pairs of footwear at 25% to 85% off regular retail price. Stocking a kitchen? Head for the Corning Factory Store or the Paul Revere Shop for discounted accessories and cookware. Kitchen Collection offers a wide variety of utensils and gadgets. American Tourister lops 40% to 70% off its luggage, and Leather Manor takes up to 60% off leather goods. Up and down this outdoor mall are bargains to be had in toys, jewelry, cosmetics, china, and linen. In the Market Place, two enclosed malls-within-malls, one can find food, respite from the elements, and more specialty shops. And if you are in the mood to do a little wine tasting, the Chateau Grand Traverse specializes in Michigan wines, which you can taste before buying.

Somerset Mall, located on Big Beaver Road at Coolidge in suburban Troy (across a highway from K Mart world headquarters), is anchored by Bonwit Teller and Saks Fifth Avenue and has 43 shops and restaurants catering to the chic tastes of shoppers from nearby Bloomfield Hills and Birmingham. This one-level enclosed mall features an array of trendy, select stores such as Gucci, Mark Cross, Brooks Brothers, and Louis Vuitton. Trees, plants, flowers, and park benches create an outdoorsy atmosphere. Cafe Jardin, which occupies the center of the mall, offers alfresco dining on contemporary California French cuisine plus a view of passing shoppers. Down the line the highly rated Sebastian's Restaurant specializes in fresh fish. Houlihan's, more downbeat and casual, completes the trio of mall restaurants. In the Sharper Image, which has been called the Yuppie toy store, you can find all sorts of technological wizardry from Go'pher It—an electronic device that promises to drive away burrowing rodents from your garden— to a Turbo Chess Computer and a talking bathroom scale. At LaCuisine Jardin, harried shoppers can pick up gourmet meals to take home. Godiva Chocolatier and Fannie May Candies compete for the sweet-toothed buyers. Somerset Mall also stages a series of events each month, among them Sunday concerts, Working Women's Lunch and Fashion Shows, Sunday and Thursday Forum Lectures, and art exhibits. All this gives Somerset the image of a part-time cultural events center.

Trappers Alley Festival Marketplace, located in downtown Detroit's Greektown on Monroe Avenue, within blocks of the Renaissance Center and Cobo Conference/Exhibition Center, symbolizes a resurgence to bring shoppers back to the city. Housed in five century-old tannery buildings, the Marketplace has been adapted into a five-level complex of shops and restaurants that capitalizes on the character of the historic buildings. Turn-of-the-century flavor has been retained with a brick-paved center alley, custom brass railings, and period lighting fixtures. The enclosed area between the buildings is topped with about 14,000 square feet of skylights, giving an overall atrium effect. Escalators, wide stairways, and pedestrian ramps give access to the multilevel shops.

About half of the marketplace's 70 tenants are restaurants, mostly ethnic. Other shops include boutiques for clothing, gifts, and houseware items. Monroe's, a trendy restaurant and nightclub, occupies the "rooftop" in the mall. The Blue Nile is a sit-down restaurant featuring Ethiopian cuisine.

Easy access to Trappers Alley is provided by the Detroit People Mover, the 13-station elevated transit system that opened in 1987. The system has almost three miles of track that loops around the Detroit central business section. In operation seven days a week, the People Mover is probably the best buy in town at 50¢, and the Greektown station is located on the third level of Trappers Alley.

3 Michigan

Introduction

Michigan is the only state abutting four of the five Great Lakes: Erie, Huron, and Michigan touch the Lower Peninsula, Huron, Michigan, and Superior the Upper Peninsula. The state has over 2,200 miles of shoreline, more than the seven other lakes states combined, and the longest shoreline—albeit not a continuous one—of any state in the continental United States.

The two segments of the state are as different as can be and, until 30 years ago, were nearly as remote from each other as if they had been islands. The UP, as the Upper Peninsula is known, became part of the state by default. When Michigan applied for statehood in 1834, the application said that the lower boundary should run from the southern tip of Lake Michigan due east to Lake Erie, as Congress had established in 1787. But neighboring Ohio, a state since 1803, had long ago defined the boundary as lying several miles to the north. At stake was a narrow strip containing Toledo, then called Port Lawrence. In the spring of 1835 the two sides raised armies that tramped through the wilderness without (to everyone's relief) finding each other. President Andrew Jackson and the U.S. Congress stepped in: The Toledo Strip belongs to Ohio, they ruled, and Michigan could have the Upper Peninsula to make up for the loss. The decision was extremely unpopular in Michigan, until the region's vast iron and copper deposits were discovered a few years later.

The Lower Peninsula, 277 miles long and 195 miles wide, is often referred to as "the mitten." Detroit lies at the outer base of the left-hand thumb and Lake Huron is on the right, with Saginaw Bay in the space between thumb and forefinger. The Straits of Mackinac (MACK-in-aw) run across the top of the fingers, and Lake Michigan begins at the little finger, running down to the left.

Lake Michigan modifies the climate of the western Lower Peninsula and provides near-perfect conditions for fruit growing. When Antoine de la Mothe Cadillac founded Detroit in 1701 he brought with him a gardener whose duty it was to lay out orchards. And while it is virtually impossible to sort fact and fiction in the life of John Chapman, who was called Johnny Appleseed, it is known that he left seeds with missionary priests in early Michigan. The Grand Traverse region leads in the production of tart red cherries; blueberries, sweet cherries, plums, and peaches, as well as grapes for a significant wine industry, are among other fruits grown in the western Lower Peninsula.

The Upper Peninsula is separated from the lower by the 4½-mile-wide Straits of Mackinac, the short, deep channel that connects Lake Michigan and Lake Huron. The straits, and Mackinac Island, at the Lake Huron entrance, were vital in the fur trade, the Indian Wars, and Jesuit missionary work with the Indians. St. Ignace, on the north shore, dates from 1671, when Père Jacques Marquette founded a mission there. Three years earlier he had built a mission on the St. Marys River at Sault Ste. Marie, the state's first permanent settlement and its oldest surviving town.

Until the five-mile-long Mackinac Bridge connected the Upper and Lower peninsulas in 1957, heavily used auto ferries ran across the straits. Lower Peninsula deer hunters allowed two days—one coming and one going—just to make the crossing, while others took a long route around the lower end of Lake Michigan, across Indiana and Illinois, and north through Wisconsin. Today the bridge crossing takes less than 15 minutes.

The UP is more than 350 miles long and is about 65 miles across on average. Because Lake Superior is nearly landlocked, for many years there was no way to ship the UP's rich mineral resources to market. The lake funnels into Whitefish Bay at its southeastern end, then empties into the 61-mile-long St. Marys River, which connects with Lake Huron. At Sault Ste. Marie a rapids in the river that drops 21 feet over half a mile prevented ships from reaching Lake Huron. Then between 1853 and 1855 a scales salesman, Charles T. Harvey, engineered the construction of the first canal and locks, which allowed ships to bypass the rapids. Today the U.S. Army Corps of Engineers operates the world's largest and busiest lockage system at Sault Ste. Marie (known as the Soo), with more than 95 million tons of cargo shipped through annually.

The UP's iron and copper mines are no longer operating; the last copper mine closed in 1968. Today the peninsula is better known for its wild beauty. It is nearly covered by state and national forests, including the Hiawatha and Ottawa National Forests, which together encompass 2,360,000 acres. Scenic rivers crisscross the UP, and there are more than 150 waterfalls, some easily accessible, others found only after long, arduous hikes. White-tailed deer, black bear, elk, moose, and the eastern timber wolf make their homes in the forests, and campers can pick wild blueberries or thimbleberries to add to their morning pancakes. The Lake Superior snow belt, in the western UP and adjoining sections of northern Wisconsin, gets over 200 inches annually. A large number of hills and resorts in the region provide some of the finest downhill skiing in the Midwest.

The products of Michigan appear in nearly every home in the country—usually an auto in the family garage or a breakfast cereal on the family table. The nation's leading cereal manufacturers have headquarters in Battle Creek. Detroit remains one of the world's great auto manufacturing cities, and Flint and Lansing are major production centers. The vast majority of the state's population live in the southern third of the Lower Peninsula, near the major cities. As for distances, they are considerable; it is 594 miles from Detroit to Copper Harbor, at the tip of the Keweenaw Peninsula, and 593 miles to Ironwood, in the west, on the Wisconsin border.

We have divided the state into four regions; after examining Detroit, the state's largest city, we will take the state one quadrant at a time, discussing the attractions in and around the major cities and towns of each section.

Michigan

N

Ferry

Copper
Harbor

Calumet
Hancock

26

Lake Superio

41

Ontonagon

*Pictured
Nat'l Lake*

45

Ironwood

41

Marquette

2

Munising

41

Iron
Mountain

2

Escanabe

41

*Green
Bay*

94

WISCONSIN

90

Ludingt

43

*Lake
Michigan*

Madison

94

Milwaukee

Mississippi River

IOWA

ILLINOIS

90

Chicago

80

0   40 miles
0   60 km

Thunder
Bay

Ferry

Isle Royale
Nat'l Park

Copper
Harbor

Sault
Ste. Marie

28

2

Manistique

St. Ignace
Mackinaw
Bridge
Mackinac Island

Mackinaw City
Cheboygan

Petoskey

75

31

131

Alpena

23

Traverse
City

Sable River

Manistee River

*Lake
Huron*

Cadillac

10

131

Muskegon River

Bay
City

53   25

Saginaw

75

Muskegon
Grand
Rapids

27

Grand River

96

Flint

69

Port
Huron

ONTARIO

Holland

Lansing ✪

23

Pontiac

Kalamazoo River

196

Battle
Creek

Ann
Arbor

96

*Lake
St. Clair*

Detroit

Kalamazoo

94

131

69

Jackson

12

127

23

75

Toledo

INDIANA

80 90

OHIO

Lake Erie

Detroit

It is appropriate that one of the newest pieces of sculpture in downtown Detroit is a four-ton, 24-foot-long bronze of the arm and fist of the late world heavyweight champion Joe Louis. An east-side Detroiter who held the heavyweight crown for 13 years, Louis was a good, tough fighter. And Detroit is a tough town, having survived as many haymakers as the "Brown Bomber" himself.

Seven decades before the American Revolution, Detroit was already on the map. The city was founded on July 24, 1701, when Frenchman Antoine de la Mothe Cadillac arrived with 50 soldiers and 50 settlers to build a stockaded fort guarding the 90-mile waterway that connects Lake Huron with Lake Erie. It was named Fort Pontchartrain d'Etroit ("on the Strait"); the Hotel Pontchartrain, at 2 Washington Boulevard, occupies the site near the river today.

The struggle between France and Britain over the lucrative fur trade eventually erupted into the French and Indian War. Detroit fell under British control in 1760 and remained so for nearly 40 years. Although the Treaty of Paris of 1783, ratified after the Revolutionary War, gave Michigan to the Americans, the British were slow to cede the frontier posts at war's end, and the Americans were not strong enough to do anything about it. Both Detroit and Michigan were incorporated into Upper Canada, and in 1792 Detroit sent its first delegates to the Canadian legislature. It was not until July 11, 1796, that the British ended their occupation.

The British held Detroit again during the War of 1812, when the city was surrendered by a terrified post commander without the firing of a shot. Only after Commodore Oliver Hazard Perry's overwhelming victory against British naval forces on Lake Erie on September 10, 1813 ("We have met the enemy and they are ours"), was Detroit returned to American control.

From the beginning Detroiters were an independent lot. As early as 1802 they incorporated the muddy frontier post as a city, gave women the vote, and held what is believed to have been the first town meeting in the Midwest.

In 1805 the city, which had a population of some 2,200, burned to the ground. With the grandiose statement "I will make this place the Paris of the Midwest," Judge Augustus Woodward, newly appointed administrator of the Michigan Territory, drew up plans for a large, beautiful city based on the design for Washington, DC. The city never followed the plan to any great extent; some downtown thoroughfares were laid out like spokes on a wheel, but the effect is lost at street level and can best be appreciated on a map.

Rising from the ashes, Detroit continued to grow. Sidewalks were required by city ordinance in 1827; street names on corner signs were ordered in 1836. The population reached 10,000 in 1837. Always a strong antislavery city, Detroit was an important stop on the Underground Railroad; slaves were hidden until they could be smuggled across the river to Canada and freedom.

The population doubled every decade from 1830 to 1860 as great waves of immigration rolled in. After the Civil War, Detroit became a leader in the manufacture of horse-drawn carriages. Then, one day, there appeared a carriage that didn't need a horse to pull it.

It is likely that the first self-propelled vehicle in Michigan was a steam-driven car built in the winter of 1884–1885 by John and Thomas Clegg of Memphis, Michigan, about 50 miles north of Detroit. Ransom E. Olds of Lansing developed a practical gasoline-driven automobile in 1894 and in 1896 organized the Olds Motor Vehicle Company. Also in that year Charles C. King, a trained engineer who dabbled in auto design in his free time, drove the first gasoline-powered horseless carriage in Detroit. In June 1896 a mechanically inclined electric company engineer named Henry Ford, who had been born on a suburban Dearborn farm during the Civil War, first tested his Quadricycle, which was built in a brick shed on Bagely Avenue in Highland Park (you can see it at the Henry Ford Museum in Dearborn). The Quadricycle ran well enough on its first test, although it had no brakes and could not be reversed.

In 1899 Olds's company was re-formed on Jefferson Avenue in Detroit as the Olds Motor Works, considered the first commercial auto factory in the world. Other pioneers followed Olds's lead and settled in the Detroit area, where there was a large pool of wealthy men willing to pump dollars into the infant industry. There were four manufacturers by 1902; Ford formed the present Ford Motor Company in 1903. The then-independent Cadillac Automobile Company soon followed. In 1907 Olds and Buick combined to form General Motors, and Ford introduced his Model T.

Detroit's population exploded as workers from around the world rushed to the city where Ford was paying an unbelievable $5 a day. By 1917, some 23 companies in Detroit and its suburbs were assembling cars; a further 132 firms provided parts and accessories. More than a million people were employed in various phases of the auto industry and almost a million cars were chugging off the assembly lines each year. Detroit had become the Motor City.

During World War II Detroit automakers switched to weapons; planes, tanks, jeeps, and other war matériel rolled off the production lines in a seemingly endless stream. War workers poured into the city in droves. No automobiles were built from 1943 to 1945, but when the war ended Americans were hungry for new cars. Because wartime shortages still existed, the 1946 line consisted for the most part of dolled-up 1941 models, but they were new, and the public loved them. New models, new designs, new engines followed.

In the 1930s and '40s few cities in America swung as did Detroit. Crowds thronged into Paradise Valley, a noisy, hot, jiving, undefined pocket of the inner city. There were "blind pigs," as after-hours establishments were known, and "black and tans," clubs where people of all races freely mingled. There was jazz, the blues, dancing, laughter. But silence began to fall after World War II. As in most large communities in the 1950s, in Detroit the middle class began to leave for the suburbs, forming rings of affluence around the neglected inner city. The exodus was spurred by the construction of freeways, and the

Detroit & Its Suburbs

central city fell victim to a domino effect: More people moved, more businesses closed, more people moved. The social and shopping aspects of downtown Detroit shriveled and nearly died.

While this was happening a young black man, Berry Gordy Jr., built a tiny studio in the basement of his house and began recording local talent. Most of the music Gordy produced and recorded under the Motown label had a steady, hard-driving beat like the city itself. By the mid-'60s artists such as Marvin Gaye, Smokey Robinson and the Miracles, Gladys Knight and the Pips, the Temptations, the Supremes, and Stevie Wonder had produced a long string of hits in that tiny studio. It was commercial black music performed by black musicians, and both blacks and whites loved it. Motown put Detroit on the map for something besides autos, and jukeboxes the world over blared out its hits.

Then came the late 1960s, years of massive unrest in this country. The summers of 1967 and 1968 saw riots in Chicago, Los Angeles, Detroit, and other major cities. Network TV films of Detroit in flames left a lasting impression on the city and the country. The crime rate soared. By the 1970s, downtown Detroit had become a nighttime desert. As Mayor Coleman Young observed then, after 6 PM you could shoot a cannon down Woodward Avenue and not hit a soul.

But a dramatic renewal has taken place in the central city in the past two decades. Acres of abandoned and run-down buildings were leveled, and new building has been extensive, especially downtown and along the riverfront. Scores of new restaurants have opened. The auto slump of the early 1980s slowed some programs and stopped others, but the work continues. Greektown, Trappers Alley, Bricktown, and Rivertown are downtown commercial areas where restored buildings have become bright new trendy places to dine, dance, shop, and party. A $200-million expansion of the Cobo Conference/Exhibition Center and Arena, Detroit's premier convention facility, will be completed in 1989, adding more than 300,000 square feet of exhibit space and drawing a projected 250,000 additional visitors to Detroit each year.

The focal point of the revitalized downtown is the Renaissance Center, four circular towers of dark reflective glass surrounding the 73-story circular glass Westin Hotel, the highest building in the city. A spectacular sight as it sparkles in the sun on the riverfront, the five-million-square-foot Ren Cen, as it is known, comprises shops, office towers, restaurants, lounges, and a 1,400-room hotel. It even has its own ZIP Code.

One of the newest downtown innovations is the People Mover. Completed in 1987, the elevated monorail transit system makes its circut around the central business district in 14 minutes.

Detroit moves to a rhythm of its own. (It's not the Motown sound; that succumbed to the glitter of Hollywood and moved west over a decade ago.) This is a big city, with a hard edge. The riverfront harbor is one of the busiest ports on the Great Lakes; every ship that moves between Lake Erie and Lake Huron passes by Detroit's doorstep. Downtown, the city bustles with a constant flow of traffic in and out of the Detroit–Windsor Tunnel, next to the Renaissance Center. But this is also a place where the line between haves and have-nots is sharply defined. In stark contrast to the gleaming Renaissance Center are dozens of abandoned, decaying buildings within its very shadow. As in all big cities, there are places where one does not go alone or at night.

By a quirk of geography (and a bend in the Detroit River), the city lies north of Canada; Windsor, Ontario, is directly across the river. Tourists can enjoy easy access to a foreign country, the favorable rate of currency exchange, and the good buys to be found in Windsor, where both the money and the postage stamps are different (*see* Excursions from Detroit).

Detroit is a sports town. Following Joe Louis, Sugar Ray Robinson, and Thomas Hearns's examples, young men still work and sweat in the gymnasiums, seeking to make their way with their fists. The Tigers play baseball downtown in Tiger Stadium (the last stadium in the American League to install lights for night games). The Joe Louis Arena, also downtown, houses the Red Wings hockey team. The Silverdome, in suburban Pontiac, has the world's largest inflated dome and has been home to the Detroit Lions and the Detroit Pistons, although the Pistons recently moved to the Palace of Auburn Hills, 15 minutes from the Silverdome.

Detroit is a melting pot, with more than 150 ethnic groups represented in a total metropolitan population of approximately 4,500,000. Almost 900,000 blacks live in the metropolitan area; the Detroit branch of the National Association for the Advancement of Colored People is the largest in the country.

Metro Detroit is also home to more than 400,000 people of Polish descent, a number approximately equal to the population of Gdansk, Poland. The city has the largest population of ethnic Bulgarians in North America, and its Chaldean community— Chaldeans are from Iraq—is the largest in the United States. Some 40,000 to 50,000 Belgians are in the area, the largest such community outside Belgium, and 280,000 Arab-Americans live there, the largest Arab population outside the Middle East. These numbers add up to a wealth of cultural diversity that's felt in language, music, food, art, and entertainment.

Above all, in its heart and soul, Detroit is a business town. Funerals are often scheduled at noon to cause the least interruption in the business day. Some 26% of the nation's automobiles, trucks, and tractors are produced here, with a new lineup of cars every year; their sales affect not only Detroit's economy but also that of the nation and the world.

Arriving and Departing

By Plane **Detroit Metropolitan Airport** (tel. 313/942–3550) is in Romulus, about 26 miles from downtown Detroit. Served by American, British Airways, Comair, Continental, Delta, Eastern, Jet America, Midway, Northwest, Pan American, Piedmont, Simmons, Southwest, TWA, United, USAir.

Between the Airport **Commuter Transportation Company** (tel. 313/941–9391) oper-
and Center City ates buses from the airport to major downtown hotels from 6 AM to 11 PM. Departures every half-hour weekdays, every hour weekends; $11 one-way fare, $20 round-trip.

Taxis to and from the airport take about 45 minutes; the fare is about $26.

By car from the airport, take I–94 east to U.S. 10 South into downtown. Going to the airport take I–94 west to Romulus.

By Train **Detroit Amtrak Station** (Vernor Hwy. and Michigan Ave.) and **Dearborn Amtrak Station** (16121 Michigan Ave.) provide rail service to all parts of the country (tel. 800/872–7245).

By Bus Two nationwide bus lines serve Detroit: **Greyhound Bus** (130 E. Congress St., tel. 313/963–9840 or 800/528–0447) and **Michigan Trailways** (1833 E. Jefferson Ave., tel. 313/259–6680 or 800/242 –2935).

By Car I–75 enters from the north and south, U.S. 10 from the north. Approaching from the west and northeast is I–94, from the west, I–96 and I–696. From the east Canadian Route 401 becomes Route 3 when entering Detroit from Windsor via the Ambassador Bridge (toll $1.25), and Route 3B when entering via the Detroit–Windsor Tunnel (toll $1.25).

Michigan law requires front-seat riders to wear seat belts. Cars are allowed to turn right on a red light after stopping to check for oncoming traffic.

Getting Around

By Car Most downtown streets are one way; a detailed map is a necessity. The main streets into downtown are Woodward Avenue (north–south) and Jefferson Avenue (east–west).

By Monorail The **People Mover** (tel. 313/962–7245) transports riders around a 2.9-mile track downtown, stopping at major hotels and attractions. *Mon.–Thurs. 7 AM–11 PM, Fri. 7 AM–midnight, Sat. 9 AM–midnight, Sun. noon–8 PM. Fare: 50¢, cash or token* .

By Trolley The **Downtown Trolley** (tel. 313/933–1330) runs along Jefferson Avenue and Washington Boulevard from Grand Circus Park to the Renaissance Center. *Weekdays 7–6, weekends 10–6; fare $1.*

By Bus The **Department of Transportation** (tel. 313/933–1300) operates bus service throughout Detroit; call for schedules and routes. *Fare $1.*

The **Southeastern Michigan Transportation Authority** (tel. 313/962–5515) provides suburban bus service; call for fare and route information.

By Taxi The taxi fare is 90¢ at the flag drop and 10¢ each ninth of a mile. Taxis can be ordered by phone or hired at stands at most major hotels. Major companies are **All American** (tel. 313/833–3800), **Blue Eagle** (tel. 313/934–2000), **Checker** (tel. 313/963–7000), **City Cab** (tel. 313/833–7060), **Lorraine** (tel. 313/582–6900), **Metropolitan** (tel. 313/869–8300), **Motor City** (tel. 313/342–8200), and **Radio Cab** (tel. 313/491–2600).

Important Addresses and Numbers

Tourist Information The **Detroit Visitor Information Center** (tel. 313/567–1170) is at 2 East Jefferson Avenue, in the Hart Plaza, just west of the Renaissance Center. Open weekdays 9–5; weekends 10:30–4:30. For a taped message on daily events in the Detroit area, phone 313/298–6262.

Guided Tours

DOT-Grayline Tours (tel. 313/341–6808) offers narrated bus tours of Detroit during the summer months. Schedules vary; call for schedule, pickup points, and fees.

Detroit Upbeat (tel. 313/341–6808) offers a variety of guided tours of ethnic neighborhoods, fall foliage, the city's transportation, and areas highlighting Detroit's economic growth.

Working Detroit (tel. 313/822–6426) offers guided tours relating to labor and the auto industry.

Kirby Tours (tel. 800/521–0711) has guided bus tours of the city during the summer months. Call for schedules, fares, and pickup points.

Lunch and dinner cruises aboard the 165-foot *Star of Detroit* leave daily from mid-May to mid-October. *20 E. Atwater St., (on riverfront behind Hart Plaza); tel. 313/465–7827 for schedules and prices.*

Walking Tours An excellent self-guided walking tour of downtown Detroit is outlined in the Detroit Yellow Pages (page 14). It covers 38 points of historical and architectural interest and takes about 2½ hours; if you get weary, hop aboard the People Mover, which closely parallels the route.

Exploring Detroit

Numbers in the margin correspond with points of interest on the Downtown Detroit map.

Orientation Downtown Detroit is bounded by the Detroit River on the south, Lodge Freeway (U.S. 10) on the west, Fisher Freeway (I–75) on the north, and Chrysler Freeway (I–375) on the east. You can reach most points of interest quite easily on foot or by using the People Mover; for attractions outside the downtown area, visitors will want to go by auto or public transportation.

❶ Start at the **Detroit Visitor Information Center** to pick up maps, brochures, and listings of events. The *Detroit Visitors Guide* has a map that will help you find attractions, but it is not detailed enough for driving. If you're driving, ask for a copy of the *Downtown Detroit Parking Guide*, which lists parking lots and garages downtown, at the Cultural Center, and at the Eastern Market. *2 E. Jefferson Ave., just west of the Renaissance Center, tel. 313/567–1170. Open weekdays 9–5, weekends 10:30–4:30; closed Christmas, New Year's, and Easter.*

On the median at East Jefferson and Woodward avenues is the sculpture of Joe Louis's arm and fist, *Monument to Joe Louis,* by Robert Graham. The statue before the City–County Building at the northeast corner of East Jefferson Avenue and Woodward is Marshall Fredericks's *Spirit of Detroit;* Detroiters may speak of it as the "Jolly Green Giant."

❷ At this point you are at the **Civic Center,** which covers 75 acres on the downtown waterfront. At its center is **Philip A. Hart Plaza** (W. Jefferson Ave., tel. 313/224–1184), designed by Isamu Noguchi. The paved downtown park with its riverfront promenade is home to summer ethnic festivals of food and entertainment, including the Stroh's Montreux Detroit Jazz Festival. In warm weather brown-bag-carrying lunchtime crowds turn up to enjoy the open spaces, the sculpture, and the $30-million computer-controlled Dodge Fountain. The plaza, which has two outdoor amphitheaters (in winter one becomes an ice rink), an underground theater, cultural galleries, and a restaurant, is a great place for people-watching and for getting a feel for the city.

The Henry and Edsel Ford Auditorium (20 Auditorium Dr., tel. 313/224–1070) was the home of the Detroit Symphony Orchestra from 1956 to 1988. The striking facade is of Swedish blue pearl granite in a basketweave design.

The lobby of the **Veterans Memorial Building** (151 W. Jefferson Ave., tel. 313/224–1060) has a collection of war scenes by battlefront artists and a memorial plaque to Detroiters who died in war.

Also part of the Civic Center, the **Cobo Conference/Exhibition Center,** covering 17 acres, is one of the world's largest exhibition buildings. Named after the late Albert E. Cobo, mayor from 1950 to 1957, the facility is just completing an expansion to 720,000 square feet of exhibition halls. In it is **Cobo Arena,** a 12,000-seat hall. *One Washington Blvd., tel. 313/224–1010. Admission free. Open weekdays 9–5.*

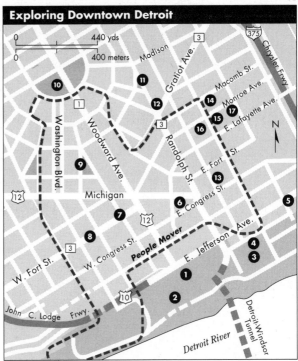

Exploring Downtown Detroit

Time Out   **Coleman's Corner** on the main floor in Cobo Hall serves cocktails in a spacious lounge overlooking the river. Named after Mayor Coleman Young. *Open weekdays noon–8.*

Just west of Cobo Center is **Joe Louis Arena** (600 Civic Center Dr., tel. 313/567–6000), where the Detroit Red Wings play hockey; it is also used for concerts and other entertainment.

At the east end of the Civic Center is the big, bold, brassy hotel-office-retail complex the **Renaissance Center.** Dedicated in 1977, this city-within-a-city, with its 12,000 employees, is the symbol of downtown revitalization. The tall center tower is the 73-story, circular **Westin Hotel,** surrounded by four 39-story office towers; the towers rise from a four-level, 14-acre podium. Immediately adjacent on the east are two 21-story office towers. The towers contain not only offices but also restaurants, bars, designer boutiques—in all, more than 80 retail outlets—as well as walkways, atriums, gardens, and an indoor lake. At the top of the Westin is the **Summit,** a revolving restaurant with full views of Detroit and Windsor; it is reached by a glass-enclosed elevator (there is a $3 fee unless you're dining).

Plan on getting lost in the Renaissance Center; everyone does, and it's part of the experience. Navigation has become somewhat easier as the result of a just-completed $27-million redevelopment program. Along with cosmetic work on the exterior, the hotel lobby was remodeled, retail stores were moved and expanded, and pedestrian walkways and shopping areas were color-coded.

4 At Renaissance Center you can board the **People Mover,** an elevated, automated monorail that makes a 14-minute, 2.9-mile circle to 13 downtown stations: Times Square, Michigan Avenue, Fort/Cass, Cobo Hall, Joe Louis Arena, Financial District, Millender Center, Renaissance Center, Bricktown, Greektown, Cadillac Square, Broadway, and Grand Circus Park. Trains run about every three minutes; the fare is 50¢. To see the most, go around twice, once on the right side of the car and once on the left. Accenting the stations are works of art, mostly large murals, many matching the surrounding neighborhood. A brochure available at most station turnstiles provides information on the art works and includes a system map.

You may continue to explore the city on foot or ride the People Mover to any of the following sites.

As you leave the Renaissance Center, you may want to take a brief detour to the right on East Jefferson Avenue to St. An-
5 toine Street, to see **Sts. Peter and Paul Roman Catholic Church.** Built in 1848, it's the oldest church structure in the downtown area.

Retrace your steps along East Jefferson Avenue to Randolph
6 Street, turn right, and head two blocks north to the end of **Cadillac Square,** site of many presidential speeches. At this end you'll find the **Old Wayne County Building,** built in the late 1890s and now undergoing a multimillion-dollar renovation; the bronze figures atop the building represent Agriculture, Commerce, Law, Mechanics, and Progress. Walk the length of Cadillac Square to look at the **Civil War Soldier's and Sailor's Monument,** erected in 1872, which was designed by Randolph Rogers, who created the bronze doors on the Capitol in Washington, DC. Beside the monument is a marker commemorating the First Michigan Regiment and the Civil War.

Turn left down Woodward Avenue to Fort Street, then turn right on Fort and walk one block to Griswold Street. On the
7 southeast corner is the **Penobscot Building,** the tallest office building in Michigan. (The blinking red light atop its 47 stories has been part of the Detroit skyline since 1928.) Two blocks farther on Fort, at the corner of Washington Boulevard, the
8 **Comerica Bank** stands on the site of Fort Lernoult, headquarters of the British when they held the city. The bank has a first-floor art exhibit that is open to the public free during business hours.

Go east one block to Shelby Street, turn left, and walk three
9 blocks north to reach triangular **Capitol Park,** the site of Michigan's first capitol (the capitol was moved to Lansing in 1846). A statue of Steven T. Mason, who was elected the first governor at age 23, stands over his grave in the park.

Walk one block west to Washington Boulevard, turn right, and
10 go north to **Grand Circus Park.** In his early plan for Detroit, Judge Woodward envisioned a complete circus (circle) here; only half was built. The park has two fountains, the larger one in the west park honoring Thomas A. Edison. The solemn figures seated at the corners are two former Detroit mayors, Hazen Pingree and William Maybury. Nearby is a statue of Christopher Columbus.

Exit from the east park onto Witherell, then walk two blocks east on Madison and make a right. Where Madison intersects **⑪** Grand River Avenue, you'll find tiny **Harmonie Park.** Named for a musical society formed in 1848, it is the site of a number of art galleries and shops. On the east side of the park, at the corner of Randolph Street and Centre Street, is the 50-year-old **⑫** **Detroit Artists Market** (1452 Randolph St., tel. 313/ 962–0337), where local artists show and sell their work.

Continue south down Randolph Street to Fort, turn left and go **⑬** one block to Brush Street to reach **Bricktown,** a collection of dining spots and bars in a refurbished corner of downtown. Characterized by brick facades on a majority of the buildings, Bricktown is a place for a leisurely lunch, a shopping spree, or cocktails. The newest addition is the **Millender Center,** which houses the 240-room Omni International Hotel, a 33-story apartment tower, restaurants and shops, and six parking levels. Millender is connected by pedestrian skywalks to the City–County Building and the Renaissance Center.

Some 70 years ago a thriving Greek community was focused on a prosperous one-block section of Monroe Street five blocks **⑭** north of the Ren Cen. The area is now known as **Greektown.** Authentic restaurants serve shish kebab, *dolmathes* (stuffed grape leaves), baklava, and *saganaki* (flaming cheese). There are bakeries, bars, markets, coffeehouses, shops and boutiques, and, in summer, mimes, musicians, and street vendors. While some spots are new and trendy, others date from the community's origins.

⑮ In the center of Greektown, at 508 Monroe, is **Trappers Alley,** which once bustled with the wagons of fur traders and trappers delivering pelts to Traugott Schmidt & Sons Co., one of the Midwest's leading fur centers. Today the marketplace is a shopping enclave, created by restoring, remodeling, and enclosing five century-old buildings under one roof. Trappers Alley features a "city market" of produce, fruit, cheese, wine, baked goods, and fresh flowers sold by vendors in individual stalls; in all the complex contains more than 45 shops and 30 restaurants. Some of the furriers' equipment is still in place.

On the adjacent corner of Monroe and Beaubien streets, the **⑯** **Second Baptist Church,** organized in 1836, is Detroit's oldest black congregation. It was here that blacks gathered to celebrate the Emancipation Proclamation. A block away, at **⑰** Monroe and St. Antoine streets, is **Old St. Mary's,** a Catholic church built in 1885 but dating from 1833 as a parish of Irish and German immigrants.

Exploring East Detroit

Numbers in the margin correspond with points of interest on the East and Near Northwest Detroit map.

In the 1880s the section east of what is now the Renaissance Center, between the river and Jefferson Avenue, blossomed with lumberyards, shipyards, and railroads. The area, known **❶** as **Rivertown,** is seeing new life today with parks, shops, and housing developments. Set in rejuvenated warehouses and carriage houses are new restaurants and night spots: the **Rhinoceros** offers dining in an old stone stable; **Soup Kitchen Saloon** has casual dining and entertainment in a former bordel-

Exploring East and Near Northwest Detroit

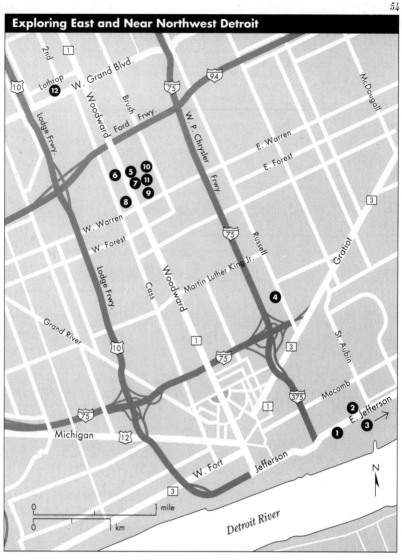

Belle Isle, **3**
Children's Museum, **5**
Detroit Public Library, **8**
Eastern Market, **4**

Historical Museum, **6**
Institute of Arts, **7**
International Institute, **10**
Museum of African-American History, **11**

New Center, **12**
Pewabic Pottery, **2**
Rivertown, **1**
Science Center, **9**

lo; **Woodbridge Tavern** is an old-fashioned speakeasy owned by the same family since 1905. The nine-acre riverside **Chene Park,** opened in 1984, has concerts, festivals, and special events. **Stroh Riverplace,** opened in 1988, is attracting new businesses, restaurants, and shops to a 21-acre site that lay empty for years. **Harbortown,** a complex of condos and apartments, is under construction on the riverfront.

Rivertown is also the home of ceramic Pewabic tiles, found in buildings throughout the nation and widely used in Detroit renovation projects. **Pewabic Pottery** was founded in 1907 by the late Mary Chase Stratton, who produced the brilliantly glazed clay tiles that became the company's hallmark. The pottery contains a ceramic museum, contemporary gallery, workshop, and learning center. *10125 E. Jefferson Ave., tel. 313/ 822-0954. Museum and gallery open Mon.–Sat. 10–5. Admission free. Guided tours by appointment Tues.–Sat. 10–5; admission: $2 adults, $1 students and over 59.*

A popular attraction, especially in summer, is **Belle Isle** (tel. 313/267-7115), a thousand–acre island park in the Detroit River three miles from the city center. (From downtown take E. Jefferson Ave. to E. Grand River Blvd. and turn onto Douglas MacArthur Bridge.) Belle Isle was granted to the French settlers by Cadillac as a public common and was called Ile au Cochon (Hog Island) until 1845. After the city purchased it in 1879 for $200,000, the landscape architect Frederick Law Olmsted was chosen to design it as a park.

Island visitors can enjoy a quiet walk in 238 acres of woods or take a scenic 5½-mile drive around the shore. There is a children's playground. A recently completed outdoor complex houses recreational facilities, including 10 lighted tennis courts; nine baseball diamonds; basketball courts; football, rugby, and soccer fields; a cinder track; bicycle trails; a putting green and a nine-hole golf course; a half-mile-long beach; and a 20-station fitness trail. The **Whitcomb Conservatory** has year-round flower shows, permanent displays of cacti, ferns, and palms, and one of the largest orchid collections in the country.

Belle Isle Aquarium (tel. 313/267-7159), one of the nation's oldest municipal aquariums, dating from 1904, exhibits more than 200 species of fish, reptiles, and amphibians. *Admission free. Open daily 10–5.*

Belle Isle Nature Center (tel. 313/267-7157) has changing exhibits and audiovisual presentations on area nature. Woodland trails offer closer looks at the island's plants and animals. *Admission free. Open Wed.–Sun. 10–4.*

Belle Isle Zoo (tel. 313/267-7160 or 398–0903) covers 25 acres. Visitors may stroll along an elevated walkway for views of animals roaming uncaged in natural settings. *Admission: $2 adults, $1 over 62, 50¢ ages 5–12. Open May 1–Oct. 31, Mon.– Sat. 10–5, Sun. and holidays 9–6.*

Dossin Great Lakes Museum (tel. 313/267–6440) has displays about the Great Lakes, from sailing vessels to modern freighters. Just inside the main door is a restored smoking lounge from the steamer *City of Detroit III*, built in 1912; called the Gothic Room, it contains more than seven tons of hand-carved oak arches, stained glass, and decorative work. Visitors can listen to ship-to-shore radio messages and view the river and city through a periscope. *100 Strand Dr., Bell Isle, Detroit, MI 48207. Admission: $1 adults, 50¢ senior citizens and children over 12. Open Wed.–Sun. 10–5:30; closed holidays.*

❹ The **Eastern Market** (tel. 313/833–1560) is a 10-acre patchwork of produce and meatpacking houses, fish markets, wholesale import shops, pubs, and restaurants. From 5 to 9 AM Monday to Saturday wholesalers do business with supermarkets, produce dealers, and restaurants. Private individuals are welcome but must be prepared to buy by the bushel or the case. Public shopping hours are Saturday 10–6. Items are displayed in gaily painted open-air sheds dating from 1892. Barter and bargain are key words; the air is filled with the scent of exotic spices and home-baked goods; peddlers shout and street musicians and tangled traffic add to the confusion.

The architecture of the district is late Victorian; most buildings are of brick. Market Street is its heart, while Riopelle Street is considered the street for produce. A majority of the meat processors are on Orleans Street. The R. Hirt Jr. Co., at 2468 Market Street for over a century, has good buys on tea, cheese, and baskets (third floor, self-service).

Time Out An early breakfast can be had at the **Farmer's Restaurant** (2542 Market St., open at 3 AM), or **Butcher's Saloon** (1489 Winder St., open at 7 AM). The **Roma Cafe** (3401 Riopelle St.) is one of Detroit's oldest restaurants, serving good Italian food in a building dating from 1855.

Exploring Near Northwest Detroit

The **Detroit Cultural Center** is a cluster of municipal, state, and private educational and cultural institutions concentrated in some 40 city blocks 2½ miles from downtown via Woodward Avenue. The **Detroit Festival of the Arts,** held there each September, is a three-day street arts fair with mimes, jugglers, musicians, dancers, and booths displaying artists' work.

Among the center's attractions are:

❺ The **Children's Museum.** A unit of the Detroit Public Schools, it contains exhibits on everything from dolls and toys to birds and life in other cultures. A planetarium shows the night sky in Detroit and faraway lands. Outdoors near the entrance is *Silverbolt,* a chrome-plated life-size horse sculpture made of automobile bumpers. *67 E. Kirby, between Woodward Ave. and John R. St., tel. 313/492–1210. Admission free. Open year-round weekdays 1–4; Oct.–May, Sat. 9–4.*

❻ The **Detroit Historical Museum.** Its exhibits allow visitors to "walk through" the city's history from 1701. "Streets of Old Detroit" depicts three historical periods: the 1840s, with cobblestone streets and wooden sidewalks; the 1870s, with cedar-block pavement and ornate Victorian storefronts; and an 1895–1905 street of brick, lined with authentically equipped stores. New is the Booth-Wilkinson Costume Gallery, which features 50,000 women's garments and accessories. Special film and educational programs are presented throughout the year. *5401 Woodward Ave., tel. 313/833–1805. Admission: voluntary donation. Open Wed.–Sun. 9:30–5; closed holidays.*

7 The **Detroit Institute of Arts.** Dating from 1885, it is among the five largest fine-arts museums in the United States. It has recently undergone extensive expansion and renovation of its 101 galleries, exterior, and grounds. Highlights of the collections are Van Gogh's *Self-Portrait,* Joos Van Cleve's *Adoration of the Magi,* and Jan van Eyck's *St. Jerome in His Study.* Notable, too, are four immense Diego Rivera frescoes titled *Detroit Industry,* the William Randolph Hearst collection of armor, the Tannahill collection of Impressionist paintings, and the G. Mennen Williams collection of African art. The Paul McPharlin Gallery of Puppets contains a large collection of historical specimens. There are also important collections of sculpture, clocks, china, silver, and other furnishings. *5200 Woodward Ave., tel. 313/833–7900. Children under 12 must be accompanied by adults. Admission free, donations accepted. Open Tues.–Sun. 9:30–5:30; closed holidays.*

Time Out The museum's **Kresge Court Cafe** offers cafeteria dining in a European-style courtyard Tuesday to Saturday from 11:30 to 4 and Sunday 1 to 4. The museum dining room has a gourmet menu Tuesday to Friday from 11 to 2 (reservations required).

8 Home to 1.3 million books, the Cultural Center branch of the **Detroit public library** is the largest of the system's 24 branches. It holds a large, thorough collection of automobile history; the Burton Historical Collection, a joint venture of the Detroit Historical Society and the library, is the state's most comprehensive on Detroit, Michigan, and Great Lakes lore. The Italian Renaissance building, constructed in 1921 of white Vermont marble, has Pewabic tiles decorating the Biography Room, murals by Edwin Blashfield and Gari Melchers, stained-glass windows designed by Frederick J. Wiley, and mosaic panels depicting *The Seven Ages of Man.* Adam Strohm Hall on the third floor has special exhibits and also murals identifying Michigan with a century of development in transportation. *5201 Woodward Ave., tel. 313/833–1000 or 833–1722 for 24–hr recorded information. Admission free. Open Tues. and Thurs. –Sat. 9:30–5:30, Wed. 9–9.*

9 The **Detroit Science Center.** A space capsule in the lobby— usually surrounded by excited youngsters—sets the tone for a museum where visitors are encouraged to touch, pull, push, and turn the controls of more than 50 exhibits. Visitors travel through a kaleidoscopic cylindrical tube to the space theater, which has 244 tilt-back seats and 180-degree films that allow one to fly over land, travel under water, and race to the limits of space. *5020 John R. St. at Warren St., tel. 313/577–8400. Admission: $4 adults, $3 children 6–12, $2 senior citizens, 75¢ children 4–5. Open Tues.–Fri. 9–4, Sat. 10–7, Sun. noon–7.*

10 The **International Institute** is a museum, working social agency for the foreign-born, and a lunchtime cafe. Its "gallery of nations" features the arts and crafts of 43 countries. Weekday cafeteria luncheons are available from 11 to 2 in the **Melting Pot Cafe.** The Tiny Shop sells ethnic crafts and gift items. *111 E. Kirby St., tel. 313/871–8600. Admission free. Open weekdays 8:30–5.*

11 The **Museum of African-American History,** the newest addition to the Cultural Center, is housed in a $3.5-million trapezoid-shape building that opened in 1987. (The institution was

founded in 1965.) The inaugural exhibit was "An Epic of Heroism: The Underground Railroad in Michigan, 1837–1870,"
depicting the history of the slave trade and the network that
sheltered and conveyed fugitive slaves to freedom. Two smaller
galleries have exhibits on African art; the entrance to the museum features the *Portals of Sankofa,* using African symbols to
tell the story of the black experience in America. *301 Frederick
Douglass, tel. 313/833–9800. Admission free. Open Tues.–Sat.
9–5.*

⑫ The **New Center,** at Woodward Avenue and Grand Boulevard,
contains the home of General Motors, the Unisys world headquarters, the Fisher Building, and a $50-million retail-office
complex, New Center One. Glass-enclosed skywalks link businesses, hotels, theaters, and restaurants. The Detroit Opera's
fall season takes place in the Fisher Theater; summer concerts
and other events are presented in the parks.

Other Points of Interest

The ornate **Fisher Mansion,** the former home of Fisher Body
Company founder Lawrence Fisher, now serves as the
Bhaktivedanta Cultural Center, a learning center operated by
members of the Hare Krishna community. Visitors can tour the
elaborately decorated Italianate mansion; the former dining
room is now a vegetarian restaurant. *383 Lenox Ave., tel. 313/
331–6740. Admission: $4 adults, $3 senior citizens and students. Open Fri.–Sun. noon–9 PM.*

The **Edsel and Eleanor Ford House,** set on 62 acres overlooking
Lake St. Clair, was the home of Henry Ford's only son. The
Cotswold-style stone mansion, with its leaded and stained-
glass windows and interior carved paneling imported from England, also contains the Fords' extraordinary art collection.
*1100 Lake Shore Rd., in suburban Grosse Pointe Shores, tel.
313/884–4222. ½ hr from downtown; follow E. Jefferson Ave. to
Lake Shore Rd. Admission: $3 adults, $2 senior citizens, $1
children under 13. Open Wed.–Sun. 1–4, with guided tours on
the hour.*

Historic Fort Wayne was built along the river in 1843 to protect
the northern U.S. border. One of the best-preserved pre-Civil
War forts in the nation, it still has its original stone barracks
and powder magazine. Walking tours, exhibits, and costumed
interpreters present the fort's history; other attractions on site
include the **Tuskegee Airmen Museum** (dedicated to America's
first black military aviation unit) and the **Great Lakes Indian
Museum.** *6325 W. Jefferson Ave. at Livernois, tel. 313/297–
9360. Admission: $1 adults, 50¢ senior citizens and children.
Open May 1–Labor Day, Wed.–Sun. 9:30–5.*

In the Detroit River between Michigan and Ontario, **Boblo
Island** is a 272-acre amusement park featuring 75 rides (three
of them roller coasters), shows, onstage reviews, and 25 food
stands and restaurants. A 314-foot Sky Tower allows a 20-mile
view from a rotating observation cabin. *Park open late May–
Labor Day daily at 11, closing times vary. Boblo Island served
by ferries from Amherstburg, Ontario (10-min ride); Gibraltar, MI (45-min ride); and Detroit (90-min ride). Detroit departures begin 9:30 AM from Boblo Dock, Clark Ave. (I–75 SW
to Clark Ave., exit 47A, follow signs to dock). Ample parking.*

Boblo Island, 151 W. Jefferson Ave., tel. 313/259–7500. Admission: $14.95 adults, $12.95 under 10; transportation, rides, and shows included.

The **Detroit Zoological Park,** in the suburb of Royal Oak, covers 122 acres and is one of the largest and most modern zoos in the country. Grouped by continents, animals appear in natural environments without bars. The zoo houses what is described as the world's largest penguinarium and has a walk-through aviary featuring tropical birds and plants and a waterfall. Other highlights are the reptile and polar-bear exhibits. *8450 W. Ten Mile Rd., 1 block west of Woodward Ave., tel. 313/398–0903. Admission: $3.50 adults, $2 over 62, $1.50 children 5–12, free under 5; parking $2. Open May–Oct., daily 10–5; Nov.–Apr., Wed.–Sun. 10–4.*

In Bloomfield Hills, **Cranbrook** was originally the 300-acre estate of the publisher of *The Detroit News*, George G. Booth, and his wife, Ellen Scripps Booth. It is now a cultural and educational center, with art and science museums, a graduate art academy, and college preparatory schools. **Cranbrook House and Gardens** preserves the heart of the original estate. Designed by the architect Albert Kahn and built in 1908, the English-style manor features leaded-glass windows, imported tapestries, and art objects. The 40-acre gardens display both casual and formal plantings, fieldstone terraces, fountains, sculpture, pine walks, and an Oriental garden. *380 Lone Pine Rd. at Woodward Ave., Bloomfield Hills, tel. 313/645–3149. Separate admission to each: $2 adults, $1.50 senior citizens and students. Cranbrook House open Apr.–Oct., 4th Sun. of each month 2–4 PM; July and Aug., select Sun. Cranbrook Gardens open June–Aug., Mon.–Sat. 10–5, Sun. 1–5; May and Sept., daily 1–5.*

The **Cranbrook Academy of Art Museum,** set amid manicured lawns, reflecting pools, and sculpture by Carl Milles, has a permanent collection including works by Eliel and Eero Saarinen, Harry Bertoia, Charles Eames, and other Cranbrook artists, architects, and designers. The galleries show changing works of contemporary art. There is a museum gift shop and a bookstore. *500 Lone Pine Rd., tel. 313/645–3312. Admission: $2.50 adults, $1.50 students and senior citizens, free under 7. Open Tues.–Sun. 1–5; closed holidays.*

The **Cranbrook Institute of Science** is a natural-history museum with an outstanding mineral collection, hands-on physics exhibits, and a Hall of Lights, with holograms and other forms of entertainment. A new dinosaur laboratory enables visitors to watch staff members as they restore specimens. There is a planetarium show on Saturday and Sunday, and an observatory open Saturday evenings. *500 Lone Pine Rd., tel. 313/645–3200. Admission: $3 adults, $2 under 18 and over 65. Laser-light show admission $1.50 additional.*

In Rochester, the castle-like mansion **Meadow Brook Hall** was built between 1926 and 1929 by Alfred Wilson and Matilda Dodge Wilson, widow of the auto pioneer John Dodge. In its 100 rooms are 24 fireplaces, a massive great hall with a carved wolf's head at the end of a banister, solariums, a large library with carved paneling, works of art, hidden staircases, antique needlepoint draperies, sculptured ceilings, courtyards, and gardens. Some 80 percent of the original furnishings remain intact. The hall is now used as a conference and cultural center for Oakland University. A summer tearoom and buffet dinners are available to guests touring the mansion. *3 mi west of Rochester via Walton Blvd. and Adams Rd. on Oakland University campus, tel. 313/370–3140. Admission: $4 adults, $3 over 64, $2 under 13. Open July–Aug., Mon.–Sat. 10–5, Sun. 1–5; Sept.– June, Sun. 1–5.*

Henry Ford Museum and Greenfield Village (*see* Dearborn in Excursions from Detroit).

Detroit for Free

On **Belle Isle** (*see* Exploring East Detroit), the Belle Isle Aquarium and Nature Center are free, as are many of the activities—hiking, the children's playground, the gardens, and picnic areas. *Tel. 313/267–7115.*

Detroit Free Press **Tours** introduce visitors to the newspaper's editorial, composing, and printing facilities. *321 W. Lafayette Blvd., tel. 313/222–8655. Tours Tues. and Thurs. 9:30 and 11 AM, Wed. 9:30 and 10:30.*

The **Detroit Garden Center** features walled gardens at the Moross House, Detroit's oldest brick home. *1400 E. Jefferson Ave., tel. 313/259–6363. Call for hours.*

The **Sibley House,** built for Mrs. Simon Sibley, widow of Detroit's first mayor, is a Greek Revival home built in 1848 and recently renovated by the Junior League of Detroit. *976 E. Jefferson Ave., tel. 313/881–0040. Call for hours.*

The **Fire Historical Museum** features exhibits on and mementos of the early days of fire fighting in Detroit. *2737 Gratiot at Chene, tel. 313/224–2035. Open weekdays 9–5.*

Many of the museums in the Cultural Center are open without charge (*see* Exploring Near Northwest), as are these nearby:

Wayne State University Museum, which features displays of the ecology of plants and animals. *319 Old Main Bldg. (Cass St. at Warren St.), tel. 313/577–2555. Open weekdays 1:30–4:30.*

The **Sarkis Galleries,** in the Yamasaki Building, College of Art and Design, present revolving exhibitions of faculty, alumni, and guest artists' works. A student-run gallery is on the lower level. *245 E. Kirby St., tel. 313/872–3118. Open weekdays 9–4.*

What to See and Do with Children

Belle Isle Aquarium, Nature Center, Zoo (*see* Exploring East Detroit).

Detroit Tigers baseball (*see* Spectator Sports).

Children's Museum (*see* Exploring Near Northwest).

Detroit Institute of Arts (*see* Exploring Near Northwest). In the red-carpet area, children can play the "Thinker's Guessing Game," a computer quiz designed to teach art appreciation. In the Rivera Court, youngsters can begin an archaeological hunt through the ancient galleries as they play the "Mystery of the Five Fragments" with the help of a clue booklet. *5200 Woodward Ave., tel. 313/833–7900. Admission free. Open Tues.– Sun. 9:30–5:30.*

Detroit Science Center (*see* Exploring Near Northwest).

Detroit Youtheater. Weekend programs designed for young folks take place in the auditorium at the Detroit Institute of Arts. *5200 Woodward Ave., tel. 313/833–7900. Admission: $3.50. Call for schedule.*

Detroit Zoo (*see* Other Points of Interest).

Boblo Island Amusement Park (*see* Other Points of Interest).

Cranbrook Institute of Science (*see* Other Points of Interest).

Detroit Historical Museum (*see* Exploring Near Northwest).

Henry Ford Museum and Greenfield Village (*see* Dearborn in Excursions from Detroit).

Dossin Great Lakes Museum (*see* Exploring East Detroit).

The People Mover (*see* Exploring Downtown).

Off the Beaten Track

The World of Ford is a product-and-technology exhibition displaying the Ford Motor Company's newest automotive products, components, and technological advances—futuristic prototype vehicles, racing machines, robots, and videos on auto racing and other automotive subjects. *Renaissance Center Level 2 in corridors between Towers 200 and 300. Admission free. Open weekdays 10–6, Sat. noon–6.*

Nearly lost in the bustle surrounding the Renaissance Center and the entrance to the Detroit–Windsor Tunnel, **Old Mariner's Church** is the Maritime Sailor's Cathedral that folksinger Gordon Lightfoot wrote about in "The Wreck of the Edmund Fitzgerald." Founded as a mission to Great Lakes sailors in 1849, it has been extensively remodeled and refurbished over the years and was moved to its present site in 1955. There are maritime scenes in some of its stained glass windows, marine carvings and models in the sanctuary, and a memorial to lost sailors. Regular services are Thursday at noon and Sunday at 8:30 and 11 AM. *170 E. Jefferson Ave., across the street to west of Ren Cen, tel. 313/259–2206. Open Mon.–Sat. 10–4. Brief tours can be arranged by calling.*

The **John K. King Bookstore,** Michigan's largest bookstore, has five floors of some 600,000 used and rare books, as well as prints, photos, and paintings, in a warehouselike setting. *901 W. Lafayette Blvd., tel. 313/961–0622. Open Mon.–Sat. 9:30–5:30.*

The **Holocaust Memorial Center** displays film clips, photos, artifacts, and video highlighting Jewish history, particularly the Holocaust. At the end of a guided tour a Holocaust survivor answers questions. *6602 West Maple Rd., West Bloomfield, tel. 313/661–0840. Admission free. Open Sun.–Tues. and Thurs. 10–3:30, Wed. 10–7:30. Guided tours Wed. 6 PM, Sun. 1 and 2:15.*

Dubbed "Hitsville USA," the **Motown Museum** is set in the house in which Berry Gordy Jr. lived and started Motown Records. On the lower level is his small recording studio. Videos and artifacts, including record album covers, top-selling records, performers' costumes, and photographs, tell the Motown story. *2648 W. Grand Blvd., tel. 313/875–2264. Admission: $2. Open weekdays 10–5, Sun. 2–5; closed holidays.*

American Coney Island is a tiny restaurant that affords a look at the real Detroit—teeming and bustling, with waiters and kitchen help shouting, and a diverse clientele. A Coney Island is a hot dog covered with chili. *114 W. Lafayette St., tel. 313/ 961–7758. No credit cards. Inexpensive.*

Shopping

Shopping Districts The downtown shopping district extends along Woodward Avenue from Grand Circus Park to the riverfront.

In the Renaissance Center is the **World of Shops,** with some 80 retail outlets. *E. Jefferson Ave., tel. 313/568–5626. Open Mon.–Sat. 10–6; some stores open Sun. 1–5.*

The shops of the new **Millender Center,** which can be reached by all-weather walkways from the Ren Cen or the City–County Building, include a bakery, bank, beauty and barber shops, bookstores, and jewelers. *340 E. Congress St., tel. 313/222–1300. Most stores open Mon.–Sat. 10–7.*

Trappers Alley Festival Marketplace in Greektown has 70 or so stores, gift shops, food booths, and restaurants. *508 Monroe St., tel. 313/963–5445. Open Mon.–Thurs. 10–9, Fri. and Sat. 10 AM–midnight, Sun. noon–9.*

The **Eastern Market** is open to the general public on Saturday from 10 to 6, and stores around it are open daily. *2934 Russell St., tel. 313/833–1560.*

New Center One Mall has weatherproof skywalks connecting its more than 50 stores, shops, galleries, and restaurants to the Fisher Building, the General Motors Building, and the Hotel St. Regis. *Grand and Second Blvds. in New Center area, tel. 313/874–0480. Open Mon.–Sat. 10–6; some stores open Sun. noon–5.*

In the **Somerset Mall** are such well-known stores as Saks Fifth Avenue, Bonwit Teller, Gucci, Brooks Brothers, Laura Ashley, Brookstone, and Ann Taylor. *2801 W. Big Beaver Rd., Troy, tel. 313/643–6360. Open Mon., Thurs., Fri. 10–9; Tues., Wed., Sat. 10–6; Sun. noon–5.*

Department Stores **Crowley's** is well known for fashions for men, women, and children, as well as home furnishings and gifts. Several locations include a new store in the New Center One Shopping Mall.

J. L. Hudson's, a leader in fashion and home merchandise, offers wardrobe and shopping services, personal services, restaurants, and bakeries at eight metropolitan locations, including the Fairlane Town Mall in Dearborn.

Specialty Stores **Alabama Antiques** deals in clocks, china, glassware, dolls, and
Antiques toys. *13207 Livernois, tel. 313/933–0300.*

Antiques on Main features 25 dealers in antiques, furniture, glassware, and collectibles. *115 S. Main, Royal Oak, tel. 313/ 545–4663.*

Art Dealers **DuMouchelle Art Galleries Co.** offers fine arts, antiques, and collectibles at auctions held the third weekend of every month. *Across from the Renaissance Center, 409 E. Jefferson Ave., tel. 313/963–6255.*

Detroit Artists Market sells contemporary works by Michigan artists. *1452 Randolph St., tel. 313/962–0337.*

Jewelry **Meyer Jewelry Co.** (1400 Woodward Ave. at Grand River Ave., tel. 313/963–1530) has been a leading jeweler for many years; watch repair.

David Wachler & Sons (Renaissance Center Tower 200, Level 1, tel. 313/963–1530) offers award-winning jewelry, designed in the shop, and rings, earrings, and watches.

Men's Apparel **Anton's** (Renaissance Center Tower 300, Level 1, tel. 313/259–9290) carries business and sportswear in designer and private labels.

La Mirage (29555 Northwestern Hwy., Southfield, tel. 313/356–7666) is a classic men's boutique.

Women's Apparel **Carnaby Shoes** (Renaissance Center between Towers 200 and 300) sells Bandolino, Capezio, Golo, Liz Claiborne fashions.

Lynn Portnoy (522 Brush St., Bricktown, tel. 313/964–0339) carries fashions for the businesswoman.

Kathy Scott (148 Pierce St., Birmingham, tel. 313/642–3064) offers select suits and dresses.

Toys **Bear Essentials** (Southland Shopping Center, Taylor, tel. 313/287–4450) carries a full line of bears and bearaphernalia.

Sports and Fitness

Beaches Many of the 13 **Metroparks** (tel. 313/227–2757 or 800/247–2757) of the Huron Clinton Metropolitan Authority offer swimming. Beaches and pools open beginning Memorial Day weekend.

Beaches with bathhouses are at **Metro Beach Metropark** (on Lake St. Clair 5 mi SE of Mt. Clemens, tel. 313/463–4581), with a beach shop, sailboard school and rental, and canoe rental; **Stony Creek Metropark** (6 mi N of Utica, tel. 313/781–4242), and **Kensington Metropark** (near Milford–Brighton, tel. 313/685–1561), with boat rental.

A half-mile-long beach with changing houses is at Belle Isle (E. Jefferson and E. Grand Aves., tel. 313/267–7115).

Bicycling Belle Island and most Huron-Clinton Metroparks have scenic bicycle trails. Rentals at Stony Creek Metropark.

Cross-country Skiing Most cross-country skiing in Detroit is done in the parks. For information on trails in the city, call the Detroit Parks and Recreation Department (tel. 313/224–1100). Many of the Huron-Clinton Metroparks have trails (tel. 313/227–2757 or 800/247–2757). Information on trails in Oakland County parks is available from its Parks and Recreation Department (tel. 313/858–0960).

Tennis Belle Isle has 10 lighted tennis courts (E. Jefferson Ave. at E. Grand Ave., tel. 313/267–7115). There are courts in Metro Beach Metropark, Hudson Mills Metropark, Lower Huron Metropark, and Willow Metropark. For information, tel. 800/247–2757. The city has several public courts, with those at Belle Isle and Palmer Park (W. Seven Mile Rd. at Woodward Ave., tel. 313/876–0428) regarded among the best.

Downhill Skiing Several downhill ski areas lie within a short drive from Detroit: phone ahead for schedules. For a recorded report on snow conditions statewide, call 800/292–5404 in Michigan, 800/248–5708 elsewhere.

Alpine Valley in Milford has 23 runs, 9 chair lifts, 14 rope tows, and snowmaking; its longest run is 1,800 feet with a vertical drop of 220 feet. Rentals, instruction, repairs, ski shop, cafeterias, lounge/bar, snack bar, entertainment. *6755 E. Highland, 10 mi west of Telegraph Rd., tel. 313/887–4183.*

Mt. Brighton Ski Area in Brighton has 22 runs, seven chair lifts, 10 rope tows, and snowmaking; its longest run is 1,500 feet with a vertical drop of 250 feet. Rentals, instruction, ski shop, restaurant, bar/lounge, entertainment. *4141 Bauer Rd., tel. 313/ 229–9581.*

Mt. Holly Inc. in Holly has 17 runs, seven chair lifts, four rope tows, and snowmaking; its longest run is 2,100 feet, with a vertical drop of 325 feet. Rental, instruction, ski shop, restaurant, lounge/bar, entertainment. *13536 S. Dixie Hwy. 18 mi north of Pontiac on U.S. 10, tel. 313/582–7256.*

Pine Knob Ski Resort in Clarkston has 20 runs, five chair lifts, eight rope tows, and snowmaking; its longest run is 3,250 feet with a vertical drop of 300 feet. Rental, instruction, ski shop, restaurant, lounge, bar, entertainment. *Box 16499, 8 mi north of Pontiac on I–75 Exit 189, ¼ mi on right, tel. 313/625–0800.*

Riverview Highlands Ski Area in Riverview has 10 runs, two chair lifts, two pomas, one rope tow, two pony tows, and snowmaking; its longest run is 1,500 feet, with a vertical drop of 195 feet. Cross-country skiing, instruction, rental, ski shop, restaurant, lounge/bar, entertainment. *15015 Sibley Rd., 18 mi south of Detroit on I–75 to Exit 34B, 2 mi west, tel. 313/ 479–2080.*

Fishing About 100 lakes in the metropolitan area offer good fishing for bluegills, crappies, walleye, bass, and northern pike. Fishing is often good in the Detroit River, especially around Belle Isle. Bait-and-tackle shops can provide information. Charter fishing for lake trout, salmon, and walleye on Lake St. Clair and Lake Erie is offered by Fun-N-Fish Charters (360 Ashland, tel. 313/ 882–3018) and Fishing Tours and Great Lakes Charters Unlimited (25218 Acacia, Southfield, tel. 313/355–0530). Huron-Clinton Metroparks have fishing (tel. 313/227–2757 or 800/247–2757); Stony Creek, Kensington, and Lake Erie Metroparks are especially popular.

Golf The metropolitan area has more than 100 golf courses. Municipal courses are at **Belle Isle Park** (tel. 313/267–7130), 9 holes; **Chandler Park** (Chandler Park Dr. at Dickerson, tel. 313/267–7150), 18 holes; **Palmer Park** (1 W. Seven Mile Rd. at Woodward Ave., tel. 313/876–0428), 18 holes; **Rackham** (10100 W. Ten Mile Rd., Huntington, tel. 313/564–4939), 18 holes; **William Rogell Park** (18601 Berg Rd., tel. 313/935–5331), 18 holes; and **Rouge Park** (11701 Burt Rd. at Plymouth, tel. 313/935–3761), 18 holes. Rackham and William Rogell are considered the best of these.

Jogging and Fitness Most joggers use the city parks. You can jog the three miles to Belle Isle from downtown (along E. Jefferson Ave. to E. Grand Ave.) or drive to and jog around the island. The Downtown YMCA (2020 Witherell, tel. 313/962–6126) has an indoor pool, running track, exercise and weights rooms, a gymnasium, and racquetball, squash, and handball courts.

Spectator Sports

Auto Racing Indy Championship cars, NASCAR stock cars, and others race at Michigan International Speedway 60 miles west of Detroit. *12626 U.S. 12, Brooklyn, tel. 313/961–1922.*

Baseball The **Detroit Tigers** play at the 50,000-seat Tiger Stadium, the oldest U.S. ballpark. *2121 Trumble Ave. at Michigan Ave., tel. 313/963–9444, or 962–4000 for recorded ticket information.*

Some 1,600 softball teams play an April–October season at **Softball City** at the Michigan State Fairgrounds. *1001 W. Eight Mile Rd., tel. 313/368–1850.*

Basketball The **Detroit Pistons** of the NBA play in the Palace of Auburn Hills (3777 Lapeer Rd., Auburn Hills, tel. 313/377–0100.) The **University of Detroit Titans** play in Calihan Hall (main campus, W. McNichols at Livernois, tel. 313/927–1700). **Wayne State University** (tel. 313/577–4280) also fields a basketball team.

Boat Racing The **Spirit of Detroit** unlimited hydroplane races in the Detroit River pit outstanding hydroplane drivers in June. *Spirit of Detroit Association, Box 8819, 48824, tel. 313/763–4423.*

Football The **Detroit Lions** play in the Pontiac Silverdome (1200 Featherstone, Pontiac, tel. 313/335–4151). Both the **University of Detroit** (tel. 313/927–1700) and **Wayne State** (tel. 313/577–4280) field football teams.

Hockey The **Detroit Red Wings** of the NHL play in Joe Louis Arena, downtown on the riverfront. *600 Civic Center Dr., tel. 313/567–6000.*

Horse Racing Four racetracks in the area provide harness racing year-round: Hazel Park Harness Raceway (1650 E. Ten Mile Rd., Hazel Park, tel. 313/398–1000); Ladbroke Detroit Race Course (28001 Schoolcraft Rd., Livonia, tel. 313/525–7300); Northville Downs (301 S. Center St., Northville, tel. 313/349–1000), and Windsor Raceway (Hwy. 18, Windsor, Ont., tel. 313/961–9545). In addition, Ladbroke Detroit Race Course has thoroughbred racing.

Dining

by Jeremy Iggers

Currently a restaurant critic for the Star Tribune *in Minneapolis, Jeremy Iggers was food writer for the Detroit Free Press from 1980 to 1987.*

The tremendous diversity of the Detroit restaurant scene may surprise first-time visitors. As the auto industry has brought waves of immigrants to the city, each wave has made its culinary mark. You'll find soul food restaurants in the inner city, a vibrant Mexican community on the west side, and America's largest Arabic community just west of Detroit in Dearborn. There are excellent Polish cafes in Hamtramck, an independent municipality surrounded by Detroit.

Detroiters often dine across the river in Windsor, Ontario, which boasts its own rich ethnic restaurant mix: Italian, Ukrainian, French, German, Hungarian, Afghani, Yugoslav, Vietnamese, and most notably, authentic and inexpensive Chinese restaurants. A favorable rate of exchange makes the Canadian restaurants excellent values.

The metropolitan area also has its share of celebrity chefs, who produce haute cuisine in very personal styles. Best known of the local talent is Jimmy Schmidt, who gained a national reputation at Detroit's venerable London Chop House, left to open the Rattlesnake Club in Denver, and recently returned as partner and chef in the new Detroit Rattlesnake Club. Czech-born Milos Cihelka of the Golden Mushroom in Southfield is known as a wild game and wild mushroom specialist; Ed Janos of Chez Raphael in Novi and Keith Famie of Les Auteurs in Royal Oak both cook in an eclectic "nouvelle American" style.

The most highly recommended restaurants in each price category are indicated by a star ★.

Category	Cost*
Very Expensive	over $25
Expensive	$20–$25
Moderate	$12–$20
Inexpensive	under $12

per person, excluding drinks, service, and sales tax (4%)

The following credit card abbreviations are used: AE, American Express; CB, Carte Blanche; DC, Diners Club; MC, MasterCard; V, Visa.

American **Chez Raphael.** No expense was spared in converting this former automobile showroom into a luxurious suburban assemblage of wood and stone in country French style. New chef Ed Janos, who gained recognition for his imaginative regional American cuisine while working in a more modest establishment, is now showing what he can do with (almost) unlimited resources. Typical dishes include stuffed breast of pintelle guinea hen with truffles and vegetables in Champagne sauce, and Alaskan halibut rolled in lobster mousse and sealed in phyllo pastry. *27000 Sheraton Dr., Novi, tel. 348–5555. Reservations recommended. Jacket and tie recommended. AE, CB, DC, MC, V. No lunch. Closed Sun. Very Expensive.*

The London Chop House. Don't be fooled by the basement setting and the informal decor. Once Detroit's premier restaurant, the legendary Chop is still where the elite meet to eat in downtown Detroit. The traditional clientele is mostly content with simpler fare, of the highest quality and flawlessly presented: steaks, chops, seafood, even "a mess of perch." But talented chef Grant Brown is also capable of more creative cuisine, from sautéed venison medallions with wild mushrooms to basil-jalapeño pasta with warm peppered beef. *155 W. Congress, downtown Detroit, tel. 313/926–0277. Reservations recommended. Jacket and tie required. AE, CB, DC, MC, V. Closed Sun. Very Expensive.*

★ **The Whitney.** After opening Van Dyke Place (*see Continental, below*), partners Fox and McCarthy decided to transform the Whitney mansion, once the home of lumber baron David Whitney, into an outrageously opulent palace of gastronomy. The detailed craftsmanship and the quality of the restoration are worth a visit in themselves, but the cuisine is a match for

Central Detroit Dining and Lodging

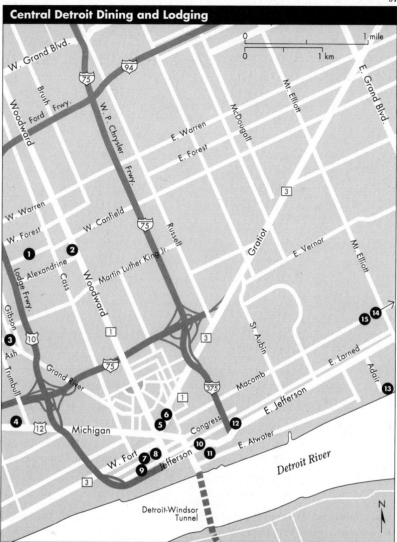

Dining

Blue Nile, **5**

Carl's Chop House, **3**

Caucus Club, **7**

London Chop House, **8**

Maxie's Left Field Deli, **4**

Pegasus Taverna, **6**

Rattlesnake Club, **13**

Royal Eagle, **14**

Summit, **11**

Traffic Jam and Snug, **1**

Van Dyke Place, **15**

Whitney, **2**

Lodging

Hotel Pontchartrain, **9**

Omni International, **10**

Shorecrest Motor Inn, **12**

Westin Hotel Renaissance Center Detroit, **11**

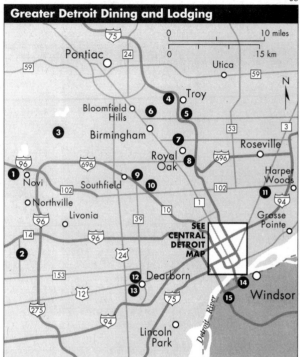

Greater Detroit Dining and Lodging

the setting: an imaginative, eclectic menu, ranging from lobster and salmon in brioche to chicken pot pie, flawlessly prepared and strikingly presented. A fun spot for Sunday brunch. *4421 Woodward Ave., Detroit, tel. 313/832–5700. Reservations recommended. Jacket and tie recommended. AE, MC, V. No lunch Sat. Very Expensive.*

The Caucus Club. This venerable Detroit institution is a period piece, dating to the era when elegant restaurants had cocktail lounges, piano bars, and boardroom decor with lots of wood and oil paintings. The menu is of similar vintage: corned beef hash, steaks, chops, Dover sole, and famous baby back ribs. Cuisine and service are of the highest standard. A favorite lunch spot for the old guard among Detroit's power elite. *150 W. Congress, Detroit, tel. 313/965–4970. Reservations recommended. Jacket and tie recommended. AE, CB, DC, MC, V. Closed Sun. Expensive.*

The Rattlesnake Club. The Detroit branch of Denver's Rattlesnake Club, a partnership of Santa Monica celebrity chef Michael McCarty and local star Jimmy Schmidt, is a showcase for Schmidt's imaginative style of cooking: crawfish wontons, salmon carpaccio with mustard and capers, roast chicken with endive, preserved lemon and chives. The decor is contemporary—Italian green marble and Brazilian cherrywood chairs. The adjoining Rattlesnake Grill offers a more casual menu. Good for Sunday brunch. *300 River Pl., Detroit, tel. 313/567–4400. Reservations recommended. Jacket and tie required in main dining room, jeans acceptable in grill. AE, CB, DC, MC, V. Main dining room closed for lunch on weekends. Expensive.*

The Summit. This revolving restaurant on the 71st floor of the Westin Hotel has a superb view of Detroit. The menu includes charbroiled steaks, chops, prime rib, and seafood, all served in quite generous portions. The quality is very good, but what you're really paying for is the view. *In the Westin Hotel, Renaissance Center, Detroit, tel. 313/568–8600. Reservations recommended. Jacket and tie recommended. AE, CB, DC, MC, V. Expensive.*

Carl's Chop House. Remember the old days, when fine dining meant going someplace with dark paneling and valet parking, where waitresses in polyester uniforms and white shoes would bring you relish trays and plastic-wrapped crackers and big juicy steaks? It's still that way at Carl's. The steaks are U.S.D.A. Prime, and the restaurant has a reputation for buying blue-ribbon winners at the Michigan State Fair. The menu also offers an extensive selection of seafoods. *3020 Grand River, Detroit, 313/833–0700. Reservations recommended. Jacket and tie recommended. AE, CB, DC, MC, V. Moderate.*

Les Auteurs. Brash, talented young Keith Famie pays homage to the giants of the culinary world in the decor of his trendy and popular new suburban cafe. His menus offer Chinese barbecued baby back ribs side by side with lamb osso bucco and confit of duck pizza topped with onions, shiitakes, lingonberries, and Camembert. *222 Sherman Dr., Washington Square Plaza, Royal Oak, tel. 313/544–2887. No reservations. Dress: casual. MC, V. Moderate.*

★ **Maxie's Left Field Deli.** The decor badly needs a face-lift, but the cops and robbers, judges and vagrants who congregate at the counter of Max Silk's deli could care less. They're there for Max's sandwiches and superb homemade soups, and to shoot the breeze with the legendary octogenarian owner. Max's career during Prohibition is a subject he is still reluctant to discuss; these days, he's better known as a tireless fund-raiser for local charities. Best bets include the chicken soup, beef barley soup, and short ribs; the potato pancakes on Wednesdays are definitive. *1266 Michigan Ave., Detroit, tel. 313/961–7968. No reservations. Dress: casual. No credit cards. No dinner. Closed Sun. Inexpensive.*

Traffic Jam & Snug. In 20 years this popular hangout near the Wayne State campus hasn't stopped growing and owners Ben Edwards and Richard Vincent haven't stopped experimenting. The sprawling kitchens turn out an exotic selection of breads, cheeses, ice creams, and sausages, and Vincent and Edwards have ambitious plans to open an on-premises brewery someday. Die-hard carnivores can find chicken, fish, or even a hamburger here, but TJ's strong suit is natural foods: everything from tofu fettucine Stroganoff to superb soups and criminally good desserts. Lots of funky charm. *511 W. Canfield, Detroit, tel. 313/831–9470. No reservations. Dress: casual. MC, V. No dinner Sun. and Mon., no lunch weekends. Inexpensive.*

Continental **Golden Mushroom.** Master chef Milos Cihelka has gradually transformed this from a casual suburban spot into one of the area's most ambitious restaurants, but in spite of the linen, china, and tuxedoed servers, the restaurant retains a boisterous informal flavor. Offerings vary seasonally but can include fungi ranging from black-and-white truffles to chanterelles, hedgehog mushrooms, lobster mushrooms, oyster mushrooms, brown trumpets, cepes and shiitakes, as well as such game choices as pheasant, wild boar, and axis venison. Other staples include rack of lamb, Dover sole, and free-range chicken. Service is personable but highly professional. *18100 W. Ten Mile Rd., Southfield, tel. 313/559–4230. Reservations recommended. Jacket and tie recommended. AE, CB, DC, MC, V. Closed Sun. Very Expensive.*

★ **The Lark.** Millionaire real-estate developer Jim Lark plays maitre d' for an evening of gastronomic fantasy, re-creating a traditional Spanish country inn. Prix-fixe dinners, priced from $37.50 to $47.50, include unlimited samplings from the hors d'oeuvres trolley, a hot appetizer, soup or pasta, and a choice of entrees that ranges from rack of lamb Genghis Khan to free-range hen with wild mushrooms. *6430 Farmington Rd., West Bloomfield, tel. 313/661–4466. Reservations recommended. Jacket and tie recommended. AE, CB, DC, MC, V. No lunch. Closed Sun. and Mon. Very Expensive.*

Van Dyke Place. Partners Ron Fox and John McCarthy have restored a turn-of-the-century mansion in Detroit's stately Indian Village neighborhood to its former glory. The evening ritual starts with dinner in main-floor dining rooms, followed by dessert and coffee in the upstairs drawing rooms. The menu, billed as an American perspective on French cuisine, offers dishes such as roasted boneless quail in potato nest and veal sweetbreads in brown butter sauce. The wine list is one of the best in the Midwest. *6549 Van Dyke, Detroit, tel. 313/821–2620. Reservations recommended. Jacket and tie recommended. AE, MC, V. Closed Sun.; no lunch Sat. Very Expensive.*

Ethnic **Nippon Kai.** For visiting Japanese auto industry executives,
★ this restaurant with traditional Japanese decor offers the next best thing to being home. First-rate renditions of tempura, sukiyaki, and shabu-shabu are offered, but the real action is at the sushi bar, where chef Seiji Ueno creates presentations of raw fish and vinegared rice that go light years beyond the salmon roll. *511 W. 14 Mile Rd., Clawson, tel. 313/288–3210. Reservations recommended. Dress: casual. AE, DC, MC, V. Expensive.*

★ **Park Terrace.** If you think Canadian cuisine is an oxymoron, you're in for a pleasant surprise. This rather formal hotel dining room offers a stunning view of Detroit across the river, and serves a menu of Canadian specialties ranging from buffalo and caribou to fiddlehead ferns and morels, creatively prepared and strikingly presented. Not cheap, but a comparable meal across the border could cost much more. Best values are the three-course seasonal heritage dinners. *In the Hilton International Windsor, 277 Riverside Drive W, Windsor, Ontario, tel. 519/973–5555; toll-free from Detroit 962–3834. Reservations recommended. Jacket and tie recommended. AE, DC, MC, V. Expensive.*

★ **Blue Nile.** Silverware is optional when you dine Ethiopian style; richly seasoned meats and vegetables are served on communal trays covered with *injera*, a pancake-like flatbread, chunks of which are torn off to be used as scoops for the other foods. Menu choices include mild and spicy stews of chicken, lamb, and beef, with accompaniments of well-spiced lentils, beans, and cabbage. Your best bet is to order a couple of different combination dinners and share them (there's no limit on seconds). Ethiopian food served at dinner only; fresh fish menu at lunch. Simple but stylish casual decor features native handicrafts. *In Trappers Alley, 508 Monroe St., Detroit, tel. 313/ 964–6699. Reservations recommended. Dress: casual. AE, MC, V. Moderate.*

★ **Koreana.** This modest but hospitable Korean eatery, in what was once a pizzeria, invariably wins a spot on local critics' top-10 lists. Korean cuisine has its own characteristic combinations of flavors: sweet and spicy, salty and sometimes sour. If you've never had it before, start with the *bulgogi* (broiled marinated beef) and *chap chae* (beef with glass noodles and vegetables); if you're feeling more adventuresome, try the *chop tang* (mixed meats and seafoods in a savory sauce) or the *be bim bop* (a garnished rice bowl). *14537 Gratiot, Detroit, tel. 313/372–6601. No reservations. Dress: casual. AE, DC, MC, V. Closed Sun., no lunch Sat. Moderate.*

The Royal Eagle. The heart of the city's Polish dining is at modestly priced little cafes such as Under the Eagle and the Polonia in Hamtramck, Detroit's Polish neighborhood. But for a special occasion, the more formal Royal Eagle in Indian Village offers a level of creature comfort and gastronomy Hamtramck can't match. Typical dishes include *czarnina* (duck blood soup), veal Daniel, and roast duckling. *In the Parkstone Hotel, 1415 Parker, Detroit, tel. 313/331–8088. Reservations recommended. Jacket and tie recommended. DC, MC, V. No lunch. Closed Mon. and Tues. Moderate.*

Pegasus Taverna. Take your pick: the Pegasus, the New Hellas, the Old Parthenon, the Grecian Garden, the Laikon—the mass-produced cuisine is pretty much the same wherever you eat along Monroe Street, heart of Detroit's Greektown. Staples include moussaka, pastitio, roast leg of lamb, stuffed grape leaves, and baklava, all served in generous portions at very reasonable prices. This isn't great cooking, but it's consistent, and besides, the throngs of diners who pack Greektown's restaurants mostly come just to have a good time. With the help of a little retsina or ouzo to drink, they usually succeed. The Greektown experience isn't complete without an order of saganaki—flaming kasseri cheese ignited at tableside. A second Pegasus location in the Fisher Building in Detroit's New Center area lacks the Greektown ambience but offers a striking Art Nouveau decor and identical food. *585 Monroe St., Detroit, tel. 313/964–6800. Reservations recommended. Dress: casual. AE, CB, DC, MC, V. Inexpensive.*

★ **Wah Court.** Right across the river from downtown Detroit in Windsor, Ontario, this popular no-frills Cantonese restaurant can rival the best that the Chinatowns of New York and Toronto have to offer. The large population of Chinese students at the nearby University of Windsor are sticklers for authenticity, so the menu is full of such offerings as pork and duck in hot pot, fish maw with shredded duck soup, and shrimp and chicken in a taro root bird's nest. Dim sum, the traditional Chinese tea snacks, are served daily, with the biggest selection on Sundays. *2037 Wyandotte Ave. W, Windsor, tel. 519/254–1388. No reservations. Dress: casual. MC, V. Inexpensive.*

Lodging

Accommodations in and around the Motor City range from the pricey high-rise room-with-a-view to the more moderate and closer to the ground. Downtown, near Cobo Center, the Renaissance Center, and Joe Louis Arena, you'll find Detroit's luxury mega-hotels—the Omni, the Westin, and the Pontchartrain. Accommodations in suburban Troy, with its high concentration of corporate businesses, and Dearborn, where the Ford Motor Company has its headquarters, are quickly and easily accessed by freeways and expressways. Most of the hotels, motels, and inns offer price-reduced weekend packages.

The most highly recommended lodgings in each price category are indicated by a star ★ .

Category	Cost*
Very Expensive	over $100
Expensive	$75–$100
Moderate	$50–$75
Inexpensive	under $50

All prices are for a standard double room for two, excluding 11% tax.

The following credit card abbreviations are used: AE, American Express; CB, Carte Blanche; DC, Diners Club; MC, MasterCard; V, Visa.

Downtown
★ **Hotel Pontchartrain.** The Pontch, as it is familiarly known, has been recently renovated—and it shows. Light, airy, spacious rooms each have a wonderful view of the city and the river. The staff gives you a feeling that you are family. Do not, however, accept a room in the back of the hotel—which is across the street from the fire station—unless you are a heavy sleeper. A real plus here is the location, just minutes by foot from Cobo Hall and a short People Mover ride to the Ren Cen and Greektown. *2 Washington Blvd., 48226, tel. 313/965–0200 or 800/537–6624. 420 rooms. Facilities: restaurants, lounge, bar, concierge, heated outdoor pool, health club, complimentary limo service within city. AE, CB, DC, MC, V. Very Expensive.*

★ **Omni International.** Detroit's newest hotel, the Omni is connected by skywalk to the Renaissance Center. The standard rooms reflect the newness of the hotel; they are bright, large, and decorated in soothing blues and whites, with luxurious and unscuffed furniture. Each has three (count them) telephones and two TVs, one of each in the bathroom. Part of the Millender Center, which also houses an apartment-and-shopping complex, the Omni is right where the action is with a People Mover station on site. *333 E. Jefferson Ave., 48226, tel. 313/222–7700. 253 rooms. Facilities: indoor pool, sauna, whirlpool, putting green, health club, 2 lighted tennis courts, racquetball court, restaurant, lounge, concierge, valet parking, barber and beauty shop. AE, CB, DC, MC, V. Very Expensive.*

★ **The Westin Hotel–Renaissance Center Detroit.** With its 1,404 rooms and 73 stories, this hotel is best summed up as mega-big with mega-buck prices. The rooms themselves are neither large nor special, but the view is to die for. Overlooking the Detroit River, each room commands a waterfront view of the city and neighboring Windsor, Ontario. Shopping in the Ren Cen is right at hand, although it can be confusing with so many levels, aerial walkways, and towers. The newly remodeled lobby's granite, marble, brass, and earth tones set an ambience that is not, unfortunately, followed through in its standard rooms. Location-wise, however, the Westin is tops, within People Mover distance from everything downtown. *Renaissance Center, Jefferson Ave. at Randolph St., 48243, tel. 313/568–8000 or 800/228–3000. Facilities: indoor pool, health club, ½-mi outdoor jogging track, lounges, arcade shopping, valet parking, and the revolving Summit Restaurant on top. AE, CB, MC, V. Very Expensive.*

Shorecrest Motor Inn. This two-story hotel is conveniently located, two blocks east of the Renaissance Center and within walking distance of downtown attractions. *1316 E. Jefferson Ave., 48207, tel. 313/568–3000 or 800/992–9616. 54 rooms. Facilities: restaurant. AE, DC, MC, V. Inexpensive–Moderate.*

Near Northwest ★ **Hotel St. Regis.** The St. Regis has recently undergone expansion and renovation, adding 110 guest rooms, a restaurant, a lounge, and a health club, and renovating all other guest rooms. When the hotel first opened in 1967, it was designed to cater to the likes of the European jet set. Reality has set in, and now the St. Regis has downgraded its prices and upgraded (or Yuppie-graded) its decor and facilities to attract more of the business and tourist trade. New guest rooms are roomy, light, and tastefully decorated with simple modern furniture. The hotel is linked by skywalks to the General Motors Building, New Center One shopping and office complex, and the Fisher Building. *3071 W. Grand Blvd., 48202, tel. 313/873–3000 or 800/223–5560. 225 rooms. Facilities: valet parking, minibars, health club, restaurants, lounges. AE, CB, DC, MC, V. Very Expensive.*

Dearborn ★ **Hyatt Regency Dearborn.** Opposite the Ford Motor Company's world headquarters, this large hotel adjoins a shopping mall and is only five minutes from the Henry Ford Museum and Greenfield Village. Its public spaces are attractive, and many of its rooms have been renovated recently. *Fairlane Town Mall, ¼ mi east of Rte. 39 on Michigan Ave., ¼ mi north on Evergreen Rd., 48126, tel. 313/593–1234. 766 rooms. Facilities: indoor pool, sauna, whirlpool, valet parking, 2 restaurants, coffee shop, lounge. AE, CD, DC, MC, V. Very Expensive.*

The Dearborn Inn. Located across from the Henry Ford Museum and Greenfield Village, this property features five replicas of historic Colonial homes, honoring famous Americans such as Patrick Henry, Edgar Allan Poe, and Walt Whitman. *20301 Oakwood Blvd., 48124, tel. 313/271–2700 or 800/221–7236. 179 rooms. Facilities: outdoor pool, 2 tennis courts, children's playground, 2 restaurants, lounge. AE, CB, DC, MC, V. Expensive.*

Mayflower Bed and Breakfast Hotel. Guest rooms, many of which have been recently renovated, are comfortable; 16 of them have whirlpool baths. Guests receive a complimentary full breakfast. Shopping, golf, and cross-country skiing are nearby. *827 W. Ann Arbor Trail, Plymouth, 48170, tel. 313/453–1620. 100 rooms. Facilities: 3 restaurants, lounge. AE, DC, MC, V. Moderate–Expensive.*

Southfield **Michigan Inn.** This 14-story hotel, which is adjacent to the Northland Shopping Center, is popular with locals for its Red Parrot Lounge. Shopping, theaters, and the Detroit Zoo are nearby. *16400 J. L. Hudson Dr., 48075, tel. 313/559–6500 or*

800/521-1709. 412 rooms. Facilities: indoor-outdoor pool, sauna, putting green, 2 tennis courts, exercise room, restaurant, coffee shop. AE, CB, DC, MC, V. Expensive.

Troy **Guest Quarters.** Opened in May 1987, this suite hotel is a feast for the eyes, with an eight-story atrium full of foliage, trees, flowers, ivy, a small fountain, and miniwaterfalls. All the decor, from carpeting to upholstery to cafe tablecloths, combine to create an outdoors feeling. Each minisuite has a living room, with sofa bed and console TV, a kitchen area with refrigerator and microwave, and a bedroom with a king-size bed and remote-control TV. All rooms, including the bathroom, have a phone. A complimentary full American breakfast is served daily. The hotel is very close to the I-75 expressway and the Pontiac Silverdome. *850 Tower Dr., 48098, tel. 313/879-7500 or 800/424-2900. 251 suites. Facilities: indoor pool, health club, cafe, lounge. AE, CB, DC, MC, V. Very Expensive.*

Somerset Inn. Located in the heart of Troy's corporate and financial district, the Somerset is a favorite with the business set. It is close to the I-75 expressway and only 25 miles north of Detroit. Right next door is the posh Somerset Mall, with its Fifth Avenue-style shopping and prices. Adjacent to the inn is a full-service Vic Tanny spa whose facilities are available to guests at no charge. Guest rooms here are nothing special—rather small and "hotel standard"—but were renovated in late 1988. The entry level is lovely, with marble floors, greenery, and several small sitting rooms tucked around the perimeter. *2601 W. Big Beaver Rd., 48084, tel. 313/643-7800 or 800/228-TROY. 250 rooms. Facilities: outdoor pool, indoor pool, valet parking, 2 restaurants, bar, full-service health and racquet facility. AE, CB, DC, MC, V. Expensive.*

The Drury Inn. Conveniently located close to the Troy business corridor and only 10 minutes from the Pontiac Silverdome, the Drury has surprisingly spacious and well-appointed rooms for so moderate a price. Decorated mostly in earth tones, the rooms include brick and stucco walls and neat and clean furnishings. The hotel offers a complimentary breakfast buffet. Herschel's American Deli restaurant, adjacent to the inn, serves such delicacies as a chocolate egg cream and bagels with lox and cream cheese. *575 W. Big Beaver Rd., 48084, tel. 313/528-3330 or 800/325-8300. 154 rooms with bath. Facilities: outdoor pool, cable TV, small pets allowed, valet and laundry service available weekdays. AE, CB, DC, MC, V. Moderate.*

The Arts

The city magazine *Detroit Monthly* has a comprehensive calendar of events, as does *Metro Times*, a free weekly tabloid available in downtown stores. "What's Line" (tel. 313/298-6262) gives you a recorded message from the visitors and convention bureau that includes information on the arts. And check the arts sections of *The Detroit News* and *Free Press.*

Theater **Actors Alliance Theater Company** (30800 Evergreen Rd., Southfield, tel. 313/642-1326) presents Michigan and world premieres of contemporary and classical comedies, musicals, and dramas.

Attic Theater (2990 W. Grand Blvd., tel. 313/875-8284). This highly acclaimed troupe performs contemporary off-Broadway plays and the works of new playwrights year-round.

Birmingham Theater (211 S. Woodward Ave., tel. 313/644–3533) is home to musicals, comedies, and dramatic productions by professional casts and big-name performers.

The Bonstelle Theater (3424 Woodward Ave., tel. 313/577–2960) is Wayne State University's highly regarded undergraduate studies theater, housed in a historic former synagogue.

Detroit Institute of the Arts Theater (5200 Woodward Ave., tel. 313/832–2730) offers a year-round schedule of informal chamber concerts, travel-adventure film series, live performances, and performances for youth.

Detroit Repertory Theater (13103 Woodrow Wilson Ave., tel. 313/868–1347), one of the city's oldest resident professional theaters, stages four to five plays each year in a season running from September to June.

Fisher Theater (Fisher Bldg., W. Grand Blvd. at Second, tel. 313/872–1000). Broadway touring companies, drama, and musicals play in this intriguing space, where the theater stage and rigging are seven stories high.

Hillbery Theater (4743 Cass Ave., tel. 313/577–2972) is the center for Wayne State's graduate theater program.

Meadow Brook Theater (on the Oakland University campus, Rochester, tel. 313/370–3310) presents musicals and contemporary and classic drama in an intimate 608-seat theater from October to May.

Music Hall Center for the Performing Arts (350 Madison Ave., tel. 313/963–7680) presents theater, dance, and modern music.

Studio Theater (4001 W. McNichols, tel. 313/927–1130), on the University of Detroit's main campus, is home to the university's theatrical troupe.

Concerts **Fox Theater** (2211 Woodward Ave., tel. 313/965–7100), an ornate Byzantine/Babylonian-style theater first built in 1927 and re-opened after extensive renovation in 1988, presents musical performers, touring Broadway shows, and other nationally known acts in a 4,800-seat auditorium.

Macomb Center for the Performing Arts (44575 Garfield Rd., Mt. Clemens, tel. 313/286–2222) presents symphony, classical, jazz, and big-band performances in a 1,200-seat theater noted for its acoustics.

Masonic Temple (500 Temple St., tel. 313/832–7100) has a 4,600-seat theater offering entertainment ranging from Broadway productions to ballet and music.

Meadow Brook Music Festival (on the Oakland University campus, Rochester, tel. 313/377–2010) offers classical, variety, and popular music outdoors in summer; it is the summer home of the Detroit Symphony.

Pine Knob Music Theater (7773 Pine Knob Rd., Clarkston, tel. 313/625–0800) has top-name pop, rock, and country stars at an outdoor amphitheater all summer.

Orchestra Hall (3711 Woodward Ave., tel. 313/833–3700), recently renovated and designated a national and state historic site, boasts superior acoustics and stages world-class chamber, symphonic, and solo recitals. It is home to the Chamber Music Society of Detroit as well as the Detroit Symphony.

Opera **Michigan Opera Theater** (tel. 313/874–7850), one of the largest professional companies in the United States, produces classical and untraditional fare. The fall season, October to December, is at the Fisher Theater in the New Center while the spring season is at the Music Hall Center on Madison Avenue.

Nightlife

Bars and Nightclubs

Bouzouki Lounge in Greektown presents traditional Greek music, belly dancers, folk dancers and singers, and food. *432 E. Lafayette Ave., tel. 313/964–5744. Open Tues.–Sun. 5:30 PM– 2AM. AE, CB, DC, MC, V.*

Dakota Inn Rathskeller. Beer, food, and song in a German *bierstube* setting. The octogenarian Basil Oliver brings down the house with his rendition of "Sunrise, Sunset." There are piano-accompanied sing-alongs. *17324 John R. St., tel. 313/ 867–9722. Music begins at 7:30 PM; no cover. AE, MC, V.*

Monroe's Restaurant and Nightclub. In addition to the food in this Trappers Alley night spot, a pianist plays in the dining room until 9 PM, followed by dancing, a DJ, and a light show. *508 Monroe St., tel. 313/961–5577. AE, DC, MC, V. Open Mon.– Sat. to 2 AM, Sun. to 4 AM; cover charge.*

Mykonos Supper Club. Another Greektown night spot with nightly entertainment by a bouzouki band, singers, and belly dancers. *454 E. Lafayette St. at Beaubien St., tel. 313/965– 3737; no cover, with 2-drink minimum. Open daily 5:30 PM–2 AM. AE, CB, DC, MC, V.*

Pinkey's Boulevard Club. A friendly piano bar where strangers join the sing-alongs. *110 E. Grand Blvd. at E. Jefferson Ave., tel. 313/824–2820. Open until midnight. AE, MC, V.*

Premier Center. Popular nightclub entertainers (Aretha Franklin, Barry Manilow, etc.) perform in this small club. *33970 Van Dyke in Sterling Heights, tel. 313/978–3450. Shows at 7:30 and 10:30; call for specifics.*

Taboo Nightclub. A trendy, upbeat light show in a New York– style nightclub, with three bar areas, DJ, large dance floor, fog machines. *1940 Woodbridge in Rivertown, tel. 313/567–6140. Open daily 9 PM–2 AM; cover charge. AE, MC, V.*

Folk Clubs

Om Cafe. A vegetarian restaurant from the '60s, complete with flower children and a statue of Buddha. Folk music Thurs.–Sat. evenings. *23136 Woodward Ave., tel. 313/548–1941. No credit cards.*

Jazz

Alexander's. A leading jazz spot, especially on weekends. Comedy on Wednesday and occasional open-mike poetry readings. *4265 Woodward Ave., tel. 313/831–2662. Weekend music starts at 9:45 PM; $6 cover. AE, MC, V.*

All That Jazz. A glitzy club with mirrors, tiny lights, and black and white floor tiles. *111 Cadillac Sq., Cadillac Sq. Apartment Bldg., tel. 313/961–6760. Open Mon.–Sat. 9 PM–2 AM; $3 cover charge. MC, V.*

Baker's Keyboard Lounge. A landmark institution, called the world's oldest jazz club, it is dimly lit and smoke-filled and features jazz greats. Call for schedule. *20510 Livernois, tel. 313/ 864–1201. Open Thurs.–Sun., shows at 9:30 PM; $5 cover. No credit cards.*

Dummy George Jazz Room. Big-name acts, primarily vocalists. The club is comfortably elegant. *10320 W. McNichols, tel. 313/ 341–2700. Open daily, shows at 10 PM and midnight; cover charge varies. AE, DC, MC, V.*

The Gnome. A Middle Eastern restaurant where top jazz musicians perform. Sunday brunch with classical pianists. *4160 Woodward Ave., tel. 313/833–0120. Open daily at 11 AM, jazz Fri.–Sat. 8:30 PM–1 AM; cover charge varies. AE, DC, MC, V.*

Old Detroit. Nostalgic photos, exposed brick, and overhead fans provide the atmosphere. *655 Beaubien St., tel. 313/222–7972. Open daily, performances at 10 PM; $2 cover charge Fri. and Sat.*

Sierra Station. A Tex-Mex bar and restaurant offering jazz on weekends. *15110 Mack, Grosse Pointe Park, tel. 313/822–1270. Open daily; no cover. Jazz Fri. and Sat. at 9 PM. AE, CB, DC, MC, V.*

Soup Kitchen Saloon. An old saloon, home of the Detroit blues. *1585 Franklin, Rivertown, tel. 313/259–2643. Open daily, music Tues.–Sat. 9:30 PM–2 AM, Sun. 7 PM–midnight; cover $4–$9 weekends. AE, CB, DC, MC, V.*

Rock Clubs

Alvin's Detroit Bar. Raucous and casual, a Wayne State hangout. *5756 Cass St., tel. 313/832–2355. Rock Fri. and Sat. 9 PM–2 AM; $2–$7 cover. No credit cards.*

Doug's Body Shop. Lined with classic cars converted into booths, benches, and wall decorations. *22061 Woodward Ave., Ferndale, tel. 313/399–1040. Rock Wed.–Sat. at 9 PM; $1 cover weekends. AE, DC, MC, V.*

Paycheck's Lounge. Neighborhood bar by day, New Wave rock club by night. *2932 Caniff, Hamtramck, tel. 313/872–8934. Music Thurs.–Sun. 9 PM–2 AM; cover $3–$5. For the younger set. AE, MC, V.*

St. Andrews Hall/Clutch Cargos. Some top rock bands made their Motor City debuts in this former Scottish meeting hall in Bricktown. *431 E. Congress St., tel. 313/287–8090. Call for schedule and prices.*

Comedy Clubs

Bea's Comedy Kitchen. Local acts and nationally known comedians. *541 E. Larned St., tel. 313/961–2581. Shows Fri. and Sat. at 8:30 and 11 PM; cover charge $10. AE, MC, V.*

Chaplin's. A new club featuring mostly local acts. *34244 Groesbeck, Fraser, tel. 313/792–1902. Shows Wed.–Thurs. 8:30 PM, Fri. and Sat. 8:30 and 10:30 PM. Dancing after each show; cover $5–$8. AE, DC, MC, V.*

Northwood Inn and Mark Ridley's Comedy Castle. One of the first comedy clubs in the Midwest pairing local talent and top performers. Bar and dining area. *2593 Woodward Ave. north of Eleven Mile Rd., Royal Oak, tel. 313/542–9900. Open Mon.–Sat., shows at 8:30 PM, late show at 11 Fri.–Sat.; cover $3–$10. AE, CB, DC, MC, V.*

Dance Clubs

Cracker Jax. Features top-40 music, new music, and vintage disco. *18696 Mack, Grosse Pointe Farms, tel. 313/884–3710. Open daily 8 PM–2 AM; Sun. is teen night; $3 cover Fri. and Sat. AE, MC, V.*

Woodward Jukebox. A dance club where waitresses wear bobby sox and letter sweaters. *4616 N. Woodward Ave., Royal Oak, tel. 313/549–2233. Open Tues.–Fri. 8 PM–2 AM, Sat. 7 PM–2 AM, Sun. 9 PM–2 AM; $3 cover after 9. AE, MC, V.*

Wooly Bully's. Oldies dance bar with a record-shape floor and a go-go cage. To beat the weekend line arrive before 8. *11310 Hayes at Kelly, tel. 313/839–8777. Music Mon.–Sat. 9 PM–2 AM, Sun. 5 PM–2 AM; $3 cover weekends. AE, MC, V.*

Ballrooms

New Grande Ballroom. Local bands play big-band hits from the '30s, '40s, and '50s. *31186 Warren at Merriman, Westland, tel. 313/421–7630. Open Sun. and Tues. 7 PM–midnight, Thurs. noon–5 PM. Admission: $5, $3 for Thurs. matinee. No credit cards.*

Excursions from Detroit

Price categories for restaurants are the same as in Detroit Dining.

Numbers in the margin correspond with points of interest on the Greater Detroit and Southeastern Michigan map.

Windsor, Ontario

❶ Like Detroit, **Windsor** is an industrial city—Ford, GM, Chrysler, and Champion Spark Plugs have manufacturing plants here, and the Hiram Walker Distillery is the third largest in Canada. Yet it is known as the City of Roses and is famous for its miles of riverfront parks and gardens. **Dieppe Gardens,** named in memory of members of the Essex Scottish Regiment who fell during the assault on Dieppe, France, in 1942, is set in the heart of the city and affords a view of the Detroit skyline. It is a favorite spot for downtown workers to eat lunch, and bands frequently perform for the crowd. To the east along the river is **Coventry Gardens,** with a large computer-controlled floating fountain. Away from the river, **Jackson Park** (south on Ouellette Ave.) has a six-acre garden displaying more than 12,000 roses in 450 varieties surrounding a World War II veterans memorial.

Windsor's large multicultural population has established ethnic restaurants serving French, Italian, Turkish, Greek, Mexican, and Asian cuisine. In summer the downtown area is dotted with outdoor cafes.

Several festivals are held during the year, the largest being the International Freedom Festival, a two-week event shared with Detroit, celebrating the two countries' national days (July 1 in Canada, July 4 in the United States). The fête, starting in late June, includes cultural and sporting events and ends with a big fireworks display.

You can reach Windsor by car via the 1.8-mile **Ambassador Bridge** (accessed by either I–96 or I–75), or through the **Detroit–Windsor Tunnel,** which you enter from Randolph Street on the west side of the Renaissance Center. The toll is $1.25 ($1.50 Canadian) for bridge or tunnel, and you will have to pass through Customs. The **Windsor–Detroit Tunnel Bus** (tel. 519/944–4111) provides frequent service, leaving from either the corner of Fort and Woodward avenues or the Tunnel Plaza adjacent to the Renaissance Center. The Windsor depot is just east of 500 Ouellette Avenue. The fare is $1 (U.S. or Canadian).

To enter Canada, U.S. citizens need proof of citizenship; a birth certificate or voter registration card is fine, though a passport is usually the best form of ID. Naturalized citizens should have their papers. Returning U.S. residents are allowed to bring back $400 worth of personal or household merchandise every 30 days, provided they have been out of the country for at least 48 hours. If you stay 24 hours or less, $25 worth of merchandise may be brought back duty-free.

Most establishments in Windsor will accept American currency, but you will receive the most up-to-date exchange rate at a bank. American currency can be exchanged at branches of

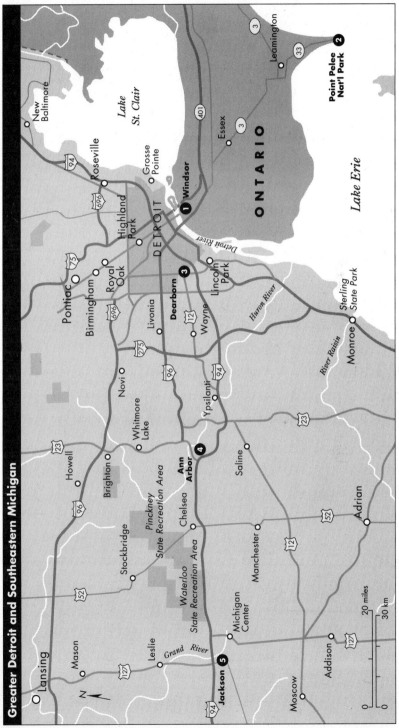

Greater Detroit and Southeastern Michigan

Bluewater Currency Exchange Ltd. in the Ontario Travel Information Bureau, 110 Park Street at Goyeau (turn right at the tunnel exit), and at 1235 Huron Church Road, half a mile from the bridge exit. **Tunnel Money Exchange** is to the right of the toll booths at the tunnel entrance on Goyeau.

When shopping, determine whether the price quoted is in Canadian or American dollars; depending on the rate of exchange, the difference can be substantial on high-priced items.

Exploring Information on Windsor attractions is available at the Convention and Visitors Bureau of Windsor, Essex County, and Pelée Island, 80 Chatham Street East, tel. 519/255–6530, weekdays 8:30–4:30. Ontario Travel Centres are at 110 Park Street East and 1235 Harbor Church Road, open daily 8:30–4:30, until 8 PM mid-May–Labor Day.

Many visitors go to Windsor to shop and take advantage of a favorable exchange rate. You'll find especially good buys in jewelry, china, and furs. The British import shops are well known, and designer apparel for men and women—especially clothing made of Scottish wool—ranks high. Some boutiques are tucked away in restored Victorian houses or in sleek buildings along Ouellette Avenue, the main street downtown, and along Pelissier Street, a block west. Erie Street, which crosses Ouellette Avenue, offers a touch of Italy with clothing and specialty shops. Wyandotte Street East, which also crosses Ouellette, has shops and boutiques selling European and Canadian designs.

The newly renovated **Art Gallery of Windsor,** housed in a former brewery, has 15 areas presenting changing displays of contemporary and historic art from across Canada and abroad. The permanent collection of more than 3,000 paintings, graphics, and sculptures highlights achievements of Canadian artists from the 18th century on. *445 Riverside Dr. W, tel. 519/258–7111. Admission free. Open Tues.–Sat. 10–5, Wed. until 10, Sun. 1–5.*

The **Hiram Walker Historical Museum** is named after the distiller who, in 1858, established the first large-scale industry on the Canadian shore. Collections include Indian artifacts, firearms, tools, household items, glassware, maps, and newspapers; a reference library holds many original documents relating to the history of southwestern Ontario. *254 Pitt St. W, tel. 519/253–1812. Admission free. Open Tues.–Sat. 9–5, Sun. 2–5.*

Willistead Manor, a mansion built in 1906 by Edward Chandler Walker (Hiram's son), is a 40-room Tudor-style mansion designed by the Detroit architect Alfred Kahn and set in a 15-acre park. Carved paneling is found throughout, as are Carrera marble fireplaces. The manor is used for public and private cultural, business, and social events. *1899 Niagara St., tel. 519/255–6545. Admission: $1.75 adults, $1.25 senior citizens, 75¢ children. Open 1st and 3d Sun. 1–4 PM Sept.–Nov. and Jan.–June,; Dec., Sun. 1–6 and Wed. 7–9 PM; July–Aug., Sun.–Wed. 1–4.*

Farmers, butchers, and bakers from southwestern Ontario bring their fresh produce and goods to sell at the **Windsor City Market,** which has more than 500 stalls. *Chatham St. E between McDougall and Market Sts., tel. 519/255–6260. Open 6 AM Mon.–Sat., most active Wed. and Sat.*

Windsor Raceway features harness racing. *6 mi south of downtown on Rte. 18. Racing Oct.–June, Tues. nights and Fri.–Sun. nights. Dinner in clubhouse. Bets made in U.S. currency are paid in U.S. currency. Tel. 519/969–8311; in Detroit 313/961–9545.*

The **North American Black Historical Museum** has a permanent exhibit on the Underground Railroad as well as displays on black origins in Africa, the years of slavery, and settlement and emancipation in North America. *227 King St., Amherstberg, 18 mi south of Windsor, tel. 519/736–56433. Admission: $1 adults, 50¢ senior citizens and under 17, $3 family. Open Wed.–Fri. 10–5, weekends 1–5.*

Dining **Mason-Girardot Alan Manor.** One of Windsor's notable restau-
★ rants, featuring Turkish and Continental cuisine in six dining rooms in a restored 1865 manor. Specials include Sheftalia kebab, filet of sole Meunière, steak Diane, unusual desserts. *3203 Peter St. (no restaurant sign), tel. 519/253–9212 or 973–9536. Reservations advised. Jacket and tie advised. AE, MC, V. No lunch Sat. Closed Sun. and Mon. Expensive.*

Chez Vin Bistro. An intimate place featuring lobster, linguini, and beef satay, among other dishes. Extensive wine list. *26 Chatham St. W, tel. 519/252–2801. Reservations advised. Jacket and tie advised. MC, V. Open Mon.–Sat. for dinner. Moderate.*

The **Old Fish Market.** Windsor's original seafood restaurant, featuring fresh fish and shellfish, oysters on the half-shell, clams, and mussels. Nonseafood items also available. Maritime atmosphere and decor. *156 Chatham St. W, tel. 519/253–2670. Reservations advised. Dress: casual. AE, DC, MC, V. Open for lunch Mon.–Sat., dinner daily. Moderate.*

Runner Bar & Grill. A richly appointed period room featuring sandwiches, light dinners, and late-evening snacks. Live entertainment and dancing. *Hilton International Hotel, 277 Riverside Dr. W, tel. 519/973–5555. Reservations advised. Dress: casual. AE, DC, MC, V. Open Mon.–Sat. 4 PM–1 AM. Moderate.*

T.B.Q.'s Other Place. Three informal dining rooms with a business atmosphere (there are tableside telephones and calculators). Specials include home-cured prosciutto and melon, fresh Atlantic salmon, lobster, steak. *3067 Dougall Rd., tel. 519/969–6011. Reservations advised. Dress: casual. AE, CB, DC, MC, V. Open Mon.–Sat. 11 AM–1 AM, Sun. till 10. Moderate.*

Maxwell's Riverside Restaurant. Steak and seafood are specialties in a riverside room offering a view of Detroit. *480 Riverside Dr. W, in the Holiday Inn, tel. 519/253–4411. Reservations suggested. Dress: casual. AE, DC, MC, V. Open for dinner daily. Inexpensive.*

Milano Restaurant and Tavern. A favorite luncheon haunt of auto bosses. Italian cuisine served in the chandeliered Verdi and LaScala Rooms. Pasta and veal specialties, flaming coffee, daily specials. *1520 Tecumseh Rd. E, tel. 519/254–5125. Reservations suggested. Jacket and tie advised. AE, DC, MC, V. Inexpensive–Moderate.*

Wong's Eatery. An outstanding Oriental restaurant featuring Szechwan, Cantonese, and Hong Kong cuisine. *1457 University Ave. W, tel. 519/252–8814. Reservations suggested. Dress: casual. AE, MC, V. Open Mon.–Thurs. 11 AM–11:30 PM, Fri. and Sat. till 1 AM, Sun. 11–9:30. Inexpensive.*

❷ Point Pelée National Park

Situated 34 miles (56 kilometers) southwest of Windsor, Point Pelée National Park is the southernmost point in mainland Canada, at about the same latitude as Chicago. A sandspit jutting into Lake Erie, the six-square-mile park is noted for its spring and autumn bird migrations and for Monarch butterfly migrations, in which millions of the insects stop on their way to Mexico each autumn.

Ancient Indian tribes traveling along the lake established a portage across the sandspit to bypass dangerous currents. French explorers 300 years ago named the peninsula *Point Pelée*, meaning Bald Point. By the beginning of the 20th century naturalists recognized the point as an important stopover for migrating birds and began efforts to preserve it.

To reach the park, take Route 3 from Windsor (the Ambassador Bridge exits onto Rte. 3 in Windsor) to Leamington and follow Route 77 south to the junction with Route 33, which leads into the park. The drive takes about 45 minutes one way from Windsor.

Exploring Point Pelée is a day-use park open year-round. Spring is noted for smelt fishing and bird-watching, with 346 species sighted. In summer there is swimming and picnicking. The main beaches—Northwest, Black Willow, West, and East Point— have changing houses and beach patrols. Autumn brings the bird migration; the butterfly migration reaches its peak in September. A large skating area and a network of cross-country ski trails are open in winter.

Begin your visit at the Visitors Centre, four miles south of the entrance. It has bird-watching and wildlife exhibits, a small reference library, and displays on the formation of the park and the natural history of the region. An information desk posts a long up-to-date list of bird sightings, and a small theater presents natural-history films and audiovisual programs.

About two-thirds of the park is marshland, and five plant communities are found here, some (such as the swamp rose-mallow and prickly pear cactus) rare in Canada. The rest of the park is forested, though there are open fields remaining from early attempts at farming. The outer edges of the peninsula are ringed with sand-and-pebble beach. White-tailed deer, rabbits, and squirrels are often seen in the forests, as are the eastern mole and eastern fox snake.

Among the short hiking trails is the 1.6-kilometer **Marsh Boardwalk,** part of which is floating. A 45-foot observation tower provides a bird's-eye view of the marsh. The **Tip Trail,** 0.8 kilometers on boardwalk, is an excellent bird-watching route and, in September, is the best area for viewing the Monarchs.

A concession stand selling burgers, fries, and similar fare operates near the Marsh Boardwalk during the summer, and fast-food vending machines stand near the Tip.

Because of a relatively fragile environment and large numbers of people, the southern end of the park is closed to vehicles from early April to Labor Day, and on weekends in September and

October. During those times a free shuttle train runs between the Visitors Centre and the Tip.

Daily admission fee $4 (Canadian) per car charged to enter Point Pelée National Park Apr.–Labor Day, free rest of year. Park is open daily 6 AM–10 PM, and opens an hour earlier for bird-watchers late Apr.–late May. Visitors Centre hours reduced in winter. Shuttle tram operates Apr. and June–Labor Day 9–9; May 6 AM–9 PM; Sept. 8–8; Oct. 8–8. For additional information contact Superintendent, Point Pelée National Park, RR 1, Leamington, Ontario N8H 3V4, tel. 519/322–2365.

Dining **Tropicana Restaurant,** Leamington. Featuring Greek and Canadian food, it is known for its chicken and ribs, Greek bread, and pizza. Steaks and seafood specials also on the menu. Dining on an outdoor patio in season. *2311 Erie St. S, tel. 519/326–6071. Reservations suggested. Jacket and tie suggested for dinner. AE, MC, V. Open daily 11 AM–1 AM. Moderate.*

❸ Dearborn

Exploring The **Henry Ford Museum and Greenfield Village,** in suburban Dearborn, draws more than a million visitors a year. Ideally, allow a day for the museum and a day for the village. For those with less time, a museum map included with admission will outline the highlights. Founded by Ford in 1929 to show how rapidly and profoundly American life changed because of technological innovations, the museum occupies 12 acres and covers domestic life, communications, transportation, agriculture, and industry. Artifacts range from the first Honda auto produced in the United States to an 1850s hand-cranked washing machine. Adjoining Greenfield Village is designed to show how America used the artifacts displayed in the museum. Its 240 acres contain historical structures that Ford moved here, among them the bicycle shop where the Wright Brothers designed and built their first airplane, the house where Noah Webster wrote his dictionary, the birthplace of tire pioneer Harvey S. Firestone, an Illinois courthouse where Abraham Lincoln practiced law, and the Dearborn farm where Ford himself was born.

The museum entrance is a full-size copy of Independence Hall in Philadelphia. Here one encounters a spade belonging to the horticulturist Luther Burbank imbedded in a cube of concrete, placed there in 1928 by Ford's hero, Thomas A. Edison, who then carved his name deeply into the concrete.

The newest permanent exhibit, opened in 1987, is "The Automobile in American Life." Along with more than 100 historically significant autos, the exhibit includes a 1940s Texaco service station, a 1946 roadside diner, a 1941 tourist cabin, an early '60s Holiday Inn guest room and sign, a wooded campground with early recreational vehicles, a single-arch McDonald's sign offering hamburgers for 15¢, a drive-in theater showing "Car Culture," with an Edsel and a Studebaker parked before the screen, and rhyming Burma Shave signs. Among presidential autos is the Lincoln in which John F. Kennedy was assassinated. In a glass case near the presidential vehicles is a letter to Henry Ford by the gangster Clyde Barrow, of *Bonnie and Clyde* notoriety, in which he wrote, "I have driven Fords exclusively when I could get away with one."

Other museum highlights include the Fokker Trimotor airplane Admiral Richard E. Bryd flew over the South Pole in 1929; a cast-iron steam engine, circa 1857; the chair Lincoln was sitting in when he was assassinated in 1865; and a 1938 Massey-Harris Model 20 combine, which opened a new era in farm mechanization.

Visitors may shop at several museum stores for art postcards, books, and museum and village handcrafted objects. Guided tours are available; check at the admissions deck for details.

Visitors may tour Greenfield Village on foot, by carriage, on sleighs (in winter), by Model T in summer, or on a steam train (May–mid-October) for an additional fee. Costumed interpreters are in each building; in many, craftsmen use traditional techniques to blow glass, make pottery, or forge tools. A featured exhibit is Edison's reconstructed Menlo Park, New Jersey, laboratory, where over 400 inventions originated, including the electric light, phonograph, and mimeograph.

Village Rd. and Oakwood Blvd., Dearborn, 3 mi north of I–94 to Oakwood Blvd. and west 2 mi; tel. 313/271–1620 or 800/835–2246. A separate admission is charged for the museum and village: $9.50 adults, $4.75 children under 13, $8.50 senior citizens, free children under 5. Two-day (consecutive) unlimited admission ticket to museum and village $16 adults, $8 children 5–12. Jan. 4–mid-March, $9.50 adults, $4.75 under 13 for both museum and village (village buildings closed). Open daily 9–5; village buildings closed Jan. 4–mid-March; village and museum closed Thanksgiving, Dec. 25, Jan. 1.

The **Dearborn Historical Museum** consists of three buildings that were once part of the U.S. Government Arsenal here. The museum has an Exhibit Annex with craft shops and displays on wagons and buggies. The Commandant's Quarters and the McFadden-Ross House date from the early 1800s and contain period furnishings. *21950 Michigan Ave., tel. 313/565–3000. Admission free. Open May–Oct., Mon.–Sat. 9–5; Nov.–Apr., Mon.–Sat. 1–5; closed holidays.*

Fair Lane, set on 72 acres beside the Rouge River in Dearborn, was Henry and Clara Ford's home for more than 30 years. The 56-room mansion had its own powerhouse, which used the river to generate electricity (Edison laid the cornerstone in 1914, and Ford once dried President Herbert Hoover's hat on the boiler). The grounds were designed by the landscape architect Jens Jenson. Austere in comparison with other auto barons' estates, Fair Lane nevertheless has carved paneling, marble fireplaces, and a view of the river. Visitors may dine in the **Pool** restaurant in the mansion's original swimming-pool room. *4901 Evergreen Rd. on the University of Michigan Dearborn campus, tel. 313/593–5590. Admission: $5 adults, $4 senior citizens and children under 13. Open Mon.–Sat. 10–2:30, Sun. 12:30–4. Check for times of guided tours.*

Dining   The **American Cafe** in the Ford museum offers cafeteria dining with plate lunches, salads, and sandwiches. The **Corner Cupboard**, also in the museum, features hot dogs and other light refreshments. In the village the **Eagle Tavern** (circa 1832) serves 1850s food, spirits, and customs, and the **Suwanee Res-**

taurant offers cafeteria-style sandwiches, salad plates, beer, and wine. The **Covered Bridge Lunch Stand** sells turn-of-the-century picnic lunches and snack foods. *In Henry Ford Museum and Village, Village Rd. and Oakwood Blvd., tel. 313/271–1620 or 800/835–2246. Dress: casual. Open same hours as village and museum. Inexpensive–Moderate.*

The Waterworks, in a former Dearborn pumping station, serves soups, salads, sandwiches, beer, and an extensive selection of wines. *21031 Michigan Ave. (adjacent to Ford Museum), tel. 313/562–6080. Dress: casual. Open weekdays 11 AM–2 AM, Sat. 4 PM–2 AM. Moderate.*

Southeastern Michigan

Detroit dominates this section of the state, but two other cities, Ann Arbor and Jackson, maintain their own identity and are well worth the drive west on I–94.

Numbers in the margin correspond with points of interest on the Greater Detroit and Southeastern Michigan map.

Restaurants and hotels are listed after each city's attractions. Price categories for restaurants and hotels are the same as in Detroit Dining and Lodging.

❹ Ann Arbor

Take I–94 west from Detroit to reach Ann Arbor, home of the University of Michigan. Tradition says the town got its name in 1824 from settlers' references to a grape arbor and from the first pioneers' wives, Ann Allen and Ann Rumsey. **Kerrytown,** a complex of specialty shops housed in three restored historical buildings on North Fifth Street, occupies the site of the original village.

Exploring   Ann Arbor had fewer than 2,000 residents in 1837, when its bid for the University of Michigan was accepted; the school was moved from Detroit to 40 acres here. The university now occupies more than 1,300 acres, much of it downtown. The handsome Gothic buildings of the **Law Quadrangle,** at State Street and South University Avenue, exude a strong sense of the "hallowed halls of ivy." On the North Campus are research facilities and the School of Music building, designed by Eero Saarinen. Other campus highlights include these:

The **Gerald R. Ford Library** has rotating exhibits relating to the former president's life. *1000 Beal Ave., North Campus, tel. 313/668–2218. Admission free. Open weekdays 8:45–4:45; closed Federal holidays and whenever Ford is present.*

The **Kelsey Museum of Archaeology** exhibits pottery, glass, statues, coins, textiles, and other artifacts from ancient Rome and the Middle East. *Newberry Hall, 434 State St., tel. 313/764–9304. Admission free. Guided tours may be arranged in advance. Open weekdays 9–4, weekends 1–4 during academic year, weekends 1–4 in summer; closed academic and legal holidays and during Christmas break.*

Matthaei Botanical Gardens, a university research facility, grows plants from around the world in the Exotic Conservatory. Facility includes horticultural specialty gardens, nature trails, greenhouses, laboratories, and a gift shop. *1800 Dixboro*

Rd., 7 mi northeast, tel. 313/763-7060. Admission: $1 adults, 75¢ senior citizens, 50¢ children 6–12, free under 6. Open daily 10–4:30; closed Thanksgiving, Dec. 25, Jan. 1.

Michigan Stadium, which seats 101,000 spectators is the nation's largest college-owned stadium. Visitors may tour by entering the gates on Stadium Boulevard. *Main St. and Stadium Blvd. Open daily 9–3:30 except home football Saturdays.*

The **University of Michigan Museum of Art** holds permanent collections of Western art dating from the 6th century AD and Asian art dating from 1000 BC. Exhibits are strong in Asian sculpture, prints, and drawings, and 18th- and 19th-century European and American paintings. *525 S. State St. at University Ave., tel. 313/763-1231. Admission free. Open Tues.–Fri. 10–4, Sat.–Sun. 1–5; shorter hours in summer.*

Ruthven Exhibit Museum displays focus on natural history, with special attention to the state's prehistory. Exhibits cover evolution, astronomy, biology, anthropology, and Michigan wildlife. Planetarium. *University Museum Bldg., 1109 Geddes Ave., tel. 313/764-0478. Admission free; planetarium shows $1.50. Museum open Mon.–Sat. 9–5, Thurs. until 9, Sun. 1–5. Planetarium shows Thurs. and weekends.*

A number of bookstores and specialty shops stand in the campus area. An annual highlight is the city's **Summer Art Fair,** held for four days each July, with artists from all over the country.

Burton Memorial Tower houses the 55-bell Charles Baird Carillon, one of the largest in the world; bell weights range from 12 pounds to 12 tons. *230 S. Ingalls St. off N. University Ave., tel. 313/764-2538. Admission free. Weekly concerts Mon. at 7 PM late June–Aug. Tower open to visitors Wed. 4–5 PM, and home football Saturdays 11–noon, weather permitting.*

The **Ann Arbor Hands-On Museum** has more than 140 exhibits connecting science, art, and culture. You can step inside a bubble, watch honeybees hard at work, move a robot, or make yourself "float" at this museum housed in a renovated century-old firehouse. *219 E. Huron Ave., tel. 313/995-5437. Admission: $2.50 adults, $1.50 children, students, and senior citizens, $6 family (grandparents included). Open Tues.–Fri. 1:30–5:30, Sat. 10–5, Sun. 1–5.*

Domino's Farms, Archives, and Galleries, the corporate headquarters of Domino's Pizza, is the brainchild of the pizza chain's founder, Tom Monaghan, who is also the owner of the Detroit Tigers. Housed in a half-mile-long low-rise building called Prairie House, the headquarters is home to the **National Center for the Study of Frank Lloyd Wright,** with a collection of manuscripts, videotapes of the architect and his clients, oral histories, and monographs written by and about him. The center maintains and exhibits Monagahan's personal $30-million collection of Wright material, some 300 pieces in all, said to be the largest collection of its kind in the world. Also displayed are a high-back chair (for which Monaghan paid $198,000) and other furniture designed by the architect, as well as lamps, art-glass windows, metal works, ceramics, and drawings. *44 Frank Lloyd Wright Dr., tel. 313/995-4504. Admission: suggested donation $2 adults, $1 senior citizens and students, free under 5. Open weekdays 10–6, Thurs. till 9, weekends noon–5.*

The building also houses Monaghan's **Classic Car Museum,** with about 100 of some 250 cars on display. Included are Corvettes, T-Birds, Duesenbergs, and an $8.1-million 1931 Bugatti Royale, one of only six built. A gift shop sells auto films, original and poster art, and a collection of auto-related items. *44 Frank Lloyd Wright Dr., tel. 313/930–3000. Admission: $5 adults, $3 senior citizens and students, $1 11 and under. Open Mon.–Thurs. 11–6, Fri. and Sat. 11–9, Sun. noon–5.*

The complex also has a petting farm that enables children to learn about farm animals and farm life. *Admission free. Open weekdays 11 AM–1 PM, weekends 1–4 PM.*

Public tours of the world headquarters are offered weekend afternoons 1–4 PM. Domino's Farms complex is at 30 Frank Lloyd Wright Dr., at the junction of Rte. M–14 and U.S. 23, tel. 313/ 930–3000.

The Arts As is natural for a university town, Ann Arbor has a strong reputation in the performing arts, and in many cases tickets are free. Check out the **Power Center for the Performing Arts** (tel. 313/763–3333), the **Ann Arbor Symphony Orchestra** (tel. 313/ 994–4801), the **Ann Arbor Chamber Orchestra** (tel. 313/996– 0066), **ARS Musica** (tel. 313/662–3976), the **University Musical Society** (tel. 313/764–2538), the **Comic Opera Guild** (tel. 313/ 973–3264), and the **Ann Arbor Civic Ballet** (tel. 313/668–8066).

Dining **Gandy Dancer.** A seafood restaurant set in the 19th-century
American former Ann Arbor railroad station. High ceilings give the place
★ a palatial feel; there is a two-story cocktail lounge and a garden room. The menu lists grilled, poached, and fried fish, with stuffed clam and oyster dishes for appetizers. Extensive wine list. *401 Depot, tel. 313/769–0592. Reservations advised. Dress: casual. AE, CB, DC, MC, V. Open weekdays 11:30–4 and 5– 11, Fri. until midnight, Sat. 5–midnight, Sun. 3–10; closed holidays. Moderate–Expensive.*
Windows. This 11th-floor penthouse restaurant and lounge features a view of the city. Entrees include pheasant and quail; homemade desserts. *Ann Arbor Inn, 100 S. 4th Ave., tel. 313/ 769–9500. Reservations advised. Jacket and tie advised. AE, CB, DC, MC, V. Open for dinner Mon.–Sat., brunch Sun., call for hours. Moderate–Expensive.*

French **The Moveable Feast.** Set in a restored 1870 Victorian mansion,
★ the style falls somewhere between California and France. Specialties include breads, pastries, and beef and fowl dishes. Four-course and three-course fixed-price dinners. *326 W. Liberty, tel. 313/663–3278. Reservations suggested. Jacket and tie advised. AE, MC, V. Open for lunch and dinner Tues.–Fri., dinner only Sat. Moderate–Expensive.*

German **Metzger's Black Forest Inn.** A restaurant with German murals and beer steins that has been operated by the same family since 1929. The menu features chicken livers, wurst, Spaetzle, dark beer; servings are generous. Children's menu, cocktail lounge. *203 E. Washington, tel. 313/668–8987. Reservations advised. Dress: casual. AE, CB, DC, MC, V. Open Tues.–Sat. 11–10, Sun. 11:30–8; closed Thanksgiving, Dec. 25, Jan. 1. Moderate.*

Italian **Argiero's Italian Restaurant.** A small indoor-outdoor cafe, it serves soups, pasta, cannoli, and cappuccino. The sandwiches are extra big; no bar. *300 Detroit St., tel. 313/665–0444. Reser-*

vations not required. Dress: casual. No credit cards. Open Mon.–Sat. for lunch and dinner. Inexpensive.

Jewish **Zingerman's Delicatessen.** It's a deli but more than that: an array of carryout items includes 150 varieties of imported cheese, smoked fish, three kinds of knishes, and over 30 salads. Great sandwiches. Packed from dusk to dawn. *422 Detroit St., tel. 313/663–3354. No reservations. Dress: casual. No credit cards. Open Mon.–Sat. 7AM–8:30 PM, Sun. 9–8:30. Inexpensive.*

Lodging Ann Arbor is one of the most avid college-football towns in the Midwest, so lodging can be at a premium on home game Saturdays. Autumn visitors should check the football schedule.

Ann Arbor Hilton Berkshire. The hotel, which is two miles from Ann Arbor Stadium, serves a complimentary Continental breakfast, provides robes for guest use, and has wall-mounted hair dryers. Comfortable, spacious rooms, modern decor. *610 Hilton Blvd., at junction of I–94 and State St. (exit 177), 48104, tel. 313/761–7800. 210 rooms. Facilities: indoor pool, sauna, whirlpool, restaurant, lounge, entertainment. AE, CB, DC, MC, V. Expensive.*

Ann Arbor Inn. Close to downtown shopping and the University of Michigan campus, this hotel's well-kept rooms are bright and cheery. The rooftop lounge has views of the city. *100 S. 4th Ave., 48104, tel. 313/769–9500. 189 rooms. Facilities: indoor pool, whirlpool, pay garage, dining room, coffee shop, lounge, entertainment. AE, CB, DC, MC, V. Expensive.*

Campus Inn. Adjacent to the university, it is a favorite stopping place for Wolverine fans. Rooms are modern and comfortable. *615 E. Huron, 48104, tel. 313/769–2200. 205 rooms. Facilities: small outdoor pool, sauna, valet parking, 2 dining rooms, patio dining in summer, lounge. AE, CB, DC, MC, V. Moderate.*

Howard Johnson Motor Lodge. Situated close to the University of Michigan and Eastern Michigan University, it offers clean, comfortable rooms in the Howard Johnson fashion. Tropical decor in pool area is pleasant. *2380 Carpenter Rd., 48108, tel. 313/ 971–0700. 128 rooms. Facilities: indoor pool, sauna, whirlpool, sundeck. AE, CB, DC, MC, V. Moderate.*

---

❺ Jackson

Farther west along I–94 is the city where the Republican Party was founded in July 1854. More than a thousand Free Soilers, Whigs, and Democrats gathered here, adopted the Republican name, issued a platform, and nominated candidates for state office. The meeting was held "under the oaks" because the town had no hall large enough. A tablet marks the site on the northwest corner of Franklin and Second Streets. Jackson celebrates a **Rose Festival** each year in late May and a **Hot Air Jubilee** that draws dozens of balloonists each July.

Exploring The city also is the site of the **Cascades Falls**—15 man-made waterfalls and six large fountains on which water tumbles in continuously changing patterns, illuminated at night. The 500-foot falls, built in 1932, are described as the largest man-made falls in North America. A small museum tells the history of the falls; a miniature golf course, picnic area, and carriage and paddleboat rides are on the grounds. *Sparks Foundation County Park, 1500 S. Brown St. south of I–94, tel.*

517/788–4320. Admission: $2, free 5 and under; additional fee for carriage rides and paddleboat rental. Cascades operate Memorial Day–Labor Day, nightly 7–11.

The **Ella Sharp Museum** is a complex of buildings spanning the development of Jackson County. Visitors can view a typical settler's log cabin of the 1830s, a one-room schoolhouse, and a wealthy family's Victorian farm home filled with 19th-century furnishings. Adjacent are a craft shop, general store, and contemporary art gallery and studio, with changing exhibits. The **Peter F. Hurst Planetarium** has astronomy programs Sunday afternoons from September to mid-June and Thursday evenings in July and August. *3225 4th St., tel. 517/787–2320. Admission to farm home: $2.50 adults, $2 senior citizens, $1 under 12. Planetarium show: $1 adults, 50¢ under 12. Museum open Tues.–Fri. 10–5, weekends 1:30–5; closed major holidays and Jan.*

Called "the biggest little space center on Earth," the **Michigan Space Center** displays some $30 million worth of artifacts in a gold geodesic dome on the campus of Jackson Community College. An 85-foot Mercury Redstone rocket and several rocket engines stand outside. Exhibits from NASA, the Smithsonian Institution, and the space industry include the Apollo 9 command module, Mercury and Gemini spacecraft, space suits, a moon rock, and a lunar rover. Multimedia shows take place in the astro-theater. Youngsters can try on a space helmet and climb into a capsule. *2111 Emmons Rd., tel. 517/787–4425. Admission: $3 adults, $2 students and over 60, $9 families. Open May 26–Sept. 1, weekdays 10–7, Sat. 10–5, Sun. noon–6; Mar. 31–May 25, Mon.–Sat. 10–5, Sun. noon–5; rest of year, Tues.–Sat. 10–5, Sun. noon–5; closed Easter, Thanksgiving, Dec. 25, Jan. 1. Last visitors admitted 45 min before closing.*

The **Conklin Antique Reed Organ Museum** exhibits more than 70 reed organs and melodeons in the renovated gymnasium of the former Hanover High School (circa 1911). Many organs are more than a century old, and some date from the Civil War. Among the rarities are a "suitcase organ" used for religious services on the battlefields of World War I, a small "circuit rider" organ used by a traveling minister, and a reed organ with bells that sound the notes. *Fairview St., Hanover, tel. 517/563–2311. Exit I–94 at Rte. M–60 south to Moscow Rd., then south to Hanover Rd. and west to Fairview St. Admission: $1 adults, 50¢ students and senior citizens. Open Apr.–Oct., 1st and 3rd Sun. 1–5.*

Dining **Gilbert's Steak House** has been a Jackson tradition for more than 40 years. The warm, pleasant dining room has Tiffany-style lamps. The menu includes veal, seafood, and prime rib. Children's menu, cocktail lounge. *2323 Shirley Dr., tel. 517/782–7135. Reservations advised. Dress: casual. AE, MC, V. Open Mon.–Thurs. 11 AM–10 PM, Fri. and Sat. 11AM–11 PM, Sun. noon–7; closed holidays. Inexpensive–Moderate.*

Schuler's. The menu offers well-prepared traditional beef and seafood specialties served in a casual Old English atmosphere. Children's menu, cocktail lounge. *6020 Ann Arbor Rd., 5 mi east at I–94 exit 145, tel. 517/764–1200. Reservations suggested weekends. Dress: casual. AE, CB, DC, MC, V. Inexpensive–Moderate.*

Lodging **Colonial Inn.** Quiet pleasant rooms with modern Colonial-style decor. There aren't a lot of extras, but the motel is comfortable and well kept. *6027 Ann Arbor Rd., 49201, tel. 517/764–3820. 5 mi east at I–94 exit 145. 74 rooms. Facilities: outdoor pool, coin laundry, winter plug-ins. AE, CB, DC, MC, V. Inexpensive.*

Knights Inn. The modern rooms are typical of this motel chain —spacious, with Old English decor. *830 Royal Dr., 49202, tel. 517/789–7186. ¼ mi south of I–94 on Rte. 127. 96 rooms. Facilities: outdoor·pool, restaurant adjacent. AE, MC, V. Inexpensive.*

Southwestern Michigan

A climate modified by Lake Michigan gives this region bountiful crops, including apples, strawberries, cherries, blueberries, plums, and grapes. During the harvest season you can buy at roadside stands or cider mills, or pick your own if you're energetic. This is also wine country. Gentle hills covered with fruit trees and vineyards roll away from the lake into the wine-producing region centered around Paw Paw. Indiana borders the area to the south, with Lake Michigan on the west. We will begin in the south and work our way north and west.

Because of the distances between towns, we have treated each stop as a separate destination, listing its attractions and facilities. Price categories for restaurants and hotels are the same as in Detroit Dining and Lodging.

Numbers in the margin correspond with points of interest on the Southwestern Michigan map.

Getting Around

By Plane **Kellogg Municipal Airport,** Battle Creek (tel. 616/966–3470), is served by Air Wisconsin and Northwest Airlink.

Kent County International Airport, Grand Rapids (616/949–4500), is served by American, Delta, Midstate, Midway, Northwest, Piedmont, United, and USAir.

Kalamazoo County Airport, Kalamazoo (tel. 616/358–8177), is served by American Eagle, Northwest, Piedmont, and United Express.

Muskegon County Airport, Muskegon (tel. 616/798–4596), is served by American Eagle, Northwest Airlink, and United Express.

By Car I–94 and I–96 are principal east–west roads, U.S. 31 and U.S. 131 principal roads north–south. **Michigan–Wisconsin Ferry Service** (tel. 616/843–2521 or 800/253–0094) runs auto ferryboats between Ludington and Kewaunee, WI, year-round.

By Train **Amtrak** (tel. 800/872–7245) runs trains between Detroit and Chicago that stop at Battle Creek, Kalamazoo, Niles, and St. Joseph.

By Bus **Greyhound** and **Michigan Trailways** serve the larger communities.

Scenic Drives

Route BR–15 between Pentwater and Montague follows the Lake Michigan shoreline for about 25 miles, as does **Route A–2** between Saugatuck and South Haven.

Important Addresses and Numbers

Tourist Information
Battle Creek Visitors and Convention Bureau, 172 W. Van Buren, Battle Creek 49017, tel. 616/962–2240; weekdays 9–5.

Greater Grand Rapids Convention Bureau, the Grand Center, 245 Monroe NW, Grand Rapids 49503, tel. 616/459–8287; weekdays 9–5.

Holland Area Chamber of Commerce, 272 E. 8th St., Holland 49422, tel. 616/392–2389; weekdays 8–5.

Kalamazoo County Convention and Visitors Bureau, 128 N. Kalamazoo Mall, Kalamazoo, 49007, tel. 616/381–4003; weekdays 9–5.

Muskegon County Convention and Visitors Bureau, 349 W. Webster Ave., Muskegon, 49440, tel. 616/722–3751; weekdays 9–5.

Saugatuck–Douglas Chamber of Commerce, 303 Butler St., Saugatuck, 49453, tel. 616/857–5801; weekdays 9–4:30.

Emergencies
Michigan State Patrol (tel. 517/332–2521). 911 is the **emergency number** in most of the region.

❶ Battle Creek

Exploring
In 1894 two brothers named Kellogg developed a flaked cereal, and Battle Creek was on its way to becoming "The Cereal Capital of the World." Today the Kellogg Company, Post Cereals division of General Foods, and the Ralston Purina Company are here. A Cereal Festival in June features what is described as the world's largest breakfast.

The weeklong **Battle Creek International Balloon Championship** held each July draws up to 200 leading balloonists and features mass launches, air shows, auto shows, and entertainment. **Linear Park,** linking natural waterways and parks, extends across much of the city, with 11 miles of pathways that include boardwalks, gazebos, and bridges.

The **Art Center** comprises four galleries featuring the work of Michigan artists and craftsmen. Classes and workshops are scheduled from time to time, and a gift shop displays the work of regional artists. *265 E. Emmett St., tel. 616/962–9511. Admission free. Open weekdays 10–5, weekends 1–4; closed holidays and Aug.*

The **Kingman Museum of Natural History** is in the 72-acre **Leila Arboretum,** part of Linear Park. Throughout three floors of natural-history exhibits in the museum, visitors may touch dinosaur bones more than 65 million years old, grind corn, "race" in an authentic South American dugout canoe, and explore many other exhibits. The **Gardner Memorial Planetarium** presents films for children and young people on weekends. *W. Michigan Ave. at 20th St., tel. 616/965–5117. Admission: 50¢*

adults, 25¢ students. Planetarium shows Sat. at 11, 1:30, and 3:30, Sun. at 2 and 3:30. Museum open Tues.–Sat. 9–5, Sun. 1–5; open Mon. in July–Aug. only. The arboretum is open at all times.

The **Kellogg Bird Sanctuary,** an experimental facility of Michigan State University, has gained national recognition for its contributions to wildlife management and environmental education. It is refuge to many species of waterfowl, songbirds, and small animals; visitors can use paved walkways where wild turkeys and peafowl roam. Thousands of Canada geese stop at Wintergreen Lake each fall. There are wildlife exhibits and an observation deck. *12685 E. C Ave., Augusta, 13 mi northwest of Battle Creek, tel. 616/671–2510. Admission: $1 adults, 50¢ under 18. Open Apr. 1–Nov. 30, daily 8 AM–sunset; rest of year, 8–5.*

Dining
American

New York, New York. Pictures of more than 400 celebrities adorn the walls. Prime rib is a house specialty; other specials served tableside on Thursday and Friday evenings include steak Diane, lobster Le Havre, and scampi. Among desserts is the "original" New York cheesecake. *1399 E. Michigan Ave. at Wattles Rd., tel. 616/964–8992. Reservations advised. Jacket and tie advised. MC, V. Closed holidays. Expensive.*

McCamly's Roof. The dining room atop the Stouffer Battle Creek Hotel offers a panoramic view of the city. House specialties include veal scallopini with crabmeat and herbed roast rack of lamb. Extensive wine list, cocktail lounge. *50 Capital Ave. SW, on 16th floor, tel. 616/963–7050. Reservations advised. Jacket and tie required. AE, DC, MC, V. Moderate–Expensive.*

Countryside Inn. This rustic restaurant has antiques and crafts in the dining room. A "garden greenery" specializes in salads; menu highlights also include a seafood catch of the day and chicken-and-ribs barbecue. Cocktail lounge. *1967 E. Michigan Ave., tel. 616/965–1247. Reservations advised. Dress: casual. AE, MC, V. Open Tues.–Thurs. 11–10, Fri.–Sat. till 11 PM, Sun. 8 PM; closed Dec. 25. Inexpensive.*

Italian

Roma Cafe and Spaghetti Factory. One of Battle Creek's oldest restaurants, its specials include spaghetti, baked lasagna, veal parmigiana, and pizza. Cocktail lounge. *914 W. Columbia Ave., tel. 616/968–6377. Reservations suggested. Dress: casual. No credit cards. Inexpensive–Moderate.*

Lodging
★

Stouffer's Battle Creek Hotel. The city's largest hotel, offering luxuriously appointed rooms, and 15 suites; barrier-free rooms are available. The decor is contemporary and comfortable. *50 Capital Ave. SW, 49017, tel. 616/963–7050. 245 rooms. Facilities: indoor pool, sauna, whirlpool, rooftop restaurant and lounge, entertainment. AE, CB, DC, MC, V. Expensive.*

Comfort Inn. The spacious motel rooms are modern and, living up to the name, quite comfortable. Good quality for the money. *165 Capital Ave. SW, 49015, tel. 616/965–3976. 54 rooms. Facilities: outdoor pool, cocktail lounge; restaurant adjacent. AE, CB, DC, MC, V. Inexpensive.*

Knights Inn. Ground-level rooms, functional comfort, and Old English decor. *2529 Capital Ave. SE, 49015, tel. 616/964–2600. 96 rooms, 10 with kitchenettes. Facilities: outdoor pool, cable TV; restaurant adjacent. CB, DC, MC, V. Inexpensive.*

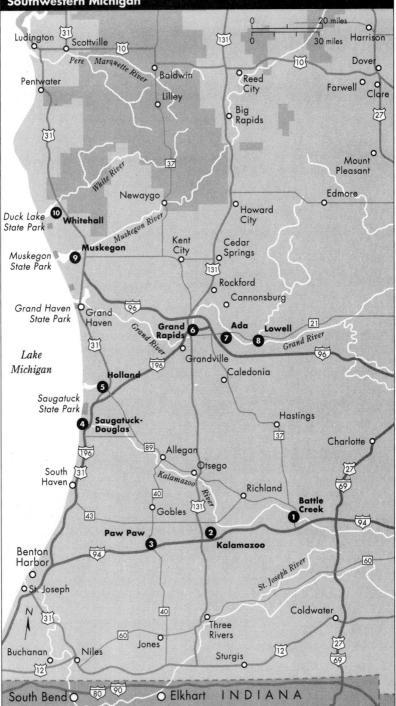

INDIANA

Bars and **Gangplank.** Sandwiches and soups are served at this watering
Nightclubs hole with nautical decor. Live entertainment and dancing Monday to Saturday evenings. *1749 E. Columbia Ave., tel. 616/962–7814. MC. V. Happy hour 4–6 PM.*

Verex Lounge. Cocktails and snacks are accompanied by live entertainment, and dancing Monday to Saturday. *Howard Johnson's Motor Lodge, 2580 Capital Ave. SW, tel. 616/965–0441. AE, DC, MC, V.*

❷ Kalamazoo

Kalamazoo, an Indian word meaning "place where the water boils," describes the springs bubbling up in the city's riverbed. The Michigan International Air Show each July draws more than 100,000 spectators. Western Michigan University is one of several colleges and universities here.

Exploring The **Kalamazoo Aviation History Museum** is also called the Kalamazoo Air Zoo because of the "cats" in its collection—a Curtis P-40 Flying Tiger and Grumman Wildcat, Hellcat, and Bearcat fighter planes. Dedicated to the contribution air power made to the Allies' World War II victory, the museum exhibits several other aircraft as well; most flew in World War II and are rare. Also displayed are aircraft engines, aviation uniforms, photo murals, and wartime artifacts donated by local citizens. Visitors can watch aircraft restoration work. *2101 E. Milham Rd. (I–94 exit 78, ¾ mi south on Portage Rd., then ½ mi east), tel. 616/382–6555. Admission: $4 adults, $3 over 59, $1 children under 13. Open Mon.–Sat. 10–5, Sun. 1–5; closed holidays.*

The **Kalamazoo Institute of Arts'** permanent collection consists of more than 2,000 prints, photos, paintings, sculptures, and ceramic pieces. The emphasis is on 20th-century American art and extensive holdings of German Expressionist art. Works by Alexander Calder, George Rickey, Helen Frankenthaler, and Ed Paschke, as well as by local artists, are in the collection. *314 S. Park St., tel. 616/349–7775 or 349–3959 for 24-hr information. Admission free. Open Tues.–Sat. 10–5, Sun. 1–5; closed Sun. June–Aug.*

The **Kalamazoo Nature Center** has 11 trails winding through 600 acres of meadows and woodlands, as well as an extensive herb garden and arboretum. A two-story glass-domed Sun-Rain Room displays historical and uncommon plants. The restored **DeLano Homestead,** built in 1858, presents demonstrations of pioneer crafts, exhibits on Michigan history, and domestic animals (May 1–Oct. 15) on a working pioneer farm. *7000 N. Westnedge Ave. (5 mi from downtown), tel. 616/381–1574. Weekend admission: $1.50 adults, $1 children, students, and over 65; weekdays $1 adults, 50¢ children, students, and over 65. Open Mon.–Sat. 9–5, Sun. 1–5; closed for 14 days after Labor Day, also Thanksgiving, Dec. 25, Jan. 1.*

The **Kalamazoo Public Library Museum** has a Pioneer Room with exhibits on local history and an Egyptian tomb, as well as on dinosaurs, computers, African cultures, and manufacturing. The **Hans Baldauf Planetarium** is part of the museum. *315 S. Rose St., tel. 616/345–7092 or 382–6873 for 24-hr information. Planetarium lectures and shows at 7 and 8 PM Wed.,*

Sat.–Sun at 2, 3, and 4. Planetarium admission: $2 adults, $1.50 children; museum free. Open Tues.–Sat. 9–5, Wed. 9–9, Sun. 1–5; closed Sun. June and Aug.

The **State Theater** (built in 1927) is host to concerts and stage productions. Of Spanish design, it has courtyards, arches, towers, balconies, and fountains. Free tours except during performances. *404 S. Burdick St.; tel. 616/344–9670 to arrange a tour.*

If architecture is your interest, Kalamazoo has two restored historic districts. The **South Street area** (tel. 616/345–7092), from Westnedge Avenue west to Oakland Drive, was the city's first suburb, more than 140 years ago. Listed on the National Register of Historic Places, it has a number of 19th- and early 20th-century building styles. The **Stuart Area Historic District** (tel. 616/346–7432), bordered by Stuart Street, Elm Street, Woodward Street, and West Main Street, includes Italian Revival and Queen Anne residences built in the 1870s and 1880s, many restored.

❸ A few miles west of Kalamazoo, just north of I–94 on Route 40, the village of **Paw Paw** has three wineries: St. Julian Winery (60902 Rte. M–51, tel. 616/657–2964), Frontenac Vineyards (39149 Red Arrow Hwy., tel. 616/657–5531) and Warner Vineyards (706 S. Kalamazoo St., tel. 616/657–3165). All offer free guided tours with tastings afterward. Call for schedules.

Dining   **Mountain Jack's.** Beef dishes are the specialty; the menu also
American   includes grilled swordfish, teriyaki chicken, stuffed shrimp, fresh fish, stuffed filet mignon, and prime rib. Children's menu, cocktail lounge, with entertainment Thursday and Friday nights. *6701 Westnedge Ave., Portage, tel. 616/327–6797. AE, DC, MC, V. No lunch weekends. Inexpensive.*

International   **Carlos Murphy's Cafe.** Casual dining with a rather unlikely combination of Mexican and Irish entrees, as well as barbecued ribs, shrimp, steak, and sandwiches. *5650 W. Main St., tel. 616/343–0330. Reservations advised. Dress: casual. AE, MC, V. Inexpensive.*

Italian   **Angelina's Ristorante.** This downtown restaurant features homemade pasta, sauces, and bread, plus veal, beef, poultry, and seafood. The contemporary dining room has a pleasant Italian air. Cocktail lounge. *109 W. Lovell, lower level of State Theater Bldg., tel. 616/344–2100. Reservations advised. Jacket and tie advised. AE, DC, MC, V. Open Mon.–Sat. 11 AM–3 PM, and 5–10 PM, until 11 Fri. and Sat., Sun. 5–10. Inexpensive–Moderate.*

Lodging   **Hilton Inn.** This Hilton, in the Kalamazoo Center downtown, offers package plans and a number of amenities. Rooms are comfortably spacious. *100 Michigan Ave., 49007, tel. 616/381–2130. 287 rooms. Facilities: indoor pool, sauna, whirlpool, health club (fee), parking ramp, movie theater, restaurants, cocktail lounge, entertainment. AE, CB, DC, MC, V. Expensive.*
Sheraton Inn. Rooms feature designer decor and are modern and spacious, with comfortable furnishings and extra touches. *3600 E. Cork St., 49001, tel. 616/385–3922. 156 rooms. Facili-*

ties: indoor pool, sauna, whirlpool, exercise room, restaurant, lounge, entertainment. AE, CB, DC, MC, V. Moderate.

Knights Inn. Oversize beds and Old English decor are offered by this chain. *3704 Van Rick Rd., 49002, tel. 616/344–9255. One mi south of I–94 at exit 80. 103 rooms, 14 with kitchenettes. Facilities: outdoor pool; restaurant adjacent. AE, CB, DC, MC, V. Inexpensive.*

Bars and Nightclubs

Bourbon Street. This night spot and restaurant has dancing Monday to Saturday evenings, with a Dixieland jazz brunch on Sunday. Reservations advised. *123 W. South, tel. 616/381–6614. AE, MC, V. Open Mon.–Sat. 11 AM–2 AM, Sun. 10 AM–3 PM.*

Cheek to Cheek and the Silver Bullet Saloon. A country bar serving Mexican and specialty sandwiches and offering country and top-40 music nightly. *3750 E. Kilgore, Portage, tel. 616/345–1608. MC, V.*

Club Soda. A downtown nightclub for the adventurous. Dancing and live entertainment by rock, blues, reggae, and jazz performers six nights a week, disco on Sunday. *340 E. Michigan, tel. 616/342–8067. MC, V.*

Cricket's Piano Bar. A quiet spot with light food—oysters, clams, fettucine, shrimp—and easy prices, plus nightly piano music. *In Dimitri's, Portage and Michigan, tel. 616/381–2700. Closed Sun.*

Holly's Bistro. This bar, styled after a 1900s bistro, serves lunch and dinner daily and presents live entertainment evenings. *5036 S. Westnedge Ave., tel. 616/345–4408. AE, MC, V. Open daily 7:30 PM–12:30 AM.*

Zanies Comedy Night Club. Live comedy featuring professionals from stage, screen, and TV. *State Theater, 404 S. Burdick, lower level, tel. 616/344–5400. MC, V. Showtimes 8 PM Thurs.–Sat. with 10:30 PM show Fri. and Sat.*

---

❹ Saugatuck–Douglas

Situated on Lake Michigan at the mouth of the Kalamazoo River, the small community of **Saugatuck** has become a trendy tourist spot with a turn-of-the-century feel. A well-known artists' colony, it is home to the **Ox-Bow Art Workshop,** the Midwest's oldest summer school of painting. The boardwalk pier, one of the longest on the Great Lakes, overlooks a harbor with all manner of boats from yachts to dinghies. Rockhounds comb the beaches in search of so-called septarian nodules, which when halved and polished display an endless array of designs.

One-and-a-half-hour cruises along the scenic Kalamazoo River and onto Lake Michigan (weather permitting) are conducted by the 82-passenger sternwheeler *Queen of Saugatuck. 716 Water St., tel. 616/857–4261. Fare: $4.50 adults, $3 children under 12. MC, V. Several times daily Memorial Day–Labor Day.*

Before a bridge linked Saugatuck to its across-the-river neighbor, Douglas, the only way to cross the Kalamazoo was aboard a hand-cranked, chain-powered ferryboat. The Chain Ferry continues to carry pedestrians and bicyclists, as it has for more than a century. *S. of Saugatuck–Douglas Bridge, tel. 616/857–2151, ext. 26. One-way fare: $1 adults, 50¢ children. Open Memorial Day–Labor Day, daily 9–9.*

The *City of Douglas* cruise ship runs 1½-hour scenic after-noon cruises and luncheon and dinner cruises. *Saugatuck–Douglas Bridge, tel. 616/857–2151, ext. 26, or 857–2107. Fare for scenic cruises: $5 adults, $2.50 children under 13; fares vary for luncheon and dinner cruises. Reservations required: call for schedule. Runs Memorial Day–Labor Day.*

The SS *Keewatin*, a former passenger vessel that sailed the Great Lakes until 1965, is moored in Douglas as a marine muse-um. One of the last of the classic steamboats, it is carefully preserved and maintained, right down to a pair of boots stand-ing in the captain's stateroom. *S. of the Saugatuck–Douglas Bridge, tel. 616/857–2151, ext. 50, or 857–2107. Admission: $2.50 adults, $1 under 13. MC, V. Guided tours Memorial Day –Labor Day, several times daily 10–4:30.*

---

⑤ Holland

Settled in 1847 by Dutch immigrants seeking religious free-dom, Holland works to retain its Dutch air. Millions of tulips provide displays of vibrant color and beauty; the **Tulip Time Festival,** held in mid-May at the peak of the bloom, draws half a million visitors each year. The community today remains Dutch right down to daily street scrubbing.

Exploring **DeKlomp Wooden Shoe and Delft Factory.** Here you can watch artisans create wooden shoes on machinery imported from the Netherlands, then buy a pair in the gift shop (about $25). You can also watch each stage in the process by which hand-painted Delftware pottery is created. *Veldheer Tulip Farm, 12755 Quincy at U.S. 31, tel. 616/399–1900. Admission free. Factory open Mon.–Sat. 8–4:30. Gift shop open daily 8–6:30. Extended hours during tulip festival.*

Over the years the Hollanders have re-created a **Dutch Village** like those in their homeland 100 years ago. Distinctive Dutch buildings, roofed with orange tiles, stand amid canals, bridges, and gardens. Live animals populate a farm. In warm weather brightly costumed girls perform *klompen* dances in their wood-en shoes to the music of a huge Amsterdam street organ. The village has carving exhibits, windmills, shops, and a restaurant with Dutch decor serving Dutch and American fare. *One mi north on U.S. 32, tel. 616/396–1475. Admission $3 adults, $2 children under 12. Open July–Aug., daily 9–6; late Apr.–June and Sept.–mid-Oct., 9–4:30.*

The **Netherlands Museum** holds a collection of artifacts on Dutch folklore and heritage. Displays include 19th-century furnishings, Delftware, and exhibits from the Netherlands Pa-vilion of the 1939 New York World's Fair. Gift shop. *12th St. and Central Ave., tel. 616/392–9084. Admission $1, under 13 free. Open May 1–Sept. 15, Mon.–Sat. 9–5, Sun. 11:30–5; Sept. 16–Dec. 31 and Mar. 1–April 30, Mon.–Sat. 9–5; rest of year, 10–4. Closed Thanksgiving, Dec. 25, Jan. 1.*

Windmill Island. This unusual municipal park, on an island in the Black River, has canals, a working drawbridge, a miniature Dutch village called Little Netherlands, and tulip gardens surrounding a huge working windmill. Called *De Zwaan*, the 200-year-old windmill was brought from Holland and still grinds a fine graham flour, which can be purchased on site. Costumed guides escort visitors. Other attractions are the

Posthouse Museum, a replica of a Dutch country inn; candle carving demonstrations; films on Dutch windmills; free rides for children on an authentic Dutch carousel; and klompen dancing during the summer. *7th and Lincoln Sts., tel. 616/396–5433. Admission: $3.50 adults, $1.75 children under 13. Open May 1–31 and July 1–Labor Day, Mon.–Sat. 9–6, Sun. 11:30–6; June 1–30, Mon.–Sat. 10–5, Sun. 11:30–5; limited hours after Labor Day to Oct. 31.*

The **Wooden Shoe Factory** conducts tours of the largest such plant in the United States. Skilled shoemakers produce klompens using hand-carving methods, century-old machines, and modern machinery. A country store and gift shops sell Dutch gift items and souvenirs. *U.S. 31 at 16th St., tel. 616/396–6513. Admission: 25¢, under 6 free. Open Mon.–Sat. 8–4:30.*

Car buffs should visit the **Poll Museum of Transportation,** with its collection of more than 30 gas, steam, and electric autos and fire engines dating from 1902. Highlights are a 1921 Pierce Arrow roadster and a 1931 Rolls-Royce. Bicycles, model trains, and traction engines are also displayed. *U.S. 31 and New Holland St., 5 mi north of downtown, tel. 616/399–1955. Admission: $1 adults, 50¢ under 3. Open Memorial Day–Labor Day, Mon.–Sat. and holidays 8–6; May 1–Memorial Day and Labor Day–Oct. 1, Mon.–Sat. and holidays 8–5.*

Dining **The Hatch.** Specialties are prime rib, fresh seafood, steaks, and a garden-fresh salad bar. The dining room is casual, with contemporary nautical decor, and in summer there's a tropical outdoor patio bar. An indoor lounge features live entertainment Wednesday to Saturday. Sunday brunch served. *1870 Ottawa Beach Rd., tel. 616/399–9120. Reservations advised. Dress: casual. AE, MC, V. Open Mon.–Thurs. 11:30 AM–2 PM and 5:30–11 PM, Fri-Sat. till 11:30, Sun. 11:30 AM–7 PM; closed for lunch on Sat. and on Thanksgiving, Dec. 25, Jan. 1. Moderate.*

Dave's Garage. A restaurant aptly named for its automobile motif. The wide-ranging menu includes crab legs and other seafood, as well as steaks and prime rib. Cocktail lounge, imorted beer, fairly extensive wine list. *478 E. 16th St., tel. 616/392–3017. Reservations advised. Dress: casual. MC, V. Open Mon.–Sat. 11 AM–2 PM and 4:45–10 PM. Inexpensive–Moderate.*

Lodging **Point West Inn and Conference Center.** Set on Lake Macatawa, the inn has luxurious rooms in modern decor, including suites and efficiency units and a four-bedroom cottage. Package plans. *2150 South Shore Dr., Macatawa, 49434, tel. 616/335–5894. 5 mi west, at west end of Lake Macatawa. 67 rooms. Facilities: pool, beach, 5 tennis courts, playground, dock (fee), paddleboat, sailboat, ski rental, restaurant, lounge. AE, DC, MC, V. Very Expensive.*

Budget Host Wooden Shoe Motel. A bright, sunny motel with some Dutch touches around the edges. Nonsmoking rooms and suites, package plans. *465 U.S. 31, 49423, tel. 616/392–8521 or 800/835–7427, ext. 630. U.S. 31 and 16th St. 29 rooms. Facilities: outdoor pool, satellite TV, tanning booth (fee), miniature golf (fee), restaurant. AE, DC, MC, V. Inexpensive.*

Comfort Inn. A newer motel with modern, comfortable, spacious rooms and public spaces. Some whirlpool rooms. Close to the Dutch Village and Windmill Island. *422 E. 32d St., 49423, tel. 616/392–1000 or 800/228–5150. 71 rooms. Facilities: outdoor pool and whirlpool, in-room movies; restaurant adjacent. AE, DC, MC, V. Inexpensive.*

❻ Grand Rapids

Exploring Established as a trading post in 1826, Michigan's second most populous city gets its name from the rapids of the Grand River, which flows through it. Grand Rapids was an early furniture-manufacturing center; that industry still flourishes. After a major overhaul and rejuvenation in the early 1980s, the downtown area is now a thriving showcase for the arts, local history, and business, with pedestrian malls, public art works, hotels, and shopping areas. **Monroe Center,** in the heart of downtown, is a landscaped outdoor pedestrian mall that features shopping, street vendors, concerts, and festivals throughout the year.

John Ball Zoological Gardens is one of the largest zoos in Michigan, with approximately 500 animals and 145 species, including several endangered ones. Don't miss the lizards and reptiles in the indoor herpetarium. Also to be seen are a children's petting zoo, primate and South American exhibits, an aquarium, and terraced zoological gardens. *Fulton and Valley SW, tel. 616/776–2591. Admission: $1 adults, 50¢ under 16. Open daily 10–4.*

The **Grand Rapids Art Museum,** set in the city's first Federal building and Post Office (circa 1879), has eight galleries housing a permanent collection and traveling exhibitions. Emphasis is on 17th-, 19th-, and 20th-century master prints, 20th-century American paintings, and German Expressionism; the collection includes furniture, paintings, drawings, prints, photographs, sculpture, and decorative arts. A children's gallery has hands-on art and color experiments, as well as film and music programs. *155 N. Division Ave., tel. 616/459–4676. Admission: $1 adults, 50¢ senior citizens and children ages 12–18. Open Mon.–Sat. 10–5, Sun. noon–5.*

Gerald R. Ford Presidential Museum provides a close look at the life of the Grand Rapids native who became the 38th president. Documents, graphics, videotapes, and slide presentations feature Ford's Congressional years, his vice-presidency, the controversial pardon of Richard M. Nixon, and related national and international issues. Exhibits also deal with the American Bicentennial and Betty Ford's role as First Lady. Personal memorabilia, gifts from world leaders, and a cartoon-laden wall explaining the lawmaking process are on display. The Oval Office in the White House during the Ford Administration is depicted. *303 Pearl St. NW, tel. 616/456–2675. Admission: $1.50 age 16 and older. Open Mon.–Sat 9–4:45, Sun. noon–4:45; closed Thanksgiving, Dec. 25, Jan. 1.*

The **Grand Rapids Public Museum** features Gaslight Village, which re-creates a Grand Rapids street of the 1880s, complete with horse-drawn streetcar and stores. A "People of the Grand" exhibit offers a historical view of the Grand River Valley and allows visitors to eavesdrop on business dealings between an Indian family and French fur traders. Exhibits also concern the history of furniture and the natural history of the area. *54 Jefferson St. SE, tel. 616/456–3977. Admission: $1 adults, 50¢ children 5–15 and senior citizens, free under 5. Open Mon.–Sat. 10–5, Sun. 1–5.*

Roger B. Chaffee Planetarium. Named for the Grand Rapids astronaut killed in the Apollo I fire in 1965, the small facility, part of the Public Museum, has an 86-seat domed theater featuring productions ranging from programs about *Star Trek* and backyard astronomy to light, music, and sky shows. The **Hall of the Universe** near the planetarium has exhibits on astronomy and space science, and striking "blacklight" murals. Call **Skyline** (tel. 616/456–3200) for information on current sky objects and upcoming astronomical and planetarium events. *233 Washington SE, tel. 616/456–3985. Shows Thurs. and Fri. 8 PM, Sat. 11:30 AM, 1:30, 8 PM; hours sometimes vary. Admission: $2 adults, $1.50 children and senior citizens. Children under 5 admitted only for special shows.*

Heritage Hill, a historic district east of downtown, has approximately 1,300 dwellings representing some 60 architectural styles. Some are downright spectacular, especially those built by lumber barons. Two Frank Lloyd Wright–designed houses are in the district—the Amberg House (505 College Ave. SE), and the May House (450 Madison Ave. SE). Brochures outlining two self-guided walking tours may be picked up at the *Heritage Hill Association office, 126 College St. SE, tel. 616/ 459–8950. First weekend in Oct. is annual Historic Homes Tour.*

The Calder. Its name is *La Grande Vitesse* (the Grand Rapids) but everyone refers to it as the Calder because it is 42 tons of streamlined strawberry-red sculpture by Alexander Calder. Controversial at first, it has become a symbol of the city. Next to the sculpture on the roof of the county building is a 127-by-127-foot abstract painting, also by Calder. *Vandenberg Center, behind City–County Buildings between Monroe and Ionia.*

The **Fish Ladder,** although called a sculpture, is a series of watery steps that help migrating salmon bypass the 6th Street dam to swim upstream in the Grand River to spawn. *Grand River at 6th St.*

Only a few 19th-century covered bridges are left in Michigan; three are close to Grand Rapids and just a few miles apart. The **❼ Ada Covered Bridge,** which crosses the Thorn Apple River, is open to foot traffic only (7507 Thorn Apple River Dr., Ada, 12 mi east on Rte. M–21, tel. 616/676–9191). Ten miles east of Ada **❽** on Route M–21 is Lowell, where the **Fallasburg Covered Bridge,** in continuous service since it was built in 1871, is one of two remaining "kissing bridges" in Michigan that you can drive across. (Fallasburg Park, 4 mi north of Lowell on Lincoln Lake Rd. to Covered Bridge Rd., then 1 mi east, tel. 616/897–8545.) Also near Lowell is **White's Covered Bridge,** a century-old structure spanning the Flat River; it is open to vehicular traffic. (White's Bridge Rd., 2½ mi east of Lowell, then 6 mi north, tel. 616/897–8545.)

Dining **The 1913 Room.** One of eight restaurants in the Amway Grand
American Plaza Hotel, it has crystal chandeliers, floor-to-ceiling mirrors,
★ beamed ceilings, fresh flowers, and red velvet circular

booths, which create a lavish 1900s mood and set the tone for excellent food and service. The menu is innovative; desserts are made with fresh fruit from the area. Very good wine list. *Amway Grand Plaza Hotel, Pearl St. at Monroe St., tel. 616/ 776–6426. Reservations required. Jacket and tie required. AE, CB, DC, MC, V. Open 11:30–2 and 5:30–11 Mon.–Fri., Sat. from 5:30 PM; closed Sun.; Closed Thanksgiving, Dec. 25, Jan. 1. Expensive.*

Churchill's. A downtown favorite, with tableside preparation of steak Diane and scampi Renaissance. A range of seafood, chicken, veal, and beef includes Chateaubriand, fresh sword-fish, and rack of lamb. Rich paneling and mahogany tables suggest an air of British dignity. *188 Monroe St. NW, tel. 616/ 456–7074. Reservations advised. Jacket and tie advised. AE, MC, V. Closed Dec. 25. Moderate–Expensive.*

Great Lakes Shipping Company. The menu highlights aged steaks, slow-roasted prime rib, and select seafood served in a comfortable dining room decorated in nautical style. Lunch features omelets and a quiche of the day; sandwiches and a lighter menu are served in the tavern. Children's menu. *2455 Burton St. SE, tel. 616/949–9440. Reservations advised. Jack-et and tie advised. AE, MC, V. Open Mon.–Thurs. 11:30 AM–2 PM and 5–10:30 PM, Fri. till 11 PM, Sat. till midnight; closed major holidays. Moderate.*

Zak's Diner. A '50s-style diner, it has a jukebox full of golden oldies, wall boxes, booths, and a lunch counter, amid a decor of chrome, stainless steel, and glass blocks. Specialties include meat loaf, hot beef sandwiches with mashed potatoes, the 3-D burger, Zak's french toast, and hash browns. Breakfast served all day. *Ledyard Bldg., Monroe Mall, 116 Monroe Center, tel. 616/235–7349. No reservations. Dress: casual. MC, V. Inexpensive.*

German **Schnitzelbank.** Fine German dining featuring Wiener schnit-zel, sauerbraten, pot roast; locals say the prime rib is among the best in town. The warm Old World rooms are richly pan-eled. Children's menu. *342 Jefferson Ave. SE, tel. 616/459– 9527. Reservations suggested. Jacket and tie advised. AE, DC. Open Mon.–Sat. 11:30 AM–8 PM; closed holidays. Moderate.*

International **Jose Babushka's.** The menu is mostly Mexican, with a Polish touch. Specials include Santa Fe barbecued ribs, flaming fajitas, tacos, kielbasa, chimichangas, goumpki, and kapusta chili dogs. Family-style dining room, separate cocktail lounge. *Two locations: 5501 Northland NE, tel. 616/364–6266, and 1820 44th St. SW, tel. 616/534–0704. Reservations advised. Dress: casual. MC, V. Music and dancing some evenings. In-expensive.*

Lodging **Amway Grand Plaza Hotel.** Far and away the best hotel in town
★ and one of the ranking hotels in Michigan, luxurious from top to bottom. Rooms in the east section have traditional furnishings and decor, while those in the west are contemporary; original works of art are displayed throughout the hotel. *Pearl and Monroe Sts., 49503, tel. 616/774–2000 or 800/323–7500. 682 rooms. Facilities: indoor pool, saunas, whirlpool, 2 lighted tennis courts, racquetball court, squash court, exercise room, tanning booth (fee). Eight restaurants in hotel, two of them outstanding. Lounges, entertainment. Weekend package plans. AE, CB, DC, MC, V. Very Expensive.*

Grand Rapids Marriott. In this luxury hotel with a host of amenities, the rooms are spacious, light, and airy, with modern decor and comfortable furnishings. Oriented to the corporate world but comfortable for families. Weekend and honeymoon packages. *5700 28th St. SE, 49506, tel. 616/957–1770 or 800/ 228–9290. ¼ mi east of I–96 Exit 43B. 319 rooms. Facilities: indoor-outdoor pool, sauna, whirlpool, exercise room, 18-hole golf course, 4 tennis courts, dining room, lounge, entertainment. AE, CB, DC, MC, V. Very Expensive–Expensive*

Harley Hotel. A low, modern motor hotel in a suburban setting eight minutes from downtown. Rooms are large and color-coordinated, with homey touches such as extra towels and swing-out lamps for each bed. Weekend packages available. *4041 Cascade Dr. SE, 49506, tel. 616/949–8800 or 800/321– 2323. 6 mi east of I–96 exit 40A. 147 rooms. Facilities: indoor-outdoor pool, wading pool, saunas, 2 lighted tennis courts, playground, restaurant, lounge, entertainment. AE, CB, DC, MC, V. Moderate–Expensive.*

Airport Hilton Inn. Plants, brass, and rich paneling grace the public spaces. Guest rooms are spacious and airy, with comfortable furnishings and large desks. Some suites. *4747 28th St. SE, 49508, tel. 616/957–0100. One mi west of I–96 exit 43A. 185 rooms. Facilities: indoor pool, sauna, whirlpool, restaurant, lounge, entertainment. AE, CB, DC, MC, V. Moderate.*

Signature Inn. The skylight and curved staircase in the lobby give this newly remodeled motor hotel a futuristic look. Room decor is modern, with oversize desks and reclining chairs (in the single rooms). Complimentary Continental breakfasts with free newspapers. Nonsmoking rooms. *5500 28th St. SE, 49508, tel. 616/949–8400 or 800/822–5252. 7 mi south on Rte. 11 at junction with I–94 exit 43B. 100 rooms. Facilities: outdoor pool, sauna, whirlpool, exercise room, playground, restaurant, lounge. AE, DC, MC, V. Moderate.*

The Arts **Grand Rapids Civic Theater** (30 N. Division St., tel. 616/456– 9301), the oldest community theater in Michigan, annually presents six productions and two plays for children.

The **Community Circle Theater** (tel. 616/456–6656), in John Ball Park (Fulton St. at Valley) gives five stage performances a year.

Music in the city dates from 1883, when the **St. Cecilia Music Society** built a performing-arts auditorium, said to be the first of its kind in the nation to be financed, built, and operated by women. The organization sponsors programs for young musicians and an adult performance group, the Grand Rapids Chamber Winds.

The **Grand Rapids Symphony** (415 Grand Plaza Place, tel. 616/ 454–9451), a leading regional orchestra, presents a full concert season in DeVos Hall, with many outstanding guest artists. The 2,400-seat hall, noted for its acoustics, is also the home of the **Grand Rapids Civic Ballet** (714 Metro Bank Bldg., tel. 616/ 454–4770) and **Opera Grand Rapids** (203D Walters Bldg., tel. 616/451–2741).

On–The–Town, a free monthly publication, prints an arts calendar of events in the region, as does *Grand Rapids Magazine*. For ticket and performance information call TicketMaster (tel. 616/456–3333); for concert information call the Concert Line (616/456–54883). And check the Fun Line (tel. 616/459–8620) for area events.

Bars and Nightclubs

Comedy Den. Comedians from across the country appear. *Shows Thurs. 9 PM, Fri. and Sat. 8 and 10:30. 2845 Thornhill, tel. 616/949–9322. Call for schedule and ticket information.*

Cottage Bar. A cozy pub with a good burger-and-sandwich menu. Piano bar Thursday from 8 to 10 PM. *8 LaGrave, SW, tel. 616/454–9088. MC, V.*

Escapades. A DJ is on hand nightly to spin top-40 tunes. Happy hour and deli bar weeknights 4–8. Nightly music, dancing, and videos. *Holiday Inn East, 3333 28th St. SE, tel. 616/949–3791; Holiday Inn North, 270 Ann St. NW, tel. 616/363–7748. AE, CB, DC, MC, V.*

Flanagan's. This pub with an Irish atmosphere is popular after work. Jazz Thursday 9 PM–1 AM. *139 Pearl St. NW, tel. 616/ 454–7852. AE, MC, V.*

Hoffman House Lounge. People of all ages mingle for contemporary rock Monday to Saturday 7–11 PM. *Best Western Midway Motor Lodge, 4101 28th St. SE, tel. 616/949–3880. AE, CB, DC, MC, V.*

Intersection. Burgers and sandwiches and live music of the '60s Tuesday to Saturday. *1520 Wealthy SE, tel. 616/459–0931. AE, MC, V. Open Mon.–Sat. 11 AM–2 AM.*

Silver Cloud Lounge. Features Chicago-style blues every weekend. *741 W. Leonard, tel. 616/454–4606. AE, MC, V. Open Sun.–Fri. noon–2 AM, Sat. 10 AM–2:30 AM. Call for show and ticket information.*

Tootsie Van Kelly's. Presenting Sunday jazz from 3 to 7 PM and jazz groups Monday to Saturday. There really is a Tootsie—she takes the stage Friday and Saturday nights. *212 Lyon NW, tel. 616/776–6495. MC, V.*

---

⑨ Muskegon

Once known as the Lumber Queen of the World, Muskegon produced 800 million board-feet in 1888 alone. The city faded badly when the lumbering era ended, but its excellent harbor, which handles millions of tons of cargo annually, maintains the vitality of the city, now the largest port on the eastern shore of Lake Michigan. The **Muskegon River** offers walleye fishing; hundreds line the channel piers and breakwalls during the annual perch and salmon runs. **Muskegon State Park** is at the north edge of the harbor entrance, **Pere Marquette Park** on the south.

Exploring

Hackley House, a Victorian mansion typical of the lifestyle of the 19th-century lumber barons, features intricately carved woodwork, ceramic tiles, stained glass windows, and elaborate fireplaces. **Hume House,** next door, is being restored. *484 W. Webster Ave., tel. 616/722–7578. Admission: $2. Open Memorial Day–Sept. 30, 1–4 PM Wed. and Sat. and Sun.*

The **Muskegon County Museum** has galleries dedicated to the lumbering industry, the fur trade, and medicine. *430 W. Clay, tel. 616/728–4119. Admission free. Open weekdays 9–4:30, weekends 12:30–4:30; closed holidays.*

The **Muskegon Museum of Art** features the works of such American artists as Homer, Whistler, Hopper, and Wyeth. A highlight is John Stuart Curry's *Tornado Over Kansas*. A foreign collection has objects ranging from Coptic tapestry fabrics to contemporary art. *296 W. Webster Ave., tel. 616/722–2600. Admission free. Open Tues.–Sat. 10–4, Sun. 12:30–4:30; closed holidays.*

Youngsters will be delighted with **Deer Park,** an amusement center with 16 rides, including roller coaster and water flume. The deer will eat from your hand. Picnic area. *8 mi north on U.S. 31, tel. 616/766–3377. Admission: $6, including rides. Open Memorial Day–Labor Day, weekdays 11–6, weekends and holidays 11–7.*

Another treat for the younger set is **Pleasure Island,** an aquatic amusement park with pools, beaches, paddleboats, bumper boats, and water slides. *6 mi south on U.S. 31, then 1½ mi west on Pontaluna Rd., tel. 616/798–7858. Admission, including rides: $9.95 adults, $8.95 ages 5–12, $7.95 under 5. Open mid-June–Labor Day, daily 10–6; extended midsummer hours.*

Twelve miles north of the city on U.S. 31, in Whitehall, is the ❿ **White River Light Station Museum.** In the lighthouse, built in 1875, a spiral wrought-iron staircase leads to the museum rooms and a view of Lake Michigan. Exhibits feature ship relics, charts, and models. *6199 Murray Rd., Whitehall, tel. 616/894–8265, Open Apr.–Sept. daily; Sept., weekends only. Call for schedule and admission prices.*

Dining **Crackers & Co. Eatery & Saloon.** A casual place serving flame-broiled baby back ribs, pasta, stir-fried vegetables, burritos, steaks, chops, seafood, salads, and sandwiches. The cocktail lounge has a happy hour from 3 to 6 PM Monday to Friday. *61 Ottawa St., tel. 616/726–4217. Dress: casual. Reservations not required. MC, V. Closed Mon. Inexpensive.*
Maxi's Restaurant and Nightspot. A daytime restaurant serving American and Mexican dishes becomes a popular night spot after 9 PM, with dancing Monday to Saturday. *576 Seminole Rd., tel. 616/733–3134. AE, MC, V. Closed Dec. 24–25. Inexpensive.*

Lodging **Muskegon Harbor Hilton.** A new hotel downtown near Muskegon Lake, it has spacious rooms with modern decor and comfortable appointments. *939 3rd St., 49440, tel. 616/722–0100 or 800/445–8667. 201 rooms. Facilities: indoor pool, sauna, whirlpool, steamroom, exercise room, parking ramp, restaurant, lounge. AE, CB, DC, MC, V. Moderate–Expensive.*
Days Inn. There are two double beds in each room as well as modern, comfortable furnishings, touch-tone phones, and cable TV. *150 E. Seaway Dr., 49444, tel. 616/739–9429. 4½ mi south on I–96 and U.S. 31. 152 rooms. Facilities: indoor pool, 24-hr restaurant. AE, CB, DC, MC, V. Inexpensive.*

The Arts **The Frauenthal Center for the Performing Arts** (407 W. Western Ave., tel. 616/722–7736), a restored 1,800-seat vaudeville-era theater with Italian columns and Victorian decor, is now home to stage productions and concerts year-round.

Participant Sports

Beaches and Water Sports **Willard Beach,** Battle Creek, at George B. Place Park (2 mi south on Goguac Lake), has a wide bathing beach, a house, and supervised swimming.

Coldbrook Park, Kalamazoo (8 mi east on MN Ave., 2 mi south of I–94, tel. 616/383–8778), has a supervised swimming beach and pedal-boat rental. **Prairie View County Park** (on U Ave. between Portage Rd. and Oakland Dr., 7 mi south of I–94, tel. 616/338–8778) has a bathing beach and bathhouse.

Grand Rapids residents usually head for a Lake Michigan beach when it's time for a swim. There are sand beaches all along the shore, with the best in the state parks.

Canoeing Southwestern Michigan has a diversity of canoeing rivers. The Kalamazoo, Paw Paw, Looking Glass, Grand, Flat, and Pere Marquette rivers are all quiet, with no rapids. The Pine and White are very fast, with some rapids, while the Little Manistique and Manistique and the Muskegon and Little Muskegon vary from medium to fast, with some rapids. Ask about specific hazards before setting out on strange waters.

Fishing Yellow perch, perhaps the most frequently caught sports fish in Michigan, are abundant in southwestern waters. You'll also find panfish and trout as well as walleye, bass, northern pike, catfish, and bullheads.

Some of the best fishing is in the heart of **Grand Rapids.** The river holds bass, trout, walleye, and catfish, not to mention chinook and coho salmon, and steelhead, which are stocked each year; the Grand also has an annual lake-trout run. Reeds Lake, in East Grand Rapids, contains largemouth bass, northern pike, bluegills, crappies, and northern pike.

Good to excellent fishing is to be found in parks. If your quarry is lake trout and salmon, fishing off Lake Michigan piers and docks sometimes brings success.

Golf Southwestern Michigan is sometimes called the Golf Coast because of its large number of courses.

Battle Creek **Bedford Valley Country Club** (2316 Waubascon Rd., tel. 616/965–3384), 18 holes; **Binder Park Municipal Golf Course** (6723 B Dr., tel. 616/966–3459), 18 holes; **Cedar Creek Golf Course** (1400 Renton Rd., tel. 616/965–6423), 18 holes; **Oakland Hills** (11619 H Dr. N, tel. 616/965–0809), 9 holes.

Grand Rapids **Alpine** (6320 Alpine Ave. NW, Comstock Park, tel. 616/784–1064), 18 holes; **Briarwood** (2900 92d St., Caledonia, tel. 616/698–8720), 18 holes; **Grand Rapids** (4300 Leonard NE, tel. 616/949–2820), 18 holes; **Indian Trails** (2776 Kalamazoo Ave. SE, tel. 616/245–2021), 18 holes; the **Pines** (5050 Byron Center Ave., tel. 616/538–8380), 18 holes; **Scott Lake** (911 Hayes NE, Comstock Park, tel. 616/784–1355), 18 holes.

Holland **Crest View** (6279 96th Ave., Zeeland, tel. 616/875–8101), 18 holes; **Holland Country Club** (51 Country Club Rd., tel. 616/392–1844), 18 holes; **West Ottawa** (6045 136th St., tel. 616/399–1678), 18 holes; **Winding Creek** (8600 Ottogan St., tel. 616/396–4516), 18 holes.

Kalamazoo **Crestview** (900 W. D. Ave., tel. 616/349–1111), 18 holes; **Milham Municipal** (4200 Lovers La., tel. 616/344–7639), 9 holes; **Ridge View** (10260 W. Main St., tel. 616/375–8821), 18 holes; **Thornapple Creek** (6415 West F Ave., tel. 616/342–2600), 18 holes.

Muskegon **Family Golf** (4200 Whitehall Rd., tel. 616/766–2217), 9 holes; **Fruitport** (6330 S. Harvey), 18 holes; **Chase Hammond** (2454 N. Putnam Rd., tel. 616/766–3035), 18 holes; **Lincoln** (4907 N. Whitehall Rd., tel. 616/766–2226), 18 holes; **Parkview** (4600 S. Sheridan Dr., tel. 616/773–8814), 18 holes.

Saugatuck-Douglas **Clearbrook** (135th Ave., Saugatuck, tel. 616/857–2000), 18 holes; **West Shore** (14 Ferry St., Douglas, tel. 616/857–2500), 18 holes.

Downhill Skiing A number of downhill ski areas operate in the region; phone ahead for hours. For a recorded report on snow conditions statewide, tel. 800/292–5404 in Michigan, 800/248–5708 elsewhere.

Bittersweet Ski Resort has 12 runs, 4 rope tows, 4 chair lifts, and snowmaking; its longest run is 2,300 feet with a vertical drop of 300 feet. Cross-country skiing also. Rentals, instruction, ski shop, restaurant, lounge/bar, entertainment. *600 River Rd., Otsego, tel. 616/694–2032.*

Cannonsburg Ski Area offers 15 runs, 3 chair lifts, 2 bar lifts, 7 rope tows, and snowmaking; its longest run is 1,800 feet, with a vertical drop of 250 feet. Rentals, instruction, ski shop, restaurant, lounge/bar, entertainment. *Box 14, Cannonsburg, tel. 616/874–6711. 10 mi northeast of Grand Rapids, 8 mi east of U.S. 131 on Cannonsburg Rd.; take West River Dr. from U.S. 131.*

Mulligan's Hollow Ski Bowl has 6 runs, 3 rope tows, and snowmaking; its longest run is 700 feet, with a vertical drop of 150 feet. Cross-country skiing also. Rental, instruction, warming hut, cafeteria. *519 Washington, Grand Haven, 3 mi west of U.S. 31 just off Harbor Dr., tel. 616/846–5590.*

Pando Ski Center offers 7 runs, 6 rope tows, and snowmaking; its vertical drop is 125 feet. Cross-country skiing also. Rentals, instruction, snack bar. *8076 Belding Rd., Rockford, 12 mi northeast of Grand Rapids on Rte. M–44, tel. 616/874–8343.*

Ski World has 15 runs, 3 chair lifts, 9 rope tows, and snowmaking; its longest run is 1,800 feet, with a vertical drop of 250 feet. Rental, instruction, ski shop, restaurant, lounge/bar, entertainment. *14547 N. Main St., Buchanan, tel. 616/695–3847 or 800/231–9420.*

Swiss Valley Ski Lodge provides 11 runs, 3 chair lifts, 4 rope tows, and snowmaking; its vertical drop is 225 feet. Rental, instruction, ski shop, restaurant, lounge/bar. *9 mi west of Three Rivers on Rte. M–60, tel. 616/224–5635 or 224–8016 for conditions.*

Timber Ridge Ski Area has 15 runs, 3 chair lifts, 1 bar lift, 3 rope tows, and snowmaking; its longest run is 2,000 feet, with a vertical drop of 250 feet. Rental, instruction, repairs, ski shop, cafeteria, lounge/bar, entertainment. *Gobles, tel. 616/694–9449, 694–9741 or 800/253–2928. U.S. 131 N. of Kalamazoo to D Ave., then west 6 mi to 23½ St., north 1 mi.*

Cross-country Skiing Most cross-country skiing is in city, county, and state parks.

Binder Winter Park, Battle Creek (11632 Six and One-Half Mile Rd., tel. 616/979–4233), has 15 miles of groomed trails, equipment rental, and special events. **Coldbrook Park** in Kalamazoo (8 mi east of MN Ave., 2 mi south of I–94, tel. 616/383–8778) has trails. Trail areas in Grand Rapids include the **Grand Rapids Marriott Trail** (5700 28th St. SE, tel. 616/957–1770) and **Palmer Park** (tel. 616/774–3697). Rentals are available at both places. In Holland, the **Hope College Biology Field Station** (near Holtz

Lake on 166th St.) has unmarked trails, and **Point West Trails** has wooded trails and scenic dune skiing near the West Point Inn (tel. 800/631–0011 in Michigan).

Spectator Sports

Baseball Battle Creek plays host to the week-long **National Amateur Baseball World Series Tournament** in late August. Call Bailey Stadium (tel. 616/979–4433) for schedule and ticket information.

Hockey The **Kalamazoo Wings,** a professional team in the International Hockey League, play home games at Wings Stadium. *3600 Van Rick Dr., Kalamazoo, tel. 616/345–1125.*

Northeastern Michigan

This is the second largest tourism region in the state, running from the northern edge of the industrialized south to the Straits of Mackinac. Much of the area is bordered by Lake Huron. We will begin in the south and move northward to the Straits of Mackinac.

Because of the distances between towns, we have treated each stop as a separate destination, listing its own attractions and facilities. Price categories for restaurants and hotels are the same as in Detroit Dining and Lodging.

Numbers in the margin correspond with points of interest on the Northeastern Michigan map.

Getting Around

By Plane **Bishop Airport,** Flint (3425 W. Bristol Rd., tel. 313/766–8620), is served by American Eagle, Comair, Northwest Airlink, and Piedmont.

Capital City Airport, Lansing (tel. 517/321–6121), is served by American Eagle, Comair, Northwest Airlink, Piedmont, and United Express.

Tri–City International Airport, Saginaw (tel. 517/695–5555), is at Freeland, midway between Saginaw and Midland, and is served by American Eagle, Northwest Airlink, and United.

By Car I–75 and Route M–27 are major north–south highways; I–69 and Routes M–46, M–55, and M–32 are east–west.

By Bus **Greyhound** and **Michigan Trailways** provide service to the larger communities.

Scenic Drives

Route M–25 follows the Lake Huron shoreline from White River to Bay City.

From just south of Tawas City **Route M–23** follows the Huron shoreline most of the way to Mackinaw City, more than 160 miles—one of the most scenic drives in the Lower Peninsula.

Important Addresses and Numbers

Tourist Information

Flint Area Convention and Visitors Bureau, 400 North Saginaw Street, Flint 48502, tel. 313/232–8900; weekdays 9–5.

Frankenmuth Chamber of Commerce, 635 South Main Street, Frankenmuth 48734, tel. 517/652–6106; weekdays 8:30–5.

Convention and Visitors Bureau of Greater Lansing, Civic Center, Suite 302, Lansing 48933, tel. 517/487–6800; weekdays 9–5.

Midland County Visitors and Convention Bureau, 300 Rodd Street, Midland 48640, 517/839–9901; weekdays 9–5.

Saginaw County Convention and Visitors Bureau, 901 South Washington, Saginaw, tel. 517/752–7164; weekdays 8:30–5.

Emergencies

Michigan State Patrol (tel. 517/332–2521). 911 is the **emergency number** in most of the region.

❶ Lansing

When the state capital was moved from Detroit to Lansing in 1847, the settlement consisted of a log cabin and a sawmill, but within a dozen years the town had a population of 4,000, a new brick capitol, two newspapers, and several small businesses. Ransom E. Olds put Lansing on the map in 1896 when he organized the Olds Motor Vehicle Company. By the turn of the century Lansing was a leading manufacturer of autos and gasoline engines.

While the economy has become more diversified, it is still heavily involved with the auto industry. Adjoining East Lansing, mostly residential, is the home of Michigan State University, whose football team won the 1988 Rose Bowl.

Exploring

The **State Capitol Building,** built in 1878 and completely restored, is a Victorian architectural gem. It was one of the first state capitols to emulate the dome and wings of the U.S. Capitol. The interior walls and ceilings reflect the work of many artisans, muralists, and portrait painters. Guided tours conducted daily. *Capitol and Michigan Aves., tel. 517/335–1483 weekdays, 373–0996 weekends and holidays. Admission free. Tours on the hour weekdays 8–4, Sat. and holidays 10–4, Sun. noon–4.*

A block northeast of the Capitol is the **Michigan Historical Museum,** established in 1879 and the official state museum, which preserves and displays the Michigan heritage. Multimedia presentations, artifacts, photos, and changing exhibits tell the story. *208 N. Capitol Ave., tel. 517/373–3559. Admission free. Open weekdays 9:30–4:30, Sat. and holidays noon–4:30; closed Thanksgiving, Dec. 25, Jan. 1.*

Three blocks east of the Capitol is the **Impression 5 Science Museum,** set in a renovated century-old building with its original floors and brick walls. This is a hands-on museum where you can look through microscopes, see rocketry experiments, and explore more than 240 exhibits on energy, physical science, and

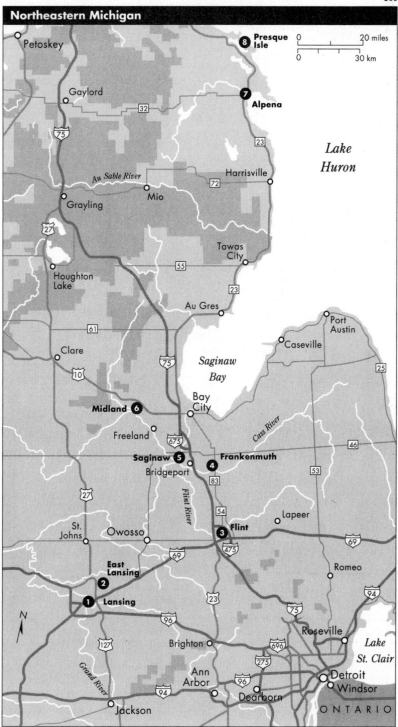

Northeastern Michigan

Petoskey

Gaylord

8 Presque Isle

0   20 miles
0   30 km

75

32

7 Alpena

Au Sable River

23

Lake Huron

Grayling

Mio

Harrisville

72

27

Houghton Lake

55

Tawas City

23

Au Gres

Clare

Saginaw Bay

Port Austin

Caseville

25

61

75

10

Bay City

Midland 6

Freeland

675

Cass River

46

Saginaw 5

4 **Frankenmuth**

Bridgeport

83

53

27

St. Johns

Owosso

Flint River

54

3 Flint

Lapeer

69

475

Romeo

East Lansing

2

69

23

94

1 Lansing

N

75

696

Roseville

127

96

Brighton

275

Lake St. Clair

Grand River

94

Ann Arbor

96

Detroit

Windsor

Jackson

Dearborn

ONTARIO

medicine. *200 Museum Dr., tel. 517/485–8115. Admission: $3 adults, $2.50 children 4–12, $2 senior citizens. MC, V. Open Mon.–Sat. 10–5, Sun. noon–5; closed major holidays.*

Just up the street is the **R. E. Olds Museum,** which exhibits vehicles produced in Lansing. You'll see the first Oldsmobile, built in 1897, and the first Toronado off the line in 1966, along with Reos (named for R. E. Olds) and autos such as Stars, Durants, and Bateses. Auto memorabilia and period clothing are also displayed. *240 Museum Dr., tel. 517/372–0422. Admission: $3 adults, $2 over 55 and ages 6–12. Open Tues.–Fri. 9:30–5, weekends and holidays noon–5; closed Thanksgiving, Dec. 25, Jan. 1.*

The **Lansing Municipal Market** (333 N. Cedar St.), open Tuesday, Thursday, and Saturday, offers fresh fruit, flowers, bread, and meat in a country-market atmosphere.

Potter Park Zoo has, in addition to a variety of animals in natural settings, special exhibits on Michigan animals, an aviary with dozens of exotic species, and fish displays. You can ride a miniature train around the grounds or rent a canoe on the Grand River; there are pony rides for children. *1301 S. Pennsylvania Ave., tel. 517/483–4222. Admission free, parking $1. Park open daily 8 AM–dusk, zoo buildings open daily 10 AM–dusk.*

❷ **Michigan State University,** in **East Lansing,** was a pioneer land-grant college, beginning as Michigan Agricultural College in 1855. It has grown from three buildings near the Red Cedar River to a 5,320-acre complex with one of the largest enrollments in the Midwest. **Beaumont Tower,** which contains a 47-bell carillon, stands on the site of one of the original buildings. To arrange walking tours, phone 517/355–8314. Among campus highlights are these:

The **Kresge Art Museum,** noted for a comprehensive collection from many cultures, has more than 4,000 works, from prehistoric to contemporary. *Auditorium Rd., tel. 517/355–7631. Admission free. Open Mon.–Wed. and Fri. 9:30–4:30, Thurs. noon–8, weekends 1–4, summer hours reduced; closed holidays and Dec. 25–Jan. 2.*

The **Abrams Planetarium** presents public programs on astronomy; it has an exhibit gallery and a gift shop. Astronomers are available to answer questions in person or by phone (tel. 517/355–4647). Programs on space-science topics are presented weekends in the 360-degree domed theater; telescopic outdoor observations are available after evening shows, weather permitting. *Shaw La., tel. 517/355–4672. Admission free. Open weekdays 8:30–noon and 1–4:30. Star shows presented Fri. and Sat. 8 PM, Sun. 4. Admission: $2.50 adults, $2 students and senior citizens, $1.50 children under 13.*

The **Michigan State Museum** has three floors of exhibits that span the development of human culture from dinosaurs to the modern age. Displays replicate the kitchens, shops, crafts, cultures, and natural environments of the world. *West Circle Dr., tel. 517/355–2370. Admission free. Open weekdays 9–5, Thurs. 9–9, weekends 1–5, home football Sats., 9 AM–1 PM.*

Dining

American

Jim's Tiffany Place and Greenhouse Cafe. The menu offers a little of everything in Greek, Cajun, and American dishes. Try the seafood. Rococo decor and genuine Tiffany lamps give this interesting restaurant its name. Children's menu. *116 E. Michigan Ave., 1 block east of capitol, tel. 517/372–4300. Reservations suggested. Jacket and tie advised. MC, V. Open 11 AM–midnight, Sun. 10:30–10; closed Dec. 25. Inexpensive–Moderate.*

Peach Tree Cafe. Lansing rib-lovers seem to agree that the Peach Tree serves the best in town. The menu also includes steaks, chicken, and seafood. Children's menu. *7216 Saginaw Hwy., tel. 517/321–6100. Reservations advised. Dress: casual. AE, MC, V. Open 11 AM–10 PM, Fri.–Sat. to 11:30, Sun. to 8. Inexpensive–Moderate.*

Pretzel Bell. The salad bar is outstanding at this East Lansing establishment, which also serves good steaks, prime rib, and seafood. Children's menu. *1020 Trowbridge Rd., East Lansing, tel. 517/351–0300. Reservations advised. Jacket and tie advised. AE, MC, V. Open 11:30 AM–10 PM, Fri. from 5 PM, Sat. 11:30 AM–2 PM and 5–10 PM, Sun. 10:30 AM–8 PM. Inexpensive–Moderate.*

Mexican

Cheddar's Restaurant. An informal spot serving Mexican and American specialties, including seafood, steaks, salads, and half-pound hamburgers. This is the home of the best hot-fudge sundae in Lansing, served in a homemade cinnamon shell. Children's menu. *5919 W. Saginaw Rd., tel. 517/323–4963. Dress: casual. AE, CB, DC, MC, V. Open until 11:30 PM Sun.–Thurs., 12:30 AM Fri. and Sat.; closed Dec. 25. Inexpensive.*

Lodging

Radisson Hotel Lansing. Situated two blocks from the State Capitol, this ultramodern motor lodge offers a variety of accommodations, including "king" rooms, whirlpool suites, and board room suites for business travelers. The rooms are spacious with elegant modern decor. *111 N. Grand Ave., 48933, tel. 517/482–0188. 260 rooms. Facilities: indoor pool, sauna, whirlpool, exercise room, valet garage (fee), restaurant, lounge. AE, DC, MC, V. Expensive.*

Sheraton Inn Lansing. A fine motor inn, it has a large atrium lobby and glass-enclosed elevators. The spacious rooms have such extras as lighted makeup mirrors and hair dryers (rooms have king-size beds). Barrier-free and nonsmoking rooms. *925 S. Creyts Rd., 48917, tel. 517/323–7100. 4 mi west on I–496 at Creyts Rd. 223 rooms. Facilities: indoor pool, sauna, whirlpool, racquetball court, exercise room, tanning bed, restaurant, lounge. AE, DC, MC, V. Expensive.*

Hilton Inn. The spacious, airy rooms have a number of amenities. Nonsmoking and specially equipped barrier-free rooms are available. *7501 W. Saginaw Hwy., 48917, tel. 517/627–3211 or 800/445–8667. 249 rooms. Facilities: outdoor pool, indoor pool, sauna, whirlpool, 2 tennis courts, indoor recreation area, dining room, lounge. AE, DC, MC, V. Moderate–Expensive.*

University Inn. Adjacent to the Michigan State campus, this well-appointed motor lodge contains suites, kitchenettes, and spacious rooms with twin beds, waterbeds, or king-size beds. It has attractive, comfortable modern decor. Weekend packages and group rates for MSU fans. *1100 Trowbridge Rd., East*

Lansing, 48823, tel. 517/351–5500 or 800/221–8466. 168 rooms.
Facilities: outdoor pool, restaurant, lounge. AE, CB, DC, MC,
V. Inexpensive.

The Arts The **Wharton Center for the Performing Arts** (tel. 517/355–6686)
is a new addition to the Michigan State campus.

The **Lansing Civic Players Guild** (2300 E. Michigan Ave., tel.
517/484–9115) is in an old firehouse, where performances take
place from fall to spring.

The **BoarsHead Michigan Public Theater** (425 S. Grand, tel.
517/484–7805) is a regional theater with a diverse agenda.

The **Michigan State University Performing Arts Company** (tel.
517/355–0148) performs all over campus with a variety of
cultural events.

The **Riverwalk Players** (tel. 517/484–9020) perform from September to June.

The **Greater Lansing Symphony Orchestra** (tel. 517/487–5001 or
355–6686) has been in existence for more than half a century.

Bars and **Omar's.** An "adult" show bar, with a businessmen's lunch
Nightclubs weekdays. *316 E. Michigan Ave., tel. 517/371–4500. MC, V.*
Hayloft Saloon. Offering home-cooked sandwiches and steaks,
live entertainment, and dancing Wednesday to Sunday until
1:30 AM. *727 E. Miller Rd., tel. 517/882–7225. AE, CB, DC, MC,*
V. Open daily.
Tango Caffe and Supperclub. A two-level atrium setting with
dining above and dining and dancing below in a cafe. Northern
Italian cuisine. *111 W. Washtenaw Ave., tel. 517/374–1100.*
Reservations advised. AE, CB, DC, MC, V. Open for lunch
and dinner.

---

❸ Flint

The city began as a river crossing on the Pontiac Trail, part of
the network of Indian trails. The 19th-century logging boom
created a need for carts and wagons, so Flint became a major
manufacturing center. The production of carriages followed,
and that industry gained Flint a national reputation. Today the
city is one of the largest auto-manufacturing centers in the
world, world headquarters for the Buick Division of General
Motors and AC Spark Plugs, with 10 plants.

Exploring One of downtown Flint's newest additions is the **Water Street
Pavilion** (One Water St., tel. 313/239–9000), a two-story festival marketplace featuring an array of shops and an outdoor ice
rink. **Antique World Mall** (303 W. Water St., tel. 313/238–6346)
features 42 antiques dealers in a restored carriage factory used
by Flint auto pioneers William C. Durant and Dallas Dort.

The **Flint Cultural Center,** two blocks from downtown, is home
to the Sloan Museum, Longway Planetarium, Flint Institute of
the Arts, Flint Institute of Music, Whiting Auditorium, Bower
Theater, and the Whaley Historical House.

The **Alfred P. Sloan Museum** displays more than 50 antique and
experimental autos, plus exhibits focusing on Flint's heritage
as the birthplace of General Motors. The cars include a 1902
Flint Roadster, 1904 Buick test car, 1910 Buick Bug, and sever-

al GM prototypes. Other exhibits trace the history of Genesee County from the Ice Age to 1900. Youngsters will enjoy the **Pierson Children's Gallery,** which displays more than 200 miniature figures dramatizing the building of the United States. *1221 E. Kearsley St., tel. 313/762–1169. Admission: $2 adults, $1 senior citizens and children 5–12, free under 5. Open Tues.–Fri. 10–5, weekends noon–5, with extended summer hours; closed major holidays.*

The **Flint Institute of Arts** has a big permanent collection, including Renaissance period furniture, decorative arts, and wall tapestries. There is an Oriental gallery and collections of 19th- and 20th-century paintings and antique French glass paperweights. *1120 E. Kearsley St., tel. 313/234–1695, 234–1692 for recorded information. Admission free. Open Oct.–May, Tues.–Sat. 10–5, Sun. 1–5, and Tues. 7–9; closed holidays.*

The **Robert T. Longway Planetarium** features astronomy exhibits and ultraviolet and fluorescent murals. The planetarium projector reproduces the night sky on a 60-foot dome. *1310 E. Kearsley St., tel. 313/762–1181. Admission: $2 adults, $1 students and over 60. Call for schedules.*

The **Children's Museum** has hands-on exhibits for those aged 3 and up. Special features include a real airplane, stagecoach, courtroom, and television studio. Educational programs on weekends. *Northbank Center Bldg., 432 N. Saginaw St., tel. 313/238–6900. Admission: $2 adults, $1 senior citizens, $9 family. Open Tues.–Fri. 10–6, Sat.–Mon. 1–6.*

Crossroads Village and Huckleberry Railroad is a restored village of the 1860s–1880s with 24 buildings and sites, consisting of a working blacksmith shop, sawmill, leather shop, cider mill, general store, church, and residences, plus a carousel and free entertainment. Special events most weekends. You'll need several hours to take it all in. Huckleberry Railroad is an authentic steam-powered narrow-gauge line with open and enclosed passenger coaches pulled by a Baldwin locomotive. Visitors can take a 45-minute, 10-mile ride through the countryside. *Just north of Flint, take I–475, I–75, or I–69 north to Carpenter Rd. (exit 11) and follow signs. G-6140 Bray Rd., tel. 313/736–7100. Admission, including village and train rides: $5.95 adults, $4.95 over 60, $3.95 ages 4–12; parking $1. Open Memorial Day–Labor Day, weekdays 10–5:30, weekends 11–6; weekend following Thanksgiving–Dec. 31, Fri.–Sun. 3–9; closed Dec. 24–25.*

Dining
American

Floogles. The decor is Art Deco and the dining is casual. Barbecued ribs are the house specialty; the large menu offers seafood, steaks, and such light dishes as soups and salads. Children's menu. Cocktail lounge with entertainment. *1174 Longway Blvd. adjacent to Hampton Inn, tel. 313/235–6661. Reservations suggested. Dress: casual. AE, DC, MC, V. Open 7 AM–11 PM, Sun. to 8 PM; closed Thanksgiving, Dec. 25. Inexpensive–Moderate.*

Mister Gibby's Inn. The Porch is a sunny, plant-filled setting amid turn-of-the-century decor, while the lounge and bar are decorated with World War I mementos. King crab and prime rib lead the menu; there are daily specials. The Pool Bar offers poolside sipping and supping from May to September. Sunday brunch. Entertainment nightly. *Best Western Gibby's Inn,*

G-3129 Miller Rd., tel. 313/235-8561. Reservations advised. Jacket and tie advised. MC, V. Open daily 6:30 AM-10 PM, weekends noon-10, Sun. brunch 11-2. Lounge open until 2 AM. Inexpensive-Moderate.

Real Seafood Company. This fresh-seafood restaurant serves well-prepared baked, broiled, and grilled fish and seafood. A few pasta and meat items are on the menu. A raw-fish bar is in the cocktail lounge. The atmosphere is casual and intimate. *866 E. Fifth Ave., tel. 313/232-5300. Reservations suggested. Dress: casual. AE, DC, MC, V. Open weekdays 11 AM-10 PM, Fri. and Sat. to 11 PM, Sun. 4-9 PM; closed Thanksgiving, Dec. 25, Jan. 1. Inexpensive-Moderate.*

Mexican **Amigos Mexican Restaurante.** Tex-Mex and New Mexico–style food: daily dinner specials, plus enchiladas, tacos, burritos, and refried beans, all made from scratch. Cocktail lounge. *3539 S. Dort Hwy., tel. 313/743-5840. Reservations not required. Dress: casual. MC, V. Open 11 AM-11 PM, Fri. and Sat. 1 AM, Sun. noon-10 PM; closed Thanksgiving, Dec. 24 and 25. Inexpensive.*

Lodging **Hyatt Regency Flint.** This plush downtown hotel has a three-story lobby atrium. The spacious rooms are bright and airy, with comfortable furnishings. *One Riverfront Center West, 48502, tel. 313/239-1234 or 800/228-9000. 369 rooms with bath. Facilities: indoor pool, sauna, whirlpool, restaurant, cafe, lounge, shops. AE, CB, DC, MC, V. Expensive.*

Day's Inn Flint. The hotel has single, standard, and king-size rooms, with modern decor. Nonsmoking rooms. *2207 W. Bristol Rd., 48507, tel. 313/239-4681 or 800/325-2525. Junction of I-75 and Bristol Rd. 142 rooms. Facilities: outdoor pool, playground, cable TV, restaurant, lounge. AE, DC, MC, V. Inexpensive.*

Knights Inn. A ground-level park-at-your-door motel. The rooms are in pleasant Old English decor. Nonsmoking rooms, rooms for handicapped, and kitchenettes available. *G-3277 Miller Rd., 48507, tel. 313/733-5910. I-75 and Miller Rd. 144 rooms. Facilities: cable TV, restaurant adjacent. AE, CB, DC, MC, V. Inexpensive.*

The Arts **Flint Community Players** (tel. 313/235-6963) stages productions featuring local talent at the Bower Theater, in the College and Cultural Center.

The Flint Institute of Music (1025 E. Kearsley St., tel. 313/238-9651) is the management company for the **Flint Symphony Orchestra, Ballet Michigan,** and the **Flint School of Performing Arts.** Performances are at the College and Cultural Center.

Flint Youth Theater (924 E. 6th St., tel. 313/762-1018) holds performances in the Bower Theater and Whiting Auditorium in the College and Cultural Center.

Star Theatre (Whiting Auditorium, tel. 313/239-1464) presents "name" talent in summer productions, Tuesday through Sunday evenings and Saturday and Sunday matinees.

Bars and Nightlife **Churchill's.** An Old English pub with a warm and inviting atmosphere. Entertainment Wednesday to Saturday. *340 S. Saginaw St., tel. 313/233-0746. Open Mon.-Sat. 11 AM-2 AM; closed major holidays.*

New Vic Supper Theater. Semiprofessional dinner theater. *755 S. Saginaw St., tel. 313/235–8866. Call for schedule, ticket prices, and reservations.*
Tommy's Peppermill. Cafeteria setting for breakfast and lunch, with a jazz bar on the lower level and entertainment six nights a week. *111 W. Kearsley St., tel. 313/235–6619. Cafeteria open Mon.–Sat. 6:45 AM–2:30 PM, jazz bar 8 PM–2:30 AM. MC, V.*

❹ Frankenmuth

When German settlers founded this town in 1845 in an attempt to spread Christianity to the Chippewa Indians, they gave it a name meaning "Courage of the Franks." Arrivals from the Old World continued to reinforce the heritage, and German was the principal language until after 1900. Known as Michigan's Little Bavaria, it retains much of its Old World architecture, culture, and attractions. Many businesses are housed in half-timbered chalets with balconies, gingerbread decorations, and flower boxes. Flowers (and gift shops) seem to be everywhere.

Exploring A 35-bell carillon in the Bavarian Inn's **Glockenspiel Tower** performs at 11 AM, noon, and 3, 6, 9, and 10 PM; wooden figures on it depict the legend of the Pied Piper of Hamelin. Nearby is a 239-foot copy of a 19th-century covered bridge, spanning the Cass River.

Bronner's Christmas Wonderland has done much to turn the community of 3,700 into a major attraction. The store, which bills itself as the world's largest ornament retailer (it covers an acre), features a selection of more than 50,000 decorations, lights, and ornaments, among them life-size Santas and wind-up elves. Prices range from under $1 for a candle to $11,000 for a life-size Hummel figurine. Two million people visit the store each year; a record was set on the day after Thanksgiving 1987: 21,759 shoppers. Business bustles even in July. *One mi south at 25 Christmas La., tel. 517/652–9931. Admission free. Open June 1–Dec. 24, weekdays 9–9, Sat. 9–7, Sun. noon–7; rest of year, Mon.–Thurs. and Sat. 9–5:30, Fri. 9–9, Sun. 1–5:30; closed Easter, Thanksgiving, Dec. 25, Jan. 1.*

The **Nickless-Hubinger Flour Mill and General Store,** on the banks of the Cass River, is a reconstructed working mill, originally established in 1848, which still produces cornmeal and flour, which you can purchase in an adjoining store. Twenty-minute tours explain mill operations, with close looks at the grindstone and 13-foot waterwheel. *701 Mill St., tel. 517/652–8422. Admission: $1 adults, 50¢ under 14. Open May 1–Oct. 15, daily 10–6; rest of year, 10–4; closed Easter, Thanksgiving, Dec. 25, Jan. 1.*

The **Frankenmuth Historical Museum** highlights local history since the missionary days. *613 S. Main St., tel. 517/652–9701. Admission: $1, free under 12. Open June–Oct., daily 10:30–5:30; Mar.–May and Nov.–Dec., Wed.–Sun. 10:30–5:30; rest of year, Sat. and Sun. 10:30–5:30.*

The **Junction Valley Railroad,** a line built to one-quarter size, consists of locomotives and such rolling stock as gondola and hopper cars traveling past bridges, depots, junction stations, and other buildings. Special events take place most weekends in summer. *7065 Dixie Hwy., Bridgeport (5 mi west of Frankenmuth), tel. 517/777–3480. Admission: $2 adults, $1.50*

*children. Open Memorial Day–Labor Day, Mon.–Sat. 10–6,
Sun. 1–6; Sept.–Oct., weekends 1–5 only.*

Michigan's Own Inc. Military and Space Museum is dedicated to
the state's 2 million veterans. Featured are uniforms, medals,
photos, and stories about Medal of Honor winners, governors
who served in the military, and the World War I "Polar Bears."
The uniforms and flight suits of Michigan astronauts James
McDivitt, Al Worden, Jack Lousma, and Brewster Shaw are on
display. *245 S. Main St., tel. 517/652–8005 or 652–3188. Admission: $2 adults, $1 over 65 and 6–18, $6 family. Open
Mon.–Sat. 10–5, Sun. noon–5.*

Dining **Bavarian Inn.** Vast is the best description of this place—seven
★ dining rooms with German themes have a total capacity of
1,200. Family-style chicken dinners (homemade bread, chicken
noodle soup, chicken, gravy, mashed potatoes, vegetables,
noodles, and homemade ice cream) are the specialty. German
entrees include Wiener Schnitzel, Sauerbraten, and Kasseler
Rippchen. Children's menu. *713 S. Main St., tel. 517/652–9941.
Reservations advised. Dress: casual. AE, MC, V. Open 11 AM–
9:30 PM; closed Mon., Jan. and Feb. Inexpensive–Moderate.*
Zehnder's Restaurant. Family-style dining in attractive Colonial rooms. Chicken dinners are featured; steaks and seafood
are available. Cocktail lounge, bakery, gift shop, golf course.
*730 Main St., tel. 517/652–9925. Reservations advised. Dress:
casual. AE, MC, V. Open daily 11 AM–9:30 PM; no dinner Dec.
24. Inexpensive–Moderate.*

Lodging **Bavarian Inn Motor Lodge.** A place with balconies and flower
boxes, hand-carved headboards, and other Bavarian touches.
All rooms have two double extra-long beds. Some poolside
rooms. *One Covered Bridge La., 48734, tel. 517/652–2651. 100
rooms. Facilities: indoor pool, whirlpool, exercise room, dining room, lounge, entertainment. AE, MC, V. Moderate–
Expensive.*
Bavarian Haus Motel. A chalet-style two-story motel with modern, spacious rooms, some with balconies. *1365 S. Main St.,
48734, tel. 517/652–6144. 114 rooms. Facilities: outdoor pool,
sauna, whirlpool, coffee shop. AE, MC, V. Moderate.*

---

❺ Saginaw

Once the 19th-century lumbering center for most of eastern
Michigan, when the logging era ended Saginaw turned to producing beans and sugar beets, iron-making, and, after the turn
of the century, auto production.

Exploring The **Rose Garden** (423 Rust Ave., west of Washington Ave.)
contains more than 1,000 bushes bearing more than 50 varieties
planted atop a 20-million-gallon landscaped reservoir. The **Old
Saginaw City Historical District** (Court–Hamilton area) consists of restored warehouses and buildings that have been
converted into trendy restaurants and shops.

The **Historical Society Museum of Saginaw County** is in a renovated post office building (circa 1897) built like a French
chateau, with towers, turrets, and a great hall. Multimedia
presentations and exhibits trace the history of Saginaw County. *500 Federal Ave., tel. 517/752–2861. Admission: $1 adults,
50¢ under 19. Open Tues.–Sat. 10–4:30, Sun. 1–4.*

The **Saginaw Art Museum,** in the turn-of-the-century Ring Mansion, has among its collections Oriental works, contemporary prints, textiles, and sculpture by John Rogers and others, some of it in the gardens. **Visionarea** is the museum's hands-on gallery for young people, with films, tours, and art classes. *1126 N. Michigan Ave., tel. 517/754–2491. Admission free. Open Tues.–Sat. 10–5, Sun. 1–5; closed Aug.*

The **Saginaw Children's Zoo,** built in 1967, contains 200 young animals, a petting zoo, an aquarium, and unusual specimens. The **Ibershoff Special,** a miniature steam train, makes half-mile tours of the zoo. *1435 S. Washington Ave. at Rtes. M–13 and M–46, tel. 517/776–1657. Admission: 50¢ adults, 25¢ children; train 50¢. Open mid-May–Labor Day, daily 10–5.*

The **Japanese Cultural Center and Tea House** is a joint project with Saginaw's sister city, Tokushima, Japan. Tours introduce Japanese culture and "the way of tea." Japanese in traditional garb guide visitors through the center and demonstrate arts and crafts. *1315 S. Washington Ave., tel. 517/776–1684. Admission: $1, children under 12 free when accompanied by adult. Tea house open from Sat. before Memorial Day to first Sun. after Labor Day, Tues.–Sun. noon–6, garden open 9–6; rest of year, Wed.–Sun. noon–4.*

Dining **West Bank Restaurant.** The dining room is in a restored bank. Rack of lamb and beef dishes are served, as are chicken and seafood. Cocktail lounge. *115 N. Hamilton, tel. 517/792–8027. Reservations suggested. Dress: casual. AE, MC, V. Open weekdays 11–10, Sat. 4–11 PM; closed Sun. Inexpensive–Moderate.*
Casa del Rey. The menu lists a large selection of Mexican favorites, including enchiladas, seafood, tostadas, and burritos, and fajitas and Texas-style barbecued beef and ribs cooked over mesquite. The tables are crafted of wood from all over the world. Children's menu. Cocktail lounge with entertainment. *2945 Bay Rd., tel. 517/792–8787. Reservations suggested. Dress: casual. AE, MC, V. Open 11 AM–midnight, Tues.–Sat. to 2 AM; closed July 4, Thanksgiving, Dec. 25. Inexpensive.*

Lodging **Montague Inn.** An elegantly restored brick two-story Georgian
★ mansion with library, sitting rooms, and dining rooms open to guests. A wide curving stairway leads to large second-floor bedrooms furnished with such period pieces as four-poster beds and wing-back chairs. Complimentary breakfast of pastry, cereal, and fruit served; other meals by reservation only. *1581 S. Washington Ave., 48601, tel. 517/752–3939. 14 rooms with private bath, 4 rooms share bath. All rooms nonsmoking. Facilities: beautifully landscaped grounds, dining room. AE, MC, V. Expensive–Very Expensive.*
Sheraton Fashion Square. A characteristic Sheraton Inn offering large, modern rooms. *4960 Town Center Rd., 48604, tel. 517/790–5050. 156 rooms. Facilities: indoor-outdoor pool, sauna, whirlpool, dining room, lounge, entertainment. AE, DC, MC, V. Expensive.*
Florentine Inn. A modern motor lodge, adjacent to the Civic Center, it has well-appointed rooms, with comfortable furnishings and views of the city. *400 Johnson St., 48607, tel. 517/755–1161 or 800/323–8909. 174 rooms. Facilities: indoor pool, sauna, whirlpool, dining room, lounge. AE, CB, DC, MC, V. Moderate.*

The Arts **Temple Theater Arts Association** (203 N. Washington Ave., tel. 517/752–2365), housed in a 1927 movie theater, presents movie classics, foreign films, and live productions.

Bars and **Jasper's River Front Saloon** presents comedy every Tuesday
Nightclubs with local and, occasionally, nationally known comedians. *108 N. Niagara, tel. 517/790–7661. Showtime 9 PM; call for prices.*

---

❻ Midland

This former lumbering community is the world headquarters of the Dow Chemical Company, the largest single chemical complex in the United States, at the junction of the Tittabawassee and Chippewa rivers; large brine deposits brought Dow here. Midland boasts a "tridge," a three-cornered walking bridge of unique design that leads to park areas.

The **Chippewa Nature Center** covers 1,000 acres, with 14 miles of walking trails. On site are a museum with hands-on exhibits, a homestead farm complex, a maple-sugar house, a log school, and an arboretum with wildflower walkway. *400 S. Badour Rd., tel. 517/631–0830. Admission: 75¢ adults, 25¢ children under 13. Open weekdays 8–5, Sat. 9–5, Sun. and holidays 1–5; closed Thanksgiving, Dec. 25.*

Dow Gardens, at the home of Dr. Herbert H. Dow, founder of the chemical company, display 600 species of flowers and shrubs on 60 acres, amid streams, waterfalls, trees, and bridges. *1018 W. Main St., tel. 517/631–2677. Admission: $1. Open daily 10 AM–dusk; closed Thanksgiving, Dec. 25, Jan. 1.*

Adjacent to the gardens is the **Midland Center for the Arts,** mid-Michigan's cultural and entertainment center. The Hall of Ideas leads visitors through exhibits on Michigan's history, depicting the American Indian, fur traders, farmers, and lumbermen. Plays, concerts, dance events, films, and lectures are presented. *1801 W. St. Andrews Dr., tel. 517/631–5930. Admission free. Open weekdays 9–5, Thurs. 7–9 PM, weekends 1–5; closed major holidays.*

Dining **Old Hickory House.** Charcoal-broiled steaks and lobster are features of this popular family restaurant. Other dishes include chicken and prime rib. Sunday brunch, children's menu. *3626 N. Saginaw Rd., tel. 517/832–8440. Reservations advised. Dress: casual. AE, MC, V. Open 11:30 AM–2 PM and 5–10 PM, Sat. from 5 PM, Sun. 10:30 AM–8 PM; closed major holidays. Moderate.*
D'Alessandro's. Veal scallopini, chicken cacciatore, scampi, and tasty pasta dishes and pizza specials are on the menu at this warm Italian place. All-you-can-eat antipasti presented from 5 to 8 PM Monday and Tuesday. *931 S. Saginaw Rd., in Eastlawn Shopping Center, tel. 517/631–3821. Reservations suggested. Dress: casual. No credit cards. Open daily 11–11, Tues.–Thurs. till midnight, Fri. and Sat. till 2 AM. Inexpensive.*

Lodging **Holiday Inn.** A light, airy motor lodge, its rooms are typical of Holiday Inn's modern decor. Weekend package plans. *1500 W. Wackerly, 48640, tel. 517/631–4220. 220 rooms. Facilities: indoor pool, sauna, whirlpool, indoor recreation area, exercise* room, 2 racquetball courts (fee), dining room, lounge, enter-tainment. AE, DC, MC, V. Moderate.

Valley Plaza Inn. A modern two-level motor lodge with rooms decorated in warm earth tones and some suites with whirlpool baths. Package plans and resort RV camping available. *5221 Bay City Rd., 48640, tel. 517/496–2770 or 800/825–2700. 163 rooms. Facilities: 3 indoor pools, wading pool, sand beach, sauna, whirlpool, 2 lighted tennis courts, indoor recreation area, health club (fee), 3 dining rooms, coffee shop, lounge, 3 movie theaters. AE, DC, MC, V. Moderate.*

➐ Alpena

Alpena, on Thunder Bay, was a lumbering boomtown in the late 19th century; stone-quarrying is an important industry to-day. The **Thunder Bay Underwater Preserve** (tel. 517/354–4181 or 800/582–1906) encompasses 288 square miles and holds about 80 shipwrecks, old and new, that are accessible to experienced divers.

The **Jesse Besser Museum and Planetarium** is a regional center for science, art, and history, with collections devoted to northern Michigan and the Great Lakes. Three galleries feature changing art exhibits. Period shops line a re-created 1890s street, and there are several restored 19th-century buildings on the grounds. *491 Johnson St., Alpena Community College campus, tel. 517/356–2202. Admission free. Open weekdays 10–5, Thurs. till 9 PM, weekends noon–5; closed holidays. Sky Theater Planetarium stages sky shows July and Aug., Thurs. at 7:30 PM; rest of year, Sun. at 2 and 4. Admission: $1.25 adults, 75¢ under 18; under 5 not admitted to planetarium.*

➑ **Old Presque Isle Lighthouse and Museum.** The lighthouse, built by the U.S. Government in 1840 and abandoned in 1870, is now a museum; visitors are allowed in the tower for a view of Lake Huron. *5295 County Rd. 405 (5 mi north of Presque Isle between Alpena and Rogers City), tel. 517/595–2787. Open May 15–Oct. 15, 9–6.*

A newer lighthouse (built in 1870) nearby is still in use; the tower is not open to the public, but the keeper's quarters are being restored and eventually will be a museum. The lighthouse is in a 100-acre park with nature trails, picnic areas, and pavilion. *County Rd. 405, 1 mi from Old Presque Isle Lighthouse.*

Participant Sports

Beaches and Water Sports
Stratford Woods, in Midland (E. Ashman and U.S. 10), has a beach and bathhouse; the **Midland Community Center** has a pool for public use.

In Lansing, **Grand River Park** (Grovenburg Rd.) has a public beach. **Lake Lansing South** (7 mi from downtown, tel. 517/676–2233) has a swimming area with a bathhouse and picnicking.

The Genesee County Parks and Recreation Commission (tel. 313/736–7100) operates public beaches near Flint at **Mott Lake, Holloway Reservoir, Byram Lake,** and the **Genesee Recreation Area,** all charging fees.

Along the Lake Huron shoreline are a number of state parks with beaches.

Canoeing   Canoeists will find the northeastern Michigan waters diverse. Much canoeing is done on the inland lakes. The Au Sable, both the main river and the south branch, have quiet waters with no rapids. The Manistee varies from quiet to fast, while the Rifle varies from medium-fast to fast, with some rapids. Canoeists should check for hazards before entering unfamiliar waters.

Cross-country Skiing   Cross-country skiing is a growing sport in northeastern Michigan; participants can be found on golf courses and arboretums and in parks. Flint's **For-Mar Nature Preserve and Arboretum** is one such area, as is **Grand River Park,** southwest of Lansing.

Downhill Skiing   A number of downhill ski areas operate in the region; phone ahead for schedules. For a recorded report on snow conditions statewide, tel. 800/292–5404 in Michigan, 800/248–5708 elsewhere.

Blintz Apple Mountain has 10 runs, 10 rope tows and snowmaking; its longest run is 1,000 feet, with a vertical drop of 200 feet. Cross-country skiing. Rental, instruction, ski shop, restaurant, lounge/bar, entertainment. *4535 N. River Rd., Freeland, tel. 517/781–0170.*

Hanson Hills has 8 runs, a bar lift, and 3 rope tows; its longest run is 1,200 feet, with a vertical drop of 200 feet. Cross-country skiing. Rental, instruction, ski shop, snacks. *2 mi west of Grayling, tel. 517/348–9266.*

Michaywe Slopes offers 9 runs, a chair lift, 2 bar lifts, and 2 rope tows; its longest run is 1,100 feet, with a vertical drop of 220 feet. Cross-country skiing. Rental, instruction, ski shop, lodging, restaurant, lounge/bar, entertainment. *1535 Opal Lake Rd., Gaylord, tel. 517/939–8919.*

Mio Mountain Ski Area has 13 runs, 5 rope tows, and snowmaking; its longest run is 1,500 feet, with a vertical drop of 250 feet. Rental, instruction, snack bar. *1282 Mountain Dr., Mio, tel. 517/826–5569.*

Mott Mountain offers 7 runs, double chair lift, 4 rope tows, and snowmaking; its longest run is 1,800 feet, with a vertical drop of 200 feet. Rental, instruction, restaurant, lounge/bar. *1½ mi south of Farwell, tel. 517/588–2945.*

Skyline Ski Area has 7 runs, a chair lift, and 7 rope tows; its longest run is 1,500 feet, with a vertical drop of 210 feet. Rental, instruction, ski shop, cafeteria. *R.R. 1, Grayling, tel. 517/275–5445.*

Snowsnake Mountain provides 14 runs, a chair lift, 5 rope tows, and snowmaking; its longest run is 2,600 feet, with a vertical drop of 220 feet. Cross-country skiing. Rental, instruction, ski shop, restaurant. *3407 E. Mannsiding Rd., Harrison, tel. 517/539–6583.*

Sylvan Resort offers 11 runs, 2 chair lifts, 2 bar lifts, rope tow, and snowmaking; its longest run is 1,800 feet, with a vertical drop of 225 feet. Cross-country skiing. Rental, instruction, night skiing, ski shop, lodging, restaurant, lounge/bar, entertainment, heated outdoor-indoor pool. *3962 Wilkinson Rd., Gaylord, tel. 517/732–6711 or 800/368–4133.*

Tyrolean Ski Resort has 14 runs, double chair lift, bar lift, rope tow, and snowmaking; its longest run is 4,100 feet, with a vertical drop of 290 feet. Cross-country skiing. Rental, instruction, ski shop, lodging, restaurant, lounge/bar, pool. *R.R. 1, Gaylord, tel. 517/732–2743.*

Fishing Northeastern waters contain panfish, trout, yellow perch, walleye, bass, northern pike, and the elusive muskellunge. Inland water provides excellent fishing. Good to excellent fishing is to be found in parks. If your quarry is lake trout and salmon, fishing off Lake Huron piers sometimes brings success.

Golf **Kearsley Lake Municipal** (4266 E. Pierson, tel. 313/736–0930),
Flint 18 holes; **Mott Park Municipal** (2401 Nolan Dr., tel. 313/766–7077), 9 holes; **Pierce Park Municipal** (2302 Brookside, tel. 313/766–7297), 18 holes; and **Schwartz Creek Municipal** (1902 Hammersburg, tel. 313/766–7043), 18 holes.

Lansing **Groesbeck Municipal** (1600 Ormond, tel. 517/374–0557), 18 holes; **Red Cedar Municipal** (203 S. Clippert, tel. 517/332–9161), 9 holes; and **Waverly Municipal** (3619 W. Saginaw, tel. 517/321–9094). Michigan State University's 36-hole **Forest Aker Golf Course** (Harrison Rd., East Lansing, tel. 517/355–1635) is open to the public.

Midland **Currie Municipal** (1006 Currie Pkwy., tel. 517/839–9600), 36 holes; and **Sandy Ridge** (2750 W. Lauria Rd., tel. 517/631–6010), 18 holes.

Saginaw **Crooked Creek** (9387 Gratiot Rd., tel. 517/781–4887), 18 holes; **Rolling Green** (5170 Weiss, tel. 517/799–1450), 9 holes; **Swan Valley** (9499 Geddes Rd., tel. 517/781–9495), 18 holes; and **Valley View Farms** (1435 S. Thomas Rd., tel. 517/781–1248).

Spectator Sports

College Sports Michigan State University, East Lansing (tel. 517/355–1610), participates in Big Ten baseball, basketball, football, and hockey.

Hockey The **Flint Spirits** (IMA Sports Arena, 3501 Lapeer Rd., Flint, tel. 313/743–1780) play an October-to-April season in the International Hockey League.

Horse Racing **Sports Creek Raceway** (4290 Moorish Rd., Schwartz Creek, tel. 313/635–3333) has an October-to-April harness-racing season.

Northwestern Michigan and Upper Peninsula

Centered on the 45th parallel, halfway between the North Pole and the equator (on the same latitudes as the great wine regions of France), the northwestern corner of the Lower Peninsula is one of the leading cherry-producing regions in the world.

The Upper Peninsula, known as UP, is an area of state and national forests, copper and iron deposits, waterfalls (more than

150), old mining towns, and ski slopes. This is Big Snow Country, where well over 200 inches fall each year. Here, too, is the "Two-Hearted River" Ernest Hemingway wrote about.

Marquette, with a population of 22,000, is the largest city in the peninsula. July and August are the big tourist months; nearly all attractions have limited hours in June and September, and most close by October 15. Snow is not uncommon in October.

We will explore the region beginning in the northwestern corner of the Lower Peninsula, then cross the Mackinac Bridge to the Upper Peninsula.

Because of the distances between towns, we have treated each stop as a separate destination, listings its attractions and facilities. Price categories for restaurants and hotels are the same as in Detroit Dining and Lodging.

Numbers in the margin correspond with points of interest on the Northwestern Michigan and the Upper Peninsula map.

Getting Around

By Plane **Delta County Airport,** Escanaba (tel. 906/786–9037), is served by American Eagle.

Houghton County Airport, Hancock (tel. 906/482–3970), is served by Northwest Airlines.

Ford Airport, Iron Mountain (tel. 906/774–9617), is served by American Eagle.

Gogebic County Airport, Ironwood (tel. 906/932–3121), is served by Northwest Airlink.

Marquette County Airport (tel. 906/475–4651) is served by American Eagle and Northwest Airlink.

Twin Cities Airport, Menominee (tel. 906/863–8408), is served by Alliance Airlines.

Chippewa International Airport, Sault Ste. Marie–Kincheloe (tel. 906/495–5656), is served by Northwest Airlink.

Cherry Capital Airport, Traverse City (tel. 616/947–2250), is served by American Eagle, Midway, and Northwest Airlink.

By Car Northwestern Michigan and the Upper Peninsula have a fairly extensive highway network. I–75 runs north–south to the Canadian border. In the UP, U.S. 2 and Rte. M–28 are principal east–west roads.

By Bus **Greyhound** and **Trailways** provide service to the larger places.

Scenic Drives

Route M–37, from Traverse City into the Old Mission Peninsula, which splits Grand Traverse Bay in two, is particularly lovely, especially in spring when the cherry orchards are in bloom.

U.S. 2 parallels the Lake Michigan shore between St. Ignace and Naubinway, a distance of 50 miles.

Important Addresses and Numbers

Tourist Information **Gogebic Area Convention and Visitor Bureau,** U.S. 2 East, Ironwood, 49938, tel. 906/932–4850; weekdays 8–5.

Grand Traverse Convention and Visitors Bureau, 900 Front Street, Suite 100, Traverse City, 49684, tel. 616/947–1120; weekdays 8–5.

Keweenaw Tourism Council, 1197 Calumet Avenue, Calumet, 49913, tel. 906/337–4579; weekdays 8:30–5.

Mackinac Island Chamber of Commerce, Box 451, Mackinac Island, 49757, tel. 906/847–3783 or 847–3761; weekdays 8–5.

Marquette Chamber of Commerce, 501 South Front Street, Marquette, 49855, tel. 906/226–6591; weekdays 8:30–5.

Upper Peninsula Travel and Recreation Association, Box 400, Iron Mountain, 49801, tel. 906/774–5480; weekdays 9–5.

Emergencies **Michigan State Patrol** (tel. 517/332–2521). 911 is the **emergency number** in some parts of the region.

---

❶ Traverse City

Set at the southern end of Grand Traverse Bay, Traverse City is the center of a region with some 500 commercial orchards and is ranked as the world's largest producer of tart cherries.

Exploring The **National Cherry Festival** each summer draws crowds estimated to be as large as 350,000. The **Interlochen Center for the Arts,** a national year-round academy of the creative arts, attracts outstanding students from around the world. **Grand Traverse Bay** offers excellent small-boat sailing.

Clinch Park has a small zoo with exhibits on the animals, birds, and fish native to Michigan—badger, gray wolf, lynx, buffalo, hawks, and owls, among others. A ministeam train carries visitors around the zoo. *West Bay, tel. 616/941–2331 or 922–4904. Admission free. Train rides: 75¢ adults, 50¢ under 12. Zoo open Memorial Day–Labor Day, daily 9:30 AM–7:30 PM; Apr. 15–Memorial Day and Labor Day–Oct. 31, 9:30–4:30. Train rides daily 10–5 on same schedule.*

The **Con Foster Museum** focuses its exhibits and programs on Grand Traverse history: Indians, blacksmithing, coopering, harvesting maple syrup, lumbering, agriculture, and Great Lakes shipping. An annual summer **Folkways Festival** is a celebration of folk art, music, and lore. *Clinch Park at 400 Boardman Ave., tel. 616/922–4905. Admission: $1 adults, 50¢ children Memorial Day–Labor Day, free rest of year. Open daily 10–6; rest of the year, Tues.–Sat. 10–5.*

 Sleeping Bear Dunes National Lakeshore, 27 miles west of Traverse City, has a 31-mile Lake Michigan shoreline and massive sand dunes that tower nearly 500 feet above the water—said to be the largest in the world outside the Sahara. The park has 35 miles of hiking trails and the 7.6-mile **Pierce Stocking Scenic Drive,** which affords great views of the dunes and lake. More than 50 species of animals, including white-tailed deer, red fox, and bobcat, call the park home, as do more than 250 species of birds. The park headquarters contains exhibits on regional his-

Northwestern Michigan and Upper Peninsula

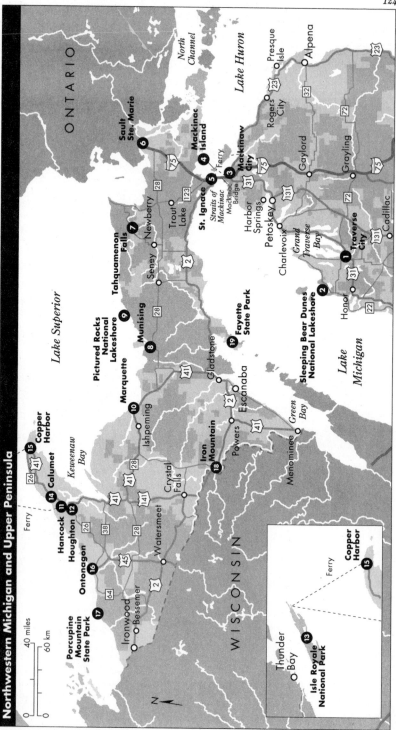

tory and a slide program on the park. *Headquarters on Rte. 72, Empire, tel. 616/326–5134. Admission free. Open daily 9– 4:30.*

Dining   **Reflections Restaurant.** Sitting atop the Waterfront Inn, the dining room overlooks East Bay and Old Mission Peninsula. House specials are seafood (from both the East Coast and the Great Lakes), premium steaks, and prime rib. Raw-fish bar. Children's menu. Cocktail lounge with entertainment. Sunday brunch. *2061 U.S. 31 N. at Four Mile Rd., tel. 616/938– 2321. Reservations suggested. Dress: casual. AE, DC, MC, V. Open daily 7 AM–3 PM and 5–10 PM; closed Dec. 24 and 25. Moderate.*

D. J. Kelly's. A popular, casual restaurant with modern decor. Seafood and pasta highlight the menu, as well as fondues and veal, chicken, and beef dishes. Children's menu. Cocktail lounge. *120 Park St., tel. 616/941–4550. Reservations advised. Dress: casual. AE, MC, V. Open Mon.–Thurs. 11–10, Fri. and Sat. till 11, Sun. 4–9; closed Thanksgiving, Dec. 25. Inexpensive–Moderate.*

Embers on the Bay. Modern, casual dining room overlooks Grand Traverse Bay. The house special is a one-pound porkchop dinner; also on the menu are seafood and beef dishes and daily early-bird specials. Children's menu. Cocktail lounge. *5 mi north of Traverse City at 5555 U.S. 31 N, in Acme, tel. 616/938–1300. Reservations advised. Dress: casual. AE, CB, DC, MC, V. Open daily 5–10 PM, Fri. and Sat. till 11, Sun. 10 AM–2 PM and 5–9; closed Dec. 24 and 25. No dinner Nov. 1–Apr. 1. Sun. and Mon. Inexpensive–Moderate.*

Lodging   **Waterfront Inn.** The inn, on Grand Traverse Bay, has a 775-foot sand beach. All rooms have a view of the water; 56 are efficiencies with kitchenettes and dining tables. Weekend packages. *Box 1736, 49685, tel. 616/938–1100 or 800/553–9328. 2061 U.S. 31 N. at Four Mile Rd. 128 rooms. Facilities: indoor pool, whirlpool, sauna, sun deck, boat dock, restaurant, lounge, jet ski, surf jet, paddleboat rental. AE, DC, MC, V. Expensive– Very Expensive.*

New Heritage Inn. The low white frame motel has a Colonial look; the spacious rooms have modern decor and all have twoperson whirlpools. Some waterbeds. The pool/patio area is pleasantly secluded. *417 Munson Ave., 49684, tel. 616/947– 9520. 39 rooms. Facilities: outdoor pool, exercise room, game room, tanning bed (fee), winter plug-ins. AE, MC, V. Expensive.*

Hampton Inn. A new motel set opposite a state park beach, with airy, comfortable rooms. *1000 U.S. 31 N, 49685, tel. 616/ 946–8900. 4 mi east on U.S. 31 and Rte. M–72. 127 rooms. Facilities: outdoor pool, whirlpool, free Continental breakfast, cable TV. AE, DC, MC, V. Moderate.*

The Arts   The **Interlochen Center for the Arts** Academy and National Music Camp (tel. 616/276–9221) draw more than 450 gifted students from around the world. Recitals, concerts, and exhibitions are presented each summer, as is an International Concert Series with nationally known performers.

The **Cherry County Playhouse** (300 E. State St., tel. 616/946– 5000) stages celebrity concerts, comedies, children's plays, and family musicals each summer.

The **Old Town Playhouse** (148 E. 8th St., tel. 616/947–2210) presents musicals, drama, and comedy.

The **Traverse City Civic Players** (tel. 616/947–2443 or 947–2210) present six plays and five studio-theater productions in a September–June season.

Bars and Nightclubs **Dill's Olde Town Saloon** has live music and entertainment on weekends. *423 S. Union, tel. 616/947–7534. No credit cards. Open until 2 AM weekends.*

JRR's serves up rock on Wednesday night, country on Thursday, and music and dancing on weekends. *205 Lake Ave., tel. 616/941–4422. Open weekends until 2 AM. AE, MC, V.*

The **Trillium Night Club** at Grand Traverse Resort has music, entertainment, and dancing year-round. *6300 U.S. 31 N. (8 miles northeast), tel. 616/938–2100. AE, CB, DC, MC, V. Open until 2 AM weekends.*

The Straits of Mackinac

Mackinaw City
3 Anchoring the southern end of the Mackinac Bridge, which connects the Upper and Lower peninsulas, this bustling tourist community of 900 residents began life as a French fur-trading post. In 1715 it became Fort Michilimackinac, remaining under French rule until 1761, when the British took control of French possessions in the Great Lakes region. In 1780–1781 the British moved to nearby Mackinac Island (town, strait, and island are all pronounced MACK-in-aw). The original fort was reconstructed in 1959 after extensive research in the United States, Canada, and Europe; it is operated by the Mackinac Island State Park Commission. Ferryboat service to the island runs from mid-May to December.

Tours of **Colonial Fort Michilimackinac** begin at a visitors center where exhibits help put this fort and the one on the island into historical context. The reconstruction consists of stockade and blockhouses, water and land entrances, commanding officer's house, barracks, guardhouse, storehouses, trader's houses, St. Anne's Church, priest's house, blacksmith shop, and powder magazine. The fort's history is brought to life by museum displays, murals, cooking and blacksmithing demonstrations by costumed interpreters, the firing of musket and cannon, performances of Colonial music, and a sound-and-light show in the church. Summer visitors can view archaeological work.

Mackinac Marine Park, reached from the visitors center, contains the restored Old Mackinac Point Lighthouse (1829), a maritime museum with Great Lakes shipping artifacts, an aquarium, several old vessels, and examples of Mackinaw boats. The reconstructed 1775 sloop *Welcome*, which sank in a storm in 1781, is anchored at the City Marina on Main Street when not sailing, and is open to the public. *Foot of Mackinac Bridge, I–75 at Exit 339, tel. 616/436–5563. Admission includes Fort Michilimackinac, Mackinac Maritime Park, and sloop* Welcome *when in port: $5 adults, $2.50 age 6–12, $15 family. Combination ticket with Old Mill Creek State Historic Park: $9 adults, $5 ages 6–12. MC, V.*

Old Mill Creek State Historic Park is the site of an 18th-century industrial complex; a sawmill built here in 1780 provided lumber for the construction of Fort Mackinac. Remnants of the complex were discovered in 1972. Now there is a working water mill, a mill dam, a museum, reconstructed buildings, and an interpretive nature trail. Visitors may watch archaeological work in progress in summer. Demonstrations by costumed guides supplement a slide show and exhibits at the visitors center. *3 mi south of Mackinaw City on Rte. M–23, tel. 616/436–7301. Admission: $2.50 adults, $1.25 age 6–12, $7.50 family. Combination ticket with Fort Michilimackinac: $9 adults, $5 age 6–12. Open June 15–Sept. 5, daily 10–7; May 15–June 14 and Sept. 6–Oct. 16, 10–4.*

The **Mackinac Bridge,** known as Mighty Mac, spans the Straits of Mackinac. Completed in 1957, it is five miles long, including approaches, making it one of the longest suspension bridges in the world. The main towers are 552 feet high and the bridge floor is 199 feet above water. The main suspension cables consist of 42,000 miles of wire. The toll for passenger cars is $1.50 each way. A **Mackinac Bridge Walk** is held each Labor Day morning, when the two east lanes are closed to auto traffic and as many as 40,000 people cross.

Before the Mackinac Bridge came into being, the Upper Peninsula was extremely isolated. The **Mackinac Bridge Museum** depicts how the bridge has changed life in the region, using exhibits, artifacts, and a short film. *Central Ave., tel. 616/436–5534. Admission free. Open May 30–Oct. 15, daily 8 AM–10 PM.*

Mackinac Island ❹ This small island—three miles by two—in the east end of the straits has high cliffs along the shore, with ravines, natural bridges, caves, and strange rock formations bearing names like **Arch Rock and Sugar Loaf.** Indians who lived here and used it as a burial ground called it *Michilimackinac*, meaning "The Turtle"; early French and British occupiers shortened and twisted the name to Mackinac. Long a fur-trading post, the island became home to John Jacob Astor's American Fur Company in 1815. Tourists began to arrive as early as the mid-1850s, and the **Grand Hotel,** still standing, was built in 1887.

The old fort is now part of the state park, which occupies about 80 percent of the island. No cars are allowed (except for a public utilities truck, a fire truck, and an ambulance), so transportation to the island is by ferryboat and on it is by bicycle, carriage, or horse. The island actively pursues tourist trade with gift and souvenir shops, tearooms and restaurants. Aside from tourism, the chief industry is the concoction of Mackinac Island fudge, made in half a dozen shops whose sweet aroma wafts about. Since nearly every one of the 700,000 tourists who visit the island each summer buys some, they have become known as Fudgies. Most are day-trippers; those who wish to stay overnight must make reservations well in advance and pay premium prices.

Route M–185 makes an eight-mile circle around the rim of the island, ideal for—and crowded with—bicycles. Island bicycle concessions rent by the hour or the day; several are near the ferry landing on Huron Street. The island can be reached by charter plane from St. Ignace (Great Lakes Air), or Pellston (Michigan Airways), but most visitors use a ferryboat. **Arnold Mackinac Island Ferry** (tel. 906/847–3351 or 643–8275) and **Shepler's Mackinac Island Ferry** (tel. 616/436–5023) operate from Mackinaw City and St. Ignace, **Star Line Mackinac Island Passenger Service** (tel. 906/643–7635) from St. Ignace. The trip takes 20 minutes. *Round-trip fare: $8.50 adults, $5.25 ages 6–12, free under 5; $3 for bicycles. Mid-April to late December, every half-hour in summer.*

Mackinac Island Carriage Tours cover the scenic and historic points of interest in 1¾–hour narrated tours. *Depart from Main St., in center of shopping district, tel. 906/847–3573. Fare: $8 adults, $5 age 5–15. Tours mid-June–Labor Day, daily 8:30–5; mid-May–mid-June, 8:30–4; after Labor Day to mid-Oct., 8:30–3.*

Marquette Park, which commemorates the work of the French priest, Père Marquette, has a statue of him that was dedicated in 1909. A reconstructed bark chapel is patterned after chapels built by the 17th-century missionaries. *Huron St., tel. 906/847–3328. Admission free. Open May 15–Oct. 20, daily 9–5.*

Old Fort Mackinac, on a bluff above the harbor, is preserved as a living-history museum. **The State Park Visitor Center,** where you obtain tickets and literature on the fort and the island, is adjacent to the ferry docks. Then it's a short walk up the hill to the fort and its 14 buildings, all dating from 1780 to 1885. Costumed guides conduct tours on the hour. There are museum exhibits and demonstrations of blacksmithing, cooking, and spinning, along with military music and the firing of musket and cannon. Lunches are available in the **Fort Tea Room** (additional charge) overlooking the straits.

Admission includes several other nearby historic buildings related to the fort, all within easy walking distance: The **Beaumont Memorial,** dedicated to Dr. William Beaumont, who pioneered studies of the human digestive system; the **Benjamin Blacksmith Shop; Biddle House,** said to be the oldest house on the island; the **Indian Dormitory,** dating from 1838; and **McGulpin House,** a French-style log house, possibly brought to the island from Fort Michilimackinac in 1780. *Old Fort Mackinac, tel. 906/847–3328. Admission: $5 adults, $2.50 age 6–12, $15 family. Combination tickets with Fort Michilimackinac or Old Mill Creek Historic Park at Mackinaw City: $9 adults, $5 age 6–12. MC, V. Fort Mackinac open June 15–Labor Day, daily 9–6; May 15–June 14 and after Labor Day–mid-Oct, daily 10–4. All other buildings open June 15–Labor Day, daily 11–5.*

The Stuart House Museum was the original headquarters of Astor's fur company. Its **Agency House and Warehouse** contain company records, furniture dating from 1824, and exhibits on the fur trade. *Market St. Admission: $1. Open Mon.–Sat. and holidays 11–5; June 1–Sept. 15, Sun. 1–5.*

The **Grand Hotel** was built by the railroads that reached Mackinaw City, where there were no rooms for their passengers. The 286-room hotel has a porch reputed to be the world's longest, at 880 feet. In a 10-year renovation program, it was remodeled from top to bottom for its 100th anniversary in 1987.

The Grand is one of the few hotels that charge visitors just to look. For years tea and cookies were served to anyone in the lobby at 4 PM, but as the hotel's fame spread, gawkers gradually outnumbered paying guests. Today it costs $3 to stroll on the porch and wander into the elegant public spaces. Those not guests may buy meals in the dining rooms or dance in the Terrace Room; after 6 PM there is no entry charge, but there is a strict dress code—ties and jackets for men, dresses for women.

St. Ignace Dating from 1671, when Père Marquette founded a mission
❺ here, the community is the northern anchor of the Mackinac Bridge and the gateway to the Upper Peninsula. The *Chief Wawatam*, one of the last hand-fired railroad-car ferries on the Great Lakes, is docked here. The St. Ignace Area Chamber of Commerce distributes a free self-guided walking-driving tour.

The **Father Marquette National Memorial and Museum** is in the Marquette unit of **Straits State Park.** A simple contemporary structure contains a bronze plaque outlining some of the pioneer priest's achievements. An adjoining museum presents slides and films each half-hour and displays artifacts relating to mission activity and 19th-century St. Ignace. There are hiking trails and outstanding views of the straits and the bridge. The park sector east of the bridge has campgrounds and a beach. *¼ mi west of I-75 at the bridge, tel. 906/643-8620. Admission to monument and museum free; $2 vehicle permit required. Open June–Labor Day, daily 8 AM–8:30 PM.*

Dining **Sinbad's of Mackinaw.** The dining room has a nautical look and
Mackinaw City affords casual dining with a view of the straits. Charbroiled steaks are a house specialty. Children's menu. *611 Huron St., tel. 616/436-7541. Reservations suggested. Dress: casual. MC, V. Open May 1–Oct. 31, daily 6:30 AM–11 PM. Inexpensive–Moderate.*

Teysen's Cafeteria. Standing opposite the Mackinac Island ferryboat docks, this popular cafeteria has been operated by the same family since 1927. Native whitefish and chicken pot pie are specialties, and sandwiches and salads are offered. Friendly employees carry trays to your table. *416 S. Huron St., tel. 616/436-7011. No reservations. Dress: casual. AE, MC, V. Open May 1–Oct. 31, daily 7 AM–9 PM; June–Sept., until 10 PM. Inexpensive.*

Mackinac Island **Cable Room.** Elegant dining in a Victorian atmosphere in the
★ Lakeview Hotel and Conference Center. Seafood, beef, and chicken are featured. Children's menu. Cocktail lounge. The hotel's Hoban St. Cafe and the Pilot House restaurant are more casual. *Main St., tel. 906/847-3384. Reservations advised. Jacket and tie advised. AE, MC, V. Expensive.*

Carriage House. The glass-enclosed dining room in the Hotel Iroquois affords a view of the Straits of Mackinac. Seafood and beef and chicken dishes are featured. Children's menu. Cocktail lounge. *Front St., tel. 906/847-3321. Reservations advised. Jacket and tie advised. MC, V. Moderate–Expensive.*

Harbor View. This dining room in the Chippewa Hotel on the lakefront overlooks the harbor. Seafood, including Lake Huron whitefish, is featured, as are New York strip steak and other beef dishes. Sunday brunch in season. Children's menu. Cocktail lounge. *Main St., tel. 906/847-3341. Reservations suggested. Jacket and tie advised. AE, MC, V. Closed Oct. 16–May 14. Moderate.*

Horn's Gaslight Bar and Restaurant. Sandwiches, salads, and Mexican dishes are served in a room with a Gay '90s atmosphere. Cocktail lounge with entertainment afternoons and evenings. *Main St., tel. 906/847–6145. Reservations not required. Dress: casual. MC, V. Inexpensive.*

St. Ignace **Blue Waters Restaurant.** Informal dining in a modern room. Specialties include fresh whitefish and lake trout, caught in nearby waters, as well as beef and poultry. Children's menu. *927 State St. (Business I–75), tel. 906/643–8494. Reservations advised. Dress: casual. MC, V. Closed Oct. 16–Apr. 30. Inexpensive–Moderate.*

The Flame. Owned by the same family for 30 years, this restaurant features seafood and prime rib. There is a daily breakfast buffet, a children's menu, and a cocktail lounge with entertainment in summer. *U.S. 2 and Church St., tel. 906/643–8554. Reservations not required. Dress: casual. CB, DC, MC, V. Inexpensive–Moderate.*

The Galley. A family restaurant overlooking Lake Huron and Mackinac Island, it has such seafood specials as broiled whitefish, trout, and deep-fried perch, along with beef and chicken dishes and homemade soups and salads. Children's menu. Cocktail lounge. *241 State St. at harbor, tel. 906/643–7960. Reservations not required. Dress: casual. MC, V. Inexpensive–Moderate.*

Huron Landing. This pleasant harborfront restaurant and bar serves Italian food. The lounge is open until 1 AM. *441 N. State St., tel. 906/643–9613. AE, DC, MC, V. Inexpensive.*

Lodging
Mackinaw City
To handle the overflow of tourists whose budgets preclude a night on Mackinac Island, the town has a large number of lodging facilities for its size. Many motels and lodges are closed in winter, however.

Ramada Inn. Standing near the Mackinac Bridge, the motel offers pleasant, comfortable rooms in the Ramada Inn style and is open year-round. *314 S. Nicolet St., 49701, tel. 616/436–5535 or 800/272–6232. ½ mi south of bridge at Exit 338 off I–75. 155 rooms. Facilities: indoor pool, sauna, whirlpool, recreation area, dining room and coffeeshop. AE, DC, MC, V. Inexpensive–Moderate.*

Traveler's Motel. This family motel on Lake Huron near the ferry docks has roomy accommodations at reasonable prices. Lakefront rooms have balconies and views of the Mackinac Bridge. Some rooms have waterbeds, Honeymoon suites. Open May 1–Oct. 31. *905 S. Huron St., 49701, tel. 616/436–5539. 3 mi southeast on U.S. 23. Facilities: indoor pool, beach, whirlpool, playground, game room, cable TV. AE, DC, MC, V. Inexpensive–Moderate.*

Big Mac Motor Lodge. The motel, three blocks from the Mackinac Island ferries and other attractions, does not have a large number of amenities but the rooms are clean and pleasant. *206 Nicolet St., 49701, tel. 616/436–8961. Exit 399, I–75. 47 rooms. Facilities: outdoor pool, cable TV, winter plug-ins; restaurant and cocktail lounge adjacent. AE, MC, V. Inexpensive.*

Mackinac Island Reservations are an absolute necessity; make them as far in advance as possible, especially for July and August.

★ **Grand Hotel.** Perched amid neatly manicured grounds on a hill overlooking the Straits of Mackinac, the gleaming white Grand expresses the elegance of a bygone era. Recently remodeled from top to bottom, it has luxurious rooms and suites that are decorated with period furnishings and antiques or are in modern style. Red-coated coachmen meet guests at the ferry landing. *Mackinac Island, 49757, tel. 906/847–3331. 286 rooms. Facilities: outdoor pool, sauna, whirlpool, playground, jogging/exercise trail, rental bicycles, golf (fee), 4 tennis courts, dining rooms, lounge, entertainment. MC, V. Closed mid-Nov.–mid-May. Very Expensive.*

Lakeview Hotel and Conference Center. This restored white frame hotel, built in 1862, has Victorian turrets and towers and a four-level porch; a new section has been added. Rooms have Victorian furnishings. Some Jacuzzi suites. *Main St., 49757, tel. 906/847–3384. 95 rooms. Facilities: indoor pool, sauna, whirlpool, dining room. Closed Nov. 1–early May. Very Expensive.*

Island House. The island's oldest hotel, built in 1852, it has large porches, Victorian turrets and towers, and spacious grounds. Recently renovated, comfortable rooms display variety in decor. *Main St., 49757, tel. 906/847–3347. 95 rooms. Facilities: radios, rental bicycles, dining room, lounge, entertainment, golf, tennis. AE, MC, V. Closed mid-Oct.–mid-May. Expensive–Very Expensive.*

Mackinac Hotel and Conference Center. A massive lobby, with heavy timbers, rustic woodwork, and fireplaces, sets the tone for this more recent hotel. Rooms range from modest to spacious, including 100 two-bedroom units. *Lake Shore Dr., Box 430, 49757, tel. 906/847–3312. 240 rooms. Facilities: outdoor pool, whirlpools, 3 tennis courts, exercise room, playground, rental bicycles. MC, V. Closed Nov. 1–May. Expensive–Very Expensive.*

Chippewa Hotel. This turn-of-the-century place has rooms ranging from modest to modern, many with a lake view. The decor leans toward Victorian. *Main St., 49757, tel. 906/847–3341. 75 rooms. Facilities: outdoor pool, rental TV, restaurant, lounge. AE, MC, V. Closed mid-Oct.–mid-May. Moderate–Very Expensive.*

St. Ignace **Heritage Inn.** A two-story Colonial-style motel overlooking Lake Huron and Mackinac Island. The large, comfortable rooms have modern decor, refrigerators, and balconies on the lake. *1020 N. State St., 49781, 2¼ mi north of bridge on Business I–75, tel. 906/643–7581. 40 rooms. Facilities: indoor pool, beach, whirlpool, playground, fishing, picnic tables and grill, restaurant. AE, DC, MC, V. Closed Nov. 1–Apr. 14. Expensive.*

Bavarian Haus Motel. A new motel with large, modern rooms done in Bavarian style, it overlooks Lake Huron and Mackinac Island; some rooms have balconies. *1067 N. State St., 49781, 3 mi north of bridge on Business I–75, tel. 906/643–7777. 27 rooms. Facilities: indoor pool, whirlpool, fishing, cable TV; restaurant adjacent. AE, MC, V. Closed Nov. 16–Apr. 14. Moderate.*

Belle Isle Motel. Set on seven acres of landscaped grounds on a hill overlooking Lake Huron and Mackinac Island, this two-story motel has large, modern, well-kept rooms. *1030 N. State St., 49781, 2½ mi north of bridge on Business I–75, tel. 906/643–8060. 47 rooms. Facilities: indoor pool, whirlpool, playground, sauna deck and patio, picnic area, cable TV; restaurant adjacent. AE, DC, MC, V. Closed mid-Oct.–early May. Inexpensive–Moderate.*

Bars and Nightlife **Audie's** has a pleasant cocktail lounge. The adjoining restaurant serves until 11 PM on summer weekends. *314 Nicolet St., Mackinaw City, tel. 616/436–5744. MC, V.*

The **Spinnaker** cocktail lounge has nautical decor and views of the Mackinac Bridge. *116 N. Huron St., Mackinaw City, tel. 616/436–5519. Open mid-May–mid-Oct. MC, V.*

The cocktail lounge of the **Embers North** features music and entertainment during the summer. The dining room serves until 10 PM; the lounge is open until 1 AM. *590 N. State St., St. Ignace, tel. 906/643–8600. MC, V.*

---

❻ Sault Ste. Marie

The oldest settlement in Michigan, Sault Ste. Marie (Soo Saint Marie) was visited by the French explorer Etienne Brule between 1618 and 1622 as he made his way along the St. Marys River, which connects Lake Superior and Lake Huron. In 1668 Jacques Marquette and Claude Dablon established a mission beside the rapids and named it in honor of the Virgin Mary. Its twin city, Sault Ste. Marie, Ontario, is across the river.

The half-mile-long rapids of the St. Marys was a barrier to Lake Superior navigation until 1855, when the first lock was completed. Today the U.S. Army Corps of Engineers operates the four parallel locks, the largest and busiest lock system in the world, raising and lowering ships the 21-foot difference between Lake Superior and Lake Huron (there is a single lock on the Canadian side).

Exploring An adjoining park has three observation platforms allowing a close view of ships in the locks. A small museum displays exhibits and films on the locks and Great Lakes shipping. Visitors center. *Portage St. Admission free. Park open Apr. 1–Nov. 1, 6 AM–midnight; visitors center open mid-May–mid-Oct., 9–9.*

Soo Locks Boat Tours provides two-hour, 10-mile narrated cruises on the St. Marys. The boats traverse the waterfront, pass through the American locks, travel up the river, and return through the Canadian lock. *Depart from 500 E. Portage Ave. (tel. 906/632–2512) and 1157 E. Portage Ave. (tel. 906/632–6301). Fare: $9.50 adults, $4.25 age 6–15, free 5 and under. Tours July–Aug., daily 9–7; May 15–June 30 and Sept. 1–Oct. 15, daily 9–5:30.*

Soo Locks Train Tours run rubber-tired, glass-enclosed cars on 1¼-hour narrated tours of points of interest in Sault Ste. Marie and cross the International Bridge for a brief stop in Sault Ste. Marie, Ontario. *315 W. Portage Ave. (across from Soo Locks), tel. 906/635–5912. Admission: $3.25 adults, $1.75 age 6–15, free 5 and under. Departures every half-hour Memorial Day–Labor Day, daily 9 AM–7:30 PM.*

The **Museum Ship** *Valley Camp* is a retired 550-foot Great Lakes freighter permanently moored at the Soo and open for tours. The hold contains a maritime museum with aquariums, a recovered lifeboat from the *Edmund Fitzgerald* (which sank in Lake Superior in 1975), shipwreck exhibits, a marine hall of fame, theaters, and exhibits on Great Lakes history. The adjoining **Port Adventure** complex has gift shops, a picnic area, and a historic home. *Johnston and Water Sts., tel. 609/632–3658. Admission: $4.75 adults, $2.50 age 6–16, free 5 and under. Open July 1–Aug. 31, daily 9 AM–8 PM; May 15–June 30 and Sept. 1–Oct. 15, daily 10–5. Last ticket sold hour before closing.*

The **Tower of History** is a modern 21-story observation tower. A small museum and a slide show on the history of Sault Ste. Marie and the Great Lakes are in the lobby; an elevator leads to the observation deck, which has views of the area. *326 E. Portage Ave., tel. 609/635–3050. Admission: $2.50 adults, $1.50 age 6–16, free 5 and under. Open July 1–Aug. 31, daily 9–8; May 15–June 30 and Sept. 1–Aug. 15, daily 10–5. Last ticket sold hour before closing.*

Dining **Cafe du Voyageur.** A family restaurant featuring seafood, including lake trout and whitefish, and beef and chicken, plus daily specials and homemade desserts. *205 W. Portage Ave., tel. 906/632–0228. Reservations not required. Dress: casual. AE, MC, V. Closed Sun., Thanksgiving, Dec. 25. Jan. 1–Mar. 1. Inexpensive–Moderate.*
Robin's Nest. The atmosphere is casual and the menu lists seafood specials, including whitefish and lake trout, and chicken, steaks, and burgers. Children's menu. Cocktail lounge. *3520 Business I–75, tel. 906/632–3200. Reservations not required. Dress: casual. MC, V. Open 8 AM–10 PM daily, 9 AM mid-Oct.– May 31; closed Dec. 25. Inexpensive–Moderate.*

Lodging **Best Western Colonial Inn.** A family motel with clean, spacious rooms and modern decor, minutes away from downtown attractions. *Box 659, 49783, tel. 906/632–2170. ¼ mi northeast of downtown on Business I–75. 58 rooms. Facilities: indoor pool, sauna, indoor recreation area. AE, DC, MC, V. Open mid-March–Nov. Inexpensive–Moderate.*
Ramada Inn. Comfortable rooms with modern decor—what you might expect from a Ramada. Some suites. *Ashmun St., 49783, tel. 906/635–1523. 1 mi northeast of Business I–75. 104 rooms. Facilities: indoor pool, saunas, whirlpool, restaurant, lounge. AE, DC, MC, V. Open year-round. Inexpensive–Moderate.*

Paradise

If you're driving west of Sault Ste. Marie on Route 28, turn north on Route 123 to visit **Tahquamenon Falls,** one of the best known of the region's many waterfalls. These are the scene of the legends of Hiawatha. Sometimes called Little Niagara, the broad upper falls is among the largest east of the Mississippi. *Tahquamenon Falls State Park, east of Paradise on Rte. M–123. $2 vehicle permit required.*

---

❽ Munising

Exploring The **Pictured Rocks National Lakeshore** extends 40 miles along Lake Superior from Munising to Grand Marais. Sandstone cliffs rising 200 feet above the lake have been carved by wind, waves, and ice into forms bearing such names as Miner's Castle, Battleship Rock, Indian Head, and Lover's Leap. Mineral seepage has painted the rocks red (iron), blue and green (copper), and white (limestone). Several drive-in campsites are along the shore. Visitors' centers near Munising Falls and Grand Marais are open in the summer. *Admission free. Open 24 hrs, year-round. Park headquarters on Sand Point Rd. near Munising (tel. 906/387–2607) open weekdays year-round.*

The rock formation known as **Miner's Castle,** the only significant one accessible on foot, is five miles northeast of Munising on Route H–13 and an easy walk from the parking lot at the end of the road. Picturesque Miner's Falls is easily reached nearby. Half a dozen or so waterfalls are in Munising itself.

Pictured Rocks Cruises takes visitors on three-hour, 37-mile cruises along the shore. *Municipal Pier, tel. 906/387–2379. Fare: $12 adults, $5 age 6–12, free 5 and under. July–Aug., daily at 9, 11, 1, 3, and 5 June and Sept. 1–Oct. 10 at 10 and 2, weather permitting.*

Dining **DogPatch.** This informal family restaurant serves such specials as "Earthquake McGoon's Rib-eye Steak Dinner" (charbroiled rib-eye, potatoes, salad, onion rings, rolls) and a "Li'l Abner" burger. Fish dishes include fresh Lake Superior trout. Children's menu. Cocktail lounge. *820 E. Superior St., tel. 906/ 387–9948. Reservations suggested. Dress: casual. MC, V. Open daily 7 AM–10 PM, Fri.–Sat. till 11; closed Dec. 25. Inexpensive.*

Ziegert's Restaurant. A family restaurant, it serves breakfast until late afternoon. Specialties are whitefish and Lake Superior trout. Children's menu. Cocktail lounge. *Rte. M–28, tel. 906/387–3124. No reservations. Dress: casual. DC, MC, V. Open weekdays 6 AM–10 PM, weekends 6:30 AM–10 PM. Inexpensive.*

Lodging **Best Western of Munising.** Munising's largest and newest motel has spacious, modern rooms. *Box 310, 49862, tel. 906/387–4864 or 800/528–1234. 3 mi east on Rte. M–28. Open year-round. 50 rooms. Facilities: outdoor pool, playground, game room, color TV, winter plug-ins, restaurant. AE, DC, MC, V. Inexpensive–Moderate.*

⑩ Marquette

This community was founded in 1849 as a shipping center for ore from the Marquette Iron Range. Northern Michigan University, which includes one of the nation's Olympic training sites, is here.

Exploring The **Marquette County Historical Society Museum** (213 N. Front St., tel. 906/226–3571) has exhibits on pioneer life, mining, and lumbering, and supplies a map outlining a historical walking tour.

Presque Isle Park, just north of the city, offers free picnicking, swimming, rock hunting, and a children's zoo.

Dining **Northwoods Supper Club.** North-country dining is set in birch- and cedar-paneled rooms with fireplaces and views of the woods. The menu includes charbroiled steaks, prime rib, chicken, and seafood; some dishes are prepared at tableside. Sunday brunch and Tuesday-evening smorgasbord. Children's menu. Cocktail lounge. *3½ mi west on U.S. 41 and Rte. M–28, tel.*

906/228–4343. Reservations suggested. Dress: casual. AE, CB, DC, MC, V. Open weekdays 11:30 AM–11 PM, Fri. and Sat. till 1 AM, Sun. 10:30 AM–10 PM; closed Dec. 24–26. Inexpensive–Moderate.

Office Bar and Restaurant. This pub in the heart of downtown features barbecued ribs and steaks and more than 30 sandwiches. Cocktail lounge. *154 W. Washington St., tel. 906/228–8722. MC, V. Inexpensive.*

Lodging **Cedar Motor Inn.** A pleasant, comfortable motel offering clean rooms decorated in north-woods modern. *2523 U.S. 41 W., 49855, tel. 906/228–2280. 44 rooms. Facilities: indoor pool, sauna. AE, MC, V. Inexpensive.*

Westwood Motel. This two-story motel recently renovated its public spaces and remodeled some rooms. The rooms are pleasant and airy, with modern decor. *2403 U.S. 41 W, 49855, tel. 906/225–1393. 65 rooms. Facilities: indoor pool, sauna, whirlpool, free Continental breakfast. AE, MC, V. Inexpensive.*

Bars and **J. T.'s Shaft.** This popular downtown bar serves deli-style sand-
Nightclubs wiches, soup, and salads until 9:30 PM. The lounge is open until 1 AM. *1125 Ridge St. (behind Shop KO), tel. 906/228–9210. AE, MC, V.*

Keweenaw Peninsula

Curving into Lake Superior like a crooked finger, Keweenaw (KEY-wa-naw) was the site of extensive copper mining from the 1840s to the 1960s. The deposits were exceptionally pure, and in its heyday Keweenaw produced a considerable part of the world's copper. The man-made Keweenaw Waterway, incorporating Portage Lake, cuts across the middle of the peninsula, providing shelter for storm-threatened vessels and enabling them to avoid the dangerous waters surrounding the peninsula.

Exploring The twin cities of Houghton and Hancock, the gateway to the Keweenaw, are connected by a double-deck lift bridge with a four-lane highway on the upper level and a railroad track
⑪ on the lower level. In **Hancock,** the **Arcadian Copper Mine** has a ¼-mile guided tour of workings no longer in operation. *1 mi east on Rte. M–26, tel. 906/482–7502. Admission: $3.50 adults, $2 age 6–12. Tours July and Aug., daily 9–6; June and Sept., 9–5.*

⑫ **Houghton** is home to **Michigan Technical University.** The **E. A. Seaman Mineralogical Museum** (in the Electrical Energy Resources Center, tel. 906/487–2572) displays minerals native to the UP. The inland headquarters of Isle Royale National Park are also in Houghton.

⑬ **Isle Royale,** the largest island in Lake Superior, is 45 miles long and 9 miles wide at its widest point. It lies 50 miles off Eagle Harbor, a tiny community farther north. Isle Royale is a wilderness park inhabited by moose, wolves, beavers, red foxes, mink, and snowshoe hares. There are 166 miles of trails and many campgrounds; travel is on foot or by boat. A small marina and two lodges are open from May to October; reservations are required well in advance. All equipment must be backpacked in; all surface water must be boiled.

The park is reached by boat or seaplane, for which reservations are also required. Boat service is available from Copper Harbor (4½ hours one way) or Houghton (6½ hours); plane service is available from Houghton mid-June to mid-September. Isle Royale is not a place where one drops in for a picnic; trips take advance planning. Those considering a visit are advised to obtain further information. *Superintendent, Isle Royale National Park, 87 N. Ripley St., Houghton 49931, tel. 906/482–0986.*

⑭ The Victorian stone architecture in **Calumet** gives just a hint of the wealth in the copper towns during the boom days. At its peak, Calumet, whose population is 1,000 today, had more than 20 churches and a 37-room school. Much of the downtown area is listed on the National Register of Historic Places. The 1,000-seat **Calumet Theater,** built in 1910, was the stage for such stars as Lillian Russell, Sarah Bernhardt, William S. Hart, and Douglas Fairbanks Sr. Restored in 1974 at a cost of $200,000, the theater presents performances and major community events throughout the year, including summer concerts by the Detroit Symphony. *3340 6th St., tel. 906/337–2610. Tours weekdays 10–4. Call for additional information.*

At **Coppertown USA,** a visitors center tells the story of the mines, towns, and people of the Keweenaw Peninsula. Exhibits of equipment trace the evolution of mining from ancient times through the boom days and the closing of the last working mine in 1968. A simulated mine affords a glimpse into the miner's world. *2 blocks west of U.S. 41, tel. 906/337–4354. Admission: $3 adults, $1.50 age 6–12. Open mid-June–mid-Oct., weekdays 10–8, Sat. 10–6; closed holidays.*

⑮ **Copper Harbor** is Michigan's northernmost community and a popular spot with campers. **Fort Wilkins State Park** contains the restored buildings of an Army post established in 1844 and abandoned in 1870. The complex also has copper mine shafts sunk in 1844 and the Copper Harbor Lighthouse. Audiovisual presentations and costumed interpreters depict the lifestyles and routines of the officers, enlisted men, and their families. Additional exhibits show the history of copper mining. The park has campgrounds and hiking trails. *3 mi east of Copper Harbor on U.S. 41, tel. 906/289–4215. $2 vehicle sticker required. Open June 1–Labor Day, daily 9 AM–10 PM; May 15–31 and day after Labor Day–Oct. 15, 8–5.*

Copper Harbor Lighthouse Tour. The trip includes a 20-minute boat ride on the *Star of Keweenaw* and an hour long visit to the lighthouse. The lighthouse museum, accessible only by boat, has exhibits on mining and the history of Lake Superior. *Tours leave from marina, tel. 906/289–4410. Admission: $3.75 adults, $2 age 4–12. Daily departures third week in June–Labor Day, on the hour 10–5, weather permitting.*

Brockway Mountain Drive climbs more than 900 feet above Copper Harbor to provide magnificent views of the peninsula and Lake Superior; if the day is clear, look to the northwest and you might see Isle Royale as a dark smudge on the horizon. Constructed as a WPA project during the 1930s, the drive, which is regarded as one of the most scenic in Michigan, runs nine miles between Copper Harbor and Eagle Harbor.

Estivant Pines, a stand of virgin white pine on the outskirts of Copper Harbor, has trees more than 500 years old and over 100 feet tall. The largest, "Leaning Giant," measures 23 feet in circumference, making it one of the largest in the continental United States.

Dining **Summer Place.** A rustic dining room overlooking Portage Lake, it serves seafood, including lake trout and whitefish, and steaks, chicken, and veal. Children's menu, cocktail lounge. *6 mi south on U.S. 41, Houghton, tel. 906/523–4915. Reservations suggested. Dress: casual. MC, V. Closed July 4, Labor Day, Dec. 25–26. Inexpensive–Moderate.*

Harbor Haus. Michigan's northernmost restaurant has a crisp dining room overlooking Lake Superior and the harbor. The menu offers fresh-caught Lake Superior whitefish and trout, plus hearty German items like Sauerbraten and Wiener Schnitzel. *1 block off U.S. 41, Copper Harbor, tel. 906/289–4502. Dress: casual. DC, MC, V. Closed mid-Oct.–May 24. Inexpensive.*

Lodging **Best Western King's Inn.** A modern, comfortable motel, with pleasant rooms, some with a view of the city and valley. *215 Shelden Ave., Houghton 49931, tel. 906/482–5000. 65 rooms. Facilities: indoor pool, sauna, whirlpool, winter plug-ins. AE, DC, MC, V. Inexpensive–Moderate.*

Keweenaw Mountain Lodge. The lodge consists of rustic duplex cabins and a modern motel set on a wooded hillside. Some cabins have fireplaces. The main lodge is of logs, with rustic public spaces. *Copper Harbor, 49918, tel. 906/289–4403. 1 mi south on U.S. 41. 41 rooms. Facilities: tennis court, 9-hole golf course (fee), cable TV, restaurant and lounge in main lodge. MC, V. Inexpensive–Moderate.*

Lake Fanny Hooe Resort. Some two-bedroom cottages and a modern motel with private balconies and kitchenettes are to be found at this establishment on the lakeshore. The decor is north-woods modern. Campground. *Box 116, Copper Harbor, 49918, tel. 906/289–4451. 4 blocks east of U.S. 41 and Rte. M–26, then 2 blocks south on Manganese Rd. 14 rooms. Facilities: beach, sauna, playground, nature trails, coin laundry, dock fishing, rental boats, motors, and canoes, rental paddleboats. MC, V. Inexpensive.*

Bars and Nightclubs The cocktail lounge in the **Main Street Inn** has a great view of the Keweenaw Waterway. *820 Shelton Ave., Houghton, tel. 906/487–1700. MC, V. Open Mon.–Sat. until 1 AM.*

⓰ Ontonagon

This small community on the shore west of the Keweenaw Peninsula was a frequent stop from the 1600s to the 1800s. It was once the site of a huge copper boulder—50 inches high and 3,708 pounds—that the Indians regarded as sacred. (It was eventually moved to the Smithsonian Institution in Washington.) The **Ontonagon County Historical Museum** (233 River St., tel. 906/883–3696) has exhibits on mining in the region and a replica of the copper boulder.

⓱ **Porcupine Mountain State Park** (23 mi west of Ontonagon) consists of waterfalls, scenic vistas, more than 85 miles of hiking trails, and five campgrounds. **Lake of the Clouds** scenic overlook, on an escarpment high above the lake at the western end of Route M–107, provides outstanding views and is easily accessible. A visitors center contains a small museum and audiovisual presentations. *$2 vehicle sticker required.*

Iron Mountain

Iron Mountain was established in 1878 after the discovery of rich iron-ore deposits. Since the mines ceased operations in the 1940s, it relies today on tourists and skiers for its livelihood.

Exploring The **Cornish Pump and Mining Museum** (2 blocks west of U.S. 2 on Kent St., tel. 906/774–1086) displays one of the largest steam engines built in North America as well as mining equipment. **Menominee Range Historical Foundation Museum** (300 E. Ludington St., tel. 906/774–4276) has exhibits on local history.

The **Iron Mountain Iron Mine** operated from 1877 to 1945, producing almost 22 million tons of ore. Guided tours by rail mine car through its 2,600 feet of underground drifts and tunnels include demonstrations of mining machinery. The lighted caverns have many strange rock formations. A jacket or sweater is a good idea; hard hats and raincoats are furnished. *8 mi east of Iron Mountain on U.S. 2, tel. 906/563–8077. Admission: $4 adults, $3 children under 12. Open June 1–Oct. 15, daily 9–6.*

Dining **Mine Shaft.** A casual restaurant featuring 10 varieties of breakfast omelets and a daily "Miner's Special" for lunch. On the dinner menu are a few Italian dishes, plus seafood, salads, pork chops, steaks, and prime rib. Children's menu. Cocktail lounge. *1601 Stevenson Ave., tel. 906/774–0201. Reservations not required. Dress: casual. AE, MC, V. Open Mon.–Sat. 7 AM –10 PM, Sun. 8 AM–1 PM. Inexpensive–Moderate.*
BJ's Food & Friends. This informal family restaurant displays a photo gallery of Iron Mountain. Specialties run from choice burgers to barbecued steak and chicken. There are soup and salad bars, a Sunday brunch and buffet, and outdoor patio dining in summer. *900 S. Stevenson Ave., tel. 906/774–1777. Reservations suggested. Dress: casual. MC, V. Open daily 6 AM–11 PM; closed Dec. 24–25. Inexpensive.*

Lodging **Northern Host Motor Inn.** A new motel with modern facilities and large comfortable rooms, it has suites and three efficiency units. *2702 N. Stevenson Ave., 49801, tel. 906/774–3400. 49 rooms. Facilities: saunas, whirlpool, winter plug-ins. MC, V. Inexpensive.*

Bars and Nightclubs The **Blind Duck Inn** serves snacks and full meals, including Mexican food. The cocktail-lounge specialties are a jumbo margarita and a view of Cowboy Lake. *Across from airport, tel. 906/774–0037. Open daily until 1 AM.*

Pine Mountain Lodge has entertainment on weekends, especially in winter. *½ mi north on U.S. 2, then 3 mi northwest on paved road, follow signs, tel. 906/774–2747. MC, V. Dining room serves until 9 PM.*

Fayette

A former iron-smelting community is preserved as a ghost town in **Fayette State Park.** Founded in 1866, Fayette prospered by smelting pig iron from ore from the Jackson Mine, 75 miles north, and shipping it to steel centers. Fayette was virtually abandoned in 1890 when its wood-fired furnaces could not profitably compete with new coke-fired smelters. A self-guided walking tour begins at the park museum and visits the ruins of the big furnaces and 19 buildings, among them the company store, hotel, boardinghouse, opera house, and jail. Walking trails pass along the Lake Michigan shore. *Rte. M–183, 17 mi south of U.S. 2 on Garden Peninsula, tel. 906/644–2603. $2 vehicle sticker required. Town site open June 1–Labor Day, daily 9–7; mid-May–June 1 and after Labor Day–Oct. 15, 9–5. Park open year-round.*

Participant Sports

Beaches and Water Sports The beaches in the vicinity of Traverse City, including Clinch Park, are considered by some to be among the finest in Michigan. Traverse City State Park (tel. 616/947–7193) and Interlochen State Park (tel. 616/276–9511) have very good beaches.

Upper Peninsula Except in the shallowest of bays, there is little swimming in Lake Superior, for even at the height of summer the waters are dangerously cold. Some unguarded Lake Michigan beaches lie along U.S. 2 between St. Ignace and Naubinway. Upper Peninsula state parks that have swimming include: Brimley (tel. 906/685–3338); Fayette (Garden Peninsula, tel. 906/644–2603); and W. J. Wells (Cedar River, tel. 906/863–9747). *$2 vehicle sticker required.*

Fishing Fishing is undoubtedly the most popular sport in the northwestern Lower Peninsula and the UP. Panfish, trout, perch, walleye, bass, northern pike, and the elusive muskellunge abound. Inland waters are excellent, and fishing is good to excellent in many parks. If your quarry is lake trout and salmon, fishing off piers sometimes brings success, especially in spring. Charter operators are found in virtually all port cities.

Golf The northwestern Lower Peninsula has a large number of courses, including these:

Interlochen **Interlochen** (10586 U.S. 31, tel. 616/275–7311), 18 holes.

Traverse City **Cedar Hills** (4 mi west on Cedar Run Rd., tel. 616/947–8237), 9 holes; **Elmbrook** (420 Hammond Rd., tel. 616/946–9180), 18 holes; **Grand Traverse Resort** (6300 U.S. 31N, tel. 616/938–1620), 36 holes designed by Jack Nicklaus; **Green Hills** (2411 W. Silver Lake Rd., tel. 616/946–2975), 9 holes; **Mitchell Creek** (2846 3 Mile Rd., tel. 616/941–5200), 9 holes.

Calumet **Calumet Golf Course** (1 mi south off U.S. 41, tel. 906/337–3911), 9 holes.

Copper Harbor **Keweenaw Mountain** (on U.S. 41, tel. 906/289–4403), 9 holes.

Mackinac Island **Grand Hotel Golf Course** (tel. 906/847–3331), 9 holes; **Wawashkamo** (tel. 906/847–3871), 9 holes.

Marquette **Marquette Golf Course** (on Grove St., tel. 906/225–0721), 18 holes.

Munising **Pictured Rocks** (east of Munising on Rte. M–58, tel. 906/387–2146), 9 holes.

St. Ignace **St. Ignace** (1 mi west on U.S. 2, tel. 906/643–8071), 9 holes.

Downhill Skiing This region has some of the finest skiing in the Midwest. Phone ahead for schedules. *For a recorded report on snow conditions statewide, tel. 800/292–5404 in Michigan, 800/248–5708 elsewhere.*

Al Quaal Recreation Area has 3 runs, 3 rope tows; its longest run is 600 feet, with a vertical drop of 100 feet. *Poplar St., Ishpeming, 1 mi north of U.S. 41, tel. 906/486–6181.*

Big Powderhorn Mountain has 23 runs, 6 double chair lifts, and snowmaking; its longest run is 1 mile, with a vertical drop of 600 feet. Instruction, equipment rental, repair shop, ski shop, ice skating, sleigh rides, lodging, indoor pool, restaurants, lounges/bars, entertainment. *N11375 Powderhorn Rd., Bessemer, tel. 906/932–4838 or 800/222–3131 (Oct. 15–Apr. 1).*

Blackjack Ski Resort has 16 runs, 4 chair lifts, 2 rope tows, and snowmaking; its longest run is 5,400 feet, with a vertical drop of 465 feet. Instruction, equipment rental, ski shop, lodging, nursery service, lounge/bar, entertainment. *3 mi northeast of Bessemer on U.S. 2, tel. 906/229–5115.*

Boyne Highlands operates 17 runs, 7 chair lifts, a bar lift, 2 rope tows, and snowmaking; the vertical drop is 535 feet. Instruction, equipment rental, ski shop, lodging, restaurant, lounge/bar, entertainment, heated outdoor pool. *Hedrick Rd., Harbor Springs, tel. 616/526–2171.*

Boyne Mountain has 17 runs, 10 chair lifts, rope tow, and snowmaking; its longest run is 1 mile, with a vertical drop of 450 feet. Services include instruction, equipment rental, ski shop, lodging, restaurant, lounge/bars, entertainment, heated outdoor pool. *Boyne Falls, 15 mi south of Petoskey on U.S. 31, tel. 800/632–7174.*

Briar Mountain has 10 runs, 2 chair lifts, rope tow, and snowmaking; vertical drop is 400 feet. Instruction, equipment rental, ski shop, restaurant, lounge/bar. *Off U.S. 2 in Norway, tel. 906/563–9719.*

Caberfae Ski Resort has 24 runs, 3 chair lifts, 5 T-bars, 3 rope tows, and snowmaking; its longest run is ½ mile, with a vertical drop of 470 feet. Instruction, equipment rental, ski shop, night skiing, lodge, restaurant, lounge/bar, entertainment. *Rte. M–55, 15 mi west of Cadillac, tel. 616/862–3301.*

Crystal Mountain Resort offers 22 runs, 3 chair lifts, rope tow, and snowmaking; its longest run is ½ mile, with a vertical drop of 375 feet. Instruction, equipment rental, ski shop, night skiing, lodging, restaurant, lounge/bar, entertainment, heated outdoor pool. *Rte. M–116 at Thompsonville, 36 mi northwest of Cadillac, tel. 616/378–2911 or 800/321–4637.*

Gladstone Sports Park has 3 runs, T-bar, 4 rope tows, and snowmaking; its longest run is 500 feet, with a vertical drop of 110 feet. Instruction, snacks. *N. Bluff Dr., Gladstone, tel. 906/428–2311.*

The **Homestead** has 11 runs, 3 chair lifts, cable tow, and snowmaking; vertical drop is 375 feet. Instruction, equipment rental, ski shop, lodging, restaurant, lounge/bar, entertainment. *Glen Arbor, 8 mi north of Empire on Rte. M–22, tel. 616/334–5000.*

Indian Mountain Resort operates 18 runs, 5 chair lifts, 2 bar lifts, poma, Mighty Mite, and snowmaking; its longest run is 1 mile, with a vertical drop of 638 feet. Instruction, equipment rental, ski shop, lodging, restaurant, lounge/bar, heated outdoor pool. *One mi west of Wakefield on U.S. 2, tel. 800/346-3426.*

Marquette Mountain has 16 runs, 2 chair lifts, bar, rope tow, and snowmaking; its longest run is 1¼ miles, with a vertical drop of 600 feet. Instruction, equipment rental, ski shop, restaurant, lounge/bar, entertainment. *One mi south of Marquette on County Rd. 553, tel. 906/225-1155.*

Missaukee Mountain has 5 runs, 3 rope tows; its longest run is 1,300 feet. Equipment rental. *2 mi north of Lake City on Rte. M-66, tel. 616/839-7575.*

Mount McSauba Ski Hill has 3 runs, 3 rope tows, and snowmaking; vertical drop is 160 feet. Instruction, restaurant. *North Pointe, 1 mi off U.S. 31, Charlevoix, tel. 616/547-3267.*

Mount Ripley has 6 runs, chair lift, and a bar lift; vertical drop is 420 feet. Instruction, equipment rental, ski shop, restaurant. *U.S. 41, ½ mi east of Houghton, tel. 906/487-2340.*

Mount Zion has 5 runs, chair lift, and 2 rope tows; its longest run is ½ mile, with a vertical drop of 300 feet. Instruction, equipment rental, chalet, snacks. *Ironwood on Greenbush Rd., ½ mi north of U.S. 2, tel. 906/932-3718.*

Nub's Nob Ski Area has 19 runs, 5 chair lifts, rope tow, and snowmaking; its longest run is ¾ mile, with a vertical drop of 425 feet. Instruction, equipment rental, ski shop, lodging, restaurant, children's room, lounge/bar. *6 mi northeast of Harbor Springs on Rte. C-81, tel. 616/526-2131.*

Petoskey Winter Sports Park has 1 run, rope tow, and snowmaking; length of run 460 feet, vertical drop 100 feet. Snack bar, sledding hills, skating rinks. *200 Division, Petoskey, tel. 616/347-4105.*

Pine Mountain Lodge operates 15 runs, 3 chair lifts, rope tow, and snowmaking; its longest run is 3,000 feet, with a vertical drop of 450 feet. Instruction, equipment rental, ski shop, lodging, restaurant, lounge/bar, indoor pool. *N3332 Pine Mountain Rd., Iron Mountain, 2 mi northwest of downtown Iron Mountain, tel. 906/774-2747.*

Porcupine Mountains State Park has 13 runs, chair lift, 3 bar lifts, and 2 rope tows; its longest run is 1.1 miles, with a vertical drop of 600 feet. Instruction, equipment rental, ski shop, restaurant. *599 Rte. M-107, 15 mi west of U.S. 45 from Ontonagon, tel. 906/885-5275.*

Schuss Mountain has 32 runs, 6 chair lifts, 3 rope tows, and snowmaking; its longest run is 1 mile, with a vertical drop of 400 feet. Instruction, equipment rental, ski shop, lodging, restaurant, lounge/bar, indoor/outdoor heated pool. *Schuss Mountain Rd., Mancelona, U.S. 131 to Rte. M-88, 5 mi west of Mancelona, tel. 616/587-9162 or 800/632-7170.*

Ski Brule/Ski Homestead has 12 runs, 3 chair lifts, a bar lift, rope tow, pony lift, and snowmaking; its longest run is 1 mile, with a vertical drop of 480 feet. Instruction, equipment rental, ski shop, lodging, restaurant, lounge/bar, entertainment. *397 Brule Mountain Rd., Iron River, tel. 906/265–4957 or 800/338–7174.*

Sugar Loaf Resort has 20 runs, 5 chair lifts, a bar lift, and snowmaking; its longest run is 1 mile, with a vertical drop of 500 feet. Instruction, equipment rental, ski shop, lodging, restaurant, lounge/bar, entertainment, heated outdoor pool. *County Rd. 651, Cedar, 18 mi west of Traverse City, tel. 616/ 228–5461.*

Cross-country Skiing Many downhill ski areas and resorts have marked, groomed trails, as do several state parks. **Fayette State Park,** Garden, has five miles of intermediate-level trails; **Porcupine Mountains State Park** is popular with cross-country skiers.

4 Wisconsin

Introduction

Like the rest of the Upper Great Lakes region, Wisconsin remains mainly rural. Here the dairy cow is queen—there are still more cows than people in the state—and the annual milk production is a whopping 24 million pounds.

Wisconsin began to draw vacationers soon after the Civil War. H. H. Bennett's outstanding photographs of the scenic dells of the Wisconsin River made Wisconsin Dells, then called Kilbourn, a popular tourist attraction. It still is, but neither Bennett nor those 19th-century tourists would recognize the place today. Bennett's studio looks the same as it did in 1865, though, and you can visit it for free.

The lakes region just to the west of Milwaukee was prime resort country, popular with Chicago visitors until the growing city began to encroach and mass production of the automobile, coupled with an improving road system, made the north country more accessible.

Winter as a tourist season gained recognition shortly before World War II, when the first ski areas were opened "up north" (Wisconsinites describe every spot north of the Illinois border as up north) and the first "snow trains" ran from Chicago and Milwaukee to places like Rhinelander and Eagle River, which were previously summer-only resort communities. The idea began to catch on, and resorts on many lakes began to make arrangements for skating, hockey, iceboating, and ice fishing.

Then the snowmobile, more than anything else, turned Wisconsin into a year-round playground. The first "snowbuggies," old autos converted to run on skis and half-track treads, had appeared in the 1920s. The snowmobile as we know it today came out of Canada in the late 1950s and took the north country by storm. Within a decade, Wisconsin was home to six of the 23 major manufacturers, and snowmobile cruising, camping, and racing brought an end to the winter solitude in the north. Snowmobilers from throughout the USA and Canada gather each January at Eagle River's World Championship Snowmobile Derby. Races on the banked half-mile ice track, where speeds approach 100 mph, draw world-famous drivers, including entrants from European Formula 1 and Indy car ranks.

Snow has become white gold in Wisconsin. More than 50 ski areas offer complete facilities for a ski vacation, and cross-country ski trails are virtually everywhere. You can climb aboard a snowmobile at the state's southern border and travel more than 10,000 miles of trails without ever leaving the state.

The majority of Wisconsin's industrial centers are located along Lake Michigan: Green Bay, Manitowoc, Milwaukee, Racine, and Kenosha are all suburbs of the megalopolis that curves around Lake Michigan and stretches far to the east. Papermaking and woodworking industries thrive in the cities along the Wisconsin and Fox rivers.

In the southern third of the state, Wisconsin is rolling green hills and fields dotted with red or white barns and neat-as-a-pin farmhouses. The summer crops are hay, corn, and oats, most of which are fed back into the complex bovine machinery that produces the milk.

The southwestern corner of the state holds the lead and zinc deposits that brought overnight wealth and a population boom in the 1830s. Jefferson Davis and Zachary Taylor spent part of their military careers here, and the lead region had a population in the thousands while the fledgling Milwaukee was little more than a frontier trading post. Lead interests had much to do with organizing Wisconsin Territory in 1836 and bringing about statehood in 1848.

Central Wisconsin has pulpwood forests for paper production, potato farms, and cranberry bogs. Chances are you ate Wisconsin cranberries on Thanksgiving, for the state ranks high in the production of the berry. Here the Wisconsin River, billed as the nation's hardest working river, wends its way through millraces at paper mills and over dozens of dams, producing energy and cooling water for the manufacture of a mountain of paper.

Northern Wisconsin is the great north woods, the country of Paul Bunyan and Babe the Blue Ox, of the Nicolet and Chequamegon National Forests. Here, too, is the Gogebic iron range, which produced millions of tons of ore in the 19th century. In the north, summers are short, autumn shines so bright as to seem unreal, winters are long and brutal. There are places where more than a hundred inches of snow falls each year, and snowmobile suits are the height of fashion from November to April.

Everywhere in Wisconsin one finds water. At last count there were 14,927 lakes, covering nearly 1 million acres, not including lakes Michigan and Superior. Rivers? The state claims 2,444 trout streams and an additional 5,002 warm-water streams. Millions of anglers, all in search of the big one, visit the state each year, and many are successful.

There is no wrong time to visit Wisconsin, although most visitors come between Memorial Day and Labor Day. Autumn Colorama, which begins in the north in mid-September and moves slowly southward through October, draws more and more people each year. Yet even then, at midweek, you might easily find yourself with an attraction, a lake, even a whole forest, all to yourself.

Wisconsinites have a lot of good reasons to like themselves and where they live. After all, they gave the world Spencer Tracy, Harry Houdini, Elroy "Crazy Legs" Hirsch, the typewriter, malted milk, and the Republican Party.

Milwaukee

It was beer that made Milwaukee famous. Although the city's first brewers were English, by the 1840s Bavarian brewmasters dominated the industry. Pabst, Schlitz, and Blatz were among the earliest German breweries, and each began in similar fashion.

Jacob Best established the Empire Brewery in 1844, making beer with his brother and son. Captain Frederick Pabst married Best's niece and eventually took over the firm, giving it his name. John Braun started Milwaukee's second brewery in 1846; when he died, his foreman, Valentine Blatz, bought the business and in time married the Widow Braun. In 1849 August Krug started a third brewery; on his death, the firm's book-

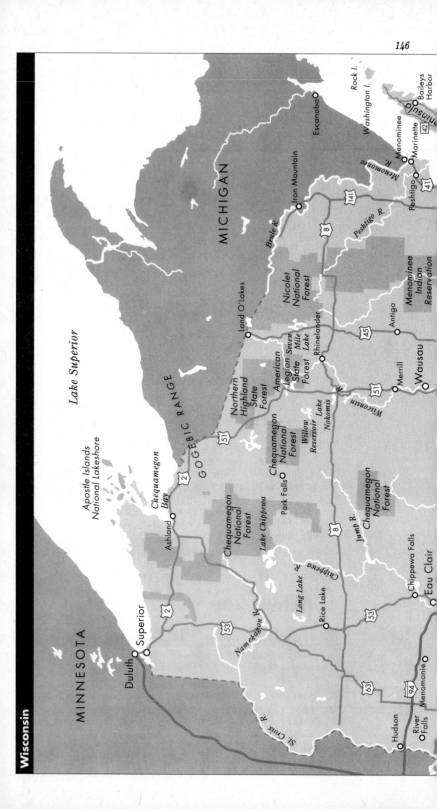

Wisconsin

MINNESOTA

Lake Superior

Apostle Islands
National Lakeshore

Duluth

Superior

MICHIGAN

Rock I.

Washington I.

Baileys
Harbor

Peninsula

Menominee

Marinette

42

Escanaba

Iron Mountain

Brule R.

Menominee R.

Peshtigo

141

41

8

Peshtigo R.

Land O'Lakes

Nicolet National Forest

Menominee Indian Reservation

GOGEBIC RANGE

Chequamegon Bay

Ashland

51

2

Northern Highland State Forest

American Legion State Forest

Seven Mile Lake

Rhinelander

45

Antigo

51

Wausau

Chequamegon National Forest

Willow Reservoir Lake Nokomis

Wisconsin R.

Merrill

Park Falls

Lake Chippewa

Chequamegon National Forest

Chequamegon National Forest

8

Jump R.

Chippewa Falls

Eau Clair

Long Lake

Chippewa R.

Rice Lake

53

Namekagon R.

63

River Falls

Menomonie

94

Hudson

St. Croix R.

53

2

keeper, Joseph Schlitz, wed Krug's widow. Meanwhile, Charles Best, Jacob Best's son, left the family enterprise to start a brewery of his own, later selling it to Frederic Miller, and, of course, the Miller name lives on.

By 1850, Milwaukee had a population of 20,061 and a dozen breweries, nearly all operated by Germans. Someone counted 255 saloons, 47 churches, and six temperance societies as well.

Although other industries have dethroned brewing as king in recent years, it remains synonymous with the city. Downtown Milwaukee still smells of malt and hops, and several lavish homes the early brewers built are now public museums. Two of the breweries, Miller and Pabst, are among the nation's largest. The city's beloved American League baseball team is named the Brewers. And not surprisingly, Milwaukee drinks more beer per capita than any other city in the nation.

Milwaukee's first settlers were Potawatomi Indians, who called the site the "Gathering Place by the Waters." The first European of record was a Northwest Fur Company agent named Jacques Vieau, who arrived with his wife and seven children in 1795. He built a cabin and trading post on the west bank of the Menominee River in what is now Mitchell Park, where he added six children to his brood.

When Vieau's daughter, 15-year-old Josette, married Solomon Juneau, a Frenchman who worked for her father, the young couple paddled a canoe more than 100 miles north to Green Bay to be married by the nearest priest. Upon returning to Milwaukee, they established a trading post on the east bank of the river. Jacques Vieau had moved on to Green Bay by the time land speculators arrived, so Solomon and Josette Juneau were credited as Milwaukee's official founders. Their home, situated at what became the intersection of Wisconsin Avenue and East Water Street, was used as an early government building; the site is now in the heart of the downtown financial district.

It is not clear when the city was first called Milwaukee. In 1679 a priest's journals mentioned a tribe of Indians living at the mouth of the "Millioki" River. Twenty years later, another priest on his way to "Chicagu" by way of Lake "Mie-sit-gan" was forced ashore in a storm and spent two days at "Melwarik." Juneau and other early settlers spelled the name of their settlement "Milwaukie." As the city grew, a controversy over the spelling caused bitter divisions between friends and relatives. As late as 1862 the post office was canceling letters with the Milwaukie spelling.

Most Indians were gone by the mid-1840s, but a few Potawatomi huts could still be found as late as 1854 in what is now downtown Milwaukee. The city's population in 1845 was about 10,000, more than half of German descent. Many Germans arrived in the 1850s, along with Italians, Poles, Scandinavians, Serbs, and Irish. By the last half of the 19th century, Milwaukee's German population was so large that the city was often called the German Athens. Only the Polish and Irish populations came close, and English was rarely heard in some neighborhoods, especially on the northwest side. Among the immigrants seeking a better life in Milwaukee late in the century was a young woman named Golda Meir; the public school at 1542 North 4th Street was renamed for her in 1979.

The German influence is still found throughout the city in architecture, in language, and especially in food, with a legacy of Old World restaurants.

With a population of about 636,000, Milwaukee is Wisconsin's largest city and the nation's 24th largest; it covers nearly 96 square miles and has more than 15 suburbs. Metropolitan Greater Milwaukee includes a four-county area with a population of nearly 1.4 million.

Thanks to the St. Lawrence Seaway, the city is an international seaport and the state's primary commercial and manufacturing center. Publishing has become a major business, and Milwaukee's graphic-arts field is considered outstanding. The city has 10 colleges and universities, including Marquette University and the University of Wisconsin–Milwaukee.

A small-town atmosphere prevails in Milwaukee, which is not so much a large city as a large collection of neighborhoods with respect for small-town values. Streets are clean, homes are tidy, parks and green spaces abound. Modern steel and glass high rises occupy much of the downtown area, but the early heritage persists in the restored and well-kept 19th-century buildings that share the city skyline.

Milwaukee is one of a handful of Midwest cities that has a skywalk system, so downtown visitors can walk from hotels to restaurants, shops, theaters, and sporting events without having to step outdoors. The Riverspan part of the system is the only skywalk in the nation built over a navigable waterway, the Milwaukee River.

The city claims over 50 ethnic groups and celebrates its "melting pot" origins with all kinds of ethnic and cultural festivals, along with the annual State Fair. Milwaukee has become known as the "city of festivals," stemming from the nationally known Summerfest, which kicks off each summer's activities on the lakefront.

Another annual highlight is the Great Circus Parade, a July spectacle that features scores of antique circus wagons from the famed Circus World Museum in Baraboo. Over a million people line the streets to watch it, and millions more view it on television.

Milwaukeeans are proud of their festivals, their 137 parks, the Brewers, the lakefront, the zoo, and the horticultural domes in Mitchell Park. There are good art and natural history museums. The Milwaukee Symphony plays at the Performing Arts Center, and there are top-notch opera, ballet, and repertory companies. The new Milwaukee Center, with its theaters, shops, office towers, and hotel (scheduled for completion in 1989) will broaden the cultural scene. Milwaukeeans will readily admit their city doesn't dazzle like Houston, or charm you like San Francisco. And they don't mind. At the same time the city lacks the hard edge of a Detroit or a Chicago, and they don't mind that, either.

Arriving and Departing

By Plane Milwaukee's **General Mitchell International Airport** (tel. 414/747–5300), six miles from downtown, is served by American, American Eagle, ComAir, Continental, Eastern, Midstate,

Midwest Express, Northwest, TWA, United, United Express, and USAir.

Between the Airport and Center City The Milwaukee County Transit System (tel. 414/344–6711) operates buses to and from the airport from 6 AM to 6:45 PM. The fare is $1.

Taxis to and from the airport take about 20 minutes; the fares range from $13 to $15. Airport limousine service fares range from $6 to downtown to about $10 to suburban hotels. Courtesy cars to many major hotels can be called by direct phones at the airport.

To travel by car from the airport, take I–94 north to the I–43 interchange and exit right at Michigan Avenue (one block), Wisconsin Avenue (two blocks), or Wells Street (three blocks) into downtown Milwaukee.

By Train **Amtrak,** 433 W. St. Paul Avenue (tel. 414/933–3081 or 800/872–7245), connects Milwaukee by rail to all parts of the USA and Canada. Daily service to Chicago and Minneapolis/St. Paul.

By Bus The **Greyhound Bus Terminal** is at 606 N. 7th Street (tel. 414/272–8900 or 800/528–0447). The **Trailways** station is at 1200 W. Wells Street (tel. 414/273–5757 or 800/242–2935).

By Car From the north, I–43 provides controlled access into downtown Milwaukee. I–94 provides direct access to downtown from Chicago and other points south. I–94 is also the controlled-access highway into the city from the west. I–894 bypasses the metropolitan area to the south and west and provides the best connection for the I–94 east–west, north–south corridor.

Getting Around

To understand Milwaukee's street system, you should know that Lake Michigan is the city's eastern boundary and that Wisconsin Avenue is the main east–west thoroughfare. The Milwaukee River divides the downtown area into east and west sections. The East–West Expressway (I–94/I–794) is the dividing line between north and south. Streets are numbered in ascending order from the Milwaukee River west well into the suburbs to the Milwaukee County line.

The speed limit in the city is 25 mph unless otherwise posted. Rush hours are from 7 to 9 AM and 3:30 to 6 PM. Right turns are permitted on red unless otherwise posted.

Many downtown attractions are situated near the Milwaukee River and can be reached by walking. The *Greater Milwaukee Dining & Visitors Guide* contains a good map of the downtown area; it is available from the Greater Milwaukee Convention & Visitors Bureau, at the airport, and at most major hotels.

By Bus All Milwaukee County buses run 24 hours a day, although less frequently after the evening rush hour on weekdays, and on weekends. Schedule and route information is available at the **Milwaukee County Transit System** (1942 N. 17th St., tel. 414/344–6711). The fare is $1; ages 6–11, 50¢. Exact fare required.

By Taxi Taxis use a meter system. The fare is $2.50 for the first mile and $1.25 for each additional mile. Taxis can be ordered by phone or at taxi stands at most major hotels. Some taxi firms accept major credit cards.

Important Addresses and Numbers

Tourist Information
The **Greater Milwaukee Convention & Visitors Bureau** (756 N. Milwaukee St., 53202, tel. 414/273–7222) is at the corner of Milwaukee Street and E. Mason Street, four blocks east of the Milwaukee River. Open weekdays 8:30–5. For a taped message on events in the area, call 414/799–1177.

The **Tourist Information Center** at Mitchell International Airport (tel. 414/747–4808) is open weekdays at 7:30 AM–9:30 PM, Saturday 10–6, and Sunday 1–9:30.

The suburban **Wauwatosa Visitor Information Center** (225 N. Mayfair Rd., tel. 414/453–1150) is open Monday–Saturday 8–5 and Sunday 8–4.

The **Milwaukee *Journal* and *Sentinel* Public Service Bureau** (333 W. State St., tel. 414/224–2120) also offers tourist information weekdays 8–5.

Emergencies
Tel. 414/765–2323.

Opening and Closing Times

Banks
Usually open weekdays 9–5.

Museums
Usually open weekdays 9–5, Saturday 10–5, Sunday 1–5. See individual listings.

Shops
Most stores are open weekdays 9–6, Saturdays 9–5, and closed Sundays. Most shopping malls are open weekdays 9–9, Saturdays 9–6, Sundays noon–5.

Guided Tours

Orientation Tours
The **Milwaukee County Transit System** (tel. 414/937–3250) offers four-hour summer sightseeing bus tours of the lakefront, historic sites, and the city's neighborhoods, with stops at the Mitchell Park horticultural domes and the Pabst or Miller brewery. Tours in air-conditioned buses leave Monday–Saturday from the Holiday Inn West (201 N. Mayfair Rd., tel. 414/771–4400); the Marc Plaza Hotel (509 W. Wisconsin Ave., tel. 414/271–7250); and the Hyatt Regency (333 W. Kilbourn Ave., tel. 414/276–1234). Fare: $9 adults, $7 senior citizens, and children under 12.

Emerald Isle Cruise Line (tel. 414/786–6886) offers narrated waterfront tours from May to November. The 250-passenger boat departs from 333 N. Water Street several times daily; Sunday brunch and weekend dinner cruises are available.

Iroquois Harbor Cruises (tel. 414/332–4194) offers daily afternoon cruises of Milwaukee's harbor on the 149-passenger *Iroquois* from late June until Labor Day. Ninety-minute tours leave at 1 and 3 PM from docks at the Clybourn Street bridge on the west bank of the Milwaukee River.

Lunch and dinner cruises aboard the 300-passenger *Star of Milwaukee* (tel. 414/273–7827) leave from the Municipal Pier, just south of the Milwaukee Art Museum, every day from May through October.

Walking Tours
Historic Milwaukee, Inc., ArchiTours (tel. 414/277–7795) conducts one-hour walking tours of the city's first settlements:

Juneautown, Kilbourntown, Walker's Point, or the east side mansion areas of Yankee Hill and Water Tower. The **Greater Milwaukee Convention & Visitors Bureau** (tel. 414/273–7222) offers free self-guided walking tour maps of downtown Milwaukee's historic Third Ward. Guided and self-guided walking tours of the suburb of West Allis are offered by **West Allis Walking Tour** (8405 W. National Ave., tel. 414/321–3687). Campus tours are offered at the University of Wisconsin–Milwaukee (tel. 414/963–4572) and Marquette University (tel. 414/224–7302).

Exploring Milwaukee

Numbers in the margin correspond with points of interest on the Milwaukee maps.

Milwaukee's central business district is a mile long and only a few blocks wide. We have divided the downtown area into two districts: east and west of the Milwaukee River. Sightseeing on foot is easy, but be sure to wait at crosswalks for the Walk signal. Some attractions are outside the downtown area, and most visitors will want to reach those by car or public transportation.

East On the east side of the river, start at the **Greater Milwaukee**
❶ **Convention & Visitors Bureau** at the corner of N. Milwaukee Street and E. Mason Street to pick up maps, brochures, and listings of events.

❷ The **Iron Block Building** at the corner of N. Water Street and E. Wisconsin Avenue is one of the few remaining iron-clad buildings in the United States. The metal facade was brought in by ship from an eastern foundry. Put up during the Civil War, the four-story building was recently restored to its original white color.

In the 1860s Milwaukee exported more wheat than any other port in the world, which gave impetus to building the **Grain Ex-**
❸ **change Room** in the **Mackie Building** (1879). The carved likeness of Mercury, the Roman god of trade and commerce (and messenger to the gods), is wedged between the granite pillars flanking the entrance. The 10,000-square-foot trading room has three-story-high columns and painted ceiling panels that feature Wisconsin wildflowers. A mural depicts classical figures representing Trade, Industry, and Agriculture. The models for the women in the mural were Milwaukee society ladies. *225 E. Michigan Ave., tel. 414/272–6230. Admission free. Open weekdays 8:30–5.*

❹ The **Milwaukee Art Museum** is in the lakefront War Memorial Center designed by Eero Saarinen. The museum's permanent collection is strong in European and American art of the 19th and 20th centuries, German Expressionism, and the Bradley collection of modern masters. There are works by Degas, Toulouse-Lautrec, Miró, Picasso, Georgia O'Keeffe, and Andy Warhol, along with designs by Frank Lloyd Wright. Programs include art films, lectures, and Sunday tours. There is a lunch room. The grounds offer an ideal view of Milwaukee's scenic lakefront. *750 N. Lincoln Memorial Dr., tel. 414/271–9508. Admission: $3 adults, $1.50 students and seniors over 59. Free, children under 12 accompanied by an adult. Open Tues., Wed., Fri., and Sat. 10–5, Thurs. noon–9, Sun. 1–6; closed Jan. 1, Thanksgiving, Dec. 25.*

⑤ On your way back to the river, rest a moment at **Cathedral Square.** This quiet park (at E. Kilbourn Ave. and Jefferson St.)
⑥ was built on the site of Milwaukee's first courthouse. **St. John's Cathedral,** across the street, was the first church built in Wisconsin specifically as a Roman Catholic cathedral. Dedicated in 1853, it is one of the city's oldest church buildings.

As you cross the river to the west side, notice that the east side and west side streets in this old section of town are not directly opposite each other and that the bridges across the Milwaukee River are built at an angle. This layout dates from the 1840s, when the area east of the river was called Juneautown and the region to the west was known as Kilbourntown. The rival communities had a fierce argument over which would pay for the bridges that connected them, and the antagonism was so intense that citizens venturing into rival territory carried white flags. The Great Bridge War was finally settled by the state legislature in 1845, but the streets on either side of the river never were aligned.

Both banks of the Milwaukee River are busy in summer, especially at noon, when downtown workers lunch in the nearby parks and public areas. It's a perfect place for people-watching
⑦ and getting a sense of everyday Milwaukee. **Pere Marquette Park,** named for the venerable Father Jacques Marquette (who may have camped here in 1674) and situated next to the river at Old World 3rd Street and W. Kilbourn Avenue, is a pleasant place to spend a summertime noon hour.

⑧ Adjacent to the park is the **Milwaukee County Historical Center.** Housed in a graceful former bank building (circa 1913), the museum features horse-drawn and early fire-fighting equipment, toys, fashions, an old-time doctor's office, an early drug store, and exhibits on military history and banking. Photographs and audiovisual presentations document Milwaukee's growth. The center houses a research library containing naturalization records and genealogical resources. *910 N. Old World 3rd St., tel. 414/273–8288. Admission free. Open weekdays 9:30–5, Sat. 10–5, Sun. 1–5. Closed holidays.*

⑨ The **Spirit of Milwaukee Theater** offers a multimedia presentation that highlights the sights and sounds of both historic and contemporary Milwaukee. It gives an especially good sense of what's going on in the city and its neighborhoods today, from the carillon bells at Marquette University to race cars at State Fair Park. *275 W. Wisconsin Ave. in the lower level of the Grand Avenue Mall, tel. 414/271–7122. Admission: $2.50 adults, $1.50 children 6–12 and seniors, $6.50 family. Half-hour shows begin at a quarter past the hour, weekdays 10:15–7:15, Sat. 10:15–5:15, Sun. 12:15–4:15.*

⑩ The **Milwaukee Public Museum,** at the corner of W. Wells and 7th streets, has the fourth largest collection of natural history exhibits in the country. The Streets of Old Milwaukee walk-through exhibit depicts the city in the 1890s, with a general store, corner saloon, and Milwaukee's earliest shops. There is also a walk-through European village, and the Third Planet (complete with full-size dinosaurs), where visitors walk into the interior of the earth to learn about its history and the forces that continue to change it. The Wizard Wing has hands-on natural and human history exhibits for children and families. *800 W. Wells St., tel. 414/278–2700. Admission: $3 adults, $1.50*

Milwaukee Metropolitan Area

Lake Michigan

SHOREWOOD

ST. FRANCIS

N. Lake Dr.

S. Lake Ave.

S. Packard Ave.

N. Downer Ave.

N. Oakland Ave.

Superior St.

S. Kinnickinnic Ave.

Pennsylvania Ave.

Whitnall Ave.

Layton Ave.

Mitchell Field

Milwaukee River

SEE DOWNTOWN MAP

S. Chase Ave.

Green Bay Rd.

W. Atkinson Ave.

N. Teutonia Ave.

W. Hopkins St.

Fond du Lac Ave.

N. 16th St.

Marquette University

S. National Ave.

S. Layton Blvd.

S. 6th St.

N. 27th St.

W. Wisconsin Ave.

S. 27th St.

Capitol Dr.

Roosevelt

Center St.

North Ave.

W. Burnham St.

W. Lincoln Ave.

S. 43rd St.

W. Oklahoma Ave.

Howard Ave.

Forest Ave.

W. Loomis Rd.

Cold Spring Rd.

W. Edgerton Ave.

N. 60th St.

W. Milwaukee

Milwaukee County Stadium

Blue Mound Rd.

Greenfield Ave.

S. 60th St.

S. 76th St.

GREENFIELD

W. Appleton Ave.

W. Lisbon Ave.

Wauwatosa Ave.

N. 92nd St.

W. Beloit Rd.

S. 84th St.

S. 92nd St.

S. 108th St.

WAUWATOSA

Plank Rd.

Watertown Plank Rd.

N. 108th St.

Zoo Fwy.

N. 124th St.

WEST ALLIS

S. 108th St.

S. 124th St.

Lilly Rd.

Burleigh St.

ELM GROVE

Sunny Slope Rd.

W. Cleveland Ave.

Pilgrim Rd.

North Ave.

Gerhardt Rd.

BROOKFIELD

Capitol Dr.

Brookfield Rd.

Blue Mound Rd.

Greenfield Ave.

Moorland Rd.

Calhoun Rd.

NEW BERLIN

Barkar Rd.

Coffee St.

N

2 miles

3 km

0

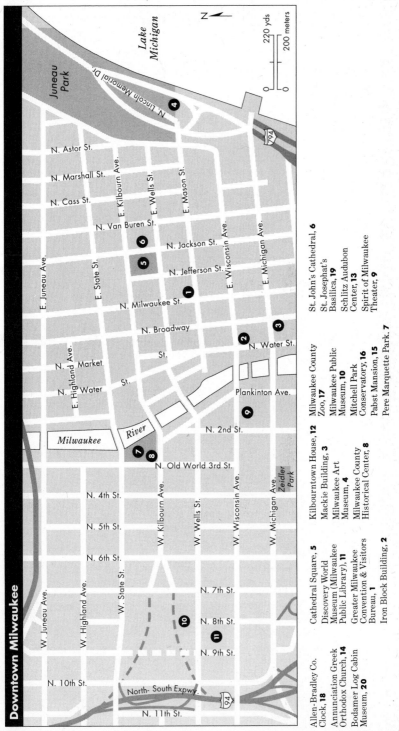

children 4–17, $8 family. Open daily 9–5 (Wizard Wing 10–3).
Closed Jan. 1, Thanksgiving, Dec. 25.

Time Out **Wales on Wells** (1508 W. Wells St.), a Marquette campus favorite, is one of the best places in town for hamburgers, served
chargrilled with sautéed onions, for just $1.39.

⓫ Anyone with a science bent will be intrigued by the **Discovery
World—Museum of Science, Economics and Technology** in the
Milwaukee Public Central Library. Here is a wide range of exhibits on magnets, motors, electricity, and computers that are
designed to be touched; it also has the Great Electric Show and
the Light Wave–Laser Beam Show on Saturday and Sunday.
The gift shop is crammed with science goodies. *818 W. Wisconsin Ave., tel. 414/765–9966. Admission: $2 adults, $1 children
under 17, students, and senior citizens, free children under 5.
Great Electric Show and Light Wave–Laser Show, $1.50
adults, $1 children under 17, students, and senior citizens.
Open Tues.–Sat. 9–5, Sun. 1–5; closed Jan. 1, Thanksgiving,
Dec. 25.*

North The **Kilbourntown House,** built in 1844, is an excellent example
⓬ of temple-style Greek Revival architecture and the light-
colored brick that gave Milwaukee its Cream City nickname.
Once slated for destruction, the building was saved and moved
from Kilbourntown, one of the city's original settlements, to its
present site in 1938. During restoration, three fireplaces were
uncovered. Doric columns and exterior walls of hand-hewn
beams and brick give the structure a feeling of strength, while
the furnishings reflect the decor of its time. Displays include an
outstanding collection of mid-19th-century furniture and decorative arts. Ice cream socials and other public events are often
held on weekends. *4400 W. Estabrook Dr., tel. 414/273–8288.
Admission free. Open late June–Labor Day, Tues., Thurs.,
and Sat. 10–5, Sun. 1–5.*

⓭ The **Schlitz Audubon Center** is a 186-acre wildlife area of forests, ponds, marshlands, and nature trails that was once the
domain of the horses of the Joseph Schlitz Brewing Co. Popular
with cross-country skiers in winter and bird-watchers year-
round, this restful spot on the Lake Michigan shoreline is only
minutes from downtown. The interpretive center offers natural
history exhibits and unadvertised drop-in nature programs on
weekends during the summer. *1111 E. Brown Deer Rd., tel.
414/352–2880. Admission: $1.50 adults, 75¢ children under 13
and senior citizens over 65. Open Tues.–Sun. 9–5; closed Mon.
and holidays.*

⓮ The **Annunciation Greek Orthodox Church** was Frank Lloyd
Wright's last major work; the famed Wisconsin architect called
it his "little jewel." As such, the blue-domed, saucer-shaped
church has drawn visitors from all over the world since it
opened in 1961. *9400 W. Congress St., tel. 414/461–9400. Tours
by appointment, $1.*

West The **Pabst Mansion,** built for the beer baron Captain Frederick
⓯ Pabst, is one of Milwaukee's treasured landmarks and a prime
example of how Milwaukee's early wealthy lived. Pabst, who
came from Germany at age 12, was a Great Lakes sailor until he
married into the Best brewing family. He became one of
Milwaukee's leading and wealthiest citizens. His castle-like,
Flemish Renaissance–style Pabst Mansion, built in 1893 for

$225,000, has a tan pressed-brick exterior, decorated with carved stone and terra-cotta ornamentation. The 37 rooms, with 12 baths and 14 fireplaces, feature carved cabinets and woodwork by the Matthews Brothers, ornamental iron work by Cyril Colnik, marble, tile, and stained glass, along with carved panels imported from a 17th-century Bavarian castle. Captain Pabst's study and a pavilion originally used at the Columbian Exposition in Chicago are a tribute to the buying power of the 1893 dollar. Friendly docents provide informative tours that take about 90 minutes. Holiday activities in December draw the largest crowds of the year. *2000 W. Wisconsin Ave., tel. 414/931–0808. Admission: $4 adults, $2.50 children 6–16, under 6 free. Open Mar. 15–Dec. 31, Mon.–Sat. 10–3:30, Sun. noon–3:30; Jan. 1–Mar. 14, Sat. 10–3:30, Sun. noon–3:30; closed major holidays.*

16 Ask for directions to the **Mitchell Park Conservatory** and you may get stares from lifelong Milwaukeeans. But ask about the "domes," and you'll get instant recognition. A unique horticultural structure, the Mitchell Park Conservatory consists of three massive glass domes housing tropical, arid, and seasonal plant and flower exhibits. The complex was built between 1959 and 1967. Each dome is 140 feet wide and 85 feet high, covering an area of 15,000 square feet. The displays of lilies at Easter and poinsettias at Christmas are spectacular. A map of the plantings and exhibits included with admission enables visitors to take a self-guided tour of the domes. *524 S. Layton Blvd., tel. 414/649–9800. Admission: $2 adults, $1 under 18. Open Memorial Day–Labor Day, Mon.–Thurs. and Sat. and Sun. 9–8, Fri. 9–5; Sept.–May, weekdays 9–5, weekends 9–8.*

17 The **Milwaukee County Zoo,** one of the finest in the world, houses about 4,000 wild animals and birds, including many endangered species. Within the zoo is a Children's Zoo (open Memorial Day to Labor Day) where youngsters can pet and feed baby and farm animals. Twenty-minute educational programs are presented several times daily, weather permitting. A schedule is provided with admission. You can take a narrated tour of the zoo aboard the Zoomobile, or enjoy a miniature train ride. Pony, camel, and elephant rides are offered. There are picnic areas and food services, and a three-mile cross-country ski trail. Rides are not included in the admission price. Allow four to six hours to see the entire zoo. *10001 W. Bluemound Rd., tel. 414/771–3040. Admission: $3.50 adults, $1.50 children under 16 and senior citizens. Parking: $2. Stroller and wheelchair rentals available. Open Memorial Day–Labor Day, Mon.–Sat. 9–5, Sun. and holidays 9–6; Sept.–May, daily 9–4:30; closed Jan. 1, Thanksgiving, Dec. 25.*

South **18** The **Allen-Bradley Co. clock** (1201 S. 2nd St.) is a Milwaukee landmark and, according to the *Guinness Book of World Records,* "the largest four-faced clock in the world." Each of its octagon-shape faces is nearly twice the area of London's Big Ben. It is actually four clocks, one in each side of the tower atop the Allen-Bradley Co. headquarters and research laboratory. The clock is some 300 feet above street level, and on a clear night the lighted faces can be seen nearly halfway across Lake Michigan. Ships sometimes use the clock as a navigational reference point.

19 **St. Josephat's Basilica,** built at the turn of the century, is adorned with a remarkable collection of relics, portraits of Polish saints and leaders, stained glass, and wood carvings. Its dome, modeled after St. Peter's in Rome, is reputed to be one of the five largest in the world. Elevated to basilica status in 1929, it is the first Polish basilica in North America. *2336 S. 6th St., tel. 414/645–5623.*

㉒ Bodamer Log Cabin Museum, built in 1833, was hidden away under layers of lath, plaster, and siding for decades. It had acquired an additional 1½ stories over the years, along with additional rooms and porches, until the original structure was unrecognizable. When restoration work began in 1966, the logs were found to be as sound as when they were first put in place. The building is furnished as it was in pioneer days. *South 56th St. and W. Layton Ave., Greenfield, tel. 414/543–3324. Admission free. Open May–Oct., Sun. 2–4:30 PM.*

Milwaukee for Free

Brewery Tours. The **Miller Brewing Co.** *4251 W. State St., tel. 414/931–2153. 1-hour tours on the hour April–Oct., Mon.–Sat. 9–3; Nov.–Mar., weekdays 9–3; closed Sun. and holidays.* **Pabst Brewery.** 915 W. Juneau Ave., tel. 414/223–3709. 40-min tours on the hour June–Aug., weekdays 10–3, Sat. 9–11 *AM; Sept.–May, weekdays 10–3.* **Sprecher Brewing Co.** *730 W. Ogden St., tel. 414/272–2337.*

If Milwaukee's **City Hall** looks vaguely familiar, it's probably because it used to be shown in the opening sequence of the *Laverne and Shirley* TV show. Built in 1895, it is striking for its soaring bell tower and the ornately carved woodwork and stenciled ceilings in the Common Council chamber and anteroom. *200 E. Wells St., tel. 414/278–2221. Open weekdays 8–4:45; guided tours by appointment; closed major holidays.*

The **Charles Allis Art Museum** occupies an elegant Tudor home designed in 1909 for the first president of the Allis-Chalmers Manufacturing Co. As you enter, look up at the three-tiered stained glass window by Louis Comfort Tiffany. The art exhibited throughout the furnished house includes Chinese porcelains dating from 300 BC, graphics by Dürer, Rembrandt, and Whistler, and landscapes by Homer, Gainsborough, and Corot. *1801 N. Prospect Ave., tel. 414/278–8295. Open Wed.–Sun. 1–5, Wed. 7–9 PM; closed holidays.*

The **American Geographical Society Collection** is exceptional—maps, old globes, atlases and charts, plus 180,000 books and 400,000 journals, all housed in the third-floor east wing of the **Golda Meir Library** on the University of Wisconsin–Milwaukee campus. *2311 E. Hartford Ave., tel. 414/963–6282. Open weekdays 8–5, Sat. 8–noon.*

The **University of Wisconsin–Milwaukee Art Museum** displays the university's permanent art collection, changing exhibits, and works by students and faculty. *3253 N. Donner Ave., tel. 414/963–5070/6509. Open weekdays 10–4, Sun. 1–4.*

The **Haggerty Museum of Art** houses the Marquette University collection and represents nearly 100 years of donations. Its highlight is the Bible series of 105 hand-colored etchings by Marc Chagall. *12th St. and Wisconsin Ave. on the campus mall between Wisconsin Ave. and Clybourn St., tel. 414/224–1669. Open weekdays 10–4:30, Sat. noon–4:30, Sun. noon–5; closed Dec. 24 and 25, Jan. 1 and 2.*

The internationally famous **Boerner Botanical Garden** is part of Whitnall Park, one of the largest municipal parks in the nation. From April through September, the formal and informal gardens are ablaze with brilliant roses, perennials, annuals, wildflowers, and herbs. Nature and hiking trails, cross-country skiing, and picnicking are available. An administrative building holds art exhibits and planting displays. During the summer, there are weekly concerts. *5879 S. 92nd St., tel. 414/425–1130. Open summer, daily 8 AM–sunset; winter, weekdays 8–4.*

The **Wehr Nature Center** in the southwest corner of Whitnall Park includes wildlife exhibits, woodlands and wetlands, a 20-acre lake, more than four miles of nature trails, and wild gardens. Seasonal hikes and lectures are conducted by naturalists. *98th and College Ave., tel. 414/425–8551. Open daily 8–4:30; closed day after Thanksgiving, Dec. 24 and 25.*

What to See and Do with Children

Discovery World Museum (*see* Exploring Milwaukee).

Milwaukee Public Museum, Wizard Wing (*see* Exploring Milwaukee).

Milwaukee Public Library Discovery World Museum (*see* Exploring Milwaukee).

First Stage Milwaukee (*see* The Arts).

Milwaukee Brewers Baseball (*see* Spectator Sports).

Milwaukee County Zoo (*see* Exploring Milwaukee).

W. K. Walthers, Inc., manufacturer of model railroad equipment since 1932, offers railroad buffs the largest single warehouse selection of trains in the world, with over 300 manufacturers represented. There is a retail counter, and warehouse tours. *N. 60th St. and Florist Ave., 4 blocks north of Silver Spring Dr. on 60th St., tel. 414/527–0770.*

Milwaukee County Parks offer a variety of ways for youngsters to let off steam. There are 39 wading pools, 17 outdoor swimming pools, and 3 indoor pools. Thirty-two parks have outdoor ice-skating on either natural lagoons or land rinks.

Wilson Recreation Center (4001 S. 20th St., tel. 414/257–6100) has indoor ice-skating year-round.

Ethnic Festivals are always in season, and many have attractions and activities for youngsters. Pick up a calendar of events at the Convention & Visitors Bureau. For a taped message on events in Greater Milwaukee, tel. 414/799–1177.

Off the Beaten Track

St. Joan of Arc Chapel, on the central mall of Marquette University campus, is a 15th-century chapel that was moved from its original site near Lyons, France, and reconstructed here in 1964. One of the stones was reputedly kissed by Joan before she went to her death, and is said to be discernibly colder than the others. *601 N. 14th St., tel. 414/224–7039. Admission free. Open daily 10–4, closed Jan. 1, Thanksgiving, Dec. 24 and 25.*

Famous Amos Cookie Studio has hand-baked cookies served in a Hawaiian atmosphere. You can get a free sample and sing along with master kazoo players. *Mitchell International Airport, 5300 S. Howell Ave., tel. 414/481–2800.*

Goldman's Department Store, right out of the 1920s with wooden floors and balcony merchandise displays, is a Milwaukee legend. *930 W. Mitchell St., tel. 414/645–9100.*

Forest Home Cemetery is the grave site of the 19th-century beer barons Joseph Schlitz, Captain Frederick Pabst, Jacob Best, and Valentine Blatz. Markers range from simple marble tablets to neoclassical monuments. A map is free at the cemetery office. *2405 W. Forest Home Ave., tel. 414/645–2632. Open weekdays 8–4:30, Sat. 8:30–noon.*

Shopping

Stores range from tiny ethnic and specialty shops to enclosed shopping malls featuring large department stores. Using the downtown skywalk system, it's possible to browse in hundreds of stores over several blocks without once setting foot outside. Large shopping malls are also situated downtown and in the outlying suburbs. The sales tax is 5%.

Shopping Districts Downtown Milwaukee's major shopping street is Wisconsin Avenue west of the Milwaukee River. The **Grand Avenue Mall** stretches east from Marshall Field's at the river to the Boston Store on Wisconsin Avenue. This four-block-long, multilevel shopping area, linked entirely by skywalks, features about 150 specialty shops and restaurants. Among the buildings in the center is the restored **Plankington Arcade,** a spacious skylighted promenade in the Old World tradition. *Open weekdays 10–8, Sat. 10–6, Sun. 12–5.*

The red brick paved streets of **Old World 3rd Street,** running north from Wisconsin Avenue to Highland Avenue, are a throwback to the streets of Old Milwaukee. The heart of Milwaukee's old German business district, this neighborhood includes many ethnic stores and restaurants, and such Milwaukee landmarks as **Usinger's Famous Sausage** and the **Wisconsin Cheese Mart.** Many stores here are closed on Sundays.

East of the river, you'll find restored 19th-century shops and ethnic stores clustered near the Pfister Hotel and along Jefferson Street between East Mason and East Wells streets. Donner Avenue between East Webster and East Park streets is another popular east-side shopping location.

Shopping centers in the metropolitan area include **Bayshore** (5900 N. Port Washington Rd.), **Brookfield Square** (95 N. Moorland Rd.), **Capital Court** (5500 W. Capitol Dr.), **Mayfair** (2500 N. Mayfair Rd.), **Northridge** (7700 W. Brown Deer Rd.), **Point Loomis** (3555 S. 27th St.), **Southgate** (3333 S. 27th St.) and **South Ridge** (5300 S. 76th St.).

Department Stores The **Boston Store** (331 W. Wisconsin Ave., tel. 414/347–4141) is one of Milwaukee's fine old stores, offering quality merchandise and service. A stalwart of the Grand Avenue Mall, it has branches in most metropolitan shopping centers.

Marshall Field's. Another well-known name, a bit trendy, anchoring the east end of the Grand Avenue Mall.

Specialty Stores The **Milwaukee Antique Center** (341 N. Milwaukee St., tel. 414/
Antiques 276–0605) is a long-established center with three floors of an-

tiques and collectibles, the wares of 75 antique dealers. Great for unusual, unexpected gifts.

Apropo Antique Furniture and Consignment Center (316 N. Milwaukee St., tel. 414/272–5311) has a comprehensive selection of antique furnishings.

Art Dealers The **David Barnet Gallery** (1024 E. State St., tel. 414/271–5058) specializes in 19th- and 20th-century European and American masters and Wisconsin artists.

Katie Gringrass Gallery (714 N. Milwaukee St., tel. 414/289–0855) has a varied selection of works by Wisconsin artists and others.

Auctions and Flea Markets Offerings range from fabulous estate sales to backyard junk. Auctions are held regularly at **Broadway Auction Gallery** (513 N. Broadway St., tel. 414/276–3620), **Milwaukee Auction Galleries Ltd.** (4747 W. Bradley Rd., tel. 414/355–5054), **New Berlin Auction and Sales Barn** (17655 W. National Ave., tel. 414/679–0780), and **Travis Auction Galleries** (1422 Underwood Ave., tel. 414/453–0342).

The garage or yard sale has become a weekend participant sport in residential neighborhoods. The offerings range from treasure to trash. It's best to concentrate on one region and go early. Check the *Journal* or *Sentinel* newspapers for listings.

Books **Harry W. Schwartz Booksellers** (209 W. Wisconsin and Grand Aves., tel. 414/274–6400) is Milwaukee's largest, most complete bookstore.

Renaissance Book Shop (834 N. Plankinton Ave., tel. 414/271–6850) has five floors of secondhand books. There is a branch at the airport.

Cheese The **West Allis Cheese and Sausage Shop** (6832 W. Becher St., West Allis, tel. 414/543–4230) is a country-style store offering 40 Wisconsin cheeses and gift packages.

Wisconsin Cheese Mart, Inc. (215 W. Highland Ave. at Old World 3rd St., tel. 414/272–3544) offers Wisconsin cheese, honey, jellies, mustard, and other delicacies.

China **George Watts and Son, Inc.** (761 N. Jefferson St., tel. 414/276–6352), offers china, silver, crystal, stoneware, stainless steel, casual glass, and art objects.

Chocolate **Ambrosia Chocolate Co.** (6th St. and Highland Ave., tel. 414/271–5774), established by Otto Schoenleber in 1894, is called the world's biggest manufacturer of bulk chocolate. The largest selection of chocolate and candies in Wisconsin can be found at the company's outlet store here.

Royale Gourmet Products (11308 W. Greenfield Ave., West Allis, tel. 414/771–8448) is a "turn-of-the-century" candy shop. Watch them make fudge, chocolate-covered potato chips, and candies.

Clocks **Alpine Boutique & Christmas Chalet** (8400 Capitol Dr., tel. 414/461–3322) has a wide variety of Alpine items: beer steins, nutcrackers, cuckoo clocks, Christmas ornaments.

Cosmetics **Natural Cosmetics** (Grand Ave. Mall, tel. 414/765–9121) offers an extensive cosmetics and treatment line, including beauty aids, manicures, and pedicures.

Crafts The **Mitchell Street Cooperative** (812 Mitchell St., tel. 414/672–3998) sells the work of more than 25 local artisans and immigrant crafts people, including hand-knit woolens, embroidery, porcelain dolls, and stained glass.

Easter Seal Home Craft Shop (623 N. Milwaukee St., tel. 414/272–0378) offers handmade gifts and toys, country crafts, and hard-to-find wooden toys. The shop features the work of Wisconsin's homebound disabled.

Cutlery **Arenz Cutlery** (101 E. Wells St., tel. 414/272–2217) offers fine German cutlery.

Jewelry **Schmitter Burg Co.** (324 E. Wisconsin Ave., tel. 414/273–7760) has good values.

Schwanke Kasten Co. (324 E. Silver Spring Dr., tel. 414/964–1242) has been in business since 1899.

Leather and **Mitchell Manufacturing** (249 N. Water St., tel. 414/272–5942)
Luggage supplies leather jackets, handbags, and luggage.

Meats **Usinger's Famous Sausage** (1030 N. 3rd St., tel. 414/276–9100) sells more than 75 kinds of cold cuts and fine sausages.

Men's Apparel **Polacheck's Clothiers** (227 E. Wisconsin Ave., tel. 414/271–1007) provides a fine line of traditional men's clothing.

Roger Stevens (428 E. Wisconsin Ave., tel. 414/277–9010), on the ground floor of the Pfister Hotel, is Milwaukee's leading men's store.

UOMO, Inc. (777 N. Jefferson St., tel. 414/273–2340), offers a wide selection of contemporary men's wear.

Outdoor Equipment **Laacke & Joys** (1433 N. Water St., tel. 414/271–7878) supplies outdoor clothing and equipment for skiing, camping, fishing, and specialized sports. The company manufactures Wildwood tents and canvas products.

Women's Apparel **Clothes Rack** (203 N. Water St., tel. 414/224–4951) has fine women's apparel with designer labels as well as sportswear, suits, and accessories.

The **Executive Gallery** (1026 E. State St., tel. 414/273–7788) sells sophisticated business clothing for professional women in an 1875 Victorian mansion near Lake Michigan.

Talbots Sale Store (8320 W. Brown Deer Rd., tel. 414/354–3044) discounts women's clothing, accessories, and footwear. This is the final selling point for the firm's catalogue overbuys and excess merchandise.

Sports and Fitness

Beaches and Lake Michigan is the place to swim, but be prepared: The mid-
Water Sports summer water temperature is only in the 50s and 60s and the wind adds to the chill. Among the most popular beaches are **Bradford Beach** (2400 N. Lincoln Memorial Dr., tel. 414/961–9799), **Doctors Beach** (1870 E. Fox Ln. in Fox Point, tel. 414/352–9949), **Grant Beach** (100 Hawthorne Ave., South Milwaukee, tel. 414/762–9907), **McKinley Beach** (1750 N. Lincoln Memorial Dr., tel. 414/257–6100), and **South Shore Beach** (2900 South Shore Dr., tel. 414/747–9108).

Bicycling A 76-mile bike trail encircles the city, and several bike tour maps have been produced by the Milwaukee County Department of Parks (tel. 414/257–6100).

Fishing Lake Michigan offers trout and salmon as big as 30 pounds. A Wisconsin fishing license and Great Lakes stamp are required. While some fishing is done from piers and breakwaters, anglers on boats equipped with the latest in fishing and electronic gear seem to land the big ones. **Associated Fishing Charters of Milwaukee** (tel. 414/272–7344) can help you hire licensed professional captains.

Golf There are 18-hole golf courses at the following county parks: **Brown Deer** (7835 N. Green Bay Rd., tel. 414/352–8080), **Currie Park** (3535 N. Mayfair Rd., tel. 414/453–7030), **Dretzka Park** (12020 W. Bradley Rd., tel. 414/354–7300), **Grant Park** (100 Hawthorne Ave., tel. 414/762–4646), **Greenfield Park** (2028 S. 124th St., 414/453–1750), and **Whitnall Park** (5879 S. 92nd St., tel. 414/425–2183).

Jogging and Fitness Most joggers use the city parks. The area along the lakefront off North Lincoln Memorial Drive just north of the Art Museum is a favorite of downtown joggers.

The **YMCA** (610 N. Jackson St., tel. 414/271–1030) offers a pool, track, sauna, weights, and massage.

Skiing Downhill **Whitnall Park** offers an 1,100-foot run, with a 65-foot vertical drop and rope tow. Equipment rental available. *5879 S. 92nd St., Hales Corners, tel. 414/425–9703. Open weekends 1–5.*

Crystal Ridge, 10 minutes from downtown, has 6 runs, 2 surface lifts, a double chair, and snowmaking; longest run 1,300 feet; maximum vertical drop 200 feet; cross-country skiing, rentals, instruction, chalet, bar, cafeteria, ski shop. *7900 W. Crystal Dr., Franklin, tel. 414/529–7676. Open weekdays 10 AM–10:45 PM; Sat., Sun. and holidays 9 AM–10:45 PM; closed Dec. 24.*

Little Switzerland, 20 miles north of Milwaukee on Highway 41, has 16 runs, 3 rope tows, 4 double chairs, a quad chair, and snowmaking. Rentals, repairs, instruction, ski shop, bar/lounge, snack bar. *105 Hwy. AA, Slinger, tel. 414/644–5271 or 644–5020. Open Mon. 4–10 PM; Tues.–Sun. and holidays 10–10; closed Dec. 24, Jan. 1.*

Olympia Resort, 26 miles west of Milwaukee on I–94, has a 2,200-foot run with a 196-foot vertical drop, 2 rope tows, 2 double chairs, and snowmaking; cross-country skiing, equipment rental, repair, instruction, chalet, 3 bar/lounges, live entertainment, 3 restaurants, 380 rooms, pool, sauna, whirlpool, health spa. *1350 Royale Mile Rd., Oconomowoc, tel. 414/567–0311. Open weekdays 2–8, Sat. and Sun. 10–8.*

Sun Burst, 35 miles north of Milwaukee, has 10 runs, a T–bar, 4 rope tows, 2 double chairs, and snowmaking; longest run 2,600 feet; maximum vertical drop 214 feet; rentals, repairs, instruction, chalet, bar/lounge, ski shop, cafeteria. *5 mi north of West Bend off Hwy. 45, tel. 414/626–4605. Open weekdays 4–10, Sat., Sun. and holidays 10–10; closed Dec. 24 and 25, Jan. 1.*

Cross-country **Brown Deer Park** has 3.9 miles of marked, groomed trails; equipment rental, skating, tobogganing, sledding. *7835 N. Green Bay Rd., tel. 414/352–8080. Open daylight hours.* **Dretzka Park** offers 3.2 miles of marked, groomed trails; equipment rentals, downhill skiing, tobogganing. *12020 W. Bradley*

Rd., tel. 414/354–5340. Open daylight hours. **Grant Park** has 4.1 miles of marked, groomed trails; equipment rental. *100 E. Hawthorne Ave., South Milwaukee, tel. 414/762–4646. Open daylight hours.* The **Milwaukee County Zoo** offers 2.5 miles of marked, tracked trails; trail fee; equipment rentals. *10001 W. Bluemound Rd., 1 blk. north of interchange of I–94–45–894, tel. 414/771–3040. Open weekdays 9–4:30, lighted night skiing Fri. and Sat. 4:30–10.*

Tennis   There are outdoor tennis courts in 34 county parks. For information call the Parks Department (tel. 414/257–6100).

Indoor tennis courts outside the park system are available at the **North Shore Racquet Club** (5750 N. Glen Park Rd., tel. 414/351–2900) and **Le Club** (2001 W. Good Hope Rd., tel. 414/352–4900).

Spectator Sports

Auto Racing   Championship Indy cars and stock cars race in summer at the famed **"Milwaukee Mile"** at **Wisconsin State Fair Park** in West Allis (84th St. Exit and I–94, tel. 414/453–8277).

Baseball   The **Milwaukee Brewers** play at County Stadium (201 S. 46th St., tel. 414/933–1818 for ticket information, 414/933–9000 for credit-card purchases).

Basketball   The **Milwaukee Bucks** play their NBA home games at the Bradley Center (4th and State Sts., tel. 414/227–0500). The **Marquette Warriors** (tel. 414/224–7127), a top college basketball team, play at the MECCA Arena (500 W. Kilbourn Ave., tel. 414/272–8080).

Football   The **Green Bay Packers** play three home games each year at Milwaukee County Stadium (tel. 414/342–2717).

Hockey   The MECCA is home to the **Milwaukee Admirals** (tel. 414/225–2400) of the International Hockey League.

Soccer   The **Milwaukee Wave** (tel. 414/962–9283) plays professional soccer in the MECCA. The **University of Wisconsin–Milwaukee Panthers** (tel. 414/963–5151) play major college soccer on campus.

Both **Marquette University** (tel. 414/224–7127) and the **University of Wisconsin–Milwaukee** (tel. 414/963–5151) offer men's and women's college athletic events at reasonable prices.

Dining

by Anne Schamberg

Anne Schamberg is a freelance writer whose stories appear frequently in the Milwaukee Journal.

Milwaukee's culinary style was shaped to a great extent by the Germans who first settled here. Many restaurants—whether or not they are German—offer Wiener schnitzel or the meringue-based desserts called "schaumtortes." County Stadium, home of the Milwaukee Brewers, is not famous for hot dogs, but for bratwurst. And rye bread, sometimes crusted with coarse salt, is as common on Milwaukee tables as robins are on a spring lawn.

The Poles were next to provide stock for Milwaukee's ethnic flavor. The city's South Side is dotted with shops that turn out fresh Polish sausage and restaurants that pride themselves on *pierogi*.

Many other ethnic groups, including Italians, Serbs, Mexicans, Armenians, Chinese, Greeks, Russians, Norwegians, Swiss, and most recently, Southeast Asians, have also donated their specialties to Milwaukee's tradition of *gemütlichkeit*, or fellowship and good cheer, in German.

Food produced on local farms and fish from nearby lakes and streams also contribute to the city's eating habits. Restaurants frequently feature cheese, veal, duck, and freshwater fish, especially whitefish, walleye pike, and lake perch.

Milwaukee people like to relax and socialize when they eat out. Fashion isn't as important as in more sophisticated, fast-paced cities. Jackets and ties are customary at the most expensive restaurants, but only a few actually require them.

Fridays rival Saturdays as the busiest nights in Milwaukee's restaurants. Most places, from VFW halls to fancy eateries, offer Friday-night fish fries, inexpensive all-you can-eat, family-style affairs. Call for a reservation, or plan to arrive before 6 P.M.

A word of caution to visitors ordering drinks: In Milwaukee, scotch and soda means scotch mixed with 7-Up. Ask for seltzer or club soda to avoid confusion with what the locals call sweet or white soda.

Many shops and markets make their own sausage, but Usinger's Fine Sausage, located downtown on 3rd Street, is the most famous. It's worth a visit just to view the bewildering assortment. Gift boxes can be shipped year-round.

You'll encounter the following terms on menus throughout Milwaukee:

bratwurst (brat rhymes with hot)—commonly referred to as "brats," these are flavorful pork sausages.
burek—an entree made with layers of flaky pastry and filled with meat, cheese or spinach.
pierogi—flour dumplings filled with meat, cheese, or sauerkraut, and usually served with sour cream.
rouladen—beef or pork slices rolled around a stuffing.
sauerbraten—beef that has been pickled in vinegar and spices.
schaumtorte—a meringue-based dessert topped with vanilla ice cream and strawberry or chocolate sauce.
Wiener schnitzel—breaded veal cutlet.

The following price categories are based on the average cost of a three-course dinner for one person, food alone, not including beverages, tax, and tip.

Category	Cost*
Very Expensive	over $30
Expensive	$20–$30
Moderate	$10–$20
Inexpensive	under $10

per person, without 5% state sales tax, service, or drinks

The following credit card abbreviations are used: AE, American Express; CB, Carte Blanche; DC, Diners Club; MC, MasterCard; V, Visa.

The most highly recommended restaurants are indicated by a star ★.

American **Boder's on the River.** Tie-back curtains, fireplaces, and lots of knickknacks give the dining rooms in this suburban restaurant a cheerful, country look. The menu offers Wisconsin favorites, including roast duckling and baked whitefish. The food is prepared in a straightforward manner, and dinner comes with lots of extras, including relish, fresh fruit, and warm muffins. The tables are usually crowded, and diners are apt to be bumped by the waitresses. On a busy night, the service is uneven, but friendly. There's a good selection of international beers, and a disappointing wine list. You can buy muffins, fritters, and dressings at the mini-deli gift shop. *11919 N. River Rd., Mequon, tel. 414/242–0335. Dress: informal. Reservations recommended, especially on weekends. AE, DC, MC, V. Closed Mon. Expensive.*

Clock Steak House. The food isn't bad, the prices are reasonable, and it's within walking distance of the downtown theater district. Booths and dark paneling contribute to a relaxing atmosphere. Try the Guayma shrimp or the Sicilian steak. On a busy night the service can be slow. *800 N. Plankinton Ave., tel. 414/272–1278. Dress: casual. Reservations recommended. AE, DC, MC, V. No lunch. Closed Sun. Moderate.*

Elsa's on the Park. Located across from Cathedral Square Park, this is a chic but casual place where talkative young professionals go to eat big, juicy hamburgers and pork chop sandwiches. The decor is crisply stylish with a gray, white, and black color scheme. *833 N. Jefferson St., tel. 414/765–0615. No credit cards. No lunch Sat. and Sun. Inexpensive.*

Mr. Bear's. This is a casual place with ceiling fans and exposed brick walls located two blocks north of the Performing Arts Center. The menu includes sandwiches and light lunch and dinner entrees, including fettucini verdi and stir-fried chicken. The soups are homemade, and so is the Oreo cheesecake. There's a good selection of beer, and music Wednesdays through Saturdays. *1247 N. Water St., tel. 414/272–8868. Dress: casual. AE, MC, V. No lunch Sun. Inexpensive.*

Watts Tea Shop. A genteel spot for breakfast or lunch located above George Watts & Sons, Milwaukee's premier store for china, crystal, and silverware. It features simple breakfast, sandwiches, a juice bar, and special custard-filled sunshine cake. Ask for a table by the window. *761 N. Jefferson St., tel. 414/276–6352. Dress: casual. No shorts. Reservations accepted. AE, MC, V. Closed Sun. Inexpensive.*

Continental **The English Room.** Milwaukee's premier hotel restaurant, in ★ the Pfister Hotel, has a dark, Victorian elegance. Executive chef Edouard Becker has put together a specialty menu that includes roast rack of lamb Provençal, escalope of veal, and seafood dishes. The service is formal, with plenty of tableside cooking. The wine list is very good. *424 E. Wisconsin Ave., tel. 414/273–8222. Jacket required. Reservations advised. AE, DC, MC, V. No lunch Sat. and Sun. Very Expensive.*

★ **Grenadier's.** Knut Apitz, chef-owner of this fine restaurant, serves some of the most elegant food in Milwaukee. The menu includes imaginative dishes that combine classical European style with Oriental or Indian flavors. Changing "chef's choices" (such as tenderloin of veal with raspberry sauce and angelhair pasta) and nouvelle cuisine selections (such as turban of fresh sea scallops and Norwegian salmon on pesto sauce) transport diners into enviable indecision. There are three small rooms with an air of matter-of-fact refinement, and a handsome, darkly furnished piano bar with tables. *747 N. Broadway St., tel. 414/276–0747. Jackets required. Reservations advised. AE, CB, DC, MC, V. No lunch Sat. Closed Sun. Very Expensive.*

John Byron's. One of Milwaukee's best restaurants for nearly a decade, John Byron's is in a period of transition. Although nationally acclaimed executive-chef Sanford D'Amato plans to open his own restaurant, the assumption is that the tradition of excellent, sophisticated cuisine will continue. Situated downtown on the second level of the First Wisconsin Building, the restaurant offers a beautiful view of the city. *777 E. Michigan St., tel. 414/291–5220. Reservations recommended. AE, CB, DC, MC, V. No lunch Sat. Closed Sun. Very Expensive.*

Claus on Juneau. Chef-owner Claus Bienek changes the menu daily at this chic little restaurant close to the theater district. It features ambitious selections like fresh tuna steak grilled with fresh coriander and served with tangerine sauce, fresh vegetable, and young dill rice; and grilled loin of lamb served in garlic butter sauce with potatoes and fresh vegetables served with crushed tomato. The food is usually very good, but there are overcooked or heavy-handed exceptions. Peach and forest green walls and furnishings contribute to a pleasant, contemporary atmosphere. Upstairs, **Claus on Top** serves light entrees in a more casual setting. *134 E. Juneau Ave., tel. 414/272–8558. Reservations recommended. AE, CB, DC, M, V. No lunch on Sat. Closed Sun. Claus on Top: no lunch, closed Sun. Expensive.*

Harold's. Velvet-backed booths, low lighting, and quiet piped-in music set a romantic, if slightly generic, mood at this restaurant in the Red Carpet Hotel across from the airport. Cream of wild mushroom soup, breast of capon with pistachio nuts, and warm duck salad are representative of the ambitious but sometimes heavy-handed choices on the menu. There is also a selection of "traditional favorites," including steaks and fresh fillet of white fish. The service is friendly but unpolished. The adequate wine list offers few bargains. *4747 S. Howell Ave., tel. 414/481–8000. AE, DC, MC, V. No lunch Sat. Closed Sun. Expensive.*

★ **Mike and Anna's.** This small, trendy restaurant is located in a working-class neighborhood on Milwaukee's South Side. The changing board menu features excellent nouvelle-inspired selections like fresh king salmon with basil, tarragon, beurre-blanc sauce or roast duck breast with caramelized onions and lingonberry sauce. Paper and crayons are provided for doodling at the dark maroon covered tables. The service is friendly, but bumbling and disorganized. *1978 S. 8th St., tel. 414/643–0072. Dress: informal. Reservations recommended. MC, V. No lunch. Expensive.*

Steven Wade's Cafe. This 38-seat restaurant, located in a former paint and wallpaper store in the southwestern suburbs, has received good reviews from the moment it opened. Chef and co-owner Steven Wade Klindt offers a changing board menu that might include Norwegian salmon fillet poached with vanilla sauce or coconut curried lamb. The tiny restaurant has a light green and apricot decor and is so small that intimate conversation is impossible. *17001 W. Greenfield Ave., New Berlin, tel. 414/784–0774. Reservations required. AE, DC, MC, V. No lunch Sat. Closed Sun. Expensive.*

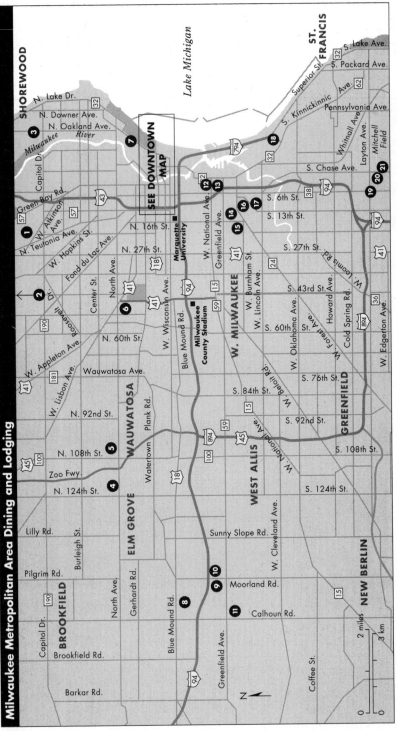

Milwaukee Metropolitan Area Dining and Lodging

169

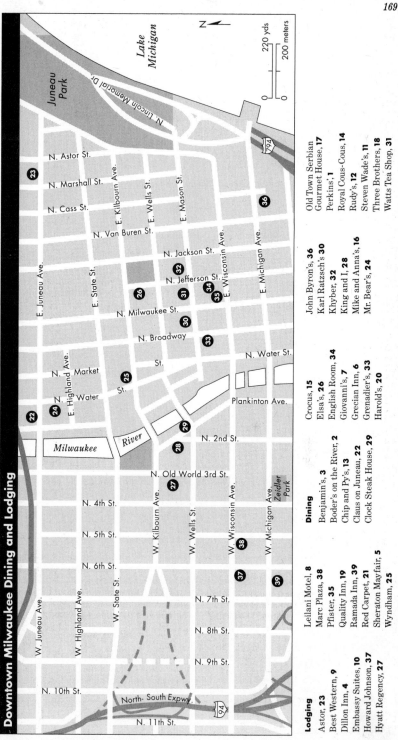

Downtown Milwaukee Dining and Lodging

Lake Michigan

Juneau Park

N. Lincoln Memorial Dr.

Milwaukee River

Zeider Park

Lodging

Astor, **23**
Best Western, **9**
Dillon Inn, **4**
Embassy Suites, **10**
Howard Johnson, **37**
Hyatt Regency, **27**

Leilani Motel, **8**
Marc Plaza, **38**
Pfister, **35**
Quality Inn, **19**
Ramada Inn, **39**
Red Carpet, **21**
Sheraton Mayfair, **5**
Wyndham, **25**

Dining

Benjamin's, **3**
Boder's on the River, **2**
Chip and Py's, **13**
Claus on Juneau, **22**
Clock Steak House, **29**

Crocus, **15**
Elsa's, **26**
English Room, **34**
Giovanni's, **7**
Grecian Inn, **6**
Grenadier's, **33**
Harold's, **20**

John Byron's, **36**
Karl Ratzsch's, **30**
Khyber, **32**
King and I, **28**
Mike and Anna's, **16**
Mr. Bear's, **24**

Old Town Serbian
Gourmet House, **17**
Perkins', **1**
Royal Cous-Cous, **14**
Rudy's, **12**
Steven Wade's, **11**
Three Brothers, **18**
Watts Tea Shop, **31**

★ **Chip and Py's.** Located in Walker's Point, a neighborhood that is home to both the down-and-out and the up-and-coming, this Art Deco restaurant serves nicely presented bistro-type fare. Try either soup or escargot for starters, then continue with sea scallops or shrimp Bordelaise. The specials are usually excellent and often include dishes that are a Continental-Oriental hybrid. There is regular jazz piano entertainment. *815 S. 5th St., 414/645–3435. Dress: informal. Reservations recommended. AE, CB, DC, MC, V. No lunch. Closed Mon. Moderate.*

Delicatessen **Benjamin's Delicatessen and Restaurant.** You'll find a wide selection of tasty specialties such as matzo ball soup, corned beef sandwiches, and brisket of beef at this classic neighborhood deli. There are booths, tables, and a counter where the TV is usually tuned to the latest sporting event. *4156 N. Oakland Ave., Shorewood, tel. 414/332–7777. MC, V. Closes 8 PM. Inexpensive.*

German **Karl Ratzsch's Old World Restaurant.** People daunted by excess amounts of German food still visit Ratzsch's to enjoy the authentic German atmosphere at this family-owned restaurant. Specialties such as schnitzel à la Ratzsch, roast duckling, and sauerbraten are served by dirndl-skirted waitresses, while a string trio schmaltzes it up. The tables in the main dining room are crowded but near the music, and provide the best vantage point for viewing the murals, antler chandeliers, and antique beer steins. Upstairs is quieter and somewhat less crowded. A pleasant alternative to an almost unavoidably heavy meal is to sit at the bar for a German beer or a glass of wine from one of the city's finest wine cellars. *320 E. Mason St., tel. 414/276–2720. Reservations recommended. Sun. brunch. AE, CB, DC, MC, V. No lunch Mon. Expensive.*

Greek **Grecian Inn Restaurant.** Delicious Greek food and cheerful decor have won lots of devotees for this restaurant. The menu goes beyond gyros to moussaka, pastitso, spanakotiropita, and a number of lamb and seafood dishes. *4831 W. North Ave., tel. 414/442–4872. AE, DC, MC, V. No lunch Sat. Closed Mon. Inexpensive–Moderate.*

Indian **Khyber.** There are candles on the tables and a subdued blue-gray decor in this fashionable restaurant on the lower level of a small downtown shopping complex. The curries are flavorful, but not fiery hot, and the tandoori chicken is very good. *770 N. Jefferson St., tel. 414/277–7777. Reservations recommended. AE, DC, MC, V. Dinner only weekends. Moderate.*

Italian **Giovanni's.** An Old World–style Sicilian place where one finds flocked wallpaper, crystal chandeliers, and large portions of rich Italian food. Veal steak Giovanni is excellent, and so is the Sicilian combination, which includes spiedini, shrimp, and eggplant Parmesan. The pasta is disappointing. *1683 N. Van Buren St., tel. 414/291–5600. Reservations recommended. AE, CB, DC, MC, V. No lunch weekends. Expensive.*

Mediterranean **Royal Cous-Cous.** Its not hard to spot this unpretentious 30-
★ seat restaurant with its red and white tent-striped exterior. It does a nice job of preparing its namesake; be sure to try some hot sauce with it. The menu also includes shish kebab, and not-too-sweet baklava. *1558 Mitchell St., tel. 414/672–8088. No credit cards. No lunch. Closed Mon. Inexpensive.*

Mexican   **Rudy's Mexican Restaurant.** Located in Walker's Point, an area south of downtown inching toward gentrification, Rudy's serves standard Mexican fare including chile rellenos, enchiladas, and guacamole. The decor is pleasant, and the food is freshly prepared. *625 S. 5th St., tel. 414/291–0296. AE, DC, MC, V. Inexpensive.*

Polish   **Crocus Restaurant and Cocktail Lounge.** Tucked away on Milwaukee's South Side, this is a friendly neighborhood restaurant that serves homemade Polish food. The decor is accented with ethnic paintings and artifacts. Braised beef roll-ups, stuffed potato dumplings, pierogi, or the special Polish Plate are all good choices. Try one of the Polish beers. *1801 S. Muskego Ave., tel. 414/643–6383. No credit cards. No lunch weekends. Inexpensive.*

Serbian   **Old Town Serbian Gourmet House.** It's fun to eat dinner here; strolling musicians and a hustle-bustle atmosphere provide the background for good ethnic cooking. Try *burek*, stuffed pastries the size of Frisbees, or Serbian shish kebab. The service can be somewhat harried on busy nights. *522 W. Lincoln Ave., tel. 414/672–0206. Reservations recommended. AE, MC, V. No lunch weekends. Closed Mon. Moderate.*
Three Brothers Bar & Restaurant. In an 1887 tavern, this is one of Milwaukee's revered ethnic restaurants. Chicken paprikash, roast lamb, Serbian salad, and homemade desserts are served at old metal kitchen tables. It's about 10 minutes from downtown on Milwaukee's near South Side. *2424 S. St. Clair St., tel. 414/481–7530. Reservations recommended. No credit cards. No lunch. Closed Mon. Moderate.*

Soul Food   **Perkins' Family Restaurant.** Located on Milwaukee's tough North Side, this unpretentious neighborhood diner is the place to go for homemade ham hocks, catfish, turnip greens, and black-eyed peas. The food is served on divided plastic plates to clientele ranging from neighborhood regulars to politicians and professional athletes. *2001 W. Atkinson Ave., tel. 414/447–6660. No credit cards. Closed Sun. Inexpensive.*

Thai   **The King and I.** Food is nicely prepared here, and you can fine-tune the degree of spiciness by stating your preference. Starters include jumping squid or pork satay; *Pud Thai* (Thai noodles) and steamed red snapper follow. The attractive front room, with its glossy wooden bar, combines the look of a European cafe with traditional Thai decor. The main dining room is darkly paneled and hung with Thai artwork. *823 N. 2nd St., tel. 414/276–4181. AE, V, MC. No lunch weekends. Moderate.*

Lodging

by Anne Schamberg

Milwaukee offers a number of different options for accommodations, ranging from cozy bed-and-breakfast rooms to executive suites overlooking Lake Michigan and the city. Most of the downtown hotels are within walking distance of the theater district, the Convention Center and Arena, and plenty of shopping and restaurants.

Bed & Breakfast of Milwaukee, Inc., keeps a list of some 25 homes in the Milwaukee area, from downtown penthouses to charming country homes. It is recommended that you make reservations three weeks in advance, but it is sometimes possible to make them on shorter notice. When calling indicate your preferences regarding smoking, children, pets, etc. *320 E. Buffalo St., Milwaukee, 53202, tel. 414/271–2337. MC, V. All price ranges.*

Milwaukee is a city of summer festivals, major league sports, music, and a thriving and diversified group of theaters. During the summer, accommodations should be booked well ahead, especially for weekends.

There are many weekend or festival packages, so be sure to ask about special prices when calling for reservations.

Category	Cost*
Very Expensive	over $90
Expensive	$70–$90
Moderate	$40–$70
Inexpensive	under $40

*double room (add 11% tax in Milwaukee)

The following credit card abbreviations are used: AE, American Express; CB, Carte Blanche; DC, Diners Club; MC, MasterCard; V, Visa.

The most highly recommended hotels are indicated by a star ★.

Downtown
Very Expensive

Hyatt Regency. This centrally located 484-room high-rise hotel has a revolving restaurant on top. The rooms are airy and bright. *333 W. Kilbourn Ave., 53203, tel. 414/276–1234. Facilities: garage parking, gift shop, health club privileges. AE, DC, MC, V.*

Marc Plaza. Crystal chandeliers, marble-based columns, and dark woodwork in the lobby give this gracious hotel built in 1929 a handsome appearance. The traditionally decorated rooms vary quite a bit in size. *509 W. Wisconsin Ave., 53203, tel. 414/271–7250. Facilities: barber shop, restaurants, indoor pool, sauna, shopping arcade. AE, DC, MC, V.*

★ **Pfister Hotel.** Many of the rooms in Milwaukee's grand old hotel, built in 1893, have been combined to make suites, with enlarged bathrooms. A collection of 19th-century art hangs in the elegant Victorian lobby. The rooms in the Tower, built in 1975, are decorated traditionally, in keeping with furnishings throughout the hotel. *424 E. Wisconsin Ave., 53202, tel. 414/273–8222. Facilities: indoor pool. AE, DC, MC, V.*

Wyndham Hotel. A 221-room hotel perched atop the Milwaukee Center. The opulent lobby is tiled with Italian marble; the rooms are traditionally styled with mahogany furniture. *139 E. Kilbourn Ave., 53202, tel. 414/276–8686. Facilities: health club, jogging track. AE, CB, DC, MC.*

Moderate–Expensive

Astor Hotel. Only half of this 200-room hotel built in 1920 is available for transient guests. Located just a few blocks from Lake Michigan, it has the not unpleasant air of a hotel past its heyday. The large lobby has comfortable seating, a handsome grandfather's clock, and a display of photographs of illustrious people who have stayed here. Many of the rooms and studio apartments have been remodeled, but they still contain old bathroom fixtures. *924 E. Juneau Ave., 53202, tel. 414/271–4220. AE, DC, MC, V.*

Moderate **Howard Johnson Downtown.** This 10-story downtown hotel provides basic accommodations; the west-side rooms are quietest. *611 W. Wisconsin Ave., 53203, tel. 414/273–2950. Facilities: outdoor pool, free valet parking, health club privileges, restaurant. AE, CB, DC, MC, V.*

Ramada Inn Downtown. Rough knotty-pine paneling gives the lobby of this 152-room hotel a casual feeling. Rooms are clean and standard-looking. *633 W. Michigan Ave., 53202, tel. 414/272–8410. Facilities: outdoor pool, restaurant, valet service, gift shop, rental car. AE, CB, DC, MC, V.*

Away from Downtown
Expensive– Very Expensive
Embassy Suites Hotel. The atrium lobby and glass elevators give this 203-suite hotel in the western suburbs a big-city feeling. *1200 S. Moorland Rd., Brookfield, 53005, tel. 414/782–2900. Facilities: indoor pool, sauna, steam room, whirlpool, exercise room, restaurant, game room. AE, DC, MC, V.*

Moderate– Expensive
Red Carpet Hotel. Across from Mitchell Field, this 510-room hotel is the largest in the state. *4747 S. Howell Ave., 53207, tel. 414/481–8000. Facilities: indoor and outdoor pool, fitness center, indoor track, travel agency, 24-hr. airport transportation, barber shop. AE, DC, MC, V.*

Sheraton Mayfair. Recently remodeled, this 150-room high rise is convenient to the County Medical Complex, the Milwaukee County Zoo, and the Mayfair Shopping Mall. The rooms have a bright contemporary look, and the top floors offer fine views. *2303 N. Mayfair Rd., Wauwatosa, 53226, tel. 414/257–3400. Facilities: indoor pool, sauna, restaurant. AE, DC, MC, V.*

Moderate **Best Western Midway Motor Lodge.** The rooms are standard-looking and clean in this 125-room facility. The rooms on the west side have a view of the golf course. *1005 S. Moorland Rd., Brookfield, 53005, tel. 414/786–9540. Facilities: pool, game room, restaurant, bar. AE, DC, MC, V.*

Dillon Inn. The lobby of this three-story brick motel, with a fireplace and hanging plants, is more homey than most. *11111 W. North Ave., 53207, Wauwatosa, 53226, tel. 414/778–0333. Facilities: complimentary breakfasts, restaurant adjacent. AE, DC, MC, V.*

Quality Inn Airport. Opposite Mitchell Field, this well-kept motel recently opened a new 3-story, 60-room wing, and also remodeled the original section, for a total of 138 rooms. *5311 S. Howell Ave., 53207, tel. 414/481–2400. Facilities: indoor pool, restaurant, travel agency, car rental, parking, 24-hr. airport shuttle to and from the airport. AE, DC, MC, V.*

Leilani Motel. In an area west of Milwaukee that has gone from farmland to fast food in the last 15 years, this family-owned motel retains the flavor of the late 1950s. The 60 rooms are clean but outdated in appearance. The indoor pool is crystal clear and kept at 86 degrees all year long. *18615 W. Bluemound Rd., Brookfield, 53005, tel. 414/786–7100. Facilities: playground, tennis courts, fishing pond, free Continental breakfast. AE, DC, MC, V.*

The Arts

Milwaukee's theaters are in a two-block area bounded by the Milwaukee River, E. Wells Street, N. Water Street, and E. State Street. With the recent renovation of several fine old theaters and the completion of the Milwaukee Center, which houses three theaters, an office tower, restaurants, retail space, parking, and a hotel, this area is becoming the cultural center of the city.

The calendar section of the monthly *Milwaukee Magazine* has the most complete listing of events. The Greater Milwaukee Calendar of Events, put out twice a month by the Greater Milwaukee Convention & Visitors Bureau, contains helpful information. Also check the Arts section of the Sunday Milwaukee *Journal*.

Most tickets are sold at box offices, although for some events tickets can be charged by phoning Ticketron (tel. 414/273–6400). Some events offer rush tickets at substantial savings, especially for seniors and students.

Theater   The **Milwaukee Repertory Theater** (108 E. Wells St., tel. 414/224–9490) is one of the top resident theaters in the nation. The Rep is in the new Milwaukee Center, with a 720-seat main auditorium, the 216-seat Stiemke Theater, and the 120-seat Stackner Cabaret. The season is October–June.
First Stage Milwaukee. An arts-in-education program, with productions geared to elementary, middle, high school, and adult audiences. *Todd Wehr Theater, Performing Arts Center, 929 N. Water St., tel. 414/273–7206.*
Acacia Theater Company (2844 N. Oakland Ave., tel. 414/926–2380) presents both musicals and dramas at a variety of locations.
Hansberry Sands Theater Company (tel. 414/272–2787) performs at Lincoln Center for the Arts (820 E. Knapp St.).
Next Generation Theater for children and the **Milwaukee Chamber Theater,** which presents an annual Shaw festival and other productions, both perform at Skylight Music Theater (813 N. Jefferson St., tel. 414/271–8815).

Concerts   **Milwaukee Symphony Orchestra** (tel. 414/291–6000). This famous orchestra's season runs September–June and includes a Superpops series. *Uihlein Hall, Performing Arts Center, 929 N. Water St.*
The **Bel Canto Chorus** (tel. 414/276–8533). This distinguished oratorio chorus is accompanied by the Milwaukee Symphony Orchestra. *Uihlein Hall, Performing Arts Center.*
"Music Under the Stars" Programs (tel. 414/278–4389). Free summer evenings of music at two parks: *Humboldt Park and Band Shell, 3000 S. Howell Ave., and Washington Park and Band Shell, 1859 N. 40th St.*
Pabst Theater (144 E. Wells St., tel. 414/271–3773). Built by beer baron Frederick Pabst, this is both a historic landmark and a center for theatrical productions, concerts, and dance by touring artists, Broadway productions, and local professional and amateur groups.
Riverside Theater (116 W. Wisconsin Ave., tel. 414/271–2000). Wisconsin's largest landmark theater, recently renovated, seats 2,500; a showplace for touring Broadway productions, symphony, pop, and country artists.

Opera   **Florentine Opera Co.** (tel. 414/273–1474). An outstanding regional company for over a half century. Their home is the Performing Arts Center.
Skylight Comic Opera (Skylight Music Theater, 813 N. Jefferson St., tel. 414/271–8815). Vivid productions ranging from Mozart to Gilbert and Sullivan.

Dance **Milwaukee Ballet Company** (tel. 414/643–7677) offers both classical and contemporary dance at the Performing Arts Center.
Lincoln Center for the Arts (820 E. Knapp St., tel. 414/272–
2787) is home to three dance groups: the **Bauer Dance Company, Dancecircus,** and **J.U.M.P. Dance Theater.**

Ethnic and folk dances are presented in the city and suburbs
nearly every weekend. Check calendars of events for listings.

Film **Oriental Landmark Theater** (2230 N. Farwell Ave., tel. 414/
276–8711). Movie buffs flock to the foreign and hard-to-find
films at this 1927 theater whose East Indian–style decor,
onion-shape domes, and terra-cotta lions are worth seeing in
themselves.

Nightlife

Milwaukee isn't likely to be your first choice when you think of
an exciting place to spend an evening. Yet the city offers a variety of nightlife in one of the country's safest downtown areas.
There are friendly saloons all over the city; some have a very
cosmopolitan feel, others seem to take you back a hundred
years. The music scene varies greatly, and one establishment
may offer country, jazz, and rock music in the same week.

Bars and **Bombay Bicycle Club.** One of the best piano bars in town; a re-
Nightclubs laxing and friendly atmosphere. *In the Marc Plaza, 509 W.
Wisconsin Ave., tel. 414/271–7250. AE, DC, MC, V. Closed
Sun.*

Gas Lite East. Hot sandwiches, soups, salads, and a friendly
neighborhood tavern atmosphere. *775 N. Jackson St., tel. 414/
784–4574. No credit cards.*

La Playa. A South American atmosphere combines the ambience of a Rio nightclub and the glamour of a supper club. Live
bands on Fridays and Saturdays. *In the Pfister Hotel, 414 E.
Wisconsin Ave., tel. 414/273–8222. AE, DC, MC, V. Closed
Sun.*

Polaris. Milwaukee's only revolving rooftop restaurant and
lounge, atop the Hyatt Regency Hotel. Spectacular views of
downtown and Lake Michigan. *333 W. Kilbourn Ave., tel. 414/
276–1234. AE, DC, MC, V.*

Major Goolsby's. *USA Today* called it one of the country's top 10
sports bars. Cocktails, soft drinks, burgers, and fries. *340 W.
Kilbourn Ave., across from the Hyatt and the Sports Arena,
tel. 414/271–3414. AE, MC, V.*

Oscar's Video Dance Lounge. DJ entertainment and dancing six
nights a week. Happy-hour cocktails with complimentary buffet nightly. *In the Midway Motor Lodge, 251 N. Mayfair Rd.,
Wauwatosa, tel. 414/774–3600. No credit cards.*

Safe House. One of the city's most unusual clubs. A James Bond
decor makes this "spy hideout" a favorite. Enter through the
"International Exports" office. *779 N. Front St., tel. 414/271–
2007. AE, DC, MC, V.*

Von Trier. A quiet watering hole with Black Forest decor,
steins, and murals, and a large selection of imported beers.
2235 N. Farwell Ave., tel. 414/272–1775.

Jazz Clubs **Brass's.** A large hall with red wallpaper and carpeting and For-
mica tables. Music varies from 1960s and 1970s rock and
Dixieland jazz to polkas, waltzes, and ballroom dancing. *16755
Lisbon Rd., Brookfield, tel. 414/781–3680. No credit cards.*

Sardino's on Farwell has featured jazz entertainment for over 50 years. *1617 N. Farwell Ave., tel. 414/273–7983. Open weekdays 3 PM–2 AM, Sat. 6 PM–3:30 AM, Sun. 6 PM–2 AM.*

Up and Under Pub has jazz or rhythm and blues 8 PM–midnight various nights. *1216 E. Brady St., tel. 414/276–2677. No credit cards.*

Comedy **ComedySportz.** Improvisational comedy sports teams compete against each other at Kalt's Bar and Restaurant. *2856 N. Oakland Ave., tel. 414/332–6323. Thurs. 7:30 PM; Fri.–Sat. 7:30 and 10 PM; Sun. 3 and 4:30 PM. Admission: $2 adults, $1 students.*

The **Funny Bone Comedy Club.** Stand-up comedy with TV performers. *1434 N. Farwell Ave., tel. 414/273–1330. Tues.–Thurs. 9 PM; Fri.–Sat. 8:30 and 10:30 PM. Admission: Tues. $1; Wed.–Thurs. and Sun., $3; Fri.–Sat. $5. Reservations recommended.*

Excursions from Milwaukee

Price categories for restaurants and hotels are the same as in Milwaukee Dining and Lodging.

Numbers in the margin correspond with points of interest on the Excursions from Milwaukee map.

❶ Cedarburg

When the first settlers saw what is now Cedarburg, Indians were still passing through on a trail between Milwaukee and Green Bay. By the 1830s most of the Indians were gone. Relics and mounds, some of them 1,500 years old, are still being found.

The source of Cedarburg's vigor from its birth was the creek that German and Irish immigrants found here. They built five dams and mills, and the life of the town flowed along the banks of Cedar Creek.

The pioneer settlers carved their history in limestone. Two local quarries provided the Niagara limestone that was used to build many of the churches, homes, businesses, and shops still in use.

Today Cedarburg has a population of 10,000, and its entire downtown district has been placed on the National Register of Historic Places. The community celebrates its heritage with an annual Stone and Century Houses Tour of private historic homes and buildings in early June.

Arriving and Departing Take I–43 north to the Cedarburg exit (15 mi) and county highway C west three miles into Cedarburg. The drive from Milwaukee takes about 25 minutes.

Exploring The Cedarburg Chamber of Commerce offers *A Walk Through Yesterday*, a self-guided walking and driving tour that covers 59 buildings. Pick up a tour booklet ($1) at the **Visitor Information Center** (W63 N645 Washington Ave., tel. 414/377–9620). Those interested in antiques should ask for the free list of dealers.

Cedar Creek Settlement is a historic village of shops in the Wittenberg Woolen Mill, which was built in 1864 and operated until 1969. The restored mill now holds over 35 businesses, including

Excursions from Milwaukee

restaurants, antique shops, pottery shops, art galleries, and specialty shops. With several levels, wooden floors, and lots of nooks and crannies, it's fun to explore. *N70 W6340 Bridge Rd., tel. 414/377–8020. Open Mon.–Sat. 10–5, Sun. noon–5.*

The Stone Mill Winery offers 45-minute guided tours including the winery museum and the cellars where the wine is fermented, aged, and bottled. Some guides will show you how one crawls through the tiny openings of the wine barrels to clean inside. *Lower level of the Cedar Creek Settlement, tel. 414/377–8020. Tours: $2. Open Mon.–Sat. 10–5, Sun. noon–5; closed Jan. 1, Easter, Thanksgiving, Dec. 25.*

The **Uihlein Antique Racing Car Museum** exhibits restored racing cars from the 1930s and 1940s. Race fans will enjoy the beautiful restorations; the museum is situated in a lovely stone building. *236 Hamilton Rd., tel. 414/375–4032. Admission: $2 adults, 75 cents children under 17 and senior citizens. Open Memorial Day–Labor Day, Wed.–Sat. 10–5, Sun. 1–5; Labor Day–Oct., Sat. 10–5, Sun. 1–5.*

The **Stagecoach Inn,** a beautiful restoration of a stone hotel of 1853, is now a bed-and-breakfast inn with nine guest rooms. The inn has a small but well-stocked bookstore for gifts and browsing, a cozy pub, and a chocolate shop offering handmade treats. *W61 N520 Washington Ave., 53012, tel. 414/375–0208. The shops are open Mon.–Sat. 10–5; pub opens at noon.*

Wisconsin's last remaining historic **covered bridge** crosses Cedar Creek three miles north of Cedarburg. The 120-foot bridge was built in 1876 and retired in 1962. Its white pine was cut and squared at a mill near Baraboo and hauled 75 miles to the bridge site. A small park beside the bridge is pleasant for viewing and picnicking. Follow Washington Avenue north to Highway 143; at the junction with Highway 60, take Covered Bridge Road north to the bridge. About three miles from town.

Dining **Bath's at the Bridge.** Early American decor and good soups, salads, chicken, and seafood distinguish this restaurant with a children's menu and cocktail lounge. *N58 W6 194 Columbia Rd., tel. 414/337–0660. Reservations advised. AE, DC, MC, V. Closed Mon. and major holidays. Moderate.*
Woolen Mill Inn. This restaurant is of the Cedar Creek shopping and historical settlement, located in the former woolen mill office. Mill artifacts are on display in the bar and two dining rooms; the menu includes salads, sandwiches, and seafood, chicken, and beef entrees. *W63 N706 Washington Ave., tel. 414/377–7111. Reservations suggested. AE, DC, MC, V. No dinner. Moderate.*

---

❷ Racine

The city was founded in 1834 by French missionaries who named the region "racine" (meaning root) because of the roots that grew from the banks of the Root River, which snakes through the city and empties into Lake Michigan.

In its heyday, Racine was a bustling harbor, once the fifth-busiest port on the Great Lakes. Shipbuilding was a major 19th-century industry.

Now heavily industrialized, the city of 90,000 is working at becoming a resort city, and recently it added a 110-acre recreational boating marina, the largest on Lake Michigan. A new lakefront park and building complex designed to house the community's many ethnic festivals and artistic events has brought new life to the waterfront. Salmon-O-Rama, a nine-day fishing contest held the second week of July, draws 300,000 participants from the USA and Canada.

Arriving and Departing Take I–94 south to the Highway 20 exit into Racine. It's 26 miles and about 35 minutes from downtown Milwaukee.

Exploring Thirty-minute guided tours of the **Johnson Wax Administration Building,** designed by Frank Lloyd Wright, are offered on weekdays. Although conceived and built in the 1930s, the Art Deco building looks as modern as many of today's structures. The center for the S.C. Johnson Company's public tour programs is the adjacent **Golden Rondelle Theater** (1525 Howe St., tel. 414/631–2154). Originally built in New York City as the company's pavilion at the 1964–65 World's Fair, the Rondelle offers acclaimed film programs that include regular showings of *On The Wing, Living Planet,* and *To Be Alive.* Tours and films are free, but reservations must be made in advance.

The **Charles A. Wustum Museum of Fine Arts** is a small museum with one of the Midwest's largest collections of Works Project Administration art. Selected from paintings, sculpture, and photographs of the 1930s, the permanent collection provides a graphic look at the Great Depression. The grounds are lovely, with 13 acres of park and formal gardens, plantings, and sculptures. *2519 Northwestern Ave., tel. 414/636–9177. Admission free. Open Tues., Wed., Fri.–Sun. 1–5, Mon. and Thurs. 1–9.*

It's hard to think of a furniture store as a tourist attraction, but the 130-year-old **Porters of Racine** is one. Housed in seven old restored buildings, the pricey store, a city block long, has four floors of furniture. *Main entrance at Sixth St. and Wisconsin Ave., tel. 414/633–6363. Open Tues.–Thurs., Sat. 10–5:30, Mon. and Fri. 10–9; closed Sun.*

Racine Zoological Gardens occupy 32 acres on the shore of Lake Michigan. The zoo has about 350 specimens, and the grounds are pleasant for strolling. *2131 Main St., tel. 414/636–9189. Admission free. Grounds open 6 AM–8 PM daily year-round; zoo building open weekdays 10–5, weekends 10–6.*

Sunbathers and cold-water swimmers will like **North Beach,** with over a mile of white sandy beach. There are lifeguards in season, a concession stand, picnic area, bathhouse, and showers. *Michigan Blvd. at the lake, just north of the harbor, tel. 414/636–9233. Admission free.*

Picturesque **Wind Point Lighthouse,** built in 1880, is in the village of Wind Point on the north edge of Racine. The 112-foot tower is one of the tallest on Lake Michigan. The light is still in operation, but the tower is closed to visitors, and the former keeper's quarters are now used as a village hall; the scenic grounds are open daily. *On Lighthouse Dr.; from downtown take Hwy. 32 north to Three Mile Rd., turn right to Lighthouse Dr.*

Any visit to Racine must include a sample of *kringle,* the famous Danish coffee cake known for its delicate, flaky texture and delightful fillings. You'll have to stand in line to buy one.

The pastries cost about $3. Try **Lehmann's Bakery** (2210 16th St., tel. 414/632–4636), **Larsen Bakery** (3311 Washington Ave., tel. 414/633–4298), or **O & H Danish Bakery** (1841 Douglas Ave., tel. 414/637–8895). All three will ship kringles.

Dining   **The Packing House.** One of Racine's best restaurants, serving
★   typical American fare, including ribs, steaks, veal, poultry, and seafood. *6825 Washington Ave., tel. 414/886–9866. Jacket and tie required. Reservations suggested. AE, DC, MC, V. Expensive.*

Gatsby's Speakeasy & Eatery. There's roaring '20s decor and Mexican, Italian, and American food at this restaurant and cocktail lounge. *3932 Douglas Ave., tel. 414/639–0910. Dress: informal. Reservations suggested. AE, MC, V. Moderate.*

The Chart Room offers meals with a view of the Root River. There's outdoor dining in summer, and a cocktail lounge. *209 Dodge St. at Main St. Bridge, tel. 414/632–9901. Dress: informal. Reservations suggested. MC, V. Closed major holidays. Inexpensive.*

Old World Wisconsin

❸ The State Historical Society's living museum, **Old World Wisconsin,** celebrates the state's ethnic heritage in architecture. Set on 576 acres in the beautiful Southern Kettle Moraine State Forest near Eagle, the museum has over 50 historic buildings.

Arriving and   Take I–94 west to the Highway 67 exit at Delafield and drive
Departing   approximately 12 miles south to the village of Eagle. The museum is another mile south on Highway 67. The drive from Milwaukee takes about one hour.

Exploring   This living museum of restored farm and village buildings has been gathered from across the state to depict 19th- and 20th-century rural Wisconsin. All were originally built and inhabited by European immigrants; they are grouped into ethnic farms.

On display are a rural crossroads village of the 1870s, a Yankee farm, and German, Norwegian, Danish, and Finnish farmsteads. Costumed interpreters relate the story of immigration to Wisconsin along with each ethnic group's role in the state's history. They also perform the routine chores necessary to rural life a century ago, and visitors are sometimes invited to help feed animals, make soap, or wield a hoe in a 19th-century garden. Special seasonal events take place most weekends.

Self-guided tours begin with a 15-minute slide orientation on 19th-century Wisconsin in the lower level of the Ramsey Barn Visitors Center. The program is highly recommended for an overview of the museum before you start.

Old World Wisconsin takes time to see. You'll have to walk two and one half miles to see all the exhibits. Allow four to six hours, and wear comfortable shoes and clothes. Tram service between the farmsteads is available, but walking is still required. *S103 W37890 Hwy. 67, 1 mi south of Eagle, tel. 414/594–2116. Admission: $6 adults, $4.80 over 65, $2.50 under 18, $10 family. Shuttle tram ride: $1 per person. Open May–Oct., daily 10–5. MC, V.*

Dining   **The Clausing Barn Restaurant,** on the lower level of a large octagonal barn on the museum grounds, offers sandwiches, hot and cold plates, and soft drinks, wine, and beer. A plate lunch of a different ethnic origin is featured each week, and dinner is served on weekends. *MC, V. Inexpensive.*

Southern Wisconsin

Southern Wisconsin is bounded by Lake Michigan on the east, the Mississippi River on the west, and Illinois on the south. Although it is the state's most populous region, it remains rural. This was one of Wisconsin's earliest regions to be settled; its second- and third-oldest communities are here, along with one tiny hamlet, Belmont, which in the territory's formative days was the capital of a huge part of the Upper Midwest.

Getting Around

By Plane Madison's **Dane County Regional Airport** (tel. 608/246–3380) is served by American Eagle, Midstate Connection, Midway Airlines, Midwest Express, Northwest, TWA, United, and United Express.

By Car Most travel in southern Wisconsin is by car on an extensive network of good roads.

By Bus Greyhound and Trailways serve the larger cities and towns.

Scenic Drives **U.S. 12.** The 70-mile drive from Lake Geneva to Madison, lovely at any time of year, takes you through some of the region's most productive farmland.
U.S. 18–151. Extending from Blue Mounds west to Prairie du Chien (approximately 70 mi), this road follows the route of the Old Military Road, constructed by soldiers from Fort Crawford in 1836.
Route 35. Part of the Great River Road, the 55-mile drive between Prairie du Chien and La Crosse offers many scenic vistas and the autumn colors are spectacular.

Important Addresses and Numbers

Tourist **Fort Atkinson Chamber of Commerce** (89 N. Main St., 53538,
Information tel. 414/563–3210). Open weekdays 8–4:30.
La Crosse Convention & Visitor's Bureau (Riverside Park, 54602, tel. 608/782–2366). Open weekdays 8:30–5; Sat.–Sun. 10–4 in summer.
Lake Geneva Convention & Visitors Bureau (201 Wrigley Dr., 53147, tel. 414/248–4416). Open daily 9–5.
Madison Convention & Visitor's Bureau (425 W. Washington Ave., 53703, tel. 608/255–0701). Open weekdays 8–5.
Mineral Point Chamber of Commerce (114 High St., 53565, tel. 608/987–2277). Open weekdays 9–5.
Platteville Chamber of Commerce (97 E. Main St., 53818, tel. 608/348–8888). Open weekdays 9:30–12:30 and 2–4.
Prairie du Chien Chamber of Commerce (211 S. Main St., 53821, tel. 608/326–8555). Open weekdays 9–4:30.
Wisconsin Tourist Information Centers are situated near Beloit on I–90 at Rest Area #22; Kenosha on I–94 at Rest Area #26; La Crosse, I–90 at Rest Area #31; and Prairie du Chien at the Highway 18 Mississippi River Bridge; open May–Oct. In Madison, one block from the Capitol Square (123 W. Washington Ave., 53703, tel. 608/266–2161 or 800/372–2737); open weekdays 8–5.

Emergencies **Wisconsin State Patrol** (tel. 608/246–3220). Emergency numbers vary. Dialing "0" will get an operator.

Exploring Southern Wisconsin

Numbers in the margin correspond with points of interest on the Southern Wisconsin map.

Most visitors who come to the region are driving and seeking scenic areas and attractions. We begin southwest of Milwaukee in Lake Geneva and move across southern Wisconsin from east to west.

❶ **Lake Geneva** is a year-round resort on spring-fed Geneva Lake. The region is actually not especially well known by Wisconsinites, whose travel orientation is mainly to the north. Recreational features include beaches, boat ramps, golf courses, excursion boats, and horseback riding. There are also numerous hiking, bicycle, snowmobile, and cross-country ski trails. Bigfoot Beach State Park is a mile south of Lake Geneva on Highway 120, and the villages of Fontana and Williams Bay are on the lake.

Gage Marine and Boat Tours (101 Broad St., tel. 414/248–6206 or 800/558–5911) offers pleasant sightseeing trips on Geneva Lake and Bay aboard restorations or replicas of historic yachts. Boats leave Riviera Docks downtown daily 10–3:30 from mid-June to Labor Day, operating on a limited schedule during May and early June and September and October. Luncheon, dinner, and Sunday brunch cruises are available; fares vary.

More than 100,000 Canada geese are counted each year at the **❷** **Horicon Marsh Wildlife Refuge** (about 40 mi northwest of Milwaukee). Follow the roads officially marked Wild Goose Parkway to drive around the 32,000-acre marsh and view the spring and autumn migrations. Information on hiking trails is provided at the Marsh Headquarters. Trails are open all year, dusk to dawn, except during resting and migration seasons. You'll see the most geese in October and November; a good viewing area is along the northern edge of the marsh, just east of Waupun on Highway 49. Almost anyone can produce good wildlife photos here. *Headquarters, 1210 N. Palmatory St., Horicon, tel. 414/485–4434. Admission free. Headquarters open weekdays 8–4.*

Horicon Marsh Boat Tours. One-hour boat tours of the inner marsh leave from the Highway 33 bridge from May through October. *101 S. Main St., Horicon, tel. 414/485–4663 or 485–2942.*

❸ The city of **Madison** existed only on paper when it was chosen as the territorial capital in 1836, and there were but three settlers. Named after President James Madison, the town was known in the early days as Four Lakes, after the lakes that surround it.

The center of the city lies on an eight-block-wide isthmus between Lakes Mendota and Monona. Here the State Capitol dominates the skyline. Built between 1906 and 1917, the building looks similar to the Capitol in Washington. Capitol Square is connected to the University of Wisconsin campus by State Street, a tree-lined shopping district of import shops, ethnic restaurants, galleries, and artisans' studios. A Farmer's Market, with several hundred vendors offering baked goods,

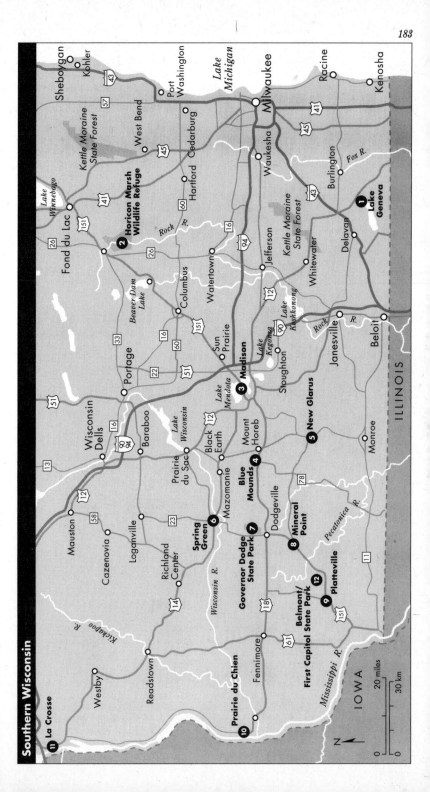

Southern Wisconsin

1 Lake Geneva
2 Horicon Marsh Wildlife Refuge
3 Madison
4 Blue Mounds
5 New Glarus
6 Spring Green
7 Governor Dodge State Park
8 Mineral Point
9 Platteville
10 Prairie du Chien
11 La Crosse
12 First Capitol State Park
12 Belmont/First Capitol State Park

ILLINOIS

IOWA

N

0   20 miles
0   30 km

flowers, and fresh produce is held on the square each Saturday from 6 AM to 2 PM May through October. The Art Fair on the Square in July draws hundreds of artists and thousands of visitors.

Wisconsin State Capitol. Tours of this magnificent Roman Renaissance structure take you through the Rotunda, Supreme Court Room, Senate and Assembly chambers, and Governor's Conference Room. *Free tours from the information desk in the Rotunda, tel. 608/266–0382 Memorial Day–Labor Day, daily 9–11 and 1–4; Sept.–May, Mon.–Sat. 9–11 and 1–3, and Sun. 1–3; closed holidays.*

The **G.A.R. Memorial Hall Museum** is an attractive small museum of special interest to Civil War buffs. Displays include uniforms, flags, swords, and other paraphernalia of Wisconsin's Civil War units and exhibits on the Spanish-American War. *Room 419 North, State Capitol, tel. 608/266–1680. Admission free. Open Memorial Day–Labor Day, weekdays 9–4:30, Sat. and Sun. 9–4:30; closed holidays.*

State Historical Society Museum. The society predates statehood, and the museum's permanent displays cover the history of the region's Indians from prehistoric times to the 20th century. There are also exhibits on fur trading and pioneer life. *30 N. Carroll St. on the Capitol Square, tel. 608/262–7700. Admission free. Open Tues.–Sat. 10–5, Sun. noon–5; closed Jan. 1, Thanksgiving, Dec. 25.*

The Madison Art Center, in the lobby of the Civic Center, features more than 25 exhibitions annually and has a permanent collection of more than 4,000 works. *211 State St., tel. 608/257–0158. Admission free. Open Tues.–Thurs. 11–5, Fri. 11–9, Sat. 10–5, Sun. 1–5; closed Mon. and holidays.*

Elvehjem Museum of Art. This University of Wisconsin museum is one of the state's best. There is a permanent collection of more than 12,000 paintings, sculpture, graphics, furniture, and decorative arts dating from 2300 BC to the present in five floors of galleries. Collections of Russian icons and of Egyptian, Greek, and Roman sculpture, ceramics, and coins are especially noteworthy. *On the university campus, 800 University Ave., tel. 608/263–2246. Admission free. Open Mon.–Sat. 9–4:45, Sun. 11–4:45; closed holidays.*

University of Wisconsin. The college opened in 1849 with 20 students. Today, with an enrollment of 46,000, it occupies a 1,000-acre campus on the shores of Lake Mendota. Visit the Memorial Union terrace (800 Langdon St.) on the lakefront and you'll see why this is one of the most beautiful campuses in the nation. A mile-long path along the lakeshore is a pleasant place for a stroll. *Free guided walking tours of the campus can be arranged at the visitor information center of the Memorial Union, tel. 608/262–1331. Open weekdays 7:45 AM–8 PM, Sat. and Sun. 12:30–3.*

The **University Arboretum** has more than 1,200 acres of natural plant and animal communities and horticultural collections of the Upper Midwest. The large lilacs and apple tree gardens are spectacular in spring, usually in early May. *1207 Seminole Hwy., tel. 608/263–7888. McKay Information Center open Mon.–Sat. 9:30–4, Sun. 12:30–4; closed holidays. Free arboretum tours May–Oct., Sun.*

Henry Vilas Park Zoo (tel. 608/266–4732). Youngsters get free camel rides during the summer at this zoological park with nearly 200 species of animals. A Children's Zoo, where youngsters can pet and feed animals, is open from Memorial Day through Labor Day. Adjoining Vilas Park has tennis courts, ball diamonds, a children's playground, a swimming beach, and large picnic areas. It is one of Madison's most popular family spots. *Situated on Lake Wingra via S. Park St. to Drake St.; watch for the signs. Admission free. Open daily 9:30–4:45; buildings closed Jan. 1, Thanksgiving, and Dec. 26.*

Olbrich Park Botanical Gardens. A 14-acre botanical garden in this lakefront park features herb and rock gardens and wildflower plantings. Flower shows and plant sales are held several times a year in the Botanical Center. The adjoining park has boat launching ramps, children's playground, and picnic areas. *3330 Atwood Ave., tel. 608/246–4551. Admission free. Open Oct.–May, daily 9–8; June–Sept., weekdays 9–5; closed Jan. 1, Thanksgiving, Dec. 25.*

Landmarks for the early settlers, the two blue hills 25 miles west of Madison mark the eastern extremity of Wisconsin's lead-mining region and can be seen from many points in southern Wisconsin. In 1828 Ebenezer Brigham established a lead mine and smelter, and the community of **Blue Mounds took shape.**

❹ Blue Mounds State Park, situated on 1,716-foot-high Blue Mound, has hiking trails, picnic areas, a large campground, and a swimming pool; viewing towers on the summit offer glorious vistas. Many varieties of birds can be seen from the hiking trails; markers point out where to look for them. *One mi northwest of the village, tel. 608/437–5711. Admission: park sticker. Open daily.*

Cave of the Mounds. A small but colorful limestone cave famous for its diverse mineral formations. Situated on the old Brigham Farm, the cave was discovered only during quarrying operations in the late 1930s. Guides point out the lifeline where the cavern had its beginnings nearly a million years ago; the formations are highlighted by artificial lighting. The cave temperature is in the low 50s year-round, and a sweater or jacket is recommended. Hourlong guided tours along concrete walkways leave every 15 minutes in summer. *Cave of the Mounds Rd., tel. 608/437–3038. Admission: $6 adults, $5 children 5–12 and senior citizens over 65. Open mid-Mar.–mid-Nov., daily 9–5; June–Aug., daily 9–7; mid-Nov.–mid-Mar., Sat. and Sun. 9–5.*

Nestled in a picturesque valley nearby is **Little Norway,** or *Nissedahle* (Valley of the Elves). This restored 1856 Norwegian homestead with its original log buildings has an outstanding collection of Norse antiques and pioneer arts and crafts. One building is topped by a growing sod roof; a spring house has three cupolas. Most of the buildings are trimmed in blue, which is typically Norwegian. Here, too, is a large *Stavekirke,* or stave church, complete with dragon heads at the gable peaks. The replica of the 12th-century church was built in Norway and exhibited at the 1893 World's Columbian Exhibition. *3576 Hwy. JG North, tel. 608/437–8211. Admission: $4 adults, $3.50 senior citizens, $1.75 under 12. Open May–Oct., daily 9–5; July and Aug., daily 9–7.*

The beauty of the **Hidden Valleys** region west of Madison is woven into rolling hills and deep dales. Wisconsin got its nickname, the Badger State, from the early lead miners who burrowed into these hills like badgers. The area is rich in history and therefore in state historical sites. One of the most charming spots in this region is the Old World village of **New Glarus.** Founded by Swiss from the canton of Glarus in 1845, New Glarus retains its Swiss character in language (many residents are bilingual), food, architecture, and festivities. Summer events include a Heidi Festival the last full weekend in June and the Volksfest on the first Sunday in August. The Wilhelm Tell Festival attracts thousands on Labor Day weekend for its German and English-language presentations of Friedrich Schiller's drama.

The **Chalet of the Golden Fleece,** an authentic mountain-style chalet, was built as a private residence in 1937. The white plaster foundation, brown-stained wooden walls, and rocks and logs on the roof to keep the slate shingles in place are typical of construction in the Berne canton. The chalet is now a Swiss museum filled with historical items. Displays include Swiss stamp, coin, and doll collections, wood carvings, and a porcelain tile stove from 1760. *618 2nd St., tel. 608/527–2614. Admission: $2.50 adults, $1 under 19, 50¢ under 12. Open May–Oct., daily 9–4:30.*

Twelve reconstructed buildings at the **Swiss Historical Village** depict the homes, trades, and skills of the Swiss who first settled here. Descendants of those settlers donated land for the museum. There are exhibits on Swiss immigration, a replica of the first long church constructed in 1849 (the churchyard contains tombstones of many of the original settlers), and tools, furnishings, and equipment from early New Glarus businesses. *612 7th Ave., tel. 608/527–2317. Admission: $3 adults, $1 children 6–13. Open May–Oct., daily 9–5.*

Frank Lloyd Wright chose the farming community of **Spring Green** on the Wisconsin River for his home "Taliesin" and his architectural school. **Tower Hill State Park,** across the river, has a restored Civil War shot tower, the last sign of the pioneer village of Helena. Wright's influence is evident in a number of buildings in the village of Spring Green; notice the use of geometric shapes, low flat-roof profiles, cantilever projections, and steeple-like spires. On Jefferson Street, the bank, medical office, pharmacy, and facade of the Robert E. Gard Theater all show strong Wright influence.

Tours of the Taliesin Fellowship buildings, designed and built by Wright, include the 1903 Hillside Home School, galleries, drafting studio, and theater. *3 mi south of Spring Green on Hwy. 23, tel. 608/588–2511. Admission: $5 adults, $2 children under 12. Open mid-May–mid-Oct., daily 10–4.*

The **House on the Rock** is one of Wisconsin's biggest tourist attractions. The extraordinary multilevel stone home, which stands on a chimney-like rock 450 feet above the Wyoming Valley, was begun by the artist Robert Jordan in the early 1940s. Jordan actually hauled materials to the site in baskets on his back, climbing a shaky rope ladder to the top of the rock. Built mainly of stone, the house contains pools, waterfalls, massive fireplaces, trees growing through floors and ceilings, and rooms with canted windows jutting out over the valley. The home was opened to the public in 1961; seven years later, Jordan built a Mill House to hold his vast collection of paperweights, dolls, mechanical banks, music boxes, and armor. Other buildings followed, and today the complex includes **Artists Village,** with 18 specialty and artists' shops in a garden setting; **Streets of Yesterday,** re-creating 19th-century buildings, shops, and businesses; the **Cannon Building,** housing a huge cannon and doll collections; and the **Music of Yesterday,** which houses an extensive collection of animated musical machines and a giant carousel, with 269 animals and over 18,000 lights. Other buildings contain exhibits on circuses, dolls, console theater organs, and Oriental arts. Self-guided tours are available and a restaurant and picnic area are on the grounds. Allow most of a day to see it all. *9 mi. south of Spring Green on Hwy. 23, tel. 608/935–3639. Admission: $10 adults, $6 children 7–12, $1 children 4–6. Open 8 AM–dusk; ticket sales end 2 1/2 hours before closing.*

❼ **Governor Dodge State Park** (near Dodgeville, about 15 mi south of Spring Green) is Wisconsin's second-largest state park with more than 5,000 acres, two manmade lakes, fishing, campgrounds, picnic areas, and hiking trails. *2 mi north of Dodgeville on Hwy. 23, tel. 414/935–2315. Admission: park sticker. Open daily.*

❽ Just south of Dodgeville along U.S. Highway 151, **Mineral Point** was once the metropolis of southwest Wisconsin's lead-mining region. It dates from 1828, when lead was discovered, and it is Wisconsin's third oldest community. Beginning in the mid-1830s, Cornish miners skilled in hard-rock mining and stone masonry arrived. Their English heritage survives in the town's old stone houses and in the meat pies called "pasties" and the saffron cakes served in local restaurants. Today the community is home to many artists and galleries, and studios are open to visitors.

Booklets outlining a self-guided driving tour of Mineral Point's historical and architectural attractions are available. *Tour Information Center in Water Tower Park on U.S. Hwy. 151. Open May–Oct., daily 9–5.*

The Gundry House, a Victorian Italianate house dating from 1868, contains Victorian furnishings and mineral exhibits and artifacts relating to the early days of Mineral Point. *234 Mason St., tel. 608/987–2991. Admission: $1 adults, 50 cents children under 18. Open Memorial Day–Labor Day, daily 10–4.*

Pendarvis (named after a town in Cornwall) is the State Historical Society's complex of six carefully restored rock and log houses built by Cornish miners in the 1840s. The homes are filled with exhibits of mining tools and equipment as well as furniture and antiques. They are excellent examples of the Cornish stone mason's art and of what life was like in the lead region in the 1830s and '40s. *114 Shake Rag St., tel. 608/987–2122. Admission: $4 adults, $3.20 over 65, $1.50 ages 5–17, $10 family. Costumed guides give tours May–Oct., daily 9–5.*

Shake Rag Alley. This restored craft community includes stone and log buildings of Mineral Point's early craftsmen where today local artists create and sell their products. The name Shake Rag comes from the custom of Cornish wives of shaking a rag to summon their men from the hillside mines. Browse the grounds on self-guided tours. *18 Shake Rag St., tel. 608/987–2808. Admission: $1.75 adults, $1.25 students. Open May–Oct., daily 9–5.*

9 Named for the "plats," or ingots, into which lead was melted in the 19th century, the old mining town of **Platteville** has recently gained fame as the training camp of the National Football League's Chicago Bears. Lead and zinc were mined until just a few years ago, but there are few signs of the mines; the hills and earth beneath the community are honeycombed with tunnels. A branch of the University of Wisconsin is situated here.

The Mining Museum and Rollo Jamison Museum. The Mining Museum traces the region's mining history through dioramas, models, artifacts, and photos. A guided tour includes a walk into the 1845 Bevans Mine, a visit to a mine hoist house, and a train ride around the museum grounds in ore cars pulled by a 1931 locomotive. The Jamison Museum features farm implements, carriages, and a turn-of-the-century kitchen and parlor. *405 E. Main, tel. 608/348–3301. Admission: $3 adults, $2 over 65, $1 5–15, includes both museums. Open Memorial Day–Labor Day, daily 9–4; Labor Day–Nov. 1, Sat. and Sun. 9–4.*

10 Wisconsin's second oldest community, **Prairie du Chien,** dates from 1673, when Marquette and Jolliet reached the confluence of the Wisconsin and Mississippi rivers six miles south of here. The name is French for "prairie of the dog," which referred to an Indian chief whose name meant dog.

The oldest part of town is St. Feriole Island, which became a flourishing fur market in the late 17th century, attracting Indians from the upper regions of the Wisconsin and Mississippi as well as traders and settlers. Between 1685 and 1831, four forts were built and occupied at various times by French, British, and Americans. A skirmish in the War of 1812 was fought here, and Jefferson Davis and Zachary Taylor were stationed at Fort Crawford in the late 1820s.

Prairie du Chien today is a bustling river community where the Mississippi steamers *Delta Queen* and *Mississippi Queen* call in summer.

The **Villa Louis Mansion** was built in 1870 by H. L. Dousman, a fur trader and agent of the American Fur Co. who was Wisconsin's first millionaire. The home, a State Historical Society site, stands on an ancient Hopewell Indian mound and contains one of the finest collections of Victorian decorative arts in the country. The Astor Fur Warehouse on the grounds has exhibits on the fur trade of the upper Mississippi, and the carriage house has been converted into a museum. Displays include artifacts from the days when the city was a military outpost, and a blockhouse from Fort Crawford has been reconstructed on the grounds. *521 Villa Louis Rd., tel. 608/326–2721. Admission: $4 adults, $3.20 over 65, $1 under 17, $9 family. Open May–Oct., daily 9–5.*

The **Fort Crawford Medical Museum** contains 19th-century medical displays with exhibits on Indian cures, an 1890s pharmacy, dioramas, and artifacts. The museum is in the reconstructed hospital of the second Fort Crawford, built in 1828. One exhibit is a barred window from the Fort Crawford guardhouse where Chief Black Hawk was held prisoner in 1832. *717*

S. Beaumont St., tel. 608/326–6960. Admission: $2 adults, 50 cents children under 12, $5 family. Open May–Oct., daily 10–5.

Scenic cruises on the Mississippi River are offered from May through October aboard a new 150-passenger sidewheeler packet boat. Dinner and dance cruises are available. *Box 279, Genoa, WI 54632, tel. 608/689–2140 or 326–4234.*

Wyalusing State Park, 2,650 acres on the bluffs nearly 600 feet above the Mississippi, is at the spot where Marquette and Jolliet reached the Upper Mississippi. There are unusual rock formations and lookouts throughout the park, and camping, hiking trails, and a boat landing. *On Hwy. 18–151, 7 mi south from Prairie du Chien, then right at Hwy. C, tel. 608/996–2261. Admission: park sticker. Open daily 6 AM–11 PM.*

Situated on the Mississippi where the Black and La Crosse rivers meet, **La Crosse** was founded in 1842 as an Indian trading post. Lumbering and sawmill products were its chief industries until the forests were ravaged; breweries then became an important part of the area's economic base. Today the city serves a trading area that extends into northeastern Iowa and southeastern Minnesota. The summer Riverfest celebrates the city's river heritage, and autumn's Oktoberfest recalls La Crosse's German and Norwegian heritage. There is a branch of the University of Wisconsin here.

A self-guided tour of buildings of architectural and historical significance begins at the **Hixon House** (429 N. 7th St.). Information, brochures, and maps are available at the **La Crosse Historical Society** in the Swarthout Museum of the Main Library (9th and Main Sts.), and at the **La Crosse Convention and Visitors Bureau** in Riverside Park (tel. 608/782–2366). There are also tours of the **University of Wisconsin–La Crosse** (tel. 608/785–8067).

Granddad's Bluff towers 530 feet above the city; the summit offers a panoramic view of three states. This is a fine place for photos of the river, but in the afternoon, you'll be shooting into the sun.

The Hixon House and Museum is an Italianate-style house built in the mid-1800s by the businessman and philanthropist George Hixon. The original contents include ceramics from Europe and the Orient, and Empire and Victorian period furniture. This is a good example of the affluent lifestyle of the Upper Mississippi Valley in the mid-19th-century. *429 N. 7th St., tel. 608/784–9080. Admission: $3 adults, $1.50 children under 15. Open June 1–Labor Day, daily 1–4.*

Mississippi River cruises are offered aboard the *La Crosse Queen,* a 150-passenger paddlewheeler. Dinner, fish boil, happy-hour, and luncheon cruises are available. *Riverside Park, 3 blks. west of U.S. Hwy. 53, tel. 608/784–2893. Sightseeing cruises depart Memorial Day–Labor Day, at 11 AM, 1:30, and 3:30 PM; mid-May–Memorial Day and after Labor Day– mid-Oct., daily at 11 AM. Fare: $6.95 adults, $6.45 over 62, $4.25 children under 12. AE, MC, V.*

Myrick Park Zoo includes a children's zoo and a small collection of domestic and wild animals and birds. The park has picnic areas, a wading pool, boat ramps, and a nature trail. *2000 La*

Crosse St., tel. 608/784–5886. Admission free. Open May–Oct., daily 9–6.

The Pump House is a former pumping station of Romanesque Revival design that has been renovated into a home for the visual and performing arts. The art gallery features changing exhibits of work by local and regional artists. *119 King St., tel. 608/785–1434. Open weekdays 9–5, Sat 1–5; closed Sun.*

Swarthout Museum, operated by the La Crosse County Historical Society, is in a wing of the Main Library. Displays include changing exhibits on local history, social customs, transportation, river life, agriculture, and commerce. *Corner of 9th and Main Sts., tel. 608/782–1980. Admission free. Open Tues.–Fri. 11–5, Sat. 1–5; closed Sun. and Mon.*

What to See and Do with Children

Blue Mounds **Cave of the Mounds** (*see* Exploring Southern Wisconsin).

La Crosse **La Crosse Queen Cruises** and **Myrick Park Zoo** (*see* Exploring Southern Wisconsin).

Lake Geneva **Gage Boat Tours** (*see* Exploring Southern Wisconsin).

Madison **Vilas Park Zoo** (*see* Exploring Southern Wisconsin).

Prairie du Chien **J & D Livery** (tel. 608/326–6475) offers narrated horse-drawn carriage tours of the city. *Tours depart from 531 N. Marquette Rd. (the Country Kitchen restaurant) late May–early Oct., daily 1 PM–dusk, weather permitting.*

Lock & Dam No. 9, Highway 35 near Lynxville, 20 miles north of Prairie du Chien. There's an observation deck for watching the large riverboats and their barges pass through the lock. If there's no boat, ask one of the lockworkers when one is due. Also Lock & Dam No. 7, 12 miles south of La Crosse.

Off the Beaten Track

When Wisconsin achieved territorial status on July 3, 1836, Governor Henry Dodge selected tiny **Belmont,** then barely two months old, as the capital. A Council House and Supreme Court Building were hastily constructed in Pittsburgh and shipped here by steamboat and overland transport. When the legislators met in October 1836, they held jurisdiction over a region that included all of present-day Wisconsin, Iowa, Minnesota, and North and South Dakota as far west as the Missouri River. After a stormy 46-day session, the legislature chose Madison as the permanent capital, agreed to hold the 1837 legislative session in Burlington, Iowa, and adjourned. In the 1860s the railroad passed three miles to the south, and most of the remaining town went with it, leaving Belmont and its capitol complex behind.

First Capitol State Park. After several moves and checkered lives as homes, barns and other farm buildings, the Council House and Supreme Court Building were returned to their original site. The Council House has been refurbished to look as it did in 1836. A stove and a secretary's desk are from the 1836 legislative session. The Supreme Court Building contains a small museum with exhibits on tools, crafts, and agriculture of the 1830s. Picnic areas on the grounds. *3 mi north of Belmont*

on Hwy. G, tel. 608/523–4427. Admission free. Open Memorial
Day–Labor Day, daily 9–5.

Forest Hill Cemetery, Madison (tel. 608/266–4720). 140 Confederate prisoners of war who died in Madison during the Civil
War are buried in this northernmost Confederate cemetery.
"Confederate Rest" is 1/4 mile inside the cemetery entrance on
the left. *1 Speedway Rd, about 1 mi west of Camp Randall, the
university's football stadium.*

Shopping

Madison's **State Street** in the area between Capitol Square and
university campus offers ethnic and unusual shops. Street vendors near the campus have a variety of goods for sale.

Rowe Pottery Works (217 Main St., Cambridge, 15 mi east of
Madison on Hwy. 18, tel. 608/423–3935) produces traditional
American salt glaze stoneware, handmade and decorated.
There are excellent buys at the factory outlet.

You can watch lace being made on 19th-century machinery at
the **Upright Embroidery Factory** in New Glarus, then purchase
it along with woolens and other imported fabrics at the **Swiss
Miss Textile Mart** (1101 Hwy. 69, tel. 608/527–2514). New
Glarus stores feature Swiss imports.

Items from Norway and other Scandinavian countries can be
found in the village of Mount Horeb, where many of the residents are of Norwegian heritage. Norwegian hand-painting on
wooden items, a process called *rosemalling*, is especially lovely. The village offers an outstanding selection of antiques, with
shops and malls featuring the wares of more than 100 dealers.

Sports and Fitness

Beaches The numerous beaches in the Lake Geneva region include **Big
Foot State Park** (Hwy. 120 south of Lake Geneva, tel. 414/248–
2528), **Fontana Beach** (Fontana Blvd. in Fontana), **Lake Geneva
Beach** (downtown Lake Geneva), and **Williams Bay Beach** (Williams Bay). Most cater to an under-30 crowd, although there is
room for all.

Beaches in Madison parks include **Olbrich** (3330 Atwood Ave.),
Tenney (1300 Sherman Ave.), and **Vilas** (1939 Vilas Park Dr.).
All are family beaches, free, with changing houses and life-
guards.

Governor Dodge State Park has two family beaches with changing houses and lifeguards.

Hundreds of unsupervised beaches along the Mississippi are
available for picnics, sunbathing, and relaxing. Most are accessible only by boat. Swimmers at these beaches should use
caution; there are dangerous drop-offs and undercurrents in
the river.

Bicycling Dozens of miles of bicycle trails in the Lake Geneva area include
hills that the normally desk-bound should prepare for.

There are several state bicycle trails in southern Wisconsin.
The 23-mile **Sugar River State Trail** runs from New Glarus to
Brodhead, crossing the Sugar River and its tributaries 14
times. There is a trail fee. *Sugar River State Trail, Box 256,
Monroe 53566, tel. 608/527–2334 in summer; 608/325–4844 in
winter.*

The **Military Ridge State Trail,** Wisconsin's newest, traces the path of the Old Military Ridge Trail of the mid-1800s. The 47-mile trail runs from Verona, 5 miles southwest of Madison, to Dodgeville. There is a trail fee. *Governor Dodge State Park, Box 42, Dodgeville 53533, tel. 608/935-2315.*

The **Elroy–Sparta State Trail,** the granddaddy of Wisconsin's bicycle trails, treats cyclists to a 33-mile roll through wooded hills and valleys. It begins at Sparta, 25 miles northeast of La Crosse, and traverses 3 old railroad tunnels on the way to Elroy. There is a trail fee. *Elroy–Sparta State Trail, Box 98, Ontario 54651, tel. 608/337-4775; or Elroy–Sparta National Trail, Box 153, Kendall 54638, tel. 608/463-7109.*

Canoeing Wisconsin rivers come in all sizes and challenge beginners and experts alike.

Southern Gateway The **Yahara River** flows from Madison's lakes to the Rock River. Access is available on Lake Mendota in Madison and along the river at road crossings. Locks lead through a series of lakes, and some dams need portaging. The current is slow, and additional portages may be necessary during low water.

The **Rock River** flows leisurely through southern Wisconsin's farmlands and urban areas. Access is available at road crossings and cities along the way.

The **Fox River,** known as the Little Fox or Illinois Fox to differentiate it from the north-flowing Fox that empties into Lake Michigan, is a slow-current waterway that meanders from southeast Wisconsin into Illinois. Access is available at county and state highway crossings; there are several dams to portage.

Hidden Valleys Because of its currents and heavy traffic, the Mississippi River is not known as a canoeing river, although canoeing is possible in some of the sloughs and backwaters.

The **Kickapoo,** said to be "the crookedest river in the world," is navigable all the way to its confluence with the Wisconsin River. Access is available at numerous road crossings. The current is relaxing, but be prepared to portage several dams and the occasional fallen tree.

Pine River. A popular and relaxing canoe trip, through farmland to the Wisconsin River. Access at Richland Center and on a number of country roads.

Pecatonica and **East Branch of the Pecatonica.** Mild current and picturesque scenery, including farmland, woods, and marsh. There is no rough water, but it may be necessary to skirt an occasional fallen tree. The river's branches join near Browntown in Green County and head south into Illinois.

The **Sugar River** flows gently through rich southern Wisconsin farmland. You must portage two dams on the upper river, but it is entirely navigable below Brodhead to the Wisconsin border.

Fishing Northern pike, walleye, smallmouth and largemouth bass, bullheads, catfish, and a variety of panfish are all found in southern Wisconsin waters. Rainbow, brown, and brook trout are stocked in specially designated streams. Local bait and tackle shops or resorts will tell you where to look for the fish, or help you obtain a professional guide.

Golf There are scores of public golf courses in the southern Wisconsin.

Lake Geneva **Abbey Springs Country Club** (S. Shore Dr., Fontana, tel. 414/275–6111), 18 holes; **Alpine Valley Resort** (Hwy. G, East Troy, tel. 414/642–7374), 27 holes; **American Lake Geneva Resort** (Hwy. 50 E., Lake Geneva, tel. 414/248–8811), 36 holes; **George Williams College** (Hwy. 67, Williams Bay, tel. 414/245–9507), 18 holes; **Hillmoor Country Club** (Hwy. 50 E., Lake Geneva, tel. 414/248–4570), 18 holes; **Lakelawn Lodge** (Hwy. 50, Delevan, tel. 414/728–5511), 18 holes.

Madison Madison offers 11 public courses, including three municipal ones. **Glenway Golf Course** (3747 Speedway Rd., tel. 608/266–4737) is a nine-hole executive course. **Monona Municipal Golf Course** (111 E. Dean Ave., tel. 608/266–4736) is a nine-hole regulation course; **Yahara Hills** (67001 E. Broadway on Hwy. 12/18, tel. 608/838–3126) is a 36-hole regulation course.

La Crosse La Crosse has several courses within a few minutes' drive, including **Walsh Golf Center** (4203 Hwy. B, tel. 414/782–0838), a nine-hole executive course, and **Maple Grove Country Club** (Rte. 1, West Salem, tel. 414/786–0340), an 18-hole championship course.

Skiing Downhill skiing has become increasingly popular in southern
Downhill Wisconsin with facilities ranging from just some snow and a slope to lavish resorts complete with saunas, whirlpools, restaurants, bars and music.

Alpine Valley has 9 runs, 4 rope tows, 9 double chairs, snowmaking; longest run 3,330 feet, vertical drop 386 feet. Cross-country skiing, rentals, repair, instruction, ski shop, restaurant, bar, motel. *3 mi south of East Troy on Hwy. G, then 1½ mi west on Hwy. D, tel. 414/642–7374. Open weekdays 10 AM–11 PM, weekends and holidays 9 AM–11 PM; closed Dec. 24.*

Americana offers 13 runs, 2 rope tows, 3 double chairs, snowmaking; longest run, 1,320 feet, vertical drop 211 feet. Cross-country skiing, rentals, repairs, instruction, ski shop, 3 bar/lounges, cafeteria, 3 restaurants, 342-room hotel, health spa. *3 mi from Lake Geneva on Hwy. 50, tel. 414/248–8811. Open weekdays 10–10, weekends 9–11.*

Majestic has 9 runs, 4 rope tows, 2 double chairs, quad chair, snowmaking; longest run 1/4 mile, vertical drop 235 feet. Rentals, instruction, chalet, bar/lounge, ski shop, cafeteria. *8 mi south of Lake Geneva on Hwy. 120 to Hwy. BB to S. Shore Dr., tel. 414/248–6128. Open daily 9:30 AM–11 PM.*

Wilmot Mountain has 30 runs, 6 rope tows, 4 double chairs, quad chair, snowmaking; longest run 2,500 feet, vertical drop 230 feet. Rentals, repairs, instruction, chalet, 2 bar/lounges, ski shop, restaurant, 2 cafeterias. *1 mi south of Wilmot on Hwy. 20, tel. 414/862–2301. Open weekdays 10 AM–11 PM; weekends, and holidays 9:30 AM–11 PM; closed Dec. 24.*

Mt. La Crosse offers 14 runs, 3 rope tows, 3 double chairs, snowmaking; longest run 5,300 feet, vertical drop 516 feet. Cross-country skiing, rentals, repairs, instruction, chalet, bar/lounge, ski shop, snack bar. *2 mi south on Hwy. 35, tel. 608/788–0044. Open Mon. 10–5, Tues.–Sat. 9–9, Sun. 9–5; closed Dec. 25.*

Cross-country Cross-country skiing is perhaps the Midwest's most rapidly growing sport, and skiers can be found crossing golf courses, parks, arboretums, and even city streets. Many city, township, county, and state parks in southern Wisconsin offer cross-country ski trails, and many alpine ski resorts provide facilities for the Nordic skier.

Spectator Sports

Auto Racing   "Fender bender" auto races are held at many small tracks in the summer. The **Great Lakes Dragway** at Union Grove (15 mi west of Racine on Hwy. 11, Box 154, tel. 414/878–3783) has drag racing Wednesdays, weekends, and holidays from April through November.

Baseball   The **Madison Muskies** (1511 Northport Dr., tel. 608/271–0010), a Midwest League club affiliated with the Oakland A's, play their home games at Warner Park in Madison.

Basketball   The **La Crosse Catbirds** (300 Harborview Plaza, tel. 608/782–4500), a professional team in the Continental Basketball Association, play 24 home games from December through March at the La Crosse Center.

Football   The **University of Wisconsin–Madison** plays its home games at Camp Randall Stadium (1430 Monroe St., tel. 608/262–1440). University branch campuses at **Whitewater, Platteville,** and **La Crosse** also field football teams.

The **Racine Raiders** minor league team plays from July through November at Horlick Field (1648 N. Memorial Dr., tel. 414/634–3293).

Dining and Lodging

Dining in southern Wisconsin runs the gastronomical gamut from burger joints and meat-and-potatoes places to elegant restaurants. The most variety, of course, is found in larger communities and resort areas. Steaks are big everywhere, and prime rib is on nearly every menu. The Friday-night fish fry is ubiquitous—you'd have to search to find a restaurant that doesn't serve one. Here and there you'll find ethnic fare.

The variety of accommodations ranges from quaint bed-and-breakfasts and plush and elegant resorts to utilitarian places with comfortable beds, clean linens, and plenty of hot water.

Price categories for restaurants and hotels are the same as in the Milwaukee Dining and Lodging sections.

Fontana   **The Abbey on Lake Geneva.** 320 luxurious rooms; 2-day mini-
Lodging   mum stay weekends, package plans. *Fontana Blvd., 53125, tel.*
★   *414/275–6811 or 800/558–2405. Facilities: 4 outdoor pools, indoor pool, saunas, whirlpool, 6 tennis courts, health club, bowling, bicycle rentals, water skiing, and boat rentals, fishing; 2 dining rooms, coffee shop, cocktail lounge, entertainment. AE, DC, MC, V. Expensive–Very Expensive.*

La Crosse   **The Freight House Restaurant.** This restored railroad freight
Dining   house is a National Historic Site. Steaks, Alaska king crab, and prime rib are the specialties. There's a lounge and entertainment. *107 Vine St., tel. 608/784–6211. Dress: informal. Reservations suggested. AE, DC, MC, V. No lunch. Closed Easter, Thanksgiving, Dec. 24–25. Moderate.*

Lodging   **The Radisson Hotel.** 170 rooms, many with river view. *200 Harborview Plaza, 54601, tel. 608/784–6680 or 800/228–9822.*

Facilities: indoor pool, whirlpool, dining room, cocktail lounge. AE, DC, MC, V. Moderate.

Exel Inn. 103 well-kept rooms with queen-size beds; nonsmoker's rooms available. *2150 Rose St., 54601, tel. 608/781–0400 or 800/356–8013. Facilities: free satellite movies, restaurant opposite. AE, MC, V. Inexpensive.*

Super 8 of La Crosse. 80 rooms. *1625 Rose St., 54601, tel. 608/781–8880. Facilities: whirlpool. AE, MC, V. Inexpensive.*

Lake Geneva
Dining

The Red Geranium Restaurant. Specializing in steaks and lobster, this restaurant features an attractive setting with sun porch and an open hearth grill. There's a children's menu and cocktail lounge. *West of U.S. 12 on Hwy. 50 E, tel. 414/248–3637. Dress: informal. Reservations suggested. AE, MC, V. Closed Thanksgiving, Dec. 25. Moderate.*

Popeye's Gallery & Grog. Excellent sandwiches and Greek and Mexican dishes are served at this casual place overlooking Geneva Lake. There's outdoor dining and a barbecue pit in summer. *811 Wrigley Dr., tel. 414/248–4361. Dress: casual. Reservations recommended. AE, MC, V. Inexpensive–Moderate.*

Lodging
★

Americana Lake Geneva Resort. 350 large, well-kept rooms with bath, many with a view of the golf course, 2-day minimum stay on weekends. *Hwy. 50 E at junction with U.S. 12, 53147, tel. 414/248–8811. Facilities: 2 pools (1 indoor), sauna, whirlpool, exercise room, health club, 12 tennis courts (4 indoor), 5 racquetball courts, 36-hole golf course, lighted airstrip, paddleboats, miniature golf, skeet and trapshooting, riding, cross-country and downhill skiing, 2 restaurants, cocktail lounge, entertainment. AE, DC, MC, V. Very Expensive.*

Hilton Inn. 107 rooms, some with lake view. *300 Wrigley Dr., 53147, tel. 414/248–9181. Facilities: small indoor pool, whirlpool, sauna, dining room, cocktail lounge, entertainment; beach and boat rental nearby. AE, DC, MC, V. Expensive.*

Diplomat Motel. 23 rooms. *1060 Well St., 53147, tel. 414/248–1809. Facilities: outdoor pool, picnic area; snowmobile trails nearby. AE, MC, V. Moderate.*

Madison
Dining
★

Fess Hotel Dining Room. Excellent American and European cuisine in elegantly restored dining rooms; garden dining in season. *123 E. Doty St., 1 block off Capitol Square, tel. 608/256–0263. Jacket and tie recommended for dinner. Reservations recommended. AE, DC, MC, V. Closed Dec. 25. Moderate.*

Cafe Palms. European and American food served in a refurbished historic hotel. *636 W. Washington Ave., tel. 608/256–0166. Dress: informal. AE, MC, V. Inexpensive–Moderate.*

Porta Bella. Specializing in homemade pasta, pizza, steaks, and seafood in a quiet, intimate atmosphere near the UW campus. *425 N. Francis St., tel. 608/256–3186. MC, V. Dinner only. Inexpensive–Moderate.*

Chi-Chi's. The Mexican food is mild but tasty. The cocktail lounge is a favorite with the west side under-30 crowd. *414 Grand Canyon Dr., tel. 608/893–9200. Reservations recommended. AE, DC, MC, V. Closed Thanksgiving, Dec. 24 and 25. Inexpensive.*

Heritage House Smorgasbord. Large daily smorgasbord with dessert section, children's menu. *3858 E. Washington Ave., tel. 608/249–7687. No credit cards. Closed Sat. and Dec. 25. Inexpensive.*

Lodging
★

Mansion Hill Inn. This 1858 stone mansion has 11 elegant rooms with baths and a Victorian parlor. Each room has a different decor; some have fireplaces and four-poster beds. *424 N. Pinckney St., 53703, tel. 608/255–3999. Children under 12 not accepted. AE, MC, V. Very Expensive.*

The Edgewater Hotel. This is one of Madison's most elegant motor hotels; most of the 143 rooms have a view of Lake Mendota. *666 Wisconsin Ave., 53703, tel. 608/256–9071. Facilities: lake swimming, dock, fishing, pier bar, dining room, cocktail lounge. AE, MC, V. Expensive.*

Best Western Inn on the Park. On Capitol Square, the hotel has 222 units. *22 S. Carroll, 53704, tel. 608/257–8811. Facilities: indoor pool, whirlpool, exercise room, off-street parking, two dining rooms, cocktail lounge, entertainment. AE, DC, MC, V. Moderate.*

Red Roof Inn. 109 rooms. *4830 Hayes Rd., 53704, tel. 608/241–1787. Facilities: restaurant opposite. AE, DC, MC, V. Inexpensive.*

West Town Motor Inn. 95 rooms. *6900 Sebold Rd., 53719, tel. 608/274–6900. Facilities: coffee shop adjacent. AE, DC, MC, V. Inexpensive.*

Mineral Point
Dining

Red Rooster Cafe. There are booths and a lunch counter at this cafe offering Cornish pasties, hearty soups, and other stick-to-the-ribs food. *158 High St., tel. 608/987–9936. Dress: casual. No reservations. No credit cards. Inexpensive.*

Royal Inn. Cornish fare, including pasties, and American food make up the bill of fare at this restored turn-of-the-century hotel. Cocktail lounge. *43 High St., tel. 608/987–2770. Dress: casual. MC, V. Inexpensive.*

Lodging

The Duke House This B&B is listed on the National Register of Historic Places. There are four rooms with private baths in a Colonial-style house furnished with period pieces. *618 Maiden St., 53565, tel. 608/987–2821. AE, MC, V. Inexpensive–Moderate.*

Redwood Motel. 27 well-kept rooms in a quiet motel with an expansive country view. *Box 43, 53565, tel. 608/987–2317, 1 mi north on U.S. 151. Facilities: restaurant opposite. AE, MC, V. Inexpensive.*

New Glarus
Dining

The Glarner Stube. Sandwiches, fondues, and other Swiss/German delicacies served in an attractive chalet atmosphere. *518 1st St., tel. 608/527–2216. Dress: casual. Weekend reservations recommended. AE, DC, MC, V. Inexpensive–moderate.*

New Glarus Hotel. Authentic Swiss food is served in an Old World atmosphere. Luncheons, dinners, buffet dinners. There are several dining rooms and a cocktail lounge. Entertainment Friday and Saturday nights. *518 1st St., tel. 608/527–2216. Dress: informal. Weekend reservations recommended. AE, MC, V. Closed Tues. Inexpensive–Moderate.*

Lodging

Chalet Landhaus Motel. 42 spacious rooms, some with whirlpool baths. The comfortable lobby has a chalet atmosphere, with a stone fireplace and beamed ceilings. *801 Hwy. 69, 53574, tel. 608/527–5234. Facilities: dining room, cocktail lounge, coffee shop, close to the Sugar River bike trail. AE, MC, V. Inexpensive–Moderate.*

Swiss-Aire Motel. 26 rooms. *1200 Hwy. 69, 53574, tel. 608/526–2138. Facilities: 1 block from Sugar River Bike Trail and adjoining snowmobile trails, restaurants nearby. MC, V. Inexpensive.*

Platteville **The Timber Supper Club.** This attractive dining room has a
Dining large theater organ. The extensive menu features steaks and
seafoods, there's a children's menu and a cocktail lounge. ¼ *mi
east of junction of U.S. 151, and Hwy. 80 and 81, tel. 608/348–
2406. Jacket and tie for dinner. Reservations recommended.
MC, V. Closed major holidays. Inexpensive–Moderate.*

Lodging **Best Western Governor Dodge Motor Inn.** 74 units. *Box 658,
53818, tel. 608/348–2301. 1 mi south on U.S. 151. Facilities: indoor pool, sauna, restaurant, cocktail lounge. AE, DC, MC,
V. Moderate.*

Prairie du Chien **The Barn.** Rustic dining room with beautiful bluff view.
Dining Standard fare, Sunday brunch, noon buffet, children's menu;
cocktail lounge. *3 mi north on Main St., tel. 608/326–4941.
Dress: casual. Reservations recommended. AE, MC, V. No
lunch Sat. Moderate.*

Lodging **Brisbois Motor Inn.** 37 rooms. *533 N. Marquette Rd., 53821, tel.
608/326–8480 or 800/356–5850. Facilities: indoor pool, restaurant adjacent. AE, DC, MC, V. Inexpensive.*

Spring Green **The Spring Green.** Designed by Frank Lloyd Wright, the stone
Dining and wood construction and towering spire are typical of his
famed Prairie-style architecture. Steaks, prime rib, and sea-
food are served in dining rooms overlook the Wisconsin River.
Children's menu, cocktail lounge. *2½ mi south of Spring Green
on Hwy. 23 at the Wisconsin River bridge, tel. 608/588–2571.
Jacket and tie required. Reservations recommended. AE, MC,
V. Moderate–Expensive.*
Arthur's. This contemporary dining room specializes in steaks.
There's a children's menu and a cocktail lounge. *On U.S. 14, at
junction of Hwys. 60 and 23, tel. 608/588–2521. Dress: infor-
mal. Reservations recommended. MC, V. No lunch. Closed
Sun. Moderate.*

Lodging **The Prairie House.** 31 rooms. *Junction of U.S. 14 and Hwy. 23,
53588, tel. 608/588–2088. Facilities: sauna, whirlpool, exercise
room, restaurant opposite. AE, MC, V. Inexpensive.*

The Arts

Blue Mounds *The Song of Norway,* a light opera based on the life of the Norwegian composer Edvard Grieg, is presented on the grounds of
Cave of the Mounds several weekends each summer. *1 mi east
on U.S. 18–151, then ½ mi north on Cave of the Mounds Rd.,
tel. 608/437–4600.*

Madison **The Madison Civic Center** (211 State St., tel. 608/266–9055) is
host to such resident groups as the Madison Repertory Thea-
ter, Children's Theater of Madison, and Madison Symphony
Orchestra. Touring shows include Broadway productions, big
bands, ballet and dance companies.
The **Madison Opera Guild** (tel. 608/238–8085) presents several
operas each season.
The **Madison Symphony** presents free outdoor concerts on the
Capitol Square Wednesday evenings at 7 in July. Spread a blan-
ket on the lawn and picnic. Go early; the best spots are taken by
5 PM.
The University of Wisconsin's **Union Theater** (800 Langdon St.,
tel. 608/262–2201) offers a travel/adventure film series and a
concert series each year. Performers have included the Mil-

waukee Symphony Orchestra and the Polish Chamber Orchestra.

Many film societies on the University of Wisconsin campus show art films and revivals. For schedules, call Memorial Union Information (tel. 608/262–6333).

Platteville The annual **Wisconsin Shakespeare Festival** is held at the University of Wisconsin–Platteville's Center for the Arts one month each summer. Shakespeare's works are presented on a rotating basis. *Center for the Arts, UW–Platteville, tel. 608/ 342–1298.*

Spring Green The **American Players Theater** is described as the only professional drama company in the USA devoted solely to classical productions. Performances are in a wooded outdoor amphitheater. *Hwy. C to Golf Course Rd., tel. 608/588–7401 June–Oct, Wed.–Sun.*

Central Wisconsin

The Central Wisconsin River Country gets its name from the scenic Wisconsin River. This hardworking waterway runs through the heart of the region and offers a wide range of recreational opportunities. Camping, canoeing, fishing, and boating are popular summer activities—skiing and snowmobiling rule in winter. Millions upon millions of board feet of lumber were rafted down the Wisconsin in the last century, and many communities owe their beginnings to the lumbering industry.

It was this southern section of the waterway, where the river bends sharply and heads west toward the Mississippi, that Marquette and Jolliet explored on their way to discovering the Mississippi.

Getting Around

By Plane **Central Wisconsin Airport** at Mosinee (Hwy. 153 at Hwy. 51, tel. 715/693–2522) serves Wausau, Wisconsin Rapids, and Stevens Point. Air Wisconsin, American Eagle, Mesaba, and Midstate Airlines provide daily air service.

By Car Most travel in central Wisconsin is by car on an extensive network of good state and county roads. Interstate 90–94 runs through the southern section of the region; U.S. 51 is the major north–south highway.

By Train **Amtrak** runs between Milwaukee and Minneapolis/St. Paul, with stops at Portage and Wisconsin Dells in the southern sections of the region.

By Bus **Greyhound** and **Trailways** stop in the larger cities and towns.

Scenic Drives **County Highway Z,** from Nekoosa (just south of Wisconsin Rapids) south to the junction with Highway 13, runs for 45 miles along the east bank of the Wisconsin River and past the Petenwell and Castle Rock Flowages.

Important Addresses and Numbers

Tourist Information **Baraboo Chamber of Commerce** (124 2nd St., 53913, tel. 608/ 356–8333). Open weekdays 10–4.
Portage Chamber of Commerce (301 W. Wisconsin Ave., 53901, tel. 608/742–6242). Open weekdays 8–noon and 1–5.

Reedsburg Chamber of Commerce (127 Main St., 53959, tel. 608/524–2850). Open weekdays 9:30–noon and 1–2:30.

Stevens Point Convention & Visitors Bureau (600 Main St., 54481, tel. 715/344–2556). Open weekdays 9–5, Sat. 9–noon.

Wausau Area Convention & Visitors Bureau (427 4th St., 54401, tel. 715/845–6231). Open weekdays 8–4:30.

Wisconsin Dells Visitors & Convention Bureau (115 Wisconsin Ave., 53965, tel. 608/254–8088 or 800/223–3557 in the Midwest). Open weekdays 9–5; daily 9–5 in summer.

Wisconsin Rapids Chamber of Commerce (211 4th Ave. N, 54494, tel. 715/423–1830). Open weekdays 9–5.

Emergencies **Wisconsin State Patrol** (tel. 608/246–3220). While emergency numbers vary, dialing "0" will bring an operator on the line.

Exploring Central Wisconsin

Numbers in the margin correspond with points of interest on the Central Wisconsin map.

Some of Wisconsin's most popular tourist attractions lie in the southern part of the Central Wisconsin River Country. We begin our journey here and work northward—upstream.

 The city of **Portage** is situated at the point where the Fox River, flowing northward toward the waters of Green Bay, and the Wisconsin River, working its way toward the Mississippi, come within a mile of each other. In June of 1673, Father Jacques Marquette counted off 2,700 paces as he and Louis Jolliet crossed the portage between the two rivers. The junction soon became an important trade route, a key link between the Great Lakes and the Gulf of Mexico, and in 1829, with the help of a young Jefferson Davis, Fort Winnebago was built on the banks of the Fox. Portage grew up around the fort. In 1850 a canal was dug between the two rivers. Modern Portage is a busy community of 8,000 and the trade center of the surrounding farmland.

The Old Indian Agency House was built in 1832 by the U.S. Government for its agent, John Kinzie. The house has been carefully restored and furnished with period antiques. *1¼ mi east on Hwy. 33, then ½ mi north along the canal, tel. 608/742–6362. Tours start at the visitors center. Admission: $2.50 adults, $2 senior citizens with ID, 50¢ children under 15. Open mid-May–mid-Oct., daily 10–4.*

The Surgeon's Quarters, built between 1819 and 1828, is the only remaining building from Fort Winnebago. The restored building contains period furnishings, some artifacts from the fort, documents, and plans of the fort. At the site is the Garrison School, in use from 1850 to 1960, with original furnishings. *2 mi east on Hwy. 33, tel. 608/742–2949. Admission: $2.50 adults, $2 senior citizens, 50¢ children 4–14. Open mid-May–mid-Oct., daily 10–4.*

The river and pleasant little city of **Baraboo** both took their name from a French fur trader, Baribault, whose trading post stood here in the early 19th century. More recognizable is the name Ringling. Although born in Iowa, the five Ringling Brothers began their circus careers here. Their "Classic and Comic Concert Company" show (first presented in 1882) grew into "the Greatest Show on Earth"—Ringling Bros. and Barnum & Bailey Circus. From 1884 to 1912 Baraboo was winter

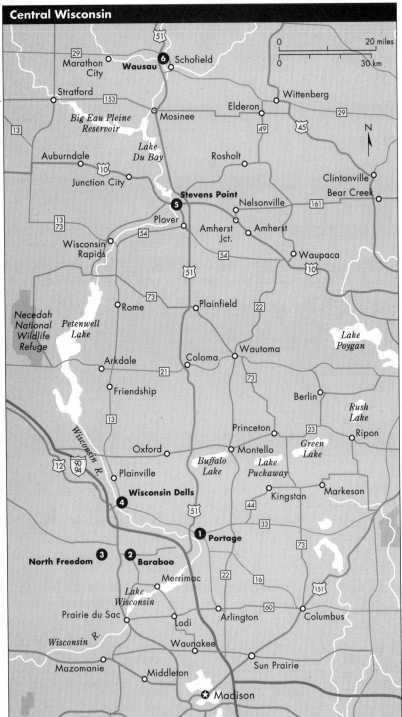

Central Wisconsin

quarters for the Ringling Brothers Circus. Many buildings from those days are still in use along Water Street.

Circus World Museum is a State Historical Society site situated in the original Ringling Bros. winter quarters. Wisconsin gave birth to more than 100 circuses, and circus history is preserved with an outstanding collection of antique circus wagons (the basis for Milwaukee's Great Circus Parade each July) along with big-top performances featuring circus stars of today. There's always something happening, with calliope and circus instrument concerts, parades, high-wire acts, train-loading demonstrations, and exhibits. Allow most of a day to savor it all. Food service and picnic area on the grounds. *426 Water St., tel. 608/356–8341. Admission: $7.95 adults, $4.95 children 8–13, $2.95 children 3–7, $6.95 age 65 and older, $27 family. Open early May–early Sept., daily 9–6; mid-July–mid-Aug., daily 9–9.*

Devil's Lake State Park, with 7,716 acres, is one of the region's most popular parks. Ringed by the quartzite bluffs of the Baraboo Range, Devil's Lake has no visible outlet. There are several prehistoric Indian mounds in the park. Activities include hiking, camping, rock climbing, swimming, and fishing. *3½ mi south of Baraboo on Hwy. 123, tel. 608/356–8301. Admission: park sticker.*

The International Crane Foundation is a world famous center for the study, propagation, and preservation of endangered crane species. There are chick-hatching exhibits, nature walks, films, and videos. *5 mi north on U.S. 12, ¼ mi east on Shady Lane Rd., tel. 608/356–9462. Admission: $3.50 adults, $3 over 62, $1.75 under 12. Open Memorial Day–Labor Day, daily 9–5; May 1–Memorial Day and Labor Day–Oct. 31, weekends 9–5. Guided tours at 10, 1 and 3.*

❸ The **Mid-Continent Railway Museum** in **North Freedom** features a nine-mile ride on turn-of-the-century trains pulled by vintage steam locomotives, a 1894 depot, a wooden water tower, and rolling stock from the "golden era of railroading." There are exhibits on locomotive construction and identification, a chance to board a caboose and other cars, and many hands-on exhibits. There is a concession stand and picnic area. *5 mi west of Baraboo on Hwy. 136 and 2¼ mi southwest on Hwy. PF, tel. 608/522–4261. Admission: $6 adults, $5 over 61, $3 under 16, $18 family. Open mid-May–Labor Day, daily 9–5; mid-Sept.– mid-Oct., weekends. Trains run at 10:30, 12:30, 2, and 3:30.*

Time Out | **Freedom Inn** (200 E. Walnut St., North Freedom). Great for a brew and the best burgers around. *Open Mon.–Sat. 11 AM–2 AM, Sun. noon–7. No credit cards.*

The scenic dells of the Wisconsin River are one of the state's foremost natural attractions. Created over thousands of years by the river cutting through soft limestone to a depth of 150 ❹ feet, the Upper and Lower **Wisconsin Dells** are nearly 15 miles of fantastic soaring rock formations.

Inspired by the photographs of the pioneer 19th-century photographer H. H. Bennett, families have been coming here to see the majestic scenery since the 1860s. They still flock to the Dells by the thousands, but now the area is filled with manmade attractions. In summer, this town of 2,500 is a children's paradise. Ride the bumper boats, challenge the Tidal Wave Pool, try one of dozens of water slides. Ride a helicopter, visit Robot World, see the Standing Rock Indian Ceremonials, visit Storybook Gardens, see the water-ski shows, tour the Royal Wax Museum, ride in a hot air balloon—the list goes on and on. It would take days—and a fortune—to see it all.

River sightseeing trips are among the most popular attractions. **Dells Boat Tours** (11 Broadway, tel. 608/253–1561),**Olson Boat Line** (815 River Rd., tel. 608/254–8500), and **Riverview Boat Line** (31 Broadway, tel. 608/254–8751) offer tours to the Upper and Lower Dells, which are separated by a dam. Boats leave about every 30 minutes from mid-April through October. The **Dells Ducks** (tel. 608/254–8751) has land and water tours aboard "ducks," World War II amphibious vehicles.

If you need a break, **Mirror Lake State Park** (8 mi south on Hwy. 12) offers camping, swimming, hiking and solitude. *Admission: park sticker.*

There are free tours of H. H. Bennett's photo studio (215 Broadway, tel. 608/253–2261), founded in 1865, each afternoon, from Memorial Day through Labor Day.

❺ Founded as a trading post on the Wisconsin River in 1838, **Stevens Point** became the "Gateway to the Pineries," as the great northern forests were called. Now a manufacturing community, Stevens Point is headquarters for major insurance companies and for Stevens Point Brewery, producer of Point Beer.

A branch of the **University of Wisconsin** is situated here, and campus tours can be arranged (tel. 715/346–4242). A planetarium and observatory in the Science Building are open year-round; so is the world's largest mosaic mural created with computer assistance.

The **Museum of Natural History** features one of the country's most comprehensive collections of preserved birds and bird eggs. *Albertson Learning Resources Center, University of Wisconsin–Stevens Point (tel. 715/346–2858). Admission free. Open Sept. 1–May 15, Mon.–Thurs. 7:45 AM–9 PM, Fri. 7:45–4:30, Sat. 9–5, Sun. 10–9. Hours vary during semester breaks and summer.*

❻ **Wausau,** which began as a sawmill settlement called Big Bull Falls, now ranks as one of Wisconsin's major industrial and insurance centers. Rib Mountain is the third-highest point in Wisconsin. Rib Mountain State Park is one of the Midwest's finest ski areas. The parks observation tower offers spectacular views of the river valley. *Admission: park sticker.*

The **Leigh Yawkey Woodson Art Museum** has a permanent collection of wildlife art, glass, and porcelain. It is a world leader in bird art, with an acclaimed annual bird show in September. *Franklin St. at 12th St., tel. 715/845–7070. Admission free. Open Tues.–Fri. 9–4, weekends 1–5.*

The **Marathon County Historical Museum,** in a restored Victorian mansion, traces the development of the region's lumber industry. There is a model railroad exhibit in the basement; trains run the first and third Sunday of each month. *403 McIndoe St., tel. 715/848–6143. Admission free. Open Tues.–Thur. 9–5, weekends 1–5; closed holidays.*

What to See and Do with Children

Baraboo **Circus World Museum** and **International Crane Foundation** (*see* Exploring Central Wisconsin).

North Freedom **Mid-Continent Railway Museum** (*see* Exploring Central Wisconsin).

Wisconsin Dells (*see* Exploring Central Wisconsin).

Merrimac Ferry (*see* Off the Beaten Track).

Off the Beaten Track

The **Merrimac Ferry** holds 12 autos and takes about 10 minutes to cross the Wisconsin River. Service has existed at this spot since 1844. Around-the-clock free service is provided daily from about mid-April to mid-November. On summer weekends the wait can exceed an hour. *Hwy. 113, Merrimac, tel. 608/266–3722.*

The **Wollersheim Winery** dates from 1840, when the first vineyards were planted on the high bluffs above the Wisconsin River by Count Auguston Haraszthy, who later established the American wine industry in California. Tours include a slide show on the history of the winery, the modern winemaking process, visits to the wine cellars, the vineyards, and the tasting room. *¼ mi east of Prairie du Sac on Hwy. 60, then north ¾ mi on Hwy. 188, tel. 608/643–6515 or 800/847–9463 in WI. Admission: $2, children under 12 free. Open daily 10–5; closed Easter, Thanksgiving, Dec. 25.*

Shopping

Items made by Native Americans including baskets, beadwork, jewelry, rugs, and other crafts, are popular in the Wisconsin Dells area.

The **Direct Mall** in Plover offers over 40 specialty shops selling brand-name merchandise at discount prices. *3 mi south of Stevens Point on Hwy. 51, tel. 715/341–7980.*

Sports and Fitness

Beaches and Water Sports Hundreds of unsupervised beaches along the Wisconsin River are available for picnics, sunbathing, and relaxing. Most are accessible only by boat.

Some state parks offer excellent beaches. **Devil's Lake State Park** (3½ mi south of Baraboo on Hwy. 123) has two sand beaches and changing houses: There are sailboard rentals at the North Shore Concession Stand (tel. 608/356–8301). **Mirror Lake State Park** (tel. 608/254–2333), near Wisconsin Dells, has a 200-foot sand beach and changing houses. *Exit I–90–94 at Hwy. 12, east ½ mi, then right on Fern Dell Rd. for 1½ mi.* **Buckhorn State Park** (tel. 608/565–2789) has a beach and bathhouse. *8 mi south of Necedah on Hwy. G.* **Hartman Creek State Park** (tel. 715/258–2372) has a pleasant beach and changing house. *6 mi west of Waupaca on Hwy. 54.*

Dozens of this region's county and city parks on lakes and rivers offer swimming and sunning beaches.

Bicycling The back roads and the byways of the Central Wisconsin River Country offer bikers a variety of terrains. The southeastern terminus of the Elroy–Sparta Bike Trail is in the village of Elroy.

Canoeing The **Wisconsin River** flows 430 miles across the state from Lac Vieux Desert to the Mississippi. Traveling the entire river is popular with canoeists who have the time. The lower river, with its beautiful scenery and numerous islands, is also popular, especially the stretch of water between Sauk City and Spring Green.

The **Lemonweir River** is navigable from western Juneau County to its mouth on the Wisconsin River. The current is generally moderate to slow; a portage is necessary at two dams.

The **Baraboo River** offers a relaxing canoe outing with no rapids or falls. A portage is necessary at three dams. Access is at road crossings.

Canoeists in the Stevens Point region use the **Wisconsin, Tomorrow,** and **Little Eau Pleine** rivers. Near Wausau, the casual canoeist will enjoy the Wisconsin and its tributaries—the **Big Rib, Eau Claire, Big Eau Pleine,** and **Plover.**

Fishing The Wisconsin River, the flowages created by damming the river, and the thousands of lakes and streams in the Central Wisconsin River Country provide excellent fishing. The elusive muskellunge is found here, along with walleye, northern pike, largemouth and smallmouth bass, and a variety of panfish. Local bait shops, resorts, and other fishermen can tell you where to find which fish or put you in contact with local guides.

Golf Central Wisconsin River Country has public golf courses to challenge golfers at all levels.

New Lisbon **Castle Rock Golf Course** (2 mi north of Mauston on Hwy. Q, tel. 608/847–4658), nine holes.

Portage **Swan Lake Village Golf Club** (4 mi east on Hwy. 33, tel. 608/742–2181), nine holes.

Stevens Point **Sentry World Sports Center** (601 N. Michigan Ave., tel. 715/345–1600), 18 holes; **Wisconsin River Country Club** (705 W. River Dr., tel. 715/344–9152), 18 holes.

Wausau **American Legion Golf Course** (Golf Club Rd., tel. 715/675–3663), nine holes; **Pine Valley** (8 mi west on Hwy. 29, tel. 715/443–2848), nine holes; **Rib Mountain Golf Club** (3 mi south on Hwy. 51 at foot of Rib Mountain, tel. 715/845–5570), nine holes; **Trapp River Golf Course** (northeast on Hwy. WW, tel. 715/675–3044), 18 holes.

Wisconsin Dells **Christmas Mountain** (Hwy. H between Wisconsin Dells and Reedsburg, tel. 608/254–3971), 18 holes; **Coldwater Canyon Golf Course** (2 mi north on River Rd., tel. 608/254–8489), nine holes; **Dell View Resort** (Hwy. 12, Lake Delton, tel. 608/253–1261), 18 holes; **Pinecrest Par III Golf Course** (4 mi east on Hwy. 23, tel. 608/254–2165), nine holes.

Skiing
Downhill You'll find a wide range of downhill skiing facilities and services in the Central Wisconsin River Country.

Cascade Mountain (3 mi west of Portage on Hwy. 33, then left on Cascade Mt. Rd., tel. 608/742–5588). 14 runs, T-bar, rope tow, cable tow, double chair, 2 triple chairs, quad chair, snowmaking, NASTAR program; longest run 5,300 feet, vertical drop, 460 feet. Rentals, instruction, chalet, bar/lounge, entertainment, ski shop, restaurant, cafeteria, snack bar, child care. *Open weekdays 10–10, weekends and holidays 9 AM–10 PM; closed 3 PM Dec. 24, open 4:30–10 Dec. 25.*

Christmas Mountain (4 mi west of Wisconsin Dells on Hwy. H, tel. 608/253–1000). 7 runs, rope tow, 2 double chairs, snowmaking; longest run, 2,800 feet, vertical drop 205 feet. Cross-country skiing, rentals, instruction, bar/lounge, entertainment, ski shop, restaurant, snack bar, lodging in villas and log cabins. *Open weekdays 10–10, Sat. 9 AM–10 PM, Sun. 9–5:30.*

Devil's Head (south of Baraboo, 10 mi west of I–90–94 on Hwy. DL, tel. 608/493–2251 or 800/472–6670 in WI, 800/338–4579 in neighboring states). 13 runs, 3 rope tows, 6 double chairs, triple chair, quad chair, snowmaking; longest run, 1 mile, vertical drop 500 feet. Cross-country skiing, rentals, repairs, instruction, chalet, 3 bar/lounges, nonalcoholic teen bar, music, ski shop, 3 outdoor hot tubs, 238-room motel, condos, hostel, pool, sauna, whirlpool, exercise area. *Open weekdays 10–10, Sat., Sun., holidays 9 AM–10 PM; closed Dec. 24 at 3 PM.*

Powers Bluff (17 mi northwest of Wisconsin Rapids, tel. 715/421–8422). 3 runs, 2 rope tows; longest run 1,320 feet, vertical drop 250 feet. Cross-country skiing, snow tubing, rentals, snack bar. *Open weekends noon–8; closed Dec. 24–25.*

Rib Mountain (3 mi southwest of Wausau on Hwy. 51, 1 mi west on Hwy. NN, tel. 715/845–2846). 11 runs, 2 T-bars, rope tow, 2 double chairs, snowmaking; longest run 3,880 feet, vertical drop 624 feet. Rentals, instruction, chalet, bar/lounge, ski shop, cafeteria. *Open weekdays noon–10, Sat. and holidays 9 AM–10 PM, Sun. 9–5; closed Dec. 24–25.*

Sky Line (1 mi northwest of Friendship off Hwy. 13, tel. 608/339–3421). 7 runs, rope tow, double chair, triple chair, snowmaking; longest run ½ mile, vertical drop 335 feet. Cross-country skiing, rentals, repairs, instruction, chalet, bar/lounge, entertainment, ski shop, restaurant, snack bar. *Open weekends and holiday period 9–4:30 and 5:30–10; closed Dec. 25.*

Standing Rocks (10 mi southeast of Stevens Point on Hwy. 51, then east on Hwy. B, tel. 715/346–1433 or 824–3949). 5 runs, 3 rope tows; longest run 1,200 feet, vertical drop 125 feet. Cross-country skiing, rentals, repairs, instruction, chalet, ski shop, snack bar. *Open weekends and Dec. 26–Jan 1, 10–4; closed Dec. 25.*

Sylvan Hill Park (off N. 6th St. at end of Sylvan St., Wausau, tel. 715/842–5411 or 847–5235). 4 runs, 3 rope tows; longest run 1,800 feet, vertical drop 90 feet. Cross-country skiing, snowshoeing. Rentals, instruction, chalet, snack bar. *Open Fri. 6–9 PM, Sat. 10:30–4:30 and 5–9, Sun. 11–4:30, Christmas holiday period 10–4:30; closed Dec. 24 and 25.*

Woodside Ranch Resort (4 mi east of Mauston on Hwy. 82, tel. 608/847–4275). Rope tow, snowmaking; 800-foot run, vertical drop 100 feet. Cross-country skiing, rentals, instruction, chalet, bar/lounge, snack bar, motel and cabins. *Open weekends and holidays 9–9.*

Cross-country Many parks in the Central Wisconsin River Country offer cross-country ski trails; several alpine ski areas provide facilities for the Nordic skier.

Spectator Sports

Auto Racing   Stock car racing at **State Park Speedway** Thursday evenings Memorial Day through Labor Day (tel. 715/842–4777, Hwy. NN west of U.S. 51 at Rib Mountain, Wausau).

There is stock car racing at **Dells Motor Speedway** Saturdays at 8 PM in summer (tel. 608/254–7822, 5 mi west of Wisconsin Dells).

Baseball   **The Wausau Timbers** (tel. 715/845–4900), a class-A team affiliated with the Seattle Mariners, play from April through August at Athletic Park (corner of 5th St. and Wausau Ave.).

Football   University of Wisconsin–Stevens Point (tel. 715/346–4212).

Dining and Lodging

Although you'll find a fairly wide range of restaurants, steaks, prime rib, and seafood tend to dominate most menus. Dining is more casual than in the metropolitan areas.

Price categories for restaurants and hotels are the same as in the Milwaukee Dining and Lodging sections.

Baraboo   **Dombroski's.** The nightly specials here include chicken, steaks,
Dining   and prime rib. Friday-night fish fries, children's menu, cocktail lounge. *135 Walnut St., tel. 608/356–5757. Dress: casual. Reservations recommended on weekends. MC, V. No lunch. Closed Mon. Inexpensive.*
Pappa's Place. There are good soups and all-you-can-eat Friday night fish fries in a pleasant casual resort atmosphere. Children's menu and cocktail lounge. *630 W. Pine (Hwy. 12), tel. 608/356–4869. Dress: casual. Reservations recommended on weekends. MC, V. Closed major holidays. Inexpensive.*

Lodging   **The Barn Motel.** 20 well-kept rooms. *Box 31, 53913, 2 mi south on Hwy. 123, tel. 608/356–5511. Facilities: rural setting next to Devil's Lake State Park, bicycling, hiking, swimming, fishing, boating nearby. MC, V. Inexpensive.*
Spinning Wheel Motel. 25 attractive rooms. *809 8th St., 2 mi east of U.S. 12, tel. 608/356–3933. Facilities: cable TV, restaurant adjacent. AE, DC, MC, V. Inexpensive.*

Portage   **Dave's Porterhouse.** The steaks and the resort atmosphere are
Dining   special here. Cocktail lounge, entertainment. *2 mi north on U.S. 51, 1721½ New Pinery Rd., tel. 608/742–5431. Dress: casual. Dinner reservations recommended. AE, MC. Closed Dec. 25. Inexpensive–Moderate.*
Blankenhaus. Owned and operated by the same family for 50 years, this restaurant serves standard American fare, seafood, and steaks. Wednesday buffet, children's menu, cocktail lounge. *1233 E. Wisconsin St., 1 mi southeast on U.S. 51, tel. 608/742–7555. Dress: informal. Reservations recommended. MC, V. Closed Sun., Thanksgiving, Dec. 25. Inexpensive.*

Lodging   **Porterhouse Motel.** 35 rooms. *U.S. 51N, 1721 New Pinery Rd., 53901, tel. 608/742–2186. Facilities: coin-operated laundry, restaurant adjacent. AE, MC, V. Inexpensive.*

Stevens Point   **The Restaurant.** In SentryWorld headquarters, this attractive
Dining   dining room has a view of the wildlife feeding station. Soups, salads, seafood, and steaks make up the bill of fare. Children's menu, cocktail lounge. *1800 N. Point Dr., tel. 715/341–1755. Jacket and tie required. Reservations recommended. AE, MC,*

V. No lunch Sat.; no dinner Sun. Closed Mon. and major holidays. Moderate–Expensive.

Antlers Supper Club. Prime rib, steaks, seafood, and Sunday brunch, served in a resort atmosphere with a lake view. Cocktail lounge. *12 mi north on U.S. 51, ¼ mi west on Hwy. DB., tel. 715/344–3091. Dress: informal. Reservations recommended. AE, DC, MC, V. No lunch. Closed Dec. 25. Moderate.*

Lodging **Holiday Inn.** 295 large, well-kept rooms. *1501 N. Point Dr., 54481, tel. 715/341–1340. Facilities: coin laundry, indoor pool, sauna, whirlpool, miniature golf, winter plug-ins, restaurant, cocktail lounge. AE, DC, MC, V. Moderate.*

Roadstar Inn. 67 well-kept rooms. *159 N. Division St., 54481, tel. 715/241–9090. Facilities: dining room opposite, nearby golf, fishing. AE, DC, MC, V. Inexpensive.*

Wausau **Michael's.** This warm, attractive dining room specializes in
Dining veal, seafood, and steaks. Cocktail lounge, entertainment. *2901 Rib Mountain Dr., exit U.S. 51 S at Hwy. NN, tel. 715/842–9856. Jacket and tie required. Reservations recommended. AE, DC, MC, V. No lunch; closed Sun. Moderate–Expensive.*

Iozzo's. Ravioli, spaghetti, and lasagna are the specialties here. Cocktails. *3115 Camp Phillips Rd., Hwy. 51N to 29E, tel. 715/848–2202. Dress: informal. Reservations recommended. MC, V. No lunch; closed Mon., Dec. 25. Inexpensive–Moderate.*

Chicos. The specialties here include chimichangas, steaks, and seafood. Cocktails. *5704 Hwy. 52 E, tel. 715/842–9851. Dress: casual. Reservations recommended on weekends. No credit cards. No lunch; closed Mon., Dec. 25. Inexpensive.*

Lodging **Rib Mountain Howard Johnson.** 120 rooms. *2001 N. Mountain Rd., 54401, U.S. 51S at Hwy. NN, tel. 715/842–0711. Facilities: indoor pool, sauna, whirlpool, putting green, winter plug-ins, restaurant, cocktail lounge, entertainment, ski hill and snowmobile trails nearby. AE, CB, DC, MC, V. Moderate.*

Exel Inn. 124 exceptionally well-kept rooms; nonsmoker's rooms. *116 S. 17th Ave., 54401, northeast of U.S. 51, Hwy. 29 exit, tel. 715/842–0641 or 800/356–8013. Facilities: free satellite movies, restaurant opposite. AE, MC, V. Inexpensive.*

Wisconsin Dells Although Wisconsin Dells has only 2,500 permanent residents, it draws so many visitors that there are more than 100 motels, hotels, and resorts and as many restaurants. Some, however, are open only seasonally.

Dining **Fisher's Restaurant.** Resort decor distinguishes this restaurant, operated by the same family since 1950. Serves steaks, prime rib, and seafood. Children's menu; cocktail lounge, dancing. *In Lake Delton, 1 mi north of I–90–94 on U.S. 12, tel. 608/253–7531. Dress: informal. Reservations recommended. MC, V. No lunch; closed Dec. 24–26. Moderate–Expensive.*

Field's Steak & Stein. This large restaurant with several dining rooms serves steaks and seafood and has excellent service. Children's menu; cocktail lounge. *¾ mi east on Hwy. 13, 16 and 23, then 2 mi north on 13, tel. 608/254–4841. Dress: informal. Reservations recommended. AE, DC, MC, V. No lunch. Closed Thanksgiving, Dec. 24 and 25. Moderate–Expensive.*

Patio Restaurant. This unpretentious downtown restaurant in the same family since 1925 serves home-cooked food. *208 Broadway, tel. 608/254–7176. Dress: casual. No credit cards. Closed Oct.–Apr. Inexpensive.*

Paul Bunyan Lumberjack Meals. All-you-can-eat logging camp meals are served in a setting where a lumberjack would feel at home. Children's menu; beer. *¼ mi east of I–90–94 on Hwy. 13, tel. 608/254–8717. Dress: casual. No credit cards. Closed Oct.– May 14. Inexpensive.*

Lodging **Chula Vista Resort.** 130 rooms on exceptionally attractive
★ grounds on the Upper Dells of the Wisconsin River. *N. River Rd., 53965, tel. 608/254–8366. Facilities: outdoor pool, wading pool, sauna, whirlpool, steam room, exercise room, miniature golf, 2 tennis courts, nature trails, restaurant with 4 dining rooms, cocktail lounge, entertainment. AE, DC, MC, V. Closed Dec. 21–Mar. 31. Very Expensive.*

Inn of the Dells. 132 rooms. *Box 190, 3 mi south of Lake Delton, 53940, tel. 608/253–1511. Facilities: indoor pool, sauna, whirlpool, miniature golf, snowmobile trails, restaurant, cocktail lounge, entertainment. AE, DC, MC, V. Moderate– Expensive.*

Holiday Inn. 132 rooms. *Box 236, I–90–94 at exit 87, 53965, tel. 608/254–8306. Facilities: indoor pool, sauna, whirlpool, domed recreation area, dining room, coffee shop, cocktail lounge. AE, DC, MC, V. Moderate.*

The Arts

Stevens Point **The University of Wisconsin–Stevens Point Fine Arts Center** is home to the **Edna Carlsten Art Gallery** and **Michelsen Hall.** There are art exhibits and concerts, theater, and dance productions all year. For information, contact the University Information Desk (tel. 715/346–4242). Stevens Point's **Central Wisconsin Symphony Orchestra** (tel. 715/334–1420), now over 40 years old, presents concerts all year.

The **Central Wisconsin Area Community Theater** (tel. 715/341– 5502) offers three or four productions a season.

Wausau **The Grand Theater** (415 4th St.) was recently restored to its 1926 splendor at a cost of over $2 million; the Greek Revival structure is now home to the performing arts in the Wausau area. Contact the Performing Arts Foundation (407 Scott Ave., tel. 715/842–0988) for a schedule.

Wausau's annual arts weekend includes the **Wausau Festival of the Arts, Art in the Park,** and **Art World,** on the second weekend in September. Contact Wausau Area Convention & Visitors Bureau (427 4th St., Wausau, 54401, tel. 715/845–6231) for complete schedule.

Nightlife

There are no jazz clubs, discos, and rock clubs. Bars, large restaurants, and lounges, particularly in resort areas, generally have music and entertainment, especially on weekends. One might find country and western music on a Wednesday, rock music on Friday, country again on Saturday, and a piano player on Sunday, all in the same establishment. Nightlife is liveliest in the Wisconsin Dells, at least from April through October.

The Wisconsin Opry is a live country music show, where Nashville stars occasionally appear. *Wisconsin Dells, Hwy. 12, just south of I–90–94, tel. 608/254–7951. May–Sept., Mon.–Sat.*

Eastern Wisconsin

You're never far from water in the East Wisconsin Waters region. Life here is closely related to the lakes. In some places people still fish Lake Michigan for a living, and the water sets the tone for the lifestyle.

Getting Around

By Plane Appleton's **Outagamie County Airport** (tel. 414/735–5268), which covers the Fox River Valley cities of Appleton, Neenah, and Menasha, is served by Midwest Express, Northwest, and United Express.

Austin-Straubel Airport at Green Bay (tel. 414/498–4800) is served by Chicago Air, United, and United Express.

Wittman Field in Oshkosh (tel. 414/233–1720) is served by Northwest Airlink and United Express.

By Car Most travel in the region is by car. I–43 and U.S. 41 are major north–south roads, while U.S. 151 is an east–west link.

By Bus **Greyhound** and **Trailways** buses service the larger cities and towns.

Scenic Drives **Route 42.** The road runs along Lake Michigan most of the way between Manitowoc and Gill's Rock, at the tip of the Door County Peninsula. A lovely drive any time of the year, but best in autumn.

Important Addresses and Numbers

Tourist Information **Fox Cities Chamber of Commerce** (Box 2427, Appleton, 54913, tel. 414/734–7101). Open weekdays 8:30–5.
Door County Chamber of Commerce (Box 346, Sta. A, Sturgeon Bay, 54235, tel. 414/743–4456). Open weekdays 8:30–4:30; limited hours on Saturdays from mid-May to mid-Oct.
Fond du Lac Convention & Visitors Bureau (207 N. Main St., 54935, tel. 414/923–3010). Open weekdays 8–5.
Green Bay Visitor & Convention Bureau (1901 Oneida St., 54307-05596, tel. 414/494–9507 or 800/236–3976 in WI). Open weekdays 8–5.
Manitowoc–Two Rivers Chamber of Commerce (1515 Memorial Dr., Manitowoc, 54220, tel. 414/684–3678 or 800/262–7892 in WI, 800/922–6278 in the Midwest). Open weekdays 8–5.
Oshkosh Convention & Tourism Bureau (2 N. Main St., 54903-3001, tel. 414/236–5250). Open weekdays 8–4:30.
Sheboygan Convention & Visitors Bureau (631 New York Ave., 53082-0687, tel. 414/457–9495). Open weekdays 8:30–5.

Emergencies **Wisconsin State Patrol** (tel. 608/246–3220). Emergency numbers vary; dialing "0" will bring an operator to the line.

Exploring Eastern Wisconsin

Numbers in the margin correspond with points of interest on the Eastern Wisconsin map.

This is a bustling region, with water everywhere. Lake Winnebago, Wisconsin's largest inland lake, is here, as are hundreds of miles of Lake Michigan shoreline. We begin in the southern part of the region, on the west side of Lake Winnebago, then move to the Lake Michigan shore and head north.

❶ A former French trading post, **Fond du Lac** is a popular resort at the southern end of Lake Winnebago. Sailing, boating, and fishing are favorite pastimes. For a brief season in winter, fishermen cut holes in the ice and spear sturgeon that weigh as much as a hundred pounds. The **Walleye Weekend Festival** (second week in June) draws thousands to fishing clinics, boat, motor and tackle demonstrations, music, and dancing.

Lakeside Park, at the north end of Main Street, has a petting zoo, boat ramps, a picturesque lighthouse, picnic areas, and scenic walks and drives. See the lighthouse at sunset and bring your camera.

Restored and refurnished to mid-Victorian grandeur, the 30-room **Galloway House** is now surrounded by a village of 20 authentic turn-of-the-century buildings from elsewhere in the county. *336 Old Pioneer Rd., exit U.S. 41 at Hwy. 175, ¾ mi to Pioneer Rd., tel. 414/922–6390. Admission: $3 adults, 50 cents under 19. Open Memorial Day–Labor Day, daily 1–4; Labor Day–Sept. 30, weekends.*

St. Paul's Episcopal Cathedral has magnificent wood carvings from Oberammergau, West Germany, beautiful stained glass windows, and other ecclesiastical art. It's worth seeing even if you're only vaguely interested. *51 W. Division St., tel. 414/921–3363.*

❷ Once a lumbering town nicknamed "Sawdust City," **Oshkosh** is a modern manufacturing center on the west shore of Lake Winnebago. It's home to Oshkosh B'Gosh Clothing and the world-famous Experimental Aircraft Association. The **EAA Fly-In and Convention** in August draws nearly 15,000 planes and hundreds of thousands of visitors. The **University of Wisconsin–Oshkosh** is here.

Allen Priebe Gallery. Exhibitions during the school year present local, college and national works. *Corner of Elmwood and Woodland Ave., tel. 414/424–0147. Admission free. Open Sept.–May, Mon.–Thurs. 10:30–3 and 7–9, Fri. 10:30–3, Sat. and Sun. 1–4.*

The **EAA Air Adventure Museum** exhibits 80 full-size aircraft, including World War II fighter planes, homebuilts, aerobatic planes, racing, antique, and classic aircraft, along with films, models, and art and photo galleries. **Pioneer Airport,** whose grass runways take you back to the open cockpit planes of the 1920s and '30s, is open on selected weekends in the summer. The museum's films and videos put you in the cockpit and have you hanging on to your seat. Displays include "Solar Riser," the world's first solar-powered plane, the "Stits Sky Baby" (with its seven-foot wingspan the world's smallest plane), the gondola from Double Eagle V, the first and only manned balloon to have made a Pacific crossing, and an XP-51, prototype of the famed Mustang fighter of World War II. A major exhibit on Voyager, which flew around the world nonstop, will be completed in early 1989. Aside from the Smithsonian, with which the EAA works closely, this is the nation's premier air museum. *3000 Poberenzy Rd., junction of U.S. 41 and Hwy. 44, tel. 414/426–4818. Admission: $4.50 adults, $3.50 over 65 and*

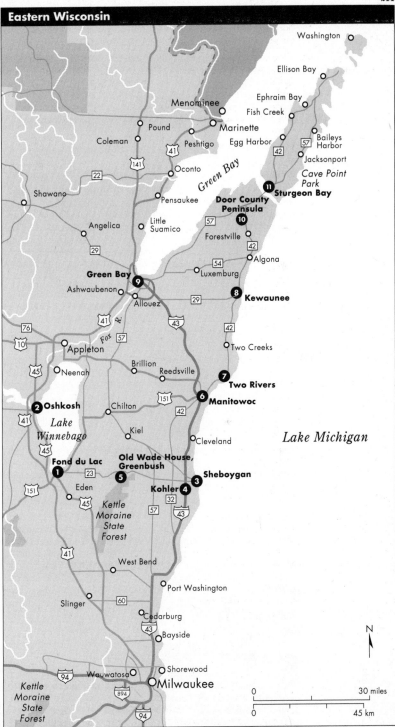

Eastern Wisconsin

Washington

Ellison Bay

Ephraim Bay

Fish Creek

Menominee

Pound

Marinette

Coleman

Peshtigo

Egg Harbor

Baileys Harbor

141

Oconto

Jacksonport

22

Green Bay

Cave Point Park

Shawano

Pensaukee

Door County Peninsula ❿

Sturgeon Bay ⓫

Angelica

Little Suamico

57

29

Forestville

Algona

54

Luxemburg

Green Bay ❾

Ashwaubenon

Allouez

29

Kewaunee ❽

76

41

Fox R.

43

42

10

57

Appleton

Two Creeks

45

Neenah

Brillion

Reedsville

Two Rivers ❼

151

Manitowoc ❻

Lake Michigan

❷ **Oshkosh**

Chilton

42

41

Kiel

Lake Winnebago

45

Cleveland

❶ **Fond du Lac**

Old Wade House, Greenbush

23

❺

Sheboygan ❸

151

Eden

Kohler ❹

45

32

43

57

Kettle Moraine State Forest

41

West Bend

Slinger

60

Port Washington

Cedarburg

43

Bayside

N

Kettle Moraine State Forest

94

Wauwatosa

Shorewood

Milwaukee

894

94

0   30 miles

0   45 km

under 18, free under age 8. Open Mon.–Sat. 8:30–5, Sun. 11–5; closed Jan. 1, Easter, Thanksgiving, Dec. 25.

Oshkosh Public Museum. Housed in an English-style mansion, the museum has exhibits in art and natural sciences and very good collections of pressed glass and meteorites. A 19th-century railroad station and fire station are on the grounds. *1331 Algoma Blvd., tel. 414/236–5150. Admission free. Open Tues.–Sat. 9–5, Sun. 1–5; closed Mon., holidays.*

Paine Art Center and Arboretum is an elegant museum with period rooms, Oriental rugs, American impressionist paintings, and a 14-acre arboretum–botanical garden. *1410 Algoma Blvd., tel. 414/235–4530. Open Tues.–Sat. 10–4:30, Sun. 1–4:30; closed Mon. and holidays.*

Tour Wisconsin's largest inland lake aboard the 350-passenger *Valley Queen II.* Narrated sightseeing tours of Lake Winnebago and the historic Fox Waterway and dining and other cruises are available. *1000 Pioneer Dr. at the Pioneer Inn Marina, tel. 414/231–2131. One-hr cruises depart late May–Labor Day, Sat. 10, Sun. at 4; 1½-hr cruises Mon.–Sat. at 2. Reduced schedule in early May, Sept., and Oct. Fare: 1-hr cruise, $6 adults, $3 under 13; 1½-hour cruise, $7.50 adults, $4.50 under 13.*

Walking tours of the **University of Wisconsin–Oshkosh** campus are available (Admissions Office, 800 Algoma Blvd., tel. 414/424–0202).

③ Situated on Lake Michigan at the mouth of the Sheboygan River, the community of **Sheboygan** evokes thoughts of tasty bratwurst, sausage, and cheese for many people. An active Lake Michigan port, Sheboygan also turns out furniture, clothing, and leather goods.

The **John Michael Kohler Arts Center** incorporates the original home of J. M. Kohler (of plumbing-products fame), an Italianate villa built in 1882 and listed on the National Register of Historic Places. Exhibits of contemporary American art are displayed in five galleries and include sculpture, crafts, and photography. There's a gift shop and sales gallery. *Corner of 6th and New York Ave., tel. 414/458–6144. Admission free. Open Tues.–Thurs. noon–5; Mon. noon–5 and 7–9; closed holidays.*

The **Sheboygan County Museum's** collections are housed in a stately brick house (1850). Each room has a theme: musical instruments, toys, medicine, Indian artifacts, and country kitchen. There is also an 1862 log cabin and a barn with antique farm machinery. *3110 Erie Ave., tel. 414/458–1103. Admission: $1 adults, 50 cents under 13. Open Tues.–Sat. 10–5, Sun. 1–5; closed Mon. and Oct.–Mar.*

Indian Mound Park. Situated on the south side, off Panther Avenue, the park has about a dozen burial mounds built in a variety of rare-animal effigies. They are believed to have been built by woodland Indians between AD 500 and 1,000. A hiking trail provides easy viewing. *Admission free.*

④ Built to house employees of the Kohler Co. (manufacturers of plumbing products), the small, planned village of **Kohler** surrounds the company's factories. The **Kohler Design Center,** a three-level exhibition hall, features a product pavilion, a designer showcase of 26 kitchen and bath interiors, a village museum, a ceramic art collection, and a multimedia theater. Waterfalls, working spas, and greenery share space with the "Great Wall of China," a three-story-high wall of bathroom fixtures in more colors and designs than you imagined possible. Factory tours can be arranged at the information desk. *101 Upper Rd., tel. 414/457–4441. Admission free. Open weekdays 9–5, 10–4 weekends.*

Waelderhaus. This "house in the woods" is a replica of the Kohler ancestral home in Bregenzerwald, Austria, and contains original furnishings. Fascinating features include candle-reflected water-globe lighting fixtures, a tile stove, and secret hiding places for family valuables. *W. Riverside Dr., tel. 414/452–4079. Free guided tours daily at 2, 3, and 4; closed holidays.*

❺ The **Old Wade House** in **Greenbush** is a stagecoach inn built in 1851 along a plank road that linked Sheboygan and Fond du Lac. Restored by the State Historical Society, it contains many of the original American furnishings, including Betsy Wade's rare spatterware in the pea fowl design. The **Jung Carriage Museum,** one of America's finest carriage collections, with over 70 vehicles, is next to the inn. Included are delivery wagons, coaches, gigs, fire wagons, ladies' phaetons, and sleighs dating from 1870 to 1910. Costumed guides conduct tours of the inn and museum and handle daily chores such as cooking, weaving, and blacksmithing. *On Hwy. 23, 20 mi west of Sheboygan, tel. 414/526–3271. Admission: $4 adults, $2.80 over 65, $1.25 under 18, $10 family. Open May–June and Sept.–Oct., daily 10–4; July and Aug., daily 10–5; closed Nov.–Apr.*

❻ The lakeshore community of **Manitowoc** is known as the Clipper City because of the hundreds of wooden ships local shipyards produced in the 19th-century. During World War II submarines and other warships were built here. Still an important Lake Michigan port, Manitowoc is home to a large sport fishing fleet.

Set on the banks of the Manitowoc River, the **Manitowoc Maritime Museum** is one of the largest marine museums on the Great Lakes. Exhibits depict the history of Manitowoc and Great Lakes shipping through models (some up to 12 feet long), artifacts from scrimshaw to ship engines and tools. The Richard Young Collection of ship models is outstanding. There is a full-size cross-section of the hull of a wooden sailing ship, with exhibits showing how it was built. The Port of Old Manitowoc exhibit includes three-story facades of businesses involved in 19th-century shipping. Several displays are dedicated to Manitowoc shipbuilding during World War II, and especially the 28 submarines built by local yards. The largest exhibit is the USS *Cobia,* a WW II submarine open for tours during warm-weather months. This may be the best maritime museum in the Great Lakes region. *75 Maritime Dr., tel. 414/684–0218. Admission: $5 adults, $2.50 under 13, $13 family. Open daily 9–5; closed holidays.*

Pinecrest Historical Village is a pre-1900 village with 14 restored buildings relocated to a 40-acre site. There is a law office, school, operating blacksmith shop, sawmill, harness shop, and train depot with an 1887 engine. Special weekend events are scheduled during the summer. *927 Pinecrest La., 5* *mi west on Hwy. JJ to Pinecrest La., tel. 414/684–5110. Admission: $3 adults, $2 under 18. Open Memorial Day–Labor Day, daily 10–5.*

The **Rahr-West Museum,** in a fine Victorian mansion (1891), exhibits 19th-century art and furniture as well as artifacts on the region's prehistoric Indians, and Chinese ivories, dolls, and porcelains. A modern exhibition wing presents changing art exhibits. *610 N. 8th St., tel. 414/683–4501. Admission free. Open weekdays 9–4:30, weekends 1–4; closed holidays.*

❼ Commercial fishermen still work on Lake Michigan in **Two Rivers,** the community where the American ice cream sundae was invented by a soda jerk in 1881.

The **Rogers Street Fishing Village,** on the East Twin River, is a small museum that tells the story of commercial fishing over the past 150 years and displays artifacts recovered from shipwrecks. *2102 Jackson St., tel. 414/794–7771. Admission: $1. Open June–Aug., daily 10–4.*

Point Beach Nuclear Plant–Energy Information Center features a tour of a simulated nuclear reactor, alternative energy displays, computer games, observation tower, and nature trail. *660 Nuclear Rd., 10 mi north of Two Rivers, tel. 414/755–4334. Admission free. Open daily 8:30–5; closed major holidays.*

Car ferry service, the system of shipping loaded railroad cars across Lake Michigan on specially designed boats, began in **❽** **Kewaunee** on November 27, 1892. The service, which also carries passengers and autos between Kewaunee and Ludington, Michigan, continues to this day. The ferry is the largest passenger vessel in regular service on the Great Lakes and can carry 500 passengers, 23 rail cars, or 150 autos. *Michigan–Wisconsin Ferry Service, tel. 616/843–2521 or 800/253–0094.*

Kewaunee County Jail Museum. Built in 1876, this jail, sheriff's office, and home was in use until 1969. Exhibits include antiques, artifacts, and memorabilia. There is a large basswood carving depicting Custer's Last Stand and life-size wood carvings of Father Marquette and Indians. *Courthouse Sq., corner Vliet and Dodge Sts., tel. 414/388–4906. Admission: $2 adults, $1 under 19, $4 family. Open Memorial Day–Labor Day, daily 10:30–4:30.*

❾ Best known for its football team, **Green Bay** is Wisconsin's oldest city. Permanent settlement dates from 1669 when Father Claude Allouez established a mission by the rapids of the Fox River at what is now the suburb of De Pere. Situated at the head of the strategic Fox-Wisconsin waterway, Green Bay under French control was an important outpost of fur trade and mission activity. British troops occupied the community and the French fort at the mouth of the river during the French and Indian War; the region remained under British dominance until the War of 1812. The United States did not gain control until 1816. Green Bay was a major lumbering and fishing center in the latter half of the 19th century and is today a manufacturing center for paper and related products. Using the St. Lawrence Seaway, ships of many nations call at Green Bay. A branch of the University of Wisconsin is here, and the city claims to be bowling capital of the world, with more alleys per capita than anywhere else.

Bay Beach Park has been a family amusement park for more than 60 years. Midway amusements, including rides on bumper cars, a miniature train, and children's rides, cost 10¢ each. *1313 Bay Beach Dr., on the Green Bay shore, tel. 414/497–3677. Open Memorial Day–Labor Day, daily 10–9; late Apr., May, and Sept., weekends.*

Bay Beach Wildlife Sanctuary is a 700-acre city park with a wildlife refuge and a nature education center. *Sanctuary Rd., across from the amusement park, tel. 414/497–0684. Admission free. Open mid-Apr.–mid-Sept., daily 8–8; mid-Sept.– mid-Apr., daily 8–6.*

The **Green Bay Packer Hall of Fame** tells the history of the National Football League's only city-owned team. Exhibits start with mementos from the days of Curly Lambeau, who founded the club with funds borrowed from a meat-packing firm. Films and videos of Packer game highlights are shown; the trophy from Super Bowl I is here. Of note are the Vince Lombardi collection and hands-on exhibits that allow you to throw a pass or kick a field goal. There is a gift shop with scads of green-and-gold Packer items for sale. *1901 S. Oneida St., across from Lambeau Field, tel. 414/499–4281. Admission: $4 adults, $3.50 over age 62, $2.50 under 13, $14 family. Open daily 10–5; closed Dec. 25.*

Hazelwood was the elegant frontier home of Morgan Martin, where much of the early work on Wisconsin's constitution was done. The home contains original furnishings. *1008 Monroe St., tel. 414/497–3768. Admission: 50¢ adults, 25¢ under 19. Open May 1–Sept. 30, Wed.–Sun. 1–5; Oct.–Apr., Tues.–Sat. 1–5; closed holidays.*

Heritage Hill State Park, within the city, is not a typical state park, but a complex of furnished historical buildings grouped into theme areas. There is a 1762 fur trader's cabin, Tank Cottage (1776), the oldest standing home in Wisconsin, buildings from Fort Howard used during the 1830s, and a Belgian farmstead. A tiny bark chapel, representing the first missions in the region, shows the hardships of 17th-century Wisconsin life. *2640 S. Webster Ave., tel. 414/497–4368. Admission: $4 adults, $3 over 65, $2 under 19, $10 family. Open Memorial Day–Labor Day, Tues.–Sun. 10–5; May and Sept., weekends 10–5.*

Neville Public Museum has six galleries of art and science exhibits that illustrate Green Bay and Wisconsin history. Of special note are a silver monstrance used at the Green Bay mission in 1686 and the exhibit "On the Edge of the Inland Sea," which traces 13,000 years of northeast Wisconsin's geologic development. *210 Museum Pl., tel. 414/497–3767. Admission free. Open Tues.–Sat. 9–5, Sun. and Mon. noon–5.*

For those who wish to learn more about northeastern Wisconsin Indians, the **Oneida Nation Museum** traces the history of the Oneida Nation as it moved from New York to Wisconsin. Exhibits include a full-scale reconstruction of an Oneida longhouse. *5 mi east of Green Bay on Hwy. 54, then south 5 mi on Hwy. E, tel. 414/896–2768. Admission: self-guided: $1 adults, 50¢ under 18; guided: $2 adults, $1 under 18. Open Apr. 1–Nov. 30, Mon.–Sat. 9–5; Dec.–Mar., weekdays 9–5; closed holidays.*

Rail America has locomotives dating from 1910 and rolling stock from 1880. Exhibits include General Eisenhower's World War II staff train, Winston Churchill's traveling car, a "Big

Boy" steam locomotive, and 40 locomotives and cars from the steam and diesel era. Admission includes a 1½-mile ride on an 1890s train. *2285 S. Broadway, on the bank of the Fox River, tel. 414/435-7245 or 437-7623. Admission: $4 adults, $3.50 over 62, $2.50 under 13, $4 family. Open May-Oct., daily 9-5.*

Narrated sightseeing cruises on the Fox River are available on the *River Queen*, along with entertainment and dinner cruises. *Cruises leave the docksite in Ashwaubomay Park on S. Broadway adjacent to Rail America, tel. 414/432-4450 or 336-0900. Fare: $6.25 adults, $3.50 under 13. Cruises late May-mid-Oct., daily noon-1:30 and 2-3.*

⑩ Jutting into Lake Michigan like the thumb on a mitten, **Door County** is a 42-mile-long, 13-mile-wide peninsula that is often called the Cape Cod of the Midwest. And not without reason; quaint coastal villages dot 250 miles of shoreline, with the waters of Green Bay on the west and Lake Michigan on the east. There are lighthouses, wide sand beaches, apple and cherry orchards, commercial fishermen, and offshore islands.

More than a million people flock to Door County each summer, with substantial numbers coming to view the brilliant colors in autumn. Regardless of the season, a visit to the peninsula can include stops at a half-dozen towns, each with its own flavor. First-time visitors often make a circle tour via Highways 57 and 42.

This is not the place to arrive without confirmed reservations, especially between June and October when even the state park campgrounds are filled. If you should find yourself without a place to stay, the **Door County Chamber of Commerce** has a 24-hour, computerized telephone information plaza at Highways 57 and 42, at the southern edge of Sturgeon Bay. You'll find pictures and descriptions of accommodations, a display to indicate which has space, and phone lines to motel, resort and campground offices throughout the county. The service is free.

⑪ **Sturgeon Bay,** with a population of about 9,000, is the region's largest community and the gateway to the peninsula. It is the sixth largest shipbuilding port in the nation, where Navy vessels, Great Lakes freighters, commercial fishing boats and luxury yachts have all been built.

At **Bailey's Harbor,** on the Lake Michigan side, the **Ridges Sanctuary,** an 800-acre nature and wildlife area, has hiking trails. Guided tours are conducted in summer and early fall.

The Cana Island Lighthouse, on a point about four miles northeast of Bailey's Harbor on Highway Q, was built in 1851; it is still in service and a favorite with photographers. About four miles south of Bailey's Harbor, you cross the 45th parallel, halfway between the Equator and North Pole.

Northport, at the tip of the peninsula, is the port of departure for the daily car ferries to Washington Island, six miles away. The island, with 600 inhabitants, is the oldest Icelandic settlement in the United States. Here a tram takes you on a narrated tour of the island; there are museums, restaurants, and accommodations. There is also ferry service to the Rock Island State Park.

On the Green Bay side of the peninsula are the villages of **Ellison Bay, Sister Bay, Ephraim, Fish Creek,** and **Egg Harbor.**

The **Peninsula Players Summer Theater,** called America's oldest professional resident summer theater, makes Fish Creek its home; performances run from June through October. Here, too, is **Peninsula State Park,** where in summer you can tour the 19th-century Eagle Bluff Lighthouse, which is still in use. The park is the state's busiest, drawing over a million visitors each year.

No visit to Door County would be complete without sampling the region's famed fish boil, which originated more than 100 years ago. It is a simple but delicious meal that has reached legendary status in the Upper Great Lakes region. A huge caldron of water is brought to a boil over a wood fire. A basket of red potatoes is then cooked in the caldron, followed by a basket of whitefish steaks. At the moment the fish is cooked to perfection, kerosene is dumped on the fire, and the flames shoot high in the air. The intense heat causes the caldron to boil over, carrying away most of the fish oils and fat. The steaming whitefish is then served with melted butter, potatoes, cole slaw, and another favorite, Door County cherry pie.

What to See and Do with Children

Fond du Lac **Lakeside Park** (*see* Exploring Eastern Wisconsin).

Green Bay **Bay Beach Park, Packer Hall of Fame, Heritage Hill Park, Rail America, River Queen cruises** (*see* Exploring Eastern Wisconsin).

Manitowoc **Maritime Museum** (*see* Exploring Eastern Wisconsin).

Oshkosh **EAA Air Museum** and ***Valley Queen II* cruises** (*see* Exploring Eastern Wisconsin).

Sturgeon Bay **Lollipop Boat Tours.** Narrated boat tours of marinas, shipyards and the Door County shoreline. *12 N. Madison St., tel. 414/ 743–4377. Memorial Day–Oct., daily; June–Aug. at 1:30, 2:30, and sunset.*

Two Rivers **Rogers Street Fishing Village** (*see* Exploring Eastern Wisconsin).

Off the Beaten Track

Door County **Cave Point County Park.** Waves have worn caves into the 30-foot-high limestone cliffs here; picnic area, lakeshore hiking. *North of the village of Valmay off Hwy. 57.*

Sturgeon Bay **Sturgeon Bay Marine Museum.** Contains the office of a steamship company and exhibits on area shipbuilding. *At the foot of Florida St. by the bay, tel. 414/743–8139. Open Memorial Day–Labor Day, daily 10–noon and 1:30–4.*

Kewaunee **Svoboda Industries, Inc.** This is the home of the "world's largest grandfather clock." Enough clocks for a lifetime. *Hwys. 42 and 29, north of the city limits, tel. 414/388–2691. Open daily 9–5; closed Jan. 1, Easter, Dec. 25.*

Manitowoc **Beerntsen Candies.** An old-fashioned ice cream parlor and candy store, founded in 1932 and in the same family for a half-century. Marble-topped counters, soda fountain booths, homemade candies, ice cream, and delicious hand-dipped chocolates; light lunches are available. *108 N. 8th St., downtown, tel. 414/ 684–9616. Open daily 10–10.*

Shopping

Door County There are artists, sculptors, potters, weavers and craftspeople working in wood and metal here, with good buys in many shops and galleries.

Manitowoc **The Factory Outlet.** Very good buys on MIRRO cookware and bakeware. *814 Jay St., tel. 414/684–5521. Open Mon. and Fri. 9–9, Tues.–Thurs. and Sat. 9–5.*

Mishicot **The Old School** was the community's first consolidated school (1905). It now hosts a dozen shops and stores. There is a vast Norman Rockwell collection and shops with antiques, clocks, dolls, quilts, and Swedish gifts and crafts. *315 Elizabeth St., tel. 414/755–4014. Open Mon.–Sat. 10–4, Sun. 1–4.*

Oshkosh **The Genuine Article.** This is the factory outlet for Oshkosh B'Gosh clothing. *206 State St., tel. 414/426–5817. Open Mon.–Thurs. and Sat. 9–5, Fri. 9–8, Sun. 11–4:30.*

Sports and Fitness

Beaches and Water Sports
Lake Winnebago
Many lake communities have beaches, although some are unsupervised. In Fond du Lac, there's a beach and changing house at **Lakeside Park West.** In Oshkosh, there's **Menominee Park Beach** at the end of Merritt Avenue. **High Cliff State Park,** near the community of Sherwood, on the northeast side of the lake, has swimming beaches and a marina (park sticker required).

Lake Michigan's waters are cold, but its beaches are popular. **Kohler-Andrae State Park** (tel. 414/452–3457), seven miles south of Sheboygan, has two miles of beach. **Point Beach State Forest** (tel. 414/794–7480), six miles north of Two Rivers, has a large beach. Park sticker required at both. Farther north, **Kewaunee** and **Algoma** have small beaches.

Virtually every community in the Door County Peninsula has a beach. There are sand beaches at **Peninsula State Park** at Fish Creek (tel. 414/868–3258); **Whitefish Dunes State Park** near Sturgeon Bay (tel. 414/823–2400); and **Newport State Park,** near Ellison Bay (tel. 414/854–2500). Park stickers are required.

Watercraft Rental
Ephraim
South Shore Pier (tel. 414/854–4324), sailboards, sailboats; **Windsurf Door Co., Inc.** (9876 Water St., tel. 414/854–4071), sailboards.

Fond du Lac **Lakeside Park** (487 Garfield St., tel. 414/922–5930), paddleboats, rubber rafts.

Oshkosh **Fox River Marina, Inc.** (501 S. Main St., tel. 414/235–2340), sailboats, sailboards.

Bicycling There are hundreds of miles of bicycle trails in city parks and arboretums, and much riding in state parks. Door County's **Peninsula State Park** has a trail from Fish Creek to Ephraim.

Canoeing The Waupaca Chain O'Lakes and the Crystal and Waupaca rivers attract many beginners.

The Lower Wolf River has a steady current and wild appearance, but it lacks the rough-water characteristic of its upper stretches (*see* Northern Wisconsin). There are public landings in Shawano, and the trip can be continued through Lakes Poygan and Butte des Morts to Lake Winnebago.

The Fox River flows northward across central and eastern Wisconsin to Green Bay. The current is slow with large areas that are good for lake and marsh canoeing. Access is available at many parks along the river. Below Lake Winnebago, recreational boat traffic is very heavy.

Fishing Big water fishing, inland lake fishing, and stream fishing are all available in East Wisconsin waters. Local resorts, bait and tackle shops, or other fishermen will steer you to the best spots. Some Lake Michigan trout and salmon fishing is done from docks and piers, but the really big fish are caught from well-equipped boats, whose skippers know the waters. Charter boats abound on the lakeshore, with over a hundred in Manitowoc and Two Rivers. The short-lived but frantic spring smelt run, where the tiny fish are dipped from the lake by the basketful, must be seen to be believed.

Golf There are well over 50 golf courses in the East Wisconsin Waters region, most open to the public.

Door County **Alpine Resort & Golf Club,** Egg Harbor (tel. 414/868–3232), 27 holes; **Bay Ridge Golf Course,** Sister Bay (tel. 414/854–4085), 9 holes; **Maple Grove Golf Course,** Washington Island (tel. 414/847–2017); **Peninsula State Park Golf Course,** Ephraim (tel. 414/868–3258), 18 holes; **Pepperdine Golf Course,** Sturgeon Bay (tel. 414/743–7246), 18 holes.

Fond du Lac **Ledgewood Golf** (U.S. 151 N to Golf Course Rd., then 4 mi east, tel. 414/921–8053), 9 holes; **Rolling Meadows Golf Course** (U.S. 151 S, tel. 414/921–9369), 18 holes.

Green Bay **Brown County Golf Course** (897 Riverdale Dr., Oneida, tel. 414/497–1731), 9 holes; **Crystal Springs Golf Course** (2 mi northwest of Seymore on French Rd., tel. 414/833–6348), 18 holes; **Hilly Haven Ski and Golf** (6 mi southeast of De Pere on Hwy. PP, tel. 414/336–6204), 9 holes; **Mid Valley Golf Course** (Hwy. 41, De Pere, tel. 414/432–0034), 18 holes; **Mystery Hills Golf Course** (3 mi east of De Pere on Hwy. G, tel. 414/336–6077), 18 holes; **UW-Green Bay Shorewood Golf Course** (2420 Nicolet Dr., tel. 414/465–2118); **Woodside Country Club** (530 Erie Rd., 1½ mi off I–41, tel. 414/468–5729), 18 holes.

Kohler **Blackwolf Run** at the American Club (1111 W. Riverside Dr., tel. 414/457–4446), 27 holes.

Manitowoc **Meadow Links Golf Course** (1540 Johnson Dr., tel. 414/682–6842), 18 holes; **Fairview Golf Club** (5805 River View Dr., Two Rivers, tel. 414/794–8726), 9 holes.

Oshkosh **Far-VU Golf Course** (4985 Van Dyne Rd., tel. 414/231–1570), holes; **Lake Shore Municipal Golf Course** (2175 Punhoqua St., tel. 414/236–5090), 18 holes; **Utica Golf Club** (3350 Knott Rd., tel. 414/233–4446), 9 holes; **Westhaven Golf Club** (1400 Westhaven Dr., tel. 414/233–4640).

Sheboygan **Riverdale Country Club** (5008 S. 12th St., tel. 414/458–2561), 18 holes; **Town & Country Club** (6521 Hwy. J, tel. 414/458–8724), 27 holes.

Skiing There's a wide range of alpine skiing facilities in the East Wisconsin Waters region.
Downhill

Bear Valley (3 mi south of De Pere on Hwy. 52, tel. 414/336–0656) has 4 runs, T-bar, 2 rope tows, snowmaking; longest run 1,200 feet, vertical drop 140 feet. Rentals, instruction, chalet, bar/lounge, entertainment, ski shop, snack bar. *Open Wed.–Sun. 11–4:30, Tues.–Fri. 6–10 PM.*

Hidden Valley (13 mi north of Manitowoc, I–43 exit 91 to Hwy. R, then 1 mi south, tel. 414/863–2713 or 682–5475) offers 3 runs, 4 rope tows, double chair, snowmaking; longest run 3,600 feet, vertical drop 200 feet. Rentals, repairs, instruction, chalet, bar/lounge, ski shop, snack bar. *Open Tues.–Fri. 10–4, and 6–10 PM; weekends 10–4:30; closed Dec. 25.*

Calumet County Park (2 mi north of Stockbridge on Hwy. 55, then 2 mi west on Hwy. EE, tel. 414/439–1008) has 5 runs, 5 rope tows, snowmaking; longest run 980 feet, vertical drop 180 feet. Cross-country skiing, rentals, chalet, snack bar, sledding, snowmobiling, snow tubing, ice fishing, winter camping, snowshoeing. *Open weekends 11–4; closed Dec. 25.*

Narvino Hills (15 mi south of Shawano on Hwy. 187, 30 mi west of Green Bay, tel. 414/758–2221) provides an open slope, 2 rope tows, double chair, snowmaking; longest run 1,500 feet, vertical drop 106 feet. Cross-country skiing; rentals, repairs, instruction, chalet, bar/lounge, ski shop, snack bar. *Open Wed.–Fri. 6:30–10, weekends 9:30 AM–10 PM.*

Nordic Mountain (8 mi north on Hwy. W at town of Mt. Morris, 40 mi west of Oshkosh, tel. 414/787–3324 or 249–5703) has 10 runs, T-bar, rope tow, triple chair, poma lift, snowmaking; longest run 1 mile, vertical drop 265 feet. Rentals, repairs, instruction, chalet, bar/lounge, cafeteria, ski shop. *Open Jan. and Feb., Tues.–Thurs. 6 PM–10 PM, Fri. noon–10, Sat. 10–10, Sun. 10–8; Mon. 6 PM–10 PM, closed Dec. 25.*

Potawatomi State Park (4 mi southwest of Sturgeon Bay off Hwy. 42/57 to Park Dr., tel. 414/743–8869) offers 3 runs, 2 rope tows, double chair, snowmaking; longest run 2,000 feet, vertical drop 120 feet. Cross-country skiing, instruction, chalet, snack bar, 2 warming shelters, winter camping. *Open weekends and holidays 10–4:30, Wed. 6–10.*

Cross-country Many city, township, and county parks, and especially the state parks in the Eastern Wisconsin Waters, offer cross-country ski trails, and several alpine ski areas also provide facilities for Nordic skiers.

Spectator Sports

Auto Racing **Road America.** There's big-time racing at this four-mile, 14-turn track, with sports cars, Indy cars, and motorcycles. *2 mi south of Elkhart Lake on Hwy. 67, tel. 414/876–3366.*

Football The **Green Bay Packers** play half of their home football games at Lambeau Field, where the spirit of Vince Lombardi lives on. Tickets are sometimes available (tel. 414/499–2351). High school football is played in most communities, and the University of Wisconsin branches at Oshkosh and Green Bay field football teams, as does Lawrence University in Appleton.

Dining and Lodging

Dining tends to be casual in the region, and the Friday-night fish fry is as much a way of life as a meal. Prime rib and steaks are popular.

You'll find a wide variety of accommodations, ranging from state park campgrounds to plush resorts, where prices are as high as in big cities.

Price categories for restaurants and hotels are the same as in the Milwaukee Dining and Lodging sections.

Bailey's Harbor
Dining

The Common House. Sandwiches, steaks, and seafood are served in small dining rooms with library decor. Cocktails and entertainment. *Hwy. 57, downtown, tel. 414/839–2708. Dress: casual. Reservations required for Thurs.–Sat. fish boils. AE, MC, V. Inexpensive.*

Lodging
★

Gordon Lodge. 40 rooms including cottage and motel accommodations, some with fireplaces, on Lake Michigan. *Box A, 54202, tel. 414/839–2331, 6 mi northwest on Hwy. Q. Facilities: outdoor pool, beach, putting green, 2 lighted tennis courts, rental bicycles and boats, marina, fishing, dining room, cocktail lounge. 3-day minimum stay summer weekends. MC, V. Closed mid-Oct.–mid-May. Expensive–Very Expensive.*

Egg Harbor
Lodging
★

Landmark Resort. 160 modern rooms with lake or wood view and pleasant public area with fireplace. *Box 260, 54209, tel. 414/868–3205, 1 mi southwest on Hwy. G to Hillside Trail. Facilities: indoor and outdoor pools, saunas, whirlpools, coin laundry, 3 tennis courts, exercise room, adjacent to 27-hole golf course. AE, MC, V. Expensive–Very Expensive.*

Ellison Bay
Dining

The Viking. There are nightly outdoor fish boils, from late May through mid-October; the regular menu features sandwiches, steaks, and seafood. *Hwy. 42, center of town, tel. 414/854–2998. Dress: casual. Reservations suggested. AE, MC, V. Closed Easter, Thanksgiving, Dec. 25. Inexpensive–Moderate.*

Lodging

Grand View Motel. 30 rooms with spectacular view of Green Bay and village. *Box 30, 54210, tel. 414/854–5150, 1 mi south on Hwy. 42. Facilities: bicycle rentals, ski and snowmobile trails, beaches, golf, restaurants nearby. AE, MC, V. Moderate.*

Ephraim
Lodging

The Edgewater Motel. 40 rooms overlooking waters of Green Bay. Three-day minimum stay from mid-June through Labor Day. *Box 143, 54211, tel. 414/854–2734, Hwy. 42, center of town. Facilities: outdoor pool, restaurant, beach, golf, boating nearby. AE, MC, V. Closed late Oct.–Apr. Moderate.*

Fish Creek
Dining
★

White Gull Inn. This 1896 country inn is noted for its fish boils, held Wednesday nights and weekends in summer, and Wednesday and Saturday evenings in winter. The regular menu features steaks and seafood. *On Main St., ¼ mi west of Hwy. 32, tel. 414/868–3517. Reservations recommended. MC, V. Closed Thanksgiving, Dec. 23–25.*

Lodging

The Whistling Swan. 7 rooms with turn-of-the-century furnishings and modern conveniences. *Box 193, 54212, tel. 414/868–3442, on Main St., just west of Hwy. 42. Facilities: restaurant opposite, beach, golf, boating, skiing nearby. AE, MC, V. Moderate–Expensive.*
The Peninsula Motel. 17 rooms, including 6 two-bedroom units. *Box 246, 54212, tel. 414/868–3281, ¼ mi north at entrance to Peninsula State Park. Facilities: golf, beach, boating, restaurants nearby. AE, MC, V. Moderate.*

Sister Bay
Dining
★

Al Johnson's Swedish Restaurant. Swedish specialties and decor distinguish this sod-roofed log building with goats on its roof in summer. *Center of town on Hwy. 42, tel. 414/854–2626. Dress: casual. Reservations required. AE, MC, V. Closed Thanksgiving, Dec. 25. Inexpensive–Moderate.*

Lodging **Open Hearth Lodge.** 30 rooms. *1109 S. Bay Shore Dr., 54234, tel. 414/854–4890, ¾ mi south on Hwy. 42. Facilities: indoor pool, whirlpool, snowmobile trails, skiing, beach, boating, golf nearby. AE, MC, V. Moderate.*

Sturgeon Bay **White Lace Inn.** 15 rooms in two Victorian homes and a con-
Lodging verted coach house. Some have fireplaces, 4 have whirlpool baths, and all are furnished with antiques and period pieces. Children not welcome. *16 N. Fifth Ave., 54235, tel. 414/743–1105, 2 blocks north of business hwys. 42 and 57. Facilities: restaurants nearby. MC, V. Moderate–Very Expensive.*

Best Western Maritime Inn. 91 large well-kept rooms. *1001 N. 14 Ave., 54235, tel. 414/743–7231, 1 mi north on business hwys. 42 and 57. Facilities: indoor pool, whirlpool, cafeteria opposite. AE, DC, MC, V. Moderate.*

Fond du Lac **The Gazebo at the Dartmoor.** Friday's seafood buffet and Sun-
Dining day brunch are this comfortable restaurant's claim to fame. *925 Forest Ave., tel. 414/922–6030. Dress: casual. AE, DC, MC, V. Inexpensive–Moderate.*

Schreiner's Restaurant. American fare and excellent pies are the specialties here. *168 N. Pioneer Rd., tel. 414/922–0590. Dress: casual. AE, MC, V. Closed Thanksgiving, Dec. 25. Inexpensive.*

Lodging **Holiday Inn.** 145 rooms. *625 Rolling Meadows, 54935, tel. 414/923–1440, southwest of junction of U.S. 41 and 151. Facilities: indoor pool, whirlpool, dining room, cocktail lounge. AE, MC, V. Moderate.*

Retlaw Plaza Hotel. 138 large, comfortable rooms in a recently renovated 1922 hotel. *1 N. Main St., 54935, tel. 414/923–3000. Facilities: indoor pool, sauna, whirlpool, dining room, cocktail lounge, adjoining parking ramp. AE, DC, MC, V. Moderate.*

Green Bay **Mariner Supper Club & Motel.** The nightly specials here include
Dining prime rib, roast duck, and braised lamb; cocktail lounge. *2222 Riverside Dr., ½ mi north of Hwy. 172, tel. 414/437–7107. Dress: informal. AE, MC, V. No lunch weekends. Moderate.*

River Room. Overlooking the Fox River, this restaurant specializes in prime rib, seafood, and steaks. *In Holiday Inn City Centre, 200 Main St., tel. 414/437–5900. Dress: informal. AE, DC, MC, V. Moderate.*

Carlton Inn. Fish, steaks, and prime rib in a setting overlooking Green Bay. *607 N. Nicolet Rd., tel. 414/468–1086. Dress: informal. Reservations recommended. AE, MC, V. Closed Mon. Inexpensive–Moderate.*

John Nero's. This family restaurant specializes in soups and pastries. *2040 Velp Ave., just west of U.S. 41, tel. 414/434–3400. Dress: casual. MC, V. Closed major holidays. Inexpensive.*

Lodging Green Bay adds nearly 60,000 to its population on weekends when the Packers play at home, and lodging is at a premium. If you plan to visit in autumn, check the NFL schedule in advance.

Ramada Inn. 152 rooms. *2750 Ramada Way, 54304, tel. 414/499–0631, ½ mi southwest on U.S. 41 at Oneida St. exit. Facilities: indoor pool, sauna, whirlpool, putting green, coffee shop, restaurant, cocktail lounge. AE, DC, MC, V. Moderate.*

Best Western Downtowner Motel. 138 rooms. *321 S. Washington St., 54301, tel. 414/437–8771. Facilities: indoor pool, sauna,* *whirlpool, large recreation area, winter plug-ins, dining room, cocktail lounge, entertainment. AE, DC, MC, V. Inexpensive–Moderate.*

Bay Motel. 55 rooms. *1301 S. Military Ave., 54304, tel. 414/494–3441, 3½ mi west on U.S. Business 41. Facilities: winter plug-ins, restaurant. AE, MC, V. Inexpensive.*

Exel Inn. 106 rooms, some nonsmoking. *2870 Ramada Way, 53404, tel. 414/499–3599 or 800/356–8013, 6½ mi southwest on U.S. 41 at Oneida St. exit. Facilities: free satellite movies, restaurant adjacent. AE, MC, V. Inexpensive.*

Mariner Motel. 21 rooms with river view. *2222 Riverside Dr. on Hwy. 57, 54301, tel. 414/437–7107. Facilities: winter plug-in, good restaurant. AE, MC, V. Inexpensive.*

Kohler
Dining
★

The Immigrant Room in the American Club provides exceptional dining and service in one of Wisconsin's finest restaurants. There are six intimate, ethnic-theme dining rooms. *Highland Dr., tel. 414/457–8888. Jacket and tie required. Reservations recommended. AE, DC, MC, V. Dinner only; closed Easter, Dec. 25. Expensive.*

The **Lean Bean Restaurant** at the American Club Health Center overlooks a small lake, and has outdoor dining during the summer. *Highland Dr., tel. 414/457–4445. Dress: casual. Reservations recommended. AE, DC, MC, V. Closed Easter, Dec. 25. Inexpensive.*

Lodging
★

The American Club. 165 large rooms with whirlpools in a recently renovated building listed in the National Register of Historic Places. *Highland Dr., tel. 414/457–8000. Facilities: indoor pool, beach, sauna, golf, rental canoes and bicycles, 4 racquetball courts, 12 tennis courts (6 indoor), health club, tanning room, massage; dining room, restaurant, and coffee shop. AE, DC, MC, V. Expensive–Very Expensive.*

Manitowoc
Dining

The Breakwater. Good steaks and seafood are served in a nautical setting; the dining room has an outstanding harbor view. Cocktails, lounge. *In the Inn on Maritime Bay, 101 Maritime Dr., tel. 414/682–7000. Jacket and tie suggested. Reservations recommended. AE, DC, MC, V. Moderate–Expensive.*

Colonial Inn. This local restaurant serves seafood, steaks, and home-style desserts. *1001 8th St., tel. 414/684–6495. Dress: casual. No credit cards. Closed Dec. 25. Inexpensive.*

Lodging

Holiday Inn. 204 rooms, some with balcony or patio overlooking an atrium, some for nonsmokers. *4601 Calmet Ave., 54220, tel. 414/682–6000 or 800/465–4329, junction of I–43 and U.S. 151. Facilities: indoor pool, whirlpool, sauna, dining room, cocktail lounge. AE, DC, MC, V. Moderate.*

Inn on Maritime Bay. 109 rooms, most with lake views; nautical themes in public areas. *101 Maritime Dr., 54220, tel. 414/682–7000. Facilities: indoor pool, sauna, whirlpool, cocktail lounge, restaurant, YMCA nearby. AE, DC, MC, V. Moderate.*

Budgetel Inn. 53 rooms. *908 Washington St., 54220, tel. 414/682–8271. Facilities: cocktail lounge, coffee shop adjoining. AE, DC, MC, V. Inexpensive.*

Oshkosh
Dining

Marco's Italian Gardens. Italian, Greek, and American specialties are served in a dining room with a garden view; cocktail lounge. *2605 Jackson, 3½ mi north on U.S. 45, tel. 414/236–5360. Reservations recommended. AE, DC, MC, V. Moderate–Expensive.*

Butch's Anchor Inn. Good food served in nautical atmosphere; children's menu, cocktail lounge, Sunday buffet. *225 W. 20th St., 1 mi south on U.S. 45, tel. 414/236–5360. Reservations recommended. Dress: casual. AE, DC, MC, V. Moderate.*

Lodging Every available space for miles around is booked months in advance for the EAA Fly-In held during the end of July and the beginning of August.

The Pioneer Inn. 200 large, comfortable rooms. *1000 Pioneer Dr., 54901, tel. 414/233–5000. Facilities: indoor and outdoor pools, wading pool, whirlpool, putting green, 2 tennis courts, miniature golf, waterskiing, boat rental, dining room, coffee shop, cocktail lounge, entertainment. AE, MC, V. Moderate.*
Radisson Hotel at Park Plaza. 180 rooms, most with a view of the Fox River. *1 N. Main St., 54901, tel. 414/231–5000. Facilities: indoor pool, whirlpool, adjoining parking ramp, dining room, cocktail lounge. AE, DC, MC, V. Moderate.*

Sheboygan **City Streets.** Steaks, seafood, and prime rib served with a su-
Dining perb view of downtown Sheboygan and Lake Michigan shoreline; cocktail lounge. *607 N. 8th St., tel. 414/457–9050. Dress: informal. Reservations recommended. AE, MC. No lunch Sat.; closed Sun. Inexpensive–Moderate.*

Lodging **Budgetel Inn.** 97 rooms. *2932 Kohler Memorial Dr., 53081, tel. 414/457–2321, 1 mi north of I–43 at Hwy. 23 exit. Facilities: winter plug-ins, restaurant adjacent. AE, MC, V. Inexpensive.*
Parkway Motel. 32 rooms. *Rte. 3, 53081, tel. 414/458–8383, on Hwy. V, just east of I–43 at exit 48. Facilities: winter plug-ins, restaurant opposite, cross-country skiing, hiking, swimming nearby. AE, MC, V. Inexpensive.*

Two Rivers **Lighthouse on the Lake.** Steaks and seafood are featured in a
Dining dining room with a lake view. Children's menu, cocktails, and lounge. *In the Lighthouse Inn, 1515 Memorial Dr., tel. 414/793–4524. Dress: informal. Reservations recommended. AE, MC, V. Inexpensive–Moderate.*

Lodging **Lighthouse Inn.** 68 rooms, some with Lake Michigan view. Weekend packages available. *1515 Memorial Dr., 54241, tel. 414/739–4524. Facilities: indoor pool, sauna, whirlpool, cocktail lounge, restaurant, fishing, fish freezer. AE, MC, V. Inexpensive.*

The Arts

Door County **The Clearing** is an adult school with courses covering experiences with nature, the arts, and the humanities in a natural setting. Classes run from October through May. *Box 65, Ellison Bay, 54210, tel. 414/854–4088.*

The Peninsula Players, called America's oldest professional resident summer theater, offers Broadway plays and musicals from June through October in an all-weather pavilion. *Hwy. 42, Fish Creek, tel. 414/868–3287.*

The Heritage Ensemble (tel. 414/868–3258) presents musical entertainment in Peninsula State Park's amphitheater in summer.

The **Birch Creek Music Center and Performing Arts Academy** offers concerts and other summer performances. *Box 36, Egg Harbor, 54209, tel. 414/868–3763.*

In July the three-day **Door County Folk Festival** is held in Sister Bay; Sunset Concert Cruises aboard an excursion steamer leave Gills Rock in July and August; *Handverks, 10055-C Hwy. 57, Sister Bay, 54234, tel. 414/854-2986.*

The **Peninsula Music Festival** is held each August at Gibraltar Auditorium in Fish Creek (tel. 414/743-4456).

Green Bay There are many opportunities to enjoy music, theater, and art here. **City Centre Theatre** offers nationally known performers in dance, theater and music. The **Green Bay Symphony** (tel. 414/435-9151) presents a yearly subscription concert series and special performances for young people. The **Civic Music Association** (tel. 414/432-4432) brings visiting artists to the city, and the **City Band,** one of the oldest city bands in the nation, gives weekly summer concerts. Regular concerts and recitals are also offered at **St. Norbert College** (tel. 414/337-3181) and the **University of Wisconsin–Green Bay** (tel. 414/465-2256).

The **Community Theater** (tel. 414/437-8707) presents a variety of modern plays, as does **St. Norbert, UW–Green Bay,** and the **Harlequin Players.** For calendar of events, contact the Green Bay Area Visitor and Convention Center (tel. 414/494-9507).

Oshkosh **Milwaukee's Skylight Comic Opera** gives several performances each year in the remodeled Grand Opera House (100 High Ave., tel. 414/236-5290). The **Oshkosh Symphony,** founded in 1940, presents five concerts a year, some featuring nationally known artists, at the Oshkosh Civic Auditorium. The **University of Wisconsin–Oshkosh** (tel. 414/424-2345) has many music, art, and special events open to the public.

Sheboygan The **Sheboygan Symphony Orchestra** (tel. 414/452-1985) plays five concerts a year at Kohler Memorial Theater. **Concerts in the Park** (tel. 414/459-3773) by local municipal bands are held in Fountain Park on Wednesday evenings between July 4 and Labor Day. **Footlights** (tel. 414/458-6144), an annual series highlighting regional dance and theater groups, vocalists and musicians, takes place at **John Michael Kohler Arts Center Theater. Lakeland College** (tel. 414/565-1283) and the **University of Wisconsin Center–Sheboygan** (tel. 414/459-3750) offer music and theater from September through May. Film classics are shown on Friday nights, from September through April at the UW Center–Sheboygan Fine Arts Theater (tel. 414/459-3750).

Nightlife

Nightlife is better in larger cities, but one still finds few jazz clubs, discos, or rock clubs. Bars, large restaurants, and lounges, particularly in resort areas, generally have music and entertainment, especially on weekends.

Fond du Lac **Backstage** (1 S. Main St., tel. 414/922-3585) offers live rock, country and western, blues and jazz. **County Woods Pub** at the Holiday Inn has dance bands Tuesdays through Saturdays. (U.S. 41 at U.S. 151 S, tel. 414/923-1440). **Roaring '20s** (1 N. Main St., tel. 414/923-3000) at the Retlaw Plaza has live music for dancing on weekends.

Green Bay Live jazz is offered at **Floyd's** (1139 Main St., tel. 414/432-4530) and **Top Shelf** (417 Pine St., tel. 414/432-9324). You'll find live country music at **D & B Midway Bar** (17577 Velp Ave., tel. 414/494-5443), **Jim & Bonnie's Haystack** (730 N. Quincy St., tel.

414/432–7206), the **Downtowner Motel** (347 S. Washington St., tel. 414/437–8771), and the **Tuxedo Lounge** (1313 S. Broadway, tel. 414/435–6699). You can listen to rock music at **Brogan's** in the Ramada Inn (2750 Ramada Way, tel. 414/499–0888).

Northern Wisconsin

Northern Wisconsin is the land of endless green pine forests, sky-blue lakes, and crystal-clear streams. Here you can shoot the rapids in a whitewater raft, enjoy some of the best fishing anywhere, or discover a waterfall along a wilderness trail. It's hunting, fishing, and, in the winter, snowmobiling country. Families come back to the thousands of small lakeside resorts year after year.

Northern Wisconsin is divided into two tourist regions—Northwoods and Indian Head Country.

Getting Around

By Plane **Rhinelander Oneida County Airport** (3375 Airport Rd., tel. 715/369–1955) is served by Midwest Express, Northwest Airlink, and United Express.

By Car Almost all travel in the region is by car. U.S. Highway 8 is the major east–west road. U.S. Highway 51, Highway 13, and U.S. Highway 53 are the north–south roads.

By Bus **Greyhound** and **Trailways** provide bus service to the larger cities and towns.

Scenic Drives **Highway 13.** Starting at Ashland, the road follows the Chequamegon Bay–Lake Superior shoreline for 25 miles to Red Cliff.

Highway 103. For 23 miles between Merrill and Tomahawk, the highway winds along the banks of the Wisconsin River. It's scenic anytime, but spectacular in autumn.

U.S. 51. From Rhinelander to Hurley, the 80-mile road winds through some of Northwoods' most scenic lake country.

Important Address and Numbers

Tourist **Ashland Chamber of Commerce** (Box 746, 54806, tel. 715/682–Information 2500). Open weekdays 8:30–5.
Bayfield Chamber of Commerce (42 Broad St., 54814, tel. 715/779–3334). Open weekdays 8:30–5.
Eau Claire Convention & Tourism Bureau (2127 Brackett Ave., 54701, tel. 715/836–7680). Open weekdays 9–5.
Hayward Chamber of Commerce (121 W. 1st St., 54843, tel. 715/634–8662, 800/472–3474 in WI, or 800/826–3474). Open Sun.–Thurs. 8–7, Fri. and Sat. 9–8 in summer; weekdays 9–3 in winter.
Madeline Island Service Organization (Box 274, La Pointe, 54840, tel. 715/747–2801). Open weekdays 9–4:30.
Marinette Chamber of Commerce (601 Marinette Ave., 54143, tel. 715/735–6681). Open weekdays 8–4:30, Sat. 8–12.
Minocqua Chamber of Commerce (Box 1006, 54548, tel. 715/356–5266 or 800/336–6784 in WI). Open weekdays 8:30–5.
Rhinelander Chamber of Commerce (135 S. Stevens St., 54501,

tel. 715/362–7464). Open weekdays 8–5, Sat. 10–5 in summer; weekdays 8:30–noon, Sat. 1–5, Oct.–May.

Superior Area Chamber of Commerce (1419 Tower Ave., 54880, tel. 715/394–7716). Open weekdays 8:30–5.

Emergencies **Wisconsin State Patrol** (tel. 608/246–3220). Emergency numbers vary, but dialing "0" will bring an operator to the line.

Exploring Northern Wisconsin

Numbers in the margin correspond with points of interest on the Northern Wisconsin map.

This is the land of waterfalls, lakes, and national forests. Vilas, Oneida, and Iron counties alone have more than 2,800 lakes. We begin in Northwoods Country in the northeastern corner of the state and work our way west.

❶ On October 8, 1871, a massive forest fire destroyed the community of **Peshtigo** and some 1,280,000 acres of forest on both sides of Green Bay. So intense was the fire that the heat produced a fire storm. The death toll has been estimated at 1,200 to 1,300 people. It was the worst fire in the nation's history, but is overshadowed by the great Chicago Fire, which occurred the same night. The Peshtigo Fire Museum contains a collection of miscellany, most having little to do with the fire, although there are a few artifacts that survived the conflagration. Adjacent is the **Oconto Cemetery,** which contains graves of the fire victims, and a monument marking the mass grave of unidentified dead. *Oconto Ave., tel. 715/582–9995. Admission free. Open June–Oct., daily 9–5.*

❷ The **Lumberjack Special and Camp Five Museum Complex** in **Laona** features steam-powered train rides aboard the Laona and Northern Railways' *Lumberjack Special* to the Camp Five complex. The logging museum includes blacksmith and harness shops, transportation and logging displays, and exhibits on Northwoods life in lumbering days. The complex includes a vintage 1900 country store and offers nature walks and forest tours. Passengers board trains at the historic depot in Laona. *U.S. Hwy. 8 and Hwy. 32, tel. 715/674–3414. Admission: $8 adults, $3.75 children under 13. Open late June–Labor Day, Mon.–Sat.; trains at 11, noon, 1 and 2.*

❸ **Rhinelander** is the home of Hodag, a fearsome fictional creature from the 1880s created by the author Gene Shepard. The city's high school teams are named after the Hodag, as are several area businesses; a Hodag festival is held each July.

Rhinelander was a major logging center in the 19th century; today its mainstays are paper manufacturing and tourism, with hundreds of lakes and resorts in the area.

The **Logging Museum** is a reproduction of a camp with bunkhouse, cook shack, blacksmith shop, sawmill, displays of logging equipment, and hundreds of artifacts and photos from lumbering days. It gives examples of the number and size of the huge logs taken from the forest, a remarkable feat considering that virtually all logging was done with hand tools. Nearby is one of Rhinelander's first public schools, furnished as it was in the days of the *McGuffey Reader*. Also on the grounds is a museum filled with memorabilia of the Civilian Conservation Corps, offering a fascinating account of the men who planted

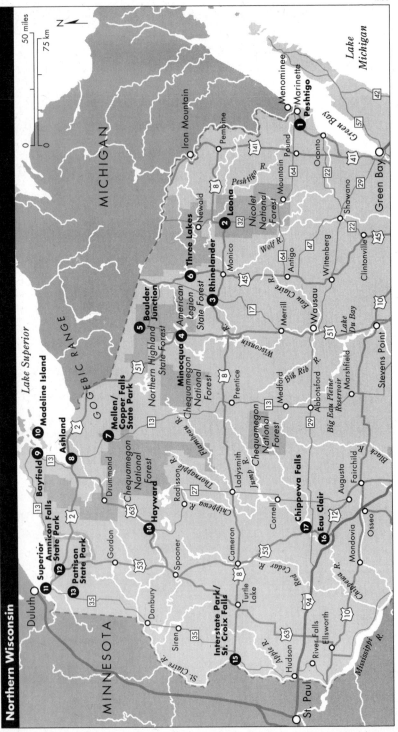

Northern Wisconsin

50 miles
75 km

MINNESOTA

MICHIGAN

Lake Superior

Lake Michigan

Green Bay

GOGEBIC RANGE

Duluth

Superior
11 Amnicon Falls State Park
12 Partison State Park
13

Bayfield **9**
8 Ashland
10 Madeline Island

7 Mellen/Copper Falls State Park

Chequamegon National Forest

Drummond

14 Hayward

Northern Highland State Forest

5 Boulder Junction

4 Minocqua

American Legion State Forest

6 Three Lakes

3 Rhinelander

Nicolet National Forest

2 Laona

Iron Mountain

Pembine

Newald

Monico

Pound

Mountain

Menominee
Marinette
1 Peshtigo

Oconto

Green Bay

Shawano

Clintonville

Wittenberg

Antigo

Merrill

Wausau

Lake Du Bay

Stevens Point

Marshfield

Abbotsford

Medford

Big Eau Pleine Reservoir

Chequamegon National Forest

Ladysmith

Prentice

Cornell

Chippewa Falls

Eau Claire **16**
17

Augusta

Fairchild

Osseo

Mondovia

Ellsworth

River Falls

Hudson

St. Paul

Interstate Park/St. Croix Falls **15**

Siren

Danbury

Gordon

Spooner

Cameron

Turtle Lake

Radisson

Ladysmith

Wolf R.

Peshtigo R.

Wisconsin R.

Eau Claire R.

Big Rib R.

Jump R.

Chippewa R.

Flambeau R.

Thornapple R.

Red Cedar R.

Black R.

Chippewa R.

Apple R.

St. Croix R.

Mississippi R.

Radisson R.

trees and built roads and parks here during the Great Depression. *Pioneer Park, Oneida Ave., tel. 715/369–5004. Admission free. Open Memorial Day–Labor Day, daily 10–6:30.*

Rhinelander Paper Co. is one of the largest mills under one roof in the country; tours are offered. *515 Davenport St., tel. 715/369–4100. Admission free; no children under 12. Open June 1–Aug. 31, Tues.–Fri. at 10, 11, 1:30 and 2:30.*

4 An all-year resort, **Minocqua** is known for musky fishing and boating in summer, skiing and snowmobiling in winter. **Circle M Corral** amusement and theme park features go-karts, bumper boats, miniature golf, kiddy rides, horseback riding, a shooting gallery, and video games. *10295 Hwy. 70 W, tel. 715/356–4441. Admission free; prices vary for rides and activity packages. Open May–mid-Oct., daily 9 AM–10 PM.*

Jim Peck's Wildwood has more than 100 varieties of wildlife, including tame deer. There is a fishing pond and nature walk; visitors may pet and hold animals. Boat rides and food are available. *Hwy. 70 W, tel. 715/356–5588. Admission: $3.95 adults, $2.75 children under 13. Open May 1–mid-Oct., daily 9–5:30.*

Time Out **The Peacock** (Hwy. 70 W at the bridge at St. Germain, 9 miles east of Minocqua, tel. 715/542–3483). A great Northwoods bar, made of real logs, that serves sandwiches and dinner.

5 **Boulder Junction** offers access to the woodlands and lakes of the Northern Highlands–American Legion State Forest. Fishing for the elusive muskellunge is excellent.

Aqualand Wildlife Park contains most species of the state's fish and wildlife, and visitors can feed many of the animals. There's a petting area for youngsters, as well as trout fishing and picnicking. *8 mi southeast on Hwy. K, tel. 715/385–2181. Admission: $3.50 adults, $2.50 children under 13. Open late May–early Oct., daily 9–5:30.*

6 **Oneida Princess Boat Tours** at **Three Lakes** provides excursions on 50-passenger boats on the Chain of Lakes situated south of Eagle River. *Board the 50-passenger boat at Three Lakes Campground, 2½ mi south of Three Lakes on Hwy. 32, tel. 715/546–3373. Tours June–Sept. daily at 2:30.*

Marinette County is known for its many scenic **waterfalls** on the Pemebonwon, Pike, Peshtigo, and Thunder rivers. **Long Slide Falls**, 60 feet high, is 5 miles north of Pembine, off Highway 141, east of Spike Horn Road. **Dave's Falls** (named after a logger who lost his life trying to clear a logjam) can be seen at Dave's Falls County Park just south of Amberg. For a list of falls and directions to them, contact *Marinette County UWEX Office, Box 320, Marinette 54143, tel. 715/735–9661.*

If you're adventurous, discover one of the nearly inaccessible falls of the Montreal River in northern **Iron County.** Four of Wisconsin's highest waterfalls are on the Montreal and its west fork. Or explore the wild river setting of the Potato River Falls, which are just south of Gurney. For a list of waterfalls and directions to them, contact *Iron County UWEX Office, Courthouse, Hurley, 54535, tel. 715/561–2695.*

7 **Copper Falls State Park** at **Mellen** epitomizes the phrase "up north." Here Brownstone and Copper Falls plunge more than

30 feet into the Bad River gorge. Foot bridges and well-maintained trails give easy access to these spectacular cascades; there are camping and picnic areas. *50 mi south of Ashland on Hwy. 13. Copper Falls State Park, Box 348, Mellen, tel. 715/ 274–5123. Park sticker required.*

Wisconsin's **Indian Head Country** stretches from Lake Superior's scenic shore to the Mississippi River. Here you can take a boat cruise through the international seaport of Superior, tour the beautiful Apostle Islands, and fish the waters of Gitche Gumee. The region has easily accessible waterfalls, including the fourth-highest falls east of the Rocky Mountains.

8 Gateway to the scenic Bayfield Peninsula, **Ashland** was a lumbering and iron-mining center in the 19th century. The fur traders Radisson and Groseilliers spent the winter of 1659 here; the site is marked along Lake Superior at the western edge of the city. The iron-ore docks, huge trestle-like structures where railroad cars unloaded ore into lake boats, still stand. A brochure outlining a walking tour of Ashland's 2nd Street Historic District is available from the Ashland Chamber of Commerce.

9 Situated near the northern tip of the Bayfield Peninsula, the Lake Superior fishing community of **Bayfield** has mansions made of the brownstone quarried here in the 19th century, the same brownstone used in the elegant town houses of Chicago and New York. Although Bayfield's population is less than 1,000, the community has some 50 buildings listed on the National Register of Historic Places. The chamber of commerce offers a free brochure outlining a self-guided walking tour. The community draws many visitors from June through the Apple Festival in mid-October. The peninsula has attracted a variety of artists; there are art galleries, pottery studios, woodworking shops, and artists' studios open to visitors. A directory of artists is available at the chamber of commerce information center and at some local shops. There's also a guide to apple orchards that welcome visitors.

The **Apostle Islands National Lakeshore Visitors Center,** in the old Bayfield County Courthouse, has films and exhibits introducing tourists to the region and the National Lakeshore. The missionaries chose the name Apostle, thinking there were 12 islands. In reality, there are 22, ranging from less than an acre to more than 14,000 acres. Activities include hiking, boating, fishing, and primitive camping. There are naturalist programs on some islands in summer. *415 W. Washington St., tel. 715/ 779–3397. Admission free. Open June–Sept., daily 8–6; Oct.– May, Mon.–Sat. 8–6; closed Dec. 25.*

Apostle Islands Cruise Service offers narrated sightseeing cruises of many islands from mid-June to early September. Camper shuttle service to some islands is available. *City Dock at the end of Rittenhouse Ave., tel. 715/779–3925.*

The **Cooperage Museum** is Wisconsin's only working barrel factory; barrels for storing and shipping fish have been made here since the last century. Today you can watch a cooper assembling barrels around a huge open hearth. A slide presentation is shown when the cooper is not at work. There are also exhibits on making barrels and a gift shop. The site is listed on the National Register of Historic Places. *1 Washington Ave., tel. 715/ 779–3400. Admission free. Open Memorial Day–early Oct.,* *daily 9:30–3:30. Guided tours at 4 PM, $1.75 adults, $1 children, $4 family.*

⑩ Because it is inhabited by approximately 175 people, **Madeline Island** is not part of the Apostle Islands National Lakeshore. The first French explorers reached this island—the largest of the Apostle Islands group—between 1618 and 1622. Trading posts were established by the French in 1693, by the British in 1793, and by the American Fur Trading Co. in 1816. The island has one settlement, the village of La Pointe, which serves the thousands of summer visitors.

Madeline Island Ferries (tel. 715/747–2051) shuttle tourists and their autos between Bayfield and La Pointe from April to December, depending on the winter freeze. In winter residents drive back and forth across the bay on a marked and maintained ice road. There are 45 miles of roads on the island, but beyond La Pointe they are extremely rough.

Guides on Madeline Island Bus Tours (tel. 414/747–2051) will show you points of interest and explain the history of the islands in a one-hour tour aboard an air-conditioned bus. *Tours leave several times a day from the ferry landing in La Pointe from early June through early October.*

The **Madeline Island Historical Museum** (tel. 414/747–2415) is a small State Historical Society site consisting of a 19th-century fur company building, jail, barn, and sailor's home. Surrounded by a log stockade, the museum's exhibits provide excellent insight into early fishing, logging, and the fur trade. It's one of those museums that has a little of everything; tools, photos, religious artifacts, fishing gear, ship models, a lighthouse lens, even a glass-sided hearse on runners. *Near the ferry landing. Admission: $1.50 adults, $1.20 over 65, 50¢ under 18, $4 family. Open mid-June–mid-Sept., daily 10–5.*

Stop at the old **Indian Cemetery,** ½ mile from the ferry landing at the south edge of La Pointe near the marina. Some of the gravestones are 200 years old. Michael Cadotte, an 18th-century French trader who married the Indian woman after whom the island is named, is buried here.

Big Bay State Park has 60 campsites, picnic areas, five miles of hiking trails, and a mile-long sand beach. Swimmers be warned: Lake Superior's waters are extremely cold. At Big Bay Point there are picturesque sandstone bluffs and caves at the water's edge. *5 mi east on Hwy. H., tel. 715/373–2015. Admission: park sticker.*

The Town of La Pointe operates **Big Bay Island Park,** with 44 rustic campsites on the north side of Big Bay. Campsites are rented on a first-come basis; the park has a picnic area and sandy beaches.

⑪ Situated 2,342 miles from the ocean, **Superior** is one of the farthest-inland seaports in the world. Along with its sister city of Duluth, Minnesota, it is one of the nation's busiest harbors, shipping millions of tons of iron ore and grain each year. Superior has 28 miles of shore lined with shipyards, grain elevators, heavy industry, and some of the world's largest docks. The **University of Wisconsin** has a branch campus here.

Vista King and Queen Harbor Cruises of Superior–Duluth Harbor leave from Barker's Island. Passengers can view close up the huge grain elevators and ore docks and see ships from many nations on the two-hour narrated cruise. *2 mi east on Hwy. 53 and U.S. 2, tel. 715/394–6846. Fare: $6.50 adults, $3 children under 12. Departures July 1–Sept. 15, daily every hour 10:30–6:30; June 1–30 and Sept. 16–Oct. 15, every two hours 10:30–4:30.*

The SS *Meteor*, built in 1896, is the sole survivor of 43 round-hulled Great Lakes freighters known as whalebacks built at Superior in the late 19th century. Guided tours take you through the ship from engine room to pilothouse. The vessel sailed until the late 1960s, and much of its equipment is intact. There is a museum and gift shop in the cargo hold. *Barker's Island, 2 mi east on Hwy. 53 and U.S. 2, tel. 715/392–5742 or 392–1083. Admission: $2.50 adults, $2 over age 62 and under age 13, $9 family. Open Memorial Day–Labor Day, daily 10–5; Sept.–Oct., weekends.*

Fairlawn Mansion and Museum. Overlooking Barker's Island and Lake Superior, this 42-room Victorian mansion was the estate of a Superior industrialist and mayor, Martin Pattison. Built in 1890 and styled after a French chateau, the home also contains the collection of the Douglas County Historical Society. First-floor rooms have been restored to Victorian splendor; carved wood, marble fireplaces, decorative brass, stained glass, and tile abound. Most of the woodwork is quarter-sawed oak, with mahogany, birch, and maple in some rooms. The upper floors contain exhibits on Great Lakes shipping, Lake Superior Indians, and 19th-century fashions. *906 E. 2nd St., tel. 715/394–5712. Admission: $3 adults, $2 over 57 and under 19, $1 under 13. Open Memorial Day–Labor Day, daily 10–5, 10–4 rest of the year, Tues.–Sun. 10–4; closed Jan. 1, Thanksgiving, Labor Day.*

Wisconsin Point is a miles-long sandbar that, along with Minnesota Point, forms the entrance to Superior's harbor. There is a wildlife preserve on the point, a lighthouse, great views of Lake Superior, and many sand beaches. *4 mi east on U.S. 2 and 53 to Moccasin Mike Rd., then 1 mi to Minnesota Point Rd.*

As it rushes northward to Lake Superior, the Amnicon River
⑫ thunders through **Amnicon Falls State Park.** Two major unnamed falls roar around a quarter-mile-long island that is reached by a charming covered bridge. You can picnic beside a waterfall, or swim under one if you've got the courage. *13 mi east of Superior on U.S. 2, Box 125, Brule, tel. 715/274–5123. Admission: park sticker.*

⑬ **Pattison State Park** is home to Big Manitou Falls, the state's largest falls and the fourth largest east of the Rocky Mountains. Here the Black River plunges 165 feet into a 10,000-year-old gorge. About a mile upstream, Little Manitou Falls drops 30 feet over giant boulders in a brilliant cascade. Both falls are easily reached on foot. *15 mi south of Superior on Hwy. 35. Box 435, tel. 715/399–8073. Admission: park sticker.*

⑭ Recalling its 19th-century logging days, **Hayward** is host to the Lumberjack World Championships in mid-July, with events including tree chopping, log rolling, climbing, and sawing by the top lumberjacks. The event draws contestants from several nations and has been nationally televised.

The **National Fresh Water Fishing Hall of Fame** is housed in a 4½-story building in the shape of a muskellunge, complete with an observation deck in the fish's mouth! Other buildings exhibit more than 400 mounted fish from around the world, antique and classic outboard motors, over 5,000 fishing lures, rods, reels, trophies, and record fish. *½ mi east at junction of Hwy. 27 and B, tel. 715/634–4440. Admission: $3 adults, $2 under 18, 50¢ under 10. Open Apr. 15–Nov. 1, daily 10–5.*

⑮ Interstate Park (tel. 715/483–3747), created in 1900, is Wisconsin's oldest state park. It lies on the east side of **St. Croix Falls**, just across the river from Minnesota's Interstate Park. Over the centuries the National Scenic Riverway has cut a 200-foot gorge, leaving rocky cliffs, towering bluffs, and formations named Devil's Chair, the Maltese Cross, and Old Man of the Dalles. There are hiking and nature trails, naturalist programs, picnic areas, campgrounds, and an interpretive center. *Admission: park sticker.*

Set at the confluence of the Eau Claire and Chippewa rivers, **⑯ Eau Claire** was a riproaring logging town in its heyday. Like many such boomtowns, Eau Claire turned to diversified manufacturing when the timber was exhausted. With a population of just over 50,000, it is the largest city in Indian Head Country, and its location at the junction of the rivers makes it the gateway to the region's resort areas. A branch of the University of Wisconsin is located here.

The **Chippewa Valley Museum** is in Carson Park, a 135-acre peninsula on Half Moon Lake. The museum presents the history of the Chippewa River valley, with exhibits that include period rooms, antique autos, Eau Claire's role in the Civil War, and an operating 1890s ice cream parlor. The Sunnyview School (1880) and a log cabin (1860) on the grounds have period furnishings. There are Woodland Indian artifacts and natural history exhibits. *Carson Park Dr., tel. 715/834–7871. Admission free. Open Tues.–Sun. 1–5; closed Mon., Dec. 25, Jan. 1.*

The **Paul Bunyan Logging Camp** is a re-created 1890s camp. Statues of the legendary lumberjack and his faithful blue ox, Babe, stand at the entrance. Equipment from the logging days is exhibited in a cook shanty, bunkhouse, stable, and blacksmith shop. The museum transports us into the days when the Chippewa and Eau Claire rivers were filled with logging rafts headed for the Mississippi, St. Louis, and points farther south, and rival logging companies battled each other on midnight logging drives. *In Carson Park, tel. 715/839–5032. Admission free. Open May 1–Labor Day, Tues.–Sun. 9:30–5:30; after Labor Day, Tues.–Sun. noon–5; closed Jan. 1, Thanksgiving, Dec. 25.*

Hibernia Brewing Ltd., formerly the Walters Brewery, was founded by John Walter in 1899. There are free guided tours and a beer garden. *318 Elm St., tel. 715/836–2337. Admission free. Tours May 15–Aug. 15, weekdays 10–2.*

⑰ Leinenkugel Brewing Company, Chippewa Falls. *Newsweek* called Leinenkugel one of the nation's most distinctive beers. Tours of the brewery include a stop in the hospitality center. *1 Jefferson Ave., Chippewa Falls, tel. 715/723–5557. Reservations required. Admission free. Tours June–Aug., weekdays 10–3.*

The **L.E. Phillips Planetarium** (tel. 715/836–3148) at the University of Wisconsin–Eau Claire has heavenly shows and lectures from September through May.

What to See and Do with Children

Augusta **Dells Mill Museum** (*see* Off the Beaten Track).

Bayfield **Apostle Islands Cruises** and **Madeline Island Ferry** (*see* Exploring Northern Wisconsin).

Boulder Junction **Aqualand Wildlife Park** (*see* Exploring Northern Wisconsin).

Eau Claire **Paul Bunyan Logging Camp** (*see* Exploring Northern Wisconsin).

Laona **Lumberjack Special and Camp Five Museum** (*see* Exploring Northern Wisconsin).

Mellen **Copper Falls State Park** (*see* Exploring Northern Wisconsin).

Minocqua **Circle M Corral** and **Jim Peck's Wildwood** (*see* Exploring Northern Wisconsin).

Rhinelander **The Logging Museum** (*see* Exploring Northern Wisconsin).

Superior **Vista King Harbor Cruises** and **SS Meteor Museum** (*see* Exploring Northern Wisconsin).

Three Lakes **Oneida Princess Boat Tours** (*see* Exploring Northern Wisconsin).

Off the Beaten Track

Augusta **Dells Mill Museum.** Built in 1864, this five-story flour mill has been in the same family since 1894. The mill is built of hand-hewn timber held together with wooden pegs, and contains 3,000 feet of belting and 175 pulleys powered by water. It was used until 1968, when it was converted into a museum. Exhibits include 19th-century farm wagons, tools, and an English naval cannon. *20 mi southeast of Eau Claire on Hwy. 12, 3 mi north of Augusta on Hwy. 27, then west on Hwy. V, tel. 715/286–2714. Admission: $4 adults, $2 under age 19, $1 children under 7. Open May–Oct., daily 10–5.*

Bayfield **Memorial Park** is a great spot to relax and watch the sunset. There's a gazebo, benches, and a fine view of the marina and Madeline Island in the distance.

Osseo **The Norske Nook.** Pie is the big seller here, 14 kinds, ranging from sour cream raisin and banana to standards like apple and blueberry. Helen Myhre reigns in the kitchen, turning out over a hundred delicious pies a day, and she swears that all the calories are removed. She also serves home-style specials including stuffed pork chops and biscuits. *Two blocks south of the water tower in Osseo, 20 mi south of Eau Claire on I–90–94. Open daily at 6 AM; closed Sundays.*

Poplar **Richard I. Bong Memorial.** Bong, flying a P-38 fighter plane, shot down 40 enemy planes during World War II to become the leading American ace of all time. The memorial, which is dedicated to WW II veterans, features a P-38 "Lightning" like the one Bong flew in combat, plus his medals, ribbons and other memorabilia. *U.S. 2, 20 mi west of Superior, tel. 715/364–2623. Admission free. Open June–mid-Aug., Mon.–Sat. 9:30–6; rest of the year, weekdays 8–4.*

Star Lake **The Star Lake Saloon and Eatery** is run by Jim and Foxy DeMuth, who turn out great food, and lots of it. Crusty potato pancakes and pan-fried steak are favorites. Come as you are and bring an appetite. *18 mi northeast of Eagle River on Hwy. K, tel. 715/542–3652 or 542–9316.*

Shopping

If you shop carefully, you'll find Indian arts and crafts at good prices. A good place to start is the **Buffalo Art Center** in Red Cliff (tel. 715/779–5858).

Antiques are no cheaper here than anywhere else, but there's always the excitement of shopping "new territory." Dealers are scattered throughout the Northwoods and Indian Head Country; **Eau Claire's Antique Emporium** (300 Main St., tel. 715/832–2494) offers the wares of 20 dealers on three floors.

Eagle River The **Cranberry Gift House** (Hwy. 70, tel. 715/479–4944) sells only cranberry-related items: jams, jellies, candy, juice, and sauces. The store will ship gift boxes.

Eagle River shops have good buys on Indian moccasins, too.

Minocqua **Storr's Pond Sweater Co.** (422 Oneida Ave., Hwy. 51, tel. 715/356–3322). This is the outlet for Winona Knits sweaters.

Superior **Berger Hardware** (525 Tower, tel. 715/394–3873) is an old-fashioned hardware store that still carries lamp chimneys, horse collars, farm machinery belting, toys, and furniture. If you need it, Berger has probably got it.

Sports and Fitness

Beaches and Water Sports With all the lakes and rivers in northern Wisconsin, beaches abound; you will be hard pressed to find a community, park, or resort that does not have one. One of the nicest is the 1½-mile sand beach at Big Bay State Park on Madeline Island (*see* Exploring).

Bicycling There are hundreds of miles of back roads where bicyclists can ride. Much biking is done in state parks.

The **Bearskin Trail** is a 12-mile state trail that winds through the woods from Minocqua past lakes, bays, and remote forests to Bearskin Lake. The area, once the domain of the Indian, the logger, and the fur trader, retains much of its wilderness beauty. Trail fee.

Red Cedar Trail. In Indian Head Country, the trail follows the valley of the Red Cedar River, taking bikers 14 miles from Menomonie through the historic lumbering town of Downsville, and on to the Chippewa River Valley. Trail fee.

Canoeing Northwoods The **Tomahawk River** offers a medium to fast current including two difficult rapids on the lower river. Access is at dams and road crossings.

The **Wolf River** has relatively calm stretches above the community of Lily. Below Lily the river is recommended for experienced canoeists only. Check local regulations before entering the Menominee Indian Reservation south of Markton.

The northernmost section of the **Oconto River** features 15 rated rapids and should not be attempted by a novice. The lower river has a moderate current.

The upper part of the **Peshtigo River** has some of the most difficult whitewater in the Midwest and requires considerable canoeing skill. The river widens and slows below Crivitz.

The **Brule River,** a boundary river between Wisconsin and Michigan, has long stretches of slow water and low-hazard rapids. There is potential hazard at the junction with the Michigamme; check local conditions.

The **Menominee River,** another river separating Wisconsin and Michigan, has stretches of fast water and difficult rapids. Parts of the upper river are extremely dangerous and should be run only by experts in decked boats.

Canoes can be rented locally from many sources; because of the difficult and sometimes dangerous nature of many Northwoods rivers, it is suggested you contact a local chamber of commerce or visitors bureau for additional information.

Indian Head Country The **Bois Brule River** is famous for trout, scenery, and exciting rapids. Some sections contain dangerous rapids, which you should not attempt unless accompanied by a knowledgeable guide.

The **St. Croix** is designated a National Scenic River, and contains low- to medium-hazard rapids. Below St. Croix Falls, the river is open to commercial traffic.

The **Namekagon River** provides lake and river canoeing with some low-hazard rapids. Low water is sometimes an obstacle, and levels should be checked locally.

The **Yellow River** offers a slow to moderate current and gentle rapids. Aquatic growth may hinder navigation in midsummer.

The **Chippewa River** is rich in history and scenic beauty, but water levels fluctuate and should be checked locally. Long portages may be necessary.

The **Flambeau River** provides one of the best whitewater trips in the Midwest. The most traveled stretch is from Nine Mile Creek (in Flambeau River State Forest) to Ladysmith.

While portions of the upper **Black River** are considered too rocky for navigation, canoeing is possible on the stretch through Jackson and Clark counties.

The rivers in Indian Head Country are generally not as wild as those in the Northwoods; however, it is suggested that you check local information before starting out.

Fishing It really doesn't get much better than this. Virtually every tourism publication here has color photos of huge fish held high by grinning fishermen or small children. And they don't exaggerate; there's good fishing for almost every species found in Wisconsin. Fishing is serious business here; many motels and resorts include fish freezing as part of their service. Bait and tackle shops, resorts, and tourist agencies can help you get a fishing guide, which may well be worth the money if you're a serious fisherman. For information on Lake Superior charter-boat fishing in the Superior region, contact *Lake Superior Sport Fishing Charter Captains Association, Box 812, Superior, 54880, tel. 715/394–4449.* The Bayfield Trollers Association (Box 406, 54814, tel. 715/779–3330) will provide information on charter fishing in its area.

Golf **The Elks Club** (Rte. 5, Chippewa Falls, tel. 715/723–7363), 9
Eau Claire holes; **Hallie Golf Course** (Rte. 7, Chippewa Falls, tel. 715/723–
8524), 18 holes; **Lowes Creek** (1714 Golf Rd., tel. 715/832–6011),
18 holes; **Mill Run** (3905 Kane Rd., tel. 715/834–1766), 9 holes;
Ojibway (Rte. 5, Chippewa Falls, tel. 715/723–8823), 9 holes;
Princeton Valley (2300 W. Princeton Ave., tel. 715/834–3334), 9
holes.

Hayward Golf & Tennis Club (3 blocks north of Main St. on
Wittwer Ave., Hayward, tel. 715/634–2760), 18 holes.

La Pointe **Madeline Island Recreation** has an 18-hole course designed by
Robert Trent-Jones (tel. 715/747–3212).

Minocqua **Jim Peck's Wildwood** (2 mi west on Hwy. 70, tel. 715/356–3477),
9 holes; **Pinewood Country Club** (Lakewood Rd., Harshaw, tel.
715/282–5500), 18 holes; **Trout Lake Golf and Country Club** (9
mi north of Woodruff on Hwy. 51, tel. 715/385–2730), 18 holes.

Rhinelander **Pinewood Country Club** (12 mi west on Hwy. K, right on Lakewood Rd. 3 ½ mi, tel. 715/282–5550), 18 holes.

Sayner **Plum Lake Golf Club** (Golf Course Rd., tel. 715/542–9315), 9
holes.

Superior **Nemadji Golf Course** (N. 58th St., tel. 715/394–9022), 27 holes;
Pattison Park (Hwy. B, tel. 715/399–2489), 9 holes; **Poplar Golf
Course** (Hwy. 2 and D, Poplar, tel. 715/364–2689), 9 holes.

Skiing **Camp 10.** 7 runs, 2 T-bars, 2 rope tows, snowmaking; longest
Northwoods run 2,000 feet, maximum vertical drop 255 feet. Rentals, instruction, chalet, cafeteria, cross-country skiing, family racing
program. *6 mi south of Rhinelander on Hwy. 17, right 2 mi on
Hwy. A, tel. 715/362–6754. Open weekends, holidays 10–4:30,
closed Dec. 25.*
Kettlebow. 5 runs, 5 rope tows, longest run 2,000 feet, maximum vertical drop 200 feet. Chalet (no indoor plumbing), snack
bar. *15 mi northeast of Antigo on Hwy. 52, tel. 715/623–3560.
Open weekends noon–4.*
Keyes Peak. 4 runs, 3 rope tows, bunny hill; longest run 1,750
feet, maximum vertical drop 200 feet. Rentals, snack bar,
cross-country skiing, snowmobiling, ice fishing. *4 mi south of
Florence on Hwy. 101, tel. 715/528–3207. Open Fri. noon–9,
weekends 10–9.*
Paul Bunyan. 5 runs, T-bar, 4 rope tows, snowmaking; longest
run 1,600 feet, maximum vertical drop 120 feet. Rentals, repairs, instruction, chalet, bar/lounge (beer only), ski shop,
snack bar, snowmobiling. *Near Lakewood, off Hwy. 32, 2 mi
north on North Rd., tel. 715/276–7610 or 276–7143. Open Fri.–
Sun., holidays 10–4:30.*
Whitecap. 36 runs, 2 rope tows, 4 double chairs, quad chair,
snowmaking; longest run 5,000 feet, maximum vertical drop
400 feet. Rentals, repairs, instruction, chalet, ski shop, restaurant, snack bar, child care, cross-country skiing, ice fishing.
Accommodations for 600 in 3 motels, condos, electrical hookups
for campers. *7 mi west of Hurley on Hwy. 77, 3 mi east on Hwy.
E, tel. 715/561–2227. Open daily 9–4.*
Winterset. Open slope, cable grip tow, 2 rope tows; longest run
1,785 feet, maximum vertical drop 180 feet. Rentals, instruction, chalet, ski shop, snack bar. *5 mi west of Crivitz on Hwy. A
to Shaffer Rd. and ¼ mi south, tel. 715/854–7935. Open weekends and holidays 10–4:30.*

Indian Head Country

Bruce Mound Winter Sports Area. 7 runs, 2 T-bars, 2 rope tows, snowmaking; longest run 2,500 feet, maximum vertical drop 325 feet. Rentals, instruction, chalet, restaurant, cross-country skiing, snow tubing. *9 mi north of Black River Falls on Hwy. 12–27, 2 mi east on Hwy. 95, tel. 715/743–2296 or 743–3241. Open Fri.–Sun. 11–4:15.*

Christie Mountain. 6 runs, T-bar, rope tow, double chair, snowmaking; longest run 4,000 feet, maximum vertical drop 350 feet. Rentals, repairs, instruction, chalet, bar/lounge, snack bar. *7 mi northwest of Bruce on Hwy. O, 60 mi north of Eau Claire, tel. 715/868–7800. Open Fri. 4:30–9:30, Sat. 9:30–9:30, Sun. 9:30–4:30.*

Deepwood. 16 runs, 2 T-bars; longest run 3,200 feet, maximum vertical drop 300 feet. Rentals, instruction, chalet, bar/lounge, snack bar, cross-country skiing. *9 mi west of Colfax off Hwy. 170, right on Hwy. N, 25 mi west of Eau Claire, tel. 715/658–1500. Open daily.*

Mt. Ashwabay. 11 runs, T-bar, 4 rope tows; longest run 3,000 feet, maximum vertical drop 317 feet. Rentals, repairs, instruction, chalet, bar/lounge, live entertainment, ski shop, cafeteria, cross-country skiing. *3 mi south of Bayfield on Hwy. 13, tel. 715/779–3227 or 779–5494. Open Wed. 9:30–4, weekends and holidays 9:30–4:30, Wed. and Sat. nights 6:30–10.*

Mt. Hardscrabble. 9 runs, 2 T-bars, 2 rope tows, double chair, snowmaking; longest run 4,000 feet, maximum vertical drop 400 feet. Rentals, repairs, instruction, chalet, bar/lounge, ski shop, cafeteria, cross-country skiing, NASTAR racing. *5 mi east of Rice Lake on Hwy. C, 60 mi north of Eau Claire, tel. 715/234–3412 or 234–8681. Open Tues.–Fri. 6–10 PM, weekends and holidays 9–4:30, daily during Christmas vacation.*

Telemark. 10 runs, 2 T-bars, rope tow, 3 double chairs, snowmaking; longest run 2,600 feet, maximum vertical drop 370 feet. Rentals, repairs, instruction, chalet, bar/lounge, ski shop, restaurant, cafeteria, shopping, snowshoeing, cross-country skiing, ice fishing, hotel, condos, pool, sauna, whirlpool, child care, 4 indoor tennis courts. *3 mi east of Cable on Hwy. M, tel. 715/798–3811, 800/472–3001 in WI, 800/826–4011 in surrounding states. Open daily 9–4:30.*

Trollhaugen. 21 runs, 6 rope tows, double chair, 2 quad chairs, snowmaking (100%); longest run 2,500 feet, maximum vertical drop 270 feet. Rentals, repairs, instruction, chalet, bar/lounge, entertainment, ski shop, year-round full-service restaurant and snack bar. *1 mi east of Dresser on Hwy. F, 80 mi northwest of Eau Claire, tel. 715/755–2955, 612/433–5141 in Twin Cities, or 800/826–7166 in upper Midwest. Open Mon.–Thurs. 10–10, Fri. 10–5, Sat. 9:30 AM–10 PM, Sun. 9:30–9, closed 3 PM Dec. 24–noon Dec. 25.*

Cross-country skiing is very popular in the Northwoods and Indian Head Country. Some alpine ski areas listed here offer cross-country trails, and there are many trails in state parks and state and national forests. For information on skiing in national forests, contact *Chequamegon National Forest, 157 N. 5th Ave., Park Falls, 54552, tel. 715/762–2461; Nicolet National Forest, 68 S. Stevens St., Rhinelander, 54501, tel. 715/362–3415.*

Spectator Sports

Baseball The **Eau Claire Cavaliers,** one of the top amateur teams in the Midwest, play their home games at Carson Park Stadium (tel. 715/839–5032).

Football The **University of Wisconsin** campuses at **Eau Claire** and **Superior** both field football teams, as well as teams in other sports.

Dining and Lodging

Dining is an informal proposition up north. Generally speaking, the food is hearty, and dress is casual.

Accommodations vary widely, probably more so than elsewhere in the state. Hundreds of small resorts offer cottages on the housekeeping plan; rental includes use of a boat and kitchenware. Larger hotels with many amenities usually offer European plan or modified American plan. Resort stays are generally a week or two, although off season some resorts welcome overnighters. Reservations are usually required months in advance. Hotel and motel accommodations are on a par with those elsewhere in the state.

Price categories for restaurants and hotels are the same as in the Milwaukee Dining and Lodging sections.

Ashland **Hotel Chequamegon.** 64 rooms in a new hotel with 19th-century
Lodging graciousness and decor. *101 W. Front St., 54806, tel. 715/682–9095. Facilities: indoor pool, sauna, whirlpool, dining room, cafe, coffee shop, cocktail lounge. AE, MC, V. Inexpensive–Moderate.*

Bayfield **Old Rittenhouse Inn.** Elegant six-course meals are served in
Dining this 1890s mansion. Wine. *301 Rittenhouse Ave., tel. 715/779–*
★ *5111. Jacket and tie required. Reservations recommended. AE, MC, V. Closed Sunday Sept.–June. Expensive.*
Greunke's Inn. This restaurant built in the 1860s specializes in poached whitefish and whitefish livers, trout, steaks. *17 Rittenhouse Ave., tel. 715/779–5480. MC, V. Closed Nov.–Mar. Inexpensive.*
Pier Plaza Restaurant. The dining room has a lake view at this family restaurant that's especially good for breakfast. Try the Friday fish fry and box lunches, too. *Corner Rittenhouse and Front Sts., tel. 715/779–3330. MC, V. Closed Dec. 25. Inexpensive.*

Lodging **Old Rittenhouse Inn.** 9 rooms with fireplaces in an antique-
★ furnished 1890s mansion with all the modern conveniences. Make reservations well in advance. *301 Rittenhouse Ave., 54814, tel. 715/779–5111. Facilities: elegant restaurant, boating, swimming, fishing nearby. MC, V. Moderate–Expensive.*
Bay Villa Motel. 25 rooms, many with a lake view. *Box 33, 54814, tel. 715/779–3252, ½ mi north on Hwy. 13. Facilities: cross-country and snowmobile trails at the door, restaurant, lounge, boating, swimming, fishing nearby. MC, V. Inexpensive.*
Harbor Edge Motel. 17 rooms opposite the ferry landing, some in a historic waterfront home. *33 Front St., 54814, tel. 715/779–3962. Facilities: restaurant, boating, fishing, swimming nearby. MC, V. Inexpensive.*

Eau Claire **Fanny Hill Supper Club and Dinner Theater.** Ribs, chicken, and
Dining seafood served with entertainment and a scenic view. *Crescent*

Ave., tel. 715/836–8184. Reservations required. AE, DC, MC, V. Closed Monday. Moderate.

Sweetwaters. Cajun specialties, sandwiches, salads, steaks, and seafood are served in a contemporary setting. *1104 W. Clairemont Ave., tel. 715/834–5777. Reservations recommended. AE, MC, V. Inexpensive–Moderate.*

Camaraderie. There are several rustic dining rooms here; wide selection of soups and sandwiches as well as steaks and seafood. *442 Water St., tel. 715/834–5411. MC, V. Closed Dec. 25. Inexpensive.*

Lodging **Civic Center Inn.** 124 large, comfortable rooms in a downtown motor hotel. *205 S. Barstow St., 54701, tel. 715/835–6121. Facilities: indoor pool, sauna, parking ramp, restaurant, coffee shop, cocktail lounge, entertainment. AE, DC, MC, V. Moderate.*

Howard Johnson Motor Lodge. 140 rooms. *809 W. Clairemont Ave., 54701, tel. 715/834–6611, 1½ mi north of I–94 exit 65. Facilities: 2 pools (1 indoor), sauna, whirlpool, winter plug-ins, restaurant, cocktail lounge. AE, DC, MC, V. Inexpensive.*

Maple Manor Motel. 34 clean, pleasant rooms. *2507 S. Hastings Way, 54701, tel. 715/834–2618, 2½ mi north of I–94 exit 65. Facilities: coffee shop, beer, winter plug-ins. AE, MC, V. Inexpensive.*

Hayward **Chippewa Inn.** German specialties and American food are
Dining served in a country dining room. *15 mi east on Hwy. B at junction with A, tel. 715/462–3648. Reservations recommended. MC, V. Moderate.*

Tony's Fireside. Steaks, chicken, ribs, and seafood specialties are served in intimate dining rooms in a Northwoods setting. *Rte. 2, 7½ mi south on Hwy. 20, 4 mi east on Hwy. K, tel. 715/634–2710. Reservations recommended. MC, V. Closed Mon.–Wed. Nov.–May. Inexpensive–Moderate.*

Minocqua **Stresing's Red Steer.** The specialties here are charcoal-broiled
Dining steaks, veal, ribs, and seafood. *Hwy. 51S, tel. 715/356–6332. Reservations recommended. AE, MC, V. No lunch; closed Dec. 24–25. Moderate.*

Paul Bunyan Lumberjack Meals. This family restaurant serves prime rib, chicken, spaghetti, and fish in a logging camplike setting. *On U.S. 51 between Minocqua and Woodruff, tel. 715/356–6270. Reservations recommended. MC, V. Closed Oct.–May 15. Inexpensive.*

Lodging **Northwoods Inn.** 34 rooms with queen-size beds. *Box 325, 54548, tel. 715/356–9451. At junction of U.S. Hwy. 51 and Hwy. 70W. Facilities: snowmobile trails; restaurants nearby. MC, V. Moderate.*

Lakeview Motor Lodge. 33 comfortable rooms. *Box 575, 54548, tel. 715/356–5208, 311 Park St., adjacent to lake. Facilities: fireside lobby, boat and snowmobile rental, winter plug-ins, lake swimming, fishing, restaurant adjacent. AE, MC, V. Moderate–Inexpensive.*

Rhinelander **Pied Piper Supper Club.** This attractive contemporary dining
Dining room with views of the woods serves up steaks, chicken, and seafood. *1305 Lincoln Ave., tel. 715/369–3646. Reservations recommended. AE, DC, MC, V. No lunch weekends; closed Easter, Thanksgiving, Dec. 24–25. Moderate–Inexpensive.*

Rhinelander Cafe and Pub. There's standard American fare and very good Greek specialties at this downtown restaurant and supper club owned by the same family since 1911. *33 N. Brown St., tel. 715/362–2918. Reservations recommended. MC, V. Moderate–Inexpensive.*

Lodging **Holiday Acres Resort.** 28 motor-lodge rooms and lakeshore cottages, some with fireplaces. *Box 460 C, 54501, tel. 715/369–1500, 4½ mi east on U.S. 8 and Hwy. 47, 2¼ mi north on Lake George Rd. Facilities: indoor pool, beach, rental boats, rental bicycles, 3 tennis courts, fishing, putting green, wind-surfing, waterskiing, good dining room, coffee shop, cocktail lounge. MC, V. Closed mid-Mar.–May 1. Moderate.*

Claridge Motor Inn. 80 well-kept rooms. *70 N. Stevens St., 54501, tel. 717/362–7100 or 800/528–1234. Facilities: indoor pool, whirlpool, winter plug-ins, restaurant, cocktail lounge. AE, DC, MC, V. Moderate–Inexpensive.*

Superior **Constrom's Supper Club.** Prime rib and seafood are served at
Dining this restaurant owned by the same family for 30 years. *Tower and 33rd St., 2 mi south on Hwy. 35, tel. 715/392–2237. Reservations recommended. MC, V. Closed July 4, Dec. 24–25. Moderate.*

The Shack Supper Club. American favorites such as steaks and ribs are the specialties here. *3301 Belknap St., 1½ mi west on U.S. 2, tel. 715/392–9836. MC, V. Moderate–Inexpensive.*

Lodging **Quality Inn Barker's Island.** 115 rooms with water views. *300 Marina Dr., 54880, tel. 715/392–7152. 1½ mi east on U.S. 2, 53 and 35. Facilities: indoor pool, sauna, whirlpool, 3 lighted tennis courts, coin laundry, restaurant, cocktail lounge. AE, DC, MC, V. Moderate.*

Superior Inn. 72 rooms. *525 Hammond Ave., 54880, tel. 715/394–7706, 1 block south of U.S. 53 and the bridge. Facilities: winter plug-ins, restaurant adjacent. AE, MC, V. Inexpensive.*

The Arts

There is a wide variety of arts and entertainment on the **University of Wisconsin–Eau Claire campus,** including the Forum **Lecture Series** and the **Artist Series,** which features symphony and chamber music by internationally recognized names. The **Foster Art Gallery** presents two major shows and several smaller ones annually. The **Foreign Film Society** has art and revival films. For information contact University Activities and Programs (tel. 715/836–4833).

Nightlife

Since only one city in the region has a population of 50,000, nightlife is somewhat limited. Offerings include Saturday night sing-alongs at mom-and-pop resorts, piano bars in cozy pubs, and rock, country, and polka bands in larger motels, supper clubs, and lounges. Nearly all large resorts have some live entertainment, especially in summer.

The Cabin, a University of Wisconsin–Eau Claire coffee house, has folk music, jazz, blues, and comedy performances. *Davis Center, tel. 715/836–2637. Open Thurs.–Sat.*

5 Minnesota

Introduction

Although its early history parallels that of Michigan and Wisconsin—French exploration followed by the development of the fur trade—Minnesota was settled last. The U.S. Government established its westernmost outpost, Fort Snelling, at the confluence of the Minnesota and Mississippi rivers in 1819. It wasn't until 1839, though, that the fort grew into the settlement that was renamed St. Paul in 1841. St. Anthony, which became Minneapolis, was established in 1848. In 1868 Duluth was a village with six or seven frame houses and a land office, while its nearby sister city of Superior, Wisconsin, had a population of 300. Much of northern Minnesota was not settled until late in the 19th century, and there are communities on the Lake Superior shore that were not established until the middle and late 1950s.

History is vague about the first Frenchman to set foot in what is now Minnesota. Etienne Brule reached western Lake Superior between 1618 and 1622. Father Claude Allouez built a mission adjacent to Allouez Bay, at what is now Superior, Wisconsin, in 1655, and it is hard to imagine that he did not paddle a canoe across the bay to the mouth of the St. Louis River where it empties into Lake Superior or explore the great sandbar that is now called Minnesota Point. The fur traders Radisson and Groseilliers came to the region from Quebec in search of fortune in 1659. They almost certainly followed the Grand Portage at Pigeon River in their quest for furs.

History does record that Daniel de Greysolon, Sieur du Luth, the man after whom Duluth is named, arrived in 1679. Following a council meeting with leaders of the Chippewa Indians and the establishment of a fur-trading post not far from present-day Duluth, he pushed on to the Sioux Indian village by Mille Lacs, where on July 2, 1679, he claimed the country for France.

A year later, while a captive of the Sioux, the Belgian priest Father Louis Hennepin saw a small cataract at the future site of Minneapolis and named it St. Anthony Falls, in honor of his patron saint.

By the beginning of the 18th century there were trading posts at Lake Pepin on the Mississippi, on the Minnesota River near present-day Mankato, and at Duluth. France controlled the fur trade in Minnesota until the French and Indian War. After 1763 England commanded the land east of the Mississippi, and the British post established at Grand Portage, on Lake Superior near the mouth of the Pigeon River, became the fur-trading capital of the West.

The American Revolution gained British-held Minnesota for the United States, and the Louisiana Purchase of 1803 brought the part of Minnesota west of the Mississippi into the fold. John Jacob Astor founded the American Fur Company in 1808 and became one of the giants in the industry. By the early 1840s, the fur trade had declined in the Upper Great Lakes area, but there were other resources to turn to.

Lumbering came to northern Minnesota after the forests to the south had been exhausted, and the results were just as devastating. "Clear the forest and farm the land" was the north-woods philosophy, and millions of acres better suited to grow-

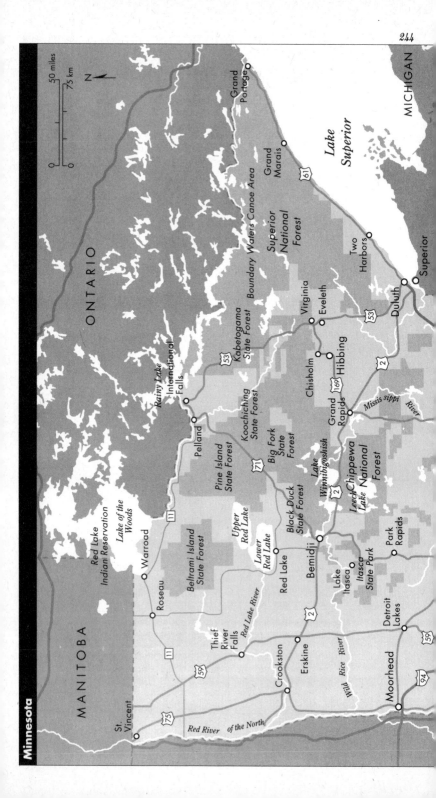

Minnesota

MANITOBA

ONTARIO

MICHIGAN

Lake Superior

50 miles
75 km
N

Red Lake Indian Reservation

Lake of the Woods

Beltrami Island State Forest

Pine Island State Forest

Kabetogama State Forest

Koochiching State Forest

Big Fork State Forest

Black Duck State Forest

Chippewa National Forest

Superior National Forest

Boundary Waters Canoe Area

Grand Portage

Grand Marais

Two Harbors

Duluth

Superior

Virginia

Eveleth

Chisholm

Hibbing

Grand Rapids

Rainy Lake

International Falls

Pelland

Upper Red Lake

Lower Red Lake

Lake Winnibigoshish

Leech Lake

Bemidji

Red Lake

Red Lake River

Park Rapids

Lake Itasca

Itasca State Park

Detroit Lakes

Thief River Falls

Crookston

Erskine

Wild Rice River

Moorhead

St. Vincent

Red River of the North

Warroad

Roseau

Mississippi River

Lake Superior

75

59

11

59

53

71

53

169

61

2

2

2

94

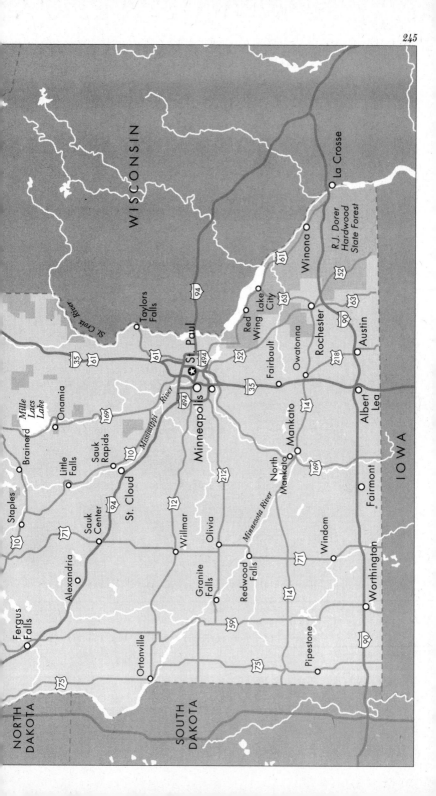

ing trees than crops were stripped clean. In 1899, 462 million board feet of lumber was shipped through Duluth, although after that the volume declined steadily. Although only one lumber mill was in operation in the city in 1925, the damage had already been done. Long hot summers turned the brush and debris that was left into dry tinder that would feed devastating fires along Minnesota's north shore in 1850, 1878, 1910, and annually from 1913 to 1925. The beautiful drive along Lake Superior from Duluth to the Canadian border passed through forests of blackened stumps. The light, sandy soils and short growing seasons of the upper lakes region were never able to support farming. Today, much of the land is county, state, and national forest that has gradually returned to the wild state. Second growth has covered many of the scars of the big cut and the ensuing forest fires.

When Minnesotans speak of "the range," they mean the great Mesabi iron range located some 75 miles northwest of Duluth near Hibbing, Chisholm, Virginia, and Eveleth. Originally it was the Vermilion Range, just west of present-day Ely, that was thought to be the most promising for development. In the early 1880s, the underground Soudan mine began operations, and by 1884 a railroad had been built to ship the ore to Two Harbors, on Lake Superior. That was just the beginning. The riches of the Mesabi Range were confirmed in 1890, and mining began as soon as a rail line was built to Duluth–Superior and ore docks constructed in the harbor. The first Mesabi Range ore was shipped from Duluth in 1892. Financial giants such as John D. Rockefeller, Andrew Carnegie, Henry W. Oliver, and James J. Hill, of the Great Northern Railroad, provided the money that developed the Mesabi Range. In 1901, J. Pierpont Morgan, the New York financial magnate, consolidated the Carnegie, Rockefeller, and Oliver interests into the U.S. Steel Corporation.

Mining in the 137-square-mile Mesabi Range is open-pit surface mining. Giant shovels scoop and load the ore into railroad cars for shipment to processing plants and, eventually, to the country's steel centers. In nearly a century of operation, billions of tons of ore have been shipped from the Mesabi mines, and their wealth promises to last for an additional 200 years.

A diverse group of people came to work in the mines—Americans from the Eastern mining communities, Cornishmen, Swedes, Italians, Slovenes, Croats, Romanians, Norwegians, Irish, Finns, Poles, Germans, and French Canadians. At the turn of the century, at least half the people living in the Mesabi region were foreign-born. Their ethnic legacy lives on, not only in Minnesota, but throughout the northern Upper Great Lakes region.

Minnesota is quite correctly thought of as a land of forests and lakes. There are millions of acres of second-growth forest, and 15,291 lakes, including Lake Itasca, where the Mississippi River rises. But parts of the state seem more closely tied to the Great Plains than the Great Lakes. The broad, flat valley of the Red River along the Dakota border, and the Tall Grass Prairie near Pipestone, in the southwest, could easily be taken for Kansas or Nebraska.

But Minnesota is a Great Lakes state, make no bones about it. There are 180 miles of Lake Superior shoreline, and Duluth/

Superior is the nation's farthest inland deep-water port, 2,342 miles from the Atlantic Ocean. Before the steel and shipping industries fell on hard times in the early 1980s, it was ranked among the 10 busiest ports in the nation. Even today, it is one of the busiest ports on the Great Lakes.

When southern Minnesotans say they are going "up north," they most likely mean someplace located in the middle of the state, like Brainerd, or perhaps Duluth. But if their destination is farther north, like International Falls or Baudette, Minnesotans are going "up on the boundary." The boundary with Canada was not legally determined until 1842, having been set through the Pigeon River and along the historic traders' route to the northwest point of Lake of the Woods. This left Minnesota with the Northwest Angle, a peninsula jutting into Lake of the Woods from the Manitoba, Canada, shore. The Northwest Angle is the northernmost point in the contiguous United States, but can be reached only by driving into Manitoba, or traveling by boat from Minnesota or Ontario, Canada. The boundary was not marked east of Lake of the Woods until early in the 20th century, and then only after conflicting claims between Americans and Canadians in the region.

Finally, a word about Minnesota's weather. Minnesotans like to tell the story, *possibly* apocryphal, about the Minnesota farmer who, upon being told that a land resurvey placed his farm in Wisconsin, wrote in his diary, "Thank God, no more cold winters." After the severe winter of 1971–1972, icebreakers were used to get ships in and out of Duluth harbor as late as June, and the record low in the Twin Cities is −41°F. Nevertheless, there have been years when the ice sculptures at St. Paul's Winter Carnival melted because of unseasonably high temperatures.

Minneapolis and St. Paul

Drawing comparisons between Minneapolis and St. Paul is much like comparing two favorite aunts—it's a difficult task, at best. St. Paul has been described as the last of the Eastern cities, while Minneapolis has been called the first of the Western ones. Indeed there is a western rambunctiousness about Minneapolis that is not found in St. Paul. Although both cities span the Mississippi River, St. Paul has been *the* river town since the first riverboat arrived at Fort Snelling in 1823. The river makes a huge loop as it cuts through the city, giving St. Paul 29 miles of waterfront and thoroughly confusing tourists who try to use the river as a north–south indicator. Towboats chug back and forth near the city's center, assembling grain-laden barges into strings to be pushed downstream to St. Louis or New Orleans. What little river traffic there is in Minneapolis is headed for St. Paul to be assembled into tows and moved southward.

There are 2.2 million people in the Greater Minneapolis/St. Paul region, but Minneapolis wins the population race by a round-figure score of 360,000 to 270,000. Both communities have miles-long skyway systems. Residents can drive downtown, park, walk to work, go to lunch, shop, see a show, and return to their car without once setting foot outdoors—a blessing in the long Minnesota winters. Both cities have tall, gleaming glass skylines. St. Paul's is designed to blend with the city's Art Deco and Victorian architecture, while Minneapolis's is more eclectic. St. Paul has preserved its architectural heritage (Summit Avenue is a magnificent five-mile stretch of residential Victorian buildings), while much of downtown Minneapolis is new. The professional baseball and football teams are the Minnesota Twins and the Minnesota Vikings; both play at the Hubert H. Humphrey Metrodome, in downtown Minneapolis, within easy walking distance of the heart of the city. Minneapolis boasts the University of Minnesota, while St. Paul is the state capital. St. Paul has a slightly reserved air about it; Minneapolis is brasher, noisier, and busier. Culture and the arts abound in the Twin Cities. There are more than 90 theaters in the metro area and the Twin Cities are considered the nation's premier theater community outside New York. And it goes on. Minneapolis has this, while St. Paul offers that. But rather than compare apples and oranges, let's go exploring.

For a community that began life with the disadvantage of a name like "Pig's Eye," St. Paul has done quite well. The first non-Indian settlement in the region was Fort Snelling, built in 1819 at the confluence of the Minnesota and Mississippi rivers, northernmost of a thin string of government forts and Indian agencies that stretched into the Old Northwest. In 1839 the commandant of the fort evicted a group of French Canadian *voyageurs* from an adjacent settlement. Among them was a former fur trader named Pierre "Pig's Eye" Parrant, who was accused of selling whiskey to the local Indians. Pig's Eye and his friends moved downstream and settled in at various landings along the river. One of the settlements was called Lowertown, and even today St. Paul has a section known by that name. The straggling collection of crude log cabins was known as Pig's Eye Landing. In 1841 a French priest, Father Lucien Galtier, built a rough log chapel dedicated to St. Paul and asked that the village's name be changed to that of the saint. The citizens agreed, and Pig's Eye Landing became St. Paul. There is to this day, however, a Pig's Eye Lake.

When Minnesota became a territory in 1849, St. Paul became the capital. More settlers began to move into the region, coming upriver or along the 233-mile Point Douglas Military Road, which linked St. Paul with Fort Crawford at Prairie du Chien, Wisconsin. In 1851 work began on the first bridge across the river, and seven professional actors from Placide's Varieties in New Orleans played a standing-room only, two-week engagement at Mazurka Hall. St. Paul was incorporated as a city in 1854 and remained the capital when Minnesota became a state in 1858.

Between 1860 and the turn of the century, thousands of immigrants arrived from Europe, in particular from Sweden, Norway, Denmark, Germany, and Great Britain, giving the city a diverse ethnic base. During those years St. Paul became the hub of an enormous railroad empire established by James J. Hill. The Great Northern Railroad (now the Burlington Northern), opened the northwest to settlement, made Hill a fortune, turned St. Paul into a major transportation center, and brought banking, insurance, and warehousing to the thriving city. Hill, along with the last of the 19th-century lumber barons and other merchants, built the city's commercial base and the mansions that line Summit Avenue. During the second and third decades of this century, when Art Deco was the architectural rage, St. Paul followed the trend. The 20-story St. Paul City Hall/ Ramsey County Courthouse, built in American Perpendicular style with an interior finished in gleaming blue marble, bronze, and gold leaf is an excellent example.

World War I, Prohibition, the Depression, World War II, and the social changes of the 1960s brought about urban decay in St. Paul, as it did in larger cities throughout the country. But by the late 1970s, the city was well into a program of reconstruction and renewal. Three and one-half miles of second-level all-weather skyways were built, connecting more than 200 downtown businesses. The old merchandising and warehouse district of Lowertown was refurbished and restored, and today the Victorian brick buildings house an assortment of shops, boutiques, and restaurants that have become one of the city's shopping and nightlife centers. The 40-story Minnesota World Trade Center with its St. Paul Center shopping mall, which opened in 1987, is a notable addition to St. Paul's skyline.

Perhaps no corner of the city better reflects the St. Paul of today than Rice Park, a small block-square park in the heart of downtown where the ice sculptures of the city's famed Winter Carnival are created. In summer it provides fountains, shade trees, hot dog vendors, and restful green spaces. The park is flanked by one of the city's newest landmarks, the architecturally acclaimed Ordway Music Theater, and by one of its oldest, the 1892 Gothic-style Landmark Center. Turn-of-the-century hotels and other public buildings surround the park and are reflected in the glass of towering skyscrapers.

Although more than a decade has passed since the last episode of the "Mary Tyler Moore Show" was filmed, the Minneapolis Convention and Visitor's Bureau still gets inquiries about the house where Mary and Rhoda lived. Set in a fictitious Minneapolis TV station, the series was filmed in Hollywood, although the stars and a film crew occasionally came to Minneapolis to shoot exterior scenes of "Mary's house." It stands on a street corner in a pleasant neighborhood in a western suburb of the city, looking just as it did on the show, although the front yard seems smaller than it appeared on TV, and the trees have grown taller. The exact location is a closely guarded secret, since tourists are inclined to knock on the door and ask if they can have a peek at Mary's room.

Some 300 years ago French explorers searching for the Northwest Passage to the Orient reached the banks of the Mississippi. In 1680 a Belgian priest, Father Louis Hennepin, was the first to see the 16-foot cataract in the Mississippi that he named St. Anthony Falls. One hundred and forty years later, soldiers from nearby Fort Snelling built a sawmill and flour mill at the falls. The village of St. Anthony was established on the east bank of the Mississippi near the falls in 1848, and was soon linked by a suspension bridge to a small community on the opposite shore.

Industry came to the rough little towns following the Civil War. In 1872 St. Anthony was combined with the village on the west bank to form Minneapolis, a name that combines the Dakota Indian word for water ("minne") with the Greek word for city ("polis"). The power-producing Falls of St. Anthony were harnessed and milling houses built along the river, eventually becoming the international giants of Pillsbury, General Mills, and Cargill.

There are 22 lakes in Minneapolis. Early in the city's history the land around the largest lakes was set aside as parkland for public use, and today Minneapolis has a sparkling collection of 153 parks and parkways used by walkers, joggers, bicyclists, sunbathers, and picnickers. Loring Park, named after the founder of the Minneapolis park system, borders the southern edge of downtown and offers green spaces, a small lake, and jogging and biking trails.

A building boom has revitalized downtown Minneapolis in the last two decades, changing the skyline so much that people who moved away only 20 years ago barely recognize it. Seventeen blocks of ramshackle downtown structures were torn down to make way for new buildings, gleaming glass and steel skyscrapers, climate-controlled plazas, and a three-mile-long, glass-enclosed skyway system. The newest additions to the skyline are the glass, swirl-topped, 36-story Opus Building and the 57-story, 772-foot-high Norwest Center, both completed in late 1988. The city's historic Warehouse District, dating from the turn of the century, is several blocks of restored buildings that now house popular restaurants, bars, shops, galleries, and nightclubs.

Downtown Minneapolis is centered on the Nicollet Mall in the heart of the shopping district. The mile-long mall is the nation's longest downtown pedestrian stroll-way. Regular auto traffic is prohibited, but buses and taxis traverse the mall from 1st to 13th streets. An extensive system of skywalks connects many of the buildings via enclosed, second-story pedestrian bridges.

From its early days, Minneapolis was a center of culture and the arts. The famed Guthrie Theater, the Walker Art Center, the Minnesota Orchestra, and the North West Dance Theater, have made the city, along with St. Paul, one of the cultural bright spots in the nation. It is rapidly becoming one of the nation's top pop-music centers, due in large measure to the popularity and success of rock-music superstar Prince, a Minneapolis native who still lives and records in the city.

Arriving and Departing

By Plane **Minneapolis/St. Paul International Airport** (tel. 612/726–1717) lies between the cities on Route 5, eight miles from downtown St. Paul and 10 miles from downtown Minneapolis. It is served by **American** (tel. 800/223–5436), **Braniff** (tel. 800/272–6433), **Continental** (tel. 800/525–0280), **Delta** (tel. 800/221–1212), **Eastern** (tel. 800/323–7323), **Midway** (tel. 800/621–5700), **Norcan Air** (tel. 800/426–7000), **Northwest** (tel. 800/441–1414), **Pan Am** (tel. 800/221–1111), **Piedmont** (tel. 800/251–5720), **Trans World** (tel. 800/221–2000), **United** (tel. 800/241–6522), and **USAir** (tel. 800/428–4322).

Between the Airport and Downtown Buses of the **Metropolitan Transit Commission** (tel. 612/827–7733) serve the airport from both communities, although service to and from St. Paul is somewhat limited. The fare is $1 during peak hours and 85¢ the rest of the day. Call for schedule information.

Taxis to and from the airport take about 20 minutes from either city. The fare to downtown St. Paul is about $10; to downtown

Minneapolis $12.50–$16. Taxi starters at the airport will assist visitors.

Limousine service between the airport and downtown hotels runs approximately every half hour between 5 AM and 9 PM. For St. Paul, call 612/726–5479, for Minneapolis, 612/827–7777. One-way fare to St. Paul is $5.50, $9 round-trip. Fare to Minneapolis is $7.50, $10 round-trip.

By car from the airport, take W. 7th Street or Shepard Road to downtown St. Paul. Route 55 or Route 62 to I–35W leads to downtown Minneapolis.

By Train   The Twin Cities **Amtrak** depot in St. Paul (730 Transfer Rd., tel. 612/339–2382 or 800/872–7245) serves both cities with daily service to Chicago and the east, and to Seattle and other points west.

By Bus   **Greyhound/Trailways** serves the Twin Cities. The Greyhound terminal in St. Paul is on 7th Street at St. Peter Street (tel. 612/222–0509 or 800/528–0447). The St. Paul Trailways Terminal is at 469 St. Peter Street (tel. 612/222–0681 or 800/242–2935). The Minneapolis Greyhound depot is at 29 N. 9th Street (tel. 612/371–3320 or 800/528–0447). The Trailways station is at 400 S. 3rd Street (tel. 612/332–3273 or 800/242–2935).

By Car   I–35 and I–94 intersect in downtown Minneapolis. I–35 divides within the Twin Cities, becoming I–35E in St. Paul and I–35W in Minneapolis. Only a portion of I–35E is complete in St. Paul, while I–35W goes north–south through Minneapolis. I–94 goes east–west through both cities. A belt line highway circles the Twin Cities, with I–494 looping through the southern suburbs and I–694 cutting through the north. Belt line interchanges connect with all major routes.

I–494 marks the northern edge of the Twin Cities suburb of Bloomington, which recently replaced Duluth as the state's third largest city. The "I–494 strip" is a rapidly growing area of restaurants, hotels and motels, and new office towers. I–694 marks the border with the North Metro region, a booming area of high-tech and medical manufacturing industries.

Getting Around

Both Minneapolis and St. Paul are laid out on a square grid system, and streets run north–south and east–west. However, since many downtown streets parallel the Mississippi and run on a diagonal, and since not all streets cross the river, a good street map would be helpful.

Following the river, 7th Street is St. Paul's principal downtown street. University Avenue and Wabasha Street divide the city into east, west, north, and south quadrants, and all addresses begin from this point. In Minneapolis east and west numbering begins at Nicollet Avenue. Many St. Paul attractions are located in the downtown area and can be reached easily by foot, while many Minneapolis attractions are farther than walking distance from downtown.

By Bus   Buses of the **Metropolitan Transit Commission** (tel. 612/827–7733) serve the metropolitan area with a full schedule. Fares range from 60¢ to $1.25, depending on the time of day and distance traveled. Exact change or bus tokens are required. Route maps, pocket schedules, and tokens are available in Minneapolis at IDS Crystal Court (7th St. and Nicollet Mall), or the MTC Transit Store (719 Marquette St.).

By Taxi Cabs must be ordered by phone or hired at cabstands. The fare is $1.95 for the first mile and $1.10 for each additional mile. The largest taxi companies in St. Paul are **Yellow** (tel. 612/222–4433) and **City Wide** (tel. 612/292–1616). In Minneapolis, **Blue and White** (tel. 612/333–3331) and **Yellow** (tel. 612/824–4444) are the largest companies. **Town Taxi** (tel. 612/331–8294) serves both cities and all suburbs.

Important Addresses and Numbers

Tourist Information The **St. Paul Convention and Visitors Bureau** (tel. 612/297–6985 or 800/328–8322, ext. 983) maintains a Visitor Information Booth on the street level of St. Paul Center at 445 Minnesota Street (tel. 612/223–5409). Open weekdays 9:30–6, Sat. 11–6.

Visitor information booths are also located in the state capitol (University Ave. between Wabasha and Cedar sts.), the Science Museum (30 E. 10th St.), the Landmark Center (75 W. 5th St.), and the City Hall/Courthouse (4th and Wabasha sts.). All are open weekdays 9–5.

The **Minneapolis Convention and Visitors Bureau** (15 S. 5th St., tel. 612/348–4313 or 800/445–7412). Open weekdays 9–5. There is also a visitor information booth at the IDS Center (7th St. and Nicollet Mall, tel. 612/372–1563). Open weekdays 9–5, Sat. 10–5.

The **Minnesota Office of Tourism** (375 Jackson St., 250 Skyway Level, St. Paul, 55101, tel. 612/296–5029 or 800/652–9747). Open weekdays 9–5.

Emergencies Dial 911 for assistance.

Opening and Closing Times

Banks Open weekdays 9–5.

Museums Open Tuesday–Sunday 9–5; closed Monday. See individual listings.

Shops Most stores are open Monday–Saturday 9:30–6; selected stores are open Sunday noon–5. Most shopping malls are open Monday–Saturday 10–9, Sunday noon–6.

Guided Tours

Orientation Tours The **Gray Line** offers 3½-hour tours of the Twin Cities from Memorial Day to October 1. *Tel. 612/591–0999 or 338–6164. Fares: $14 adults; $7 children 6–14, free under 6 if not occupying a seat to the exclusion of another passenger. Tours depart Tues.-Sat. from the Radisson Hotel St. Paul at 8:30 AM and the Holiday Inn Town Square at 8:35 AM. In Minneapolis tours leave the Holiday Inn Downtown at 9 AM, Hello Minnesota (7 S. 7th St.) at 9:10 AM, and the Radisson University Hotel at 9:30 AM.*

Twin Cities Sightseeing Tours offers 2½-hour tours that will take you to many landmarks in both cities, with a stop at Minnehaha Falls. Passengers can leave their cars in the parking lot free of charge. *3920 Nicollet Ave., tel. 612/827–7777. Fare: $13.*

Tour Du Jour (tel. 612/823–0291) offers 3½ hour tours of the Twin Cities in 10-passenger vans with one 20-minute stop. Call for pickup locations and times.

Metro Connections offers guided tours of the Twin Cities from mid-June to Labor Day. Highlights of the three-hour tour include Nicollet Mall, the mansion and cathedral areas, parkways and lakes, the gravesite of Hubert H. Humphrey, Minnehaha Falls, Summit Avenue, the State Capitol, and Ordway Music Theater. Tours originate in Minneapolis with stops at the Normandy Inn and Marriott City Center (10 and 10:05 AM) and at the Radisson Hotel St. Paul and Holiday Inn Town Square (11 and 11:05 AM). *Tel. 612/644–7152 for reservations. Cost: $13 adults, $12 senior citizens, $7 children under 14.*

Boat Tours   Sightseeing tours of the Mississippi between downtown St. Paul and Fort Snelling are offered aboard the *Jonathan Padelford* and *Josiah Snelling*, modern sternwheelers modeled after 19th-century Mississippi riverboats. Excursions lasting 1¾ hours leave from Harriet Island, ¼ mile southwest of the Wabasha Street Bridge off Nagasaki Road. *Tel. 612/227–1100. Cost: $6.50 adults, $5.50 over 60; $4 children under 12. Excursions Memorial Day–Labor Day at 10, noon, 2; May and Sept., weekends at 2.*

Twenty-five-minute cruises of Minneapolis's Lake Harriet are offered aboard the sternwheeler *Queen of the Lakes. Tel. 612/ 348–4825 or 348–2248. Cost: $1.75 per person. Cruises Memorial Day–Labor Day. Call for schedule information.*

Walking Tours   Two cassette-guided walking tours of downtown Minneapolis are available in English and Swedish. One describes the skywalk system, the other the Nicollet Mall; both provide one-hour commentaries about buildings, architectural features, history, and art. *Hello Minnesota, 7 S. 7th St., tel. 612/332–1755.*

Information on self-guided walking tours of St. Paul is available at visitor information booths in the city.

Exploring St. Paul

Numbers in the margin correspond with points of interest on the St. Paul maps.

Visitors can easily explore downtown St. Paul on foot, walking either on the streets or through the all-weather, climate-controlled skyway system that runs for 3½ miles, connecting more than 200 stores, shops, and restaurants. The skyway reaches nearly all of downtown St. Paul and is bounded by Kellogg Boulevard at the river, and 8th, Wacouta, and St. Peter streets. The skyway is open from 6 AM to 2 AM. We begin exploring at the Minnesota Museum of Art, at Kellogg Boulevard and St. Peter Street, and work northward to the state capitol.

❶ The **Minnesota Museum of Art** is housed in the Jemne Building, one of St. Paul's impressive Art Deco structures. The museum's permanent collection is strong in Asian art and 19th- and 20th-century American artists, and there are changing exhibits of contemporary sculpture, paintings, photography, and drawings. A branch of the museum is located in the nearby Landmark Center. *305 St. Peter St., tel. 612/292–4355. Admis-*

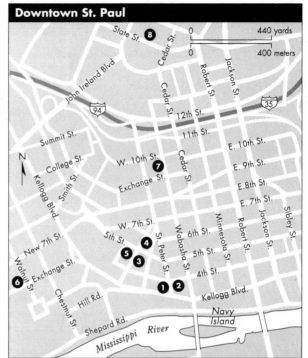

Downtown St. Paul

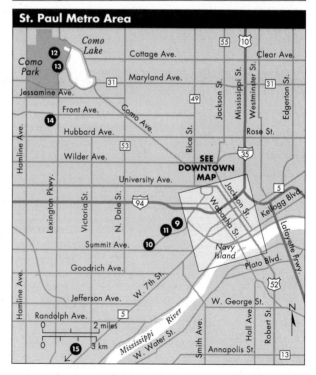

St. Paul Metro Area

sion free. Open Tues.–Sat. 10:30–4:30, Thurs. 10:30–7:30,
Sun. 11:30–4:30; closed Mon. and holidays.

Time Out Tucked away on the fourth floor of the Jemne Building in the
Minnesota Museum of Art, the **Deco Restaurant** features a view
of the Mississippi along with soups, salads, desserts, a buffet,
and Scandinavian specialties prepared by Finnish chef Soile
Anderson. The presentation is excellent. *305 St. Peter St., tel.
612/228–0520. Reservations recommended. AE. Open Tues.–
Fri. 11:30 AM–2 PM, Sun. brunch 11 AM–2 PM; closed Mon. and
Sat. Inexpensive–Moderate.*

From the museum head north one block and then east on 4th
Street for a half-block to the **City Hall** and **Ramsey County
Courthouse,** which are located in the same building. Dating
from 1931, the 20-story building is of a design known as American Perpendicular, while the interior is done in Zigzag
Moderne, an Art Deco style that originated in Paris in the
1920s. Paintings in the third-floor council chambers depict the
founding and growth of St. Paul. Most impressive is **Memorial
Hall** (4th St. entrance), 85 feet long and three stories high, finished in gleaming dark blue Belge marble with a gold-leaf
ceiling, and 16 bronze shafts set into marble columns. At the far
end of the hall is the towering *Indian God of Peace* statue, designed by the noted Swedish sculptor Carl Milles. It is the
largest carved onyx figure in the world, standing 36 feet high
and weighing 60 tons. The figure oscillates on a turntable, moving 66 degrees to the right and left to show detail. Four small
statues submitted by Milles as prototypes are also on exhibit.
In the first-floor lobby there are six elevator doors with bronze
reliefs depicting the growth of the region. *4th St., between St.
Peter and Wabasha sts., tel. 612/298–4012. Admission free.
Open weekdays 8:30–4:30.*

Follow 4th Street west two blocks to **Rice Park.** One block
square, it is St. Paul's oldest urban park and one of its finest.
Designated a public square in 1849, the park has seen everything from circuses and presidential speeches (Chester A.
Arthur) to women using the grassy areas to bleach laundry in
the sun. Rice Park was re-landscaped in 1965, and the streets
around it were paved with brick in 1985. The 7½-foot-high
bronze sculpture in the center of the fountain is called *The
Source* and is by the St. Paul sculptor Alonzo Hauser. The park
is a favorite with downtown St. Paulites, who eat lunch here in
warm weather, and is an excellent place to stop and enjoy the
flavor of the city. *Free guided tours of the park Sun. at 3, tel.
612/292–3272.*

The Landmark Center, the restored Old Federal Courts Building, is the most impressive of the buildings facing Rice Park.
Designed in 1892 and completed in 1902, the structure is of towering Romanesque Revival design; the south tower is modeled
after Trinity Church in Boston. The building was scheduled for
demolition in 1967, but saved in 1970, just one week before the
wrecker's ball was to destroy it. Fully restored, its features include a skylighted six-story indoor courtyard, stained glass
skylights, and a marble tile foyer. Several restored courtrooms
and chambers are open to the public. The center houses the offices of many of St. Paul's cultural organizations and a branch of

the **Minnesota Museum of Art.** *75 W. 5th St., tel. 612/292–3225. Admission free. Free guided tours Thurs. at 11, Sun. at 2, tel. 612/292–3272. Open weekdays 8–5, Thurs. 8–8, Sat. 10–5, Sun. 1–5; closed holidays. The Minnesota Museum of Art is open Tues.–Sat. 10–5, Sun. 1–5; closed Mon. and holidays.*

Time Out The **Gladstone Cafe,** just inside the Landmark Center's main entrance and overlooking the courtyard, is a cafeteria serving soups, salads, and sandwiches, wine and beer. *Open weekdays 9:30–2:30 PM; outdoor dining in summer. No credit cards. Inexpensive.*

The center's next-door neighbor on the east side of the square is the **Saint Paul Hotel,** one of the city's finest, built in 1910. Fully refurbished in the late 1970s, the luxury hotel is a favorite with notables from presidents to Hollywood stars. The adjacent 26-story Amhoist Tower reflects the hotel's image in its gleaming mirrored glass.

On the south side of Rice Park is the block-long Italian Renaissance Revival **St. Paul Public Library,** which was donated to the city in 1916 by railroad magnate James J. Hill. The library has a collection of 500,000 volumes and several special rooms including the James J. Hill Reference Library, which was Hill's personal collection.

❺ The **Ordway Music Theater** (345 S. Washington St., tel. 612/224–4222) is the most recent addition to Rice Park and one of St. Paul's most exciting theaters. It opened on January 1, 1985. Designed by the Boston architect Benjamin Thompson, the state-of-the-art theater has faceted glass walls set in a facade of brick and copper. It blends well with its Victorian neighbors, yet is as modern as tomorrow. It is home to the St. Paul Chamber Orchestra and the Minnesota Opera, and has two performing theaters that offer chamber music, opera, jazz, popular music, and dance. The glass-fronted public spaces provide lovely views of Rice Park.

❻ Four blocks west, at the corner of Exchange and Walnut streets, is the **Alexander Ramsey House,** home of the first governor of the Minnesota Territory. Built in 1872, the French Second Empire mansion has been restored to appear as it did more than a century ago. Its 15 rooms contain black walnut woodwork, marble fireplaces, crystal chandeliers, rich collections of china and silver, and period furnishings that belonged to the Ramseys. Tours by costumed guides begin on the hour in a reconstructed 1883 carriage house with a video on Ramsey's life and career. *265 S. Exchange St., tel. 612/296–8760. Admission: $2 adults, $1 children 6–16 and senior citizens. Open April–Dec., Tues.–Fri. 10–4, weekends 1–4:30; closed Mon. and major holidays.*

Return to Rice Park and follow Washington Street two blocks north until it runs into St. Peter Street at W. 7th Place, then north one block to W. 7th Street.

Time Out **Mickey's Diner** is an internationally famous example of a streamlined 1930s lunch-counter diner. It's not fancy, but it's a St. Paul classic, and serves great breakfasts. The diner is listed on the National Register of Historic Places. *36 W. 7th St., tel. 612/222–5633. No credit cards. Inexpensive.*

The tall brown granite building with the angled glass top one block to the east is St. Paul's **World Trade Center,** a towering complex of offices at 7th Street between Cedar and Wabasha streets. Completed in the late summer of 1987, it is a clearing-house for international trade and is the tallest building on the St. Paul skyline.

Time Out **Bailey's Bar and Grill** (6th and Wabasha Sts., tel. 612/222–7855), with its free popcorn, a brass rail at the bar, and high tables and chairs, is a good place to sit by a window, enjoy a drink and a sandwich, and watch downtown St. Paul. The menu includes gourmet hamburgers, Mexican entrees, steak and seafood (evenings only), and more than 30 brands of beer. *AE, MC, V. Inexpensive.*

7 From here continue north to 10th Street and the **Science Museum of Minnesota.** The museum offers exhibits on archaeology, technology, and biology. Youngsters will love Technology Hall where they can operate mechanical arms, make computers talk and play games, whisper into parabolic dishes that project voices the length of the galleries, and use many other fun and educational hands-on exhibits. The second-level Hall of Anthropology features exhibits on the way different peoples of the world live and work. Cross the skyway to the east building of the Science Museum where there are exhibits on dinosaurs and land use in Minnesota. In Biology Hall, models of DNA and a transparent woman allow a look inside living organisms. There is a Science Explore Store in the east building and two other "explore stores" in the west building. The museum houses the William L. McKnight Omnitheater, where 70-mm films are projected overhead on a massive tilted screen that brings a sense of total involvement in the movie. *30 E. 10th St., tel. 612/221–9488. Combination admission for the exhibit halls and Omnitheater: $5.50 adults, $4.50 children 2–12 and senior citizens. Exhibit Hall: $3 adults, $2 children 3–12, $1.50 seniors over 64. Omnitheater: $4.50 adults, $3.50 children 3–12 and seniors over 64. Open Mon.–Sat. 9:30–9, Sun. 11–9; closed Mon. from Labor Day through Easter, and Dec. 25.*

Leave the museum by the Exchange Street exit. On Exchange Street between Wabasha and Cedar streets is the World Theater (10 E. Exchange St., tel. 612/298–1300), where Garrison Keillor spun his weekly tales about mythical Lake Wobegon on the "Prairie Home Companion Radio Show." Built in 1910 and completely refurbished in 1986, it is St. Paul's oldest surviving theater space. The two-balcony proscenium theater is currently home to public radio's nationally broadcast "Good Evening" from Minnesota with Noah Adams.

Go east to Cedar Street and continue north five blocks to the **8** **Minnesota State Capitol.** This is the state's third capitol building. The original, built in 1853, was destroyed by fire in 1881, and a second building completed the following year proved to be too small. Designed by the St. Paul architect Cass Gilbert, the building contains more than 25 varieties of marble, sandstone, limestone, and granite. The grounds are exceptionally beautiful, especially when approached from the south. The capitol dome is 223 feet high and is the world's largest unsupported marble dome. At its base is a magnificent sculpture group titled *The Progress of the State*, featuring golden horses and a charioteer holding a horn of plenty. In the middle of the first floor under the rotunda is a large glass and brass star, a symbol of Minnesota as the North Star State. Flags carried by Minnesota soldiers in the Spanish-American, Civil, and Dakota Indian Wars are displayed in cases along the walls of the rotunda. Near the south entry are cases containing Minnesota's two constitutions and artifacts from early statehood years. *University Ave. between Wabasha and Cedar Sts., tel. 612/296–2881. Free guided tours of the capitol weekdays 9–4, Sat. 10–3, and Sun. 1–3. 45-min. tours leave from the rotunda on the hour.*

9 Located about a half-mile west of the capitol at the corner of Selby and Summit avenues is the **Cathedral of St. Paul.** Construction on the church, which is styled after St. Peter's in Rome, was begun in 1906 and completed in 1915. The Classical Renaissance domed church is built of Minnesota granite and seats 3,000 people. There are beautiful stained glass windows, statues, paintings, and other works of art in the cathedral, with a small historical museum, three assembly halls, and a chapel on the lower level. *239 Selby Ave., tel. 612/228–1766. Admission free. Open daily 6–6.*

10 **Summit Avenue,** long one of St. Paul's most prestigious addresses, runs four and one-half miles from the cathedral to the Mississippi, and is the nation's longest stand of intact residential Victorian architecture. F. Scott Fitzgerald lived at 599 Summit Avenue in 1918 when he wrote *This Side of Paradise*. The **Governor's Mansion** is at 1006 Summit Avenue. **Mount Zion Temple,** home of the oldest Jewish congregation in Minnesota (1856), is located at 1300 Summit Avenue.

11 Here, too, you'll find the **James J. Hill House,** home of Minnesota's transportation pioneer and builder of the Great Northern Railroad. Constructed of red sandstone and completed in 1891, the Richardsonian Romanesque mansion has carved woodwork, stained glass, tiled fireplaces, cut-glass chandeliers, and a skylit art gallery with changing art exhibits. It is administered by the Minnesota Historical Society. *240 Summit Ave., tel. 612/297–2555. Admission: $2 adults, $1 children 6–15 and seniors over 62, children under 5 free. Reservations suggested for guided tours. Open Wed.–Thurs. and Sat. 10–3:30.*

Como Park is home to a zoo and conservatory, as well as picnic areas, walking trails around the lake, children's playgrounds, and tennis and swimming facilities. *Admission free. Take I–94 to Snelling Ave., north to Midway Pkwy., then east to the park.*

12 The **Como Park Zoo** is a midsize zoo with large cats, land and water birds, primates, and aquatic animals. There are daily shows by Sparky, the performing seal. Arctic wolves are displayed in a natural setting and there is a children's zoo and zoological society gift shop. Amusement rides, refreshments, and souvenir stands are located nearby in the park. *Tel. 612/488–5572. Admission free. Zoo grounds open Apr.–Sept. 8–8, bldgs. 10–6; Oct.–Mar., grounds 8–5, bldgs. 10–4.*

13 The adjacent **Como Park Conservatory,** dating from 1913, has more than 200 permanently planted species, sunken gardens, a fern room, and Biblical plantings in the conservatory and adjoining greenhouses. There is a spring and winter flower show, a chrysanthemum show in autumn, and special summer displays. Adjacent is a traditional, formal Japanese outdoor garden, which is open limited hours from May through the end of summer. *Tel. 612/489–1740. Admission free; a fee may be*

*charged for special exhibitions. Open daily 10–6 in summer,
10–4 in winter.*

⑭ The **Children's Museum** is a place where youngsters get a
chance to try their hand at grown-up activities, including driving a bus and playing banker, dentist, clerk, or computer
operator. Two floors of simulated settings include a TV station,
railway station, doctor's office, automotive shop, working mag-
netic crane, and soda fountain. There are frequent special
events and activity days. *1217 Bandana Blvd., tel. 612/644–
3818. West on I–94 to Lexington Ave. exit, then 1 mi north to
Energy Park Dr. and west to Bandana Blvd. Admission: $2.25
adults, $1.75 children 2–17 and senior citizens. Open Tues.–
Thurs. and Sat. 10–5, Fri. 10–8, Sun. 11–5, and Mon. 10–5 in
July and Aug. Closed Mondays Sept.–June, and holidays.*

⑮ Historic **Fort Snelling** was built in 1819 at the junction of the
Mississippi and Minnesota rivers just south of what is now St.
Paul. Once the northernmost outpost in the old Northwest Ter-
ritories, it was an active military post until after World War II.
There are 17 restored buildings, including officer's quarters,
enlisted men's barracks, a school, hospital, store, and commandant's house. Costumed guides portray life at the fort in the
1820s with demonstrations of blacksmithing, carpentry, and
baking. There are infantry drills, musket firing demonstrations, and military ceremonies daily. A History Center has
exhibits and short films on the fort. A variety of special events
are held in spring and summer. *Junction of I–494 and Rte. 55
near the Minneapolis/St. Paul Airport, tel. 612/726–1171. Admission: $2 adults, $1 children 6–15 and seniors over 62. Fort
open May–Oct., daily 10–5. History Center open Nov.–Apr.,
weekends 9–4:30.*

Exploring Minneapolis

*Numbers in the margin correspond with points of interest on
the Minneapolis maps.*

Like St. Paul, downtown Minneapolis is easily walkable in any
season. The climate-controlled skyway system connects hundreds of stores, shops, and restaurants. It reaches much of
downtown Minneapolis and at present is bounded by S. 1st,
5th, and 9th streets and Hennepin Avenue, although new buildings and new additions are frequently being added. In general,
the Minneapolis skyways remain open during the business
hours of the buildings they connect.

We begin exploring where Father Hennepin started three centuries ago, at the **Falls of St. Anthony.** Harnessed by dams and
diminished in grandeur from the time Hennepin saw them, the
① historic falls are bypassed by the **Upper St. Anthony Lock.** The
lock, with a lift of 49 feet, allows river traffic to reach railheads
and industrial and commercial sections of Minneapolis. The river channel extends some three miles above the falls, which
mark the practical head of navigation on the Mississippi River.
An observation deck in a small visitor center permits good
views of lock operations and contains exhibits about the Mississippi River and locks and dams. *Foot of Portland Ave., tel. 612/
333–5336. Admission free. Observation deck open April–Oct.,
daily 8 AM–10 PM.*

The **University of Minnesota** was established in 1851. It has an
enrollment of more than 50,000, and is the fourth largest cam-

American Swedish Institute, **8**

Como-Harriet Street Car Line, **10**

Foshay Tower, **5**

Hubert H. Humphrey Metrodome, **6**

James Ford Bell Museum of Natural History, **2**

Minneapolis Institute of Arts, **7**

Minneapolis Planetarium/Public Library, **4**

Minnehaha Park, **11**

The Minnesota Zoo, **12**

University Art Museum, **3**

Upper St. Anthony Lock, **1**

Walker Art Center/ Guthrie Theater, **9**

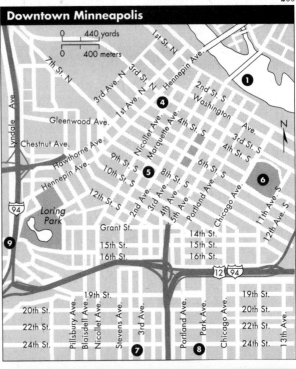

Downtown Minneapolis

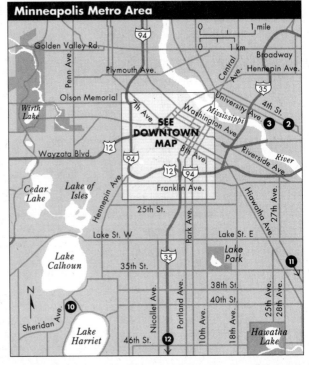

Minneapolis Metro Area

pus in the country, sitting astride the Mississippi on the edge of downtown Minneapolis. The east and west banks of the campus are joined by an unusual bridge on Washington Avenue that features an enclosed pedestrian walkway above the bridge floor where auto traffic crosses. **Dinkytown,** on the east bank in the area of 14th Avenue SE and 4th Street SE, is an area of campus bars, night spots, university shops, and record and book stores. **Seven Corners,** on the west bank, features the West Bank Theater District with popular after-hours hangouts, theaters, and night spots. Guided tours of the campus can be arranged on weekdays by calling the University Tour Office (tel. 612/624-6868).

2 Among campus highlights is the **James Ford Bell Museum of Natural History,** the oldest museum in Minnesota, famed for its dioramas of Minnesota wildlife. There is a "Touch and See" room where youngsters can handle the skins, bones, and skulls of a variety of animals, including mammoths and dinosaurs. An art gallery features paintings, sketches, and watercolors by wildlife artist Francis Lee Jacques. *University Ave. and 17th Ave. SE, tel. 612/624-7083. Admission: $2 adults, $1 children 3-16 and senior citizens, free on Thurs. Open Tues.-Sat. 9-5, Sun. 1-5.*

3 The **University Art Museum** has a varied collection that features changing exhibits, including student and faculty work, and a permanent collection of American art from 1900 to 1950. *84 Church St. SE, on the 3rd and 4th floors of Northrop Memorial Auditorium, tel. 612/624-9876. Admission free. Open Mon., Wed., and Fri. 11-5, Thurs. 11-8, Sun. 2-5, closed Sat. and university holidays.*

4 The **Minneapolis Planetarium,** in the public library, offers sky shows in which more than 2,000 stars, the visible planets, and other celestial phenomena are projected onto the 40-foot dome of the planetarium. Presentations range from tours of the night sky to investigations of the latest discoveries in space science and technology. Each program includes a 15-minute review of what to look for in the Minneapolis sky that evening. *300 Nicollet Mall, tel. 612/372-6644. Admission: $3 adults, $1.50 children 2-12. Programs mid-June-Labor Day, Mon.-Sat. at 11 and 1:30, Thurs. at 11, 1:30, and 7:30 and Sun. at 1:30; Sept.-mid-June, Thurs. at 7:30, Sat. at 11, 1:30, and 3, and Sun. at 1:30 and 3.*

5 The **Foshay Tower,** Minneapolis's first skyscraper, was built in 1929. For decades the 447-foot-high tower was the highest building in Minneapolis and the upper Midwest. While it has since been dwarfed by its gleaming glass neighbors, the tower received national attention in 1981 when a huge yellow ribbon was draped around its upper portion as a welcome-home greeting to Americans who were hostages in Iran. The building's observation deck on the 31st floor provides spectacular views of downtown Minneapolis. *821 Marquette Ave., tel. 612/341-2522. Admission to observation deck: $1.50. Open Thurs. noon-10, Fri. noon-6, Sat. 9-4.*

Much of downtown Minneapolis is a new city, constructed in the past 25 years, with more new buildings rising each year. The new 11-story Federal Reserve Bank Building (250 Marquette Ave.) is one of the first American buildings designed on a cantilevered suspension system like a bridge and is said to be strong enough to support another building of the same size as well. The mirrored 51-story **Investors Diversified Building** on Nicollet Mall is a landmark that reflects much of the downtown skyline. It contains **Crystal Court,** a focal point of the skyway system, with shops, restaurants, and offices. The aqua-blue glass 42-story **Piper Jaffray Tower** (222 S. 9th St.) and the copper-colored glass of the 17-story **Lutheran Brotherhood Building** (4th Ave. between 6th and 7th Sts.) are sparkling additions to the downtown skyline.

Time Out **Jose's American Grill** (100 N. 6th St., tel. 612/333–5665), a Southwestern-themed pub, features chili, Mexican entrees, and a wide selection of burgers and beers. A good spot for something tall and cool while you're taking a break from shopping or sightseeing. *AE, MC, V. Inexpensive–Moderate.*

6 Tours of the inflated **Hubert H. Humphrey Metrodome,** where the Minnesota Twins baseball team and the Minnesota Vikings and University of Minnesota Golden Gophers football teams play, are available. Tours visit the locker rooms, playing field, press box, and other behind-the-scenes areas. The locals seem to have their reservations about the toadstool-shaped stadium, but tourists and visiting teams love it. *501 S. Chicago Ave., tel. 612/332–0386. Admission: $2.50 adults, $1.50 children, students, and senior citizens. Call for tour times and to make reservations.*

7 The **Minneapolis Institute of Arts** has more than 70,000 works on display from every age and culture. There are exhibits of sculpture, photography, painting, drawings, and prints. The collection includes a 2,000-year-old mummy, Rembrandt works, rare Chinese jade, French impressionist paintings, and exotic African masks. "Must see" exhibits include Rembrandt's *Lucretia* (1666), Poussin's *Death of Germanicus,* and Tintoretto's *Raising of Lazarus.* The institute houses a major collection of 16th- and 17th-century Asian art. A new exhibit is the *Doryphos,* a Roman copy of an 8th-century BC Greek statue, valued at $2.5 million. The museum has free tours daily, as well as frequent concerts, films, lectures, and art classes. *2400 Third Ave. S (1 mi south of downtown), tel. 612/870–3046. Admission: $2 adults, $1 children 12–18 and students, free Thurs. 5–9 PM. Open Tues.–Sat. 10–5, Thurs. 5–9, Sun. 12–5; closed Mon., July 4, Thanksgiving Day, and Dec. 25. Studio Restaurant offers lunch and snacks Tues.–Sun. 11:30–3.*

8 The **American Swedish Institute** is a museum, meeting place, school, library, and information center for those interested in Swedish heritage. Built at the turn of the century by Swan J. Turnblad, publisher of *Svenska Amerikanska Posten,* one of the largest Swedish language newspapers in the United States, the 33-room mansion is of Romanesque château design, with soaring towers and turrets. Eighteen woodcarvers were employed on the site for two years during the building's construction, and many of the rooms are filled with carved paneling or other decorative woodwork. The first-floor Grand Hall is paneled in African mahogany and has a two-story wooden fireplace mantel with a large built-in clock. Two carved female figures flanking the clock (one with eyes open, one with eyes closed) represent day and night. The mansion contains 11 unique porcelain tile fireplaces known as *kajkelugnar.* The institute's exhibits include an art collection, pioneer items,

Swedish glass, ceramics, textiles, and furniture. A new exhibit in an upstairs alcove is a glass beaker that predates the Viking era. Film programs are presented Sunday at 2. *2600 Park Ave., tel. 612/871–4907. Admission: $3 adults, $1 students under 21 and senior citizens. Open Tues.–Sat. noon–4, Sun. 1–5; closed Mon.*

❾ The **Walker Art Center** was founded in 1879 by Thomas Barlow Walker and was established at its current location in 1927. It has been described by *The New York Times* as "one of the best contemporary art exhibition facilities in the world." The permanent collections are strong on 20th-century American and European art, especially paintings, sculpture, prints, and photography from the last two decades. The center offers regular programs of dance, music, theater, and films. In the autumn of 1988 the Walker opened the **Minneapolis Sculpture Garden,** the largest urban sculpture garden in the nation. Outstanding pieces include Frank Gehry's *Standing Glass Fish* and a fountain, *Spoonbridge and Cherry*, by Claes Oldenburg and Coosje van Bruggen. The garden is linked to Loring Park and downtown Minneapolis by a footbridge. *Southwest edge of the loop at Hennepin Ave. and Vineland Pl. adjoining the Guthrie Theater, tel. 612/375–7600. Admission free, except for special events. Open Tues.–Sat. 10–8, Sun. 11–5; closed Mon. and holidays.*

❿ One of Minneapolis's best transportation buys is the Minnesota Transportation Museum's **Como–Harriet Street Car Line,** a restored trolley that runs between Lake Harriet and Lake Calhoun. *42nd St. and Queen Ave. S, tel. 612/349–7690. One–way fare: 50¢ adults, 25¢ children. Operates daily Memorial Day–Labor Day, weekends in May, Sept., and Oct.*

⓫ **Minnehaha Park,** on the Mississippi near Minneapolis/St. Paul International Airport, contains the charming Minnehaha Falls. Above the waterfall, made famous by Longfellow's *The Song of Hiawatha*, is a statue of Hiawatha and Minnehaha. The **Minnehaha Parkway,** which follows Minnehaha Creek, provides 15 miles of jogging, biking, and roller-skating trails running westward to Lake Harriet. It is one of Minneapolis's most popular parks.

⓬ The **Minnesota Zoo** in suburban Apple Valley has been built to resemble the natural habitat of the wild animals that reside there. The zoo contains some 1,700 animals and more than 2,000 plant varieties. Exhibits are arranged in six separate year-round trail systems. The Tropics Trail, one of the most exotic areas of the zoo, features exhibits of gibbons, bears, bats, leopards, and reptiles, along with a magnificent selection of tropical plant life and Asian birds. The Minnesota Trail features animals native to Minnesota, including otters, lynx, owls, weasels, and a world-famous beaver exhibit. The Sky Trail (additional fee) allows you to ride a monorail train and observe treetop views of musk ox, trumpeter swans, and American bison. Other features are a Zoo Lab, children's seasonal zoo, bird and animal shows, camel rides in summer, and daily films and slide shows. There are eating facilities, picnic areas, rest areas, and stroller rentals. *12101 Johnny Cake Ridge Rd., Apple Valley, tel. 612/432–9200. From Minneapolis take Cedar Ave. S to Cliff Rd. and follow zoo signs. Admission: $4 adults, $1.50 children 6–16, $2 seniors over 62; Sky Trail monorail: $2 over 6; parking $1; open Apr.–Sept., daily 10–6; Oct.–Mar., daily 10–4.*

Minneapolis and St. Paul for Free

St. Paul The **Stroh Brewery Co.** has free tours followed by hospitality in the Stroh Haus. *707 Minnehaha Ave., tel. 612/778–3275; weekdays 1–4.*

The **Jacob Schmidt Brewing Co.** offers free guided tours followed by hospitality in the Rathskeller. *822 W. 7th St., tel. 612/228–9173; weekdays at 10, 2, and 3.*

The **Governor's Residence,** formerly the Horace Irvine home, is located among the Victorian splendor of Summit Avenue. The Minnesota Garden Memorial on the grounds of the mansion has a sculpture by Paul Granlund commemorating the service of Minnesotans in Vietnam. *1006 Summit Ave., tel. 612/224–9735. Admission free. Tours on the third Thurs. of each month 10–2.*

KSTP-TV offers free tickets to anyone over 18 for their two locally produced talk shows, *Good Company* and *Twin Cities Live. 3415 University Ave. W, tel. 612/641–1298. Call for details.*

The **Minnesota Air Guard Museum** displays photos, artifacts, memorabilia, and airplanes that tell the story of the Minnesota Air National Guard. It was the first air militia unit federally recognized (Jan. 21, 1917) in the United States National Guard. *Minnesota Air National Guard base, northeast corner of Minneapolis/St. Paul International Airport. Enter the base by driving south from the intersection of 62 Crosstown and Hiawatha Aves., tel. 612/725–5609. Admission free. Open mid-April–mid-Oct., Sat. 10–4, Sun. noon–4.*

The **Minnesota Historical Society** tells the story of Minnesota's history through artifacts, photos, and exhibits. A library reading room offers visitors an extensive research collection including audiovisual, map, newspaper, and reference areas. The museum gift shop features local history books and regional crafts. *690 Cedar St., tel. 612/296–6126. Admission free. Open Mon.–Sat. 8:30–5, Sun. 1–4; closed holidays.*

Minneapolis **Lake Harriet** is one of the Minneapolis chain of lakes; its park offers opportunities for outdoor recreation. The **Lake Harriet Rose Garden's** annual display features colorful, fragrant blooms. The **Lake Harriet Rock Garden** has been popular since it was established in 1929; it was redone in 1985. Community concerts and performances are held in the **Lake Harriet Bandshell** throughout the summer. *E. Lake Harriet Pkwy., tel. 612/348–2243. Admission free. Open all summer.*

The **Federal Reserve Bank of Minnesota** is one of only 12 Federal Reserve banks in the county. You can see money being counted and sorted, and unfit currency being shredded. *250 Marquette Ave., tel. 612/340–2446.*

At the **Minneapolis Grain Exchange,** one-hour tours include a film about how the exchange functions and observation of activity in the Futures Pit and on the Trading Floor. *400 S. 4th St., tel. 612/338–6212. Admission free. Tours Mon.–Fri. at 8:45 AM and 10 AM.*

The **University of Minnesota School of Music** presents a variety of free concerts during the school year at **Northrop Auditorium.** *84 Church St. SE, tel. 612/626–2200.*

The **Eloise Butler Wildflower Garden and Bird Sanctuary** offers 20 acres of natural wildflower habitat, along with hiking and bicycle trails. There are naturalist-led tours of the grounds on summer evenings and weekends. *Theodore Wirth Park, Wirth Pkwy., tel. 612/348–5702. Open daily 7:30 AM–sunset.*

The **International Design Center** offers changing exhibits on worldwide design trends. *100 2nd Ave. N, tel. 612/341–3441. Open Mon.–Sat. 9:30–6, Thurs. 9:30–9, Sun. noon–5.*

What to See and Do with Children

Unless otherwise indicated, the sites and activities listed below are covered in the preceding Exploring sections.

St. Paul
Mississippi River excursions
Rice Park
Landmark Center
Science Museum of Minnesota
Minnesota State Capitol
Como Park Zoo
Como Park Conservatory
Children's Museum
Historic Fort Snelling
Twin Cities Model Railroad Club. *See* Off the Beaten Track.
Town Square Park. *See* Off the Beaten Track.

Minneapolis
Minnesota Twins Baseball. *See* Spectator Sports.
Upper St. Anthony Lock
James Bell Ford Museum
Minneapolis Planetarium
Foshay Tower
Hubert H. Humphrey Metrodome
Minneapolis Institute of Arts
Walker Art Center
Como–Harriet Street Car Line
Minnehaha Park
Children's Theater
Minnesota Zoo
Firefighter's Memorial Museum. *See* Off the Beaten Track.
Queen of the Lakes cruises

Off the Beaten Track

St. Paul
Charles A. Lindbergh, the first pilot to make a nonstop solo flight across the Atlantic in 1927, was a native of Little Falls, Minnesota. The two bronze **Lindbergh statues** by the sculptor Paul Granlund depict Lindbergh as a young man observing passers by and as a small boy looking toward downtown St. Paul and the Mississippi. *On the slope between the capitol and the Cathedral of St. Paul.*

The **Schubert Club's Piano Museum,** in the lower level of the Landmark Center, features a collection of keyboard instruments of historical significance, including a piano signed by Franz Liszt. Museum curators often play and demonstrate the instruments, and there is a gallery with changing exhibits relating to music. *Room 301 of the Landmark Center, 75 W. 5th St., tel. 612/292–3267. Admission free. Open weekdays 11–3.*

Town Square Park, on the upper levels of the St. Paul Center shopping center, is the world's largest indoor city park. There are lots of shrubs and trees, man-made waterfalls, interesting nooks and crannies, places to sit and rest, and a small playground. The entire park is under a skylight. *445 Minnesota St., tel. 612/227–3307. Free musical concerts daily at noon. Open weekdays 9–9, Sat. 9–6, Sun. noon–5.*

The **Twin Cities Model Railroad Club** has a large, scale-model layout of railroading in the United States during the 1930s and 1950s. Models include many famous trains, and a variety of scale-model towns and cities, train yards, and rural areas. Some layouts are under continuous construction. It's a fascinating place for big and little children. *Second level, Bandana Square shopping mall at 1021 Bandana Ave. E, tel. 612/647–9628. Admission: 50¢. Open Mon.–Sat. 1–9, Sun. 1–5.*

Minneapolis The **Playwright's Center** offers regular Monday-night readings of new plays by regional playwrights. *2301 Franklin Ave. E, tel. 612/332–7481. Readings 7 PM.*

The **Firefighter's Memorial Museum** is your chance to ride a fire engine, ring its bells, and blow its sirens. The museum has a collection of more than 40 pieces of firefighting equipment, including various engines, water pumps, and hose carts. Exhibits include a 1796 Merrick and Agnew hand-drawn pumper, a collection of hand and horse-drawn equipment from the late 1880s, a 1935 Seagrave pumper, and a 1951 Pirsch 85-foot hook-and-ladder truck. *1100 Van Buren St. NE (off Central Ave. and Broadway St.), tel. 612/623–3817. Admission: $2 adults, $1 children. Rides: $2 adults, $1 children. Open Sat. 10–3.*

Walk-in tours of the **Guthrie Theater** on Saturday mornings at 11 include backstage areas, dressing rooms, prop rooms, and other areas. No reservations; meet your tour guide at the ticket office in the lobby. *725 Vineland Pl., tel. 612/347–1111 or 347–1112. Cost: $1.*

Shopping

Stores in the Twin Cities range from tiny specialty shops to enclosed shopping malls featuring large department stores. The skyway systems in each city connect hundreds of stores, shops, theaters, and restaurants. Large shopping malls are located downtown and in the outlying suburbs. The sales tax is 6%; there is no sales tax on clothing.

Shopping Districts The main downtown shopping district is bounded by Robert, **St. Paul** 5th, St. Peter, and 7th streets.

Bandana Square is located in the former Great Northern Railroad repair shops, where passenger coaches and locomotives were maintained during the turn of the century. Exposed beams, skylights, and railroad tracks from the old building have been left in place. There are more than 50 specialty shops and restaurants, as well as the Children's Museum and Sunwood Inn. *North of I–94 between Snelling Ave. and Lexington Pkwy., tel. 612/642–1509.*

Galtier Plaza in Lowertown offers three levels of shops, theaters, restaurants, and underground parking. *Sibley St. between 5th and 6th Sts., tel. 612/292–0600. Stores open weekdays 10–5.*

Saint Paul Center is decorated with an early 1900 flair, while the stores and shops are contemporary and upbeat. In the heart of downtown St. Paul, it features Dayton's, Carson Pirie Scott (formerly Donaldson's), and more than 100 specialty shops and restaurants, along with the 1/2-acre Town Square Park. *In the Minnesota World Trade Center, between Minnesota, Wabasha, 6th, and 8th Sts., tel. 612/291–1715. Stores open weekdays 10–9, Sat. 9:30–6, Sun. noon–5.*

Victoria Crossing is a collection of small shops, specialty bookstores, and restaurants housed in three brick buildings with the respective names Victoria Crossing East, West, and South (857 Grand Ave.). They provide an anchor for dozens of shops that span Grand Avenue from Dale Street to Prior Avenue, about one mile south of I–94.

Minneapolis **Nicollet Mall** is a mile-long pedestrian mall in the center of downtown Minneapolis. Regular auto traffic is prohibited, but buses and taxis traverse the mall from 1st through 13th streets. An extensive system of skywalks connects many of the buildings via enclosed, second-story pedestrian bridges.

Calhoun Square houses two levels of shopping and entertainment in an old school building and features more than 80 specialty shops, restaurants, and services. *At the corner of Lake St. and Hennepin Ave., tel. 612/824–1240. Stores open Mon.–Sat. 10–9, Sun. noon–6.*

City Center encloses more than 60 shops and stores on three levels. *33 S. 7th St., tel. 612/372–1234. Open weekdays 9:30–9, Sat. 9:30–6, Sun. noon–5.*

The **Conservatory on Nicollet** is downtown's newest shopping complex with more than 40 upscale stores and two restaurants. *808 Nicollet Mall, tel. 612/332–4649. Open weekdays 9:30–7:30, Sat. 9:30–5:30, Sun. noon–5.*

The **Crystal Court** encompasses two levels of sophisticated shops and specialty stores in the IDS Tower. *7th St. and Nicollet Mall, tel. 612/372–1660. Stores open Mon.–Sat. 9:30–6; closed Sun.*

Riverplace is designed in the atmosphere of a European village. The center contains more than 90 luxury and specialty shops and restaurants on the historic east bank of the river. *25 Main St. SE, tel. 612/378–1969. Open Mon.–Thurs. 10–9, Fri. and Sat. 10 AM–11 PM, Sun. noon–6.*

St. Anthony Main, made up of refurbished limestone buildings on the east bank of the Mississippi, houses a wide selection of shops, stores, and restaurants. *201 Main St. SE, tel. 612/379–4540. Stores open Mon.–Sat. 10–9, Sun. noon–6.*

The **Warehouse District,** west of Hennepin Avenue between 6th Street and the river, has a collection of art galleries, antique shops, and restaurants in restored turn-of-the-century buildings.

Department Stores Dayton's and Carson Pirie Scott (formerly Donaldson's) are the two largest department stores, anchoring malls in both St. Paul and Minneapolis. They are the Twin Cities' equivalents of Macy's and Gimbels.

Specialty Stores **Stanley and Livingston's** (514 Nicollet Mall, Skyway Level,
Adventurewear Minneapolis, tel. 612/333–1040) has a wide selection of outdoor wear for men and women.

Antiques   **Aardvark Treasures Antiques** (1332 Randolph Ave., St. Paul, tel. 612/698–6995) offers a wide selection of antiques and collectibles.
Touch of the Past (12 W. 26th St., Minneapolis, tel. 612/872–7775) specializes in pottery from the 1930s and 1940s.

Art Dealers   **Asian Fine Arts** (825 2nd Ave. S, Minneapolis, tel. 612/333–4704) offers a selection of antique and contemporary Asian art.
The Raven Gallery (3827 W. 50th St., Minneapolis, tel. 612/925–4474) has a selection of work by contemporary Inuit and American Indian artists.

Books   **Odegard Books** (Calhoun Sq., Minneapolis, tel. 612/825–0336) is one of the city's best bookstores.

Crafts   **Park Square Court** (400 Sibley St., St. Paul, tel. 612/225–3322) houses a variety of craftspeople, including artists you can watch creating candles, pottery, jewelry, and leather items.

Food   **Byerly** (1959 Suburban Ave., St. Paul, tel. 612/735–6340) has food and much more, including chandeliers, china, crystal, women's apparel, and gold-plated bird cages. There are eight Byerly stores in the Twin Cities, each an attraction in itself.

Games   **Grand Games** (Bandana Sq., 1021 Bandana Blvd. E, St. Paul, tel. 612/641–0957) has board and other games for all ages.

Jewelry   **Charlemagne Jewelers** (1276 Grand Ave., St. Paul, tel. 612/699–1431) offers original and custom designs.
Ingrid Lenz (the Conservatory, 800 Nicollet Mall, Minneapolis, tel. 612/338–0939 or 333–4421) presents a large selection of designer jewelry imported from Europe.

Linens   The **Linen Center** (1869 Roberts St., St. Paul, tel. 612/451–3665) offers a large selection of table linens for casual and formal dining.

Men's Apparel   **Dayton's** (St. Paul Center, E. 7th and Cedar Sts., St. Paul, tel. 612/292–5222) stocks traditional menswear and accessories.
Charlie's (811 LaSalle Ct., Minneapolis, tel. 612/343–0421) offers menswear in traditional and contemporary styling.

Women's Apparel   **Albrechts** (680 S. Cleveland Ave., St. Paul, tel. 612/690–1567) offers stylish clothes for women.
Saffran (Victoria Crossing East, 857 Grand Ave., St. Paul, tel. 612/292–0030) has traditional and contemporary clothes for women.
Connie's (3133 Hennepin Ave. S, Minneapolis, tel. 612/822–2019) has designer shoes at discount prices.
Carson Pirie Scott (formerly Donaldson's, City Center, 33 S. 7th St., Minneapolis, tel. 612/347–7613) offers classic and contemporary clothes for women.

Toys   **F.A.O. Schwarz** (the Conservatory, 800 Nicollet Mall, Minneapolis, tel. 612/339–2233) is a wonderland of toys for all ages.

Sports and Fitness

Beaches **St. Paul**   **Como Park** (N. Lexington Pkwy. at Como Ave., tel. 612/292–7400) has both swimming beaches and a pool. The pools at **Highland Park** (Montreal and Hamline Aves., tel. 612/292–7400) include a 50-meter outdoor pool, wading pool, and diving well. **Phalen Park Lake** provides swimming beaches, changing house, snack bar, and canoe, sailboard, and boat rentals.

Minneapolis With 22 lakes, the city has scores of beaches. Try the beach at **Cedar Lake. Thomas Beach,** at the south end of Lake Calhoun, is very popular with folks in Minneapolis. For more information, call the Minneapolis Parks and Recreation Board (tel. 612/348–2243 or 348–2226).

Bicycling There are 37 miles of biking, hiking, and jogging trails within
St. Paul St. Paul, including Summit Avenue, Mississippi River Boulevard, Como Park, and Phalen Lake. Free brochures providing trail information and a map of the system are available from St. Paul Parks and Recreation (300 City Hall Annex, 25 W. 4th St., 55102, tel. 612/292–7400).

Minneapolis Minneapolis offers 36 miles of bituminous bike paths. One of the most popular is the Minnehaha Parkway, which runs from Minnehaha Park to Lake Harriet. The Lake Calhoun Parkway and Lake of the Isles Parkway are favorites, too. There are separate marked paths for joggers and bicyclists, so be certain you're on the correct one. Joggers share space with roller skaters. For more information, call the Minneapolis Parks and Recreation Board (tel. 612/348–2243 or 348–2226).

Fishing Depending on water levels, fishing is sometimes good just below the locks and dams on the Mississippi River. In St. Paul, Lake Phalen (Phalen Park, Wheelock Pkwy. at Arcade St., tel. 612/292–7400) is a favorite spot. You can fish on most Minneapolis lakes. Hyland Lake Park Reserve in suburban Bloomington (10145 E. Bush Lake Rd., tel. 612/941–4362 or 941–7993) is popular.

Golf One of the region's most challenging golf courses is **Edinburgh U.S.A.** in suburban Brooklyn Park, designed by Robert Trent Jones II in the Scottish tradition.

St. Paul There are four municipal golf courses: **Phalen Park** (1615 Phalen Dr., tel. 612/788–0413), 18 holes; **Highland Park** (1403 Montreal Ave., tel. 612/699–3650), 18 holes; **Highland Park** (1797 Edgecombe Rd., tel. 612/699–6082), 9 holes; and **Como Park** (1431 N. Lexington Pkwy., tel. 612/488–9673).

Minneapolis There are three municipal golf courses: **Francis A. Gross Golf Course** (2201 St. Anthony Blvd., tel. 612/789–2542), 18 holes; **Meadowbrook Golf Course** (300 Meadowbrook Rd., Hopkins, tel. 612/929–2077), 18 holes; and **Hiawatha Golf Course** (4553 Longfellow Ave. S, tel. 612/724–7715), 18 holes.

Jogging There are 37 miles of hiking and jogging trails in the city. Sum-
St. Paul mit Avenue is a quiet place to jog or run and begins close to downtown. For a free brochure providing trail information and a map of the system, contact St. Paul Parks and Recreation (300 City Hall Annex, 25 W. 4th St., 55102, tel. 612/292–7400).

Minneapolis There are 36 miles of bituminous jogging paths in the city. One of the most popular is the Minnehaha Parkway, which runs from Minnehaha Park to Lake Harriet. Loring Park, downtown, is also a favorite with joggers. For more information, call the Minneapolis Parks and Recreation Board (tel. 612/348–2243 or 348–2226).

Skiing Several ski hills and areas are within a short drive of the Twin Cities.

Downhill **Afton Alps Ski Area** offers 36 runs, with 18 chair lifts, two rope tows, and snowmaking; longest run 3,000 feet, vertical drop

350 feet. Services include rental and instruction. *6600 Peller Ave., Rte. 4, Hastings, tel. 612/436–5245 or 800/328–1328. Open daily 9 AM–10 PM.*

Buck Hill Ski Area has 10 runs with four chair lifts, one J-bar, three rope tows, and snowmaking; longest run 2,500 feet, vertical drop 306 feet. Rental and instruction are offered. *15400 Buck Hill Rd., Burnsville, tel. 612/435–7187 or 435–7174. Open weekdays 10–10, weekends 9 AM–10 PM.*

Hyland Hills Ski Area has 14 runs with three chair lifts, three rope tows, and snowmaking; longest run 1,600 feet, vertical drop 175 feet. Services include rental, instruction, a chalet with cafe and lounge, and ski corral. *8737 E. Bush Lake Rd., Bloomington, tel. 612/835–4604 or 841–7993. Open daily 10–10.*

Theodore Wirth Regional Park offers three runs, three rope tows, and snowmaking; longest run 350 feet, vertical drop 150 feet. Services include cross-country skiing, rental, instruction, and chalet. *Glenwood Pkwy., Minneapolis, tel. 612/522–4522. Open Mon.–Thurs. 6–10 PM, weekends 10 AM–6 PM.*

Cross-country Cross-country skiing can be done on golf courses, and in parks and arboretums. **Como Park, Wirth Park, Phalen Park,** and **Crosby Farm Park** are St. Paul favorites. For additional information contact St. Paul Parks and Recreation (300 City Hall Annex, 25 W. 4th St., 55102, tel. 612/292–7400).

In Minneapolis, you can cross-country ski at **Minnehaha Park** (tel. 612/348–2243), **Columbia Park and Golf Course** (3300 Central Ave. NE, tel. 612/789–2627), and **Gross Golf Course** (St. Anthony Blvd. and 22nd Ave. NE, tel. 612/789–2542).

Fort Snelling State Park has nearly 19 miles of mostly beginner-level trails (Rte. 5 and Post Rd., Eagan, tel. 612/727–1961).

For a free copy of the 50-page booklet *Explore Minnesota on Skis, a Guide to Cross Country Ski Trails,* contact Minnesota Office of Tourism (375 Jackson St., 250 Skyway Level, St. Paul, 55101, tel. 612/296–5029 or 800/328–1461).

A state ski trail pass is required to ski in Minnesota state parks. *Cost: $1 daily, $5 annual, $7.50 husband and wife annual, free under 16 and over 65.*

Tennis The most popular of the more than 100 public courts around St. Paul are those at **Como** and **Phalen Lake parks.** For information on municipal courts contact St. Paul Parks and Recreation (tel. 612/292–7400).

In Minneapolis, **Kenwood Park** (north end of Lake of the Isles) and **Loring Park** (Hennepin Ave. and Harmon Pl.) are favorites. For information on municipal courts, call the Park Board (tel. 612/348–2226).

Eagandale Racquet and Swim Club (3330 Pilot Knob Rd., Eagan, tel. 612/454–8790) has indoor and outdoor courts available for use by nonmembers.

The **Nicollet Tennis Center** in Martin Luther King Park (4500 Nicollet Ave., tel. 612/825–6844) has indoor and outdoor courts available for use by the public.

Spectator Sports

Baseball The 1987 World Champion **Minnesota Twins** play their games at the Hubert H. Humphrey Metrodome (501 Chicago Ave., Minneapolis, tel. 612/375–1116). The University of Minnesota baseball team plays home games at Siebert Field (1606 8th St. SE, tel. 612/624–8080).

Basketball The **Minnesota Timberwolves** (5525 Cedar Lake Rd., St. Louis Pk., tel. 612/544–3865), one of the National Basketball Association's newest teams, are scheduled to begin playing in the fall of 1989. The University of Minnesota team plays at Williams Arena (1901 University Ave. SE, tel. 612/624–8080).

Football The **Minnesota Vikings** of the National Football League play their home games in the Hubert H. Humphrey Metrodome in Minneapolis (501 Chicago Ave., Minneapolis, tel. 612/333–8828), as do the **University of Minnesota Golden Gophers** (tel. 612/624–8080).

Hockey The **Minnesota North Stars** play in the Metropolitan Sports Center (better known as the Met Center) (7901 Cedar Ave., Bloomington, tel. 612/853–9310).

Horse Racing Pari-mutuel quarter horse and thoroughbred racing is held at **Canterbury Downs**, with the Saint Paul Derby at the end of June. The track is about 15 miles south of the Twin Cities. *1100 Canterbury Rd., Shakopee, tel. 612/445–7223. Open Wed.–Sun. May–mid-Oct.*

Volleyball The **Minnesota Monarchs**, a professional women's team, play a February–May season at Augsburg College Gymnasium (7101 York Ave. S, Minneapolis, tel. 612/921–3335).

Dining

by Karen Winegar

Karen Winegar is travel editor of Twin Cities *magazine and a feature writer for the* Minneapolis Star Tribune.

Dining out in the Twin Cities is both more and less diverse than outsiders might imagine. The new immigrant population has introduced gastronomic traditions ranging from Mongolian barbecue and Cambodian seafood to Vietnamese spring rolls and Tuscan pasta, from French croissants to Indian tandoor. But the majority of Minnesotans of Scandinavian and German descent still demands things "toned down a bit" and are somewhat wary of any seasonings more exotic than salt and pepper.

Surprisingly, Scandinavian food is not a specialty of area restaurants; German restaurant fare is also somewhat unusual. What the region has in abundance, however, is a growing number of northern Italian and southeast Asian eateries, and seafood and chop houses.

No matter what the cuisine, Minnesotans rarely dress up when they eat out. At all but the most stellar restaurants the unofficial dress code is urban casual-but-tidy attire.

The restaurant price categories are based on the average cost of a three-course dinner (à la carte) for one person, food alone, not including beverages, tax, and tip.

The most highly recommended restaurants are indicated by a star ★ .

Category	Cost*
Very Expensive	over $20
Expensive	$12–$20
Moderate	$8–$12
Inexpensive	under $8

per person; add 5% tax

The following credit card abbreviations are used: AE, American Express; CB, Carte Blanche; DC, Diners Club; MC, MasterCard; V, Visa.

Afghani **Khyber Pass Cafe.** In a corner storefront in a sleepy St. Paul neighborhood, the Khyber Pass has barely a dozen tables. The Afghani immigrant family that runs it serves a small menu of its sometimes-spicy native cuisine, including warm, buttery flatbreads. Among the appetizers are rich beef dumplings flavored with yogurt and mint, and eggplant with tomato sauce and yogurt. Entrees include chicken broiled on a skewer, and served with coriander chutney; spinach with leeks, onions, spices, and lamb; lentil and lamb simmered with garlic and onions; lamb kebabs; chicken stew; and lamb with basmati rice. Like the entrees, desserts are hearty, and close to Afghani native style: milk pudding laced with cardamom, rosewater, and crushed pistachios, and a baklava-like pastry with walnuts and syrup. Beverages are limited to beer, wine, and dogh, a yogurt drink with diced cucumber and mint. *1399 St. Clair Ave., St. Paul, tel. 612/698–5403. MC, V. Closed Sun. Moderate.*

American **The Fifth Season.** Hotel restaurants often mean indifferent food served to captive diners, but that's not so at the Fifth Season. The menu has a regional American slant, and includes Maine lobster, sautéed Oregon venison, prime New York sirloin, grilled salmon and swordfish, rack of lamb, veal medallions, and a Wellington of the day. Desserts run to the rich and ornate: Key lime pie, carrot cake, hazelnut cake, a variety of fruit flans, cassis cake, chocolate mousse cake, Bavarian cream cake, and cheesecake. *Marriott Hotel, City Center, Minneapolis, tel. 612/349–4077. Jacket and tie suggested. Reservations recommended. AE, CB, DC, MC, V. Very Expensive.*

★ **Goodfellow's.** The emphasis here is on regional American cuisine and painterly presentation. The menu ranges from carpaccio of Texas black buck antelope with papaya-avocado relish to grilled rare squab with ginger yam waffle and scallion pear sauce; ragout of lobster and sweetbreads in Creole sauce with smoked pheasant sausage; herb-breaded razor clams with roasted pepper relish and horseradish sauce; golden gazpacho with grilled shrimp and daikon noodles; and bay-seasoned soft-shell crab with yellow tomato sauce and red chili glazed asparagus. Desserts are equally imaginative, and include fresh blackberry buckle with vanilla ice cream, and a lace cookie cup with raspberries, cream, and caramel. The service is pleasantly professional, and there's an extensive and innovative all-American wine list. *Fourth floor of the Conservatory, 800 Nicollet Mall, Minneapolis, tel. 612/332–4800. Jacket sug-*

gested. Reservations recommended. AE, MC, V. Closed Sun. Very Expensive.

★ **Primavera.** This might be the longest and most expensive lunch in Minnesota, but the presentation is lovely, and the cuisine superb. The menu is new American: rock lobster with mixed coastal greens and tomato orange butter; chicken breast with ginger rice and balsamic vinegar; feuilleté of grilled swordfish in a confetti of fresh vegetables with a sweet red pepper cream sauce; grilled lobster salad with avocado, papaya, lime, and mint vinaigrette; and espresso crème brulée with candied orange. *International Market Square, Glenwood and Lyndale Aves. N, Minneapolis, tel. 612/339–8000. Reservations recommended. AE, MC, V. No dinner. Closed weekends. Expensive.*

★ **Whitney Grille.** The Grille is one of the few restaurants in the Twin Cities on the Mississippi River. Its flower-filled garden plaza overlooks St. Anthony Falls, and the hushed main dining room is decorated in rich woods, with ivory, sage, and green floral upholstery. Specialties include veal T-bone steak in Oregon crepes and cognac demiglaze; filet of salmon in citrus champagne sauce with bay shrimp; and shrimp and scallop in lemon tarragon sauce. The dessert list includes bête noire with berry-enhanced rum crème Anglaise and special cheesecake of the evening: either chocolate Grand Marnier, or poppyseed, raisin, and honey. *150 Portland Ave., Minneapolis, tel. 612/339–9300. Jacket required. Reservations recommended. AE, CB, MC, V. Expensive.*

Kincaid's Steak, Chop and Fish House. Kincaid's purports to be "behind the times and proud of it." But its imposing marble, brass, glass, and wood decor combined with its eclectic cuisine makes it very up to date. The kitchen does competent interpretations of Continental and all-American entrees, from mesquite-grilled mahimahi, Cajun chicken, and spicy Cajun shrimp, to steamed clams, four kinds of fresh oysters, tagliatelle Bolognese, and baked chicken Dijon. The house specialty is aged Nebraska beef T-bone steak and prime rib. The choice of imported and domestic beers is noteworthy. *8400 Normandale Lake Blvd., Bloomington, tel. 612/921–2255. Jacket and tie suggested. Reservations recommended. AE, MC, V. Moderate–Expensive.*

★ **Tejas.** Sunlight pours down a great curved rose marble staircase into this chic cafe, where the noise level is high and the entrees include sautéed breast of chicken with pasilla cream sauce and whipped sweet potatoes; duck empanada with black bean puree; green chili sage salsa with grilled scallions; and lamb stew with pineapple, pumpkin seeds, and anchos on tomatillo rice. The Southwestern theme carries equally successfully into dessert: sweet potato flan with caramel sauce; black bottom pecan pie with whiskey butter sauce; and dark chocolate ancho cake with cherimoya sauce. *The Conservatory, 800 Nicollet Mall, Minneapolis, tel. 612/375–0800. Reservations recommended. AE, MC, V. Moderate–Expensive.*

Blue Point Restaurant. Here's a subdued imitation of an East Coast roadhouse of the 1940s. The chef offers six to eight varieties of fresh fish daily, plus stone crab, soft-shell crab, stuffed lobster, shrimp gumbo, crab cakes, and Maine lobsters. For lighter fare, there's spinach and bacon salad, ocean cobb salad, shrimp Louis, and Caesar salad. The desserts sustain the road-

Dining

Caffe Latte, **9**
Khyber Pass Cafe, **8**
Old City Cafe, **7**
Tulips, **10**

Lodging

Embassy Suites-
St. Paul, **1**
Excel Inn of St. Paul, **12**
Holiday Inn St. Paul
Center, **2**
The Lowell Inn
(Stillwater), **11**
Radisson Hotel
St. Paul, **4**
The Saint Paul Hotel, **3**
Sheraton Midway
St. Paul, **5**
Sunwood Inn Bandana
Square, **6**

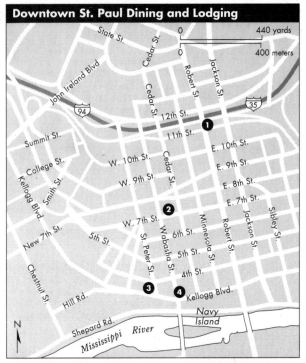

Downtown St. Paul Dining and Lodging

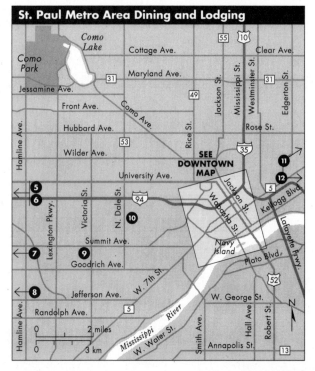

St. Paul Metro Area Dining and Lodging

Dining

Atrium Cafe, **2**
Black Forest Inn, **34**
Blue Point, **24**
Chez Bananas, **9**
Chez Paul, **17**
D'Amico Cucina, **8**
The Fifth Season, **11**
Goodfellow's, **14**
The Great Wall, **26**
Hosteria Fiorentina, **15**
It's Greek to Me, **33**
Kebabi, **18**
Kikugawa, **10**
Kincaid's, **27**
Loring Cafe, **3**
Lucia's, **32**
Pam Sherman's, **31**
Ping's Szechuan, **16**
Primavera, **1**
Tejas, **19**
Whitney Grille, **22**

Lodging

Embassy Suites-
Airport, **40**
Embassy Suites-
Bloomington, **30**
Embassy Suites-
Centre Village, **21**
Holiday Inn, **4**
Hotel Luxeford, **6**
Hotel Sofitel, **28**
Hyatt Regency, **5**
Marriott, **12**
Minneapolis Hilton
Inn, **36**
Minneapolis/St. Paul
Airport Hilton, **39**
Nicollet Island Inn, **35**
Omni Northstar, **20**
Radisson Hotel
Minnetonka, **25**
Radisson Hotel South
and Plaza Tower
(Bloomington), **29**
Radisson Plaza Hotel, **7**
Radisson University
Hotel, **37**
Sheraton Airport Hotel
(Bloomington), **38**
Vista Marquette, **13**
The Whitney, **23**

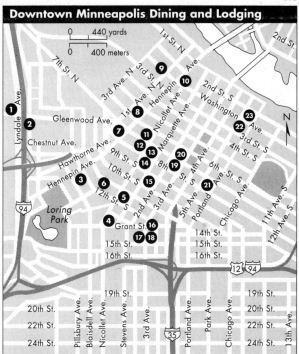

Downtown Minneapolis Dining and Lodging

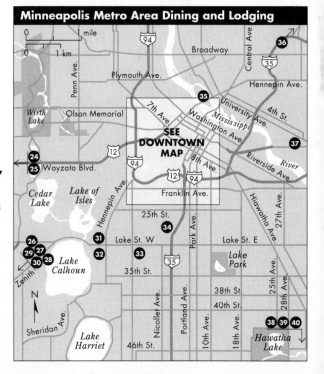

Minneapolis Metro Area Dining and Lodging

house theme with specialties including pecan pie, blueberry ice cream, strawberry shortcake, and chocolate mousse pie. *739 E. Lake St., Wayzata, tel. 612/475–3636. Reservations suggested. AE, DC, MC, V. Moderate.*

Atrium Cafe International. Housed in a former knitting factory, the Atrium Cafe is an inexpensive and informal lunch spot. It has a salad bar and serves fruit and cheese, omelets, pasta, stir-fry dishes, and a rotating selection of soups including clam chowder, split pea and ham, and vegetable beef. Desserts include half a dozen choices each day, including chocolate cheesecake, lemon tart, and apple pie. *International Market Square, Glenwood and Lyndale Aves., Minneapolis, tel. 612/339–8000. AE, MC, V. No dinner. Closed weekends. Inexpensive.*

Caribbean   **Chez Bananas.** Caribbean food served in a warehouse storefront by Yuppies with a sense of humor. There are windup toys
★ on each table, rubber bats dangle from the ceiling, and the waitstaff offer after-dinner Pez. The menu includes savory garlic-laced black beans and rice with chicken or fish, jerk chicken or beef, Creole chicken, red leaf salad with chicken or pork, and moist cornbread with green chilis. There's a selection of fruit juices, wines, and some funky brands of ethnic beer to wash it all down. *129 N. 4th St., Minneapolis, tel. 612/340–0032. MC, V. Closed Sun. Moderate.*

Chinese   **The Great Wall.** Decorated in the usual red, black, and gilt, the Great Wall is a popular suburban Szechuan-Peking restaurant with just three small rooms. Waiters zip through them at high tempo, slapping down hot plates of Mandarin chicken, sizzling duck, Chinese utopia, Mongolian beef, crispy shrimp, sesame noodles, hot and sour soup, and shrimp with spicy garlic sauce. Dessert is limited to Häagen Dazs ice cream pie, or fried toffee bananas or apples. Wine and beer are served. *4515 France Ave. S, Minneapolis, tel. 612/927–4439. Reservations recommended for groups over 4. AE, MC, V. Moderate.*

Ping's Szechuan Bar and Grill. Ping's is a sleek, pink and gray corner cafe in an area of Nicollet Mall that is quickly becoming gentrified. The Cantonese, Szechuan and Hunan food is modified for midwest taste, but still appealing and diverse. Best bets include fried or steamed pot stickers, Peking duck, Ping's special Vietnamese-style egg rolls, Hunan beef, chicken wings, and moo shoo pork. *1401 Nicollet Ave. S, Minneapolis, tel. 612/874–9404. AE, MC, V. Moderate.*

Continental   **Lucia's.** The nouvelle European and American cuisine is light and imaginative at this small cafe where wall and ceiling murals of pale clouds envelop a slightly haughty club of food devotees. The tiny menu changes every day or two, and includes imaginative dishes such as cucumber rondele sandwich, flank steak salad with sesame vinaigrette, chicken breast with goat cheese, and shrimp and wild rice salad. Desserts may include ginger tart with walnuts, mixed berries with Grand Marnier sauce, frozen praline ice cream cake with rum chocolate sauce, and ginger, brown sugar, and pecan cookies. *1432 W. 31st St., Minneapolis, tel. 612/825–1572. Reservations recommended. AE, MC, V. Closed Mon. Moderate–Expensive.*

★ **Loring Cafe.** One of the few good eating spots in the metro area that keeps late-night hours, the Loring Cafe is also the only restaurant with a view of handsome Loring Park. A young urban crowd hangs out in the decor-less single room, lingering over lemon caper chicken in tarragon sauce, chicken with basil, arugula, pesto, and gorgonzola, manicotti with lamb, and Chinese chicken salad with sesame ginger dressing. The rich, hot artichoke ramekin and foccacia hors d'oeuvres are meals in themselves. Desserts vary daily, but may include chocolate pâte laced with rum, carrot cake, white poppyseed cake, amaretto cheesecake, mascarpone with berry sauce and brown sugar, and unusually flavored homemade ice creams, perhaps apple curry, banana, pink peppercorn, or lavender. *1624 Harmon Pl., Minneapolis, tel. 612/332–1617. Reservations recommended. AE, MC, V. Moderate.*

★ **Caffe Latte.** A furiously successful and almost always jammed cafeteria for discerning diners, Caffe Latte offers an eclectic selection of soups, salads, scones, breads, and stews. Rosemary shrimp chowder, Japanese ginger salad, tuna basil tortellini, and Greek lamb stew are specialties. The post-theater crowd assembles for the Caffe's forte, desserts including chocolate turtle cake, cheesecakes, chocolate chocolate cake, and towering whipped cream fruit tortes. Seasonal hot or cold espresso drinks laced with liqueurs and whipped cream, and a small selection of wines by the glass, are also available. *850 Grand Ave., St. Paul, tel. 612/224–5687. AE. Inexpensive.*

Delicatessen **Pam Sherman's Bakery & Cafe.** Chef Pam Sherman, one of the founders of the upscale New French Cafe, goes informal with this uptown bakery and delicatessen. Her light international dishes run from fresh fruit salad, omelets, and French toast to vegetarian chili, fish cakes with tartar sauce, fettucine Alfredo, vegetarian lasagne, curried vegetables, and cod Provençal. But it's lemon cake, carrot cake with cream cheese, triple chocolate layer cake, chocolate raspberry Genoise, and her heart-stopping Reine de Saba chocolate cakes and cupcakes that make her famous. In summer, Sherman's supplies picnic baskets with cheeses, cold salads, and entrees including stuffed chicken breast with tarragon, spinach and ricotta filling, ham and Jarlsberg with mustard sauce, or smoked salmon. *2914 Hennepin Ave. S, Minneapolis, tel. 612/823–7269. No credit cards. Inexpensive–Moderate.*

French **Chez Paul.** The newest French cafe in the metro area overlooks Nicollet Mall. The menu includes poached salmon in butter cream sauce with carrots, onion and bay leaf; sautéed veal sweetbreads with capers and croutons; warm garlic sausage in puff pastry; braised chicken breast stuffed with lobster in a wild mushroom cognac sauce; and roast breast of duckling with apple brandy. The desserts are rich: éclairs, profiteroles, frozen strawberry soufflé, poached pears with Grand Marnier sauce, chocolate and Grand Marnier fondue with fresh fruit, and a novel chocolate and pistachio pâté. *1400 Nicollet Ave. S, Minneapolis, tel. 612/870–4212. Reservations suggested on weekends. AE, MC, V. Moderate–Expensive.*

Tulips. A spare, contemporary look and spare, contemporary menu characterize this small elegant storefront cafe in St. Paul's Historic Hill District. The fare is French with some northern Italian dishes, and the small menu changes daily. There is usually a selection of soups such as cream of asparagus, lemon broccoli with chive, crème de Crécy carrot, or a chilled gazpacho with grapes, sour cream, and cayenne. There are usually four entrees, typically veal in ciboulette sauce, chicken breast with sun-dried tomato butter, entrecote with béarnaise, and pink sea bass with French mustard sauce. Seafood specials such as marlin with escargot butter or red snapper with caper sauce are offered daily. Desserts include chocolate cake, lemon almond tart, crème caramel, chocolate mousse, raspberry hazelnut torte with layers of fried meringue, and Marjolaine cake. There is a small wine and beer selection. *452 Selby Ave., St. Paul, 612/221-1061. MC, V. Closed Sun. Moderate-Expensive.*

German Black Forest Inn. This student and artists' hangout is famed for its huge selection of bottled and tap beer and hearty German cuisine. The owner, Erich Christ, is the real thing, and so are his plates of no-nonsense Wiener schnitzel with potato pancakes and applesauce, sauerbraten, hasenpfeffer, homemade bratwurst, and deep-fried sauerkraut-and-cheese balls. The small grape arbor with its abstract sculpture fountain is usually packed all summer. *1 E. 26th St., Minneapolis, tel. 612/872-0812. AE, CB, DC, MC, V. Moderate.*

Greek It's Greek to Me. Small, noisy, and unpretentious, this bustling storefront cafe serves some of the best Greek food in town. The *mezes* appetizer plate with feta cheese, Greek olives, eggplant spread, taramosalata (made from fish eggs, potatoes, and olive oil), plus tomatoes and peppers is big enough for two, maybe three. The menu also includes shawirma, calamari, spanakopita, stuffed grape leaves, and roast leg of lamb. Tooth-achingly sweet homemade desserts include *galaktobouriko* with sugar, honey, and cinnamon syrup, baklava and its cousins *kadafi* and *saragli*, and *dipla*. Retsina and other Greek wines, and regular and nonalcoholic beers are served. *626 W. Lake St., Minneapolis, tel. 612/825-9922. Reservations required on weekends for groups over 6. No credit cards. Inexpensive.*

Indian Kebabi Bar and Restaurant. In the Riverplace shopping center at St. Anthony Falls, this Indian restaurant specializes in tandoor-broiled meats. You can watch the chef at his stone oven through a glass pane in the tiny kitchen. The menu also includes chicken, lamb, beef, seafood, and vegetarian curries, an especially notable kathi kebab appetizer, and a substantial buffet lunch. Desserts include homemade *kulfi*, an Indian ice cream flavored with cinnamon, saffron, cardamom, and fresh ground pistachios, mango ice cream, and pastries in butter syrup. *1424 Nicollet Ave., Minneapolis, tel. 612/871-4849. MC, V. Moderate.*

Italian D'Amico Cucina. Although D'Amico brothers insist they want
★ the "jeans crowd" as well as those in Armani suits, this isn't a casual cafe. From the *faux marbre* plates and peach and gray linens to the black marble floors and black leather chairs, it's haute urban nouvelle. Artistic presentations include carpaccio of venison with juniper-berry mayonnaise; goat-cheese dumplings with walnut sauce; pan-fried pork chop with prosciutto; fontina and fig sauce; vegetable terrine; special pizza of the day; and fresh fish. *Butler Square, 100 N. 6th St., Minneapolis, tel. 612/338-2401. Jacket and tie suggested. Reservations recommended. AE, MC, V. Closed Sun. Very Expensive.*
Hosteria Fiorentina. Owner Giorgio Cherubini's culinary talents are showcased in this purple and gold cafe in the business district. Best choices include risotto with porcini mushrooms and prosciutto; spicy cacciucco fish stew with octopus; red snapper and sea bass; five different foccacia with herb, meat or cheese toppings; tagliatelle with wild boar and wild mushrooms; fettucine with a sun-dried tomato and walnut pesto

sauce and a brunch of eggs scrambled with tomatoes, wild boar sausage, roasted potatoes, toast and jam. Desserts include spuma di cioccolato, tira misu, zuccotto, mele in gabbia, gelato al porto and tropical fruits with crushed ice and liqueurs. There are Chiantis or Tuscan wines to accompany the meal. *119 S. 10th St., Minneapolis, tel. 612/332–5200. Reservations suggested on weekends. AE, CB, DC, MC, V. Moderate.*

Japanese Kikugawa. Light and airy, this restaurant is constructed in traditional Japanese style with natural woods and maroon upholstery. A deck and a greenhouse room overlook the cobblestone street and St. Anthony Falls. The sushi bar is so popular that owner John Omori is adding a second sushi chef. There are no surprises on the menu, just nicely executed bento, teriyaki steak, seafood tempura, sukiyaki, and sashimi. The house specialty is a gourmet sampler that begins with otoshi. Omori's kitchen also turns out octopus with miso dressing and deepfried soft-shell crab in season. The desserts include unauthentic but tasty tempura ice cream, fresh fruits, green tea, and ginger ice cream. There's full bar service. *Riverplace, Main St. at Hennepin Ave., Minneapolis, tel. 612/378–3006. Reservations suggested. AE, MC, V. Moderate.*

Middle Eastern Old City Cafe. The only kosher restaurant in the Twin Cities, the tiny Old City Cafe is also one of the few vegetarian restaurants in the area. The menu features Israeli and Middle Eastern dishes including falafel, baba ghanouj, tabouli, hummus, assorted vegetable salads, ratatouille, potato knish, fried salmon, gefilte fish, and New York–style cheese and vegetable pizza or pizza with soybean sausage topping. Dessert choices are usually cherry cheese knish, cheesecake, baklava, or cookies. *1571 Grand Ave., St. Paul, tel. 612/699–5347. No credit cards. Closed 2 PM Fri. and all day Sat. Inexpensive.*

Lodging

by Karen Winegar

There is no shortage of lodging in the Twin Cities. Accommodations are available in the downtowns of either city, along U.S. 494 in the suburbs and industrial parks of Bloomington and Richfield (known as "the strip"), and near the Twin Cities International Airport. A number of hotels are attached to shopping centers as well, the better to ignore Minnesota's legendary winters and summer heat.

The two most elegant and distinguished hotels are the oldest structures, the Whitney Hotel on the rapidly developing downtown Minneapolis riverfront, and the Saint Paul Hotel in the heart of historic downtown St. Paul. There are sleek glass and steel towers, ivy-covered clapboard bed-and-breakfasts, and a variety of lodgings in between. There are also traditional inns: the Nicollet Island Inn, on an island in the Mississippi River, and the Lowell Inn in Stillwater, near the St. Croix River. The Radisson Hotel Saint Paul, the Nicollet Island Inn, and the Whitney Hotel overlook the Mississippi River.

Outside the Twin Cities, along the St. Croix and Mississippi rivers from St. Croix Falls to Winona, there are more than two dozen bed-and-breakfasts in farmhouses and restored Victorian homes. Laura Zahn's *Room at the Inn/Minnesota* published by Down to Earth Publications (1426 Sheldon Ave., St. Paul, MN 55108) profiles 60 B&Bs throughout the state.

Ratings

Category	Cost*
Very Expensive	over $120
Expensive	$90–$120
Moderate	$50–$90
Inexpensive	under $50

per room, double occupancy, without 6% state sales tax and nominal tourist tax

The following credit card abbreviations are used throughout this book: AE, American Express; CB, Carte Blanche; DC, Diners Club; MC, MasterCard; V, Visa.

The most highly recommended hotels are indicated with a star ★.

St. Paul **Embassy Suites–St. Paul.** Built in 1980, this hotel is decorated in neo-New Orleans Garden District style, with terra cotta, brick work, tropical plants, and a courtyard fountain. It is close to U.S. 35 and within walking distance of all major downtown businesses. *175 E. 10th St., 55101, tel. 612/224–5400. 210 suites. Facilities: pool, sauna, steam room, whirlpool, free airport pickup, and a restaurant. AE, DC, MC, V. Expensive.*

★ **The Saint Paul Hotel.** Built in 1910, this stately stone hotel overlooks the axis of power and culture in genteel old St. Paul: Rice Park, the Ordway Music Theater, the James J. Hill Library, the Minnesota Club, and the Landmark Center. It's also just one block from the Minnesota Museum of Art and City Hall. The hotel was completely renovated in 1979; the rooms have an eclectic traditional decor, with Oriental touches. *350 Market St., 55102, tel. 612/292–9292 or 800/457–9292. 236 rooms, 18 suites. Facilities: restaurant, coffee shop, and a lounge. AE, CB, DC, MC, V. Expensive.*

Holiday Inn St. Paul Center. This 17-story hotel has a dramatic sweep of glass that allows sunlight into an 11-story atrium that houses La Rotisserie, a formal French-American restaurant. The rooms are standard, with contemporary furnishings in autumnal green, gold, red, and tan. There's a direct connection to the Town Square shopping mall, and skyway link to Dayton's, Donaldson's, and the St. Paul World Trade Center. *411 Minnesota St., 55102, tel. 612/291–8800. 240 rooms, 10 suites. Facilities: indoor swimming pool, piano bar, 2 restaurants, and a cafe. AE, CB, DC, MC, V. Moderate–Expensive.*

Radisson Hotel Saint Paul. This 23-story riverside tower was completely renovated in 1988. The rooms are decorated in traditional American style with Oriental touches in the lobby. Almost all of the rooms have a river view. *11 E. Kellogg Blvd., 55101, tel. 612/292–1900. 423 rooms, 52 suites. Facilities: indoor pool, parking ramp, and 2 restaurants. AE, DC, MC, V. Moderate–Expensive.*

Sheraton Midway St. Paul. This contemporary four-story hotel is in the busy Midway district centered at Snelling and University avenues. Hallways decorated in green and gold lead into bright, comfortable rooms with contemporary oak woodwork. There's a tiny exercise room, and the largest sauna in town, both off the indoor pool. Rooms for handicapped guests feature safety rails, king-size beds, and adjustable shower nozzles. *400 Hamline Ave., 55104, tel. 612/642–1234. 185 rooms, 12 suites, some designated no smoking. Northwest Airlines desk in lobby. Facilities: indoor pool, sauna, whirlpool, exercise room, restaurant and lounge. AE, DC, MC, V. Moderate– Expensive.*

Sunwood Inn Bandana Square. In what was once a paint shop for the Pacific Northern Railroad, this hotel is connected by skyway to Bandana Square, a former railroad engine repair yard renovated in the early 1980s into a two-story shopping center. Rooms have king- or queen-size beds, and are decorated with contemporary furnishings. There's no restaurant in the hotel, but several Bandana Square restaurants are within walking distance. *1010 W. Bandana Blvd., 55108, tel. 612/647–1637. 103 rooms, 6 suites. Facilities: indoor pool, wading pool, whirlpool, and a sauna. AE, DC, MC, V. Inexpensive– Moderate.*

Excel Inn of St. Paul. A three-story hotel located near the Sun Ray shopping center on the eastern side of St. Paul off I–94 and White Bear Avenue. It was remodeled in 1988. *1739 Old Hudson Rd., 55106, tel. 612/771–5566 or 800/356–8013. 101 rooms, some designated no smoking. Facilities: free satellite TV, HBO. Senior discount for 55 and older. AE, DC, MC, V. Inexpensive.*

Minneapolis **Hyatt Regency Hotel.** A wide, sweeping lobby with a fountain, potted trees, and piano bar is the focal point of this hotel, which lies within easy walking distance of downtown businesses and shopping. It's close to Orchestra Hall and the YWCA and linked by a landscaped walkway to the Greenway residential area and Loring Park. The 22nd-floor Regency Club has upgraded rooms with hair dryers, terry-cloth robes, clothes valet, and luxury toiletries. There's also concierge service from 6:30 AM to 9 PM, complimentary hors d'oeuvres, and Continental breakfast. Bedrooms are the same size throughout this busy convention hotel, and decorated in contemporary jade, peach, and gray fabrics and carpeting. The hotel has very slow elevators and cold, dark hallways decorated in deep plum colors and oak, but redecorating is planned for each floor and the lobby in the next year or two. *1300 Nicollet Mall, 55403, tel. 612/370–1234. 534 rooms, 21 suites. Facilities: TV movies, parking ramp, restaurant, coffee shop, and lounge. Greenway Health Club: $8.75 fee for weights room, aerobics classes, sauna, whirlpool, massage, tennis and racquetball courts. AE, DC, MC, V. Very Expensive.*

Marriott City Center Hotel. This sleek, 31-story hotel is located within the City Center shopping mall, minutes from the IDS Center, Nicollet Mall, Dayton's, the Conservatory, and other downtown shops and offices. Rooms are contemporary in design, with peach and jade color decor. Two concierge floors at the top of the hotel provide Continental breakfast and evening hors d'oeuvres, as well as more deluxe rooms and furnishings. *30 S. 7th St., 55402, tel. 612/349–4000. 584 rooms including 23 bilevel suites, an apartment-style presidential suite. Facilities: 2 restaurants, 2 lounges, valet parking, and a coffee shop. Health club: $5 fee for sauna and whirlpool. AE, CB, DC, MC, V. Very Expensive.*

Vista Marquette Hotel. A modern 19-story hotel in the 51-story IDS Center, the tallest building in the Twin Cities. The center is linked by skyway to Dayton's and other downtown shopping and business complexes. A much-needed renovation is planned for January 1989; a health club and lobby bar will be added. *IDS Center, 710 Marquette Ave., 55402, tel. 612/332–2351. 259 rooms, 20 suites. Facilities: in-room movies, underground parking ramp, restaurant, and lounge. AE, CB, DC, MC, V. Very Expensive.*

★ **The Whitney Hotel.** A flour mill of the 1880s recently converted into an elegant, genteel, small hotel, the Whitney is near the St. Anthony Falls lock and dam. All the accommodations are suites, and about half overlook the Mississippi. Bilevel suites are connected by spiral staircases; penthouse suites have three bedrooms, baths with Jacuzzis, parlors with a fireplace, and a baby grand piano, and a patio deck overlooking the river. The lobby features rich woods and a graceful staircase flowing into a parlor with a grand piano. There are brass fixtures, marble appointments, mahogany Chippendale furniture, and 15-foot ceilings throughout the hotel. *150 Portland Ave., 55401, tel. 612/339–9300 or 800/248–1879. 97 suites. Facilities: terry bathrobes, fine toiletries, hair dryers, valet parking, restaurant, garden plaza and lounge. AE, DC, MC, V. Very Expensive.*

Embassy Suites–Airport. Minutes from the Minneapolis/St. Paul International Airport, this all-suite hotel boasts Art Deco throughout. The lobby is pale pink marble, with turquoise, fuchsia, and black Deco-style furnishings. The rooms, which surround a glass-roof atrium with bridges and tropical plants, feature calla lily motif fabrics and lamps. Jet noise is completely masked by thick wall construction and by the murmur of the garden's waterfalls. Executive rooms on the corners of the building feature large, curving picture windows. The room rate includes complimentary full breakfast and two hours of complimentary cocktails each evening. *7901 34 Ave. S, 55425, tel. 612/854–1000. 311 suites, some designated no smoking. Facilities: airport shuttle, indoor swimming pool, sauna, steam room, restaurant, and a lounge. AE, CB, DC, MC, V. Expensive–Very Expensive.*

Embassy Suites–Bloomington. Over the past decade, Bloomington has become a full-fledged business district; much of the Fortune 500 business takes place here, rather than in the older downtown areas. The look of this all-suite hotel is neo–Spanish Colonial. There's a courtyard with a fountain, potted trees, and Spanish tile. Each suite has two telephones and two televisions; the room rate includes complimentary breakfast and two hours of complimentary cocktails each evening. *2800 W. 80th St., Bloomington, 55431, tel. 612/884–4811. 219 suites. Facilities: indoor swimming pool, sauna, whirlpool, steam room, and a restaurant. AE, CB, DC, MC, V. Expensive–Very Expensive.*

Embassy Suites–Centre Village. The 6-story hotel occupies the 8th through 14th floors of the Marquette Bank Building, well up from street noise, and close to shopping and entertainment. Deco-style etched glass, pink marble, and obsidian and pastel tiles set the art deco theme that begins in the atrium lobby, and runs through the suites as well. Deco embellishes everything from hall sconces, room numbers, and elevator housings to the slash of two-tone neon around the lobby lounge. The rooms are furnished in pale pinks and greens, with Deco floral wallpapers, and cream-colored dressers, vanities, and headboards. Each suite has a microwave and minirefrigerator. *425 S. 7th St., Centre Village, 55415, tel. 612/333–3111. 219 suites. Facili-*

ties: indoor pool, sauna, Jacuzzi, restaurant, and a lounge. AE, CB, DC, MC, V. Expensive–Very Expensive.

Minneapolis/St. Paul Airport Hilton. The two-story waterfall in the lobby helps mask airport traffic noise in this 12-story contemporary hotel close to the International Tower, the Met Center, and the Control Data world headquarters. The Royal Suite is the most luxurious room, with two bedrooms, a parlor, and dining area decorated in pastel neo-Asian contemporary style. Standard rooms are decorated in bright pastels, and overlook either the Minnesota Valley or the airport and downtown areas. *3800 E. 80th St., 55420, tel. 612/854–2100 or 800/445–8667. 289 rooms, 11 suites. Facilities: indoor swimming pool, 2 whirlpools, sauna, exercise room with weights and bicycles, concierge floor, and 2 restaurants. AE, CB, DC, MC, V. Expensive–Very Expensive.*

Omni Northstar Hotel. Guest rooms run from the 7th to the 17th floor of the Northstar Center office complex, with easy access to shops. The lobby is decorated in an Oriental style with antique screens; rooms have contemporary American decor. The hotel is linked by the skyway system to the IDS Center. *618 2nd Ave. S, 55402, tel. 612/338–2288. 222 rooms, 2 suites. Facilities: restaurant and a lounge. AE, DC, MC, V. Expensive–Very Expensive.*

Radisson Plaza Hotel Minneapolis. The hushed backlit pale pink hallways of this contemporary luxury hotel lead to rooms decorated in one of three schemes: Oriental, contemporary, or European traditional. Half the rooms face out across the city, the others face a dramatic white atrium ornamented by recessed alcoves set with outsize Thai and Chinese pottery and baskets. The three Plaza Club concierge floors offer a generously proportioned gentlemen's club–style lounge with TV and newspapers; these floors feature complimentary Continental breakfast and hors d'oeuvres each day. Each Plaza Club suite offers a king-size carved four-poster bed, terry robe, dual sink, bidet, bathroom phone, hair dryer, and luxury toiletries. There are complimentary apples at the check-in desk in the lobby, where the marble fountain is somewhat deafening. The staff is professional, attentive, and well versed in the hotel's facilities. The hotel is connected directly to Dayton's, and by skyway to the City Center shopping mall. It's just opposite the Paramount Cafe and the IDS Center, and one block from the Conservatory. *35 S. 7th St., 55402, tel. 612/339–4900. 344 rooms, 13 suites; some designated no smoking. Facilities: fitness center with sauna, Jacuzzi, and weights, 2 restaurants. AE, CB, DC, MC, V. Expensive–Very Expensive.*

Hotel Luxeford. This is a warm and informal hotel, with a self-service kitchen-lounge area off the low-ceilinged lobby with its dhurries, torcheres, and fireplace. Suites in the 12-story hotel are decorated in a mixture of Queen Anne and contemporary styles, with mint, coral and ivory color schemes. Each has TV movies, a microwave oven and a minibar. It lies a few minutes' walk from Orchestra Hall, MacPhail Center for the Arts, and Nicollet Mall, as well as other downtown business and entertainment centers. *1101 La Salle Ave., 55403, tel. 612/332–6800. 230 suites. Facilities: parking ramp, exercise room with whirlpool, weights, exercise bikes, sauna, shuttle van around the downtown area, complimentary Continental breakfast, coffee shop, and a lounge. AE, DC, MC, V. Moderate–Very Expensive.*

Radisson University Hotel. One of the newest members of the Minnesota-based Radisson chain, this contemporary style eight-story brick hotel is located in the east bank area of the University of Minnesota campus. Its U-shaped courtyard is filled with flower beds. The lobby is rich in gray marble, burgundy carpet, and dark wood paneling. Rooms facing west and south have the best views. The hotel is close to the University of Minnesota hospitals, Northrop Auditorium, Stadium Village, Dinkytown, and Coffman Memorial Union, and minutes from downtown via the Washington Avenue bridge spanning the Mississippi. The desk, restaurant, and bell staff are especially courteous and helpful. *615 Washington Ave. SE, 55414, tel. 612/379–8888. 299 rooms, 7 suites. Facilities: 2 restaurants, 2 lounges and a game room. AE, CB, DC, MC, V. Moderate–Very Expensive.*

Hotel Sofitel. The Sofitel is known more for its bustling bistro-style restaurants than its rooms, which are standard-issue contemporary, arranged around an airy but cool and impersonal atrium. The hotel is just off the U.S. 494 strip at U.S. 494 and Highway 100, close to the Bloomington business centers and restaurants. *5601 W. 78th St., Bloomington, 55435, tel. 612/835–1900. 276 rooms, 11 suites. Facilities: concierge, valet parking, indoor pool, sauna, whirlpool, weights room, 2 lounges, 3 restaurants, and a take-out bakery. AE, DC, MC, V. Moderate–Expensive.*

Minneapolis Hilton Inn. Located in an industrial park near U.S. highways 280 and 35W, this Hilton has a sleekly contemporary decor that's brass, glass, green, and gold. There's golf and jogging nearby. *1330 Industrial Blvd., 55413, tel. 612/331–1900. 241 rooms, 13 suites. Facilities: indoor swimming pool, sauna, whirlpool, in-room movies, parking, restaurant, coffee shop, and a lounge. AE, CB, DC, MC, V. Moderate–Expensive.*

Nicollet Island Inn. This limestone-walled inn is in a restored 1893 door and sash factory located among 19th-century residential and commercial buildings on Nicollet Island in upper St. Anthony Falls. The rooms and lobby are decorated with updated Victorian-style furnishings—floral fabrics, wallpapers, brass appointments, and natural wood. Upper south-facing floors have the best views of the lock and dam, the falls, and the urban skyline. The inn is connected to the St. Anthony Main shopping center by an old wrought-iron bridge and to downtown Minneapolis by the Hennepin Avenue bridge (now under reconstruction). *95 Merriam St., 55401, tel. 612/331–1800. 24 rooms. Facilities: lounge and a restaurant. AE, CB, DC, MC, V. Moderate–Expensive.*

Radisson Hotel Minnetonka. A contemporary hotel with neo-Renaissance-style decor using natural woods, plants, and stained glass window inserts. There's room service until 11 PM; the V.I.P. floor provides complimentary newspaper, Continental breakfast, and happy hour each day. The hotel is close to the Ridgedale and Bonaventure shopping centers. *12201 Ridgedale Dr., Minnetonka, 55343, tel. 612/593–0000. 214 rooms, 8 suites. Facilities: indoor pool, whirlpool, sauna, parking, 2 restaurants, and a lounge. AE, CB, DC, MC, V. Moderate–Expensive.*

Holiday Inn Downtown Nicollet Mall. The desk staff is cheery enough, but the lobby, halls, and dimly lighted bar and restaurant are filled with dark brown velvet chairs, black marble, and autumnal colored carpeting that lends a somber gloom to the place. Rooms with contemporary-style furniture provide sweeping views of downtown Minneapolis. The 12-story hotel is located directly opposite the Hyatt Regency, close to the Minneapolis Auditorium and Convention Center, Loring Park, the Guthrie Theater, the Walker Art Center, Orchestra Hall, and the IDS Center, as well as many downtown businesses. *1313 Nicollet Mall, 55403, tel. 612/332–0371. 320 rooms, 5 suites. Facilities: indoor swimming pool, sauna, free HBO, and a restaurant. AE, DC, MC, V. Moderate.*

Radisson Hotel South and Plaza Tower. It's not uncommon to meet boisterous conventioneers in plastic leis and Hawaiian shorts in the lobby or halls of this big, angular convention hotel. It was renovated in contemporary style with pale pinks, plums, and greens in 1981. The Plaza Tower has larger, more elegant rooms, but rooms throughout the hotel complex are overheated, and the elevators smell of cigar smoke. *7800 Normandale Blvd., Bloomington, 55435, tel. 612/835–7800. 567 rooms, 18 suites. Facilities: lounge, indoor swimming pool, sauna, whirlpool, in-room movies, and 3 restaurants. AE, CB, DC, MC, V. Inexpensive–Very Expensive.*

Sheraton Airport Hotel. This four-story contemporary hotel was renovated in 1988. It has a shady north-woods interior design, featuring fiber wall hangings, brick, wood panels, and red and green carpets and furniture. *2525 E. 78th St., Bloomington, 55425, tel. 612/854–1771 or 800/325–3535. 227 rooms, 8 suites. Facilities: airport shuttle, Showtime TV, 2 restaurants, a lounge with live entertainment, indoor pool, Jacuzzi, and exercise rooms. AE, CB, DC, MC, V. Inexpensive–Very Expensive.*

Stillwater **The Lowell Inn.** A historic inn done in an eclectic "roadhouse Greek Revival" style, the Lowell Inn is filled with real and ersatz antiques. It's located in the business and restaurant area of downtown Stillwater, within walking distance of many renovated historic homes. *102 N. 2nd St., Stillwater, 55082, tel. 612/439–1100. 13 rooms, 8 suites. Facilities: 3 restaurants. No credit cards; AE, MC, V in the restaurants only. Moderate–Very Expensive.*

The Arts

The Twin Cities are the cultural center of the Upper Great Lakes area, with more than 90 theaters. There's hardly a night without a concert, stage, or dance production in the metro area.

The calendar sections of the monthly *Mpls. St. Paul* and *Twin Cities* magazines have extensive listings of events, as does the free monthly *Twin Cities Directory*. Calendars of events are available at tourist information locations, and are published in the Arts sections of the *St. Paul Pioneer Press* and *Dispatch* and the *Minneapolis Star* and *Tribune*.

Most tickets are sold at box offices, but they can also be purchased at Tickets-to-Go outlets in each city. Some events offer last-minute reduced-price "rush" tickets at substantial savings. *Tickets-to-Go in St. Paul, St. Paul Center, 445 Minnesota St., tel. 612/223–5408; in Minneapolis, IDS Crystal Court, 7th St. and Nicollet Mall, tel. 612/333–0159.*

Theater The **Actor's Theater of Saint Paul** (28 W. 7th Pl., tel. 612/227–
St. Paul 0050) is one of the city's premier professional theater compa-

nies, presenting contemporary drama and comedy, and the classics during the October–April season.

The **Great American History Theater** (75 W. 5th St., tel. 612/292–4323) presents plays about people and events that shaped Minnesota and Midwestern history. The season runs from October through May.

The **Park Square Theater Company** (253 E. 4th St., tel. 612/291–7005) performs classics from September through May at the Jemne Auditorium of the Minnesota Museum of Art (305 St. Peter St., tel. 612/292–4355).

The **Penumbra Theater Company,** Minnesota's only black professional theater company, performs August–May at the Hallie Q. Brown Theater (270 Kent St., tel. 612/224–4601).

The **Women's Theater Project** (203 N. Howell St., tel. 612/647–1953) produces new plays by women about issues important to them, and employs women in all aspects of production. Performances are at the Hennepin Center for the Arts (528 Hennepin Ave., tel. 612/333–6200 in Sept., Oct., Apr., and May).

The **West Bank Theater District** (2000 S. 5th Ave., tel. 612/332–6910) has the highest concentration of theaters in Minneapolis. Theater bills range from avant-garde comedy and improvisation to traditional performances. Among the companies and theaters located here are the **Theater in the Round Players** (tel. 612/333–3010), **Mixed Blood** (tel. 612/338–6131), **At the Foot of the Mountain** (tel. 612/375–9487), **Dudley Riggs, Etc.** (tel. 612/332–6620), **Southern Theater** (tel. 612/340–0155), **Theatre in the Round** (tel. 612/332–3010), and **University of Minnesota Theater** (tel. 612/625–4001).

The **Guthrie Theater** (725 Vineland Pl., tel. 612/377–2224 or 800/328–0542), founded by Sir Tyrone Guthrie in 1963. The Guthrie was awarded a Tony in 1982 for its outstanding contribution to American theater. Performances include Shakespeare, the classics, contemporary drama, comedy, and musicals.

At the Foot of the Mountain (People's Center, 2000 S. 5th St., tel. 612/375–9487) is a theater company specializing in plays about women's issues.

Charters Academy and Showcase Theater (411 1st Ave. N, tel. 612/338–0063) offers intimate, off-Broadway-type theater.

The Children's Theater Company (2400 3rd Ave. S, tel. 612/874–0400) presents adaptations of classics and contemporary children's literature during its autumn–spring season.

The **Cricket Theater** (1407 Nicollet Ave., tel. 612/871–2244) offers contemporary American theater and new works.

The **Old Log Theater** (5175 Meadville St., Excelsior, tel. 612/474–5951) presents Broadway shows and English comedy staged by the oldest continuously running stock theater in the country.

Theatre de la Jeune Lune (Box 25170, Minneapolis 55458, tel. 612/333–6200) is an international avant-garde theater company that offers the best of American and French theater performed in English. The company presents four different plays in its September through June season. (Performance locations include the Hennepin Center for the Arts, 528 Hennepin Ave., and the Southern Theater, 1420 Washington Ave. S).

The **University of Minnesota Theater** (330 21st Ave. S, tel. 612/625–4001) offers a variety of productions throughout the academic year. The company presents melodrama aboard a showboat throughout the summer.

Concerts The **Saint Paul Chamber Orchestra** (75 W. 5th St., tel. 612/292–
St. Paul 3248) is the first and only full-time chamber orchestra in the United States. Directed by Pinchas Zuckerman, the orchestra features both national and international talent in more than 85 concerts each year. The **Minnesota Chorale,** a symphonic chorus of 125 voices, is the official choir of the St. Paul Chamber Orchestra. The orchestra and chorale perform in the Ordway Music Theater and other locations.

The **Saint Paul Civic Symphony** (75 W. 5th St., tel. 612/735–6091) performs in the Weyerhaeuser Auditorium in the Landmark Center, where the public radio "Live from the Landmark" series is produced.

The **Ordway Music Theater** (345 Washington St., tel. 612/224–8537) is fashioned in the image of the classic opera houses of Europe and has been described as "one of the handsomest public spaces for music in America" by *Time* magazine. Classical, jazz, and popular music, as well as dance, theater, and mime are presented in the 1,819-seat main theater and the 315-seat McKnight Theater.

The **World Theater** (10 E. Exchange St., tel. 612/298–1300) is St. Paul's oldest surviving theater, dating from 1910. In addition to hosting Minnesota Public Radio's "Good Evening" variety radio show, the theater schedules classical, jazz, country, and pop music events, and theatrical performances.

Minneapolis The **Minneapolis Chamber Symphony** (515-B Butler Square Bldg., 100 N. 6th St., tel. 612/339–0236) offers both classical and contemporary music concerts during summer and winter.

The **Minnesota Orchestra,** an acclaimed symphony orchestra under the direction of Edo de Waart, performs in Orchestra Hall (1111 Nicollet Mall, tel. 612/371–5656), a major concert hall with year-round events.

The **University of Minnesota's Northrop Auditorium** (84 Church St. SE, tel. 612/624–2345) hosts special events and concerts.

The **Orpheum Theater** (901 Hennepin Ave., tel. 612/338–7968) occasionally offers touring productions of Broadway shows.

Opera The **Minnesota Opera** (400 Sibley St., Suite 20, tel. 612/221–
St. Paul 0256) presents four main stage operas and one summer musical each year. The season opens in September with additional productions in October, November, and June. Performances are in the Ordway Music Theater (345 Washington St., St. Paul, tel. 612/224–4222).

The **North Star Opera** (614 Portland Ave., tel. 612/224–1640) features young, rising, Upper Midwest area singers in professionally produced, fully staged operas. Performances are held at the O'Shaughnessy Auditorium (College of St. Catherine, 2004 Randolph Ave., tel. 612/690–6700).

Dance The **Minnesota Dance Alliance** (tel. 612/340–1900) provides information on dance presentations in the Twin Cities.

St. Paul **O'Shaughnessy Dance Series,** a six-week program offered each spring, spotlights local professional dance companies with performances in the O'Shaughnessy Auditorium (College of St. Catherine, 2004 Randolph Ave., tel. 612/690–6700).

Minneapolis **Northrop Dance Series** (84 Church St. SE, tel. 612/624–2345), sponsored by the University of Minnesota, is one of the major showcases for dance in the Upper Midwest region.

Hennepin Center for the Arts (528 Hennepin Ave., tel. 612/339–9150) is home to several dance companies, including the 20-year-old **Minnesota Dance Theater,** the **NorthWest Ballet,** and the **New Dance Ensemble,** which present a variety of classical, contemporary, jazz, and tap dancing.

Other noted Minneapolis dance companies include the **Ethnic Dance Theater** (1807 Elliot Ave. S, tel. 612/872–0024), the **Minnesota Jazz Dance Company** (1815 E. 38th St., tel. 612/721–3031), the **Nancy Hauser Dance Company** (1313 5th St. SE, tel. 612/623–4296), and the **Zenon Dance Company** (324 5th Ave. S, tel. 612/338–1101).

Film Art films and revivals are shown at the **Jerome Hill Theater**
St. Paul (First Trust Center, 5th and Jackson Sts., tel. 612/291–0801), the **Minnesota Museum of Art** (305 St. Peter St., tel. 612/292–4355), and the **College of St. Thomas** (Murray Hall, 2115 Summit Ave., tel. 612/647–5000).

Minneapolis Art films and revivals are shown at the University of Minnesota's **Coffman Memorial Union** (300 Washington Ave., tel. 612/625–4177), **Intermedia Arts** (413 1st Ave. N, tel. 612/627–4444), the **Minneapolis Institute of Arts** (Pillsbury Auditorium, 2400 3rd Ave. S, tel. 612/870–3131), the **University Film Society** (auditorium of the Bell Museum, 17th St. and University Ave. SE, tel. 612/627–4430), and **Walker Art Center** (southwestern edge of the loop at Hennepin Ave. and Vineland Pl., tel. 612/375–7600).

Nightlife

There's no "in the wee small hours" in the Twin Cities. Nightlife takes place in the nighttime, with closings at 1 AM. But even though things end on the early side, Minneapolis and St. Paul have no lack of fun places to visit. Most night spots are trendy and upscale and attract youngish people.

Bars and **Champps Sports Bar and Gourmet Hamburger Grill.** One of the
Nightclubs top sports bars in the Midwest with six large-screen TVs and
St. Paul two bars. Great burgers. Sports celebrities and local sports figures often hang out here. *2431 W. 7th St. at Sibley Plaza, tel. 612/698–5050. AE, MC, V.*
Gallivan's. A downtown St. Paul classic with a cozy fireplace and leather booths. *354 Wabasha St., tel. 612/227–6688. Piano bar Mon.–Sat. 9 PM–1 AM. No cover. AE, DC, MC, V.*
Gatsby's. Calling itself a nightclub where time stands still, this ultramodern casual club has dancing, dining, and drink specials. *2554 Como Ave., tel. 612/646–1339. Closed Sun. and Mon. No cover. AE, DC, MC, V.*
Grand Central. There's dancing to DJ music week nights and Saturday evening; local bands perform on Sunday nights. *788 Grand Ave., tel. 612/227–7328. Open 11 AM–1 AM Mon.–Sat., 11 AM–midnight Sun. Food served until 11 PM daily. Piano bar 11 AM–9 PM daily. Cover: $2 Fri.–Sun. AE, MC, V.*

Heartthrob Cafe and Philadelphia Bandstand. The place has a vintage '50s atmosphere combined with 1980s high-tech lights and music. There's a heart-shaped bar, a 30-foot-long Happy Hour picnic buffet, and a two-tier dance floor. The crowd is young. *St. Paul Center, 30 E. 8th St., tel. 612/224–2783. Cover. AE, MC, V.*

Plums. For the late-night crowd, this place bustles from 9 to midnight every evening. There are dinner and drink specials, and dancing nightly. *480 S. Snelling Ave., tel. 612/699–2227.*

Saint Paul Hotel. A warm and elegant bar, perfect for a nightcap after an evening at the Ordway. *In Rice Park, 350 Market St., tel. 612/292–9292. Live entertainment Mon–Sat. AE, MC, V.*

Minneapolis **Fine Line Music Cafe.** A "new music" cafe with live jazz, folk, rock, and pop music seven nights a week. The cafe features fresh fish, pasta, homemade bread, and desserts. *318 1st Ave. N, tel. 612/338–8100. Cover.*

Normandy Inn Piano Bar. This is a warm, old-country French-style pub with extensive selection of hors d'oeuvres during the cocktail hour. The atmosphere is pleasant and relaxed, and there's low-key live entertainment on week nights. *405 S. 8th St., in the Normandy Inn, tel. 612/370–1400. AE, MC, V.*

Northern Lights. The lounge presents a great light show and has a large dance floor. There are "Hungry Hour" buffets and nightly specials. *Holiday Inn North at I–694 and Shingle Creek Pkwy., tel. 612/566–8000. No cover. AE, DC, MC, V.*

Pacific Club. A new and plush downtown hot spot in the beautifully restored Lumber Exchange. There is a lavish dinner buffet with fresh seafood, homemade breads, desserts, and hot and cold dishes. Four separate bars and two dance floors round out the picture. *Lumber Exchange Bldg., 10 S. 5th St., tel. 612/339–6100. Cover charges vary. Dress: no denim or athletic wear. Over 23 for admission. AE, CB, DC, MC, V.*

Pracna Underground. This "subterranean urban escape" under the Pracna restaurant offers contemporary and classic dance music in an intimate setting. It's small, cozy, and very pleasant. *On east bank of the Mississippi in the St. Anthony Main shopping center at Pracna and Main Sts., tel. 612/379–3200. AE, MC, V.*

Rupert's Cafe and Nightclub. This is a place to see and be seen. There is a huge complimentary buffet and live music ranging from big band to contemporary sounds. *5410 Wayzata Blvd., St. Louis Park, tel. 612/544–4993. Dress: no jeans. Cover charge $2–$5. Closed Sun. and Mon. MC, V.*

William's Nightclub. William's boasts the largest light-and-sound show in the Midwest. Four bars in the two-level club cater to 20–40-year-old Yuppie/preppy/trendy types. *2911 Hennepin Ave. S, tel. 612/823–6217. Cover: Fri.–Sat. $3; Tues.–Thurs. $1. Closed Mon. MC, V.*

Jazz Clubs Call the Twin Cities Jazz Society Jazzline (612/633–0329) for local jazz events.

St. Paul **Blues Saloon.** Live blues music is presented Friday and Saturday nights and on occasional Sunday evenings; blues show and jam sessions on Monday evenings. *601 Western Ave., tel. 612/228–9959. Cover. AE, MC, V.*

Dakota Bar and Grill. Set in the Bandana Square shopping mall, the Dakota is recognized as having one of the best jazz bars around and features some of the Twin Cities' finest performers. It's also a very good restaurant. *1021 E. Bandana Blvd., tel. 612/642–1442. Shows 8:30 nightly. Cover. AE, DC, MC, V.*

Sweeney's Saloon and Cafe Cafe. This is actually two establishments in one, with live jazz at the Cafe Cafe Friday and Saturday nights. It's a dressy crowd. *96 Dale St., tel. 612/221–9157. No cover. AE, MC, V.*

Minneapolis **Artist's Quarter.** This club features food all day long and local performers or jazz greats in the evening. Showtimes vary, but the entertainment usually begins about 8 on Sunday nights, 9 on other evenings. *14 E. 26th St., tel. 612/872–0405. Food 8 AM–1 AM daily. Cover: $1–$8. No credit cards.*

Emporium of Jazz. The club features Dixieland music by the Hall Brothers Dixieland Band Friday and Saturday nights and other groups afternoons and evenings. *1351 Sibley Memorial Hwy., Mendota, across the Mississippi from the International Airport, tel. 612/452–1830. Cover: $3; patrons of the adjoining Mariner Restaurant $1.50. No credit cards.*

Live at the Hennepin Center. The lower level of the building has a comfortable and intimate club with live jazz Friday and Saturday evenings at 9, and live big band jazz on Sunday evenings at 8. *Hennepin Center for the Arts, 528 Hennepin Ave., tel. 612/339–7800. Cover: $3–$4. No credit cards.*

Rock Clubs **Alleygaters.** There's a special going on every night, plus re-
St. Paul corded music and a bowling alley next door. Diversions include "Magnificent Man Hunts" and swimsuit competitions. *Spectrum Lanes, I–494 and Bass Lake Rd., Maple Grove, tel. 612/553–9111. Cover: Fri. and Sat. No credit cards.*

Minneapolis **First Avenue Club.** Once a bus depot, this huge 1,200-seat club is the Twin Cities' largest, busiest, and most famous night spot. The club was the setting for the Minneapolis rock star Prince's movie *Purple Rain.* Prince still makes occasional appearances; a huge purple Caddy parked near the club is a sign the star may be appearing that night. There's recorded music some nights, and appearances by fast-rising local and national groups. *701 1st Ave. N, tel. 612/332–1775.*

7th St. Entry. This club is a regular stop for scouts seeking new musical talent; it's actually the 7th Street entrance to the First Avenue Club. Local and nationally known bands on their way up appear here; the music is loud and the audience young. *701 1st Ave., tel. 612/338–8388 or 612/332–1775.*

Country **Palomino Club.** A place for hard-core country fans to kick up
St. Paul their heels. Live music featured nightly. *I–94 and McKnight Rd., tel. 612/735–3757.*

Minneapolis The **Alternative.** This adult, alcohol-free club has a sound-and-light show on Wednesday nights and live country (and occasionally rock) music on Friday and Saturday evenings. The activities usually start around 9. *2533 Harding St. NE, tel. 612/781–8879. No credit cards.*

Comedy Clubs **Comedy Gallery East.** Offering regular stand-up comedy per-
St. Paul formances featuring local talent and nationally known comedians. *In the Days Inn, 1780 E. County Rd., Maplewood, tel. 612/770–2811. Performances Wed.–Sat. 8:30 PM; Fri.–Sat. 8:30 PM and 10:30 PM. Tickets $6. No credit cards.*

Minneapolis **Comedy Gallery.** Nationally known comedians perform in this state-of-the-art nightclub Wednesday, Friday, Saturday, and Sunday evenings; Thursday nights are for new talent. *Riverplace, 25 Main St. SE, tel. 612/331–5653. Shows Wed.– Thurs. and Sun. 8:30 PM; Fri.–Sat. 8:30 PM and 10:30 PM. Cover: $8.75; $2 Thurs.; $1 for women on Wed.; $2 for men on Thurs.*

Funny Bone Comedy Club. Nationally known stand-up comics take the stage at the newest of the Twin Cities' comedy clubs. *2911 Hennepin Ave., tel. 612/824–1981. Shows Wed.–Thurs. and Sun. 8:30 PM; Fri. 8:30 PM and 10:30 PM; Sat. 8 PM, 10 PM, and midnight.*

Dave Wood's Rib Tickler and Magic Club. The shows here feature a house MC and guest magicians, along with a comedian. A beautifully appointed club with top-notch comedy entertainment. *Lower level of the Itasca Bldg., 716 N. 1st St., tel. 612/ 339–9031. Shows Wed.–Sun. 8 PM; Fri.–Sat. 8 PM and 10:30 PM. Cover. No credit cards.*

Dudley Riggs' Brave New Workshop. This is a Twin Cities comedy institution. Scripted revues are followed by special aftershow improvisation sessions. *2605 Hennepin Ave., tel. 612/ 332–6620. Shows Tues.–Sat. 8 PM; Fri.–Sat. 8 PM and 10:30 PM. Tickets: Tues.–Sat. $10; Sun. $6. Reservations recommended. No credit cards.*

Southern Minnesota

The lush countryside of southern Minnesota stretches from wooded bluffs high above the Mississippi River westward across rolling pastures and prairies to the South Dakota border. Tens of thousands of years ago, the region was scoured by glaciers that carved hundreds of lakes, streams, and rivers. Today the countryside is dotted with tranquil communities rich in ethnic heritage, historic Indian sites, and centers of art and recreation.

Getting Around

By Plane **Rochester Municipal Airport** (tel. 507/282–2328) is served by **American** (tel. 800/433–7300), **Northwest** (tel. 800/225–2525), and **TransWorld Express–Air Midwest** (tel. 800/221–2000).

Mankato Municipal Airport (tel. 507/387–8268) is served by **Bemidji Airlines** (tel. 800/221–8877).

Fairmont Municipal Airport (tel. 507/235–6609) is served by **Great Lakes Aviation** (tel. 800/554–5111).

By Car Most travel in southern Minnesota is by car; federal, state, and county highways provide easy access to points of interest. I–90 runs east–west through the extreme southern sections of the region, while I–35 runs north–south to the Twin Cities. Route 52, Route 15, U.S. 71, and U.S. 59 traverse the region north to south.

By Train **Amtrak** (tel. 800/872–7245) runs between the Twin Cities and Chicago and provides daily services to Winona and Red Wing.

By Bus **Greyhound** and **Trailways** provide service to the larger cities and towns.

Scenic Drives **U.S. 61.** The drive between Red Wing and Winona along the Mississippi River is one of the most scenic in the Midwest, often compared to the Rhine River in beauty.

Important Addresses and Numbers

Tourist Information

Faribault Chamber of Commerce (228 Central Ave., 55021, tel. 507/344–4381). Open weekdays 8–4:30.

Mankato Area Convention and Visitors Bureau (120 S. Front St., Suite 200, 56002, tel. 800/426–6025, ext. 262). Open weekdays 8–5.

New Ulm Chamber of Commerce (220 N. Minnesota St., 56073, tel. 507/354–4317). Open weekdays 8:30–5. Visitors Center (3rd St. N and Broadway). Open Mon. 8 AM–9 PM, Tues.–Fri. 8–6, Sat. 8–5, Sun. 10–4.

Pipestone Chamber of Commerce (117 S.E. 8th Ave., tel. 507/825–3316). Open weekdays 8:30–5.

Rochester Convention and Visitors Bureau (220 S. Broadway, Suite 100, 55904, tel. 507/288–4331). Open weekdays 9–5.

Winona Convention and Visitors Bureau (67 Main St., 55987, tel. 507/452–2272). Open weekdays 8–5.

Emergencies

Minnesota State Highway patrol (tel. 612/452–7473). Emergency telephone numbers vary throughout the region, but dialing "0" will bring an operator onto the line.

Exploring Southern Minnesota

Numbers in the margin correspond with points of interest on the Southern Minnesota map.

Most visitors who come to the region are driving and seeking scenic areas and attractions. We begin our exploration of southern Minnesota on the banks of the Mississippi and move westward to the Dakota border.

❶ Red Wing, located in the heart of the Hiawatha Valley, a 90-mile stretch of the Mississippi noted for its scenic bluffs, was founded in 1836 as a missionary outpost. Its name comes from the Dakota Indian chiefs who once occupied the area; they were called *Koo-poo-hoo-sha,* meaning "wing of the wild swan dyed scarlet," which was the symbol of leadership they wore.

Self-guided one-half hour walking or driving tours of Red Wing's historic district begin at the former Milwaukee Road Depot, at the corner of Broad and Levee streets. Information and a free brochure are available at the Visitor Information Center, Chamber of Commerce, the depot, most hotels, and the Pottery.

The **Goodhue County Historical Museum** has exhibits on the geology, archaeology, and Indian history of the region, along with displays depicting county history. *1166 Oak St., tel. 612/388–6024. Admission: 50¢ adults, 25¢ children. Open Tues.–Sun. 1–5.*

The **Pottery** is a restored turn-of-the-century factory where the famed Red Wing pottery was manufactured. The firm began production in the late 1880s as the Minnesota Stoneware Co., using local clay sources, and closed its doors in 1967 after a prolonged labor dispute. Displays include kilns, molds, and exhibits that present a pictorial history of pottery production. *200 W. Old Main St., tel. 612/388–1420. Admission free. Open Mon.–Wed. and Sat. 9–6, Thurs. and Fri. 9–9, Sun. 10–6.*

Red Wing River Excursions offers two-hour narrated Mississippi River cruises aboard a flat-bottomed paddlewheel boat. *Levee Park at the end of Broad St., tel. 612/388–7530. Fare: $5 adults, $3 children under 12. Departures mid-May–late Oct., daily 1–4.*

② **Winona** stands on a giant sandbar created centuries ago by the meandering Mississippi River. Behind the city of 25,000, massive limestone bluffs reach more than 500 feet above the river. The name comes from a legend in which an Indian maiden named *We-No-Nah* leapt to her death from a high bluff near the sandbar when she was denied marriage to the Indian brave she loved.

Two years after its founding in 1851, Winona was a full-fledged river town with a population of 300. Today Winona celebrates its river heritage with a Steamboat Days Festival during the week of the Fourth of July. By the 1860s, wheat was the top money crop in the region, and hundreds of thousands of bushels were shipped from Winona annually. At the end of the 19th century, Winona was one of the major timber processing and shipping centers in the nation. Large numbers of German and Polish immigrants had come to work in the lumber mills, and by 1900 Winona had the largest concentrations of Kashubian Poles in the U.S.A.

The city is headquarters for the Upper Mississippi River National Wildlife and Fish Refuge, an area extending about 300 miles along the river.

Visitor's guides, as well as brochures describing self-guided tours of Winona's historic sites and bird-watching areas, are available free of charge. *Visitor Information Center, Huff St. off U.S. 14 and U.S. 61, tel. 507/452–2278. Open May–Oct., daily 8–5. Winona Convention and Visitor's Bureau, 67 Main St., tel. 507/452–2272. Open weekdays 8–5.*

The **Julius C. Wilkie Steamboat Center** is a full-scale replica of an old-time steamboat. The first deck contains a museum with river history and steamboat artifacts and a slide presentation prepared by Winona State University. The elegant Grande Salon on the second deck recaptures the splendor of the Victorian era. The pilot house on the third deck offers views of the river and the city. *In Levee Park on Main St. at the river, tel. 507/454–6880. Admission and 30-min. guided tours: $1.50 adults, $1 children 5–11 and senior citizens. Open May–Oct. 9–5 daily. Lunch daily 11–2 Memorial Day–Oct.*

The **Winona Armory Museum**—also known as the Main Museum—is one of the largest historical society museums in the state. Displays in the 1915 brick fortress include a stained glass window exhibit and a replica of an old-fashioned Main Street. The museum gift shop offers a wide selection of traditional handicrafts, local products, and historical reproductions, as well as books and toys of the past. *160 Johnson St., tel. 507/454–2723. Admission free. Open weekdays 10–5, weekends 1–5.*

The **Polish Cultural Institute of Winona** was founded in 1976 to preserve the rich Polish history of the region. The institute houses Kashubian artifacts, family heirlooms, religious articles, and folk art. *102 Liberty St., tel. 507/452–2141. Admission free. Open May–Oct., Wed. and Sun. 2–4.*

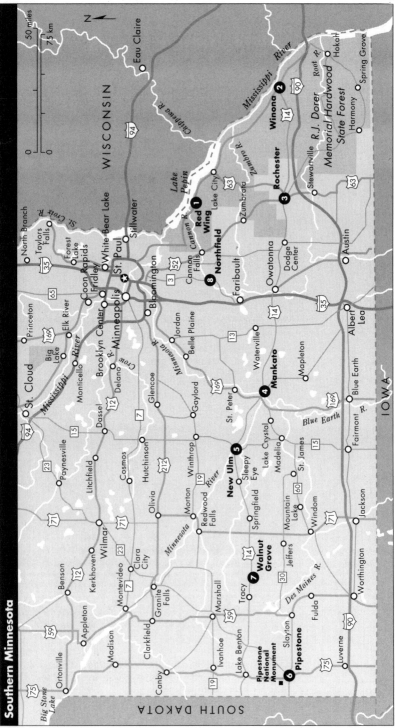

Southern Minnesota

50 miles

75 km

WISCONSIN

Eau Claire

Chippewa R.

94

Mississippi River

Winona **2** 90

14

Root R. Hokah

Spring Grove

Harmony

R.J. Dorer Memorial Hardwood State Forest

Stewartville

63

Rochester **3**

Zumbro R.

Zumbrota

63

Lake City

Lake Pepin

83

North Branch

Taylors Falls

St. Croix R.

Forest Lake

Stillwater

White Bear Lake

35

Red Wing **1**

Cannon R.

Cannon Falls

Northfield **8**

Faribault

Owatonna

Dodge Center

Austin

35

Princeton

65

Coon Rapids

Fridley

St. Paul

Bloomington

52

3

Albert Lea

Elk River

169

Big Lake

Monticello

Mississippi River

Brooklyn Center

Minneapolis

Crow R.

Jordan

Belle Plaine

13

Waterville

14

Mapleton

St. Cloud

94

Dassel

12

Glencoe

Gaylord

Minnesota R.

St. Peter

Mankato **4**

Blue Earth

169

Blue Earth

Fairmont R.

IOWA

Delano

Paynesville

23

Litchfield

15

Cosmos

Hutchinson

212

Winthrop

Morton

19

Olivia

Redwood Falls

Minnesota River

New Ulm **5**

Sleepy Eye

Springfield

Lake Crystal

Madelia

St. James

60

Mountain Lake

Windom

71

15

Fairmont

Jackson

Benson

112

Kerkhoven

Wilmar

23

Clara City

7

Montevideo

Granite Falls

Marshall

Walnut Grove **7**

14

30

Jeffers

Des Moines R.

Tracy

Worthington

90

Appleton

Madison

Clarkfield

59

Lake Benton

Ivanhoe

19

Canby

Pipestone National Monument

Pipestone **6**

75

Slayton

Fulda

Luverne

Big Stone Lake

Ortonville

75

SOUTH DAKOTA

71

Garvin Heights Park (straight south on Huff St. past U.S. 14 and U.S. 61) offers hiking trails 500 feet above the city and a scenic drive and overlook with splendid views of the city, the Mississippi, and Wisconsin on the opposite shore.

Sugar Loaf Mountain towers more than 500 feet above the river, and is lighted at night. An early Indian legend has it that the mountain was the cap of Chief *Wa-pah-sha*, but it was early quarrymen removing limestone from the bluff who were responsible for Sugar Loaf, which towers more than 85 feet above the remainder of the bluff.

The **Burnell House,** built in the 1850s by the first permanent non-Indian settler in Winona County, is considered one of the finest examples of Gothic Revival architecture in Minnesota. Run by the Winona County Historical Society, it is listed in the National Register of Historic Places. *5 mi south of Winona off U.S. 14 and U.S. 61, Homer, tel. 507/454–2723. Admission: $1.50 adults, 75¢ children. Open Memorial Day–Labor Day, Mon.–Sat. 10–5; Labor Day–Mid-Oct., Sat. 10–5, Sun. 1–5.*

❸ **Rochester** was settled in the 1850s by immigrants from Rochester, New York who named the new community after their former home. In 1863 Dr. William Worrall Mayo came to Rochester to examine Civil War army recruits and stayed. Two sons, William and Charles, both became doctors and joined their father in practice. In 1915 they incorporated the Mayo Clinic.

While Rochester is a center for dairy farming and the production of electronic data-processing equipment, it is the Mayo Clinic that has made the community of 58,000 world-famous. More than 200,000 patients visit the Clinic's 800 doctors each year, and most of the community's attractions are related to the clinic.

Mayo Park (2nd St. SE at 2nd Ave.) includes the Mayo Memorial, Mayo Civic Auditorium, Civic Theater, Rochester Art Center, and statues of the founders of the clinic.

The 56-bell **Rochester Carillon,** in the tower of the Mayo Clinic's Plummer Building, is dedicated to the American soldier. The carillon is said to be the most complete carillon in North America, covering a range of 4½ octaves. Concerts are presented Mondays at 7 PM and Wednesdays and Fridays at noon, with additional recitals for holidays and special events.

The **Mayo Clinic** complex has nine buildings, including the 19-story Mayo Building of diagnostic facilities, laboratories, libraries, and patient-care and medical training facilities. Films and guided tours tell the past and present Mayo story. *Mayo Bldg., 2nd Ave. SE and 2nd St. SW, tel. 507/284–2511. Free guided tours weekdays at 10 and 2.*

The **Mayo Medical Museum** offers films and exhibits about health, medicine, and surgical procedures. Displays include life-size anatomical models of the human body, a heart-lung machine, and an artificial kidney, along with vivid models of body parts mangled in farm accidents and a display of accidentally swallowed objects. *In the Damon Bldg., 200 1st St. SW, tel. 507/284–3280. Admission free. Open weekdays 9–9, Sat. 9–5, Sun. 1–5; closed holidays.*

Maywood, the 55-room former home of Dr. Charles Mayo, is furnished with French, Spanish, English, and American antiques. Built in 1911, the warm, elegant home sits on a hillside overlooking the Zumbro River and is listed in the National Register of Historic Places. Luminaries such as Franklin D. Roosevelt, Helen Keller, and the king of Saudi Arabia visited Dr. Mayo here. *1½-hour guided tours leave from the Olmstead County Historical Society, 122 County Rd. SW, tel. 507/282–9447. Admission: $4 adults, $3 children 5–16. Tours Apr.–Oct., Tues.–Thurs. and Sat.–Sun. 1 and 2. Reservations required.*

The **Rochester Arts Center** brings exhibits of contemporary arts and crafts from throughout the country to Rochester. *320 E. Center St., tel. 507/282–9692. Admission free. Open Tues.–Sun. 10–5, closed Mon. and holidays.*

④ **Mankato** is set on a bend in the Minnesota River where it joins the Blue Earth River. The name comes from the Dakota Indian word for "blue earth," referring to the clay found in the riverbanks here. The Old Town section contains restored buildings along Front Street in Mankato's first business district. A feather-shape granite marker at the corner of Front and Main streets marks the spot where 38 Dakota Indians were hanged for their part in an 1862 uprising.

Mankato State University's **Conkling Art Gallery** on Maywood Avenue (tel. 507/389–6412), features a changing schedule of art exhibits, including works by students and faculty.

The **Blue Earth County Historical Society** is housed in the restored 18-room Hubbard Mansion built in 1871. A restored 1873 log cabin, a 1900 schoolroom, pioneer shops and exhibits, and Victorian gardens adjoin the home. Horse-drawn vehicles and early autos are located in an adjacent carriage house. *606 S. Broad St., tel. 507/345–4154. Admission free. Open Tues.–Sun. 1–5; closed Mon. and holidays.*

Minneopa State Park contains more than a thousand acres of scenic river valley and prairie lands. Two spectacular waterfalls within a deep gorge add to the beauty, and there is a Dutch-style, wind-driven grist mill dating from 1864. The park offers camping, hiking, picnicking, and fishing. *6 mi west of Mankato on Rte. 68, tel. 507/625–4388. Admission: $3.50 vehicle permit.*

⑤ About 30 miles northwest of Mankato, **New Ulm** was named by immigrants who settled the community in 1854 after their home city in Germany. The Great Sioux Indian Uprising in 1862 climaxed with two major battles that nearly destroyed the town; a monument next to the courthouse square commemorates the bravery and heroism of the town's defenders.

Brochures outlining self-guided tours of New Ulm's historic sites and a free visitor's guide are available at the Visitor Center. *3rd St. N and Broadway, tel. 507/354–4217. Open weekdays 8–6. Sat. 8–5, Sun. 10–4.*

The **Glockenspiel,** a 45-foot-high musical clock tower, is one of the few carillon clocks in the world. Its 37 bells, which were cast in the Netherlands, weigh a total of two and one-half tons. Animated figures in the tower depict the history of New Ulm. *Schonlau Park Plaza, 5th and Minnesota Sts. The bells chime on the hour; the figures perform at noon, 3, and 5.*

The **Hermann Monument** stands on a high bluff to the west overlooking the city. The statue (known locally as Herman the German) is similar to one in the Teutoburg Forest of Germany, which commemorates the deeds of Hermann the Cheruscan, a prince who saved Germany from Roman domination in the 9th century AD. A stairway leads 102 feet to a platform atop the monument that provides a breathtaking view of the city and surrounding countryside. *Admission: 25¢. Open Memorial Day–Labor Day, daily 1–5.*

The **Brown County Historical Museum** has a large number of exhibits, manuscripts, documents, and photos that tell the history of the town and county. The 1862 Sioux uprising is heavily documented. *Center St. and Broadway, tel. 507/354–2016. Admission free. Open Memorial Day–Labor Day, weekdays 10–5, Sat. 1–5; Sept.–May, Mon.–Sat. 1–5; closed Sun. and holidays.*

Dannheim's Kuhlstall sells 35 flavors of homemade ice cream. You can watch the manufacturing process Tuesday, Wednesday, and Thursday mornings. *105 S. Minnesota St., tel. 507/354–2131.*

❻ The **Pipestone** area of southwestern Minnesota once contained seemingly endless expanses of grassy prairies and was known as the Tall Grass Prairie. It was home to the Dakota (Sioux) Indians, who considered the region near the South Dakota border sacred. With Indians from many other tribes, they quarried the soft red stone to make peace pipes. The Dakotas believed that their tribe originated here, and that the red color of the stone came from the blood of their ancestors.

The **Pipestone County Museum** is housed in the former city hall, which was constructed in 1896 of hand-hewn quartzite blocks. Exhibits on the heritage of the Pipestone area include Native American clothing, quillwork, beadwork, and weapons. There are hands-on exhibits, interpretive programs, and a library. Free brochures outlining self-guided tours detailing points of interest in the Pipestone Historic District are distributed here. *113 Hiawatha Ave., tel. 507/825–2563. Admission: 50¢ adults, children under 13 free. Open daily 10–5.*

The **Pipestone National Monument** contains quarries the Dakotas have used for centuries and protects the red rock used by today's tribal members. A Visitor Center offers slide shows and films depicting the history of the area and Indian pipes. In summer, Indian craftsmen can be seen working with the stone. A self-guided, three-quarter-mile trail takes visitors to the quarries, glacial rock formations, a waterfall, and remnants of the virgin prairie. The Upper Midwest Indian Cultural Center provides demonstrations by Indian craftsmen and items for sale. *1 mi north of Pipestone on U.S. 75, then ½ mi west, tel. 507/825–5463. Admission free. Open Memorial Day–Labor Day, Mon.–Thur. 8–6, Fri.–Sun. 8–8; Sept.–May, daily 8–5; closed Jan. 1, Dec. 25.*

The **Song of Hiawatha Pageant** is performed outdoors near the entrance to Pipestone National Monument on weekends in late July and early August. *Tel. 507/825–3316 for schedule, ticket prices, and reservations.*

What to See and Do with Children

Mankato: Minneopa State Park
New Ulm: Glockenspiel
Pipestone: Pipestone National Monument
Red Wing: Red Wing Excursions
Walnut Grove: Laura Ingalls Wilder Museum. *See* Off the Beaten Track.

Off the Beaten Track

Wabasha This picturesque river town along the Mississippi is the site of the **Anderson House,** a restored 51-room hotel in operation since 1856. It is furnished throughout with original Victorian furniture and handmade comforters; hot bricks are provided on cold winter nights, and there's a big jar of home-baked cookies on the front desk 24 hours a day. You can also rent a cat to spend the evening in your room. Grandma Anderson's Dutch Kitchen dining room serves giant cinnamon rolls, caramel pecan rolls, Dutch dumplings, home-cured hams, and mountains of other delectable edibles. An ice cream parlor features luscious concoctions for those who aren't counting calories. *333 W. Main St., 55981, tel. 612/565-4524 or 800/325-2270. Reservation deposit required. No credit cards. Inexpensive–Moderate.*

⑦ Walnut Grove. This tiny town's (population 700) most famous resident was Laura Ingalls Wilder, author of a series of children's books relating her adventures crossing the prairie and settling in South Dakota in the late 1800s, which were the basis for the highly popular TV series, "Little House on the Prairie."

The **Laura Ingalls Wilder Museum** has exhibits that depict the life of the author and her family and the early history of Walnut Grove. Memorabilia includes Laura's hand-stitched quilt, her calling cards, a bench from the Congregational Church attended by the Ingalls family, and family photos and records. *330 8th St., tel. 507/859-2358. Admission free. Open Memorial Day–Labor Day, daily 10–7; Apr.–May and Sept.–Oct. daily 11–4; closed Nov.–March except by appointment.*

The **Ingalls Homestead** is located nearby, on the Gordon farm. A footbridge crossing Plum Creek takes you to the dugout, now little more than a depression in the bank, where the Ingallses first lived. A barn stands on the site of their farmhouse. *1½ mi north of Walnut Grove on County Rd. A. Admission: $2.*

⑧ Northfield. On September 7, 1876, eight members of the infamous James–Younger band of outlaws rode into this community 40 miles south of the Twin Cities with the intent of robbing the First National Bank. Word of the gang's appearance quickly spread through town, and as the robbers left the bank, they were greeted with a withering cross fire laid down by the townspeople. Only Jesse and Frank James escaped; it was the end of years of robbery by this legendary gang from Missouri. Northfield holds a "Defeat of Jesse James Celebration," reenacting the seven-minute bank raid and shoot-out, on the weekend after Labor Day.

The First National Bank is now the **Northfield Historical Society Museum.** Its exterior and main room have been carefully restored to look just as it did on that fateful day in 1876. The clock's hands rest at the time of the robbery attempt, a few minutes before two o'clock. *408 Division St., tel. 507/645–9268. Admission: $1 adults, 50¢ children under 13. Open weekdays 9–5, Thurs. till 9, Sat. 10–4, Sun. 1–5.*

Shopping

Donmeirer's German Store (corner of 10th and Minnesota Sts., tel. 507/354–4231) in New Ulm is one of several stores selling items reflecting the community's German heritage. It has a large selection of wood carvings, European candies and cookies, ornaments, beer steins, and other Old World items.

The **Upper Midwest Indian Cultural Center** (Pipestone National Monument) has excellent buys on Native American Indian crafts, including baskets, leatherwork, and pipes.

At **Red Wing Pottery Sales** (1995 W. Main St., Red Wing, tel. 612/338–3562) you can find remaining inventory of original Red Wing pottery, along with collectibles from around the world.

Participant Sports

Beaches You can swim at the following state park beaches: **Sakatah Lake** (Waterville, tel. 507/362–4438), **Lake Shetek** (Currie, tel. 507/763–3256), **Split Rock Creek** (Jasper, tel. 507/348–7908), and **Whitewater** (Altura, tel. 507/932–3007).

Bicycling The back roads and bike trails of southern Minnesota offer scenic rides through rolling terrain. The state operates a series of trails on abandoned railroad right-of-ways surfaced with crushed limestone that are open only to bicyclists and pedestrians.

Cannon Valley Trail runs 19 miles from Red Wing to Cannon Falls, following the Cannon River through a scenic region of rocky cliffs, wooded slopes, farmland, and hardwood forests. The *Douglas Trail* between Rochester and Pine Island passes through 13 miles of lush farmland, skirting lakes and forests. The *Root River Trail* near Lanesboro is currently under construction.

There are also a number of mapped bicycle routes on public roads. The **Mississippi Bluffs** route is an 80-mile circular route through Winona that offers challenging biking through the wooded and steep bluffs along the Mississippi. The **Pipestone Countryside** tour is a 68-mile, figure-eight loop through the relatively flat countryside around Pipestone.

Canoeing The rivers and lakes of southern Minnesota offer a variety of canoeing opportunities. State canoe routes have been designated on seven rivers—the Mississippi, Minnesota, Des Moines, Straight, Cannon, Root, and Zumbro. All are considered navigable by novices except during high water season. Commercial traffic on the Mississippi can create unsafe conditions at any time, and canoeists are warned to stay well clear of the navigation channel.

Minnesota requires that all canoes be licensed, either in Minnesota or your home state. For license information, contact the DNR Information Center. *500 Lafayette Rd., Box 40, St. Paul, 55146, tel. 612/296–6157, weekdays 8–4:30.*

Fishing The backwater sloughs of the Mississippi River offer excellent fishing for walleye, bass, catfish, and a wide variety of panfish. The lakes in southern Minnesota provide fishing for walleye, northern pike, muskellunge, bass, and panfish. Local bait shops, resorts, and other fishermen can provide information on hot spots.

Golf Southern Minnesota offers a variety of courses that will challenge players of all skill levels.

Chaska. Dahlgreen Golf Club (4½ mi west of Chaska on Rte. 212, tel. 612/448–7463), 18 holes.
Chatfield. Chosen Valley Golf Club (1801 S. Main, tel. 507/867–4305), 18 holes.
Faribault. Faribault Golf and Country Club (1700 17th St. NW, tel. 507/334–5559), 18 holes.
La Crescent. Pine Creek Golf Course (4 mi west of La Crescent on County Rd. 6, tel. 507/895–2410), nine holes.
Mankato. Minneopa Golf Club (½ mi south of Mankato on Rte. 169, tel. 507/625–5777), nine holes.
Northfield. Northfield Golf Club (707 Prairie St., tel. 507/645–7694), 18 holes.

Skiing
Downhill **Coffee Mill Ski Area** has 9 runs with 2 chair lifts, 1 rope tow, and snowmaking; longest run 4,000 feet, vertical drop 425 feet. Services include cross-country skiing, equipment rentals, weekly races. *Junction of U.S. 61 and Rte. 60, Wabasha, tel. 612/565–4527 or 507/288–3923. Open weekdays 1–10, weekends 10–10.*
Hole-in-the-Mountain County Park offers 3 runs with 3 rope tows; longest run 1,400 feet, vertical drop 175 feet. Services include cross-country skiing, equipment rental, and snow tubing. *3/4 mi west of Lake Benton on U.S. 14, tel. 507/363–9350. Call for hrs.*
Mt. Frontenac Ski Area has 9 runs with 1 chair lift, 2 T-bars, 2 rope tows, and snowmaking; longest run 5,000 feet, vertical drop 420 feet. There's cross-country skiing, equipment rental, and a children's program. *9 mi south of Red Wing on U.S. 61, tel. 612/388–5826. Open weekdays 4:30–10, weekends and holidays 9 AM–10 PM.*
Mt. Kato Ski Area has 17 runs with 8 chair lifts and snowmaking; longest run 2,800 feet, vertical drop 240 feet. Services include equipment rental and a children's program. *1 mi south of Mankato on Rte. 66, tel. 507/625–3363. Call for hrs.*
Welch Village Ski Area offers 30 runs, 5 chair lifts, 2 T-bars, 1 rope tow, and snowmaking; longest run 4,000 feet, vertical drop 350 feet. Services include equipment rental and children's programs. *3 mi south of Welch Village Rd. on U.S. 61, tel. 800/421–0699. Open daily 9 AM–10 PM.*

Cross-country The southern Minnesota climate and terrain offer excellent cross-country skiing, and the sport is one of the most popular winter activities in the state. Some downhill ski areas offer cross-country trails, as do many local and state parks.

Sibley State Park (15 mi north of Willmar on U.S. 71, tel. 612/354–2055) has about eight miles of groomed trails ranging from novice to advanced, a sliding hill, a heated trail center, and interpretive programs.
D. L. Kipp State Park (12 mi south of Winona on U.S. 61, tel. 507/643–6849) has about 8½ miles of groomed trails on bluffs overlooking the Mississippi River. Trails range from beginner to intermediate.

Spectator Sports

Auto Racing The **Elko Speedway** features NASCAR stocks, late models, and thunder cars racing on a banked asphalt oval. *26350 France Ave., 612/461-3321. Racing mid-April-mid-Sept. Sat. at 7 PM.* **Raceway Park** in Shakopee is a paved quarter-mile track with figure-eight and NASCAR racing. *6528 Rte. 101, tel. 612/445-2257. Racing late April-early Oct. Sun. and holidays at 7 PM.*

College Sports **Mankato State University** (tel. 507/389-6111) has athletic programs in baseball, men's and women's basketball, and ice hockey. The Mavericks are especially competitive in baseball and women's basketball.

Horse Racing Pari-mutuel quarter horse and thoroughbred races are held at **Canterbury Downs**, with the Saint Paul Derby at the end of June. *15 mi south of the Twin Cities, 1100 Canterbury Rd., Shakopee, tel. 612/445-7223. Open May-mid-Oct. Wed.-Sun.*

Dining and Lodging

You'll find a wide variety of restaurants in southern Minnesota, with offerings ranging from hearty German fare to the standard steak, seafood, and prime rib. Dining is more casual than in metropolitan areas.

Variety is the key word in describing lodging in southern Minnesota. Accommodations range from small motels to large hotels with lots of tiny inns in between.

Price categories for restaurants and hotels are the same as in the Minneapolis and St. Paul Dining and Lodging sections.

Mankato
Dining **Cubs of Mankato.** This is a popular spot offering a large variety of Chinese specialties with some American dishes. There is a children's menu and cocktail lounge. The decor is modern with an Oriental flavor. *1430 2nd Ave., tel. 507/387-7000. MC, V. Closed Dec. 25. Inexpensive.*

Lodging **Holiday Inn-Downtown.** The motel offers the reassurance of a typical Holiday Inn—comfortable rooms and lots of amenities. The decor is Midwestern modern. *101 E. Main St., 56001, tel. 507/345-1234. 151 rooms. Facilities: indoor pool, sauna, whirlpool, putting green, garage, coin laundry, restaurant, cocktail lounge. AE, DC, MC, V. Moderate.*

New Ulm
Dining **Glockenspiel Haus Restaurant.** German specialties such as sauerbraten are featured in this Old World restaurant that bakes its own German pastries and lip-smacking, handmade candy creations. American fare is provided for the less adventurous. There is a cocktail lounge. *400 N. Minnesota St., tel. 507/354-5593. Reservations recommended. MC, V. Moderate.*
Veigel's Kaiserhoff. Barbecued ribs are the house specialty at this restaurant which has been owned and operated by the same family since 1938. You'll find steaks and fowl as well. There's a children's menu and a cocktail lounge with weekend entertainment. *221 N. Minnesota Ave., tel. 507/359-2071. Reservations recommended. No credit cards. Closed Thanksgiving, Dec. 24-25. Inexpensive-Moderate.*

Lodging **Colonial Inn Motel.** There aren't a lot of extras, but this small motel is well kept and comfortable. *1315 N. Broadway, 56073, tel. 507/354-3128. 24 rooms. Facilities: winter plug-ins, cable*

TV; *restaurants, lounges nearby. AE, CB, DC, MC, V. Inexpensive.*

Red Wing   **Port of Red Wing.** This restaurant in the St. James Hotel offers
Dining   a variety of daily specials such as scallops Provençal, along with
★   a traditional Midwest menu featuring steak, poultry, and seafood. The baked goods, all produced in the restaurant kitchens,
are a real treat. There's a cocktail lounge and entertainment.
The dining room has been decorated to recall the riverboat era.
The limestone walls are original, and the wine cellar is an old
safe deposit vault. *406 Main St., 612/388–2846. Jacket and tie
suggested. Reservations recommended. MC, V. No lunch Sun.
Moderate–Expensive.*

Lodging   **St. James Hotel.** This 1875 hotel was restored to its 19th-
★   century elegance by the Red Wing Shoe Co. in 1977 and enlarged in 1981. The individually decorated rooms feature
period wallpaper and furnishings updated with modern
touches, including Victorian wardrobes that open to reveal
television sets. The public spaces recall the heyday of the
riverboats. *406 Main St., 55066, tel. 612/388–2846. 60 rooms,
some with Mississippi River view. Facilities: 2 dining rooms,
coffee shop, parking ramp; Port of Red Wing restaurant, cocktail lounge, entertainment. AE, DC, MC, V. Expensive–Very
Expensive.*
Red Carpet Inn. This small motel offers clean and comfortable
surroundings at budget prices. The rooms are bright and
cheery with modern decor. *235 Withers Harbor Dr., 55066, tel.
612/388–1501. 37 rooms. Facilities: outdoor pool, winter plugins, cable TV. AE, CB, DC, MC, V. Inexpensive.*

Rochester   The **Elizabethan Room.** In the Kahler Hotel, this restaurant of-
Dining   fers the ambience of the era its name evokes. There are dark
★   paneled walls, coats of arms, red velvet hangings, wrought-
iron chandeliers, stained glass, and occasionally, strolling violinists. Menu offerings include breast of chicken and rack of
lamb, along with beef and seafood dishes. There is a cocktail
lounge. The service is excellent. *20 2nd Ave. SW, tel. 507/282–
2581. Jacket and tie required at dinner. Reservations advised.
Open weekdays 11–2 and 5:30–9:30, Sat. from 5:30 PM. No
lunch Sun. AE, CB, DC, MC, V. Closed holidays. Moderate–
Very Expensive.*
Aviary Restaurant. The accent is on spice at this restaurant
that serves southern and southwestern American regional cuisine. Try the chili. Takeouts are available. The cocktail lounge
will help cool down your taste buds. *4320 Rte. 52 N., tel. 507/
281–5141. AE, CB, DC, MC, V. No lunch Sun. Inexpensive–
Moderate.*
Michael's Restaurant. A very attractive restaurant serving traditional Greek fare, including delicious pastries baked on the
premises. A variety of American dishes, including chicken and
seafood, are offered as well. There's a children's menu, cocktail
lounge, and valet parking. *15 S. Broadway, tel. 507/288–2020.
Jacket and tie at dinner. Reservations recommended. AE, CB,
DC, MC, V. Closed Sun., major holidays. Inexpensive–
Moderate.*

Lodging   **Kahler Hotel.** People from around the world come to the Mayo
★   Clinic, and many famous names have been registered at this
comfortable hotel. The rooms are spacious and very well appointed. There are some suites. *20 2nd Ave. SW, 55902, tel.*

507/282–2581. 705 rooms. Facilities: domed recreation center with saunas and whirlpool, rooftop indoor pool, parking ramp, 4 restaurants, coffee shop, cocktail lounge, entertainment, convenient subway connections to Mayo Clinic and hospitals. AE, CB, DC, MC, V. Moderate–Very Expensive.

Holiday Inn Downtown. Like virtually every other lodging establishment in the city, this hotel caters to those who come to the Mayo Clinic. The rooms are contemporary and comfortable in typical Holiday Inn fashion. Services include courtesy transportation to the clinic and hospitals. *220 S. Broadway, 55904, tel. 507/288–3231. Located 2½ blocks from Mayo Clinic. 172 rooms. Facilities: restaurant, cocktail lounge, cable TV, coin laundry, parking ramp. AE, DC, MC, V. Moderate–Expensive.*

Friendship Inn Center Towne. Just three blocks from the Mayo Clinic, the inn offers Continental breakfasts and a courtesy van to the clinic and hospitals. *116 5th St. SW, 55901, tel. 507/289–1628. 54 rooms. Facilities: indoor pool, sauna, cable TV. AE, CB, DC, MC, V. Inexpensive.*

Winona Dining

Yesterdays. Located in a restored hotel in Winona's Historic District, the dining room has antique decor that carries out the historic theme. The varied menu includes salads and steak and seafood specialties. There is a children's menu and cocktail lounge. *129 W. 3rd St., tel. 507/452–5460. Reservations suggested. AE, MC, V. Closed Sun. Inexpensive.*

Zach's on the Tracks. This contemporary restaurant and cocktail lounge offers a salad bar, buffets, Sunday brunch, and family dining. The fare includes daily specials, prime rib, steak, and seafood; there are children's and senior citizens' menus. *Front and Center Sts., tel. 507/454–6939. Dress: informal. Reservations suggested. AE, MC, V. Inexpensive.*

The Arts

Mankato The **Cherry Creek Theater** (120 S. Broad St., tel. 507/345–7885) is a professional regional company presenting classics and original theater in an intimate 60-seat theater. **Mankato State University Theater Arts Department** (tel. 507/389–2118) offers a variety of musicals and light entertainment in the Performing Arts Building on Maywood Avenue.

Rochester The **Rochester Repertory Theater** (314½ S. Broadway, tel. 507/289–1737) specializes in contemporary productions in an "off Broadway"–type theater. There are 11 productions each year.

The **Rochester Civic Music Association** (tel. 507/285–8076) sponsors the Rochester Symphony Orchestra, Symphony Chorale, and String Quartet. There are performances at various locations throughout the year.

Nightlife

The lounges of the large hotels and motels in the big cities often feature live music, especially on weekends, and live entertainment can be expected in most resort areas and the larger ski lodges. Most nightlife in the region centers on the bar scene.

Bars and Nightclubs Mankato

Mettler's Bar and Restaurant. A pleasant campus bar offering light snacks and occasional musical entertainment. *117 S. Front St., tel. 507/625–9660. Closed Sun. AE, MC, V.*

Susan's Spirits and Sustenance is a popular spot with the college crowd for late-night snacks and drinks. Music is offered most weekends. *200 Walnut St., tel. 507/625-2337. No credit cards.*

Rochester **Broadstreet Cafe and Bar.** This bistro-style bar housed in a historic building is a pleasant, laid-back spot for a drink. *300 1st Ave. NW, tel. 507/281-2451. AE, CB, DC, MC, V.*

Hoffman House. The lounge in this restaurant in the Midway Motor Lodge has Bavarian decor and musical entertainment on weekends. *1517 16th St. SW, tel. 507/289-8866. AE, CB, DC, MC, V.*

The **Penthouse.** A rooftop lounge and dining room offering music and spectacular views of the city. *Kahler Hotel, 20 2nd Ave. SW, tel. 507/282-2581. AE, CB, DC, MC, V.*

Vikingland

Occupying the far northwestern corner of the state, Vikingland runs northward along the North Dakota border from Alexandria to Manitoba, Canada. Here, in the broad flat valley of the Red River, which separates North Dakota and Minnesota, there are large wheat farms, much like those on the Great Plains. Elsewhere the region is dense with lakes, forests, and wildlife refuges as well as resorts and ski areas.

The first tourists apparently stopped here early on, for a runestone found in the south, near Alexandria, indicates the possible presence of Viking explorers more than 100 years before Columbus made his first journey to the New World.

In the late 19th century, loggers cut millions of board feet of Vikingland's timber, and farmers broke the western prairie to plant wheat. Both groups pushed the native Dakota (Sioux) Indians farther west in the process.

Today, much of Vikingland's economy is dependent on tourism —boating, camping, and fishing. There are scores of resorts catering to fishermen, who come to enjoy some of the best inland lake fishing to be found in the Midwest.

Getting Around

By Plane Moorhead and Thief River Falls have commercial air service. Moorhead-bound passengers arrive at Fargo, ND, Moorhead's twin city.

Fargo Municipal Airport (tel. 701/241-1501) is served by **Northwest** (800/225-2525) and **United** (tel. 800/241-6522).

Thief River Falls Regional Airport (tel. 218/681-7680) is served by **Northwest Airlink** (tel. 800/225-2525) and **Bemidji Airlines** (tel. 800/221-8877).

By Car Most tourists travel through Vikingland by car. I-94 crosses the southern half of the region. U.S. 2 and U.S. 10 are major east-west arteries, while U.S. 59 is a north-south route.

By Train **Amtrak** (tel. 800/872-7245) provides passenger service to Detroit Lakes and Moorhead on its daily runs from the Twin Cities to Seattle.

By Bus **Greyhound** and **Trailways** provide service to the larger cities and towns.

Scenic Drives **Route 59.** The 50-mile drive from Fergus Falls to Detroit Lakes takes you through some of the region's prime lake country.

Important Addresses and Numbers

Tourist **Alexandria Resort Association** (206 N. Broadway, 56308, tel.
Information 612/763–3161). Open weekdays 8:30–5.

Detroit Lakes Regional Chamber of Commerce (700 Washington Ave., 56501, tel. 218/847–9202). Open weekdays 8–7, Saturday 8–5, Sunday 11–4; Labor Day–Memorial Day, weekdays 8–5.

Fargo/Moorhead Convention and Visitors Bureau (701 Main Ave., Fargo, ND 58107, tel. 701/237–6134). Open weekdays 8–5.

Fergus Falls Chamber of Commerce (202 S. Court St., 56537, tel. 218/736–6951). Open weekdays 8:30–5.

Thief River Falls Chamber of Commerce (413 N. 3rd St., 56701, tel. 218/681–3720). Open weekdays 8:30–5.

Emergencies Emergency numbers vary throughout the region; dialing "0" will bring an operator onto the line. Minnesota State Highway Patrol (tel. 612/452–7473).

Exploring Vikingland

Numbers in the margin correspond with points of interest on the Vikingland map.

Most visitors who come to the region drive to scenic areas and attractions. We begin exploring Vikingland in the south and move north to the Canadian border.

❶ It is possible that Viking explorers visited **Alexandria** in the 14th century. The first fur traders found the region to be a main camping ground for the Sioux and Chippewa Indians. Today Alexandria is in the center of a tourism and lakes region.

The **Runestone Museum** houses the Kensington Runestone, which reads: "[We are] 8 Goths and 22 Norwegians on [an] exploration journey from Vinland through the west . . ." Some studies appear to have confirmed the stone's authenticity, but its improbable location has also caused doubts. Other museum exhibits include 14th-century Viking implements, as well as pioneer and Indian artifacts. The **Fort Alexandria Agricultural Museum,** with displays depicting life in rural communities in the 19th and early 20th centuries, is in an adjacent building. Exhibits include antique autos and farm machinery. *206 N. Broadway, tel. 612/763–3161. Admission to both museums: $3 adults, $2 seniors over 65, $1 children 11–17. Open June–Aug., Mon.–Sat. 9–5, Sun. 10–5; Sept.–May, weekdays 9–5; closed holidays.*

❷ **Moorhead,** a city of nearly 30,000, is a regional service and agricultural center on the border of North Dakota. Moorhead State University is located here.

The **Comstock House** is the restored 1883 home of Solomon Comstock, founder of Moorhead State University. Furnishings, exhibits, and artifacts document the history of the surrounding Red River Valley. *506 8th St. S, tel. 218/233–0848. Admission: $2 adults, $1 children 6–16 and senior citizens. Open May 30–Sept. 30, weekends 1–5.*

The **Heritage Hjemkomst Interpretive Center** features the *Hjemkomst,* a 77-foot replica of an ancient Viking ship built by

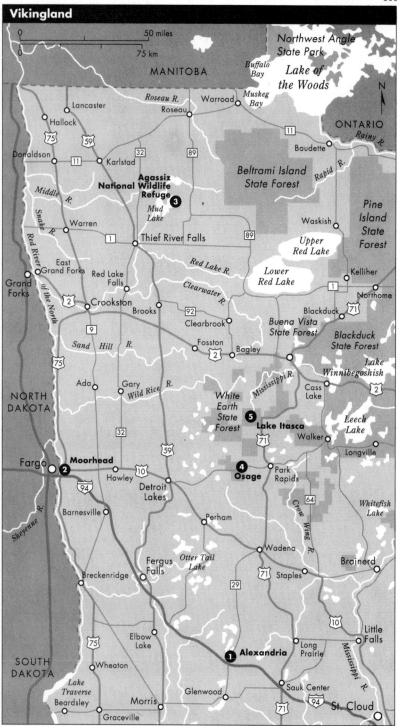

Moorhead junior high school counselor Robert Asp. Asp died of leukemia in 1980, before his dream of sailing the ship to Norway could come true. But in 1982, a 13-member crew, including three of Asp's sons and a daughter, sailed the ship 6,100 miles from Duluth to Bergen, Norway, in his memory. The voyage is documented through photos and a 30-minute video. The center also houses the **Clay County Historical** museum, which offers local history exhibits. *202 1st Ave. N, tel. 218/233–5604. Admission: $3.50 adults, $3 seniors over 60, $1.50 children 3–17. Open Memorial Day–Labor Day, Mon.–Sat. 9–5, Sun. noon–5; Sept.–May., daily noon–5.*

The **Plains Art Museum** offers changing exhibits of contemporary works by local and regional artists. The permanent collection includes both American Indian and West African art in a variety of media. *512 Main Ave., tel. 218/236–7171. Admission free. Open Tues.–Sun. noon–5.*

The **Rourke Art Gallery,** housed in a restored 1894 house, has collections of ceramics, photography, and 19th-century art. Special events and classes are held regularly. *523 S. 4th St., tel. 218/236–8861. Admission free. Open Wed.–Sun. noon–5.*

❸ The **Agassiz National Wildlife Refuge** is 61,000 acres of forest, lake, and marshland and is home to more than 245 species of birds and 41 species of mammals. There are self-guided auto tours of the refuge. *23 mi northeast of Thief River Falls on Rte. 32, then east on County Rd. 7, tel. 218/449–4115. Admission free. Open daily. Call for hrs.*

What to See and Do with Children

Alexandria: Runestone Museum
Moorhead: Heritage Hjemkomst Center
Osage: Village of Smoky Hills. *See* Off the Beaten Track.
Lake Itasca: Itasca State Park. *See* Off the Beaten Track.

Off the Beaten Track

❹ **Osage.** The **Village of Smoky Hills** is a re-created pioneer village where handicrafts including candle-dipping, spinning, paper-making, glassblowing, stenciling, blacksmithing, and quilting are demonstrated. Hands-on participation is encouraged. A lookout tower provides breathtaking views of the Smoky Hills State Forest. There are two restaurants. *Hwy. 34, tel. 218/573–3000. Admission: $4.75 adults, $2.50 children 6–16. Open Memorial Day–Labor Day, daily 10–6; Sept.–Oct., weekends 10–5.*

❺ **Lake Itasca.** The community and the lake have the same name. The source of the Mississippi River is here, in Itasca State Park. The Big Muddy is crystal clear, and so small that you can easily step across as it begins a 2,552-mile journey south to the Gulf of Mexico.
Itasca State Park was established in 1891 to preserve the region's remaining stands of virgin pine and to protect the headwaters of the Mississippi River. The park offers camping, a lodge, swimming beaches, biking and hiking trails, and in winter, cross-country skiing, and snowmobiling. Park naturalists lead hikes to view the flora and fauna and Indian burial mounds. *U.S. 71 and Rte. 92, tel. 218/266–3656. Admission: $3.50 vehicle permit. Open daily 8 AM–10 PM.*

Shopping

Good buys on craft items can be found in many communities. The **Village of Smoky Hills** is a good bet for blankets, candles, glassware, and other old-fashioned craft items. *In Osage, tel. 218/573–3700. Open Memorial Day–Labor Day, daily 10–6; Sept.–Oct., weekends 10–5; Thanksgiving weekend 10–5.*

Sports and Fitness

Beaches There are vast numbers of beaches in Vikingland to choose from. The region's state parks with swimming beaches include: **Buffalo River State Park** (Glyndon, tel. 218/498–2124), **Glacial Lakes** (Starbuck, tel. 612/239–2860), **Itasca State Park** (Lake Itasca, tel. 218/266–3656), **Lake Bronson State Park** (Lake Bronson, tel. 218/754–2200), **Maplewood State Park** (Pelican Rapids, tel. 218/863–8383), and **Old Mill State Park** (Argyle, tel. 218/437–8174). Admission: $3.50 vehicle permit.

Bicycling The peaceful woodland roads in the Alexandria, Detroit Lakes, Fergus Falls, and Lake Itasca areas offer excellent bicycling. There are 17 miles of biking trails within Itasca State Park.

Canoeing The lakes and rivers of Vikingland provide canoe waters to suit virtually any taste. The state canoe trail on the Red Lake River is 195 miles long and has campsites, accesses, and portages. The river passes through Thief River Falls, Crookston, and East Grand Rapids. The canoe trail is passable by novices except during high water.

Many state and local parks offer canoe campsites and trails traversing chains of lakes.

Minnesota requires that all canoes be licensed, either in Minnesota or your home state. Contact the DNR Information Center for license information. *500 Lafayette Rd., Box 40, St. Paul, 55146, tel. 612/296–6157. Open weekdays 8–4:30.*

Fishing Fishing throughout Vikingland is excellent; the waters contain muskellunge, walleye, bass, trout, and panfish. Local bait and tackle shops and resorts can recommend good fishing spots and help you contact local guides.

Contact DNR Information Center for fishing license information. *500 Lafayette Rd., Box 40, St. Paul, 55146, tel. 612/296–6157.*

Maps of more than 3,500 Minnesota lakes are available for $3 each, plus 6% tax and $1.50 for postage and handling, from the Minnesota State Document Center. *117 University Ave., St. Paul, 55135, tel. 612/297–3000.*

Golf There are numerous public golf courses in the Vikingland region.

Hawley Golf Club (Rte. 10 in Hawley, tel. 218/483–4808), 18 holes.
Village Green Public Golf Course (3240 Village Green Blvd., Moorhead, tel. 218/299–5366), nine holes.
Perham Lakeside Country Club (1½ mi north of Perham on County Rd. 8, tel. 218/346–6070), nine holes.

Skiing Downhill skiing is becoming increasingly popular in Minnesota;
Downhill the state's climate guarantees plenty of snow.

Andes Tower Hills Ski Area has 11 runs with 2 chair lifts, 2 rope tows, and snowmaking; longest run 1,320 feet, vertical drop 275 feet. There is equipment rental, a chalet, and food service. *15 mi west of Alexandria, tel. 612/965–2455 or 886–5420. Open Wed.–Fri. 1–9, weekends 10–9.*

Detroit Mountain Ski Area offers 11 runs with 1 chair lift, 1 T-bar, 1 rope tow, and snowmaking; longest run 1,720 feet, vertical drop 235 feet. Services include equipment rental and a chalet. *3 mi east of Detroit Lakes on Rte. 34, then 1 mi south on the township road, tel. 218/847–1661. Open Mon.–Wed. 11–5, Thurs. 11–9, Fri. 11–5, weekends 9:30–5.*

Old Smoky Ski Hill has 4 runs with 2 rope tows and snowmaking; longest run 600 feet, vertical drop 90 feet. *Fergus Falls, south on Union Ave., then west on Adolphus Ave., tel. 218/739–2251. Open weekdays 6–9 PM, weekends 1–9 PM.*

Cross-country Cross-country ski trails are found in city, county, and state parks throughout Vikingland, offering terrain that tests every level of skiing expertise.

Detroit Lakes maintains 42 miles of groomed trails around the community. Trail maps are available at the Detroit Lakes Regional Chamber of Commerce. *Box 348, 56501, tel. 218/847–9202.*

Itasca State Park (Lake Itasca, tel. 218/266–3656) has 31 miles of groomed trails ranging from beginner to expert level.

Maplewood State Park (Pelican Rapids, tel. 218/863–8383) offers 10½ miles of groomed trails.

Tennis Many resorts offer tennis facilities for their guests. Public tennis courts are usually found in local parks.

Spectator Sports

Baseball The Detroit Lakes Angels, an amateur baseball team, play several games each week at Washington Park (tel. 218/847–6106) during the summer.

College Sports Moorhead State University (1104 7th Ave. S, tel. 218/236–2622) fields baseball, men's and women's basketball, and football teams.

Curling The **Detroit Curling Club** (1/2 mi north of Detroit Lakes on U.S. 59, tel. 218/847–8186) has curling matches (roughly equivalent to shuffleboard played on ice) that are open to the public throughout the winter.

Dining and Lodging

Dining in the region, geared mainly to vacationers and tourists, is generally quite casual.

Lodging provides considerable variety. You'll find standard motels, hotels in the larger cities, and a good number of resorts, which range from minimal-amenity cabins for fishermen to plush facilities offering golf, tennis, saunas, whirlpools, indoor pools, private beaches, fine dining, and a host of other diversions.

Price categories for restaurants and hotels are the same as in the Minneapolis and St. Paul Dining and Lodging sections.

Alexandria **Fireside Steakhouse.** The dining room is a former railroad din-
Dining ing car. Charbroiled steaks are the house specialty. Salads, seafood, and chicken dishes round out the menu. *4417 Rte. 27*

E, tel. 612/763–6434. MC, V. No lunch; closed Feb., Easter, Thanksgiving, Dec. 24–25. Inexpensive–Moderate.

Travelers Inn Restaurant. Home cooking is featured in this newly redecorated cafe run by the same family since 1968. The menu includes light lunches, salads, sandwiches, chicken, and beef specials. *511 Broadway, tel. 612/763–4000. No credit cards. Closed Jan. 1, Thanksgiving, Dec. 25. Inexpensive.*

Lodging **Arrowwood Radisson Resort.** Set on the shores of Lake Darling, this luxury resort offers a host of amenities and diversions, and is open year-round. Overnight guests are welcome, but most people come for longer stays. *3½ mi north of I–94 exit 103, then ¾ mi west on County Rd. 82, and 2½ mi north on County Rd. 22, Box 639, 56308, tel. 612/762–1124. 170 rooms. Facilities: extensive grounds, 1 indoor pool, 1 outdoor pool, beach, sauna, whirlpool, rental boats, motors, and canoes, ski trails, rental snowmobiles, rental bicycles, playground, hay rides, sleigh rides, restaurants, cocktail lounge, entertainment; fee for water skiing, golf, tennis, skiing and equipment, riding and instruction. AE, CB, DC, MC, V. Very Expensive.*

Lake Itasca **Douglas Lodge.** This rustic state park lodge is set among the
Lodging green pines near the headwaters of the Mississippi. A fun place to stay, with facilities spread throughout the park. *2 mi west of the junction of U.S. 71 and Rte. 200 on Park Rd. in Itasca State Park. Lake Itasca, 56460, tel. 218/266–3656. Admission: $3.50 vehicle permit. 36 rustic rooms, 27 with bath. Common shower area. Facilities: playground, cafe nearby, grocery 2 mi, beach 3 mi, hiking trails, naturalist programs. Open Memorial Day–early Oct. No credit cards. Inexpensive.*

Moorhead **Tree Top Restaurant.** Located on the top floor of the Moorhead
Dining Federal Building, the dining room provides a panoramic view of the Moorhead/Fargo area. The luncheon menu offers sandwiches and salads; the dinner menu features a variety of traditional items with beef and seafood specialties. There is a cocktail lounge and entertainment. *403 Center Ave., tel. 218/ 233–1393. Reservations recommended. AE, DC, MC, V. No lunch Sun; closed major holidays. Moderate.*

Speak Easy Restaurant and Lounge. The restaurant re-creates a 1930s gangster theme with a 1931 Auburn roadster that once belonged to a notorious mob leader. The atmosphere is casual. The menu features American and Italian dishes, including pasta specials, along with steaks and seafood. There is a children's menu and a cocktail lounge. *1001 30th Ave., tel. 218/ 233–1326. Reservations recommended. AE, DC, MC, V. No lunch Sun.; closed Easter, Thanksgiving, Dec. 24–25. Inexpensive–Moderate.*

Lodging **Ramada Inn.** Conveniently located just off I–94, the inn offers numerous amenities. The public spaces are pleasant, and the rooms spacious and well kept. *600 30th Ave. S, 56560, tel. 218/ 233–6171. 175 rooms. Facilities: indoor pool, sauna, winter plug-ins, coffee shop, dining room, cocktail lounge, entertainment. AE, DC, MC, V. Moderate.*

The Arts

Theater L'Homme Dieu (tel. 612/846–3150), a summer theater affiliated with St. Cloud State University, presents a program of eight plays from June through August. *Located one mi north* *of Alexandria on Hwy. 29 to County Rd. 42, then west 3 mi to County Rd. 20, and north one-quarter mi, tel. 612/846–3150.*

Fargo–Moorhead Community Theater (333 S. 4th St., Fargo, tel. 701/235–1901) presents five main-stage and two children's plays annually.

The **Straw Hat Players** offer a variety of summer theater at the Center for the Arts (9th Ave. and 11th St., tel. 218/236–2271) on the Moorhead State University campus.

The **Fargo–Moorhead Symphony Orchestral Association** (810 4th Ave. S, tel. 701/233–8379) presents concerts featuring noted guest artists during its October through April season. Performance locations vary.

The **Fargo–Moorhead Civic Opera** (429 E. Main St., Fargo, tel. 701/282–3703) is the only full-time professional opera company between Minneapolis and Seattle. The company presents three operas during its October through May season.

Nightlife

Nightlife in Vikingland is centered on bars and cocktail lounges, many of which offer music and dancing. Larger resorts usually have some kind of musical entertainment during the summer. The music varies from polkas to country to rock, all played by the same group during the course of the evening.

Alexandria **Arrowwood.** This plush resort cocktail lounge offers live music and entertainment in the evenings. Most patrons are resort guests, but the public is welcome. *3½ mi north of I–94 exit 103, then ¾ mi west on County Rd. 82, and 2½ mi north on County Rd. 22, tel. 612/762–1124. Open to 1 AM. AE, CB, DC, MC, V.*
Bronc's on Broadway, Inc. A pleasant piano bar done in English decor. The adjoining restaurant serves Continental cuisine. *319 Broadway, tel. 612/763–3999. AE, MC, V.*

Moorhead **Speak Easy Restaurant and Lounge.** The decor is 1930s Chicago gangster chic and the bar claims to serve 300 specialty drinks. The restaurant serves Italian and American food. *1001 30th Ave. S, tel. 218/333–1326. Open to 1 AM. AE, DC, MC, V.*
Tree Top Restaurant. The cocktail lounge of this restaurant located atop the Federal Building offers music and entertainment evenings and a spectacular view of Moorhead/Fargo. A very pleasant spot. *403 Center Ave., tel. 218/233–1393. AE, DC, MC, V.*

Heartland

Running in a vertical strip up the center of the state, the Heartland region stretches from just north of the Twin Cities to Lake of the Woods. The northern section borders both Manitoba and Ontario, Canada.

The Heartland encompasses thousands of lakes and millions of acres of forest. This is the land of Paul Bunyan and his faithful companion, Babe, the Blue Ox. Legend says they cut the forests into clear land for the Scandinavian and German settlers who came to Minnesota in the last half of the 19th century. The region today is best known for its many lakeside resorts, although lumbering and farming are still important. It is in the

Heartland that Lake Itasca gives birth to the Mississippi River, and it is the Heartland that produced men like Charles A. Lindbergh and Sinclair Lewis. Tourism in the northern three-quarters of the region centers on sport fishing. The far northern reaches of the Heartland are quite remote.

Getting Around

By Plane Commercial air service is available to Bemidji and Brainerd. **Bemidji Municipal Airport** (tel. 218/751–2800) is served by **Bemidji Airlines** (tel. 800/221–8877) and **Northwest** (tel. 800/225–2525). Brainerd's **Crow Wing County Airport** is served by **Northwest** (tel. 800/225–2525).

By Car Most travel in the region is by car. I–94 crosses the southern section of the region. U.S. 10, U.S. 2, and Route 11 are major east–west arteries. U.S. 169, Route 371, and Route 72 traverse the region north–south.

By Bus **Greyhound** and **Trailways** provide service to the larger cities and towns.

By Train **Amtrak** (tel. 800/872–7245) provides service to St. Cloud on daily runs between Minneapolis and Seattle.

Scenic Drives **U.S. 2.** The 65-mile drive between Bemidji and Deer River runs through the lovely lake and forest scenery of Leech Lake Indian Reservation and National Forest.
Route 371. For 83 miles from the village of Cass Lake (14 mi west of Bemidji) to Brainerd, the road traverses some of the state's most scenic lake country.

Important Addresses and Numbers

Tourist Information **Baudette–Lake of the Woods Chamber of Commerce** (108 1st St. NE, 56623, tel. 218/634–1351). Open weekdays 9–5.
Bemidji Chamber of Commerce (300 Bemidji Ave., 56601, tel. 218/751–3541). Open weekdays 9–6 June–Aug., weekdays 9–4:30 Sept.–Oct.
Brainerd Chamber of Commerce (110 N. 6th St., 56401, tel. 218/829–2838). Open weekdays 8:30–5.
St. Cloud Chamber of Commerce (26 N. 6th St., Suite 100, 56302, tel. 612/251–2940). Open weekdays 9–5.
Sauk Centre Area Chamber of Commerce (1220 S. Main St., 56378, tel. 612/352–5201). Open weekdays 8:30–5.

Emergencies Emergency numbers vary throughout the region; dialing "0" will bring an operator onto the line.

Minnesota State Highway Patrol (tel. 612/452–7473).

Exploring the Heartland

Numbers in the margin correspond with points of interest on the Minnesota Heartland map.

Most visitors to the Heartland have come to see the scenery or are on fishing or camping excursions. We begin exploring in the south and move northward to Lake of the Woods on the Canadian border.

❶ A community of 3,700 at the foot of Big Sauk Lake, **Sauk Centre** is the Gopher Prairie in which Sinclair Lewis set his novel *Main Street* in 1920. Lewis, the first American to win the Nobel Prize

Heartland

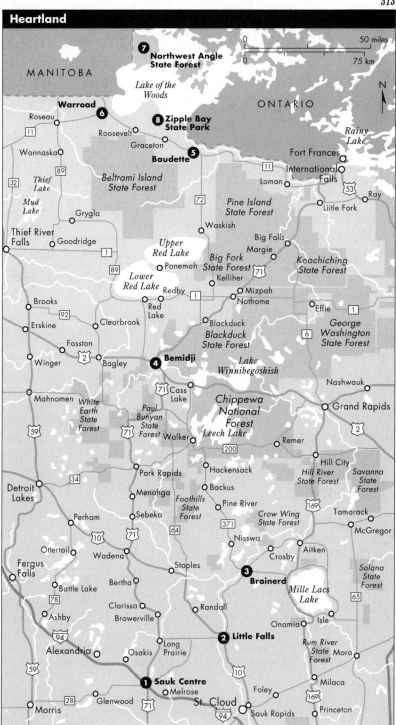

7 Northwest Angle State Forest

MANITOBA

Lake of the Woods

ONTARIO

N

50 miles

75 km

6 Warroad

Roseau

Roosevelt

8 Zipple Bay State Park

Graceton

5 Baudette

Rainy Lake

Fort Frances

International Falls

11

Loman

53

Ray

Wannaska

11

89

32

Thief Lake

Mud Lake

Grygla

Goodridge

Thief River Falls

1

89

Beltrami Island State Forest

72

Waskish

Pine Island State Forest

Liitle Fork

Big Falls

Margie

Koochiching State Forest

71

Effie

1

Upper Red Lake

Ponemah

Big Fork State Forest

Kelliher

Mizpah

Nothome

6

George Washington State Forest

Brooks

92

Lower Red Lake

Redby

1

Erskine

Clearbrook

Red Lake

Blackduck

Blackduck State Forest

Fosston

Winger

2

Bagley

4 Bemidji

Lake Winnibegoshish

Nashwauk

Mahnomen

White Earth State Forest

71

Cass Lake

Chippewa National Forest

Grand Rapids

2

59

Paul Bunyan State Forest

Walker

Leech Lake

200

Remer

Hill City

Hill River State Forest

Savanna State Forest

Detroit Lakes

34

Park Rapids

Hackensack

Menahga

Backus

Pine River

169

Tamarack

McGregor

Perham

10

71

Sebeka

Foothills State Forest

64

371

Crow Wing State Forest

Ottertail

Wadena

Nisswa

Aitken

Crosby

Solana State Forest

Fergus Falls

Battle Lake

78

Bertha

Staples

3 Brainerd

Mille Lacs Lake

65

Ashby

94

Clarissa

Browerville

Randall

Onamia

Isle

Alexandria

Osakis

Long Prairie

2 Little Falls

10

Rum River State Forest

Mora

Milaca

59

Morris

28

Glenwood

71

Melrose

1 Sauk Centre

St. Cloud

94

Foley

169

Princeton

Sauk Rapids

for literature, was born here in 1885 and grew up in a house on what is now Sinclair Lewis Avenue. Sauk Centre holds a three-day festival honoring the writer each July.

The **Sinclair Lewis Interpretive Center** exhibits old photos, memoranda, and plot notes in Lewis's own handwriting, along with the author's personal writing desk. There is a 15-minute audiovisual presentation on the author's life, and displays on the history of the area that influenced Lewis's writing. *Tourist rest stop at the junction of I–94 and U.S. 71, tel. 612/352–5201. Admission free. Open Memorial Day–Labor Day, daily 9:30–6; Sept.–May., weekdays 8–2 and by appointment.*

The **Sinclair Lewis Boyhood Home** is Lewis's restored childhood residence (circa 1900). The house contains period furniture, original artifacts and furnishings, and family memorabilia. *612 Sinclair Lewis Ave., tel. 612/352–5201. Admission: $1.50 adults, $1 senior citizens, 75¢ children 13–17, 50¢ children 6–12. Guided tours Memorial Day–Labor Day, daily 9:30–6; Sept.–May, by appointment.*

❷ Straddling the Mississippi River, **Little Falls** is named after the rapids that supplied power for the town's flour, lumber, and paper mills. Best known as the birthplace of Charles Lindbergh, Little Falls today is a center of paper-making and small boat manufacturing.

The **Charles A. Lindbergh House and Interpretive Center** is the boyhood home of the man who made the first solo nonstop trans-Atlantic flight from New York to Paris in 1927. The house has been restored to its turn-of-the-century appearance, and contains original furnishings. The center tells the story of the Lone Eagle's accomplishments. The exhibits focus on the famed New York–Paris flight, and an audiovisual program includes a recording of Lindbergh discussing the Atlantic crossing. Replicas of two of Lindbergh's planes, the *Spirit of St. Louis* and an early Jenny, hang from the ceiling. The home and center are in Charles A. Lindbergh State Park, which also has hiking trails and picnic areas. *½ mi west of Little Falls on Rte. 27, then 1 mi south on Lindbergh Dr., tel. 612/632–3154. Admission: $3.50 vehicle permit, house and center free. Open May–Oct. 15, daily 10–5; mid-Oct.–April., Sat. 10–4, Sun. noon–4, weekdays by appointment.*

Primeval Pine Grove Municipal Park contains a rare stand of virgin white pine and a small zoo with native species of animals including bear, elk, wolves, and deer. There are also picnic facilities. *1½ mi west on Rte. 27, tel. 612/632–2341. Admission free. Open daily May–Sept.*

At the park entrance is the **Dewey-Radke House,** a restored 1893 house containing 19th-century furnishings. *Located 1½ mi west on Rte. 27, tel. 612/632–5155. Free guided tours Tues.–Thurs. 11–5, Fri.–Sun. 11–6 May–Sept.*

Smuda's Zoo is a small zoo with more than 50 varieties of birds and animals from around the world, including an African lion, deer, and waterfowl. *2 mi south on Lindbergh Dr., tel. 612/632–4466. Admission: 50¢ adults, 25¢ children, under 7 free. Open May–Oct., daily 8 AM–9 PM.*

❸ **Brainerd** lies in the heart of the mythical Paul Bunyan country. Founded in 1871 when the Northern Pacific Railroad tracks were laid down, the community was named after the wife of a railroad official. The small city of 11,500 is a lumbering and paper mill center, with more than 465 lakes in the immediate area.

Visitors to the **Paul Bunyan Amusement Center** are greeted by an animated 26-foot statue of the lumberjack that spins tall tales of the north woods, along with a 15-foot statue of his faithful companion, Babe, the Blue Ox. The center offers a variety of children's rides, performing animals, a go-cart track, and picnic facilities. *2 mi west of Brainerd at the junction of Rtes. 210 and 371, tel. 218/829–6342. Admission: $3 adults, $4.75 children, $1.50 senior citizens (includes unlimited rides); additional fee for miniature golf and helicopter rides. Open Memorial Day–Labor Day, daily 10–9.*

Lumbertown USA is a re-created 1870s Minnesota logging town with more than 30 replicas and restorations of 19th-century buildings including a maple sugar plant, general store, ice cream parlor, and a pioneer home. There is also a wax museum and you can ride on a replica of a Northern Pacific train and the *Blue Berry Belle* riverboat. *4¾ mi north on Rte. 371, then 8 mi west on County Rd. 77. Admission: $2.50 adults, $2.25 seniors over 64, $1.50 children 5–11; train and boat rides are 60¢ extra. Open Memorial Day–Labor Day, daily 10–6; mid-May–Memorial Day and Labor Day–mid-Sept., 10–4.*

The **Crow Wing Historical Society Museum** has exhibits on county history, Indian artifacts, farm implements, and everyday life in late 19th-century rural Minnesota. The museum is housed in a building that was once the sheriff's house and local jail. *320 Laurel St., tel. 218/829–3268. Admission free. Open Memorial Day–Labor Day, Mon.–Sat. 1–5; Sept.–May, Tues.–Fri. 1–5.*

❹ **Bemidji** (beh-MID-jee) takes its name from a Chippewa Indian word meaning "lake with river flowing through." The community was a lumber boomtown in the late 19th century, then became a farming center when the forests were gone. New growth and controlled logging has given rise to some lumbering again, but the community is most noted as the center of a large resort area. Bemidji State University is located here.

According to legend, the biggest and strongest lumberjack ever to swing a double-bladed axe was born in Bemidji, delivered by five giant storks working in relay. His faithful companion Babe, the Blue Ox, was a birthday gift from his father on his first birthday. Babe eventually reached a size of seven axe handles between the eyes, a lot of bull, no matter how you measure it. To perpetuate the myth, the **Bunyan House Information Center** houses a collection of the fictitious lumberjack's tools and memorabilia explained with tongue-in-cheek descriptions. There is a "Fireplace of the States" built of stones from every state and Canadian province. A small historical and wildlife museum contains collections of antiques, Indian artifacts, and mounted wildlife trophies. The giant statues of Paul and Babe are reputed to be the most photographed statues in America. *Paul Bunyan Dr. (Rte. 197), tel. 218/751–3540. Admission: Information Center, free; museum, $1.25 adults, 50¢ children under 17, $2.50 family rate.*

The **Community Arts Center** features changing exhibits by local and regional artists. *426 Bemidji Ave., tel. 218/751–7570. Admission free. Open weekdays 9:30–3:30, Sun. 10–4 in summer.*

5 6 It's a 100-mile jump to **Baudette,** and slightly farther to **War-road,** the villages that are gateways to **Lake of the Woods,** the 2,000-square-mile lake that lies in the Canadian provinces of Manitoba and Ontario, and Minnesota. The lake has more than 7,000 miles of shoreline and contains some 15,000 islands.

7 **Northwest Angle State Forest,** on the massive lake's north shore, belongs to Minnesota. It is accessible only by air or water, or by road through Canada. The lake's cold blue waters are fabled fishing grounds, and there are few serious fishermen who don't dream of going "up north" to fish Lake of the Woods.

8 **Zipple Bay State Park** lies on the lake's south shore, and offers some 3,000 acres for hiking, swimming, picnicking, and snowmobiling. *1 mi East of Baudette on Rte. 11 to Rte. 172, then 12 mi north to County Rd. 8, and 9 mi west to the park. Admission: $3.50 vehicle permit.*

What to See and Do with Children

Brainerd: Paul Bunyan Amusement Center and Lumbertown USA

Bemidji: Bunyan House Information Center

Little Falls: Primeval Grove Municipal Park and Charles A. Lindbergh House and Interpretive Center

Park Rapids: Deer Town is a re-created frontier village with a large herd of deer, goats, geese, and sheep the youngsters will enjoy feeding by hand. There's a small museum, playground, observation tower, trout pond, and stagecoach rides, and performances by a trained bear. *1 mi north of Park Rapids on U.S. 71, tel. 218/732–5135. Admission: $3.50 adults, $3 seniors over 60, $2.50 children 3–11. Open Memorial Day–Labor Day, daily 9–6.*

Off the Beaten Track

Little Falls: The **Franciscan Sisters' Chapel** has beautiful Italian stained glass windows and artifacts depicting the order's history, including a collection of antique furniture. The sisters demonstrate making communion wafers. *116 8th Ave. SE, tel. 612/632–2981. Admission free. The chapel is open 1–4, or by appointment.*

Shopping

Summerhill Farm near Park Rapids features the works of more than 175 artists and craftspeople, and offers country collectibles, artwork, and handcrafted gifts. *7 mi north of Park Rapids on Rte. 71, tel. 218/732–3865. Open Mon.–Sat. 10–6, Sun. noon–4 in summer.*

Fort Milles Lacs Village offers gifts, toys, and Indian crafts along with a country store that has such Minnesota delicacies as wild rice, smoked trout, and maple syrup. *13 mi south of Garrison on U.S. 169, tel. 612/532–3651. Open daily 10–6.*

Elf Shelf and Gallery offers original wildlife paintings and limited-edition prints. *308 S. 6th St., Brainerd, tel. 218/829–2577. Open weekdays 9:30–5, Sat. 9:30–4.*

Sports and Fitness

Beaches There are literally thousands of lakeshore beaches in Minnesota's Heartland, and virtually every community in the region offers some sort of swimming beach. Among the state parks that have especially good beaches are **Milles Lacs Kathio State Park** (Onamia, tel. 612/532–3523), **Lake Bemidji State Park** (Bemidji, tel. 218/755–3843), and **Zipple Bay State Park** (Williams, tel. 218/783–6252).

Bicycling The Heartland bicycle trails and back-road routes offer varied terrain. The **Heartland Trail,** a blacktop-surfaced former railroad right-of-way, runs 27 miles between Park Rapids and Walker, passing through the eastern end of the Chippewa National Forest. A 123-mile loop route travels through Bemidji, Park Rapids, Walker, and portions of Itasca State Park.

Canoeing Canoeists have their choice of virtually every kind of water they can imagine, ranging from quiet lakes and streams, solitude on wilderness waters, to bank-to-bank canoes and companionship on some of the region's busier waters. If none of the literally thousands of lakes in the Heartland suit your fancy, Minnesota has designated a number of rivers as canoe trails, mapping them, and providing campsites and portages along the way.

River canoe trails in the Heartland region include 165 miles of the **Big Fork River** between Dora Lake and Rainy River, which has some intermediate-class rapids; 140 miles of the **Little Fork River** from Cook to Rainy River, with expert-class rapids; the **Crow Wing River,** 110 miles from Ackley to the Mississippi, suitable for novices; the **Imguadona River,** 23 miles between Lower Trelipe Lake and Leech Lake, suitable for novices; 536 miles of the **Mississippi River** from Lake Itasca to Anoka, suitable for novices; and 45 miles of the **Pine River** from Lake Hattie to the Mississippi, suitable for novices.

Golf A number of the larger resorts and several towns and cities in the region maintain golf courses. You'll have no difficulty finding courses to challenge your abilities.

Bemidji Town and Country Club (6 mi north on Birchmont Beach Rd., tel. 218/751–9215), 18 holes.
Brainerd Country Club (500 Golf Course Dr., tel. 218/751–9215), 18 holes; **Birch Bay Golf Course** (1771 Birch Dr. W, tel. 218/963–4488), 9 holes; **Madden's Resort** (Gull Lake, tel. 218/829–2811), 18 holes and 9 hole par 3.
Eagle View Golf Course (8½ mi north of Park Rapids on U.S. 71, tel. 218/732–7102), 18 holes; **Headwaters Country Club** (2 mi north on County Rd. 99, tel. 218/732–4832), 18 holes.

Skiing
Downhill **Buena Vista** offers 14 runs, 4 chair lifts, 1 rope tow, and snowmaking; longest run 1,800 feet, vertical drop 200 feet. There is cross-country skiing and equipment rental. *12 mi north of Bemidji on County Rd. 15, tel. 218/243–2231 or 751–5530.*
Eagle Mountain Resort has 11 runs, 3 rope tows, and snowmaking; longest run 2,000 feet, vertical drop 200 feet. There is cross-country skiing, equipment rental, and snow tubing. *Located 13 mi north of Freeport, tel. 612/573–2222. Open Fri. 3–10, Sat. and Sun 10–7.*
Powder Ridge Ski Area provides 9 runs, with 2 chair lifts, 2 rope tows, and snowmaking; longest run 2,400 feet, vertical drop

280 feet. Equipment rental and children's programs are offered. *15 mi south of St. Cloud on Rte. 15, tel. 612/398–7200. Open weekdays 10–10, weekends 9 AM–10 PM.*

Ski Gull Area has 7 runs with 4 chair lifts, and 1 T-bar; longest run 1,300 feet, vertical drop 200 feet. There is equipment rental. *North of Brainerd on Rte. 371, then 14 mi west on County Rd. 77, tel. 218/963–4353.*

Cross-country The wide popularity of the sport reflects both the long winters and the Scandinavian heritage of Minnesota's Heartland. Hundreds of miles of cross-country trails are maintained in state and local parks, and by private operators.

Milles Lacs Kathio State Park (Onamia, tel. 612/532–3523) offers 18 miles of groomed trails ranging from beginner to expert level. A warming shelter is available.

Lake Bemidji State Park (Bemidji, tel. 218/755–3843) has 10 miles of trails winding through virgin pine forests.

Tennis Many resorts have tennis courts for their guests; they are sometimes open to the public. Most communities have one or two courts in local parks.

Spectator Sports

Auto Racing The **Brainerd International Raceway** is the site of big-league drag and road racing. *Rte. 371, tel. 218/457–1500, racing weekends June–Aug. Call for race times.*

College Sports The St. Cloud State University Huskies play baseball, men's and women's basketball, and football. *Call 612/255–3102 for ticket information.*

Dining and Lodging

The casual resort atmosphere in the region means relaxed dining with an emphasis on home cooking.

This part of Minnesota offers a large number of resorts, with accommodations ranging from rustic cabins to plush resorts. You'll also find standard hotels and motels.

Price categories for restaurants and hotels are the same as in the Minneapolis and St. Paul Dining and Lodging sections.

Bemidji **Union Station** is a turn-of-the-century railroad depot converted
Dining to a restaurant. There are railroad artifacts and dining in a fun, casual atmosphere. The house specialty is prime rib, and a variety of Italian dishes including asparagus linguini and several kinds of pasta are served. There's a children's menu, cocktail lounge, and entertainment. *Union Sq., 1st St. and Beltrami Ave., tel. 218/751–9261. Reservations recommended. AE, DC, MC, V. Inexpensive–Moderate.*

Lodging **Holiday Inn–Bemidji.** The motel offers typical Holiday Inn modern decor, but the rooms and public spaces in this two-story motel are above average. *Box 307, 56601, tel. 218/751–9500 or 800/465–4329. 2½ mi west on U.S. 2. 119 rooms. Facilities: indoor pool, sauna, whirlpool, miniature golf, coin laundry, winter plug-ins, restaurant, cocktail lounge. AE, DC, MC, V. Moderate.*

Edgewater Hotel. True to its name, the hotel is located on the shores of Lake Bemidji. Along with standard rooms, there are housekeeping apartments and efficiency units. *1015 Paul Bun-*

yan Dr. NE, 56601, tel. 218/751–3600. 72 rooms. Facilities: 360-ft. sand beach, lake swimming, boats and canoes, dock, playground, sauna, whirlpool, steam room, winter plug-ins, restaurants nearby. AE, DC, MC, V. Inexpensive.

Brainerd
Dining

Bar Harbor Supper Club. You can make your way to this restaurant on the shore of Gull Lake by auto, boat, or snowmobile. The north-woodsy supper club specializes in charbroiled steaks, along with lobster and barbecued ribs. Luncheon menus offer lighter fare. There's a cocktail lounge with music and dancing. *6512 Interlachen Rd., tel. 218/963–2568. Located 14 mi north of Brainerd on Rte. 371 and 3 mi west on County Rd. 77. Reservations suggested. AE, DC, MC, V. Closed Easter, Thanksgiving, Dec. 24–25. Moderate.*

Pauline's Restaurant and Saloon. A popular spot, located just behind the Paul Bunyan Information Center, serving steaks, prime rib, and seafood specials. There is a children's menu, cocktail lounge, and entertainment. *1851 Excelsior Rd. N, tel. 218/829–2318. Dress: informal. Reservations recommended. MC, V. No lunch Sun; closed Jan. 1, Thanksgiving, Dec. 24–25. Inexpensive–Moderate.*

Lodging
★

Cragun's Pine Beach Lodge & Conference Center. This large, deluxe resort complex on the shore of Gull Lake offers a host of amenities and social programs. In winter there's ice fishing, cross-country and downhill skiing, dog sledding, and sleigh rides. About half the rooms have a fireplace and wet bar, others have private patios or poolside balconies. *2001 Pine Beach Rd., 56401, tel. 218/829–3591. 4¾ mi north on Rte. 371, then 6 mi west on County Rd. 77. 221 rooms. Facilities: indoor pool, beach, sauna, whirlpool, exercise room, boat, canoe and motor rentals, fishing, waterskiing, putting green, 4 tennis courts (2 lighted, 2 indoor), pony rides, 45-hole golf course, restaurant, cocktail lounge. AE, MC, V. Very Expensive.*

Paul Bunyan Motel. This medium-size motel offers more amenities than most, and is a cut above average all the way around. Some rooms have oversize beds. *1800 Fairview Dr., 56401, tel. 218/829–3571. 2 mi west at junction of Rtes. 210 and 371. 36 rooms. Facilities: indoor pool, sauna, whirlpool, winter plug-ins, 24-hr restaurant nearby. AE, MC, V. Inexpensive.*

Little Falls
Dining

Coach House Dining Room. The dining room in this comfortable restaurant is furnished in early-American decor. Walleye is a house specialty; there are beef and poultry dishes, and the baking is done on the premises. There is a children's menu and a cocktail lounge. *In the Pine Edge Inn, 308 1st St. E, tel. 612/632–6681. Dress: informal. Reservations advised for dinner. AE, MC, V. Closed Dec. 25. Inexpensive–Moderate.*

Lodging

Pine Edge Inn. The columns on the front of this pleasant motel located on the Mississippi River give it a colonial look that is carried out in the restaurant and some sleeping rooms. *308 1st St. NE, 56345, tel. 612/632–6681. 61 rooms. Facilities: outdoor pool, children's playground, cocktail lounge, restaurant. AE, MC, V. Inexpensive.*

Park Rapids
Dining

The River Room. This contemporary dining room provides views of the Fish Hook River. Steaks, seafood, salad bar, and Italian dishes are offered. There is a cocktail lounge. *In the Park Terrace Motel, U.S. 71 N, tel. 218/732–3344. Reservations suggested for dinner. MC, V. No lunch Sat., closed Dec. 24–25. Inexpensive–Moderate.*

Rapid River Logging Camp is a replica of a 19th-century logging camp dining hall featuring hearty family-style meals. Lunch and dinner offerings include chicken and beef, salads, and sandwiches, breakfast includes eggs, sausage, and pancakes. There are also logging demonstrations. *2 mi east on Rte. 34, then 4¾ mi north on Lake George Rd. (County Rd. 4), 2 mi west on County Rd. 18, then ¼ mi west on a dirt road, tel. 218/732–3444. No credit cards. Inexpensive.*

Lodging   **Park Terrace Motel.** This motel overlooks the Fish Hook River. The clean and comfortable rooms have a north-woods-modern decor; some have views of the river. Open year-round. *On U.S. 71 N, 56470, tel. 218/732–3344. 23 rooms. Facilities: boat and motor rental, beach, River Room restaurant. MC, V. Inexpensive.*

Sauk Centre   **Travel Host Motel.** This small-town motel is long on comfort, **Lodging**   easy on the budget, and open year-round. *Box 46, 56378, tel. 612/352–6581. On Rte. 71, ¼ mi north of I–94. 37 rooms. Facilities: cable TV, dining room, cocktail lounge. AE, DC, MC, V. Inexpensive.*

Warroad   The **Patch Restaurant.** Three contemporary dining areas fea-
Dining   ture fresh flowers on the table and views of the adjacent fruit orchards. The menu is strong on meat and potatoes dishes and home-baked pastries. Beer and wine are available. There is a children's menu. *In the Patch Motel, west of Warroad on Rte. 11, tel. 218/386–2082. MC, V. Inexpensive.*

Lodging   The **Patch Motel** lobby has color TV and a view of the swimming pool. It's not fancy (there's semi-truck parking) but the rooms are clean, spacious, and comfortable, as are the public spaces. *Box 501, 56763, tel. 218/836–2723. Located west of Warroad on Rte. 11. 75 rooms. Facilities: indoor pool, whirlpool, cable TV, baby-sitting service, winter plug-ins. MC, V. Inexpensive.*

The Arts

Bemidji   The **Paul Bunyan Playhouse** (530 Birchmont Beach Rd., tel. 218/751–7270) is the oldest professional summer theater in Minnesota. Eight plays are presented each summer in a 210-seat theater at Ruttger's Birchmont Lodge.

Brainerd   The **Heartland Symphony Orchestra** (1612 S. 7th St., tel. 218/829–7415) is a semiprofessional community orchestra presenting four concerts annually.

Warroad   The **Warroad Summer Theater** (Box 89, 56763, tel. 218/386–1024) offers several presentations, including drama, comedy, and musicals, during its June through August season. Performances are at the Warroad High School on Cedar Avenue.

Nightlife

Most nightlife is centered on bars and cocktail lounges.

Bemidji   The cocktail lounge in **Union Station,** an authentically converted 19th-century railroad depot, has interesting railroad decor and entertainment most nights. *At 1st St. and Beltrami Ave., tel. 218/751–9261. AE, DC, MC, V.*

Brainerd   **Madden's Resort** on Gull Lake has live entertainment in the cocktail lounge nightly during the summer season. Performers range from big bands to solo country and western artists. *On*

Pine Beach Rd., 4¾ mi north on Rte. 371 and 7¼ mi west on County Rd. 77, tel. 218/829–2811, ext. 202. No credit cards.
Pauline's Restaurant and Saloon. An upbeat cocktail lounge offering dancing nightly in summer to live bands and/or deejay music. *1851 Excelsior Rd. N, tel. 218/829–2318. MC, V.*
The **Loose Tie Saloon and Restaurant** has a fern bar with a fireplace that's a pleasant, relaxing spot for a nightcap. *501 Mall Germain (lower level), tel. 612/253–6646. Open until 1 AM. AE, CB, DC, MC, V.*

Sauk Centre The **Hayloft Lounge** is a quiet, friendly place for a drink. *At the Travel Host Motel, I–94 and Rte. 71, tel. 612/352–3786. Piano bar Wed.–Sat. 6:30–10. AE, DC, MC, V.*

Arrowhead

Slashed into a wedge shape by western Lake Superior, the Arrowhead region is a vast section of eastern and northeastern Minnesota running from just north of the Twin Cities along the Wisconsin border to Lake Superior, northeastward up the Superior shore to the Canadian border, and then westward some 300 miles. Outside of Minneapolis/St. Paul, the Arrowhead region north and east of Duluth may be the best-known section of Minnesota.

Every year, thousands travel Minnesota's famed North Shore as they drive the 1,300-mile-long Great Circle Route around Lake Superior. International Falls, on the Canadian border opposite Fort Frances, Ontario, is best known as the nation's coldest spot in winter. The Boundary Waters Canoe Area and Lake Superior National Forest draw thousands of campers and canoeists each year.

The Minnesota Iron ranges—the famed Mesabi Range, and the Virginia and Vermilion ranges—lie within the Arrowhead region, as does the bustling Great Lakes port of Duluth.

The far-northern sections of Arrowhead are among the most remote areas of the Midwest.

Getting Around

By Plane **Duluth International Airport** (tel. 218/727–2968), **Itasca County Airport** at Grand Rapids (tel. 218/326–6657), **Hibbing/ Chisholm Airport** (tel. 218/262–1268), and **International Falls International Airport** (Einerson Bros. Flying Service, tel. 218/ 283–4461), are all served by Northwest (tel. 800/225–2525).

By Car Most travel in the region is by car. I–35 connects Duluth with the Twin Cities and points south. U.S. 53 is the main north–south artery between Duluth, the Iron ranges, and International Falls, while U.S. 61 follows the Lake Superior shoreline.

By Train **Amtrak** (tel. 800/872–7245) provides rail service to Cambridge and Duluth.

By Bus **Greyhound** and **Trailways** provide service to the larger cities and towns.

Scenic Drives **U.S. 61.** The highway hugs the Lake Superior shore for 183 miles from Duluth to the Canadian border, providing spectacular views of the lake and its rocky shoreline.

Skyline Parkway Drive, Duluth. This 16-mile drive atop the 600-foot bluffs offers panoramic views of the city and harbor.

Important Addresses and Numbers

Tourist Information

Chisholm Area Chamber of Commerce (327 Lake St., 55719, tel. 218/254–3600). Open weekdays 8–4:30.

Duluth Convention and Visitors Bureau (Endion Station, 100 Lake Place Dr., 55828, tel. 218/722–4011). Open weekdays 8:30–5.

Eveleth Area Chamber of Commerce (Hat Trick Ave., 55734, tel. 218/744–1940). Open weekdays 9–5.

Grand Marais Chamber of Commerce (200 W. U.S. 61, 55604, tel. 218/387–2524). The Visitors Center in the Municipal Building is open May 15–Oct. 15, daily 8–8; mid-Oct.–mid-Apr., 9–5.

Grand Rapids Visitors and Convention Bureau (1 N.W. 3rd St., tel. 218/326–9607). Open weekdays 9–5.

Hibbing Area Chamber of Commerce (303 E. 19th St., tel. 218/262–3895). Open weekdays 8:30–4:30.

Greater International Falls Chamber of Commerce (Hwy. 53 and 19th St., tel. 218/283–9400). Open weekdays 8–5.

Two Harbors Area Development Corp. (Box 39, 55616, tel. 218/834–2600). The Information Center on U.S. 61 is open Memorial Day–Labor Day, Mon.–Thurs. 9–7, Fri. and Sat. 8–8, Sun. 8–7; Labor Day–Memorial Day, Mon.–Sat 9–5.

Emergencies

Emergency numbers vary throughout the region; dialing "0" will bring an operator onto the line.

Minnesota State Highway Patrol (tel. 612/452–7473).

Exploring Arrowhead

Numbers in the margin correspond with points of interest on the Minnesota Arrowhead map.

The region is large, and the northern sections are remote. We begin at Duluth, Minnesota's fourth largest city.

❶ With a population of 93,000, **Duluth** is Minnesota's fourth largest city and, along with its twin city of Superior, Wisconsin, a major U.S. seaport. Using the St. Lawrence Seaway, ships from around the world call at Duluth–Superior, dropping anchor 2,342 miles from the Atlantic Ocean.

The man after whom Duluth is named, explorer Daniel de Greysolon, Sieur du Luth, stepped ashore here in 1679. Duluth became an important fur-trading center and jumping-off point to the west, but the traders came and went for nearly a century and permanent settlement did not begin until 1853. Minnesota Point, a narrow, seven-mile-long sand spit, creates a natural breakwater at the mouth of the harbor. The point has beaches, marinas, a seaplane base, and excellent views of the harbor and city. With the development of the iron ranges in the late 1800s, Duluth became an important rail terminus and Lake Superior port; by the turn of the century, it was a city of wealth and power.

Although the iron and steel industries have fallen on hard times, Duluth–Superior remains an important Great Lakes port. Duluth is the cultural, economic, and recreation center of northern Minnesota. The University of Minnesota–Duluth is located here.

The symbol of Duluth is the **Aerial Lift Bridge,** which connects the mainland with Minnesota Point at the mouth of the harbor. The 386-foot bridge must be raised to allow ships in and out of port, and the entire bridge floor can be lifted 138 feet in less than a minute.

The **Canal Park Museum,** adjacent to the Aerial Lift Bridge, is Duluth's most popular waterfront attraction. Exhibits about the history of Lake Superior shipping and Duluth–Superior Harbor include models, shipwreck relics, films, and reconstructed ships' cabins. Located at the harbor entrance, the small museum and grounds offer close-up views of passing ships and the bridge rising. *1st Ave. at the foot of Main St., tel. 218/727–2497. Admission free. Open June–Aug., daily 10–9; May and Sept.–Dec. 15, daily 10–6; mid-Dec.–Apr., Fri.–Sun. 10–4:30. Hot line for up-to-the-minute information about ship schedules, tel. 218/722–6489.*

The **St. Louis County Heritage and Arts Center,** better known as the **Depot,** is in the restored Union Depot, built in 1892. There are four levels of living history and art exhibits including a replica of a fur-trading post, toy and doll collections, and exhibits on exploration and settlement. Depot Square, a re-creation of turn-of-the-century Duluth, has old-time streets and 24 period stores, including a silent-movie theater and ice cream parlor. The Immigration Room, through which many of the early settlers passed, has been restored to its original state.

The **Lake Superior Museum of Transportation,** also located in the restored Union Depot, has fine train exhibits, including the first locomotive in Minnesota and one of the most powerful steam locomotives ever built. The restored Union Depot is also home to the *Duluth Ballet, Duluth Symphony, Duluth Playhouse,* and the *Duluth Art Institute. 506 W. Michigan St., tel. 218/727–8025. Admission: $3.50 adults, $2.75 seniors over 60, $1.75 children 6–17, $10 family. Open Memorial Day–mid-Oct., daily 10–5; mid-Oct.–May, Mon.–Sat. 10–5, Sun. 1–5.*

Two-hour narrated tours of the Duluth–Superior Harbor take you past the world's largest ore docks, grain elevators, giant lake freighters, and ships from many countries. Weather permitting, the S.S. *Vista Queen* and S.S. *Vista King* pass under the Aerial Bridge for a short jaunt onto Lake Superior. When the harbor is busy, it's one of the most popular boat tours in all of Michigan, Wisconsin, and Minnesota. *Duluth–Superior Excursions, tel. 218/722–6218. Cruises from the Arena-Auditorium Dock at the foot of W. 5th Ave. Fare: $6.50 adults, $5.50 senior citizens, $3 children 3–11. Cruises late June–Labor Day, hourly 9:30–7:30; May–late June and Labor Day–mid-Oct., every 2 hrs 9:30–5:30.*

The S.S. *William A. Irvin,* a Great Lakes ore boat built in 1938, is permanently moored near the Duluth Arena-Auditorium. The 598-foot-long vessel could carry 14,000 tons of iron ore, enough to fill 200 train cars. It was retired in 1978, after 40 years of active service. Forty-five-minute guided tours take you throughout the refurbished ship, from the pilot house through crew's quarters and dining rooms, to the engine room below. The tour involves considerable walking, and

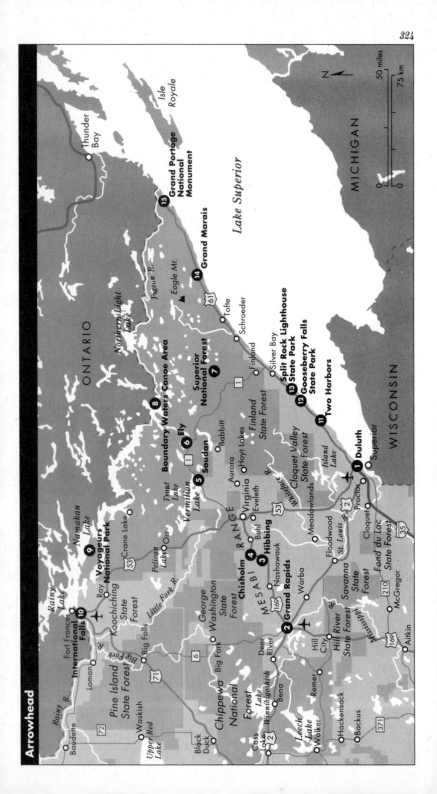

Arrowhead

there are 16 stairways aboard the ship. *350 S. 5th Ave.
W, tel. 218/722–5573. Admission: $3.50 adults, $1.50 children
under 12. Open May–Oct., daily 10–6.*

Moving away from the harbor, the University of Minnesota–
Duluth **Tweed Museum of Art** has six galleries presenting exhibits from the Tweed collection of 16th- through 20th-century
paintings, along with works by contemporary American artists, students, and faculty. *2400 Oakland Ave., tel. 218/726–
8222. Admission free. Open Tues.–Fri. 9–4:30, weekends 1–5;
closed Mon. and holidays.*

Duluth Zoological Gardens has more than 500 animals from
throughout the world. There's a zoo nursery and children's zoo
along with special exhibits of nocturnal animals. *2nd Ave. W
and Grand Ave., tel. 218/624–1502. Admission: $1.50 adults,
75¢ children 6–12. Open May 15–Labor Day, daily 9–6; mid-
Apr.–mid-May and Labor Day–mid-Oct., weekends 9–6; mid-
Oct.–mid-Apr., daily 9–4. Closed Jan. 1, Thanksgiving, Dec.
25.*

The elegance of Duluth at the turn of the century is revived at
Glensheen, the restored 39-room Jacobean-style mansion of at-
torney, mining entrepreneur, and state legislator Chester
Congdon. The house is furnished with period pieces and antiques, including some original furnishings. There are seven
and one-half acres of grounds overlooking Lake Superior, and
lovely formal gardens. The carriage house holds a collection of
carriages and sleighs. *3300 London Rd., tel. 218/724–8863. Admission: $4.75 adults, $3.50 children 13–17 and senior
citizens, $2.25 children under 13. Guided tours mid-May–mid-
Oct., Mon.–Tues. and Thurs.–Sun 9–3; mid-Oct.–mid-May,
Mon.–Tues. and Thurs.–Fri. at 1 and 2, Sun. 1–3. Closed Jan.
1, Easter, Thanksgiving, Dec. 25.*

② **Grand Rapids,** situated at the western edge of the Mesabi
Range, is a former logging town that has become a paper production and iron mining and processing center.

The **Forest History Center** is an interpretive center with exhibits explaining man's life in the forests since prehistoric times.
There is a replica of a full-size early-1900s logging camp, a 1934
Forest Service cabin and fire tower, and a modern pine planta-
tion with genetically improved trees, as well as two miles of
nature and hiking trails along the Mississippi River. *¾ mi south
on U.S. 169, then 1 mi west on County Rd. 23, and ½ mi north
on County Rd. 76, tel. 218/327–4482. Guided tours. Admission:
$2 adults, $1 children under 16 and senior citizens. Open May
15–Oct. 15, daily 10–5; mid-Oct.–mid-May, daily noon–4.*

The **Central School Heritage and Arts Center** is a restored
schoolhouse (1895) that houses gift shops, an art gallery, a museum, and a restaurant. Exhibits include a turn-of-the-century
Main Street and local history artifacts and exhibits. *At 10 N.W.
5th St., tel. 218/327–1843. Admission free. Open Memorial
Day–Labor Day, Mon.–Sat. 9:30–5:30, Sun. noon–4:30; mid-
Sept.–May, Mon.–Sat. 8:30–5:30.*

③ Founded in 1883, **Hibbing** was a logging town until the discovery of iron ore in the Mesabi Range caused the community to
pick up and move two miles closer to the ore. The Greyhound
Bus system began here in 1914, as a commuter service between
the old and the new town sites. Plants in the area develop taco-

nite, turning low-grade ore into a rich iron ore concentrate. Hibbing is also the hometown of folk singer Bob Dylan.

The **Hull-Rust Mine** covers 1,600 acres and at five miles long, two miles wide, and 500 feet deep, is one of the largest open pit mines in the world. The scale of the place is nearly overwhelming. *1½ mi north on 3rd Ave. E. Free viewing stand mid-May–Sept., open daily 9–5.*

Paulucci Space Theater has an exhibit hall and multimedia theater with a large curved screen, star projector, and computerized space effects equipment. Programs on astronomy, space exploration, and the environment are presented throughout the year. *East 23rd St. and U.S. 169, tel. 218/262–6720. Admission: $2.50 adults, $2 senior citizens, $1 children under 17. Daily shows Memorial Day–Labor Day at 2, 4, and 7; Sept.–May Fri. at 7, Sat.–Sun. at 2.*

4 **Ironworld USA** is a 15-acre park on the very edge of the Glen open-pit iron mine near Chisholm. The peaceful setting includes waterfalls, gardens, walking trails, and a 1,600-seat outdoor amphitheater that features big-name entertainment during the summer. The park's interpretive center offers presentations on the Arrowhead region's culture and heritage, and the development of the iron mining industry. There is also a research center and genealogical library. A 1920s streetcar takes visitors to an excursion train which provides a panoramic trip along the historic Glen Mine. There are ethnic food and craft demonstrations, and a variety of festivals during the summer. *½ mi southwest of Chisholm on U.S. 169, tel. 218/254–3321. Admission: $5.25 adults, $4.75 senior citizens, $3 children 7–17. Open Memorial Day–Sept., daily 10 AM; closing times vary.*

The nearby **Minnesota Museum of Mining** provides a history of 70 years of mining with indoor and outdoor exhibits of drills, ore cars, mining trucks, steam engines, and a replica of an underground drift. There are slide presentations and guided tours. *In Memorial Park, U.S. 169 at Main St., tel. 218/254–5543. Admission: $2 adults, $1 children 5–18. Open Memorial Day–Sept. 15, daily 9–5.*

5 **Tower-Soudan State Park** lies on the shores of Vermilion, Lake within the Vermilion iron range, and offers a picnic area, snowmobile trails, and self-guided walking trails. The Soudan Mine, Minnesota's largest and oldest iron mine, which operated until 1962, is within the park. Mine tours include a ride in an elevator 2,400 feet down to the 27th level, where an electric train takes you 3,000 feet through a tunnel to the area where the last of the mining was done. *½ mi north of Rte. 169, tel. 218/753–2245. Tours include the ore-crushing area and the 90-ft-high headframe. State park admission: $3.50 vehicle permit; mine tour, $3 adults, $1.50 children under 17. Tours June 1–Labor Day, daily 9–4.*

6
7 **Ely** is a small vacation and resort community serving as the gateway and supply community for those entering **Superior**
8 **National Forest** and the **Boundary Waters Canoe Area (BWCA).** The 3-million-acre forest stretches for 150 miles along the Minnesota–Canada border adjacent to Ontario's Quetico Provincial Park.

One million acres has been set aside as the BWCA, an area with several thousand lakes linked by short portages, and where motor boats are banned. The National Forest Information Center (118 S. 4th Ave., 218/365–6185) has information about travel in the BWCA and throughout the national forest. *Contact BWCA Reservations, Superior National Forest, Box 338, Duluth, 55801, tel. 218/720–5440 for permits to enter BWCA May–Sept.*

9 Dedicated in 1975, the 218,000-acre **Voyageurs National Park** commemorates the French-Canadian *voyageurs*, who were the backbone of the 17th–19th-century fur trade. These hardy men paddled the fur-laden canoes and carried them during portages from lake to lake. The 30 major lakes in Voyageurs National Park form part of the water highway that stretches from Lake Superior to Lake of the Woods. Activities within the park include hiking, canoeing, guided boat tours, motorboating, fishing, cross-country skiing, and camping. Naturalist-led boat trips and hikes are offered during the summer. Park headquarters are located at South International Falls; the Rainy Lake Visitor Center is open year-round. *Admission free. For additional information contact Superintendent, Voyageurs National Park, Box 50, International Falls, 56649, tel. 218/ 283–9821.*

10 Chances are you've heard of **International Falls** because it was mentioned on TV or radio as the coldest spot in the nation one winter day. Located nearly 300 miles north of the Twin Cities, the community of 5,600 manufactures paper and serves tourists, and is a port of entry to Ontario, Canada. Ice Box Days is a week-long festival in mid-January, which includes snow sculpture, ice fishing contests, and a Freeze Yer Gizzard Blizzard Run.

Smokey Bear Park (3rd St. and 6th Ave.) has a 26-foot-tall likeness of the well-known bear. **Koochiching County Historical Museum,** within the park, has exhibits about Indian artifacts, gold mining, early settlement, and farm machinery. There are paintings and audiovisual programs. *6th Ave. and 2nd St., tel. 218/283–4316. Admission: $1 adults, 50¢ children under 12. Open mid-May–mid-Sept., Mon.–Sat. 10–4.*

Boise Cascade offers guided tours of its paper-mill operations in the summer. Children under 10 not admitted, cameras not permitted. *2nd St., tel. 218/283–9400. Admission free. Call for days and hours of tours.*

Grand Mound Interpretive Center contains one of the largest prehistoric burial mounds in the Upper Midwest. A museum offers exhibits on early Indian cultures, wildlife, and audiovisual programs about the mounds. *17 mi west of International Falls on Rte. 11, tel. 218/279–3332. Admission free. Open May–Labor Day, Tues.–Sun. 10–5; Sept.–Apr., Sat. 10–4, Sun. noon–4.*

We return now to Duluth and travel northeast, exploring the north shore of Lake Superior. As you leave Duluth on U.S. 61, signs will urge you to leave the new highway and take "old" 61 along the lakeshore for 22 miles to Two Harbors. Do it! The scenic route goes through the tiny villages of French River and Yellow Knife, where rivers cascade down from lakeshore bluffs to Lake Superior.

11 **Two Harbors** was the first of Minnesota's Lake Superior iron ports. It earned its name from its twin harbors, Agate Bay and

Burlington Bay. **Van Haven Lake Front Park** provides views of the giant loading docks on Agate Bay; you may be able to watch a giant freighter loading ore destined for a lower lakes port.

The **Lake County Historical Museum** is in the former railroad depot (1907). It contains displays about railroading, logging, iron mining, commercial fishing, and Great Lakes shipping. Outdoor exhibits include the *Three Spot*, the first locomotive used in the area, and a Mallett, one of the world's most powerful steam locomotives. It's one of those interesting, cluttered little museums where you can spend hours. *Foot of Waterfront Dr., tel. 218/834-4898. Admission: $1 adults, 50¢ children under 12. Open Memorial Day–Oct. 15, Mon.–Sat. 9–4, Sun. 1–4.*

The Gooseberry River, which surges through the 1,600-acre **Gooseberry Falls State Park** on the shores of Lake Superior, has five waterfalls, two of which are more than 30 feet high. There are hiking trails, a park interpretive center, camping and picnic areas. *13 mi north of Two Rivers on U.S. 61, tel. 218/834-3855. Admission: $3.50 vehicle permit. Open daily 8 AM–10 PM.*

The 54-foot octagonal **Split Rock Lighthouse,** which still warns ships away from the dangerous cliffs that line the shore, is the most visited lighthouse on the Great Lakes. Built atop a 100-foot bluff in 1910, the light is 168 feet above the surface of Lake Superior. When the light was automated in 1961, the lighthouse, land, and other buildings became a state park. You can tour the light and tower, foghorn building, and keeper's quarters. An interpretive center has exhibits and videos on the construction of the lighthouse and its operation. *Split Rock Lighthouse State Park, 18 mi northwest of Two Harbors on U.S. 61, tel. 218/226-4372. Admission: $3.50 vehicle permit. Open May 15–Oct. 15, daily 9–5.*

The scenery is outstanding as you continue along U.S. 61, but you'll want to take note of two communities. The world's first large-scale taconite manufacturing plant is located in **Silver Bay,** an incorporated village built in 1955 by Reserve Mining for its employees and their families. **Tettegouche State Park** is located near Silver Bay, and **Baptism River Falls,** one of the highest waterfalls in Minnesota, is in the scenic river gorge.

Taconite Harbor was built by the Erie Mining Company. Concentrated ore pellets from the company's taconite processing plant about 65 miles to the west are loaded on Great Lakes freighters here. An observation stand offers a view of shiploading operations.

Grand Marais is a village of 1,300 located at an excellent natural harbor. It's a bustling little town, and one of the jumping-off places for trips to the Superior National Forest and Boundary Waters Canoe Area. The Gunflint Trail, a hiking and cross-country ski trail that runs northwest to Saganaga Lake on the Canadian border, begins here. Nearby **Cascade Falls State Park** features a 50-foot-high waterfall.

The **Grand Portage National Monument** marks the site of the Grand Portage, the "great carrying place," a nine-mile trail that bypasses some 20 miles of waterfalls and rapids near the mouth of the Pigeon River on Lake Superior. The trail was first used and named by French fur traders and *voyageurs* in 1722 as a route into and out of the Canadian wilderness. In 1779 the Montreal-based North West Company made the site on the south bank of the Pigeon River its inland headquarters and built a trading post here. An annual exchange of goods known as Rendezvous (the equivalent of an 18th-century north-woods block party) took place each summer, accompanied by games, drinking, fighting, and similar activities.

As the site of the earliest settlement in Minnesota, Grand Portage has been partially reconstructed on the basis of archaeological evidence. A stockade, Great Hall, kitchen, and other buildings re-create the setting of the fur-trading post that stood here more than 200 years ago and there are artifacts from the voyageur era. Ranger-historians are on duty at an information center where craft demonstrations and interpretive programs are offered. Visitors may hike an eight-and-one-half-mile trail along the portage route. *38 mi northeast of Grand Marais on U.S. 61, tel. 218/387–2788. Admission: $1 adults, children under 13 and seniors over 61 free, maximum charge $3 per car. Open mid-May–mid-Oct., daily 8–5. Additional information available from the Superintendent, Grand Portage National Monument, Box 666, Grand Marais, 55603, tel. 218/387–2788.*

What to See and Do with Children

Chisholm: Ironworld and Minnesota Mining Museum
Duluth: Aerial Lift Bridge, Canal Park Museum, The Depot, Duluth–Superior Harbor Excursions, and Zoological Gardens
Grand Portage: Grand Portage National Monument
Hibbing: Hull-Rust Mine and Paulucci Space Theater
International Falls: Voyageur National Park
Two Harbors: Gooseberry Falls State Park and Split Rock Lighthouse State Park

Off the Beaten Track

Ore Docks Observation Platform. The Duluth, Mesabi, and Iron Range Railway Company docks extend over 2,000 feet into the harbor. There's an excellent view of the ship-loading operation from the observation platform. *35th Ave. and Superior St., Duluth. Admission free. Open daily, dusk to dawn.*

Shopping

Even small communities in resort areas have boutiques, art galleries, and local craft shops. Many are open only in summer.

Fitger's in Duluth is a shopping mall built in a refurbished 19th-century waterfront brewery that has more than 30 specialty shops and restaurants. *600 E. Superior St., tel. 218/722–8826. Open Mon.–Sat. 10–9, Sun. noon–5.*
Made in the Shade in Duluth offers a collection of crafts made by American artisans from Maine to California. There are hand-blown glass, leather, metal, and fiberwork items, toys, and hand-dipped candles. *325 W. Superior St., Duluth, tel. 218/722–1929. Open Mon.–Sat. 10–9, Sun. 11–5 in summer.*
The **Pioneer Crafts Co-op** near Two Harbors has a selection of handmade crafts and art produced by local and regional craftspeople. *4½ mi northwest of Two Harbors on U.S. 61, tel. 218/834–4175. Open June–Sept., daily 9–7; Oct.–May, weekends 9–5.*

Sports and Fitness

Beaches With the thousands of lakes in the Arrowhead region, finding a swimming beach is not difficult. Many resorts and local parks offer both beaches and pools. Minnesota Point, the sand spit at the harbor entrance, has several unguarded sand beaches. There is little swimming in Lake Superior, because the water is so very cold. **St. Croix State Park** (Hinkley, tel. 612/384–6591), **McCarthy Beach State Park** (Hibbing, tel. 218/254–2411), and **Moose Lake State Park** (Moose Lake, tel. 218/485–4059) all offer swimming beaches. A $3.50 vehicle sticker is required for admission.

Bicycling Quiet back roads and beautiful scenery make biking in Arrowhead country a pleasure. The state has created a number of bike trails on abandoned railroad right-of-ways. The black-topped, 32-mile Hinkley Fire Trail runs between Hinkley and Moose Lake, winding through a now-green area that was the scene of a devastating forest fire in 1894.

In other areas, scenic roads have been designated as state bike routes. The 22-mile **North Shore Bike Route** takes cyclists along old Route 61 between Duluth and Two Harbors and provides spectacular views of the Lake Superior shoreline.

Canoeing Minnesota's Arrowhead region contains some of the finest canoe waters in the nation, including the **Boundary Waters Canoe Area (BWCA)** and other sections of the **Superior National Forest, Voyageurs National Park,** and the **St. Croix National Scenic Waterway.**

Minnesota has designated several rivers in Arrowhead country as canoe routes, and maintains portage trails, rest areas, and campsites. Among them are the Cloquet, Kettle, Mississippi, St. Croix, St. Louis, and Vermilion rivers. Maps are available.

Fishing The waters in the northern sections of the Arrowhead area are the big league of Midwest sport fishing. The thousands of lakes, streams, and rivers offer walleye, muskellunge, northern pike, bass, trout, and various species of panfish. Lake Superior offers a variety of fish including lake trout and Pacific salmon. "Big game" charter-boat operators are found in most Lake Superior ports, with more than a dozen operating out of Duluth. If you're fishing inland waters, resorts and bait and tackle shops can help you locate fishing hot spots or local guides.

The Twin Ports Fishing Guide contains information on fishing in the Duluth region, including charter fishing information, fish identification, and where and how to fish for various species. The Duluth Convention and Visitors Bureau distributes free copies.

Golf Despite the northern clime, golf is popular here, and the Arrowhead region offers excellent courses.

Duluth has three public golf courses: **Enger Park** (1801 W. Boulevard St., tel. 218/722–5044), 18 holes; **Grandview Park** (9859 Grandview Rd., tel. 218/624–3452), 9 holes; **Lester Park** (Lester River Rd. and U.S. 61, tel. 218/525–1400), 18 holes. **Sugar Hills & Lodge** (on the north shore of Sugar Lake, tel. 218/326–9461), 9 holes; **Pokegama Golf Club** (1 mi east on Rte. 23 on Pokegama Lake, tel. 218/326–3444), 18 holes.

Two Harbors. **Superior Shores Golf Course** (1 mi north on U.S. 61, tel. 218/834–5042), 18 holes.

Skiing
Downhill
Some of the best downhill skiing in Minnesota is found in Arrowhead country.

Chester Municipal Park offers 3 runs and 1 rope tow; longest run 1,000 feet, vertical drop 160 feet. Services include children's programs, free ski lessons Jan.–Feb. *1 mi west of University of Minnesota–Duluth campus off Skyline Dr., tel. 218/723–3337. Open Tues., Thurs., and Fri. 5–9, weekends 11–4:30.*

Giant's Ridge Recreation Area has 15 runs, 4 chair lifts, 1 T-bar, and snowmaking; longest run 3,500 feet, vertical drop 165 feet. Cross-country skiing, equipment rental, and children's programs are offered. *4 mi east of Biwabik on County Rd. 416, tel. 218/262–7669. Call for hrs.*

Hidden Valley Recreation Area offers 4 runs, 1 T-bar, 1 rope tow; longest run 1,800 feet, vertical drop 165 feet. There is cross-country skiing, equipment rental, and a world-class 60-meter ski jump. *Rte. 169 east from Ely, then 1 mi north on Hidden Valley Rd., tel. 218/365–3097. Open weekends 11–5; call for additional hrs.*

Lutsen Mountain Resort has 27 runs, 4 chair lifts, 2 T-bars, and snowmaking; longest run 6,000 feet, vertical drop 800 feet. Services include cross-country skiing, equipment rental, children's programs, racing programs. *Located 90 mi northeast of Duluth on U.S. 61, tel. 218/663–7281. Call for hrs.*

Quadna Mountain Resort offers 15 runs, 1 chair lift, 2 T-bars, and snowmaking; longest run 2,640 feet, vertical drop 350 feet. Services include cross-country skiing, equipment rental, snowmobile trails. *Quadna Rd. south of Hill City off U.S. 169, tel. 800/422–6649. Open daily 9–4:30.*

Spirit Mountain Ski Area has 14 runs, 4 chair lifts, 1 T-bar, 1 rope tow, and snowmaking; longest run 5,400 feet, vertical drop 700 feet. Services include cross-country skiing, equipment rental, instruction. *10 mi south of Duluth off I–35, exit 249, tel. 800/247–0146. Open weekdays 10–9, weekends 9–9.*

Sugar Hills Lodge Resort has 23 runs, 2 chair lifts, 4 T-bars, 1 rope tow, and snowmaking; longest run 2,500 feet, vertical drop 400 feet. Services include cross-country skiing, equipment rental, and a fitness center. *7 mi south of Grand Rapids on U.S. 169, tel. 218/326–9461. Call for hrs.*

Wild Mountain Ski Area offers 21 runs, 4 chair lifts, 2 rope tows, and snowmaking; longest run 500 feet, vertical drop 300 feet. *Services include equipment rental. Off U.S. 8 near Taylors Falls, tel. 612/291–7980. Call for hrs.*

Cross-country
The Arrowhead region offers excellent terrain for cross-country skiing; some of the state's finest trails are located here.

The **North Shore Trail** runs 74 miles through the Lake Superior hills between Grand Marais and Little Marais. There are a number of lodges along the trail.

The **Gunflint Trail** runs north from Grand Marais and offers more than 100 miles of trails and a variety of terrain. Many trails loop through the Boundary Waters Canoe Area.

Grand Portage Ski Trail has 43 miles of maintained trails running north to near the Canadian border. The trails range from beginner to advanced levels.

Jay Cooke State Park south of Duluth offers 32 miles of groomed trails that include spectacular overlooks of the St. Louis River Gorge.

Tennis Many of the larger resorts have tennis courts for their guests. Some are available to the public, but most public tennis courts are found in municipal parks. **Sugar Hills Lodge,** Grand Rapids (14 mi southwest on U.S. 169, tel. 218/326–9461) rents its courts to the general public. The **Duluth City Parks** (tel. 218/722–4011) have 41 public tennis courts. **Spirit Mountain Recreation Area** (9500 Spirit Mountain Pl., Duluth, tel. 218/628–2891) has public courts.

Spectator Sports

College Sports The University of Minnesota–Duluth (10 University Dr., tel. 218/726–8168) offers a full program of spectator sports including baseball, women's and men's basketball, wrestling, and hockey. The *Bulldogs* are especially competitive in hockey.

Dining and Lodging

The selection of restaurants in this region is varied, but they are uniformly casual. Look for local fish specials, along with steaks, chicken, and prime rib.

Like most everything else in the Arrowhead region, lodging is a fairly informal business. It runs the gamut from spartan fishing camps to full-service hotels, motels, and resorts.

Price categories for restaurants and hotels are the same as in the Minneapolis and St. Paul Dining and Lodging sections.

Duluth The **Chinese Lantern** offers Mandarin and Szechuan dishes and
Dining some American fare. Specialties include subgum won ton and wor shue duck. The dining room has an Oriental garden atmosphere. There's a children's menu and cocktail lounge and entertainment most nights. *402 W. 1st St., tel. 218/722–7488. AE, DC, MC, V. Inexpensive–Moderate.*

The **Pickwick Restaurant,** owned and operated by the same family since 1914, specializes in charbroiled steaks and seafood. There's a children's menu and a cocktail lounge. The contemporary dining room has views of Lake Superior. *508 E. Superior St., tel. 218/727–8901. Reservations suggested. AE, CB, DC, MC, V. Closed Sun., major holidays. Inexpensive–Moderate.*

Coney Island Deluxe is a very casual spot. Specialties include Coney Island sandwiches, gyro sandwiches, and other Greek delights. It's been a favorite with locals for nearly 50 years. *112 W. 1st St., tel. 218/722–2772. No credit cards. Inexpensive.*

Lodging **Fitger's Inn.** Part of a shopping area set in a refurbished brewery, this inn is listed in the National Register of Historic Places. It provides minisuites and elegant, spacious, individually styled rooms with period furnishings. Most rooms have a lake view. *600 E. Superior St., 55802, tel. 218/722–8826. 48 rooms. Facilities: restaurant, lounge, shopping mall and parking adjacent. AE, CB, DC, MC, V. Expensive.*

Radisson Duluth. In downtown Duluth, the hotel overlooks the harbor and Lake Superior. The rooms, typically well kept and well furnished, have city or harbor views. *505 W. Superior St., 55802, tel. 218/727–8981. 268 rooms. Facilities: indoor pool, parking ramp, complimentary beverages each evening, rooftop restaurant. AE, CB, DC, MC, V. Moderate–Expensive.*

Best Western Edgewater East Motel. Overlooking Lake Superior, this is the largest of the three Best Western inns in town. The rooms are light and airy, and many offer lake views. The moderate prices cover a large number of amenities. *2330 London Rd., 55812, tel. 218/728–3601. 119 rooms. Facilities: indoor pool, sauna, whirlpool, putting green, 2 lighted tennis courts, playground, coin laundry, winter plug-ins, restaurant adjacent. AE, DC, MC, V. Inexpensive–Moderate.*

Grand Marais
Dining

Birch Terrace Supper Club. The specialties at this family-run restaurant in a restored 1899 home include ribs and fresh Lake Superior trout. The baked goods come straight from the restaurant kitchen. Children's menu; beer and wine available. ½ *mi east on U.S. 61, tel. 218/387–2215. Dinner reservations suggested. MC, V. Open daily 5–11 PM May–mid-Oct. Inexpensive–Moderate.*

Grand Rapids
Dining

Forest Lake Restaurant and Steakhouse. The dining room in this rustic north-woods log building overlooks Forest Lake; the steak house in the lower level is open for dinner only. The upstairs menu includes Lake Superior fish specialties, plus breakfast and luncheon specials. There is a children's menu and cocktail lounge. *1201 N.W. 4th St., tel. 218/326–3423. AE, MC, V. Closed Jan. 1, Dec. 25.*

Lodging

Sawmill Inn. A modern, two-story motel with spacious rooms, contemporary decor, and lots of amenities. *2301 S. Pokegama, 55744, tel. 218/326–8501. 2½ mi south on U.S. 169. 125 rooms. Facilities: indoor pool, sauna, whirlpool, putting green, winter plug-ins, airport transportation, restaurant, cocktail lounge, entertainment. AE, CB, DC, MC, V. Moderate.*

Hibbing
Lodging

Regency Inn. This iron-range motel has a north-woodsy feeling in the lobby and public spaces, and bright, comfortable rooms and suites. *1402 Howard St., 55746, tel. 218/262–3481. 125 rooms. Facilities: indoor pool, wading pool, sauna, playground, winter plug-ins, dining room and coffee shop, cocktail lounge. AE, CB, DC, MC, V. Inexpensive.*

International Falls
Dining

Spot Supper Club. This family-owned restaurant is about as far into the north woods as you can get in the Upper Midwest. North-woods staples include steak, prime rib, and fish. There are daily specials, a children's menu, and a cocktail lounge. *1801 2nd Ave. W, tel. 218/283–2440. Dinner reservations suggested. AE, CB, DC, MC, V. Dinner only in winter. Inexpensive–Moderate.*

Lodging

Days Inn. There aren't a lot of extras, but the rooms are clean, comfortable, and well kept. The prices won't break the bank. *2 mi south on U.S. 53. Drawer O, 56679, tel. 218/283–9441. 61 rooms. Facilities: winter plug-ins, free Continental breakfast, cafe adjacent. AE, CB, DC, MC, V. Inexpensive.*

The Arts

Duluth
The **Buckhorn Theater** (506 W. Michigan St., tel. 218/722–2341) offers dramatic presentations at The Depot.

Colder by the Lake (201 E. Superior St., tel. 218/722–8492) is a comedy-satire company that uses dance, music, and visuals to lampoon life in northern Minnesota.

The **Duluth Playhouse Community Theater** (506 W. Michigan St., tel. 218/722–0349) is in its 73rd season, and presents seven productions at The Depot in an October through August season.

The **Duluth–Superior Symphony Orchestra** (506 W. Michigan St., tel. 218/727–7429) offers performances during a September through May season at the Duluth Auditorium (350 S. 5th Ave. W, tel. 218/722–5573).

The **Duluth Ballet** (506 W. Michigan St., tel. 218/722–2314) is the only Minnesota ballet company north of the Twin Cities. It performs throughout the year at The Depot.

Grand Marais The **Grand Marais Playhouse** (corner 1st Ave. and 3rd St., tel. 218/387–1036) offers a variety of little theater productions in a March through August season. The **Grand Marais Art Colony** (120 W. 3rd Ave., tel. 218/387–2737), the oldest art colony in Minnesota, offers summer classes in painting, drawing, and creative writing.

Grand Rapids The **Grand Rapids Players** offer little theater productions at the Myles Reif Performing Arts Center (Conifer Dr., tel. 218/326–8215). The **Grand Rapids Showboat** (16th Ave. W and 3rd St., tel. 218/326–3491) presents summer variety shows patterned after those on the old-time Mississippi riverboats on the last three weekends in July. **Itasca Community College** (1851 E. U.S. 169, tel. 218/327–4460) presents a Young Artists Series of six concerts in an October through April season.

Hibbing Arrowhead Regional Theater (1515 E. 25th St., tel. 218/262–7000) presents an October through May community theater season offering opera, musicals, and children's productions.

Nightlife

The night scene is more diverse in Duluth than in the rest of Arrowhead country, but much of it revolves around bars and nightclubs. Away from the city, the pub or cocktail lounge in a resort or supper club is your best bet.

Duluth The **Fond-du-Luth Gaming Casino** offers games of chance including high-stakes bingo, video poker, video blackjack, video keno, and more. *129 E. Superior St., tel. 218/722–0280 or 800/654–0714. Admission free, 18 or older.*

Club Saratoga offers Las Vegas–type showgirl revues. *331 S. 1st Ave. (2 blks. north of the Canal Park), tel. 218/722–5577. Shows nightly at 9, matinees Thur. and Fri. at 4:30.*

The **Lyric** is a popular drinking establishment offering hors d'oeuvres weekdays from 5 to 7 PM, and live Top 40 entertainment weekends at 8 PM. The club also hosts "Wicked Wednesday," a popular midweek party. *In the Holiday Center, tel. 218/722–1201. Closed Sun. No credit cards.*

Sneakers Sports Bar and Grill. An informal bar with continuous coverage of sports events on large-screen TV. There are sandwiches, gourmet burgers, homemade fries, and daily snack specials. *In the Holiday Center, tel. 218/727–7494. No credit cards.*

The **Tap Room.** An informal bar featuring burgers, hot dogs, and sandwiches. Monday is Comedy Night (8:30 PM) with local and regional comedians. There's live music Tuesday through Saturday, 9 PM to 1 AM. *In Fitger's Complex, 600 E. Superior St., tel. 218/722–5055.*

Grand Rapids The **Drumbeater Supper Club** offers weekend entertainment from 9 PM to 1 AM. *29 Crystal Springs Rd., tel. 218/327–2237.* The **Rainbow Inn** cocktail lounge offers live entertainment and dancing nightly during the summer season. *In the Best Western Rainbow Inn, 1300 U.S. 169 E, tel. 218/326–9655. AE, DC, MC, V.*

The cocktail lounge in the **Sawmill Inn** offers music and entertainment during the summer season. *2301 S. Pokegama, tel. 218/326–8501. AE, CB, DC, MC, V.*

6 Around Lake Superior

Introduction

The drive from Pigeon River at the Minnesota/Ontario border to the Canadian city of Sault Ste. Marie at the Ontario/Michigan border is part of the 1,300-mile Circle Route around Lake Superior, the largest freshwater lake in the world. Approximately 35 miles from the Minnesota border, Thunder Bay is the only major community along the 470 miles of the Circle Route that run through Ontario. Both Thunder Bay and Sault Ste. Marie have good restaurants and accommodations, shopping, and visitor attractions. Most of the towns and villages scattered along the route between these two cities are settlements that serve nearby mines, pulp mills, or hydroelectric plants.

The scenery along the route is a delight to those who enjoy north-woods vistas. Towering cliffs, deep canyons, cascading waterfalls, mountains, dark green forests, and sparkling lakes line the roadway; provincial parks provide access and guarantee that the wilderness will remain unharmed.

Admission to Ontario Provincial Parks is $4.25 per vehicle for day use, and $12 for camping.

Entry into Canada

U.S. citizens need proof of citizenship: a passport, birth certificate or voter registration card will do. Naturalized U.S. citizens should have their naturalization papers. You will be required to go through Canadian Customs when you enter Canada and through U.S. Customs when you return to the United States. It is a quick and painless procedure in almost all cases.

Getting Around

By Air   Sault Ste. Marie's **City Airport** is served by **Air Canada** (tel. 800/361–5373), **Air Ontario** (tel. 800/265–1263), and **Nordair** (tel. 800/268–7255).

Thunder Bay is served by **Air Canada** (tel. 800/361–5373) and **Northwest** (tel. 800/225–2525).

By Car   Nearly all travel in the area is by auto. Main roads are paved; most secondary roads are gravel or dirt. The Lake Superior Circle Route uses the Trans–Canada Highway from Thunder Bay to Sault Ste. Marie.

By Train   Sault Ste. Marie is served by the **Algoma Central Railway** (tel. 705/254–4331).

Thunder Bay is served by **VIA Rail Canada** (tel. 800/387–1144), Canada's version of Amtrak.

By Bus   **Greyhound** serves the region.

Scenic Drives   **Route 17.** The road follows the Lake Superior shore for 178 miles from Thunder Bay to Marathon and provides outstanding views of the big lake.

Important Addresses and Numbers

Tourist Information	**Hospitality and Travel Sault Ste. Marie,** 99 Foster Dr., Sault Ste. Marie, Ontario P6A 5X6, tel. 705/942–4001. Open daily 9–4:30.

Public Affairs—Visitors and Convention Dept., 520 Leith St., Thunder Bay, Ontario P7C 1M9, tel. 807/625–2149. Open daily 8:30–5.

North of Superior Tourism, 79 N. Court St., Thunder Bay, Ontario P7A 4T7, tel. 807/345–3322. Open daily 9–5.

Ontario Ministry of Tourism and Recreation, Queen's Park, Toronto, Ontario M7A 2E5, tel. 800/268–3735. Open daily 8–6 mid-May–Labor Day; weekdays 8–6 Sept.–mid-May.

Emergency Dial "0" and ask the operator for Zenith 50,000. The operator will connect you with the nearest unit of the **Ontario Provincial Police.**

Exploring

The following tour of the Lake Superior Circle Route's scenic areas and attractions begins at the international boundary at Pigeon River and moves east and then south to Sault Ste. Marie.

Thunder Bay This community of 112,000 is the Canadian lakehead and western terminus for Canada-bound oceangoing freighters that ply the St. Lawrence Seaway. It is Canada's third-largest port and the largest grain-handling port in the world, with storage facilities for more than 100 million bushels of grain.

Thunder Bay dates back to only 1969, when the adjacent cities of Fort William and Port Arthur were combined and named Thunder Bay by popular vote.

The **Sleeping Giant** rock formation, more than six miles long and 1,000 feet high, is part of the Sibley Peninsula that extends into Lake Superior from the forest northeast of the city. Prominent in Ojibwa Indian legend, the rock is seen as a silhouette from the city's waterfront. **Hillcrest Park** (off routes 11B and 17B on N. High St. near Red River Rd.) offers a great view of the Sleeping Giant and the harbor area.

The international **Friendship Gardens** have a variety of ethnic gardens planted by local citizens and donated as a centennial gift to Canada. *1800–2000 Victoria Ave. Admission free. Open daily.*

The cruise ship *Welcome* offers two-hour narrated tours of Thunder Bay Harbor, taking in shipping, grain elevators, docks, and offshore islands. There is also a daily 1½-hour cruise to old **Fort William.** *Cruises depart Water Front Park at the foot of Red River Rd. (Rte. 102), tel. 807/344–2512. Harbor cruise: $10 adults, $8 seniors over 65, $5 children 6–14 accompanied by an adult. Fort William cruise: $12 adults, $10 seniors over 65, $5 children 6–14 accompanied by an adult. Harbor cruises mid-May–June 25 and Aug. 22–early Oct. at 2 PM; June 26–Aug. 21 at 2, 4, and 7:30 PM. Fort William trips mid-May–mid-Oct., daily at 10 AM.*

Set on the banks of the Kaministiquia River, **Fort William** is a reconstruction of the early 19th-century inland headquarters of the North West Company. It served as a busy center for the fur trade between 1803 and 1821 and in its heyday consisted of an elaborate stockaded headquarters for 40 buildings. After 1821, when the North West Company joined the Hudson's Bay Company, Fort William fell into ruin from neglect and disuse. The 30 reconstructed buildings at Fort William include fur-trade buildings and craft shops with items typical of the period. There is also a farm, a 19th-century naval yard, an Indian encampment, and a site where birchbark canoes are made. Demonstrations of breadmaking, dancing, and musket firing, interpretive programs, and free 1½-hour guided tours, bring the old fort to life. The Rendezvous celebration in July draws large numbers of visitors. *Broadway Ave., 2½ miles south of junction of rtes. 11B, 17B, and 61 via Rte. 61, then 2½ miles southwest on Broadway, tel. 807/557–8461. Admission: $5 adults, $3 children 6–18 and seniors over 64. Open June 19–Aug. 21, daily 10–6; May 21–June 18 and Aug. 22–Sept. 25, weekdays 10–4, weekends 10–5.*

The **Centennial Botanical Conservatory** contains a wide assortment of identified foliage and flowering plants. Tropical plants, cacti, and succulents are featured, along with seasonal exhibits. *1601 Dease St., tel. 807/622–7036 or 625–2351. Admission free. Open daily 1–4; closed Good Friday and Dec. 25 and 26.*

Centennial Park is a wooded park on the banks of the Current River. An animal farm, a reproduction of a typical early-1900s northern Ontario logging camp, and a museum with exhibits about logging tools and equipment are open to visitors. There are cross-country ski trails, a picnic area, and a sand beach at nearby Boulevard Lake. *North on Boulevard Lake Park Rd. to Arundel St., then a short distance east, tel. 807/683–6511 or 625–2351. Admission free. Park and exhibits open daily 10 AM–dusk. The logging camp is open June 30–Labor Day, 10 AM–dusk.*

The **Thunder Bay Art Gallery** is the only public art gallery in all of Canada with a special focus on Canadian native art. The exhibits include pottery, sculpture, quilts, and photography, along with Indian artifacts. *Keewatin St. and Red Lake Rd. on the Confederate College campus, tel. 807/577–6427. Admission free. Open Tues.–Thurs. noon–8, Fri.–Sun. noon–5; closed Mon.*

The **Thunder Bay Historical Museum** has a good collection of pioneer, marine, and military items, Indian artifacts, along with documents, photos, and maps that describe the development and culture of the region. *219 S. May St., tel. 807/623–0801. Open mid-June–mid-Sept., daily 11–5; mid-Sept.–mid-June, Tues.–Sun. 1–5; closed Jan. 1, Dec. 25 and 26.*

A nine-foot-high statue of **Terry Fox** stands east of Thunder Bay at a scenic overlook on Route 11/17. Fox lost a leg to cancer at age 18 and began a 5,300-mile run across Canada to raise money for cancer research. He left St. John's, Newfoundland, on April 12, 1980, but was forced to stop near Thunder Bay on Sept. 1, 1980, when the disease recurred. He died the next year. The monument is about 7 miles from where Fox halted his run, facing westward, in the direction of his goal.

Thunder Bay Amethyst Mine. While land was being cleared for a fire tower, a bulldozer uncovered a vein of purple amethyst. There are guided tours of the gemstone mine operation and the cleaning processes. Rock collectors may purchase specimens or search for pieces on their own, at $1 per pound. *35 mi east on Rte. 11/17, then north 6 mi on E. Loon Rd., tel. 807/ 622–6908. Admission: $1, free for children under 9. Open June–Aug., daily 10–7; May 15–31 and Sept. 1–Oct. 15, daily 10–5.*

Sibley Peninsula and Provincial Park Located 25 miles east of Thunder Bay, this 25-mile-long peninsula was named after the president of the Silver Islet Mining Company, which operated a silver mine at the tip of the peninsula between 1869 and 1884. The mine was flooded by Lake Superior and today lies completely underwater.

In 1944 the peninsula became Sibley Provincial Park. Known for its abundant wildlife such as moose and deer, the park offers camping, hiking, fishing, and swimming. *Tel. 807/933–4332. Park open year-round; closed to cars in winter. Museum and interpretive center open mid-May–mid-Sept., daily 9–6.*

Ouimet Canyon Provincial Park Of the eight nature reserves in Ontario, this is the only one open to the public. The 500-foot-wide, 350-foot-deep canyon is a two-mile cleft in volcanic rock carved by wind, water, and ice. There are hiking trails and interpretive exhibits. Temperatures in the canyon are quite low, and some species of Arctic plants have been found there. Viewing platforms on the rim of the canyon provide spectacular scenic vistas. There are no camping or other facilities. *Located 25 mi southwest of Nipigon on Rte. 11 and 17, tel. 807/475–1531. Open mid-May–mid-Oct., daily dawn–dusk.*

Nipigon This community is the site of the first permanent non-Indian settlement on the north shore of Lake Superior and the home of the world-record brook trout (14½ lbs.). The **Nipigon Historical Museum** (Newton and 2nd Sts.) has exhibits about local history, archaeology, logging, railroads, and Finnish settlements.

Rainbow Falls Provincial Park The park is named after the series of waterfalls dropping from Whitesand Lake to Lake Superior. The park offers camping, hiking, nature trails, a sand beach, swimming, and fishing. There are showers and a laundry. Trails leading to park bluffs have spectacular views of Lake Superior. *8 miles west of Schreiber on Rte. 17, tel. 807/824–2299. Open year-round; closed to cars in winter.*

Neys Provincial Park This park has one of the finest swimming beaches on Lake Superior's north shore. Located at the site of a World War II prisoner-of-war camp, it offers campgrounds, hiking trails, picnic areas, and a resident herd of caribou. It's a fun spot for beachcombing. *20 miles west of Marathon on Rte. 17, tel. 807/ 229–1624. Open year-round; closed to cars in winter.*

Marathon One of the larger communities along the route (population: 2,271), Marathon was established as the village of Peninsula Harbor during the construction of the Canadian Pacific Railroad in the mid-1880s. The original village languished, but in 1945 a new community was built on the site and given its present name. The main industry is paper manufacturing, but gold fields were recently discovered nearby.

Pukaskwa National Park This 725-square-mile wilderness park is only accessible by canoe or hiking trail. You can reach the park entrance at Hattie Cove via Route 627, which extends south several miles from Marathon. There is a variety of plant life in the park, along with resident populations of bear, moose, wolves, and woodland caribou.

The **Visitor Center** at Hattie's Cove has interpretive programs and exhibits, along with campgrounds, showers, a laundry, picnic areas, beaches, and hiking trails. Visitors must register before going farther into the park. *Visitor Center open daily 11–6 early June–late Sept. Park open daily. Admission free. For additional information contact Superintendent, Pukaskwa National Park, Bag Service #5, Marathon, Ontario, Canada P0T 2E0, tel. 807/229–0801.*

Wawa Pronounced just as it looks, the name means "wild goose" in the Ojibwa tongue and refers to the thousands of geese that stop to rest on nearby Lake Wawa during the spring and fall migrations. A fur-trading post before 1700 and later the site of three gold rushes, Wawa now thrives on iron mining and tourism.

The ***Wawa Goose*** is a landmark sculpture in steel measuring 28 feet high and 22 feet from beak to tail, with a wingspan of 19 feet. It weighs over two tons.

High Falls (south of Wawa on Rte. 17, then 3 mi west, on a dirt road) is a 75-foot-high falls on the Magpie River. It is especially beautiful in winter.

Lake Superior Provincial Park. Route 17 runs for 50 miles through this huge and rugged National Environment Park. Camping and picnic areas are near the beach and on the headlands above Lake Superior. Park naturalists give talks and conduct nature tours. *North entrance located 5 mi south of Wawa. Open year-round; closed to cars in winter.*

Sault Ste. Marie Located directly across the St. Mary's River from its similarly named sister city in Michigan, Sault Ste. Marie was established in 1669. A French military post was established in 1750 and was garrisoned until the British took over 12 years later. The city was a major fur-trading center until 1842; many lovely old brick and stone buildings have been preserved. The Algoma steel mill and the Canadian lock in the St. Mary's River are located here. **Bellevue Park** (off Queen St. E) is a lovely waterside park with a small zoo, greenhouses, a marina, and a lighthouse.

Hiawathaland Sightseeing Tours offers two-hour narrated tours of the city aboard a bright red double-decker bus. Day trips to surrounding attractions are also offered. *Tours depart from ticket booth next to the Algoma Central Railway station at Bay and Dennis Sts., tel. 705/759–6200. Fare: $7 adults, $6.50 seniors over 65, $3.50 children 5–17, $16.50 family. Tours July–Aug., daily, on the hour 10–4; June 15–30 and day after Labor Day–Oct. 15, daily at 10:30, 1:30, and 4.*

Art Gallery of Algoma. Featuring the work of prominent Canadian artists, this gallery is housed in a striking new building along the St. Mary's River. There are two exhibition halls, an education room, and a gift shop. Special film and concert presentations are offered. Exhibits change monthly. *10 East St., tel. 705/949–9067. Admission: $1 adults, 50¢ seniors and stu-*

dents. Open Mon.–Wed. and Fri.–Sat. 10–5, Thurs. 10–9, Sun. 1:30–4:30; closed Good Friday and Dec. 25 and 26.

Ermatinger Old Stone House. Built in 1814 for Charles Oakes Ermatinger, an eminent fur trader with the North West Company, and his wife, the daughter of a chief of the Ojibwa tribe, this two-story Georgian-style residence is among the older stone homes in Ontario. The restored house contains many Ermatinger family personal belongings and period furnishings. Demonstrations of authentic pioneer cooking and baking are presented in the adjoining cookhouse. *831 Queen St. E, tel. 705/949–1488. Open June–Sept., daily 10–5; Apr.–May, weekdays 10–5; Oct.–Nov., weekdays 1–5.*

Great Lakes Forestry Centre. Ninety-minute tours of the laboratories and greenhouses are offered. There are audiovisual programs and exhibits on forest management and protection. *1219 Queen St. E, tel. 705/949–9461. Admission free. Tours mid-June–late Aug., weekdays at 10 and 2.*

The **Sault Ste. Marie Canal,** the Canadian section of the Soo Locks, is operated by Parks Canada. Built in 1895, the lock is more than 800 feet long. It is in a parklike setting, with interpretive programs, picnic facilities, and boatwatching. A walking trail and boardwalk lead out to the Soo Rapids. *On Canal Dr., tel. 705/942–6262. Admission free. The locks operate Apr.–Dec. The interpretive center is open July–Labor Day, daily 8–8; Sept.–June, weekdays 8–4:30.*

Lock Tours Canada runs two-hour narrated cruises that pass through the American and Canadian locks on the St. Mary's River. *Tours depart the Norgoma Dock, off Foster Dr., tel. 705/253–9850. Fare: $11 adults, $9 seniors and children 13–17, $5.50 children 6–12. MC, V. Daily trips July 1–Labor Day at 9:30, 11, noon, 1:30, 2:30, 4, 5, and 6:30; reduced schedule late May–June, and day after Labor Day–Oct. 15.*

The **M.S.** *Norgoma* was the last of the overnight passenger cruise ships built on the Great Lakes. The 80-foot vessel ran from Owen Sound to Sault Ste. Marie between 1950 and 1963, then served as an auto ferry to Manitoulin Island until 1974. Now it's a museum ship with stem-to-stern guided tours offered every half hour. There are marine exhibits and a film presentation, a snack bar, and rest rooms on board. *At the Norgoma Dock at Foster Dr., tel. 705/942–6984. Admission: $3.75 adults, $2.25 children 6–12. MC, V. Guided tours July 1–Labor Day, daily 9–9; June and day after Labor Day–mid-Oct., daily 10–6.*

What to See and Do with Children

Ouimet Canyon Provincial Park
Sault Ste. Marie: Agawa Canyon Wilderness Tours (*see* Off the Beaten Track below), Hiawathaland Sightseeing Tours, Soo Locks, Lock Tours Canada, and M.S. *Norgoma* Museum
Thunder Bay: Cruise Ship Welcome Tours, Centennial Park, and Old Fort William
Wawa: High Falls, and the Indian pictographs in Lake Superior Provincial Park. (*see* Off the Beaten Track)

Off the Beaten Track

Sault Ste. Marie **Agawa Canyon Wilderness Tours** offers a daylong rail trip into Agawa Canyon's scenic wilderness area with its waterfalls, mountains, ravines, and forests. There's a two-hour stop in the canyon for exploring or just enjoying the rugged scenery. Snow Train tours run weekends January–March. *Algoma Central Railway Terminal, 129 Bay St., tel. 705/254–4331. Round-trip fare: $31 adults, $15.50 ages 5–high school. Departures at 8 AM, return at 5 PM, early June–mid-Oct. Snow Train, weekends Jan.–March. Fares vary.*

Wawa The Indian pictographs at **Lake Superior Provincial Park** are among the most accessible of any on Lake Superior. A park road leads to the site on Agawa Bay; you walk out on a narrow rock ledge at the water's edge to see them. The paintings depict 50 Indians crossing Lake Superior and attacking another group of Indians, with images of canoes, birds, animals, and serpents. They were probably done by Chippewa or Cree Indians, who may well have been able to create them while still in their canoes (lake levels were known to be several feet higher in times past). The pictographs were apparently done with red ocher, an iron-oxide pigment, which the artists applied with their fingers. While it is not known exactly when these rock paintings were done, famed Michigan naturalist Henry Schoolcraft made a record of the site before 1850. A park naturalist is on duty at the paintings to answer questions.

Shopping

With the present rate of exchange favoring the American dollar, you can make some good buys in Canada, especially in native crafts and woolen products. Be certain that you understand whether prices are quoted in Canadian or American funds.

U.S. residents returning to the United States after 48 hours can bring back $400 (U.S.) worth of merchandise, duty free, every 30 days. After fewer than 48 hours, only $25 is allowed.

Sault Ste. Marie The main shopping areas are **Station Mall** (293 Bay St. on the waterfront) and **Cambrian Mall** (44 Great Northern Rd. [Rte. 17] at McNabb St). **Queenstown** is a factory outlet mall (E. Queen St. between Pim and Dennis Sts.). There is a Hudson's Bay Company store in Station Mall.

Thunder Bay The widest shopping selection in Thunder Bay is at **Intercity Mall** (1000 Fort William Rd.). The mall has more than 80 stores. The **Hudson's Bay Company Canadiana Shop** (413 E. Victoria, tel. 807/623–2241) has good buys on Hudson's Bay blankets and coats and Eskimo soapstone carvings. **Castagne Rock Shops** (420 E. Victoria Ave., tel. 807/623–5411) has amethyst jewelry and gift items.

You'll also find "trading post" gift shops at Wawa and in some of the small towns along the way.

Participant Sports

Beaches and
Water Sports

Sault Ste. Marie's **Kinsmen Park** (on 5th Line at Landslide Rd.) has a sand beach and bathhouse. The city of Sault Ste. Marie operates one indoor pool and two outdoor pools that are open to the public (tel. 705/759–5419).

There is a sand beach at Boulevard Lake (Arundel St. and Lyon Ave.) in Thunder Bay.

Swimming beaches are found in these provincial parks: **Middle Falls** (Rte. 61 on the Pigeon River at the U.S. border); **Sibley** (24 mi east of Thunder Bay on Rte. 11/17); **Rainbow Falls** (8 mi west of Schreiber on Rte. 17); **Neys** (15 mi west of Marathon on Rte. 17); **Lake Superior** (8 mi south of Wawa on Rte. 17); **Pancake Bay** (50 mi north of Sault Ste. Marie on Rte. 17); and **Batchawana Bay** (42 mi north of Sault Ste. Marie on Rte. 17).

Canoeing

Oskar's Heyden Crafts (10 mi north on Rte. 17, R.R. #2 Sault Ste. Marie, Ontario P6A 5K7, tel. 705/777–2426) provides rentals and guided canoe trips into the Algoma wilderness.
Wild Waters Wilderness Shop and Expeditions (119 N. Cumberland St., 807/345–0111) in Thunder Bay outfits and guides canoe expeditions.

Fishing

Trout, northern pike, walleye, bass, and a variety of fish are found in Ontario waters. In general, fishing is excellent. Local resorts or bait and tackle shops will tell you where to look for the big ones or help you obtain a professional guide. There is charter-boat fishing for trout and salmon in Lake Superior and float-plane service to fish camps located far beyond the ends of the roads. Nonresidents must have a license, available from most sporting goods stores, resorts, and fly-in camps and at all district offices of the Ministry of National Resources. For further information on regulations and licenses, contact the Ministry of Natural Resources. *Public Information Centre, tel. 416/965–4251. 99 Wellesley St. W, Room 1640, Whitney Block, Toronto, Ontario, Canada M7A 1W3. Open Mon.–Fri. 8:30–4:30.*

Golf

Public courses in Sault Ste. Marie include **Superior View Golf Course, Maplewood Golf Course, Root River Golf Course,** and the **Sault Ste. Marie Golf and Country Club.** For additional information contact Sault Ste. Marie Hospitality and Travel. *99 Foster Dr., Sault Ste. Marie, Ontario P6A 5X6, tel. 705/942–4001.*

There are several public courses in Thunder Bay, including **Fort William Golf and Country Club; Thunder Bay Municipal Golf Course; Centennial Golf Course; Emerald Green Golf Course; Thunder Bay Golf and Country Club;** and **Charles' Golf Course.** For additional information contact Public Affairs—Visitors and Convention Department (520 Leith St., Thunder Bay, Ontario P7C 1M9, tel. 807/625–2149).

Skiing
Downhill

Sault Ste. Marie's **Searchmont Ski Area** has 10 miles of runs with double and triple chair lifts, J-bars, and snowmaking; vertical drop 700 feet. Services include full-service base lodge, equipment rental, pro shop, ski school. *North of Sault Ste. Marie on Rte. 17 to Heyden, then northeast on Searchmont Rd. (Rte. 556) 12 mi to Searchmont, tel. 705/759–4881.*

There are four downhill ski areas in the immediate vicinity of Thunder Bay including **Mt. Baldy, Mt. McKay, Loch Lomond,** and **Candy Mountain.** For additional information contact Public Affairs—Visitors and Convention Department (520 Leith St., Thunder Bay P7C 1M9, tel. 807/625–2149).

Cross-country There are a variety of world-class trails in and around Sault Ste. Marie. **Stokely Creek Ski Touring Center** has over 62 miles of groomed, tracked trails and luxury accommodations. *North of Sault Ste. Marie on Rte. 17 at Goulais River, Ontario P0S 1E0, tel. 705/649–3421.*

Thunder Bay has five groomed and maintained trail systems close to the city.

Tennis **Sault Ste. Marie's Parks and Recreation Dept.** (tel. 705/759–5310) operates 18 neighborhood tennis courts that are open to the public free of charge seven days a week.

There are tennis courts in Thunder Bay's **Boulevard Lake Park** (off Rte. 17B on Gibson St.).

Dining and Lodging

In Sault Ste. Marie and Thunder Bay, dining and lodging facilities are on a par with those in similar-size American cities. Dining and lodging are very informal in the smaller communities along the route, but you can find clean and comfortable motels and restaurants that serve good food. Most businesses are geared to serve tourists, campers, and fishermen.

Price categories for restaurants and hotels are the same as in the Minneapolis and St. Paul Dining and Lodging sections.

Sault Ste. Marie **Cesira's Italian Cuisine.** Homemade Italian dishes include
Dining chicken, veal, and pasta. The menu includes steaks and seafood; children's menu and cocktails available. Dining is by candlelight in pleasant, attractive dining rooms. *122 Spring St., tel. 705/949–0600. Reservations suggested on weekends. AE, MC, V. No lunch Sat.; closed Dec. 25 and major Canadian holidays. Moderate.*

Giorgio's House of Fine Food. This restaurant offers a touch of old Italy with selections such as veal parmigiana, lasagna, pasta, and chicken, plus Canadian favorites like steaks and seafood. There is a children's menu, and cocktails are available. *280 Queen St. E, tel. 705/256–8241. Reservations suggested in season. AE, DC, MC, V. Inexpensive.*

Mr. M Restaurant. Mr. M's offers family dining in a friendly informal atmosphere near the St. Mary's River. Menu offerings include fresh whitefish and lake trout (in season), roast beef, barbecued ribs, chicken, steaks, and veal. There is a variety of daily luncheon and dinner specials and a children's menu. *293 Bay St., in the Station Mall behind the Algoma Central Railway Station, tel. 705/949–5637. AE, MC, V. Closed Sun. and major holidays. Inexpensive.*

Lodging **Holiday Inn.** Most rooms in this waterfront motor inn have views of the St. Mary's River or the city. The spacious rooms are done in comfortable modern decor. *208 St. Mary's Dr., P6A 5V4, tel. 705/949–0611. 193 rooms. Facilities: indoor pool, sauna, whirlpool, exercise room, restaurant, and a cocktail lounge. AE, DC, MC, V. Expensive–Very Expensive.*

Best Western Water Tower Inn. This is a spacious modern motor inn with regular and deluxe rooms; some suites have fireplaces. The furnishings are above average. A variety of weekend and winter sport packages are available. *360 Great Northern Rd., P6A 5N3, tel. 705/949–8111. 150 rooms. Facilities: indoor pool, sauna, whirlpool, exercise room, restaurant, cocktail lounge, and entertainment. AE, DC, MC, V. Expensive.*

Journey's End Motel. This Canadian chain motel offers accommodations at budget prices. There aren't a lot of extras, but the rooms are large and comfortable. *333 Great Northern Rd., P6B 4Z8, tel. 705/759–8000. 82 rooms. Facilities: cable TV, winter plug-ins, restaurant adjacent. AE, DC, MC, V. Inexpensive.*

Thunder Bay
Dining

Burgundy's. This very pleasant dining room in the Red Oak Inn offers a variety of seafood, beef, chicken, and veal dishes prepared in the best Canadian fashion. Cocktails are available. The ambience and service are excellent. *555 W. Arthur St., tel. 807/577–8481. Jacket and tie suggested. Reservations required. AE, DC, MC, V. No lunch weekends. Expensive.*

Circle Inn Dining Lounge. A rustic dining room and adjacent lounge in the Circle Inn Motel. The menu includes fresh whitefish and lake trout (in season), chicken, veal, beef, and pasta. There is a children's menu and cocktail lounge. *686 Memorial Ave., tel. 807/344–5744. Reservations suggested on weekends in season. AE, DC, MC, V. Closed Dec. 25. Moderate.*

The Elephant and Castle. This British pub and restaurant has authentic atmosphere right down to the dart boards. There's an Olde English menu (fish and chips), imported draught beer and ale, and daily Canadian luncheon and dinner specials. A children's menu is offered. *In the Intercity Shopping Center, tel. 807/623–7766. AE, DC, MC, V. Closed Sun. Inexpensive– Moderate.*

Prospector Restaurant. A modern family restaurant offering prime rib, steaks, seafood, and a large salad bar. The homemade rolls are baked fresh daily. There is a children's menu. *27 S. Cumberland, tel. 807/345–1901. MC, V. Closed Sun. Inexpensive.*

Lodging

Red Oak Inn. This Canadian Pacific Motor Hotel offers a solarium where tropical trees and greenery suggest summer year-round. The spacious rooms and suites are modern, bright, and airy. *555 Arthur St., P7E 5R5, tel. 807/577–8481. Rtes. 11B and 17B. 180 rooms. Facilities: indoor pool, wading pool, sauna, whirlpool, winter plug-ins, dining room, coffee shop, and a cocktail lounge. AE, DC, MC, V. Expensive.*

★ **The Valhalla Inn–Thunder Bay.** This motor inn has large, comfortable, and very attractive rooms and suites done in modern Scandinavian decor. It is luxurious throughout, including the large pool area. *West of the south metro district at the junction of Rtes. 11, 17, and 61, 1 Valhalla Inn Rd., P7E 6J1, tel. 807/ 577–1121. 270 rooms. Facilities: indoor pool, sauna, whirlpool, half court tennis, winter plug-ins, dining room, coffee shop, cocktail lounge. AE, DC, MC, V. Expensive.*

Airline Motor Hotel. A modern motor hotel with large comfortable rooms and bright public spaces. There are some suites. *West of the south metro area, 698 Arthur St., P7E 5R8, tel. 807/ 577–1181. 172 rooms. Facilities: indoor pool, wading pool, sauna, whirlpool, winter plug-ins, restaurant, and a lounge. AE, DC, MC, V. Moderate–Expensive.*

Landmark Inn. This pleasant, family-oriented motor inn has modern, spacious rooms and public spaces done in "Canadian modern" decor. A good buy for the money. *1010 Dawson Rd., P7B 5J4, tel. 807/767–1681. 106 rooms. Facilities: cable TV, indoor pool, sauna, whirlpool, winter plug-ins, restaurant, cocktail lounge, entertainment. AE, MC, V. Moderate.*

Wawa
Dining

Voyageur Restaurant. This modern family restaurant is part of a chain that serves the travel market. The menu includes steak, prime rib, and seafood dinners, soups, sandwiches, salads, and daily specials. A children's menu is available. *On Rte. 17, south of junction with Rte. 101, tel. 705/856–2622. MC, V. Closed Jan. 1, Dec. 25. Inexpensive.*

Lodging

Bristol Motel. This small family motel offers modern rooms. *Rte. 101 just east of Rte. 17. Box 105, P0S 1K0, tel. 705/856–2385. 21 rooms. Facilities: cable TV, winter plug-ins, restaurant adjacent. AE, MC, V. Inexpensive.*

The Arts

Sault Ste. Marie's **Algoma Fall Festival** is a monthlong mid-September to mid-October festival of drama, music, film, theater, and dance along with art and craft exhibitions. It is one of Canada's largest visual and performing arts festivals. For additional information contact the Algoma Arts Festival Association. *Box 526, Sault Ste. Marie, Ontario P6A 5M6, tel. 705/949–0822.*

The **Thunder Bay Community Auditorium** (Beverly St. and Winnipeg Ave., tel. 807/343–2300) showcases musical and dramatic presentations, traveling Broadway shows, and headline entertainment.

Index

Personal Itinerary

Departure *Date*

Time

Transportation

Arrival *Date*   *Time*

Departure *Date*   *Time*

Transportation

Accommodations

Arrival *Date*   *Time*

Departure *Date*   *Time*

Transportation

Accommodations

Arrival *Date*   *Time*

Departure *Date*   *Time*

Transportation

Accommodations

Personal Itinerary

Arrival *Date*   *Time*

Departure *Date*   *Time*

Transportation

Accommodations

Arrival *Date*   *Time*

Departure *Date*   *Time*

Transportation

Accommodations

Arrival *Date*   *Time*

Departure *Date*   *Time*

Transportation

Accommodations

Arrival *Date*   *Time*

Departure *Date*   *Time*

Transportation

Accommodations

Personal Itinerary

Arrival *Date*   *Time*

Departure *Date*   *Time*

Transportation

Accommodations

Arrival *Date*   *Time*

Departure *Date*   *Time*

Transportation

Accommodations

Arrival *Date*   *Time*

Departure *Date*   *Time*

Transportation

Accommodations

Arrival *Date*   *Time*

Departure *Date*   *Time*

Transportation

Accommodations

Addresses

Name

Address

Telephone

Name

Address

Telephone

Name

Address

Telephone

Name

Address

Telephone

Name

Address

Telephone

Name

Address

Telephone

Name

Address

Telephone

Name

Address

Telephone

Name

Address

Telephone

Name

Address

Telephone

Name

Address

Telephone

Name

Address

Telephone

Name

Address

Telephone

Name

Address

Telephone

Name

Address

Telephone

Name

Address

Telephone

Fodor's Travel Guides

U.S. Guides

Alaska
American Cities
The American South
Arizona
Atlantic City & the
  New Jersey Shore
Boston
California
Cape Cod
Carolinas & the
  Georgia Coast
Chesapeake
Chicago
Colorado
Dallas & Fort Worth
Disney World & the
  Orlando Area

The Far West
Florida
Greater Miami,
  Fort Lauderdale,
  Palm Beach
Hawaii
Hawaii (Great Travel
  Values)
Houston & Galveston
I-10: California to
  Florida
I-55: Chicago to New
  Orleans
I-75: Michigan to
  Florida
I-80: San Francisco to
  New York

I-95: Maine to Miami
Las Vegas
Los Angeles, Orange
  County, Palm Springs
Maui
New England
New Mexico
New Orleans
New Orleans (Pocket
  Guide)
New York City
New York City (Pocket
  Guide)
New York State
Pacific North Coast
Philadelphia
Puerto Rico (Fun in)

Rockies
San Diego
San Francisco
San Francisco (Pocket
  Guide)
Texas
United States of
  America
Virgin Islands
  (U.S. & British)
Virginia
Waikiki
Washington, DC
Williamsburg,
  Jamestown &
  Yorktown

Foreign Guides

Acapulco
Amsterdam
Australia, New Zealand
  & the South Pacific
Austria
The Bahamas
The Bahamas (Pocket
  Guide)
Barbados (Fun in)
Beijing, Guangzhou &
  Shanghai
Belgium & Luxembourg
Bermuda
Brazil
Britain (Great Travel
  Values)
Canada
Canada (Great Travel
  Values)
Canada's Maritime
  Provinces
Cancún, Cozumel,
  Mérida, The
  Yucatán
Caribbean
Caribbean (Great
  Travel Values)

Central America
Copenhagen,
  Stockholm, Oslo,
  Helsinki, Reykjavik
Eastern Europe
Egypt
Europe
Europe (Budget)
Florence & Venice
France
France (Great Travel
  Values)
Germany
Germany (Great Travel
  Values)
Great Britain
Greece
Holland
Hong Kong & Macau
Hungary
India
Ireland
Israel
Italy
Italy (Great Travel
  Values)
Jamaica (Fun in)

Japan
Japan (Great Travel
  Values)
Jordan & the Holy Land
Kenya
Korea
Lisbon
Loire Valley
London
London (Pocket Guide)
London (Great Travel
  Values)
Madrid
Mexico
Mexico (Great Travel
  Values)
Mexico City & Acapulco
Mexico's Baja & Puerto
  Vallarta, Mazatlán,
  Manzanillo, Copper
  Canyon
Montreal
Munich
New Zealand
North Africa
Paris
Paris (Pocket Guide)

People's Republic of
  China
Portugal
Province of Quebec
Rio de Janeiro
The Riviera (Fun on)
Rome
St. Martin/St. Maarten
Scandinavia
Scotland
Singapore
South America
South Pacific
Southeast Asia
Soviet Union
Spain
Spain (Great Travel
  Values)
Sweden
Switzerland
Sydney
Tokyo
Toronto
Turkey
Vienna
Yugoslavia

Special-Interest Guides

Bed & Breakfast
  Guide: North America
1936...On the
  Continent

Royalty Watching
Selected Hotels of
  Europe

Selected Resorts
  and Hotels of the U.S.
Ski Resorts of North
  America

Views to Dine by
  around the World

Join us in updating the next edition of your Fodor's guide

Title of Guide:

1 Hotel □ Restaurant □ *(check one)*

Name

Number/Street

City/State/Country

Comments

2 Hotel □ Restaurant □ *(check one)*

Name

Number/Street

City/State/Country

Comments

3 Hotel □ Restaurant □ *(check one)*

Name

Number/Street

City/State/Country

Comments

Your Name *(optional)*

Address

General Comments

Business Reply Mail

First Class   Permit Nº 7775   *New York, NY*

Postage will be paid by addressee

Fodor's Travel Publications

201 East 50th Street
New York, NY 10022